1 MONTH OF
FREE
READING

at
www.ForgottenBooks.com

By purchasing this book you are eligible for one month membership to ForgottenBooks.com, giving you unlimited access to our entire collection of over 1,000,000 titles via our web site and mobile apps.

To claim your free month visit:
www.forgottenbooks.com/free925420

ISBN 978-0-260-06315-1
PIBN 10925420

THE

CALENDAR

OF THE

University of Toronto

FOR THE YEAR

1921-1922

UNIVERSITY OF TORONTO PRESS

TABLE OF CONTENTS.

ADMINISTRATIVE OFFICERS

1920-1921.

THE UNIVERSITY.

President..Sir Robert Alexander Falconer, K.C.M.G., M.A., LL.D., D.Litt.
Registrar.............................James Brebner, B.A., LL.D.
Bursar...........................Ferdinand Albert Mouré, Esq.
Librarian.:......................Hugh Hornby Langton, M.A.
Director of Extension Work and Publicity....William James Dunlop, B.A.
Warden of Hart House............Walter Fletcher Bowles, B.A.
Physical Director.....................James Warren Barton, M.D.
Superintendent of Buildings and Grounds..Arthur D'Orr LePan, B.A.Sc.
Manager of the University Press..........Richard J. Hamilton, B.A.

THE FACULTY OF ARTS.

President...Sir Robert Alexander Falconer, K.C.M.G. M.A., LL.D., D.Litt.
Dean...............Arthur Philemon Coleman, M.A., Ph.D., F.R.S.
Secretary..........................James Brebner, B.A., LL.D.

UNIVERSITY COLLEGE.

Principal...........................Maurice Hutton, M.A., LL.D.
Registrar..............François Charles Archile Jeanneret, B.A.

VICTORIA COLLEGE.

President........... Rev. Richard Pinch Bowles, M.A., D.D., LL.D.
Dean.............................John Charles Robertson, M.A.
Registrar......................Arthur Leopold Langford, M.A.
Librarian.......................Augustus Edward Lang, M.A.
Secretary of the Faculty.....Norman Wentworth DeWitt, B.A., Ph.D.
Bursar.......................Rev. William Bryden Caswell, B.A.
Dean of Residence................Charles Vincent Massey, M.A.
Senior Tutor in Residence.............George Malcolm Smith, M.A.
Dean of Women Students............Miss M. E. T. Addison, B.A.

TRINITY COLLEGE.

Provost......Rev. Thomas Clark Street Macklem, M.A., D.D., LL.D.
Dean of the Faculty of Arts..Rev. Henry Thomas Forbes Duckworth,
M.A.
Dean of Residence............Archibald Hope Young, M.A., D.C.L.
Registrar..............William Alexander Kirkwood, M.A., Ph.D.
Librarian................Rupert Earle Loring Kittredge, M.A.
Bursar....................................Sydney H. Jones, Esq.
Principal of St. Hilda's College and Dean of Women Students,
Miss Mabel Cartwright, B.A.

ST. MICHAEL'S COLLEGE.

Superior.................................Rev. Henry Carr, B.A.
Assistant Superior...................Rev. Francis Gerald Powell.
Registrar..................Rev. Edmund Joseph McCorkell, M.A.
Bursar..........................Rev. Vincent Joseph Murphy.

FACULTY OF MEDICINE.

President..Sir Robert Alexander Falconer, K.C.M.G., M.A., LL.D.,
D.Litt.
Dean................Alexander Primrose, C.B., M.B., C.M., Edin.
Secretary....................Edward Stanley Ryerson, M.D.,C.M..

FACULTY OF APPLIED SCIENCE AND ENGINEERING.

President..Sir Robert Alexander Falconer, K.C.M.G., M.A., LL.D.,
D.Litt.
Dean..Charles Hamilton Mitchell, C.B., C.M.G., D.S.O., C.E., LL.D.
Secretary...........................Albert Thomas Laing, B.A.Sc.

FACULTY OF HOUSEHOLD SCIENCE.

President..Sir Robert Alexander Falconer, K.C.M.G., M.A., LL.D.,
D.Litt.
Dean..
Secretary.....................Miss Clara Cynthia Benson, Ph.D.

FACULTY OF EDUCATION.

President..Sir Robert Alexander Falconer, K.C.M.G., M.A., LL.D..
D.Litt.
Dean...........................William Pakenham, B.A., LL.D.
Secretary...........................John Thomas Crawford, B.A.

FACULTY OF FORESTRY.

President..Sir Robert Alexander Falconer, K.C.M.G., M.A., LL.D.,
D.Litt.
Dean.........................Clifton Durant Howe, M.A., Ph.D.

FACULTY OF MUSIC.

President..SIR ROBERT ALEXANDER FALCONER, K.C.M.G., M.A., LL.D., D.LITT.

Dean........................AUGUSTUS STEPHEN VOGT, MUS. DOC.

Secretary....................MISS ANNIE WILKIE PATTERSON, B.A.

BOARD OF GRADUATE STUDIES.

President..SIR ROBERT ALEXANDER FALCONER, K.C.M.G., M.A., LL.D., D.LITT.

Chairman........JAMES PLAYFAIR MCMURRICH, M.A., PH.D., LL.D.

Secretary.................................MISS NORA MCKENZIE.

COMMITTEE ON UNIVERSITY EXTENSION.

President..SIR ROBERT ALEXANDER FALCONER, K.C.M.G., M.A., LL.D. D.LITT,

Chairman.:.....................ALFRED TENNYSON DELURY, M.A.

Secretary..........................WILLIAM JAMES DUNLOP, B.A.

DEPARTMENT OF SOCIAL SERVICE.

President..SIR ROBERT ALEXANDER FALCONER, K.C.M.G., M.A., LL.D., D.LITT.

Acting Director.......:...................JAMES ALFRED DALE, M.A.

Secretary..................

DEPARTMENT OF PUBLIC HEALTH NURSING.

President..SIR ROBERT ALEXANDER FALCONER, K.C.M.G., M.A., LL.D. D.LITT.

Director......................MISS EDITH KATHLEEN RUSSELL, B.A.

Secretary.......................

NOTE—Communications relating to standing in all Faculties and Departments and to curricula, instruction and examinations in Law, Dentistry, Pharmacy, Agriculture, Gymnastics and Drill, and Veterinary Science are to be addressed to the Registrar of the University; correspondence regarding curricula, instruction and examinations in a particular Faculty is to be sent to the Secretary of that Faculty; correspondence regarding registration, curricula, instruction and examinations in Graduate Courses is to be sent to the Secretary of the Board of Graduate Studies; enquiries with reference to College instruction and residence are to be addressed to the Registrar of the College concerned.

Applications for admission to the Faculties of Arts, Medicine, Applied Science and Engineering, and Forestry, are to be sent to the Registrar of the University; applications for admission to the Faculties of Education and Music are to be sent to the Secretary of the Faculty concerned.

JANUARY	FEBRUARY	MARCH	APRIL
Sun. . 2 9 16 23 30	Sun. . . 6 13 20 27	Sun. . . 6 13 20 27	Sun. . 3 10 17 24 ..
Mon. . 3 10 17 24 31	Mon. . . 7 14 21 28	Mon. . . 7 14 21 28	Mon. . 4 11 18 25 ..
Tues. . 4 11 18 25 ..	Tues. . 1 8 15 22	Tues. . 1 8 15 22 29	Tues. . 5 12 19 26 ..
Wed. . 5 12 19 26 ..	Wed. . 2 9 16 23	Wed. . 2 9 16 23 30	Wed. . 6 13 20 27 ..
Thur. . 6 13 20 27 ..	Thur. . 3 10 17 24	Thur. . 3 10 17 24 31	Thur. . 7 14 21 28 ..
Fri. . 7 14 21 28 ..	Fri. . 4 11 18 25	Fri. . . 4 11 18 25 ..	Fri. 1 8 15 22 29 ..
Sat. 1 8 15 22 29 ..	Sat. . 5 12 19 26	Sat. . 5 12 19 26 ..	Sat. 2 9 16 23 30 ..

MAY	JUNE	JULY	AUGUST
Sun. . 1 8 15 22 29	Sun. . . 5 12 19 26	Sun. . 3 10 17 24 31	Sun. . . 7 14 21 28
Mon. . 2 9 16 23 30	Mon. . . 6 13 20 27	Mon. . 4 11 18 25	Mon. . 1 8 15 22 29
Tues. . 3 10 17 24 31	Tues. . . 7 14 21 28	Tues. . 5 12 19 26	Tues. . 2 9 16 23 30
Wed. . 4 11 18 25 ..	Wed. . 1 8 15 22 29	Wed. . 6 13 20 27 ..	Wed. . 3 10 17 24 31
Thur. . 5 12 19 26 ..	Thur. . 2 9 16 23 30	Thur. . 7 14 21 28	Thur. . 4 11 18 25 ..
Fri. . 6 13 20 27 ..	Fri. . 3 10 17 24 ..	Fri. 1 8 15 22 29	Fri. . 5 12 19 26 ..
Sat. . 7 14 21 28 ..	Sat. . 4 11 18 25 ..	Sat. 2 9 16 23 30	Sat. . 6 13 20 27 ..

SEPTEMBER	OCTOBER	NOVEMBER	DECEMBER
Sun. . . 4 11 18 25	Sun. . 2 9 16 23 30	Sun. . . 6 13 20 27	Sun. . . 4 11 18 25
Mon. . . 5 12 19 26	Mon. . 3 10 17 24 31	Mon. . . 7 14 21 28	Mon. . . 5 12 19 26
Tues. . . 6 13 20 27	Tues. . 4 11 18 25 ..	Tues. 1 8 15 22 29	Tues. . 6 13 20 27
Wed. . . 7 14 21 28	Wed. . 5 12 19 26 ..	Wed. . 2 9 16 23 30	Wed. . . 7 14 21 28
Thur. 1 8 15 22 29	Thur. . 6 13 20 27 ..	Thur. . 3 10 17 24 ..	Thur. 1 8 15 22 29
Fri. . 2 9 16 23 30	Fri. . 7 14 21 28 ..	Fri. . 4 11 18 25 ..	Fri. . 2 9 16 23 30
Sat. . 3 10 17 24 ..	Sat. 1 8 15 22 29 ..	Sat. . 5 12 19 26 ..	Sat. . 3 10 17 24 31

JANUARY	FEBRUARY	MARCH	APRIL
Sun. . 1 8 15 22 29	Sun. . . 5 12 19 26	Sun. . . 5 12 19 26	Sun. . 2 9 16 23 30
Mon. . 2 9 16 23 30	Mon. . . 6 13 20 27	Mon. . . 6 13 20 27	Mon. . 3 10 17 24 ..
Tues. . 3 10 17 24 31	Tues. . . 7 14 21 28	Tues. . . 7 14 21 28	Tues. . 4 11 18 25 ..
Wed. . 4 11 18 25 ..	Wed. . 1 8 15 22 ..	Wed. . 1 8 15 22 29	Wed. . 5 12 19 26 ..
Thur. . 5 12 19 26 ..	Thur. . 2 9 16 23 ..	Thur. . 2 9 16 23 30	Thur. . 6 13 20 27 ..
Fri. . 6 13 20 27 ..	Fri. . 3 10 17 24 ..	Fri. . 3 10 17 24 31	Fri. . 7 14 21 28 ..
Sat. . 7 14 21 28 ..	Sat. . 4 11 18 25 ..	Sat. . 4 11 18 25 ..	Sat. 1 8 15 22 29 ..

MAY	JUNE	JULY	AUGUST
Sun. . . 7 14 21 28	Sun. . . 4 11 18 25	Sun. . 2 9 16 23 30	Sun. . . 6 13 20 27
Mon. . 1 8 15 22 29	Mon. . . 5 12 19 26	Mon. . 3 10 17 24 31	Mon. . . 7 14 21 28
Tues. . 2 9 16 23 30	Tues. . . 6 13 20 27	Tues. . 4 11 18 25 ..	Tues. 1 8 15 22 29
Wed. . 3 10 17 24 31	Wed. . . 7 14 21 28	Wed. . 5 12 19 26 ..	Wed. . 2 9 16 23 30
Thur. . 4 11 18 25 ..	Thur. 1 8 15 22 29	Thur. . 6 13 20 27 ..	Thur. . 3 10 17 24 31
Fri. . 5 12 19 26 ..	Fri. . 2 9 16 23 30	Fri. . 7 14 21 28 ..	Fri. . 4 11 18 25 ..
Sat. . 6 13 20 27 ..	Sat. . 3 10 17 24 ..	Sat. 1 8 15 22 29 ..	Sat. . 5 12 19 26 ..

SEPTEMBER	OCTOBER	NOVEMBER	DECEMBER
Sun. . . 3 10 17 24	Sun. . 1 8 15 22 29	Sun. . . 5 12 19 26	Sun. . 3 10 17 24 31
Mon. . . 4 11 18 25	Mon. . 2 9 16 23 30	Mon . . . 6 13 20 27	Mon. . 4 11 18 25 ..
Tues. . . 5 12 19 26	Tues. . 3 10 17 24 31	Tues. . . 7 14 21 28	Tues. . 5 12 19 26 ..
Wed. . . 6 13 20 27	Wed. . 4 11 18 25 ..	Wed. . 1 8 15 22 29	Wed. . 6 13 20 27 ..
Thur. . . 7 14 21 28	Thur. . 5 12 19 26 ..	Thur. . 2 9 16 23 30	Thur. . 7 14 21 28 ..
Fri. . 1 8 15 22 29	Fri. . 6 13 20 27 ..	Fri. . 3 10 17 24 ..	Fri. 1 8 15 22 29 ..
Sat. . 2 9 16 23 30	Sat. . 7 14 21 28 ..	Sat. . 4 11 18 25 ..	Sat. 2 9 16 23 30 ..

CALENDAR 1921-1922

1921—July 1 Friday......University Buildings closed.

July 7 Thursday....Meeting of the Finance and Executive **Committee** of Trinity College.

Aug. 1 Monday.....Last day for receiving applications **for the** September Examinations in the Faculty of Arts.

Sept. 1 Thursday....Last day for receiving applications for the Supplemental Matriculation Examination.

Sept. 1 Thursday....Last day for receiving applications for **the** Supplemental Examinations in the Faculty of Medicine.

Sept. 5 Monday.....Labour Day. University Buildings closed.

Sept. 6 Tuesday.....Supplemental Junior Matriculation **Exami**nation begins, conducted by the University Matriculation Board.

Sept. 6 Tuesday....Supplemental Examinations in the Faculty of Medicine begin.

Sept. 7 Wednesday..Supplemental Examinations in the Faculty of Arts begin.

Sept. 8 Thursday....Meeting of the Finance and Executive Committee of Trinity College.

Sept. 15 Thursday....Last day for receiving applications for admission to the Faculty of Medicine.

Sept. 15 Thursday....Last day for receiving applications **for the** Supplemental Examinations in the Faculty of Applied Science and Engineering.

Sept. 16 Friday......Meeting of the Council of the Faculty of Medicine.

Sept. 23 Friday......Meeting of University College Council.

Sept. 23 Friday......Supplemental Examinations in the Faculty of Applied Science and Engineering begin.

Sept. 24 Saturday....Meeting of the Faculty of Arts of Victoria College.

Sept. 26 Monday.....Enrolment in classes by the various **Pro**fessors begins at 9.00 a.m.

Sept. 26 Monday.....Meeting of the Council of the Faculty **of** Arts.

Sept. 26 Monday....Meeting of the Council of the Faculty of Applied Science and Engineering.

Sept. 27 Tuesday....Academic Year begins at 9.00 a.m.

Sept. 27 Tuesday.....The opening address by the President **to** the students of all the Faculties at 3 **p.m.,** in Convocation Hall.

Sept. 27 Tuesday....Last day for receiving vacation work in the Faculty of Applied Science and Engineering.

Sept. 27 Tuesday.....Last day for the completion of registration in person for the Session 1920-1921.

Sept. 27 Tuesday.....Enrolment in classes for the Session 1920-1921 to be completed at 5 p.m.

Sept. 28 Wednesday..Lectures begin at 9.00 a.m.

Sept. 28 Wednesday..Meeting of the Faculty of Arts of Victoria College.

Sept. 29 Thursday....St. Michael's Day.

Sept. 30 Friday.....Meeting of the Senate of Victoria College.

Oct.   6 Thursday....Meeting of the Finance and Executive Committee of Trinity College.

Oct.   7 Friday......Meeting of University College Council.

Oct.   7 Friday......Meeting of the Council of the Faculty of Medicine.

Oct.   7 Friday......Meeting of the Council of the Faculty of Applied Science and Engineering

Oct.   8 Saturday....Stated meeting of the Caput to deal with requests as to social functions.

Oct. 10 Monday.....Meeting of the Council of the Faculty of Arts.

Oct. 14 Friday......Meeting of Senate.

Oct. 14 Friday......Charter Day, Victoria College.

Nov. 2 Wednesday..Meeting of the Faculty of Arts of Victoria College.

Nov. 4 Friday......Meeting of University College Council.

Nov. 4 Friday......Meeting of the Senate of Victoria College.

Nov. 4 Friday......Meeting of the Council of the Faculty of Applied Science and Engineering.

Nov. 7 Monday.....Meeting of the Council of the Faculty of Arts.

Nov. 10 Thursday....Meeting of the Finance and Executive committee of Trinity College.

Nov. 11 Friday......Meeting of Senate.

Nov. 16 Wednesday..Annual General Business Meeting of the Convocation of Trinity College.

Nov. 17 Thursday....Annual General Meeting of the Corporation of Trinity College.

Nov. 30 Wednesday..Meeting of the Faculty of Arts of Victoria College.

Dec. 1 Thursday....Last day for receiving applications for the January Examinations in Arts.

Dec. 2 Friday......Meeting of University College Council.

Dec. 2 Friday......Meeting of the Senate of Victoria College.

Dec. 2 Friday......Meeting of the Council of the Faculty of Medicine.

Dec. 2 Friday......Meeting of the Council of the Faculty of Applied Science and Engineering.

Dec. 5 Monday.....Meeting of the Council of the Faculty of Arts.

Dec. 8 Thursday....Meeting of the Finance and Executive Committee of Trinity College.

Dec. 9 Friday......Meeting of the Senate.

Dec. 12-16 Monday-Friday—
Term Examinations in the Faculty of Arts.

Dec. 16 Friday......Last day of Lectures. Term ends at 12 noon.

Dec. 26 Monday.....University Buildings closed.

Dec. 30 Friday......Meeting of the Faculty of Arts of Victoria College.

1922—Jan. 2 Monday ....University Buildings closed.

Jan. 3 Tuesday ....Supplemental Examinations in Arts begin.

Jan. 3 Tuesday.....Easter Term begins.

Jan. 3 Tuesday.....Last day for receiving Theses for the degree of B.A.Sc.

Jan. 4 Wednesday..Assembly of the Students of all Faculties of Convocation Hall at 12.10 p.m.

Jan. 5 Thursday....Meeting of the Finance and Executive Committee of Trinity College.

Jan. 6 Friday......Meeting of University College Council.

Jan. 6 Friday......Meeting of the Council of the Faculty of Applied Science and Engineering.

Jan. 9 Monday.....Meeting of the Council of the Faculty of Arts.

Jan. 13 Friday......Meeting of Senate.

Jan. 15 Sunday......Inauguration Day, Trinity College.

Feb. 1 Wednesday..Meeting of the Faculty of Arts of Victoria College.

Feb. 3 Friday......Meeting of University College Council.

Feb. 3 Friday......Meeting of the Senate of Victoria College.

Feb. 3 Friday......Meeting of the Council of the Faculty of Appl'ed Science and Engineering.

Feb. 3 Friday......Meeting of the Council of the Faculty of Medicine.

Feb. 6 Monday.....Meeting of the Council of the Faculty of Arts.

Feb. 9 Thursday....Meeting of the Finance and Executive Committee of Trinity College.

Feb. 10 Friday......Meeting of Senate.

Mar. 1 Wednesday..Ash Wednesday.

Mar. 1 Wednesday..Meeting of the Faculty of Arts of Victoria College.

Mar. 3 Friday......Meeting of University College Council.

Mar. 3 Friday......Meeting of the Senate of Victoria College.

Mar. 3 Friday......Meeting of the Council of the Faculty of
                    Applied Science and Engineering

Mar. 6 Monday.....Meeting of the Council of the Faculty of
                    Arts.

Mar. 9 Thursday....Meeting of the Finance and Executive Com-
                    mittee of Trinity College.

Mar. 10 Friday......Meeting of Senate.

Mar. 15 Wednesday..Last day for receiving applications for
                    Annual Examinations in the Faculties of
                    Arts and Medicine and in the Department
                    of Law.

Mar. 31 Friday......Last day for submitting LL.B. theses.

Apr. 4 Tuesday....Lectures and practical work close in the
                    Faculty of Applied Science and Engineer-
                    ing.

Apr. 5 Wednesday..Meeting of the Faculty of Arts of Victoria
                    College.

Apr. 6 Thursday....Meeting of the Finance and Executive Com-
                    mittee of Trinity College.

Apr. 7 Friday......Meeting of University College Council.

Apr. 7 Friday......Meeting of the Senate of Victoria College.

Apr. 7 Friday......Meeting of the Council of the Faculty of
                    Medicine.

Apr. 7 Friday......Meeting of the Council of the Faculty of
                    Applied Science and Engineering.

Apr. 10 Monday.....Meeting of the Council of the Faculty of
                    Arts.

Apr. 14 Friday......University Buildings closed.

Apr. 21 Friday......Meeting of Senate.

Apr. 21 Friday......Lectures in the Faculty of Arts end.

Apr. 24-28 Monday-Friday..Term Examinations.

May 1 Monday......Annual Examinations begin in the Faculties
                    Arts and Music and in the Departments
                    of Law, Pharmacy and Agriculture.

May 1 Monday....Last day for receiving applications for the
                    Alexander Mackenzie Fellowships in politi-
                    cal Science.

May 1 Monday.....Last day for receiving applications for the
                    June Examinations in the Faculty of Arts.

May 3 Wednesday..Meeting of the Faculty of Arts of Victoria
                    College.

May 4 Thursday....Meeting of the Finance and Executive Com-
                    mittee of Trinity College.

May 5 Friday......Meeting of University College Council.

May 5 Friday......Meeting of the Council of the Faculty of
                    Applied Science and Engineering.

May 5 Friday......Meeting of the Senate of Victoria College.

May 8 Monday.....Meeting of the Council of the Faculty of Arts.

May 8 Monday.... Annual Examinations in the Faculty of
                 Medicine begin.
May 12 Friday......Meeting of Senate.
May 15 Monday.....Last day for receiving applications from
                 candidates for Junior Matriculation
                 Scholarships.
May 24 Wednesday..University Buildings closed.
May 31 Wednesday..Session ends in the Faculty of Medicine.
June 1 Thursday....Last day for receiving applications for the
                 Alexander Mackenzie Fellowships in Politi-
                 cal Science.
June 5 Monday.....Meeting of the Council of the Faculty of
                 Arts.
June 7 Wednesday..Meeting of Senate.
June 7 Wednesday..Meeting of the Faculty of Arts of Victoria
June 8 Thursday....Meeting of the Finance and Executive Com-
                 mittee of Trinity College.
June 9 Friday......University Commencement.
June 20 Tuesday.....Senior Matriculation Examination begins.
July 1 Saturday....University Buildings closed.

University of Toronto

1920-1921

THE BOARD OF GOVERNORS

SIR EDMUND WALKER, C.V.O., D.C.L., LL.D., *Chairman*,
DONALD BRUCE MACDONALD, M.A., LL.D., *Vice-Chairman*.

Ex-officio

The Hon. SIR WILLIAM RALPH MEREDITH, LL.D., *Chancellor*,
SIR ROBERT ALEXANDER FALCONER, K.C.M.G., M.A. LL.D.,
D.Litt., *President*.

Retiring in 1920

JOHN HOSKIN, ESQ., K.C., LL.D.,
DANIEL MILLER, ESQ.,
His Honour COLIN GEORGE SNIDER, B.A.,
ALBERT EDWARD GOODERHAM, ESQ.,
SIR JOHN EATON.

Retiring in 1922

SIR EDMUND WALKER, C.V.O., D.C.L., LL.D.,
CHARLES VINCENT MASSEY, ESQ., M.A.,
The Rev. DONALD BRUCE MACDONALD, M.A., LL.D.,
EDWIN CANFIELD WHITNEY, ESQ.,
THOMAS ALEXANDER RUSSELL, ESQ., B.A.,
The Rev. HENRY JAMES CODY, M.A., D.D., LL.D.

Retiring in 1924

SIR EDMUND BOYD OSLER, M.P.,
SIR JOSEPH WESLEY FLAVELLE, BART., LL.D.,
The Rev. JAMES ALEXANDER MACDONALD, LL.D.,
The Hon. HUGH THOMAS KELLY,
REUBEN WELLS LEONARD, ESQ.,
The Hon. ROBERT ALLAN PYNE, M.D., LL.D.

Retiring in 1925

WILLIAM KERR GEORGE, ESQ.,
ROBERT HOME SMITH, ESQ.,
ERIC NORMAN ARMOUR, ESQ., B.A.,
ALEXANDER PIERREPONT DEROCHE, ESQ.

FERDINAND ALBERT MOURÉ, ESQ., BURSAR, *Secretary.*

—2

THE SENATE

Ex-officio Members.

THE HON. SIR WILLIAM RALPH MEREDITH, LL.D.,
> *Chancellor.*

SIR EDMUND WALKER, C.V.O., D.C.L., LL.D.,
> *Chairman of the Board of Governors.*

SIR ROBERT ALEXANDER FALCONER, K.C.M.G., M.A.,
LL.D., D.LITT.
> *President of the University.*

MAURICE HUTTON, M.A., LL.D.,
> *Principal of University College.*

REV. RICHARD PINCH BOWLES, M.A., D.D., LL.D.,
> *President of Victoria College.*

REV. THOMAS CLARK STREET MACKLEM, M.A., D.D., LL.D.,
> *Provost of Trinity College.*

REV. HENRY CARR, B.A.,
> *Superior of St. Michael's College.*

REV. ALFRED GANDIER, M.A., D.D., LL.D.,
> *Principal of Knox College.*

REV. THOMAS ROBERT O'MEARA, LL.D.,
> *Principal of Wycliffe College.*

ARTHUR PHILEMON COLEMAN, M.A., PH.D., F.R.S.,
> *Dean of the Faculty of Arts.*

ALEXANDER PRIMROSE, C.B., M.B., C.M.,
> *Dean of the Faculty of Medicine.*

CHARLES HAMILTON MITCHELL, C.B., C.M.G., D.S.O., C.E.,
LL.D.,
> *Dean of the Faculty of Applied Science and En-*
> *gineering.*

WILLIAM PAKENHAM, B.A., LL.D.,
> *Dean of the Ontario College of Education.*

CLIFTON DURANT HOWE, M.A., PH.D.,
> *Dean of the Faculty of Forestry.*

AUGUSTUS STEPHEN VOGT, MUS. DOC.,
> *Dean of the Faculty of Music.*

THE HON. SIR WILLIAM MULOCK, M.A., LL.D.,
> *Ex-Vice-Chancellor.*

Representatives of the Faculties.

Faculty of Arts of the University:
FRANCIS BARCLAY ALLAN, Ph.D.,
ANDREW JAMES BELL, M.A., Ph.D.,
BENJAMIN ARTHUR BENSLEY, B.A., Ph.D.,
THOMAS HURST BLACK, M.A., B.Sc., LL.B.,
GEORGE SIDNEY BRETT, M.A.,
MILTON ALEXANDER BUCHANAN, B.A., Ph.D.,
CLARENCE AUGUSTUS CHANT, M.A., Ph.D.,
CHARLES TRICK CURRELLY, M.A.,
JAMES ALFRED DALE, M.A.,
ALFRED TENNYSON DELURY, M.A.,
JOSEPH HORACE FAULL, B.A., Ph.D.,
JOHN CHARLES FIELDS, B.A., Ph.D., F.R.S.,
JAMES GIBSON HUME, M.A., Ph.D.,
ANDREW HUNTER, M.A., B.Sc., M.B., Ch.B.,
FRANK BOTELER KENRICK, M.A., Ph.D.,
WILLIAM ROBERT LANG, D.Sc.,
WILLAM JAMES LOUDON, B.A.,
MICHAEL ALEXANDER MACKENZIE, M.A.,
JOHN CUNNINGHAM McLENNAN, O.B.E., Ph.D., D.Sc.,
    LL.D., F.R.S.,
JOHN JAMES RICKARD MACLEOD, M.B., Ch.B.,
JAMES PLAYFAIR McMURRICH, M.A., Ph.D., LL.D.,
JAMES MAVOR, Ph.D.,
WILLIAM LASH·MILLER, B.A., Ph.D.,
WILLIAM ARTHUR PARKS, Ph.D.,
JAMES EUSTACE SHAW, A.B., Ph.D.,
THOMAS LEONARD WALKER, M.A., Ph.D.,
GEORGE McKINNON WRONG, M.A.

Faculty of Medicine:
IRVING HEWARD CAMERON, M.B., LL.D.,
DUNCAN ARCHIBALD LAMONT GRAHAM, M.B.,
JOHN JOSEPH MACKENZIE, B.A., M.B.,
BENJAMIN PHILP WATSON, M.D., Ch.B.
DAVID JAMES GIBB WISHART, B.A., M.D., C.M.

Faculty of Applied Science and Engineering:
ROBERT WILLIAM ANGUS, B.A.Sc.,
JAMES WATSON BAIN, B.A.Sc.,
HERBERT EDWARD TERRICK HAULTAIN, C.E.,
THOMAS REEVE ROSEBRUGH, M.A.,
CHARLES HENRY CHALLENOR WRIGHT, B.A.Sc.

Faculty of Household Science:
ANNIE LEWISA LAIRD, M.S.,
CLARA CYNTHIA BENSON, Ph.D.

Ontario College of Education:
  HENRY JOB CRAWFORD, B.A.,
  GEORGE MALLORY JONES, B.A.

Faculty of University College:
  SAINT-ELME DE CHAMP, B.ès L. O.I.P.,
  GEORGE HENRY NEEDLER, B.A., PH.D.,
  MALCOLM WILLIAM WALLACE, B.A., PH.D.

Faculty of Arts of Victoria College:
  VICTOR DE BEAUMONT, A.M.,
  OSCAR PELHAM EDGAR, B.A., PH.D.,
  JOHN CHARLES ROBERTSON, M.A.

Faculty of Arts of Trinity College:
  .REV. HENRY THOMAS FORBES DUCKWORTH, M.A.,
  WILLIAM ALEXANDER KIRKWOOD, M.A., PH.D.,
  ARCHIBALD HOPE YOUNG, M.A., D.C.L.,

Faculty of Arts of St. Michael's College:
  REV. FRANCIS GERALD POWELL,
  SIR BERTRAM COGHILL ALAN WINDLE, M.A., M.D., Sc.D.,
  LL.D., F.R.S.

Appointed Members.

ARTHUR LEOPOLD LANGFORD, M.A.,
  Representative of Victoria University.

THE RIGHT REV. JAMES FIELDING SWEENY, M.A., D.D., D.C.L.
  Representative of the University of Trinity College.

JOHN FRANCIS POWER, M.A.,
  Representative of St. Michael's College.

REV. JAMES BALLANTYNE, B.A., D.D.,
REV. GEORGE CAMPBELL PIDGEON, B.A., D.D.,
  Representatives of Knox College.

NEWMAN WRIGHT HOYLES, B.A., K.C., LL.D.,
JOHN DELATRE FALCONBRIDGE, M.A., LL.B.,
  . *Representatives of Wycliffe College.*

EDWARD DOUGLAS ARMOUR, K.C., D.C.L.,
  Representative of the Law Society of Upper Canada.

EDWARD NORCLIFFE BAKER, M.A., D.D.,
  Representative of Albert College, Belleville.

JOSEPH BENSON REYNOLDS, M.A.,
  Representative of the Ontario Agricultural College, Guelph.

WALLACE SECCOMBE, L.D.S., D.D.S.,
> *Representative of the Royal College of Dental Surgeons of Ontario.*

CHARLES FREDERICK HEEBNER, PHM.B.,
> *Representative of the Ontario College of Pharmacy.*

CHARLES DUNCAN McGILVRAY, V.S., M.D.V.,
> *Representative of the Ontario Veterinary College.*

Elected Members.

ALFRED BAKER, M.A., LL.D.,
JAMES HENRY COYNE. M.A., LL.D.,
GERTRUDE LAWLER, M.A.,
GEORGE GALLIE NASMITH, C.M.G., M.A., PH.D., D.SC., LL.D.,
RT. HON. LYMAN POORE DUFF, B.A., LL.B.,
JOHN MURRAY CLARK, M.A., LL.D.,
WILLIAM HOUSTON, M.A.,
WILLIAM NISBET PONTON, M.A., K.C.,
EDWIN AUSTIN HARDY, B.A., D.PAED.,
EDWARD ROBERT CAMERON, M.A.,
ADAM FORDYCE BARR, M.A.,
DUNCAN BROWN GILLIES, B.A.,
> *Representatives of the Graduates in Arts of University College.*

GEORGE HERBERT LOCKE, M.A., PH.D.,
THE HON. JOHN JAMES MACLAREN, M.A., LL.D.,
THE HON. CORNELIUS ARTHUR MASTEN, B.A., LL.D.,
MARY HURD SKINNER, B.A.,
JAMES RUSSELL LOVETT STARR, B.A., LL.B.,
> *Representatives of the Graduates in Arts of Victoria College.*

JOHN AUSTIN WORRELL, M.A., D.C.L.,
HENRY BROCK, D.C.L.,
GERARD BRAKENRIDGE STRATHY, M.A.,
CONSTANCE LAING, M.A.,
JOHN ALMON RITCHIE, B.A.,
> *Representatives of the Graduates in Arts of Trinity College.*

AUGUSTA STOWE GULLEN, M.D., C.M.,
CHARLES JOHN OLIVER HASTINGS, M.D.,
ARTHUR CLINTON HENDRICK, M.A., M.D.,
ANDREW SAMUEL MOORHEAD, B.A., M.B.,
> *Representatives of the Graduates in Medicine.*

THOMAS HENRY HOGG, B.A.Sc., C.E.,
JOHN JAMES TRAILL, B.A.Sc., C.E.,
> *Representatives of the Graduates in Applied Science and
> Engineering.*

THE HON. FEATHERSTON OSLER, D.C.L.,
THE HON. WILLIAM RENWICK RIDDELL, B.A., B.Sc., LL.D.,
> *Representatives of the Graduates in Law.*

THE HON. ERNEST CHARLES DRURY, B.S.A.,
TOWNSEND GARRETT RAYNOR, B.S.A.,
> *Representatives of the Graduates in Agriculture.*

WALTER NEHEMIAH BELL, B.A., D.PAED.,
ROBERT ALEXANDER GRAY, B.A.,
EDWARD WILLIAM HAGARTY, M.A.,
ARTHUR PRESLAND GUNDRY, B.A.,
> *Representatives of the Principals of Collegiate Institutes or High
> Schools or Assistants therein.*

OFFICERS OF INSTRUCTION.

1920-1921.

The members of the staff in the Faculty of Arts are indicated as follows: (*U.*) University of Toronto; (*C.*) University College; (*V.*) Victoria College; (*T.*) Trinity College; (*M.*) St. Michael's College.

Professores Emeriti.

ALLEN MACKENZIE BAINES, M.D., C.M.,
228 Bloor Street, West.

ALFRED.·BAKER, M.A., LL.D.,
81 Madison Avenue.

GEORGE HERBERT BURNHAM, M.D.,
128 Bloor Street West.

IRVING HEWARD CAMERON, M.B., LL.D., EDIN., F.R.C.S., ENG.,
EDIN., 307 Sherbourne Street.

REV. DANIEL CUSHING, LL.D.,
St. Michael's College.

BERNHARD EDUARD FERNOW, LL.D.,
16 Admiral Road.

FREDERICK LEMAITRE GRASETT, M.B., C.M.,
7 Forest Hill Road.

JAMES FREDERICK MCCURDY, PH.D., PRINCETON, LL.D., NEW BRUNS-
WICK, (*C.*) 106 South Drive,

ALEXANDER MCPHEDRAN, M.B., M.D., C.M., LL.D.,
151 Bloor Street, West.

HENRY THOMAS MACHELL, M.D.,
459 Avenue Road.

NEWTON ALBERT POWELL, M.D., C.M., M.D., BELLEVUE, N.Y.,
167 College Street.

REV. ALFRED HENRY REYNAR, M.A., LL.D., (*V.*)
Cobourg.

GEORGE STERLING RYERSON, M.D., C.M.,
Niagara-ou-the-Lake, Ontario.

JOHN SQUAIR, B.A.,
368 Palmerston Boulevard.

JAMES ALGERNON TEMPLE, M.D., C.M., LL.D.,
186 Warren Road.

William Henry van der Smissen, Ph.D., (C.)

15 Surrey Place.

Adam Henry Wright, B.A., M.D.,

30 Gerrard Street, East.

Robert Ramsay Wright, M.A., D.Sc., LL.D.,

Oxford, England.

Professors.

William John Alexander, B.A., Lond., Ph.D., Johns Hopkins, LL.D., Queen's,
    Professor of English, (C.)

155 Spadina Road.

Francis Barclay Allan, Ph.D.,
    Professor of Organic Chemistry, (U.)

380 Brunswick Avenue.

Harry Bertram Anderson, M.D., C.M.,
    Professor of Clinical Pathology,

184 Bloor Street, East.

Robert William Angus, B.A.Sc.,
    Professor of Mechanical Engineering,

42 Howland Avenue.

James Watson Bain, B.A.Sc.,
    Professor of Chemical Engineering,

393 Brunswick Avenue.

Nelson Henry Beemer, M.B.,
    Extra-Mural Professor of Mental Diseases,

The Asylum, Mimico.

Andrew James Bell, M.A., Ph.D., Breslau,
    Professor of Comparative Philology (U.) and John Macdonald Professor of the Latin Language and Literature, (V.)

17 Avenue Road.

Rev. Henry Stanislaus Bellisle, B.A., M.A., Cath. Univ. of America,
    Professor of Logic, (M.)

St. Michael's College.

Benjamin Arthur Bensley, B.A., Ph.D., Columbia,
    Professor of Zoology and Head of the Department of Biology, (U.)
37 Admiral Road.

Thomas Hirst Black, M.A., B.Sc., LL.B., Glasgow,
    Professor of Roman Law, (U.)

205 Roehampton Avenue.

George Sidney Brett, M.A., Oxon.,
    Professor of Philosophy, (U.) and Professor of Ethics and Ancient. Philosophy, (T.)

127 Albany Avenue.

Milton Alexander Buchanan, B.A., Ph.D., Chicago,
    Professor of Italian and Spanish, (U.)

75 Heathdale Road.

JOHN HOME CAMERON, M.A.,
  Professor of French, (C.)

  96 Admiral Road.

REV. HENRY CARR, B.A.,
  Professor of Greek and of History of Philosophy, (M.)

  St. Michael's College.

ADAM CARRUTHERS, M.A.,
  Professor of Greek Literature and Archaeology, (C.)

  603 Huron Street.

CLARENCE AUGUSTUS CHANT, M.A., PH.D., HARVARD,
  Professor of Astrophysics, (U.)

  201 Madison Avenue.

CHARLES KIRK CLARKE, M.D., LL.D.,
  *Professor of Psychiatry and Director of the Psychological Depart-
    ment*, 34 Roxborough Street, East.

ARTHUR PHILEMON COLEMAN, M.A., PH.D., BRESLAU, F.R.S.,
  Professor of Geology, (U.)

  476 Huron Street.

REV. FRANCIS HERBERT COSGRAVE, M.A., TRIN. COLL. DUBLIN, B.D.,
  Professor of Hebrew, (T.)

  Trinity College.

JAMES ALEXANDER CRAIG, M.A., McGILL, B.D., YALE, PH.D., LEIPZIG,
  Professor of Oriental Languages, (C.)

  6 Glenholme Avenue.

HENRY JOB CRAWFORD, B.A.,
  Professor of Methods in Classics in the College of Education,

  310 Roncesvalles Avenue.

CHARLES TRICK CURRELLY, M.A.,
  Professor of the History of Industrial Art, (U.)

  Wychwood Park.

JAMES ALFRED DALE, M.A. OXON.,
  Professor of Social Science,

  597 Huron Street.

ALFRED TENNYSON DeLURY, M.A.,
  Professor of Mathematics, (U.)

  University of Toronto.

NORMAN WENTWORTH DeWITT, B.A., PH.D., CHICAGO,
  Professor of Latin Literature, (V.)

  108 Bernard Avenue.

MAURICE DE WULF, M.A., PH.D., LL.D., LOUVAIN,
  Member of the Royal Academy of Belgium and Madrid,
    Professor of Mediaeval Philosophy, (M.)

  St. Michael's College.

REV. HENRY THOMAS FORBES DUCKWORTH, M.A., OXON.,
  Professor of Ancient History, (T.)

  234 Crawford Street.

OSCAR PELHAM EDGAR, B.A., PH.D., JOHNS HOPKINS,
William Gooderham Professor of English, (V.)
286 St. George Street.

JOSEPH HORACE FAULL, B.A., PH.D., HARVARD,
Professor of Botany, (U.)
102 Yorkville Avenue.

JOHN CHARLES FIELDS, B.A., PH.D., JOHNS HOPKINS, F.R.S.,
Professor of Mathematics, (U.)
310 Huron Street.

JOHN GERALD FITZGERALD, M.B.,
*Professor of Hygiene and Director of the Connaught Antitoxin
Laboratory,*
186 Balmoral Avenue.

HARRY EGERTON FORD, M.A.,
Eliza Gooderham Professor of French, (V.)
131 Balmoral Avenue.

PETER GILLESPIE, B.A.Sc., C.E., M.Sc.,
Professor of Applied Mechanics,
358 Davenport Road.

DUNCAN ARCHIBALD LAMONT GRAHAM, M.B.,
Professor of Medicine and Clinical Medicine,
Alexandra Apartments, University Avenue.

GEORGE ARTHUR GUESS, M.A., QUEEN'S,
Professor of Metallurgy,
142 Spadina Road.

VICTOR JOHN HARDING, D.Sc., MANCHESTER,
Professor of Chemical Pathology,
Pathology Building, University of Toronto.

HERBERT EDWARD TERRICK HAULTAIN, C.E.,
Professor of Mining Engineering,
50 St. George Street.

VELYIEN EWART HENDERSON, M.A., M.B.,
Professor of Pharmacy,
111 Admiral Road.

SAMUEL HENRY HOOKE, M.A., OXON., B.D., LOND.,
J. W. Flavelle Professor of Oriental Languages and Literature, (V.)
20 Highview Crescent.

LEWIS EMERSON HORNING, B.A., PH.D., GÖTTINGEN,
Professor of Teutonic Philology, (V.)
31 Woodlawn Avenue, West.

CLIFTON DURANT HOWE, M.S., VERMONT, PH.D., CHICAGO,
Professor of Forestry,
66 Tranby Avenue.

JAMES GIBSON HUME, B.A., A.M., HARVARD, PH.D., FREIBURG, BADEN,
Professor of History of Philosophy, (U.)
58 Spadina Road.

ANDREW HUNTER, M.A., B.Sc., M.B., CH.B., EDIN.,
  Professor of Biochemistry, (U.)

                                           89 St. Joseph Street.

MAURICE HUTTON, M.A., OXON., LL.D.,
  Professor of Greek, (C.)

                                           50 Prince Arthur Avenue.

REV. ALFRED JOHN JOHNSTON, B.A.,
  Professor of Church History, (V.)

                                           110 Albertus Avenue.

WILLIAM PAUL MCCLURE KENNEDY, M.A., DUBLIN, OXON., LITT.D.,
  DUBLIN,
  Professor of English, (M.)

                                           110 Quebec Avenue.

FRANK BOTELER KENRICK, M.A., PH.D., LEIPZIG,
  Professor of Chemistry, (U.)

                                           77 Lonsdale Road.

DAVID REID KEYS, M.A.,
  Professor of Anglo-Saxon, (C.)

                                           87 Avenue Road.

WILLIAM ALEXANDER KIRKWOOD, M.A., PH.D., HARVARD,
  Professor of Latin, (T.)

                                           Trinity College.

RUPERT EARLE LORING KITTREDGE, M.A., HARVARD,
  Professor of French, (T.)

                                           Trinity College.

WILMOT BURKMAR LANE, M.A., PH.D., WISCONSIN,
  Ryerson Professor of Ethics, (V.)

                                           25 Dorval Road.

AUGUSTUS EDWARD LANG, M.A.,
  Professor of the German Language and Literature, (V.)

                                           104 Spadina Road.

WILLIAM ROBERT LANG, D.SC., GLASGOW,
  Professor of Chemistry, (U.) and Director of Military Studies,
                                           55 Woodlawn Avenue, West.

ARTHUR LEOPOLD LANGFORD, M.A.,
  Professor of the Greek Language and Literature, (V.)
                                           119 Farnham Avenue.

WILLIAM JAMES LOUDON, B.A.,
  Professor of Mechanics, (U.)

                                           Cooksville.

REV. ROBERT MCBRADY,
  Professor of Latin and of French, (M.)

                                           St. Michael's College.

JAMES METCALFE MACCALLUM, B.A., M.D.,
. *Professor of Ophthalmology,*

13 Bloor Street, West.

REV. EDMUND JOSEPH MCCORKELL, B.A., M.A., CATH. UNIV. OF AMERICA
Professor of Social Ethics, (M.)

St. Michael's College.

JOHN MCGOWAN, B.A., B.A.SC.,
Professor of Applied Mechanics,

Engineering Building, University of Toronto.

JOHN JOSEPH MACKENZIE, B.A., M.B.,
*Professor of Pathology and Bacteriology and Curator of the Patho-
logical Museum and Laboratories.*

56 Wychwood Park.

MICHAEL ALEXANDER MACKENZIE, M.A., M.A., CANTAB.,
Professor of Mathematics, (U.)

1 Bellwoods Park.

REV. JOHN FLETCHER MCLAUGHLIN, B.A., D.D., VIC.,
*Eliza Phelps Massey Professor of Oriental Languages and
Literature,* (V.)

58 Roxborough Street, West.

JOHN CUNNINGHAM MCLENNAN., O.B.E., PH.D.; D.SC., MANCHESTER.
LL.D., F.R.S.,
Professor of Physics, (U.)

88 Prince Arthur Avenue.

JOHN JAMES RICKARD MACLEOD, M.B., CH.B., ABERDEEN, D.P.H.,
CAMBRIDGE.
Professor of Physiology, (U.)

45 Nanton Avenue.

JAMES PLAYFAIR MCMURRICH, M.A., PH.D., JOHNS HOPKINS, LL.D.,
MICHIGAN,
Professor of Anatomy, (U.) *and Director of the Anatomical Depart-
ment,*

75 Forest Hill Road.

JOHN MACNAUGHTON, M.A., LL.D., QUEEN'S,
Professor of Latin, (C.)

10 Poplar Plains Crescent

JAMES MAVOR, PH.D.,
Professor of Political Economy, (U.)

145 Isabella Street.

WILLIAM LASH MILLER, B.A., PH.D., MUNICH,
Professor of Physical Chemistry, (U.)

50 St. Albans Street.

WILLIAM STAFFORD MILNER, M.A.,
Professor of Greek and Roman History, (C.)

74 Grenville Street.

GEORGE HENRY NEEDLER, B.A., PH.D., LEIPZIG,
Professor of German, (C.)

103 Bedford Road.

MICHAEL JOSEPH OLIVER, B.A., PH.M., CATH. UNIV. OF AMERICA,
Professor of Psychology, (M.)

St. Michael's College.

ERIC TREVOR OWEN, M.A.,
Professor of Greek, (T.)

49 Alcina Avenue.

WILLIAM PAKENHAM, B.A., LL.D..
Professor of the History and Science of Education,

106 Spadina Road.

WILLIAM ARTHUR PARKS, PH.D.,
Professor of Palaeontology, (U.)

69 Albany Avenue.

REV. FRANCIS GERALD POWELL,
Professor of Metaphysics and Logic, (M.)

St. Michael's College.

HAROLD WILBERFORCE PRICE, B.A.SC.,
Professor of Electrical Engineering,

474 Palmerston Boulevard.

ALEXANDER PRIMROSE, C.B., M.B., C.M., EDIN.,
Professor of Clinical Surgery,

100 College Street.

JOHN CHARLES ROBERTSON, M.A.,
W. E. H. Massey Professor of the Greek Language and Philosophy, (V.)

409 Brunswick Avenue.

THOMAS REEVE ROSEBRUGH, M.A.,
Professor of Electrical Engineering,

92 Walmer Road.

ROBERT DAWSON RUDOLF, C.B.E., M.D., C.M., EDIN.,
Professor of Therapeutics,

100 College Street.

PETER SANDIFORD, M.SC., MANCHESTER, PH.D., COLUMBIA,
Professor of Educational Psychology,

22 Hilton Avenue.

JAMES EUSTACE SHAW, A.B., PH.D., JOHNS HOPKINS,
Professor of Italian and Spanish, (U.)

75 Walmer Road.

GIDEON SILVERTHORN, M.B.,
Professor of Medical Jurisprudence,

266 College Street.

HERBERT CLAYTON SIMPSON, B.A., OXON., M.A., TOR., HARVARD,
· *Professor of English Literature,* (*T.*)

635 Huron Street.

CHARLES BRUCE SISSONS, B.A.,
Nelles Professor of Ancient History, (*V.*)

110 Farnham Avenue.

LOUIS BEAUFORT STEWART,
Professor of Surveying and Geodesy,

161 Admiral Road.

WILLIAM ROBERT TAYLOR, PH.D.,
Professor of Oriental Languages, (*C.*)

221 Stibbard Avenue.

FREDERICK TRACEY, B.A., PH.D., CLARK,
Professor of Ethics, (*C.*)

173 Walmer Road.

THOMAS LEONARD WALKER, M.A., QUEEN'S, PH.D., LEIPZIG,
Professor of Mineralogy, (*U.*)

20 Avondale Avenue.

MALCOLM WILLIAM WALLACE, B.A., PH.D., CHICAGO,
Professor of English, (*C.*)

91 Walmer Road.

REV. JOSEPH BASIL WALSH, M.A.,
Professor of Religious Knowledge, (*M.*)

St. Michael's College.

BENJAMIN PHILP WATSON, M.D., CH.B., EDIN., F.R.C.S., EDIN.,
Professor of Obstetrics and Gynaecology,

100 College Street.

JOSEPH STANLEY WILL,·B.A.,
Professor of French, (*C.*)

56 Ranleigh Avenue.

SIR BERTRAM COGHILL ALAN WINDLE, M.A., M.D., DUBLIN, SC.D.,
LL.D., BIRMINGHAM, F.R.S.,
Professor of Anthropology, (*M.*)

St. Michael's College.

DAVID JAMES GIBB WISHART, B.A., M.D., C.M., TOR., MCGILL,
Professor of Oto-Laryngology,

47 Grosvenor Street.

JOHN NEVILLE WOODCOCK, M.A., OXON.,
Professor of Latin, (*T.*)

220 Glen Road.

CHARLES HENRY CHALLENOR WRIGHT, B.A.SC.,
Professor of Architecture and of Drawing,

419 Markham Street.

GEORGE MCKINNON WRONG, M.A.,
Professor of History and Ethnology, (U.)
73 Walmer Road.

ARCHIBALD HOPE YOUNG, M.A., D.C.L., KING'S COLLEGE,
. Professor of German, (T.)
Trinity College.

Associate Professors

GEORGE R. ANDERSON, M.A., A.M ,. HARVARD,
Associate Professor of Engineering Physics and Photography,
72 Isabella Street.

HARRY BERTRAM ANDERSON, M.D., C.M.,
Associate Professor of Clinical Medicine,
184 Bloor Street, East.

EDWARD GOWAN RUSSELL ARDAGH, B.A.Sc.,
Associate Professor of Analytical Chemistry,
34 Sussex Avenue.

CHARLES EARL AUGER, B.A.,
Associate Professor of English, (V.)
70 Farnham Avenue.

SAMUEL BEATTY, M.A., PH.D.,
Associate Professor of Mathematics, (U.)
537 Markham Street.

MISS CLARA CYNTHIA BENSON, PH.D.,
Associate Professor of Physiological Chemistry,
157 Bloor Street, West.

ADRIAN BERRINGTON,
Associate Professor of Architecture,
66 Charles Street West.

GEORGE ARTHUR BINGHAM, M.B., M.D., C.M.,
Associate Professor of Clinical Surgery and Clinical Anatomy,
68 Isabella Street.

MAITLAND CREASE BOSWELL, B.A.Sc., M.A., HARVARD, PH.D.,
Associate Professor of Organic Chemistry,
Mining Building, University of Toronto.

ALAN GOWANS BROWN, M.B.,
Associate Professor of Medicine in Charge of Pediatrics,
423 Avenue Road.

WALTER THEODORE BROWN, M.A., PH.D., HARVARD,
Associate Professor of Ethics, (V.)
398 Eglinton Avenue, West.

HERBERT ALEXANDER BRUCE, M.D., F.R.C.S., ENG.,
Associate Professor of Clinical Surgery,
64 Bloor Street, East.

ELI FRANKLIN BURTON, B.A., CANTAB., PH.D.,
    Associate Professor of Physics, (U.)

                                      Weston.

GRAHAM CHAMBERS, B.A., M.B.,
    Associate Professor of Clinical Medicine,

                    26 Gerrard Street, East.

JAMES ROY COCKBURN, M.C., B.A.Sc.,
    Associate Professor of Descriptive Geometry,

                    100 Walmer Road.

VICTOR DE BEAUMONT, A.M., COLUMBIA,
    Associate Professor of the French Language and Literature, (V.)
              Cotswold Court, 164 Cumberland Street.

SAINT-ELME DE CHAMP, B ÈS L., LYONS, O.I.P.,
    Associate Professor of French, (C.)

                    22 Chestnut Park.

BARKER FAIRLEY, M.A., LEEDS, PH.D., JENA,
    Associate Professor of German, (C.)

                    22 Kendal Avenue.

JOHN BRIGHT FERGUSON, B.A.,
    Associate Professor of Chemistry, (U.)

                  10 Brunswick Avenue.

RALPH FLENLEY, M.A., LIVERPOOL, B.LITT., OXON.,
    Associate Professor of History, (U.)

                393 St. Clarens Avenue.

JOHN TAYLOR FOTHERINGHAM, C.M.G., B.A., M.B., M.D., C.M., LL.D.,
        QUEEN'S, TOR.,
    Associate Professor of Medicine and Clinical Medicine,
                  20 Wellesley Street.

WILLIAM GOLDIE, M.B.,
    Associate Professor of Clinical Medicine,

                  86 College Street.

PERRY GLADSTONE GOLDSMITH, C.B.E., M.D., C.M.,
    Associate Professor in Laryngology,

                  84 Carlton Street.

STEPHEN MOFFAT HAY, M.D.,
    Associate Professor of Clinical Surgery,

                  2 Spadina Road.

WILLIAM BELFRY HENDRY, D.S.O., B.A., M.B.,
    Associate Professor of Obstetrics and Gynaecology,

                154 Walmer Road.

ARCHIBALD GOWANLOCK HUNTSMAN, B.A., M.B.,
    Associate Professor of Marine Biology, (U.)

                347 Indian Road.

ROBERT STRACHAN KNOX, M.A., ABERDEEN, B.A., OXON.,
    Associate Professor of English, (C.)

                40 Willcocks Street.

MISS ANNIE LEWISA LAIRD, M.S., DREXEL,
  Associate Professor of Household Science,
                                             157 Bloor Street, West.

THOMAS RICHARDSON LOUDON, B.A.SC.,
  Associate Professor of Ferro-Metallurgy,
                                         189 Sheldrake Boulevard.

ARTHUR WELLESLEY MCCONNELL, B.A.SC.,
  Associate Professor of Architecture,
                                          36 Prince Arthur Avenue.

REV. EDMUND JOSEPH MCCORKELL, B.A., M.A., CATH. UNIV. OF AMERICA,
  Associate Professor of English, (M.)
                                             St. Michael's College.

KENNEDY CRAWFORD MCILWRAITH, M.B.,
  Associate Professor of Obstetrics,
                                          30 Prince Arthur Avenue.

ROBERT MORRISON MACIVER, B.A., OXON., M.A., D.PHIL., EDIN.,
  Associate Professor of Political Economy, (U.)
                                           38 Humberside Avenue.

PATRICK WALTER HUGHES MCKEOWN, C.B.E., B.A., M.B.,
  Associate Professor of Clinical Surgery,
              Corner Wellesley Street and Wellesley Place.

FREDERICK WILLIAM MARLOW, M.D., C.M., F.R.C.S., ENG.,
  Associate Professor of Gynaecology,
                                             417 Bloor Street, West.

REV. JOHN HUGH MICHAEL, M.A., WALES,
  Associate Professor of Religious Knowledge, (V.)
                                                127 Hilton Avenue.

WILLIS NORMAN MILLAR, B.SC., PENN., M.F., YALE,
  Associate Professor of Forestry,
                                               110 Pricefield Road.

REV. VINCENT JOSEPH MURPHY,
  Associate Professor of Latin, (M.)
                                             St. Michael's College.

MICHAEL JOSEPH OLIVER, B.A., PH.M., CATH. UNIV. OF AMERICA,
  Associate Professor of German, (M.)
                                             St. Michael's College.

ARTHUR LEONARD PARSONS, B.A., NEW YORK,
  Associate Professor of Mineralogy, (U).
                                             47 St. Vincent Street.

WILLIAM HUNTER PIERSOL, B.A., M.B.,
  Associate Professor of Histology and Embryology, (U.)
                                                35 Dunvegan Road.

WILLIAM ARTHUR POTTER, M.A., B.D.,
  Associate Professor of Oriental Languages and Literature, (V.)
                                         244 Sheldrake Boulevard.

—3

REV. FRANCIS GERALD POWELL,
   Associate Professor of Latin, (M.)

            St. Michael's College.

GILBERT ROYCE, B.A., M.B.,
   Associate Professor of Oto-Laryngology,

            100 College Street.

GEORGE MALCOLM SMITH, M.C., B.A., M.A., OXON.,
   Associate Professor of History, (U.)

            North House, Victoria College.

GEORGE OSWALD SMITH, M.A., OXON.,
   Associate Professor of Latin, (C.)

            229 Crawford Street.

WILLIAM GEORGE SMITH, B.A.,
   Associate Professor of Psychology, (U.)

            177 Westmoreland Avenue.

HORACE BRADBURY SPEAKMAN, M.SC., MANCHESTER,
   Associate Professor of Zymology, (U.)

            Scadding House, 6 Trinity Square.

CLARENCE LESLIE STARR, M.B., M.D., BELLEVUE, N.Y.,
   Associate Professor of Clinical Surgery in charge of Orthopaedics,

            224 Bloor Street, West.

FREDERICK NEWTON GISBORNE STARR, C.B.E., M.B.,
   Associate Professor of Clinical Surgery,

            112 College Street.

WILLIAM BROWN THISTLE, M.D.,
   Associate Professor of Clinical Medicine,

            171 College Street.

ROBERT BOYD THOMSON, B.A.,
   Associate Professor of Botany, (U.)

            586 Spadina Avenue.

WILLIAM MANTON TREADGOLD, B.A.,
   Associate Professor of Surveying,

            13 Woodlawn Avenue, East.

EDMUND MURTON WALKER, B.A., M.B.,
   Associate Professor of Biology, (U.)

            67 Alcina Avenue.

HARDOLPH WASTENEYS, PH.D., COLUMBIA,
   Associate Professor of Biochemistry,

            20 Howland Avenue.

JAMES HERBERT WHITE, M.A., B.SC.F., PH.D.,
   Associate Professor of Forestry,

            75 Browning Avenue.

RALPH HODDER WILLIAMS, M.C., M.A., OXON., A.M., COLUMBIA,
   Associate Professor of History, (U.)

            9 Rowanwood Avenue.

CLARENCE RICHARD YOUNG, B.A.Sc., C.E.,
  Associate Professor of Applied Mechanics,
  98 Hilton Avenue.

Assistant Professors.

EDWARD ALEXANDER BOTT, B.A.,
  Assistant Professor of Psychology, (U.)
  57 Sussex Avenue.

ALEXANDER GRANT BROWN, B.A., M.A., OXON.,
  Assistant Professor of Ancient History, (C.)
  596 Huron Street.

JAMES TRESAWNA BURT-GERRANS, PHM.B., M.A.,
  Assistant Professor in Electro-Chemistry, (U.)
  46 Dewson Street.

WILLIAM HALL CLAWSON, B.A., NEW BRUNSWICK, M.A., PH.D., HARVARD,
  Assistant Professor of English, (C.)
  96 Oakwood Avenue.

WILBERT AMIE CLEMENS, M.A., PH.D., CORNELL,
  Assistant Professor in Elementary Biology, (U.)
  215 Davenport Road.

CHARLES NORRIS COCHRANE, B.A., M.A., OXON.,
  Assistant Professor of Ancient History, (C.)
  Ainger Apartments, Bloor Street, East.

FREDERICK ETHBERT COOMBS, M.A.,
  Assistant Professor of Methods in Elementary Subjects in the College of Education,
  158 Delaware Avenue.

GEORGE AUGUSTUS CORNISH, B.A.,
  Assistant Professor of Methods in Science in the College of Education,
  38 St. Clair Avenue, East.

ALAN FREETH COVENTRY, B.A., OXON.,
  Assistant Professor of Vertebrate Embryology, (U.)
  Hart House, University of Toronto.

JOHN THOMAS CRAWFORD, B.A.,
  Assistant Professor of Methods in Mathematics in the College of Education,
  168 Walmer Road.

SAMUEL RUTHERFORD CRERAR, B.A.Sc.,
  Assistant Professor of Surveying,
  122 Grenadier Road.

ERNEST ABELL DALE, M.A., OXON.,
  Assistant Professor of Latin, (C.)
  576 Huron Street.

ROBERT DAVIES DEFRIES, M.D.,
  Assistant Professor of Hygiene,
  135 Collier Street.

DAVID DUFF, M.A., B.D., EDIN.,
  Assistant Professor of Latin, (C.)

85 Woodlawn Avenue, West.

FREDERICK CHARLES DYER, B.A.SC.,
  Assistant Professor of Mining Engineering,

233 Ashworth Avenue.

WILLIAM CHALMERS FERGUSON, B.A.,
  Assistant Professor of Methods in French and German in the College of Education,

6 Hilton Avenue.

LACHLAN GILCHRIST, M.A., PH.D., CHICAGO,
  Assistant Professor of Physics, (U.)

North House, University of Toronto.

EMILIO GOGGIO, A.B., HARVARD, M.A., TOR., PH.D., HARVARD,
  Assistant Professor of Italian and Spanish, (U.)

77 Asquith Avenue.

THURE HEDMAN, PH.B., CHICAGO,
  Assistant Professor of German, (C.)

41 Glenholme Avenue.

WILLIAM JACKMAN, M.A.,
  Assistant Professor of Political Economy, (U.)

14 Roslin Avenue.

GILBERT EDWARD JACKSON, B.A., CANTAB.,
  Assistant Professor of Economics, (U.)

Hart House, University of Toronto.

FRANÇOIS CHARLES ARCHILE JEANNERET, B.A.,
  Assistant Professor of French, (C.)

70 St. Albans Street.

GEORGE MALLORY JONES, B.A.,
  Assistant Professor of Methods in English in the College of Education,

780 Keele Street.

WILLIAM PAUL MCCLURE KENNEDY, M.A., DUBLIN, OXON., LITT.D., DUBLIN,
  Assistant Professor in History, (U.)

110 Quebec Avenue.

ALBERT THOMAS LAING, B.A.SC.,
  Assistant Professor of Applied Mechanics,

146 Balmoral Avenue.

ALEXANDER MACLEAN, B.A.,
  Assistant Professor of Geology, (U.)

22 Havelock Street.

WALTER ERNEST MACPHERSON, B.A., LL.B., QUEENS,
  Assistant Professor in the Ontario College of Education,

98 Moore Avenue.

HENRY ALLEN MCTAGGART, M.A., B.A., CANTAB.,
Assistant Professor of Physics, (U.)
397 Huron Street.

HUGH BETHUNE MAITLAND, M.B.,
Assistant Professor of Pathology and Bacteriology,
54 Simpson Avenue.

MARCEL MORAUD, B. ès L., LIC ès L.,
Assistant Professor of French, (C.)
321 Roehampton Avenue.

MISS LAURA LAVINIA OCKLEY, B.A.,
Assistant Professor of Household Science,
50 Rosemount Avenue.

JAMES MONTROSE DUNCAN OLMSTED, M.A., OXON., PH.D., HARVARD,
Assistant Professor of Physiology, (U.)
55a East House, University Residence.

JOHN HAMILTON PARKIN, B.A.SC., M.E.,
Assistant Professor of Hydraulics,
10 Columbus Avenue.

IRVINE RUDSDALE POUNDER, M.A.,
Assistant Professor of Mathematics, (U.)
Apt. 7, 399 Dupont Street.

THOMAS RUTHERFORD ROBINSON, PH.D.,
Assistant Professor of Philosophy, (U.)
464 Indian Road.

LINNAEUS JOSLYN ROGERS, B.A.SC.,
Assistant Professor of Chemistry, (U.)
29 Rosemount Avenue.

JOHN SATTERLEY, M.A., CANTAB., D.SC., LOND.,
Assistant Professor of Physics, (U.)
269 Davenport Road.

NOBLE CARMAN SHARPE, B.A., M.B.,
Assistant Professor of Pharmacology,
102 St. Leonard's Avenue.

HAROLD BOYD SIFTON, M.A.,
Assistant Professor of Research in Botany,
10 Rathnally Avenue.

JOHN LIGHTON SYNGE, B.A., DUBLIN,
Assistant Professor of Mathematics, (U.)
26 St. Mary's Street.

JAMES CRAWFORD WATT, M.A., M.D.,
Assistant Professor of Anatomy,
20 Hawthorne Avenue.

WILLIAM DUDLEY WOODHEAD, B.A., OXON., M.A., ALBERTA, PH.D.,
CHICAGO,
Assistant Professor of Greek, (C.)
138 St. Clements Avenue.

Lecturers and Associates.

CLYDE STEWART ADAMS, B.A., M.Sc.,
Lecturer in Applied Chemistry,
320 Bloor Street, West.

SINCLAIR MACLARDY ADAMS, M.A.,
Lecturer in Classics, (T.)
Trinity College.

MISS MARGARET ELEANOR THEODORA ADDISON, B.A.,
Lecturer in German, (V.)
Annesley Hall.

S. M. AGNES, B.A.,
Lecturer in French, (M.)
St. Joseph's College.

RUTH MARGARET AGNEW, B.A.,
Lecturer in English, (M.)
12 Tennis Crescent.

WESLEY AUSTIN,
Lecturer in Metallurgical Chemistry and Mining Engineering.
Engineering Building, University of Toronto.

WILLIAM HAROLD TREVORROW BAILLIE, M.A., M.B.,
Lecturer in Mammalian Anatomy,
53 Boon Avenue.

JOHN LISNEY BANKS,
Lecturer in Modelling,
178 Kingston Road.

ERNEST WALDEMAR BANTING, B.A.Sc.,
Lecturer in Surveying,
101 Farnham Avenue.

STEWART GORDON BENNETT, M.C., B.A.Sc.,
Lecturer in Commercial Engineering,
16 Howland Avenue.

MISS LUCY BROOKING,
Lecturer in the Department of Social Service,
Alexandria Industrial School.

NORMAN BURNETTE,
Lecturer in the Department of Social Service,
50 Standish Avenue.

MISS MABEL CARTWRIGHT, B.A.,
Lecturer in English, (T.)
St. Hilda's College.

MISS ALINE CHALUFOUR,
Lecturer in French, (C.)
84 St. George Street.

HARVEY CLARE,
Associate in Psychiatry,

183 Geoffrey Street.

FREDERICK ADAM CLELAND, B.A., M.B.,
Associate in Gynaecology,

131 Bloor Street, West.

ERIC CLARKE, M.B.,
Lecturer in the Department of Social Service,

34 Roxborough Street, East.

ARTHUR ROGER CLUTE, B.A., LL.B.,
Lecturer in Constitutional Law, (U.) and Lecturer in Corporation Law and Limited Liability Companies in the Faculty of Applied Science and Engineering,

47 Elgin Avenue.

WILLIAM ANDREW COOK, M.A.,
Lecturer in Phychology, (U.)

39 Head Street, Hamilton.

EDWARD HORNE CRAIGIE, B.A., PH.D.,
Lecturer in Comparative Anatomy, (U.)

40 Leopold Street.

NORMAN PERCIVAL FREDERICK DEATH, B.A.SC.,
Special Lecturer in Mechanical Engineering,

224 Pearson Avenue.

VICTOR DE BEAUMONT, A.M., COLUMBIA,
Special Lecturer in French, (T.)

Cotswold Court, 164 Cumberland Street.

REV. CHARLES PATRICK DONOVAN, B.A.,
Lecturer in Ethics, (M.)

St. Michael's College.

GEORGE HENRY DUFF, M.A.,
Lecturer in Botany, (U.)

South House, University of Toronto.

MRS. LORRIE ALFREDA DUNINGTON-GRUBB,
Lecturer in the Department of Social Service,

University of Toronto.

JOHN RICHARDSON DYMOND, M.A.,
Lecturer in Systematic Vertebrate Zoology, (U.)

307 Dupont Street.

WELLESLEY DORLAND EVANS, B.A.,
Lecturer in French, (C.)

545 Lansdowne Avenue.

WALTER SCOTT FERGUSON,
Lecturer in Accounting, (U.)

52 Tranby Avenue.

JAMES MOFFATT FORSTER, M.D.,
Associate in Psychiatry,

573 Huron Street.

HAROLD WILLIAM ALEXANDER FOSTER,
Lecturer in Commercial and International Law, (*U.*)

100 Bedford Road.

DONALD THOMAS FRASER, B.A., M.B.,
Lecturer in Hygiene,

York Mills.

HERBERT AUSTIN FRICKER, M.A., LEEDS, MUS. BAC.,
Lecturer in Choral and Orchestral Music,

12 Braemar Apartments, Wellesley Crescent.

WILLIAM STANLEY FUNNELL, M.A.,
Lecturer in Chemistry, (*U.*)

348 Davenport Road.

WILLIAM EDWARD GALLIE, M.B.,
Associate in Surgery,

143 College Street.

WALTER SCOTT GUEST, B.A.SC.,
Lecturer in Electrical Engineering,

30 McMaster Avenue.

ALBERT HAM, MUS. DOC.,
Lecturer in Church Music,

561 Jarvis Street.

MISS EVELYN MARION HICKMANS, M.SC., BIRMINGHAM,
Lecturer in Household Science,

Department of Household Science, University of Toronto.

MISS HANNAH HILL, B.S., COLUMBIA,
Lecturer in Household Science,

47 Avenue Road.

LLOYD CLIFFORD ARNOTT HODGINS, M.A., HARVARD,
Lecturer in English, (*T.*)

Trinity College.

MISS ANNIE FRANCES HODGKINS,
Lecturer in the Department of Social Service,

21 Carlton Street.

GEOFFREY ELWOOD HOLT, M.A., MUS. BAC.,
Lecturer in German, (*C.*)

280 Bloor Street, West.

SAMUEL HENRY HOOKE, M.A., OXON., B.D., LOND.,
Special Lecturer in History, (*U.*)

20 Highview Crescent.

HAROLD ADAMS INNES, M.A., MCMASTER, PH.D., CHICAGO,
Lecturer in Political Economy, (*U.*)

102 St. Vincent Street.

WILLIAM ANDREW IRWIN, M.A., D.B., CHICAGO,
Lecturer in Oriental Languages, (C.)

74 Ellsworth Avenue.

CHARLES WILLIAM JEFFERYS,
Lecturer in Freehand Drawing,

York Mills.

WILLIAM WARNER JONES, B.A., M.B., F.R.C.S., ENG.,
Associate in Clinical Surgery,

41 Avenue Road.

HUBERT RICHMOND KEMP, M.A.,
Lecturer in Economics, (U.)

Central Y.M.C.A.

JAMES THOMAS DYER KING, B.A.Sc.,
Lecturer in Mining Engineering,

60 Ashburnham Road.

JAMES ALEXANDER KINNEAR, M.D., C.M.,
Associate in Obstetrics,

267 Russell Hill Road.

F. H. KIRKPATRICK,
Lecturer in Public Speaking,

34 Admiral Road.

ALEXANDER LACEY, M.A.,
Lecturer in French, (V.)

96 Hogarth Avenue.

JOHN WOOD MACARTHUR, A.B., OBERLIN, M.A., WABASH,
Lecturer in Experimental Biology, (U.)

319 Roehampton Avenue.

VINCENT ARTHUR MCDONOUGH, M.B.,
Lecturer in Psychology, (M.)

714 Dovercourt Road.

HERBERT SUTHERLAND MCKELLAR, B.A.,
Lecturer in French, (C.)

111 Sherwood Avenue.

REV. THOMAS CLARK STREET MACKLEM, B.A., CANTAB., M.A., D.D.,
TRIN., LL.D., TOR., NEW BRUNSWICK, D.C.L., LENNOXVILLE.
Lecturer in English Bible, (T.)

Trinity College.

HENRY HARRISON MADILL, B.A.Sc.,
Lecturer in Architecture,

88 Woodlawn Avenue, West.

M. M. MARGARITA, B.A.,
Lecturer in English, (M.)

Loretto Abbey College.

HERBERT MARSHALL, B.A.,
Lecturer in Political Economy, (U.)

102 Patterson Avenue.

WILLIAM HOWARD MARTIN, M.A.,
Lecturer in Chemistry, (U.)

113 Grenadier Road.

JOHN WALLER MELSON, B.A.SC.,
Lecturer in Surveying,

69 Walmsley Boulevard.

HUMPHREY MICHELL,
Lecturer in the Department of Social Service,

University of Toronto.

MISS SUSAN GERTRUDE MORLEY, M.A.,
Lecturer in Classics, (T.)

87 Howland Avenue.

FERDINAND ALBERT MOURÉ,
Lecturer in the History of Music,

88 Walmer Road.

WILLIAM HUDSON MURRAY. B.A.,
Lecturer in French, (M.)

St. Michael's College.

ARTHUR ANGUS NORTON, B.A., CANTAB.,
Lecturer in French, (T.)

38 Metcalfe Street.

MISS ELIZABETH O'DRISCOLL, M.A.,
Lecturer in French, (M.)

St. Joseph's College.

REV. JOHN ERNEST PAGEAU,
Lecturer in French, (M.)

St. Michael's College.

GORDON CUMMINGS PATTERSON, M.C., B.A.,
Lecturer in Italian and Spanish, (U.)

342 Berkeley Street.

S. M. PERPETUA, B.A.,
Lecturer in German, (M.)

St. Joseph's College.

SAMUEL WALTER PERRY, B.A.,
Lecturer in Art and Commercial Work in the College of Education,
406 Brunswick Avenue.

EDWIN JOHN PRATT, PH.D.,
Lecturer in English, (V.) and Lecturer in the Department of Social Service,

889 Davenport Road.

GORDON EARLE RICHARDS, M.B.,
Associate in Radiology,

325 St. George Street.

THOMAS BEDFORD RICHARDSON; M.D., C.M., F.R.C.S., EDIN.,
Associate in Clinical Surgery,

128 Bloor Street, West.

HARTLEY GRANT ROBERTSON, B.A.,
Lecturer in Classics, (V.)

409 Brunswick Avenue.

JOHN DANIEL ROBINS, B.A.,
Lecturer in German, (V.)

187 Lauder Avenue.

REV. WILLIAM ROLLO, M.A., ABERDEEN,
Lecturer in Hebrew, (T.)

Trinity College.

MISS MARY COYNE ROWELL, B.A.,
Lecturer in French, (V.)

134 Crescent Road.

EDWARD STANLEY RYERSON, M.D., C.M.,
Associate in Clinical Surgery,

14 Delisle Avenue.

ALLEN NELSON SCARROW,
Lecturer in Manual Training in the Ontario College of Education,
150 Delaware Avenue.

MISS LAILA CORDELIA SCOTT, M.A.,
Lecturer in German and Reader in French, (T.)

St. Hilda's College.

WALLACE ARTHUR SCOTT, C.M.G., B.A., M.B., F.R.C.S., ENG.,
Associate in Surgery,

627 Sherbourne Street.

NORRIS EDWARD SHEPPARD, M.A.,
Lecturer in Mechanics and Mathematics, (U.)

125 Bedford Road.

CHARLES BUCKINGHAM SHUTTLEWORTH, M.D., C.M., F.R.C.S., ENG.,
Associate in Surgery and Clinical Surgery,

478 Huron Street.

GIDEON SILVERTHORN, M.B.,
Associate in Clinical Surgery,

266 College Street.

WILLIAM JAMES SMITHER, B.A.SC.,
Lecturer in Drawing,

71 Grenville Street.

FRANK NEIL STAPLEFORD, M.A., B.D.,
*Lecturer in the Department of Social Service and Special Lecturer in
the Department of Public Health Nursing,*
233 Albany Avenue.

M. M. ST. CLARE, B.A.,
Lecturer in Latin, (M.)

Loretto Abbey College.

NORMAN BURKE TAYLOR, M.B.,
> *Lecturer in Physiology, (U.) and Lecturer in Physiology for Veterinary Students,*
>
> 184 Spadina Road.

JOSEPH ELLIS THOMSON, B.A.Sc.,
> *Lecturer in Mineralogy, (U.)*
>
> 57 Queen's Park.

JAMES EDWIN TOOMER, B.S., N. CAROLINA STATE COLLEGE OF ENGINEERING,
> *Lecturer in Metallurgical Engineering,*
>
> 164 Howard Park Avenue.

JOHN FRANKLIN UREN, M.D., C.M.,
> *Associate in Surgery and Clinical Surgery,*
>
> 520 Church Street.

MISS MOSSIE MAY WADDINGTON, PH.D.,
> *Lecturer in English, (C.)*
>
> 94 St. George Street.

WILLIAM STEWART WALLACE, B.A., M.A., OXON.,
> *Special Lecturer in History, (U.)*
>
> 59 Poplar Plains Road.

REV. JOSEPH BASIL WALSH, M.A.,
> *Lecturer in Latin, (M.)*
>
> St. Michael's College.

HEALEY WILLAN, MUS. DOC.
> *Lecturer in Theory of Music,*
>
> 139 Inglewood Drive.

MISS JESSIE GERTRUDE WRIGHT, M.A.,
> *Lecturer in Botany, (U.)*
>
> 46 Avenue Road.

WILLIAM JAMES TURNBULL WRIGHT, B.A.Sc.,
> *Lecturer in Drawing,*
>
> 432 Markham Street.

MISS MARY YATES,
> *Lecturer in the Department of Social Service,*
>
> Port Credit, Ontario.

ALBERT RUSSELL ZIMMER, B.A.Sc.,
> *Lecturer in Electrical Engineering,*
>
> 80 Pine Crest Road.

Other Appointments.

FRANK BOLTON ADAMSTONE,
> *Class Assistant in Botany, (U.)*
>
> 86 Eglington Avenue East.

THOMAS DICKSON ARCHIBALD,
> *Assistant in Anaesthesia,*
>
> 90 Park Road.

ROBERT GARDINER ARMOUR, B.A., M.B.,
Clinician in Medicine,

98 St. George Street.

HAROLD GROVER ARMSTRONG, M.B.,
Demonstrator in Biology, (U.)

627a Vaughan Road.

FREDERICK ALLEN AYLESWORTH, M.D., C.M.,
Assistant in Ophthalmology,

112 College Street.

HERBERT WILLIAM BAKER, B.A., M.B.,
Assistant in Clinical Surgery,

606 Spadina Avenue.

L. C. M. BALDWIN, B.A.Sc.,
Demonstrator in Drawing,

9 Humewood Avenue.

HAROLD DE WITT BALL, M.B.,
Class Assistant in Biology, (U.)

178 Sherbourne Street.

EDWIN CHARLES BEER, M.D., C.M.,
Temporary Assistant in Surgery and Clinical Surgery,

2212 Queen Street, East.

CHARLES HERBERT BEST,
Fellow in Physiology, (U.)

Wycliffe College.

LOUIS AUGUSTE BIBET,
Instructor in French, (C, T.)

6 Vivian Street.

NORMAN KIER BIGELOW, B.Sc., IOWA,
Assistant in Systematic Biology, (U.)

158 Cumberland Street.

GEORGE MAITLAND BIGGS, M.B.,
Assistant in Oto-Laryngology,

341 Bloor Street, West.

MISS DOROTHY BIRKETT,
Class Assistant in Pharmacy and Pharmacology,

577 Jarvis Street.

EDWARD HUME BLAKE, M.A.,
Instructor in History, (U.)

47 Clarendon Avenue.

FRANK LEVER BLAKE,
Assistant in Astro-Physics, (U.)

65 Beaty Avenue.

DAVID HARVEY BODDINGTON, M.B.,
Assistant in Clinical Laboratory in the Department of Chemical Pathology,

81 Willcocks Street.

HENRY BORSOOK,
  Fellow in Bio-Chemistry, (U.)

                                        246 Lippincott Street.

EDMUND BOYD, B.A., M.B.,
  Assistant in Oto-Laryngology,

                                        143 College Street.

MISS GLADYS LILLIAN BOYD, M.B.,
  Research Fellow in Pediatrics,

                                        24 Maynard Avenue.

GEORGE FLORIAN BOYER, M.D.,
  Clinician in Medicine,

                                        143 College Street.

LIONEL GEORGE BRAYLEY, M.B.,
  Assistant in Anatomy,

                                        378 Roncesvalles Avenue.

HORACE LESLIE BRITTAIN, M.A., NEW BRUNSWICK, PH.D., CLARK
  Instructor in the Department of Social Service,

                                        20 Dalton Road.

HAROLD DUKE BROWN,
  Assistant in Botany, (U.)

                             Gate House, Victoria College.

HENRY SPEIGHT BROWN, B.A.SC.,
  Demonstrator in Electrical Engineering,

                                        Lansing, Ontario.

WILLIAM EASSON BROWN, M.B.,
  Assistant in Anatomy,

                                        10 Carlton Street.

MISS E. BURTON,
  Assistant in Psychology, (Easter Term only).

                             University of Toronto.

JOHN NASH DOUGLAS BUSH, B.A.,
  Fellow in English, (V.)

                             Burwash Hall, Victoria College.

JOHN C. CALHOUN, M.B.,
  Assistant in Oto-Larynology,

                                        99 Farnham Avenue.

GORDON CAMPBELL CAMERON, M.B.,
  Fellow in Pathology and Bacteriology,

                                        65 Hilton Avenue.

MALCOLM HECTORSON VALENTINE CAMERON, M.B.,
  Demonstrator in Surgery and Clinical Surgery,
                                11 Prince Arthur Avenue.

ANGUS ALEXANDER CAMPBELL, M.B.,
  Assistant in Oto-Laryngology,

                                        151 Bloor Street, West.

WALTER RUGGLES CAMPBELL, M.A., M.D.,
Clinician in Medicine,

149 Beatrice Street.

ALAN WOODBURN CANFEILD, M.D., C.M.,
Clinician in Medicine,

462 Avenue Road.

ROBERT CHARLES CANTELO, M.SC., QUEENS,
Research Assistant in Chemical Engineering,

68 Lappin Avenue.

GEORGE WYLIE DUNDAS CARLETON, M.B.,
Assistant in Anatomy,

1222 Gerrard Street, East.

WILLIAM HERBERT CARVETH, M.B.,
Assistant in Anaesthesia,

178 Huron Street.

HARRY ARTHUR CATES, M.B.,
Assistant in Anatomy,

249 Dovercourt Road.

ALFRED HANS WARING CAULFEILD, M.B.,
Clinician in Medicine,

13 Spadina Road.

STUART KEITH CHENEY, B.A.SC.,
Demonstrator in Electrical Engineering,

127 Givens Street.

CHARLES W. L. CLARK, M.B.,
Assistant in Oto-Laryngology,

112 College Street.

JAMES EVERETT CLARK, B.A.SC.,
Assistant in Chemistry, (U.)

140 Galley Avenue.

NORMAN ASHWELL CLARK, B.S.A., ALBERTA, M.A.,
Assistant in Chemistry, (U.)

20 Breadalbane Street.

NORMAN SAMUEL CLARK, B.A.,
Fellow in Bio-Chemistry, (U.)

121 Bernard Avenue.

FREDERICK ARNOLD CLARKSON, M.B.,
Clinician in Medicine.

421 Bloor Street, West.

ERNEST EDGAR CLEAVER, B.A., M.B.,
Clinician in Medicine,

155 Bloor Street, East.

FREDERICK ADAM CLELAND, B.A., M.B.,
Demonstrator in Clinical Surgery,

131 Bloor Street, West.

HERBERT ERNEST CLUTTERBUCK, M.D., C.M.,
  Assistant in Clinical Surgery,

148 Grace Steret.

C. EDWARD COOPER COLE, O.B.E., B.A., M.B.,
  Demonstrator in Therapeutics,

53 Indian Road Crescent.

WILLIAM ALFRED COSTAIN, M.B.,
  Temporary Assistant in Clinical Surgery,

64 Bloor Street, East.

MISS KATHLEEN MAY CROSSLEY, B.A.,
  Demonstrator in Physics, (U.)

1 Washington Avenue.

JOHN GRANT CUNNINGHAM, B.A., M.B.,
  Demonstrator in Industrial Hygiene,

154 Ellsworth Avenue·

MISS MARY ELIZABETH CURRIE, B.A., McGILL, M.A.,
  Technical Assistant in Botany, (U.)

1 Willcocks Street.

JOHN HOWARD CURZON,
  Demonstrator in Drawing,

96 Queensbury Avenue.

GORDON McINTYRE DALE, B.A., M.B.,
  Assistant in Clinical Surgery,

591 Church Street.

WILFRED ALAN DANCEY, B.A.Sc.,
  Demonstrator in Electrical Engineering,

23 Surrey Place.

HERBERT KNUDSEN DETWEILER, M.D.,
  Clinician in Medicine,

33 Regal Road.

HAMNETT ALONZO DIXON, M.B.,
  Clinician in Medicine,

122 Bloor Street, West.

ALEXANDER ROBERT DUFF, B.A.Sc.,
  Demonstrator in Applied Chemistry,

211 Fern Avenue.

CHARLES KENT DUFF, B.A.Sc.,
  Research Assistant in Electrical Engineering,
102 St. Vincent Street.

THOMAS ALEXANDER JAMIESON DUFF, M.B.,
  Assistant in Surgery and Clinical Surgery,

Abroad.

WILLIAM BOWIE DUNBAR, B.A.Sc.,
  Demonstrator in Drawing,

26 Ozark Crescent.

HOWARD KETCHUM DUTCHER, B.Sc., M.Sc., McGILL,
Special Instructor in Hydraulics,
534A St. Clair Avenue, West.

WILLIAM STAFFORD DYER, B.A.,
Research Assistant in Palaeontology, (U.)
35 Boustead Avenue.

MISS HAZEL ISOBEL EADIE,
Class Assistant in Physics, (U.)
899 Queen Street, West.

JABEZ HENRY ELLIOTT, M.B.,
Clinician in Medicine,
11 Spadina Road.

MISS FLORENCE EMORY,
Instructor in Medical Social Service,
26 Algonquin Avenue.

ISAAC H. ERB, M.B.,
Assistant in Pathology and Bacteriology,
1549 Bloor Street, West.

WALTER RAYMOND FETZER, B.A., WESLEYAN, M.A.,
Demonstrator in Electro-Chemistry,
120 Brunswick Avenue.

EDWARD FIDLAR, B.A., M.B.,
Research Assistant in Physiology,
310 Huron Street.

ROBERT OVENS FISHER, M.B.,
Assistant in Anatomy,
343 Sherbourne Street.

ANDREW ALMON FLETCHER, M.B
Clinician in Medicine,
63 Foxbar Road.

DONALD ROY FLETCHER, M.D., C.M., QUEENS,
Demonstrator in Psychiatry,
999 Queen Street, West.

MISS NORMA HENRIETTA CARSWELL FORD, B.A.,
Special Assistant in Biology, (U.)
96 Dunn Avenue.

NORMAN FOUND, B.A., M.B.,
Class Assistant in Biology, (U.)
Toronto General Hospital.

HAROLD JAMES FRANKLIN, B.A.Sc.,
Demonstrator in Drawing,
72 Delaware Avenue.

MISS CHRISTINA JANE FRASER, M.A.,
Fellow in Physiology, (U.) Assistant in Dental Research,
218 Cottingham Street.

Nicholas D'Arcy Frawley, M.B.,
　　Assistant in Obstetrics and Gynaecology,
　　　　　　　　　　　　　　　503 Markham Street.

Walter Gardner Frisby,
　　Tutor in English for First Year Students in the Faculty of Medicine.
　　　　　　　　　　　　　　　170 Glenholme Avenue.

Miss Clara W. Fritz,
　　Research Assistant in Botany,
　　　　　　　　　　　　　　　84 St. George Street.

Robert Edward Gaby, B.A., M.D., Cornell,
　　*Demonstrator in Surgery and Clinical Surgery, and Assistant in
　　　　Anatomy,*
　　　　　　　　　　　　　　　662 Bathurst Street.

Oliver H. Gaebler, A.B., A.M.,
　　Fellow in Chemical Pathology,
　　　　　　　　　　　　　　　213 Beverly Street.

L. Galbraith,
　　Research Assistant in Aeronautics,
　　　　　　　　　　　　　　　14 St. Albans Street.

John Gordon Gallie, B.A., M.B.,
　　Demonstrator in Obstetrics and Gynaecology,
　　　　　　　　　　　　　　　143 College Street.

Carl Schloss Gilbert, B.S., Akron,
　　Assistant in Chemistry,
　　　　　　　　　　　　　　　10 Maitland Street.

Miss Ila Beatrice Giles, B.A.,
　　Demonstrator in Physics, (U.)
　　　　　　　　　　　　　　　79 St. Joseph Street.

Charles Hawkins Gilmour, M.B.,
　　Temporary Assistant in Surgery and Clinical Surgery,
　　　　　　　　　　　　　　　116 St. George Street.

George E. Gollop, B.A.,
　　Research Assistant in Chemical Engineering,
　　　　　　　　　　　　　　　497 Pape Avenue.

Arthur Melville Goulding, B.A., M.D., Harvard,
　　Clinician in Medicine,
　　　　　　　　　　　　　　　88 Warren Road.

Roscoe Reid Graham, M.B.,
　　Assistant in Clinical Surgery,
　　　　　　　　　　　　　　　112 College Street.

Thomas Stewart Graham, B.A.,Sc.,
　　Demonstrator in Drawing,
　　　　　　　　　　　　　　　139 Colbeck Street.

Edward Rochfort Grange, D.S.C., B.A.Sc.,
　　Demonstrator in Drawing,
　　　　　　　　　　　　　　　34 Chicora Avenue.

MISS FLORENCE GRAPER, B.S., WISCONSIN,
Instructor in Household Science,

142 Yorkville Avenue.

WILLIAM FOSTER GREEN, M.A.,
Demonstrator in Mining Engineering,

717 Dovercourt Road.

NORMAN BEECHEY GWYN, M.B.,
Clinician in Medicine,

48 Bloor Street, East.

EUGENE HAAS, B.S., AKRON,
Assistant in Chemistry, (U.)

10 Maitland Street.

CHARLES H. HAIR, M.D., C.M.,
Assistant in Surgery and Clinical Surgery,

545 Palmerston Boulevard.

JOHN C. HALLAMORE, PHM.B.,
Class Assistant in Pharmacy and Pharmacology,

Western Hospital.

ARMOND ALLAN HALLIDAY, M.B.,
Assistant in Oto-Larynology,

143 College Street.

MISS EDITH ANZONETTA HAMES,
*Supervisor of Field Work in the Department of Public Health
Nursing,*

100 Gloucester Street.

THOMAS RICHARD HANLEY, B.A., M.B.,
Assistant in Anaesthesia,

124 Bloor Street, West.

BEVERLEY HANNAH, M.B.,
Clinician in Medicine,

589 Sherbourne Street.

WILLIAM JOHN KNOX HARKNESS,
Class Assistant in Biology, (U.)

67 Charles Street, West.

RODERICK CAMPBELL HARDIE, B.A.Sc.,
Demonstrator in Thermodynamics,

69 Walmer Road.

ROBERT INKERMAN HARRIS, M.C., M.B.,
Temporary Assistant in Surgery and Clinical Surgery,

311 Avenue Road.

HOWARD DAVIDSON HARRISON, M.D.,
Temporary Assistant in Clinical Surgery,

415 Bloor Street, West.

ALFRED PURVIS HART, M.B.,
Fellow in Chemical Pathology, Michaelmas Term,

48 De Lisle Avenue.

Miss Carlotta Maude Harwood, B.A.,
Instructor in Food Chemistry,

84 Admiral Road.

Clarence Emerson Hastings, B.A.Sc.,
Demonstrator in Drawing,

252 Russell Hill Road.

Percy Roy Hayward, B.A., B.D., Ph.D.,
Instructor in Psychology,

112 Simpson Avenue.

Clarke Robertson Hill, B.A.Sc.,
Research Assistant in Electrical Engineering,

20 Hillcrest Road, Weston.

Clarence Edgar Hill, M.B.,
Assistant in Ophthalmology,

160 Bloor Street, West.

Ubert Cecil Holland, B.A.Sc.,
Assistant in Machine Design,

93 Pacific Avenue.

Peter John Fisher Houston, M.B.,
Class Assistant in Biology, (U.)

34 Hurndale Avenue.

Goldwin William Howland, B.A., M.B.,
Clinician in Medicine,

147 Bloor Street, West.

Richard Douglas Huestis, B.A.Sc.,
Demonstrator in Electrical Engineering,

54 Huntley Street.

Chester Arthur Hughes, B.A.Sc.,
Demonstrator in Applied Mechanics,

Mimico Beach.

Miss Lillian Mary Hunter,
Assistant in Botany, (U.)

94 St. George Street.

John Joseph Hurley, M.B.,
Assistant in Anaesthesia,

995 Bathurst Street.

Henry Seaton Hutchison, M.B.,
Clinician in Medicine,

30 Walker Avenue.

Kenneth Bell Jackson, B.A.Sc.,
Demonstrator in Engineering Physics,

35 Grosvenor Street.

Ross Jamieson, B.A., M.B.,
Clinician in Medicine,

155 Bloor Street, East.

ROBERT MEREDITH JANES, M.B.,
Assistant in Anatomy,

Hospital for Sick Children.

SAMUEL JOHNSTON, M.A., M.D., C.M.,
Demonstrator in Anaesthesia,

108 Avenue Road.

WILLIAM VICTOR JOHNSTON,
Class Assistant in Biology, (U.)

155 Cumberland Street.

JAMES KELLEHER, B.A.Sc.,
Demonstrator in Electro-Chemistry,

67 Breadalbane Street.

FREDERICK WISMER KEMP, M.A.,
Class Assistant in Physics, (U.)

741 Broadview Avenue.

F. F. KIRKPATRICK,
Tutor in English Expression for Medical Students,

34 Admiral Road.

CHARLES FRASER KNIGHT, M.B.,
Fellow in Physiology, (U.)

707 Spadina Avenue.

ALEXANDER LACEY, M.A.,
Instructor in French, (T.)

96 Hogarth Avenue.

WALTER WHITNEY LAILEY, B.A., M.B.,
Assistant in Obstetrics and Gynaecology,

43 Avenue Road.

MISS JANET CARLYLE LAING, B.A.,
Instructor in the Department of Architecture,

39 MacFarland Avenue.

HARRY MILL LANCASTER, B.A.Sc.,
Demonstrator in Sanitary Chemistry,

22 Palmerston Gardens.

MISS JESSIE LANG, B.A.,
Fellow in Physiology, (U.)

20 Leopold Street.

GEORGE FRANKLIN LAUGHLIN, M.D., C.M.,
Assistant in Pathology and Bacteriology,

495 Broadview Avenue.

NELLES BOYD LAUGHTON,
Class Assistant in Biology, (U.)

Gate House, Victoria College.

ALEXANDER SMIRLE LAWSON, M.B.,
Assistant in Anatomy and Temporary Assistant in Clinical Surgery,

82 College Street.

WALTER LEAF, B.S., UTAH,
  Assistant in Chemistry, (U.)
                                    17 Bloor Street, West.

ARTHUR BAKER LE MESURIER, M.B.,
  *Assistant in Pathology and Temporary Assistant in Clinical
    Surgery,*
                                    59 Spadina Road.

JULIAN DERWENT LOUDON, B.A., M.B.,
  Clinician in Medicine,
                                    83 St. George Street.

GLADSTONE WILFRED LOUGHEED, M.C., M.D.,
  Demonstrator in Clinical Microscopy,
                                    728 Dovercourt Road.

PERCY LOWE,
  Assistant Demonstrator in Physics, (U.)
                                    442 Shaw Street.

VLADIMIR PAUL LUBOVICH,
  Demonstrator in Physics, (Û.)
                                    69 Grant Street.

WILLIAM HERBERT LOWRY,
  Demonstrator in Ophthalmology,
                                    100 College Street.

GEORGE HERBERT WILLIAM LUCAS,
  Assistant in Chemistry, (U.)
                                    34A Breadalbane Street.

MORTIMER LYON, M.D., C.M.,
  Assistant in Ophthalmology,
                                    122 Bloor Street, West.

WILLIAM JOHN MCANDREW, M.A.,
  Special Instructor in French, (C.)
                                    144 Balliol Street.

JOHN WOOD MACARTHUR, A.B., OBERLIN, M.A., WABASH,
  Demonstrator in Physiology, (U.)
                                    319 Roehampton Avenue.

JAMES CLARENCE MCCLELLAND, B.A., M.B.,
  Temporary Assistant in Clinical Surgery,
                                    151 Bloor Street, West.

JOHN ALEXANDER MCCOLLUM, M.B.,
  Demonstrator in Clinical Surgery,
                                    12 Avenue Road.

ROBERT JAMES AVERY MCCOMB, M.B.,
  Temporary Assistant in Clinical Surgery,
                                    40 Gothic Avenue.

ERNEST ALBERT MCCULLOCH, B.A., M.B.,
  Class Assistant in Biology, (U.)
                                    165 St. Clair Avenue, West.

Edward Allister McCulloch, B.A., M.B.,
Assistant in Anatomy,

165 St. Clair Avenue, West.

Miss Myrtle Victoria McCulloch, B.A.,
Technical Assistant in Botany, (U.)

682 Spadina Avenue.

Gordon Grant Macdonald,
Demonstrator in Chemical Engineering,

88 Indian Grove.

James Alexander Macdonald, Phm.B.,
Class Assistant in Pharmacy and Pharmacology,

34 Hogarth Avenue.

John MacKay Macdonald, M.D., C.M.,
Class Assistant in Biology, (U.)

687 Pape Avenue.

Norman Geddes McDonald, B.A.Sc.,
Demonstrator in Hydraulics,

16 Maitland Street.

Miss Jennie McFarlane, M.A.,
Demonstrator in Biochemistry, (U.)

162 Fairview Avenue.

Donald McGillivray, M.B., M.D., C.M.,
Clinician in Medicine,

2 Elgin Avenue.

Miss Agnes Christine McGregor,
*Director of Field Work and Instructor for Tutorial Classes in the
Department of Social Service,*

Apt. 2, The Meldrum, Brunswick Avenue.

Miss Jean McGugan, B.A.,
Fellow in Botany, (U.)

680 Spadina Avenue.

Ellet Douglas MacInnes, B.A.,
Assistant Demonstrator in Physics, (U.)

272 Major Street.

George Crarer McIntyre, M.B.,
Assistant in Clinical Surgery,

469 Parliament Street.

Angus Mackay, M.B.,
Assistant in Pathology,

606 Spadina Avenue.

William Graeme MacKechnie, M.D., C.M.,
Assistant in Oto-Laryngology,

96 College Street.

Alexander John MacKenzie, B.A., M.B., LL.B.,
Clinician in Medicine,

12 Avenue Road.

KENNETH GEORGE MCKENZIE, M.B.,
  Assistant in Anatomy,

241 Jarvis Street.

MATTHEW DONALD MCKICHAN, B.A., M.B.,
  Assistant in Anaesthesia,

686 Broadview Avenue.

DUNCAN NEIL MACLENNAN, M.D., C.M.,
  Demonstrator in Ophthalmology,

126 Bloor Street, West.

MISS MARGARET MACLENNAN,
  Research Assistant in Pathology,

2 Sultan Street.

JOHN WALKER MACMILLAN, B.A., D.D.,
  *Instructor on Industrial Legislation in the Department of Social
  Service,*

190 Dawlish Avenue.

THOMAS CREIGHTON MCMULLEN,
  Assistant in Chemistry, (U.)

7 Borden Street.

ARCHIBALD GEORGE MCPHEDRAN, B.A., M.B.,
  Class Assistant in Biology, (U.) and Clinician in Medicine,

923 College Street.

JOHN HARRIS MCPHEDRAN, M.B.,
  Clinician in Medicine,

33 Dupont Street.

WILLIAM FLETCHER MCPHEDRAN, B.A., M.B.,
  Clinician in Medicine,

15 Bernard Avenue.

WILLIAM CAVEN MCQUARRIE, B.A.,
  Assistant Demonstrator in Physics, (U.)

56 Charles Street, West.

CHARLES STANLEY MCVICAR, M.B.,
  Clinician in Medicine,

300 Roncesvalles Avenue.

OLIVER RAYMOND MABEE, PHM. B., M.D., C.M., MCGILL,
  Demonstrator in Clinical Surgery,

419 Bloor Street, West.

MISS MARY ISABEL MACKEY,
  Demonstrator in Physics, (U.)

126 Avenue Road.

MRS. JEAN PEARL SPROULE MANSON, M.B.,
  Assistant in Oto-Laryngology,

250 Huron Street.

MISS EMILIE FRANCES DUDLEY MARTIN, B.A.,
  Assistant in Food Chemistry,

29 Admiral Road.

ARNOLD DEUBOW ALFRED MASOW, D.D.S.,
Demonstrator in Dental Surgery,

2 College Street.

MISS JEAN MASTEN,
Assistant in Psychology, (U.)

29 Bedford Road.

JOHN COTTON MAYNARD, M.B.,
Assistant in Anatomy,

151 Bloor Street, West.

MISS HAZEL CLAIRE MILLAR, B.A.,
Demonstrator in Physics, (U.)

Argyll House, Queen's Park.

BEVERLEY Z. MILNER, M.D., C.M.,
Assistant in Surgery and Clinical Surgery,

100 St. George Street.

FREDERICK SIDNEY MINNS, M.B.,
Clinician in Medicine,

120 St. Clair Avenue, West.

AMBROSE BELL MOFFAT, B.A., M.B.,
Assistant in Clinical Microscopy,

1028 Logan Avenue.

PETER JOSEPH MOLONEY, M.A.,
Demonstrator in Hygiene,

3 Dawson Avenue.

ANDREW SAMUEL MOORHEAD, B.A., M.B., F.R.C.S., ENG.,
Demonstrator in Clinical Surgery,

146 Bloor Street, West.

EDWARD ARCHIBALD MORGAN, M.B.,
Clinician in Medicine,

310 Bloor Street, West.

EZRA HENRY MOSS, M.M., B.A.,
Assistant in Botany, (U.)

34 Sussex Avenue.

MISS BESSIE KATHARINE E. MOSSOP, B.A., M.A.,
Technical Assistant in Hygiene,

164 Jameson Avenue.

LAWRENCE MCCHEYNE MURRAY,
Class Assistant in Biology, (U.)

12 Maitland Place.

LEONARD M. MURRAY, M.D., C.M.,
Clinician in Medicine,

48 Bloor Street, East.

MRS. FRANCES JANE NETHERCOTT, M.A.,
Research Worker in the Department of Household Science,

18 Biggar Avenue.

WILLIAM JOHN NICHOL, B.A.Sc.,
    Demonstrator in Electrical Engineering,
                            544 Church Street.

EDWARD CLARK NOBLE,
    Fellow in Physiology, (U.)
                    216 St. Clair Avenue, West.

WILLIAM EDWARD OGDEN, M.B.,
    Clinician in Medicine,
                            9 Spadina Road.

JOHN ALLAN OILLE, M.D.,
    Clinician in Medicine,
                          69 South Drive.

WILLIAM HAROLD ORR, B.A.Sc.,
    Demonstrator in Electrical Engineering,
                    442 Gladstone Avenue.

STEWART URQUHART PAGE, B.A,.
    Fellow in Physiology, (U.)
                       941 Bathurst Street.

THOMAS JEFFERSON PAGE, M.B.,
    Clinician in Medicine,
                       941 Bathurst Street.

LAUREL COLE PALMER, M.B.,
    Assistant in Anatomy,
               1081 St. Clair Avenue, West.

MISS EDNA WILHELMENE PARK, B.A.,
    Laboratory Assistant in Household Science,
                    25 Grosvenor Street.

CHARLES BEMISTER PARKER, B.A., M.B.,
    Assistant in Clinical Surgery,
                      52 College Street.

HAROLD CAMPBELL PARSONS, M.A., M.D., C.M.,
    Clinician in Medicine,
                    6 Clarendon Avenue.

JOSEPH ALGERNON PEARCE,
    Assistant in Astro-Physics, (U.)
                    163 Collier Street.

ROBIN PEARSE, F.R.C.S., ENG.,
    Assistant in Clinical Surgery,
                206 Bloor Street, West.

LEON AMIABLE PEQUEGNAT, M.B.,
    Class Assistant in Biology, (U.) and Assistant in Anatomy,
                    741 Dovercourt Road.

ALFRED HARSHAW PERFECT, M.B., M.D., C.M.,
    Demonstrator in Clinical Surgery,
                    201 Annette Street.

PETER ARNOLD PETRIE,
  Research Assistant in Physics, (U.)

Knox College.

GEORGE ROWE PHILIP, M.B.,
  Assistant in Pathology and Bacteriology,

607 Sherbourne Street.

JOSEPH PIJOAN, L.LITT., BARCELONA,
  Instructor in Spanish, (U.)

Strathgowan Crescent.

GEORGE ROBINSON PIRIE, M.B.,
  Clinician in Medicine,

220 Bloor Street, West.

C. T. POTTER,
  Fellow in Chemical Pathology,

85 Bloor Street, East.

HAROLD WARNICA PRICE,
  Class Assistant in Biology, (U.)

351 Sherbourne Street.

MISS FLORENCE MARY QUINLAN, M.A.,
  Demonstrator in Physics, (U.)

33 Margueretta Street.

WALTER SOUTHARD QUINT, B.SC., M.B.,
  Demonstrator in Chemical Pathology,

72 Hogarth Avenue.

CECIL ALEXANDER RAE, M.B.,
  Clinician in Medicine,

Isolation Hospital.

JOHN THOMAS RANSOM, B.A.SC.,
  Demonstrator in Engineering Physics,

47 Braemore Gardens.

JAMES WALLER REBBECK, B.SC., BRITISH COLUMBIA,
  Assistant in Chemistry, (U.)

255 Brunswick Avenue.

MISS ANNIE THERESA REED, B.A.,
  Class Assistant in Physics, (U.)

613 Spadina Avenue.

MISS INA LOUISE ROBERTS, B.A.,
  Assistant in Chemistry, (U.)

Apt. 7, 67a Gloucester Street.

JAMES ALEXANDER ROBERTS, C.B., M.B., F.R.C.S., ENG,.
  Demonstrator in Clinical Surgery,

38 Charles Street, East.

MISS ALICIA ENID ROBERTSON, B.A.,
  Instructor in Sewing in the College of Education,

19 Hazleton Avenue.

DAVID EDWIN ROBERTSON, M.B.,
Demonstrator in Clinical Surgery,

112 College Street.

LAWRENCE BRUCE ROBERTSON, B.A., M.B.,
Assistant in Anatomy,

143 College Street.

THOMAS ARNOLD ROBINSON, M.D., C.M., McGILL,
Temporary Assistant in Clinical Surgery,

147 Howard Park Avenue.

WILLIAM LIPSETT ROBINSON, B.A., McMASTER, M.B.,
Demonstrator in Pathology and Bacteriology,

15 Glen Grove Avenue, West.

CHARLES HAROLD ROBSON, M.D., C.M.,
Assistant in Anaesthesia,

26 Foxbar Road.

ORVILLE ROLFSON, M.A.Sc.,
Demonstrator in Chemical Engineering,

342 Brunswick Avenue.

FREDERICK WHITNEY ROLPH, M.A., M.D., C.M.,
Clinician in Medicine,

13 Madison Avenue.

HAROLD LEE ROWNTREE, M.B.,
Assistant in Anatomy,

1203 Bloor Street, West.

MISS EDITH KATHLEEN RUSSELL, B.A., KING'S COLLEGE,
Director of Courses for Graduate Nurses,

1 Willcocks Street.

JAMES BURN RUSSELL,
Assistant in Astrophysics, (U.)

South House, University of Toronto.

WILLIAM LISTER SAGAR, B.A.Sc.,
Demonstrator and Research Assistant in Applied Mechanics,

306 Jarvis Street.

WALLACE ARTHUR SCOTT, C.M.G., B.A., M.B., F.R.C.S., ENG.,
Assistant in Anatomy,

627 Sherbourne Street.

WILLIAM ALBERT SCOTT, B.A., M.B.,
Assistant in Obstetrics and Gynaecology,

75 Bloor Street, East.

CHARLES SHEARD, JR., M.B.,
Clinician in Medicine,

52 College Street.

NORMAN STRAHAN SHENSTONE, B.A., M.D., COLUMBIA,
Demonstrator in Clinical Surgery,

196 Bloor Street, West.

EDWARD EARLE SHOULDICE, M.B.,
   Assistant in Anatomy and Temporary Assistant in Clinical Surgery,
                                                    461 Dovercourt Road.

GORDON MERRITT SHRUM,
   Research Assistant in Physics, (U.)
                                                    Victoria College.

WILLIAM ALGERNON SIBBETT,
   Demonstrator in Drawing,
                                                    56 Lyall Avenue.

FRANCIS E. SIMPSON,
   Assistant in Modelling,
                                                    14 Lakeview Avenue.

JAMES STARR SIMPSON, M.D., C.M., McGILL,
   Temporary Assistant in Clinical Surgery,
                                                    137 Avenue Road.

DAVID KING SMITH, M.B.,
   Clinician in Medicine,
                                                    22 Wellesley Street.

GEORGE EDWARD SMITH, B.A., M.B.,
   Clinician in Medicine,
                                                    244 Bloor Street, West.

ISSCHER RUEBERT SMITH, M.B., M.R.C.S., ENG.,
   Assistant in Anatomy,
                                                    124 St. George Street.

MAURICE EDWARD SMITH, B.A., NEW BRUNSWICK, M.A.,
   Assistant in Chemistry, (U.)
                                                    12 St. Joseph Street.

HOWARD CLAYTON SOEHNER, B.A.Sc.,
   Demonstrator in Applied Chemistry,
                                                    666 Spadina Avenue.

DOUGLAS SPOHN, M.B.,
   Class Assistant in Biology (U.) and Assistant in Anatomy,
                                                    20 High Park Avenue.

HOWARD SPOHN, M.B.,
   Clinician in Medicine,
                                                    20 High Park Avenue.

GEORGE STEWART STRATHY, M.D., C.M.,
   Clinician in Medicine,
                                                    143 College Street.

ARTHUR BERTRAM STEVENSON, B.A.,
   Fellow in Mathematics, (U.),
                                                    187 Howland Avenue.

ANDREW LLEWELLAND STEWART, B.A.Sc.,
   Demonstrator in Thermodynamics,
                                                    587 Palmerston Avenue.

VALENTINE FREDERICK STOCK, B.A., M.B.,
Assistant in Anatomy,

166 St. George Street.

GEORGE STEWART STRATHY, M.D., C.M.,
Clinician in Medicine,

143 College Street.

ALFRED LEOROYD TENNYSON, B.A.Sc.,
Demonstrator in Electrical Engineering,

16 Maitland Street.

ROY HINDLEY THOMAS, M.C., M.B.,
Temporary Assistant in Clinical Surgery,

167 College Street.

HARRY SCOTT THOMSON, D.M.D., TUFTS.,
Assistant in Dental Research,

20 Summerhill Gardens.

VICTOR THOMSON,
Demonstrator in Applied Chemistry,

66 Shuter Street.

ELDRED WALTON TODD, B.A.,
Research Assistant in Mineralogy,

632 Woodbine Avenue.

EMERSON JAMES TROW, M.B.,
Clinician in Medicine,

40 Avenue Road.

HOWELL ALFRED TUTTLE, B.A.Sc.,
Instructor in Thermodynamics,

605 Huron Street.

RICHARD WILLIAM IAN URQUHART, B.A.,
Fellow in Biochemistry, (U.)

26 Suffolk Place.

HERMON BROOKFIELD VAN WYCK, B.A., M.B.,
Assistant in Anatomy,

154 Danforth Avenue.

WILLIAM STEWART VAUGHAN,
Assistant in Astrophysics, (U.)

12 Cowan Avenue.

FULTON SCHUYLER VROOMAN, M.B.,
Demonstrator in Psychiatry,

999 Queen Street, West.

MISS MARY EVELYN GERTRUDE WADDELL, M.A.,
Fellow in Mathematics, (U.)

32 Madison Avenue.

ANSON ROBERTSON WALKER, B.A.,
Assistant in Botany, (U.)

77 Grenville Street.

ARTHUR WARDELL, B.A.Sc.,
Demonstrator in Drawing,

4 Willliamson Road.

WILFRED PARSONS WARNER, M.B.,
Fellow in Pathology and Bacteriology,

142 St. George Street.

WILLIAM VIRGIL WATSON, M.B.,
Assistant in Therapeutics,

120 Quebec Avenue.

FREDERICK EARLE WATTS, M.B.,
Temporary Assistant in Clinical Surgery,

155 Bloor Street, East.

JULIUS JOHN Weicher, B.A.Sc.,
Demonstrator in Hydraulics,

33 Tennis Crescent.

ROBERT WATSON WESLEY, M.B.,
Assistant in Obstetrics and Gynaecology,

548 Palmerston Boulevard.

JOHN BRABY WEST, B.A.,
Instructor in Latin, (C.)

945 Logan Avenue.

FREDERICK WILLIAM WESTON, M.B.,
Assistant in Anatomy,

45 Avenue Road.

GLENN WILLIAMS, B.S., AKRON.,
Assistant in Chemistry, (U.)

10 Maitland Street.

ALEXANDER CURRIE WILSON, B.A.Sc.,
Demonstrator in Drawing,

283 Evelyn Avenue.

GEORGE EWART WILSON, M.B., F.R.C.S., ENG.,
Demonstrator in Clinical Surgery,

205 Bloor Street, East.

OSWALD CHARLES JOSEPH WITHROW, M.B.,
Class Assistant in Biology, (U.)

38 Albany Avenue.

JAMES HENRY WOOD, D.S.O., M.B.,
Temporary Assistant in Clinical Surgery,

1062 Dovercourt Road.

ARTHUR SUTHERLAND PIGOTT WOODHOUSE, B.A.,
Assistant in English, (C.)

42 Willcocks Street.

MISS GLADYS EMILY WOOKEY, B.A.,
Assistant in English, (C.)

Lowther Apartments, Lowther Avenue.

GEORGE ROSS WORKMAN,
    .   *Demonstrator in Drawing,*

                                22 Helena Avenue.

ARTHUR BALDWIN WRIGHT, M.B.,
    Demonstrator in Clinical Surgery,

                                52 Poplar Plains Road.

WALTER WALKER WRIGHT, M.B.,
    Assistant in Ophthalmology,

                                143 College Street.

MISS MARGARET WRONG, M.A.,
    Instructor in History, (U.)

                                85 St. George Street.

ARTHUR MARSHALL WYNNE, M.A., QUEENS,
    Fellow in Biochemistry, (U.)

                                27 Lytton Boulevard.

GEORGE SILLS YOUNG, B.A., M.B.,
    Clinician in Medicine,

                                143 College Street.

ONTARIO COLLEGE OF EDUCATION.

GEORGE NEVILLE BRAMFITT, B.A.,

                                35 Munro Park Avenue.

JOHN OLIVER CARLISLE, M.A.,

                                111 Durie Avenue.

GEORGE ALTON CLINE, D.S.O., M.A.,

                                379 Huron Street.

J. B. DANDENO,

                                13 Hazelton Avenue.

PERCY DANIELS, B.A.,

                                201 Perth Avenue.

ERNEST LE ROY DANIHER, B.A.,

                                26 Page Street.

HORACE ALEXANDER GRAINGER, B.A.,

                                25 Westmount Avenue.

FRANK HALBUS, B.A., MCMASTER,

                                482 Brunswick Avenue.

DOUGLAS EWART HAMILTON, M.A.,

                                2 Dalton Road.

JOSEPH A. IRWIN,

                                60 Grace Street.

WILLIAM JAMES LOUGHEED, M.A.,

                                316 Indian Road.

Norman Leslie Murch, B.A.,

27 Northcliffe Boulevard.

Thomas M. Porter,

64 Winchester Street.

Walter Lawrence Christie Richardson,

83 Pine Crest Road.

Walter Herbert Williams, M.A.,

198 Glenholme Avenue.

James George Workman, B.A.,

Birch Cliff Post Office.

CONSTITUTION AND ADMINISTRATION OF THE UNIVERSITY.

The constitution, powers and functions of the University are defined in "The University Act, 1906." (R.S.O., 1914, Chap. 279.)

The management of the property, finances and academic business of the University is entrusted to the Board of Governors, the Senate, Convocation, the Faculty Councils, the Council of University College and the Caput. The functions of these various bodies are exercised subject to supervision and control by the Crown, as hereafter explained.

1. THE CROWN.—The Lieutenant-Governor-in-Council has the power to appoint and to remove the Board of Governors (with the exception of the Chancellor and the President); to appoint and remove the Chairman of the Board; his assent is necessary before the Board can make any expenditure which impairs the endowment of the University or College; through the Provincial Auditor or someone else appointed by himself, he audits the accounts of the Board and he requires of them an Annual Report for submission to the Legislature.

2. THE BOARD OF GOVERNORS.—The Board of Governors consists of: The Chancellor and the President, *ex-officio*, and eighteen persons appointed by the Lieutenant-Governor-in-Council, one of whom is named as Chairman of the Board. The appointed members hold office for six years, and one-third of the number retires every two years, but these members are eligible for re-election. The Board has power to appoint the President of the University; and to appoint or remove all of the officers and servants of the University or University College upon the nomination or recommendation of the President. The government, conduct, management and control of the University and University College and of the property, revenues, business and affairs thereof are vested in the Board (University Act, 1906, Section 37), but all expenditures of endowment must be authorised by the Lieutenant-Governor-in-Council. The Board makes by-laws, rules and regulations regarding the investment of the funds; the selling and leasing of University properties; the letting of contracts; the appointment and removal of the Bursar and his assistants, clerks and other officers and servants of the University; the rate of salaries to be paid to the staff and officers; the fees to be paid by students; the annual appropriations and the transaction of other business.

3. THE SENATE.—The Senate consists of four classes of members: (1) Ex-officio members; (2) Faculty members; (3) Appointed members; and (4) Elected members. The ex-officio members are the Chancellor, the Chairman of the Board of Governors, the President of the University, the Principal of University College, the President or other head of each federated university or college, the Deans of the Faculties of Arts, Medicine, Applied Science and Engineering, Household Science, Education, Forestry

and Music, all past Chancellors, Vice-Chancellors and-Presidents. Representation of the Faculties is made up as follows; The professors, not including the associate, professors, of the Faculty of Arts of the University; five members of the Faculty of Medicine; five members of the Faculty of Applied Science and Engineering; two members of the Faculty of Education; three members from each of the four Arts Colleges, University College, Victoria University, Trinity College and St. Michael's College. The appointed members consist of one representative appointed by each federated university, two by each federated college, one by the Law Society of Upper Canada and one by each federated institution, subject, however, in the latter case, to certain restrictions. The elected members number thirty-six, made up of twelve members representing the graduates in Arts who at graduation were enrolled in University College; five members each representing similar graduates in Victoria College and Trinity College; four representing the graduates in Medicine; two each representing the graduates in Applied Science and Engineering and in Agriculture; two representing the graduates in Law; and four representing the principals of collegiate institutes or high schools or assistants therein who are actually engaged in teaching in such institute or school. The graduates in Medicine and Law of Victoria University and Trinity College vote with the graduates of the University of Toronto in these same faculties.

The body thus composed is renewed once in four years, when all except the ex-officio members and the representatives of the Faculty of Arts of the University must retire, but are eligible for reappointment or re-election. The Chairman of the Senate is the President.

The Senate has the power to fill any vancacy which may occur among the elected members of the Senate and to return a final decision in any dispute which may arise in connection with the Senate elections. Among the powers and duties of the Senate are the following: To provide for the regulation and conduct of its proceedings; for the granting of degrees, including honorary degrees, and certificates of proficiency, except in Theology; for the establishment of exhibitions, scholarships and prizes; for the affiliation of any college established in Canada; for the dissolution or modification of the terms of affiliations; for the cancellation, recall and suspension of degrees; for the establishment of any faculty, department, chair or course of instruction in the University, or any department, chair or course of instruction in University College, except Theology; for the conduct of the election of members of the Senate; for the appointment of examiners and the conduct of all University examinations other than those in the faculties; for the representation on the Senate of any faculty which may hereafter be established; for the preparation and publication of the calendars; to consider and determine on the report of the faculties, the courses of study in these faculties; and all other courses of study for which no faculty is created; to consider and determine on the report of the various faculty councils, the appointment of examiners and the conduct and results of the examinations in these faculties; to consider such matters as may be reported to it by the council of any faculty and to communicate its opinion or action thereon to the council; to hear and determine appeals from decisions of the faculty councils upon applications and memorials by students and others; to make rules and regulations for the management and conduct of the Library and to prescribe the duties of the Librarian; to make such changes in its own composition as may be deemed expedient; and to make such recommendations to the Board as may be deemed proper for promoting the interests of the University and of University College or for carrying out the objects and provisions of the Act.

4. CONVOCATION.—Convocation consists of the whole body of graduates of the University, in all faculties.   Except indirectly through its elected representatives, no part of the management of the University is exercised by it as a whole.   It elects the Chancellor, and, in divisions according to faculty, itelects members of Senate, as its representatives in Arts, Medicine, Law, Applied Science and Engineering and Agriculture.   Any question relating to University affairs may be discussed by it, and a vote taken. The result of such discussion is communicated to the Senate, which must consider the representation made, and return to Convocation its conclusion thereon.

5. FACULTY COUNCILS.—The seven faculties of Arts, Medicine, Applied Science and Engineering, Household Science, Education, Forestry and Music have each a Council, the President being Chairman, ex-officio, of the first and the Deans of the respective faculties of the other five.   All professors, associate professors and assistant professors engaged in teaching students of any faculty have a seat and vote upon the council of the faculty whose students they teach; lecturers also, provided they are upon the permanent staff, have a seat but no vote in the council.   Each council is autonomous, and has the settlement in the first instance of all applications and memorials from its students, the drawing up of a curriculum of studies, and the appointment of examiners and conduct of examinations.   In the case of applications and memorials the settlement by the council is subject to an appeal to the Senate; in the case of courses of studies, appointment of examiners and conduct of examinations, the decisions of the councils are subject to the approval of and confirmation by the Senate.

The Council of the Faculty of Arts includes the Principal of University College, the President or other head of every federated university, the Dean of the Faculty of Arts, the teaching staff of University, Victoria, Trinity and St. Michael's College (except in the case of those whose appointments are temporary), and one professor in the Department of Religious Knowledge appointed by each federated university or college.

6. THE CAPUT.—The Caput is a committee composed of the President, the Principal of University College, the Heads of the federated universities, the Heads of the federated colleges, and the Deans of the faculties of the University.

It has power to authorize teaching and lectures by others than the duly appointed members of the teaching staff, to exercise discipline over students, where more than one college or one faculty is concerned, or where breaches of discipline occur outside the buildings or grounds appropriated to the several colleges and faculties.

7. THE COUNCIL OF UNIVERSITY COLLEGE.—This body is composed of the Principal and the professors, associate professors and assistant professors of the College. It has committed to it the direction and management of the College with full authority over and entire responsibility for the discipline (including the imposition of reasonable fines) of the undergraduates in relation to the lectures and other instruction of the professors, lecturers and other teachers of the College; and no lecturing or teaching of any kind may be carried on in the College by any other than the duly appointed professors or teachers without the authority of the Council.

8. FEDERATED INSTITUTIONS.—The following institutions are federated with the University, viz., Victoria College, Trinity College, St. Michael's College, Knox College and Wycliffe College. The president or other head of each is, ex-officio, a member of the Senate and of the University Council. In addition, Knox and Wycliffe Colleges each appoint two other representatives on the Senate. Victoria and Trinity Colleges each appoint one member and the graduates of each elect five more representatives to represent each College. All regular students matriculated in the University who are enrolled in University College or Victoria College or Trinity College or St. Michael's College and who enter their names with the Registrar of the University are entitled to free instruction in Arts in the University. But this provision does not include exemption from laboratory fees, nor does it apply to graduate instruction. When a federated college, by arrangement with the University Council, teaches any part of the Arts course the Board of Governors may make a reduction in the fees of students taught in such College.

9. REVENUES OF THE UNIVERSITY.—In addition to the income from the balance of the original endowment and additions made to it from time to time, the Legislature grants to the University, annually, the sum of $500,000 from the revenues of the Province. In addition, the annual deficit upon maintenance account is borne by the Province.

MATRICULATION

MATRICULATION.

Subjects.

A candidate for Pass Matriculation must write upon the examinations conducted by the Department of Education of Ontario in the following subjects of the Middle School:

LATIN (Authors, one paper; Composition, one paper).

ENGLISH (Literature, one paper; Composition, one paper).

HISTORY (British, one paper; Ancient, one paper).

MATHEMATICS (Algebra, one paper; Geometry, one paper).

Any two of:

GREEK (Authors, one paper; Composition, one paper).

FRENCH (Authors, one paper; Composition, one paper).

GERMAN (Authors, one paper; Composition, one paper).

SPANISH (Authors, one paper; Composition, one paper).

or

ITALIAN (Authors, one paper; Composition, one paper),

EXPERIMENTAL SCIENCE (Physics, one paper; Chemistry, one paper).

or

AGRICULTURE (Part I, one paper; Part II, one paper).

In certain cases foreign students may present themselves for examination in their language instead of Greek or French or German or Spanish or Italian when the language and the curriculum in that language have been approved by the Senate. The examination in an approved language consists of two years, similar in character to those in English.

A candidate for Honour Matriculation must write upon the examinations conducted by the Department of Education of Ontario in one or more of the following subjects of the Upper School:

GREEK (Authors, one paper; Composition, one paper).

LATIN (Authors, one paper; Composition, one paper).

ENGLISH (Literature, one paper; Composition, one paper).

FRENCH (Authors, one paper; Composition, one paper).

GERMAN (Authors, one paper; Composition, one paper).

SPANISH (Authors, one paper; Composition, one paper).

HISTORY (one paper.)

MATHEMATICS (Algebra, one paper; Geometry, one paper; Trigonometry, one paper).

PHYSICS (one paper).

CHEMISTRY (one paper).

BIOLOGY (Botany, one paper; Zoology, one paper).

These examinations, both Pass and Honour, are conducted by the Department at various centres throughout the Province of Ontario in June and September of each year.

Standards.

A candidate for Pass Matriculation will be allowed to write on one or more papers at a time in any order, and on obtaining at least fifty per cent. of the marks assigned to any paper will be given credit for having passed in such paper and will receive a certificate of such standing.

A candidate for Honour Matriculation will be allowed to write on one or more papers at a time in any order.

In order to secure First Class Honours in a subject a candidate must obtain at one examination at least seventy-five per cent. of the marks assigned to that subject and at least fifty per cent. in each paper of that subject.

In order to secure Second Class Honours in a subject a candidate must obtain at one examination at least sixty-six per cent. of the marks assigned to that subject and at least fifty per cent. in each paper of that subject.

In order to secure Third Class Honours in a subject a candidate must obtain at one examination at least sixty per cent. of the marks assigned to that subject and at least fifty per cent. in each paper of that subject.

A candidate who fails to obtain First, Second or Third Class Honours in a subject under the above regulations, may secure credit for the subject by obtaining at least fifty per cent. on each paper of the subject, not necessarily at one examination.

Such credit in a subject will be accepted by the University as covering the Honour Matriculation requirement with respect to that subject for admission to any faculty.

Such credit in a subject will also be accepted by the University as entitling the candidate, if registered in the Faculty of Arts, to exemption from the Pass work of the First Year in that subject, wherever the subject is included in the First Year of the Pass Course.

FACULTY OF ARTS.

A candidate for admission to the First Year in the Faculty of Arts must produce satisfactory certificates of good character and of having completed the sixteenth year of his age on or before the first of October of the year in which he proposes to register.

A candidate for admission to the First Year of the Pass Course in 1922 must present certificates giving him credit for **complete** Pass Matriculation. (See p. 7.)

A candidate for admission to the First Year of the Pass Course in 1923 must present certificates giving him credit in certain subjects of Honour Matriculation in addition to complete Pass Matriculation standing.

A candidate for admission to the First Year of an Honour Course must present, in addition to complete Pass Matriculation standing, certificates giving him credit at the Honour Matriculation examination in the subjects prescribed below for the Honour Course which he wishes to enter.

CLASSICS:—Greek, Latin, Mathematics (Algebra and Geometry) and one of French, German, Physics, Biology; preferably French or German.

GREEK AND HEBREW:—Greek, Latin, Mathematics (Algebra and Geometry) and one of English, French, German.

FRENCH, GREEK AND LATIN:—Latin, Mathematics (Algebra and Geometry) and two of Greek, English, French.

MODERN LANGUAGES:—Latin, French, Mathematics (Algebra and Geometry) and one of English, German, History.

ENGLISH AND HISTORY:—Latin, Mathematics (Algebra and Geometry) and two of English, Greek, French, German.

MODERN HISTORY: } Latin, Mathematics (Algebra and Geometry),
POLITICAL SCIENCE:}   History or English, and French or German.

COMMERCE AND FINANCE:—Latin, English, Mathematics (Algebra, Geometry and Trigonometry) and French or German.

PHILOSOPHY:—Latin, English, Mathematics (Algebra and Geometry) and one of History, Greek, French, German, Physics.

PHILOSOPHY, ENGLISH AND HISTORY:—Latin, Mathematics (Algebra and Geometry), one of History, English, Physics, and one of Greek, French, German.

PSYCHOLOGY:—Latin, Mathematics (Algebra, Geometry and Trigonometry), French or German, and one of Physics, Biology, Chemistry.

MATHEMATICS AND PHYSICS:—Latin, Mathematics (Algebra, Geometry and Trigonometry), Physics, and French or German.

PHYSICS:
BIOLOGY:
PHYSIOLOGY AND BIOCHEMISTRY:
BIOLOGICAL AND MEDICAL SCIENCES:
CHEMISTRY AND MINERALOGY:
CHEMISTRY:
GEOLOGY AND MINERALOGY:
HOUSEHOLD SCIENCE:
SCIENCE FOR TEACHERS:

Latin, Mathematics (Algebra, Geometry and Trigonometry), French or German, and one of Physics, Biology, Chemistry.

HOUSEHOLD ECONOMICS:—Latin, Mathematics (Algebra and Geometry) and two of English, French or German, Physics, Biology, Chemistry; preferably French or German and a science.

A candidate for admission to the First Year of the Course in Commerce must present certificates giving him **full** credit in the following subjects of Pass and Honour Matriculation:

Part I—Pass Matriculation.

ENGLISH (Literature and Composition).
HISTORY (British and Ancient).
MATHEMATICS (Algebra and Geometry).
Three of:
　GREEK (Authors and Composition).
　LATIN (Authors and Composition).
　FRENCH (Authors and Composition).
　GERMAN (Authors and Composition).
　SPANISH (Authors and Composition), *or*
　ITALIAN (Authors and Composition).
EXPERIMENTAL SCIENCE (Physics and Chemistry).
of which one at least must be modern language.

Part II—Honour Matriculation.

ENGLISH (Literature and Composition).
MATHEMATICS (Algebra, Geometry and Trigonometry).
One of:
　GERMAN (Authors and Composition).
　FRENCH (Authors and Composition).
　SPANISH (Authors and Composition).

FACULTY OF MEDICINE.

A candidate for admission to the First Year in the Faculty of Medicine must produce satisfactory certificates of good character and of having completed the seventeenth year of his age on or before the first of October of the year in which he proposes to register; only under exceptional circumstances will a candidate of thirty years or more be admitted.

He must also present certificates giving him **full** credit in the following subjects of Pass and Honour Matriculation:

Part I—Pass Matriculation.

LATIN (Authors and Composition).
ENGLISH (Literature and Composition).
HISTORY (British and Ancient).
MATHEMATICS (Algebra and Geometry).
EXPERIMENTAL SCIENCE (Physics and Chemistry).
Any one of:
　GREEK (Authors and Composition).
　FRENCH (Authors and Composition).
　GERMAN (Authors and Composition).
　SPANISH (Authors and Composition), *or*
　ITALIAN (Authors and Composition).

Part II—Honour Matriculation.

ENGLISH (Literature and Composition).
MATHEMATICS (Algebra, Geometry and Trigonometry).
One of:
   LATIN (Authors and Composition).
   GREEK (Authors and Composition).
   · FRENCH (Authors and Composition).
   GERMAN (Authors and Composition).

Candidates for Matriculation in this Faculty are advised to take the complete Part I at one examination, and in a subsequent year Part II.

FACULTY OF APPLIED SCIENCE AND ENGINEERING.

A candidate for admission to the First Year in the Faculty of Applied Science and Engineering must produce satisfactory certificates of good character and of having completed the seventeenth year of his age on or before the first of October of the year in which he proposes to register.

He must also present certificates giving him credit in the following subjects of Pass and Honour Matriculation:

Part I—Pass Matriculation.

ENGLISH (Literature and Composition).
HISTORY (British and Ancient).
MATHEMATICS (Algebra and Geometry).
Any three of:
   LATIN (Authors and Composition).
   GREEK (Authors and Composition).
   FRENCH (Authors and Composition).
   GERMAN (Authors and Composition).
   SPANISH (Authors and Composition), *or*
   ITALIAN (Authors and Composition).
   EXPERIMENTAL SCIENCE (Physics and Chemistry).

Part II—Honour Matriculation.

ENGLISH (Literature and Composition).
MATHEMATICS (Algebra, Geometry and Trigonometry).
One of:
   LATIN (Authors and Composition).
   GREEK (Authors and Composition).
   FRENCH (Authors and Composition).
   GERMAN (Authors and Composition).
   SPANISH (Authors and Composition).

Candidates for Matriculation in this Faculty are advised to take the complete Part I at one examination, and in a subsequent year, Part II.

In selecting the options it is recommended that students take French, German and Experimental Science. In the Department of Architecture, French is required, in the Departments of Chemical Engineering and Mechanical Engineering it is desirable that students take German.

FACULTY OF FORESTRY.

A candidate for admission to the First Year in the Faculty of Forestry must produce satisfactory certificates of good character and of having completed the seventeenth year of his age on or before the first of October of the year in which he proposes to register.

He must also present certificates giving him credit in the following subjects of Pass and Honour Matriculation:

Part I—Pass Matriculation.

ENGLISH (Literature and Composition).
HISTORY (British and Ancient).
MATHEMATICS (Algebra, Geometry and Trigonometry).
Any three of:
  LATIN (Authors and Composition).
  GREEK (Authors and Composition).
  FRENCH (Authors and Composition).
  GERMAN (Authors and Composition).
  SPANISH (Authors and Composition), *or*
  ITALIAN (Authors and Composition).
  EXPERIMENTAL SCIENCE (Ph sics and Chemistry), *or*
  AGRICULTURE.

Part II—Honour Matriculation.

ENGLISH (Literature and Composition).
MATHEMATICS (Algebra, Geometry and Trigonometry).
Any one of:
  LATIN (Authors and Composition).
  FRENCH (Authors and Composition).
  GERMAN (Authors and Composition).

Candidates for Matriculation in this Faculty are advised to take the complete Part I at one examination, and in a subsequent year, Part II.

In selecting the options it is recommended that students take French or German in Part II.

FACULTY OF MUSIC.

The subjects for Matriculation in Music are:
ENGLISH (Literature and Composition).
Any two of:
  LATIN (Authors and Composition).
  GREEK (Authors and Composition).
  FRENCH (Authors and Composition).
  GERMAN (Authors and Composition).
  SPANISH (Authors and Composition), *or*
  ITALIAN (Authors and Composition).

A candidate for the degree of Bachelor of Music must complete his Matriculation prior to admission to the examination of the final year.

The pass standard is the same as that for Pass Matriculation.

SPECIAL MATRICULATION CONDITIONS.

The new regulations outlined on page 8 by which any candidate may receive credit in one or more papers at an examination have rendered unnecessary the special regulations for the industrial candidate. Consequently such candidate will **no longer** be required to send his statement of marks, together with a certificate of employment to the Secretary of the University Matriculation Board, in order to secure credit for the papers in which he has passed.

JUNE EXAMINATION.

The examination for Pass and Honour Matriculation is held annually in June at centres in Ontario, and, if application is made to the Senate, the examination may, with the co-operation of the Department of Education, be held at centres outside Ontario.

Applications must be sent not later than the 15th of May, to the local Public School Inspector, or in the case of candidates intending to write at the University, to the Registrar.

Scholarship candidates must also send a special application by the same date to the Registrar, according to a form to be obtained from him.

The prescribed fee will be paid to the presiding officer by the candidate, when he presents himself for examination.

The Junior Matriculation examination will be held in June at such centres outside Ontario as may from time to time be authorized by the Senate. Applications for the establishment of such local centres must be made to the Registrar not later than the 15th of April in each year. Applications from candidates for this examination must be sent to the Registrar not later than the 1st of May.

The presiding examiner's fee, together with any other necessary expenses in connection with such an examination, must be met by the candidates at the centre, or by the authorities of the School or College on whose application it is held.

SUPPLEMENTAL MATRICULATION EXAMINATION.

1. The Supplemental Junior Matriculation examination is conducted by the Department of Education for the University Matriculation Board at the following centres:—

(a) The University of Toronto; Queen's University, Kingston; McMaster University, Toronto; Western University, London.

(b) Any of the following, upon request:—Windsor, Chatham, Sarnia, St. Thomas, Woodstock, Brantford, Simcoe, Cayuga, Welland, St. Catharines, Hamilton, Goderich, Stratford, Kitchener, Guelph, Walkerton, Owen Sound, Orangeville, Barrie, Whitby, Bowmanville, Cobourg, Lindsay,

Peterborough, Belleville, Picton, Napanee, Brockville, Kemptville, Morrisburg, Cornwall, Alexandria, Vankleek Hill, Ottawa, Smith's Falls, Renfrew, Bracebridge, North Bay, Sault Ste. Marie, Port Arthur, Haileybury.

(c) Elsewhere in Ontario upon request, and if approved by the University Matriculation Board.

(d) Elsewhere in Canada, upon request of one of the aforesaid Universities and with the approval of the Board.

2. Applications to write on the examination, accompanied by the necessary fee, shall be received at the office of the Secretary of the University Matriculation Board, Parliament Buildings, Toronto, as follows:—

(a) Up to September 1st, from those who wish to write at any centre authorized in Ontario.

(b) Up to August 25th, from those who wish to write elsewhere in Ontario.

(c) Up to August 1st, from those who, through one of the aforesaid Universities, make application to write outside of the Province of Ontario.

3. On payment of the required fee with one dollar additional, a candidate who has failed to make application as specified in the foregoing regulation (2) may be admitted to the examination at a centre already established, provided the accommodation is adequate and the number of question papers sufficient.

4. The subjects of the examination, the prescription of work and the standard required shall be the same as for the Midsummer Pass and Honour Matriculation examinations of the same year.

5. The following are eligible to become candidates at this examination:

(a) Those who are applicants for the complete Matriculation examination.

(b) Those who are completing the Matriculation examination under the regulations in force in any previous year.

(c) Those who are applicants for Matriculation standing in certain papers.

6. (a) Candidates may write at any one of the four University centres mentioned in 1 (a) without any additional cost to themselves.

(b) Candidates who write at any other centre, in addition to paying the fee required, must also defray the local expenses of conducting the examination. These include the cost of supplies, any charge for the examination room, express charges, and the allowance to the Presiding Officer.

7. Forms of application and copies of the time-table may be obtained after July 1st, on application to the Secretary, University Matriculation Board, Parliament Buildings, Toronto.

EQUIVALENT EXAMINATIONS.

A person who has passed the Matriculation examination of another University may be admitted *ad eundem statum* on such conditions as the Senate, on application, may prescribe.

The local examinations conducted by the University of Oxford and the University of Cambridge may be accepted *pro tanto.*

Certificates of having passed the subjects common to the Matriculation and other examination of any of the following examinations will be accepted *pro tanto*, provided always that the standards of these certificate as to subjects and percentages meet the requirements of this University.

Province of Ontario.

The examinations for Entrance to Normal Schools or for Entrance to Faculties of Education or examinations of the same standard under other names.

Candidates who have already passed Part I. of the pass Junior Matriculation, or of the Junior Leaving examination, will not be required to pass again in the subjects thereof.

Province of Quebec.

The Associate in Arts examination.

Province of New Brunswick.

The examination for Superior and Grammar School Licenses.

Province of Nova Scotia.

The Junior and Senior Leaving examinations (Grades XI. and XII.).

Province of Manitoba.

Grade XI and Grade XII Examinations.

Province of British Columbia.

The Intermediate and Senior Grade examination.

Province of Prince Edward Island.

The First Class Teachers' License examination.

Province of Alberta.

Grade XI and Grade XII Examinations.

Province of Saskatchewan.

The First and Second Class Teachers' examinations.
The Senior and Junior Matriculation examinations.

Newfoundland.

Associate in Arts Examinations.

Candidates whose certificates do not cover all the subjects may complete matriculation by passing in the remaining subjects as prescribed by the University, or by passing in the subjects of similar standard as prescribed by the Education Department of the Province by which the certificate was issued.

The Senate will consider applications for the recognition of certificates other than those mentioned, as occasion may require.

FEES.

The Fees payable are as follows:—

For registration of certificates for other than University
purposes.. $5.00

For registration of certificates other than those of
Ontario, which exempt the applicant from the full
Matriculation examination..................... 5.00

For admission *ad eundem statum*.................... 5.00

MATRICULATION SCHOLARSHIPS IN THE FACULTY OF ARTS.

Where there is no letter prefixed the scholarship is open to all competitors and is tenable in any one of the Colleges. In all other cases, the letter C. indicates University College; the letter V., Victoria College; the letter T., Trinity College; and the letter M., St. Michael's College; the student to whom one of these scholarships is awarded is required to enroll in each year of his course in the College to which the scholarship belongs.

Pass Matriculation Scholarships.

Two Scholarships, known as "The First and Second Gibson Pass Matriculation Scholarships", of the value of $120 and $100 respectively with free tuition for one year, have been endowed by Sir John M. Gibson, of Hamilton, a graduate in Arts of 1863.

They will be awarded subject to the following conditions:

1. All candidates for these Scholarships must have been bona fide students of the Hamilton Collegiate Institute for at least the two years immediately preceding the award.

2. Each candidate must state in writing that it is his intention to proceed to a degree in Arts in one of the Colleges of the University of Toronto.

3. A student who has already obtained either complete or partial Pass Matriculation is not eligible to compete for these Scholarships.

—6

4. The Scholarships shall be awarded annually to the two matriculants who rank highest at the Pass Matriculation Examination conducted in June by the Department of Education of Ontario. The subjects and standards shall be those prescribed for Pass Matriculation in the Faculty of Arts.

5. Successful candidates must register in the First Year of the Pass Course in the Faculty of Arts during the session immediately following the award, unless special permission is granted by the Senate of the University to postpone such registration.

6. The cash payment of the Scholarships shall be made in the month of February in this session. Before payment can be made the scholar must present the prescribed certificate of attendance.

7. In the event that instruction in the First Year of the Pass Course should no longer be given at the University, the scholars shall be required to attend the Hamilton Collegiate Institute for the session following the award, and to pursue the course of study prescribed for admission to the Second Year of the Pass Course. On receipt of a certificate of attendance in February of this session the University will forward to the Scholars the cash payments due them.

Honour Matriculation Scholarships.
GENERAL PROFICIENCY.

The Prince of Wales Scholarship, the gift of the late King Edward VII., of the value of $50. This scholarship shall be awarded to the candidate who, ranking first in one of the following groups, has the highest aggregate in the subjects of Latin, English, French, History, Algebra and Geometry.

GROUP I.
GREEK, LATIN, ENGLISH, FRENCH, HISTORY, MATHEMATICS (ALGEBRA AND GEOMETRY).

The First Edward Blake Scholarship, the gift of the late Hon. Edward Blake, ex-Chancellor of the University, of the value of $50, with free tuition for four years, of a total value of $210.

The Second Edward Blake Scholarship, the gift of the late Hon. Edward Blake, ex-Chancellor of the University, of the value of $35, with free tituition for three years, of a total value of $155.

GROUP II.
LATIN, ENGLISH, FRENCH, GERMAN, HISTORY, MATHEMATICS (ALGEBRA AND GEOMETRY).

The First Edward Blake Scholarship, the gift of the late Hon. Edward Blake, ex-Chancellor of the University, of the value of $50, with free tuition for four years, of a total value of $210.

The Second Edward Blake Scholarship, the gift of the late Hon. Edward Blake, ex-Chancellor of the University, of the value of $35, with free tuition for three years, of a total value of $155.

GROUP III.

LATIN, ENGLISH, FRENCH, HISTORY, MATHEMATICS (ALGEBRA, GEOMETRY, TRIGONOMETRY, PROBLEMS), PHYSICS.

The First Edward Blake Scholarship, the gift of the late Hon. Edward Blake, ex-Chancellor of the University, of the value of $50, with free tuition for four years, of a total value of $210.

The Second Edward Blake Scholarship, the gift of the late Hon. Edward Blake, ex-Chancellor of the University, of the value of $35, with free tuition for three years, of a total value of $155.

GROUP IV.

LATIN, ENGLISH, FRENCH, HISTORY, MATHEMATICS (ALGEBRA, GEOMETRY, TRIGONOMETRY), SCIENCE, (PHYSICS, CHEMISTRY, BIOLOGY).

The First Edward Blake Scholarship, the gift of the late Hon. Edward Blake, ex-Chancellor of the University, of the value of $50, with free tuition for four years, of a total value of $210.

The Second Edward Blake Scholarship, the gift of the late Hon. Edward Blake, ex-Chancellor of the University, of the value of $35, with free tuition for three years, of a total value of $155.

C. The Gibson Scholarship, the gift of the Hon. Sir John M. Gibson, of the value of $100, with free tuition for three years, of a total value of $220. This scholarship shall be awarded to the candidate who, qualifying for one of the preceding scholarships and excluding the Prince of Wales Scholar, has the highest aggregate in the subjects of Latin, English, French, History, Algebra and Geometry.

Candidates for these scholarships are required to obtain First Class Honours in at least one Department.

T. The Upper Canada College-Trinity Scholarship, the gift of Upper Canada College Old Boys, who are alumni of Trinity College, of the value of $100.

The successful candidate must obtain first class honours in at least one department. Pass papers rank at half the value of Honour papers. The sum of $60 will be paid in equal terminal instalments in the first year, and $40 in the second year.

M. The Silver, Episcopal Jubliee Scholarship, the gift of the Toronto Subdivision of the Catholic Women's League of Canada, in honour of the Silver Jubilee of the Most Rev. Neil McNeil, Archbishop of Toronto, of the value of $100.

This Scholarship open for competition only to women students residing in Toronto.

T. The F. A. Bethune Scholarship, the gift of the trustees of the F. A. Bethune Memorial Fund, of the value of $60.

This Scholarship will be awarded to the candidate from Trinity College School, Port Hope, who obtains the highest number of marks, being not less than two-thirds of the total, at the Honour Matriculation Examination, and becomes and continues a resident undergraduate of Trinity College, Toronto, for the whole of the year for which he holds the Scholarship.

PROFICIENCY IN TWO DEPARTMENTS.

CLASSICS AND MODERN LANGUAGES.

The First Edward Blake Scholarship, the gift of the Hon. Edward Blake, ex-Chancellor of the University, of the value of $60, with free tuition for four years, of a total value of $220.

The Second Edward Blake Scholarship, the gift of the Hon. Edward Blake, ex-Chancellor of the University, of the value of $55, with free tuition for four years, of a total value of $215.

The Third Edward Blake Scholarship, the gift of the Hon. Edward Blake, ex-Chancellor of the University, of the value of $40, with free tuition for three years, of a total value of $160.

The Fourth Edward Blake Scholarship, the gift of the Hon. Edward Blake, ex-Chancellor of the University, of the value of $35, with free tuition for three years, of a total value of $155.

CLASSICS AND MATHEMATICS.

The First Edward Blake Scholarship, the gift of the Hon. Edward Blake, ex-Chancellor of the University, of the value of $60, with free tuition for four years, of a total value of $220.

The Second Edward Blake Scholarship, the gift of the Hon. Edward Blake, ex-Chancellor of the University, of the value of $40, with free tuition for three years, of a total value of $160.

MODERN LANGUAGES AND MATHEMATICS.

The First Edward Blake Scholarship, the gift of the Hon. Edward Blake, ex-Chancellor of the University, of the value of $60, with free tuition for four years, of a total value of $220.

The Second Edward Blake Scholarship, the gift of the Hon. Edward Blake, ex-Chancellor of the University, of the value of $40, with free tuition for three years, of a total value of $160.

MODERN LANGUAGES AND SCIENCE.

The First Edward Blake Scholarship, the gift of the Hon. Edward Blake, ex-Chancellor of the University, of the value of $60, with free tuition for four years, of a total value of $220.

The Second Edward Blake Scholarship, the gift of the Hon. Edward Blake, ex-Chancellor of the University, of the value of $40, with free tuition for three years, of a total value of $160.

MATHEMATICS AND SCIENCE.

The First Edward Blake Scholarship, the gift of the Hon. Edward Blake, ex-Chancellor of the University, of the value of $60, with free tuition for four years, of a total value of $220.

The Second Edward Blake Scholarship, the gift of the Hon. Edward Blake, ex-Chancellor of the University, of the value of $40, with free tuition for three years, of a total value of $160.

Candidates for these scholarships must obtain first class honours in one of the specified departments and at least second class in the other.

ENGLISH, HISTORY AND CLASSICS.

T. The Bishop Strachan Scholarship, founded in memory of the first Bishop of Toronto, of the value of $40 a year for two years.

ENGLISH, HISTORY, LATIN AND FRENCH.

T. The Dickson Scholarship, the gift of the late William Dickson, Esq., of the value of $60 a year for two years.

PROFICIENCY IN ONE DEPARTMENT.

CLASSICS.

T. The Wellington Scholarship, founded by the first Duke of Wellington, of the value of $60 a year for two years.

C. The McCaul Scholarship, the gift of G. A. H. Fraser, M.A., formerly Fellow in Classics 1889-91, Andrew Melville Stewart, M.A., LL.B., Honour graduate in Classics, 1891, and Principal Hutton, of the value of $75, with free tuition for four years, of a total value of $235.

The First Mary Mulock Scholarship, the gift of the late Mrs. Mulock, of the value of $60, with free tuition for three years, of a total value of $180.

V. The Flavelle Scholarship, the gift of Sir J. W. Flavelle, BART., LL.D., of the value of $60, with free tuition for three years, of a total value of $180.

The Second Mary Mulock Scholarship, the gift of the late Mrs. Mulock, of the value of $60, with free tuition for two years, of a total value of $140.

V. The W. E. H. Massey Scholarship, the gift of the late W. E. H. Massey, Esq., of the value of $50. with free tuition for two years, of a total value of $130.

GREEK.

The George R. R. Cockburn Scholarship, the gift of the late Mary Cockburn. Awarded to the successful candidate at the scholarship examination who ranks highest in First Class Honours in Greek.

This scholarship is tenable with any other University scholarship.

Modern Languages.

T. The Dickson Scholarship, the gift of the late William Dickson, Esq., of the value of $60 a year for two years.

The First Edward Blake Scholarship, the gift of the Hon. Edward Blake, ex-Chancellor of the University, of the value of $60, with free tuition for three years, of a total value of $180.

The Second Edward Blake Scholarship, the gift of the Hon. Edward Blake, ex-Chancellor of the University, of the value of $30, with free tuition for three years, of a total value of $150.

Mathematics.

T. The Wellington Scholarship, founded by the first Duke of Wellington, of the value of $60 a year for two years.

The First Edward Blake Scholarship, the gift of the Hon. Edward Blake, ex-Chancellor of the University, of the value of $60, with free tuition for three years, of a total value of $180.

The Second Edward Blake Scholarship the gift of the Hon. Edward Blake, ex-Chancellor of the University, of the value of $30, with free tuition for three years, of a total value of $150.

T. The Professor William Jones Scholarship, founded in memory of the late Reverend William Jones, M.A., D.C.L., by relatives and other personal friends. It is open only to students matriculating from Trinity College School, Port Hope.

Science.

T. The Burnside Scholarship, founded in memory of the late Dr. Burnside, of the value of $40 a year for two years.

The First Edward Blake Scholarship, the gift of the Hon. Edward Blake, ex-Chancellor of the University, of the value of $60, with free tuition for three years, of a total value of $180.

The Second Edward Blake Scholarship, the gift of the Hon. Edward Blake, ex-Chancellor of the University, of the value of $30, with free tuition for three years, of a total value of $150.

Candidates for these scholarships must obtain first class honours in their departments.

The John McCrae Scholarships.

Two Scholarships, each known as "The John McCrae Scholarship", and of the value of at least $200 per year for four years, have been founded in memory of the late Lieutenant-Colonel John McCrae, B.A., M.D., of Montreal, one time Fellow in Biology of the University of Toronto physician, soldier, poet, who died in France in January, 1918.

The purpose of the Scholarships is to assist youths of ability, promise and approved academic standing, who desire to acquire the education represented by an Arts degree, but whose circumstances are such as to make the fulfilment of that desire impracticable without assistance. It is, moreover, desired that the Scholarships should be used to stimulate such ambition among the pupils of the Guelph Collegiate Institute; John McCrae's home and boyhood school from which he matriculated and entered the University of Toronto. The award will, therefore, be limited to Matriculants into the University of Toronto from the Guelph Collegiate Institute, or failing eligible and acceptable candidates therefrom in any year, from among other Canadian Matriculants. The award shall go to a male candidate if there be one eligible and acceptable—if not, the award may, in exceptional cases, be made to a female. A scholar may be chosen from matriculants of the year in which the award is made or the previous year. If the award is made to a matriculant of the previous year, and one year of the scholar's course for degree has already been passed, the award may be limited to the remaining three years of the course.

The selection of the scholars shall be made by a Committee composed of the President of the University, the Principal of Guelph Collegiate Institute, and a member or nominee of the family of the late John McCrae. If in any year, an acceptable candidate is not found, the award need not then be made, but may be postponed to the following year; but such postponement shall not affect the next succeeding Scholarship, which shall be offered in the year in which in due course it would otherwise have been available.

Every successful candidate shall, as a condition of the award, sign a declaration of intention to proceed to a degree in Arts in the University of Toronto, and must attend lectures for the academic year immediately following the award, unless permission is granted by the Senate upon the recommendation of the Faculty for the postponement of attendance for a year. The candidate shall also sign a promise to repay to the University any sums paid to him on account of the Scholarship, if from any cause not beyond his control he shall fail to complete the full course in Arts leading to a degree. If, during the currency of the Scholarship, the candidate shall fail to maintain a satisfactory standard of efficiency in scholarship and good conduct, the award may, as to further payments, be cancelled by the selecting body after consultation with the University authorities.

One of these Scholarships will be offered in 1922 and in every second year thereafter. Candidates are required to make a special application on a form to be obtained from the Registrar. The award will be based upon the results of the Scholarship Matriculation Examination conducted by the Department of Education of Ontario.

The Leonard McLaughlin Scholarship.

T.   This scholarship has been endowed by Mr. and Mrs. Michael Mc-Laughlin, of Toronto, in memory of their only son Leonard, who was at the time of his death, December 10th, 1899, an undergraduate of Trinity College. As he was a pupil at Upper Canada College from 1890 to 1896, only pupils of that school are eligible for the scholarship. This award will be made by a board consisting of the Provost of Trinity College with the Principal and the Classical Master of Upper Canada College to such candidate as, without written examinations, shows evidence of possessing good scholarship in Classics, as well as manliness, a sense of honour, and a strong moral character. Failing a suitable candidate in Classics, the Board may at its discretion select one in Modern Languages, though it is not under any obligation to make a selection in any given year.

Successful candidates must pursue a course of study in Classics or Modern Languages to the satisfaction of the Board. In case of necessity, to be by it determined, the Board may allow a postponement of the time of beginning the course or an interruption of the same.

The scholarship is worth $400; $100 will be paid to successive holders at the end of each Term in the First and Second Years.

The Cooper Exhibition.

T.   These two exhibitions, founded by the Rev. C. W. Cooper, of the value of $100 each, are open to any matriculated student of Trinity College not holding a scholarship, with a preference to the sons of clergymen. The exhibitioners are nominated by the Most Reverend the Lord Bishop of Toronto.

Corporation Bursaries.

T.   The Corporation has provided that five Bursaries of a value of $50 per annum be open every year for a period not exceeding three years. Any student who shall have passed the Matriculation examination, and shall have satisfied the Executive Committee that he cannot without the aid thus afforded, avail himself of the advantage of a University education, will be eligible for a bursary, provided that he is not the holder of a scholarship or exhibition. *Caeteris paribus* the sons of clergymen will be preferred.

Scholarships, exhibitions and bursaries will be forfeited if the holder fails to keep a term, or to pass any examination at the regular time.

Daughters of the Empire Bursary.

The Imperial Order, Daughters of the Empire, has established a War Memorial Bursary in each province of the Dominion, of the value of $250 a year for four years, to be awarded to the candidate in either the Junior or the Honour Matriculation examinations who, in the judgment of the Committee, best meets the purpose in view in the foundation of the Bursary. The candidate must be the son or daughter of a killed or permanently disabled soldier, sailor or member of the Air Force. In case the holder of the Bursary for the Province of Ontario elects to study at the University of Toronto his fees will be remitted to the extent of $25 a year provided the student has passed satisfactorily his examinations for the proceeding year.

Information respecting the Ontario Bursary may be obtained from Miss W. Gordon, 122 University Avenue, Kingston, Ont., from whom forms of application may be secured.

REGULATIONS REGARDING THE UNIVERSITY SCHOLARSHIPS.

The marks for all classes of scholarships will be assigned in the following proportions:

CLASSICS	Latin	600	
	Greek	600	
			1200
MATHEMATICS			1200
MODERN LANGUAGES	English	400	
	French	400	
	German	400	
			1200
SCIENCE	Chemistry	400	
	Physics	400	
	Biology (Botany, Zoology)	400	
			1200
HISTORY			300

Candidates for Matriculation Scholarships must send a special application not later than May 15th to the Registrar of the University, according to a form to be obtained from him.

Candidates for scholarships shall at the same examination pass in all the subjects necessary for Junior Matriculation.

A candidate to whom a scholarship has been awarded at a Matriculation examination may not compete for a scholarship at a subsequent Matriculation examination. This regulation does not debar the holder of a Gibson Pass Matriculation Scholarship from competing for an Honour Matriculation Scholarship.

With the exception of the Prince of Wales Scholarship, no one shall be entitled to hold more than one University scholarship; but any one who, but for this provision, would have been entitled to a second scholarship will be published in the lists.

College Scholarships may be held with University Scholarships.

Every candidate for a Junior Matriculation scholarship shall, on application for examination, sign a declaration to the effect that he intends to proceed to a degree in Arts in this University.

A candidate competing for University scholarships must indicate at the time of application for examination the College in which he intends to enrol.

No scholarship will be awarded save on condition that the candidate becomes a matriculated student in actual attendance in this University, through enrolment in one of the colleges.

Free tuition awarded will be available on the following conditions:—For the First Year on the award of the scholarship; for any year after the first on proof that the claimant has passed his examination for the preceding year with a first class in an honour course.

In case in any year any scholarship be not taken, it will be allowable to award such scholarship, or some part thereof, to a candidate who has shown special excellence in the examination in some other group and has taken scholarship rank therein, but has failed to win a scholarship therein.

These regulations are subject to change by the Senate.

REGULATIONS RESPECTING UNIVERSITY COLLEGE AND VICTORIA COLLEGE SCHOLARSHIPS.

Scholarships in University College and in Victoria College are tenable with an Edward Blake Scholarship, always providing that the winner be in first class honours in Classics at Matriculation and becomes and continues to be a registered student in attendance upon lectures either in Classics or in English and History with the Classical option in the College by which the scholarship is awarded. In the event of no eligible candidate being forthcoming at Matriculation for either of these scholarships, the scholarships will be held over until the year following, when two scholarships will be offered.

REGULATIONS RESPECTING TRINITY COLLEGE SCHOLARSHIPS.

The regulations governing University Scholarships are applicable to Trinity College Scholarships, *mutatis mutandis*, with the additional regulation that the holder is ordinarily required to reside in College, unless special permission to the contrary is given by the Executive Committee.

As a Trinity College Scholarship is generally held in conjunction with a University Scholarship, the holder in such case enjoys (a) free tuition, (b) the cash value of the University Scholarship, (c) the cash value of the Trinity College Scholarship. For example, if he holds the Wellington Scholarship in Classics and a First Edward Blake Scholarship in the same department, his University Scholarship entitles him to free tuition for four years, which is equivalent to $160, and he receives in addition $50 from the University, and $120 from Trinity College, making a total value of $330. A further advantage is that the winner is assured of accommodation in the Trinity College Residence (or in St. Hilda's in the case of women), as Scholars are given precedence over all other applicants when rooms are being assigned.

PRESCRIPTION OF COURSES.

Pass Matriculation.

Greek.

Translation into English of passages from the prescribed texts, with questions thereon.

Translation at sight of simple narrative passages similar to the Xenophon prescribed.

Questions on Greek accidence and on the common rules of Greek syntax to test the candidate's accuracy and comprehension in such matters as are needful for the intelligent reading of his texts.

The following are the prescribed texts:—

1922 and 1924: Xenophon, Philpotts and Jerram, Easy Selections from Xenophon, chaps. 3, 4, 5; Homer, Iliad, VI., 66-118 and 237 to the end.

1923: Xenophon, Philpotts and Jerram, Easy Selections from Xenophon, chaps. 3, 4, 5; Homer, Iliad, I., 1-350.

Two papers will be set: (1) Prescribed texts; (2) translation at sight, accidence and syntax.

Latin.

Translation at sight of passages of average difficulty from Cæsar, upon which special stress will be laid.

Translation, with questions, from a prescribed portion of Virgil's Æneid.

Examination upon a short prescribed portion of Cæsar, to test the candidate's knowledge of Latin Syntax.

Questions on Latin accidence.

Translation into Latin of English sentences involving a knowledge of the vocabulary and constructions found in the introductory lessons of the High School Latin Book, as reviewed in the chapters on Syntax and Composition.

The following are the texts prescribed:—

1922: Cæsar, De Bello Gallico, Book IV., chaps, 20-38; Virgil, Æneid, Book I., vv. 1-510.

1923: Cæsar, De Bello Gallico, Book V., chaps. 1-23; Virgil, Æneid, Book I., vv. 1-510.

Two papers will be set: (1) Latin Authors, including Virgil, Cæsar and Sight Translation; (2) Latin Composition and Grammar.

English.

COMPOSITION: An essay on one of several themes set by the examiners. In order to pass in this subject, legible writing, correct spelling and punctuation, and idiomatic and grammatical construction of sentences are indispensable. The candidate should also give attention to the structure of the whole essay, the effective ordering of the thought, and the accurate employment of a good English vocabulary, About two pages of foolscap is suggested as the proper length for the essay; but quality, not quantity, will be mainly regarded.

One examination paper.

LITERATURE: Such questions only will be set as may serve to test the candidate's familiarity with, and intelligent and appreciative comprehension of, the prescribed texts. The candidate will be expected to have memorized the passages prescribed below. In addition to the questions on the prescribed selections, others will be set on a "sight passage" to test the candidate's ability to interpret literature for himself.

The candidate shall produce satisfactory proof, by the certificate of the principal of the school from which he comes or otherwise, that he has read carefully, during the preceding year, at least four suitable works in English literature (both prose and poetry) in addition to those prescribed below for examination.

One examination paper.

1922: Coleridge, The Ancient Mariner; Tennyson, Lotos Eaters, Ulysses, "Of old sat Freedom," Locksley Hall, Songs from The Princess, Ode on the Duke of Wellington, Charge of the Light Brigade, Enoch Arden; Shakespeare, Julius Cæsar.

Passages for memorization: Coleridge, The Ancient Mariner, ll. 354-372; "Around, around . . . singeth a quiet tune", ll. 599-617; "O Wedding-guest . . . made and loveth all"; Tennyson, The Lotos Eaters, ll. 10-28, §§ I, III, of the Choric Song, Ulysses, ll. 18-32, ll. 44-61, "Of Old Sat Freedom", "Sweet and low", "The Splendour falls", Charge of the Light Brigade.

Shakespeare—Julius Caesar :—

Act   I, Sc. 1, ll. 40- 60.   O you hard hearts . . . on this ingratitude.
Act III, Sc. 1, ll. 148-163.   O mighty Caesar . . . spirits of this age.
Act III, Sc 2, ll. 173-196.   If you have tears . . . flourished over us.
Act IV, Sc. 2, ll. 19- 27.   Thou hast described . . . in the trial.
Act V, Sc. 5, ll. 68- 75.   This was the noblest . . . was a man.

1923: Tennyson, The Lady of Shalott, St. Agnes' Eve, "Come not when I am dead," "Break, break, break," In the Valley of Cauteretz, In Memoriam, XXXI, XXXII, XXXVI, LXXV, LXXVI, C, CXI; Browning,

"All service ranks the same with God," The Italian in England, Cavalier Tunes, My Last Duchess, The Boy and the Angel, Home Thoughts from Abroad, Up at a Villa, The Guardian Angel, Prospice; Matthew Arnold, Sohrab and Rustum; Shakespeare, Macbeth.

Passages for memorization: Tennyson, The Lady of Shalott, Part I, St. Agnes' Eve, "Break, break, break", In the Valley of Cauteretz. Browning, "All service ranks the same with God", Home Thoughts from Abroad, Prospice.

Shakespeare—Macbeth:—

Act I, Sc. 5, ll. 16-31. LADY M. Glamis thou art . . . crown'd withal.
Act I, Sc. 7, ll. 1-28. MACB. If it were done . . . on the other.
Act II, Sc. 1, ll. 33-64. MACB. Is this a dagger . . . to hell.
Act III, Sc. 2, ll. 4-26. LADY M. Nought's had . . . him further.
Act III, Sc. 2, ll. 45-56. MACB. Be innocent . . . go with me.
Act V, Sc. 3, ll. 22-28. MACB. I have lived . . . dare not.
Act V, Sc. 3, ll. 39-45. MACB. Cure her . . . the heart?
Act V, Sc. 5, ll. 16-28. SEY. The Queen . . . signifying nothing.

1924: Wordsworth, Michael, Influence of Natural Objects, Nutting, Elegiac Stanzas, To the Rev. Dr. Wordsworth, To the Cuckoo, "Bright flower, whose home," and the following eight sonnets: "It is not to be thought of," "Dark and more dark the shades of evening fell", "O friend I know not", "Milton, thou shouldst", "Surprised by joy—impatient as the wind", "Hail twilight, sovereign of our peaceful hour", "I thought of Thee, my partner and my guide", "Such age, how beautiful"; Tennyson, The Epic and Morte d'Arthur, Œnone, The Brook, and the following sections of "In Memoriam"; XXVII, LXIV, LXXXIII, LXXXVI, CI, CXIV, CXV, CXVIII, CXXIII; Shakespeare, Merchant of Venice.

Passages for memorization: Wordsworth: "To the Cuckoo"; "It is not to be thought of"; "O friend, I know not"; "Milton, thou shouldst"; "Hail twilight, sovereign of our peaceful hour"; "I thought of Thee, my partner and my guide".

Tennyson: "Morte d'Arthur, ll. 246-255; Œnone, ll. 1-15, ll. 144-150. The lyric stanzas in the "Brook"; "In Memoriam": LXIV, LXXXIII, LXXXVI, CI, CXV, CXVIII.

Shakespeare—The Merchant of Venice:—

Act I, Sc. 1, ll. 79- 99. Let me play . . . their brothers fools.
Act II, Sc. 9, ll. 36- 49. Who chooseth me . . . to be new varnished.
Act IV, Sc. 1, ll. 184-205. The quality of mercy . . . the deeds of mercy.
Act V, Sc. 1, ll. 54- 65. How sweet the moonlight . . . cannot hear it.
Act V, Sc. 1, ll. 102-108. The crow doth sing . . . true proportion.

*French.

The candidate's knowledge of French will be tested by: (1) simple questions on grammar; (2) the translation of simple passages from English into French; (3) translation at sight of easy passages from modern French, and (4) an examination on the following texts:—

The texts contained in the New High ,School French Reader. The Old Reader may be used for the examination in 1922.

1922: Daudet, la Belle Nivernaise; Meilhac et Halévy, l'Été de la Saint-Martin.

1923: Labiche, le Voyage de M. Perrichon; Theuriet, l'Abbé Daniel (Blackie's Longer French Texts).

Two papers will be set: (1) Prescribed texts and translation at sight; questions on grammar; (2) the translation of English into French.

*German.

The candidate's knowledge of German will be tested by: (1) simple questions on grammar; (2) the translation of simple passages from English into German; (3) translation at sight of easy passages from modern German; and (4) an examination on the following texts:—

The texts contained in the High School German Reader with the exception of Von Fallensleben, Deutschland über Alles.

1922: Leander, Träumereien—the following seven stories: Der alte Koffer; Der kleine Vogel; Die himmlische Musik; Die künstliche Orgel; Vom unsichtbaren Königreiche; Die Königin, die keine Pfeffernüsse backen, U.S.W.; Der Wunschring;

or

the following five stories: Der verrostete Ritter; Die Alte-Weiber-Mühle; Heino im Sumpf; Die Traumbuche; Die drei Schwestern mit den gläsernen Herzen.

1923: Hauff, Das kalte Herz; Wilhelmi, Einer musz heiraten.

Two papers will be set: (1) Prescribed texts and translation at sight; questions on grammar; (2) the translation of English into German.

*Spanish.

The candidates knowledge of Spanish will be tested by: (1) questions on grammar; (2) the translation of sentences and connected narrative from English into Spanish; (3) composition in Spanish; (4) translation at sight from Spanish; (5) an examination on the following text:—

1922, 1923: Hills, Spanish Tales (pages 1-124).

Two papers will be set: (1) Prescribed text and translation at sight; questions on grammar; (2) the translation of English into Spanish and composition.

*When the edition is not specified, any *unabridged* edition may be used.

Italian.

The Candidate's knowledge of Italian will be tested by: (1) questions on grammar; (2) the translation of sentences and connected narrative from English into Italian ; (3) translation at sight from Italian; (4) an examinatian on the following text:—

1922; Wilkins and Altrocchi, Italian Short Stories.

Two papers will be set: (1) Prescribed text and translation at sight; (2) questions on grammar and translation of sentences illustrating the grammar.

History.

BRITISH HISTORY.—Great Britain from 1768 to 1885. The geography relating to the history prescribed. One examination paper.

ANCIENT HISTORY.—General outlines of the History of Greece to the death of Alexander and of the history of Rome to the death of Augustus, with a brief outline of the art, literature, philosophy, and social life of the Greeks and Romans. The geography relating to the history perscribed. One examination paper.

Mathematics.

ALGEBRA.—Elementary rules; factoring; highest common measure; lowest common multiple; fractions; simple equations of one, two and three unknown quantities; extraction of roots; simple graphs; simple ratio and proportion; indices; surds; quadratics of one and two unknown quantities; theory of quadratics.

One examination paper.

GEOMETRY.—A.—CONSTRUCTIONS.

To construct a triangle with sides of given lengths.

To construct an angle equal to a given rectilineal angle.

To bisect a given angle.

To bisect a given straight line.

To draw a line perpendicular to a given line from a given point in it.

To draw a line perpendicular to a given line from a given point not in the line.

Locus of a point equidistant from two given lines.

Locus of a point equidistant from two given points.

To draw a line parallel to another, through a given point.

To divide a given line into any number of equal parts.

To describe a parallelogram equal to a given triangle, and having an angle equal to a given angle.

To describe a parallelogram equal to a given rectilineal figure, and having an angle equal to a given angle.

On a given straight line to describe a parallelográm equal to a given triangle, and having an angle equal to a given angle.

To find thé centre of a given circle.

From a given point to draw a tangent to a given circle.

On a given straight line to construct a segment of a circle containing an angle equal to a given angle.

From a given circle to cut off a segment containing an angle equal to a given angle.

In a circle to inscribe a triangle equiangular to a given triangle.

To find locus of centres of circles touching two given lines.

To inscribe a circle in a given triangle.

To describe a circle touching three given straight lines.

To describe a circle about a given triangle.

About a given circle to describe a triangle equiangular to a given triangle.

To divide a given line similarly to another given divided line.

To find the fourth proportional to three given lines.

To describe a polygon similar to a given polygon, and with the corresponding sides in a given ratio.

To find the mean proportional between two given straight lines.

To construct a polygon similar to a given polygon, and such that their areas are in a given ratio.

To describe a polygon of a given shape and size.

B.—THEOREMS.

The sum of the angles of any triangle is equal to two right angles.

The angles at the base of an isosceles triangle are equal, with converse.

If the three sides of one triangle be equal, respectively, to the three sides of another, the triangles are equal in all respects.

If two sides and the included angle of one triangle be equal to two sides and the included angle of another triangle, the triangles are equal in all respects.

If two angles and one side of a triangle be equal to two angles and the corresponding side of another, the triangles are equal in all respects.

If two sides and an angle opposite one of these sides be equal, respectively, in two triangles, the angles opposite the other pair of equal sides are either equal or supplemental.

The sum of the exterior angles of a polygon is four right angles.

The greater side of any triangle has the greater angle opposite it.

The greater angle of any triangle has the greater side opposite it.

If two sides of one triangle be equal respectively to two sides of another, that with the greater contained angle has the greater base, with converse.

If a transversal fall on two parallel lines, relations between angles formed, with converse.

Lines which join equal and parallel lines towards the same parts are themselves equal and parallel.

The opposite sides and angles of a parallelogram are equal and the diagonal bisects it.

Parallelograms on the same base, or on equal bases, and between the same parallels are equal.

Triangles on the same base, or on equal bases, and between the same parallels are equal.

Triangles equal in area, and' on the same base, are between the same parallels.

· If a parallelogram and a triangle be on the same base, and between the same parallels, the parallelogram is double the triangle.

Expressions for area of a parallelogram, and the area of a triangle.

The complements of parallelograms about the diagonal of any parallelogram are equal.

The square on the hypotenuse of a right-angled triangle is equal to the sum of the squares on the sides.

If a straight line be divided into any two parts, the sum of the squares on the parts, together with twice the rectangle contained by the parts, is equal to the square on the whole line.

The square on a side of any triangle is equal to the sum of the squares on the two other sides + twice the rectangle contained by either of these sides and the projection of the other side on it.

If more than two equal straight lines can be drawn from the circumference of a circle to a point within it, that point is the centre.

The diameter is the greatest chord in a circle, and a chord nearer the centre is greater than one more remote. Also the greater chord is nearer the centre than the less.

The angle at the centre of a circle is double the angle at the circumference on the same arc.

The angles in the same segment of a circle are equal, with converse.

The opposite angles of a quadrilateral inscribed in a circle are together equal to two right angles, with converse.

The angle in a semicircle is a right angle; in a segment greater than a semicircle less than a right angle; in a segment less than a semicircle greater than a right angle.

A tangent is perpendicular to the radius to the point of contact; only one tangent can be drawn at a given point; the perpendicular to the tangent at the point of contact passes through the centre; the perpendicular from centre on tangent passes through the point of contact.

If two circles touch, the line joining the centres passes through the point of contact.

The angles which a chord drawn from the point of contact makes with the tangent, are equal to the angles in the alternate segments.

The rectangles under the segments of intersecting chords are equal.

If $OA.OB = OC^2$, OC is a tangent to the circle through A, B, and C.

Triangles of the same altitude are as their bases.

A line parallel to the base of a triangle divides the sides proportionally, with converse.

If a vertical angle of a triangle be bisected, the bisector divides the base into segments that are as the sides, with converse.

The analogous proposition when the exterior angle at the vertex is bisected, with converse.

If two triangles are equiangular, the sides are proportional.

If the sides of two triangles are proportional, the triangles are equiangular.

If the sides of two triangles about equal angles are proportional, the triangles are equiangular.

If two triangles have an angle in each equal, and the sides about two other angles proportional, the remaining angles are equal or supplemental.

Similar triangles are as the squares on corresponding sides.

The perpendicular from the right angle of a right-angled triangle on the hypotenuse divides the triangle into two which are similar to the original triangle.

In equal circles angles, whether at the centres or circumferences, are proportional to the arcs on which they stand.

The areas of two similar polygons are as the squares on corresponding sides.

If three lines be proportional, the first is to the third as the figure on the first to a similar figure on the second.

Questions and easy deductions on the preceding constructions and theorems.

It is recommended that the study of formal demonstrative Geometry be preceded by a course in Practical Geometry, extending over not more than a year, and embracing the following:—

Definitions: fundamental geometric conceptions and principles; use of simple instruments, as compasses, protractor, graduated rule, etc.; measurement of lines and angles, and construction of lines and angles of given numerical magnitude; accurate construction of figures; some leading propositions in plane geometry reached by induction as a result of accurate construction of figures; deduction also employed as principles are reached and assured. At the examination, questions may be given in Practical Geometry, the constructions being such as naturally spring from the prescribed course. Candidates must provide themselves with a graduated ruler, compasses, set-square and protractor.

In the formal deductive Geometry modifications of Euclid's treatment of the subject will be allowed, though not required, as follows:—

The employment of the "hypothetical construction".

The free employment of the method of superposition including the rotation of figures about an axis, or about a point in a plane.

A modification of Euclid's parallel postulate.

A treatment of ratio and proportion restricted to the case in which the compared magnitudes are commensurable.

One examination paper.

Experimental Science.

Chemistry:—An experimental study of the following elements and their more important compounds: hydrogen, oxygen, sulphur, sodium, potassium, nitrogen, chlorine, bromine, iodine, carbon, calcium. The course of work should be arranged so as to give the pupils a knowledge of the following: Mixtures, solutions, compounds, and elements, and their various properties and reactions; acids, bases, and salts. Fundamental laws and principles, as: conservation of mass, definite proportions, multiple proportions, valency, proportions by volume in which gases react. The quantitative meaning and use of chemical symbols, formulae and equations. Chemical nomenclature. Simple quantitative experiments and problems. The application of chemistry to the industries, illustrated by an account of the commercial manufacture and use of some of the more important substances included in this course.

Physics.—A course defined as follows, the topics to be presented experimentally with mathematical applications simple and direct in character.

SOUND.—Vibratory motion illustrated with pendulums, rods, strings, membranes, and plates.

Types of wave motion illustrated by water waves, waves in a cord, and waves in a coiled spring.

Production, propagation, velocity, and reflection of sound waves; wave lengths.

Intensity, pitch.

Laws of vibration of strings; vibration of air in organ pipes; nodes and loops in vibrating strings, and in vibrating air columns, harmonies, quality, manometric flames.

Interference phenomena; beats.

Resonance.

HEAT.—Sources of heat: Transformation of other forms of energy into heat energy.

Expansion due to heat: Anomalous expansion of water and its significance; expansion of gases; Charles' Law.

Temperature and thermometers: Construction and graduation of Centigrade and Fahrenheit thermometers; measurement of temperature on absolute scale.

Quantity of heat: Temperature as contrasted with quantity of heat; heat units; specific heat; determination of the specific heat of a solid and of a liquid.

Fusion: Determination of melting point of ice; heat changes in solution; determination of heat of fusion of ice; the influence of salt in solution on the freezing point.

Vaporization: Determination of heat of vaporization of water; dependence of boiling point on pressure and on the presence of salts in solution; evaporation; practical applications of cooling by vaporization; ice machine.

Transference of heat: Conduction and convection, as illustrated in systems of heating by hot water and by steam; ventilation; radiation; radiant energy; effect of temperature and nature of surface; emission and absorption; selective absorption.

The transformation of heat energy into the energy of mechanical motion as exemplified in the steam engine and in the gas engine.

Heat in connection with meteorology; clouds; rain; winds; dew; frost; dew point; hygrometers (Regnault's and the wet and dry bulb hygrometer).

Nature of heat: Kinetic theory.

LIGHT.—Propagation: Wave theory of light; rectilinear propagation, image through a pin-hole; photometry, shadow and grease-spot photometers.

Reflection: Laws of reflection; images in plane mirrors; images in spherical mirrors, drawing image of object in any position.

Refraction: Laws of refraction; index of refraction, its measurement, and its relation to the velocities of light in media; total reflection.

Lenses: Converging and diverging; determination of focal length; conjugate foci; drawing of images produced by lenses; vision through a lens, relation of the size of the image to the size of the object.

Optical instruments: Simple microscope; camera; projection lantern.

Colour: Decomposition and recomposition of white light; spectrum; complementary colours; rainbow.

MAGNETISM AND ELECTRICITY.—Magnetism: Laws of magnetic attraction and repulsion; magnetic field, magnetic lines of force; magnetism by induction; magnetization; molecular theory of magnetization; magnetic permeability, terrestrial magnetism; mariner's compass, inclination and declination of the magnetic needle.

Electricity at rest: Two kinds of electrification; conductors and non-conductors; gold-leaf electroscope; induced electrification; electricity at points and at surfaces; lightning rods; the Leyden jar; simple notions of electrical potential.

Electric current: Production of electric current by voltaic cells; electromotive force of a voltaic cell; detection of the electric current; polarization and local action; simple notions of the relation of electromotive force, current strength, and resistance, names of units; Leclanche cell, dry cell, Daniell cell.

Effects of the electric current: Electrolysis, theory of electrolysis, electroplating, electrotyping, storage cell, laws of electrolysis, measurement of current strength by electrolysis; magnetic effects, electromagnet, relation between the direction of the current and the polarity of an electromagnet, the electric telegraph, the electric bell, the galvanometer, the D.C. motor; heating effects of the current, practical applications, electric stoves, electric irons, electric heaters, electric welding; incandescent and arc lamps.

Induced currents: Production of induced currents; laws of induced currents; Lenz's Law; the transformer; the induction coil; the telephone;

a simple type of the A.C. and of the D.C. dynamo. Reasons for the use of the A.C. current; differences in the uses of the A.C. and D.C. current; distribution of electricity as illustrated by the Hydro-Electric System.

Electric measurements: Units of current strength, resistance, and electromotive force; Ohm's Law; measurement of current strength, the ammeter; measurement of electromotive force, the voltmeter; measurement of resistance, the Wheatstone Bridge.

Special forms of radiation: Electric waves, wireless telegraphy.

Agriculture.

Part I.

AGRICULTURAL PHYSICS.

SOIL.—Classification and identification of samples of soil by the "beaker" method into clay, loam, clay loam, sandy loam and sand; comparison of two soils by the aid of a compound microscope; identification and study of soil in the fields; experiments to show the physical effects of lime on heavy and on light soil; influence of air, cultivation and drainage on the action of lime.

Tillage: Uses of plow, cultivator, scuffler, harrow and roller; experiments to show the use of mulches, and the action of frost on heavy soil.

Drainage: Methods and value; calculation of cost of tile drainage of a given area.

SURVEYING.—Use of instruments (including level and chain) for taking levels, running lines; calculation of areas.

FARM MECHANICS.—Care of tools and farm implements; experiments to show warping and splitting of wood on exposure to the weather; practice in sharpening such tools as chisel, knife and scissors; the use of levers and pulleys in machinery; principle of the internal-combustion engine.

ELECTRICITY.—Electricity at Rest: Two kinds of electrification; conductors and non-conductors; gold leaf electroscope; induced electrification; electricity at points and surfaces; the Leyden jar; lightning-rods.

Current Electricity: Principle of voltaic cells; use of dry cells; galvanometer; detection of the current; simple notions of electro-motive force, current strength and resistance including names of units; electro-magnet; relation between the direction of the current and the polarity of a magnet; telegraph; electric bell; heating devices—irons, stoves, welders, lamps; production of induced currents; laws of induced currents; the induction coil and transformer.

AGRICULTURAL CHEMISTRY.

GENERAL.—A brief study of the following elements, carbon, oxygen, hydrogen, nitrogen, phosphorus, sulphur, potassium, calcium, and the compounds of these elements used by green plants; experiments to show how these compounds are made available for plant use (e.g., the action of carbon dioxide and water on calcium carbonate); chemical symbols, formulae and equations; chemical nomenclature.

BARNYARD MANURE AND FERTILIZERS.—Care and treatment of barnyard manure; experiments to show the presence of compounds containing, respectively, nitrogen, phosphorus and potassium in manure; a discussion of the special influence of each of these three elements on plant growth; the value of humus and lime to the soil; commercial sources of nitrogen, phosphorus and potassium used to supplement barnyard manure; test of the relative solubility of commercial fertilizers; experiments to show why certain fertilizers should not be mixed; calculation of the percentage of available plant food in different mixtures of fertilizers; explanation of the commercial terms, "phosphoric acid" and "potash". The chief provision of the Fertilizer Act.

INSECTICIDES AND FUNGICIDES.—A study of the composition, comparative merits and methods of application of arsenate of lead, arsenate of lime and Paris green; lime sulphur, Bordeaux mixture and orchard "dusts"; use of insecticides and fungicides in combination.

GARDEN OR PLOT WORK.—Work in the school gardens and plots in May and June.

Or

SOIL SURVEY.—Team work in making a plan, to scale, of four square miles showing farms, roads, bridges, streams (including natural drains) and soil (locating gravel, sand, clay, muck, depending on the locality).

Part II.

BOTANY.—Calculation of the percentage of foul seed in three or four samples of clover (or alfalfa) and timothy; use of compound microscope in examining spores and mycellia; recognition, from specimens, of rusts, smuts, white rust of crucifers, brown rot of stone fruits, mildew of cherry or lilac and anthracnose of bean. Chief provision of Seed Control Act and Noxious Weeds Act.

ENTOMOLOGY.—Identification, nature of injury, life history and methods of control of any six of the most common harmful insects of the district, e.g., white grub, wire worm, plum curculio, codling moth, San José scale, oyster shell scale, cabbage maggot, cabbage worm, Hessian fly, European corn borer, potato beetle, and clothes moth.

Poultry.—Practical operation of the incubator—ventilation, moisture, candling eggs, variation in size of air chamber, blood clots, development of the embryo by examining eggs broken open every one or two days during the period of incubation; use of water-glass in preserving eggs; poultry products and marketing.

Dairying.—Principles and uses of the Babcock machine and the lactometer; testing cream and skim milk (or whey) for fat; determining whether milk has been watered by use of the formula—(L.R. at 60° plus % of fat)$+4=$% S.N.F.; food value of milk and its products; principle and use of the milk separator; making butter with a laboratory churn; use of starters.

Field Crops.—Different types of farming; crop distribution over Ontario; meaning and importance of crop rotation; influence of the keeping of live stock on the kind of rotation; germination tests of seed, e.g., oats, turnips, corn, clover; laboratory work in seed judging and seed selection; meaning and merits of pasture crops, silage crops and soiling crops; the yield and quality of crop as influenced by the time of sowing; calculation of the relative value of certain crops as "money" crops.

Animal Husbandry.—History and characteristics of the chief breeds of horses, cattle, sheep, swine; value and importance of live stock; a survey of the breeds found in the locality; meaning of pedigree stock and grade stock; disadvantage of keeping scrub stock; visit to a local farm to study the stock kept there.

Or

Horticulture.—Orchard management—spraying, pruning, grafting, cultivating; cover crops; packing and marketing apples; methods of producing early vegetables; practice in seeding, transplanting, cultivating, mulching; fruit survey for at least two kinds of fruit.

HONOUR MATRICULATION.
Greek.

Translation into English of passages from the prescribed texts, with questions thereon.

Translation at sight of prose passages of average difficulty from Xenophon's historical works.

Translation into Greek of sentences (based upon Xenophon's vocabulary) to test the candidate's scholarship in matters of accidence, syntax and phraseology.

The following are the prescribed texts:—

1922 and 1923: Xenophon, Hellenica (Philpotts' Selections, sections, I. and II.), Homer, Iliad I., 1-350; III., 121-244; VI., 66-118, and 237 to the end; Odyssey VI. and IX.

Two papers will be set: (1) prescribed texts; (2) translation at sight and Greek prose composition.

Latin.

Translation into English of passages from prescribed texts, with grammatical questions on these passages and such other questions as arise naturally from the context.

Translation at sight of a passage of average difficulty from Caesar.

Translation into Latin of English sentences to illustrate Latin syntax, and of a continuous passage of English narrative similar to Caesar.

The following are the prescribed texts:—.

1922, 1923: Cæsar, De Bello Gallico, Book V.; Cicero, In Catalinam I. and III.; Horace, Odes as follows: Book I., 1, 2, 4 5, 9, 10, 14, 22, 24, 31, 38; Book II., 3, 10, 14, 15, 16, 17, 18, 20; Book III., 1, 2, 8, 9, 13, 18, 21, 23, 29, 30; Book IV., 3, 5, 7, 12, 15.

Two examination papers

(1) Latin Prose Composition and Caesar.

(2) Cicero, Horace and Sight Translation.

English.

COMPOSITION: An essay on one of several themes set by the examiners. One examination paper.

LITERATURE: The candidate will be expected to have memorized some of the finest passages. Besides questions to test the candidate's familiarity with, and comprehension of, the following selections, questions may also be set to determine within reasonable limits his power of appreciating literary art.

The candidate shall produce satisfactory proof by the certificate of the principal of the school from which he comes or otherwise that he has read carefully, during the preceding year, at least four suitable works in English literature (both prose and poetry) in addition to those prescribed below for examination.

One examination paper.

1922: Coleridge, The Ancient Mariner; Tennyson, Lotos Eaters, Ulyssse, "Of old sat Freedom," Locksley Hall, Songs from the Princess, Ode on the Duke of Wellington, Charge of the Light Brigade, Enoch Arden; Shakespeare, Julius Cæsar, Midsummer Night's Dream.

Passages for memorization: Coleridge, The Ancient Mariner, ll. 354-372, "Around, around ... singeth a quiet tune", ll. 599-617, O Wedding-guest ... made and loveth all"; Tennyson, The Lotos Eaters, ll. 10-28,§§ I, III, of the Choric Song, Ulysses, ll. 18-32, ll. 44-61, "Of Old Sat Freedom", "Sweet and low", "The Splendour falls", Charge of the Light Brigade.

Shakespeare—Julius Caesar:—

Act I, Sc. 1, ll. 40- 60. O you hard hearts ... on this ingratitude.
Act III, Sc. 1, ll. 148-163. O mighty Caesar ... spirits of this age.
Act III, Sc. 2, ll. 173-196. If you have tears ... flourished over us.
Act IV, Sc. 2, ll. 19- 27. Thou hast described ... in the trial.
Act V, Sc. 5, ll. 68- 75. This was the noblest ... was a man.

1923: Tennyson, The Lady of Shalott, St. Agnes' Eve, "Come not when I am dead," "Break, break, break," In the Valley of Cauteretz, In Memoriam, XXXI, XXXII, XXXVI, LXXV, LXXVI, C, CXI; Browning, My Last Duchess, "All service ranks the same with God," The Italian in England, Cavalier Tunes, The Boy and the Angel, Home Thoughts from Abroad, Up at a Villa, The Guardian Angel, Prospice; Matthew Arnold, Sohrab and Rustum; Shakespeare, Macbeth, As You Like It.

Passages for memorization:—

Tennyson: St. Agnes' Eve, "Break, break, break"; In the Valley of Cauteretz. Browning: "All service ranks the same with God"; Home Thoughts from Abroad; Prospice.

Shakespeare—Macbeth:—

Act I, Sc. 5, ll. 16-31. LADY M. Glamis thou art ... crown'd withal.
Act I, Sc. 7, ll. 1-28. MACB. If it were done ... on the other.
Act II, Sc. 1, ll. 33-64. MACB. Is this a dagger ... to hell.
Act III, Sc. 2, ll. 4-26. LADY M. Nought's had ... him further.
Act III, Sc. 2, ll. 45-56. MACB. Be innocent ... go with me.
Act V, Sc. 3, ll. 22-28. MACB. I have lived ... dare not.
Act V, Sc. 3, ll. 39-45. MACB. Cure her ... the heart?
Act V, Sc. 5, ll. 16-28. SEY. The Queen ... signifying nothing.

Shakespeare—As You Like It:—

Act II, Sc. 1, ll. 1- 18. DUKE S. Now, my co-mates . . . change it.
Act II, Sc. 5.   The Songs.
Act II, Sc. 7, ll. 139-166. JAQ. All the world's . . . sans everything.
Act II, Sc. 7, ll. 174-190. AMIENS. The Song.

1924: Wordsworth, Michael, Influence of Natural Objects, Nutting Elegiac Stanzas, To the Rev. Dr. Wordsworth, "Bright flower, whose home," and the following eight sonnets: "It is not to be thought of," "Dark and more dark the shades of evening fell", "O friend I know not", "Milton, thou shouldst", "Surprised by joy—impatient as the wind", "Hail twilight, sovereign of our peaceful hour", "I thought of Thee, my partner and my guide", "Such age, how beautiful"; Tennyson, The Epic and Morte d'Arthur, Œnone, The Brook, and the following sections of "In Memoriam"; XXVII, LXIV, LXXXIII, LXXXVI, CI, CXIV, CXV, CXVIII, CXXIII; Shakespeare, Merchant of Venice, Henry IV, Part 1.

Passages for memorization: Wordsworth: "To the Cuckoo"; "It is not to be thought of"; "O friend, I know not"; "Milton, thou shouldst"; "Hail twilight, sovereign of our peaceful hour"; "I thought of Thee, my partner and my guide".

Tennyson: "Morte d'Arthur, ll. 246-255; Œnone, ll. 1-15, ll. 144-150, The lyric stanzas in the "Brook"; "In Memoriam": LXIV, LXXXIII, LXXXVI, CI, CXV, CXVIII.

Shakespeare—The Merchant of Venice:—

Act   I, Sc. 1, ll. 79- 99. Let me play . . . their brothers fools.
Act II, Sc. 9, ll. 36- 49. Who chooseth me . . . to be new varnished.
Act IV, Sc. 1, ll. 184-205. The quality of mercy . . . the deeds of mercy.
Act V, Sc. 1, ll. 54- 65. How sweet the moonlight . . . cannot hear it.
Act V, Sc. 1, ll. 102-108. The crow doth sing . . . true proportion.

French.*

The prescription of work in grammar, the translation of English into French and sight translation, is the same for honours as for pass, but the examination will be of a more advanced character.

The following are the prescribed texts:—

1922: About, le Roi des Montagnes (Blackie's Longer French Texts); Labiche, la Poudre aux yeux.

1923: Augier et Sandeau, la Pierre de Touche; Feuillet, le Roman d'un jeune homme pauvre (Oxford Press *or* Copp, Clark).

German.*

The prescription of work in grammar, the translation of English into German and sight translation, is the same for honours as for pass, but the examination will be of a more advanced character.

---

*When the edition is not specified, any *unabridged* edition may be used.

The following are the prescribed texts:—
1922: Baumbach, Der Schwiegersohn; Fulda, Unter vier Augen.
1923: Frèytag, Die Journalisten; Gerstäcker, Germelshausen.

Spanish.*

The prescription of work in grammar, the translation of English into Spanish, and sight translation, is the same for honours as for pass, but the examination will be of a more advanced character.

.The following is the prescribed text:—
1922: Marcial Dorado, España Pintoresca.
1923: Pedro Antonio de Alarcón, El Capitán Veneno.

History.

Outlines of Modern History from the death of Queen Elizabeth to the Treaty of Paris, 1603-1763. Study of Modern History in greater detail, 1763-1885. The geography relating to the history prescribed. One examination paper.

Mathematics.

ALGEBRA: Elementary rules; highest common measure; lowest common multiple; fractions; square root; simple equations of one, two and three unknown quantities; indices, surds, quadratics of one and two unknown quantities; theory of divisors; ratio, proportion and variation; progressions; notation; permutations and combinations, binomial theorem; interest forms; annuities.

One examination paper.

TRIGONOMETRY.—Trigonometrical ratios with their relations to each other; sines, etc., of the sum and difference of angles with deduced formulas; use of logarithms; solution of triangles; expressions for the area of triangles; radii of circumscribed, inscribed and escribed circles.

One examination paper.

PROBLEMS: One paper.

GEOMETRY: A.—Exercises on the course prescribed for the pass examination, with special reference to the following topics:—loci; maxima and minima; the system of inscribed, escribed and circumscribed circles of a triangle, with metrical relations; radical axis.

B.—The following additional propositions in Synthetic Geometry, with exercises thereon:—

To divide a given straight line internally and externally in medial section.

To describe a square that shall be equal to a given rectilineal figure.

To describe an isoceles triangle having each of the angles at the base double of the third angle.

---

*When the edition is not specified any *unabridged* edition may be used.

To inscribe a regular pentagon in a given circle.

The squares on two sides of a triangle are together equal to twice the square on half the third side and twice the square on the median to that side.

If ABC be a triangle, and A be joined to a point P of the base such that BP: PC = m : n, then $nAB^2 + mAC^2 = (m+n) AP^2 + nBP^2 + mPC^2$.

In a right-angled triangle the rectilineal figure described on the hypotenuse is equal to the sum of the similar and similarly described figures on the two other sides.

If the vertical angle of a triangle be bisected by a straight line which also cuts the base, the rectangle contained by the sides of the triangle is equal to the rectangle contained by the segments of the base, together with the square on the straight line which bisects the angle.

If from the vertical angle of a triangle a straight line be drawn perpendicular to the base, the rectangle contained by the sides of the triangle is equal to the rectangle contained by the perpendicular and the diameter of the circle described about the triangle.

The rectangle contained by the diagonals of a quadrilateral inscribed in a circle is equal to the sum of the two rectangles contained by its opposite sides.

Two similar polygons may be so placed that the lines adjoining corresponding points are concurrent.

If a straight line meet the sides BC, CA, AB, of a triangle ABC in D, E, F, respectively, then BD, CE, AF = DC, EA, FB, and conversely. (Menelaus' Theorem.)

If straight lines through the angular points A, B, C of a triangle are concurrent, and intersect the opposite sides in D, E, F, respectively, then BD, CE, AF = DC, EA, FB, and conversely. (Ceva's Theorem.)

If a point A lie on the polar of a point B with respect to a circle, then B lies on polar of A.

Any straight line which passes through a fixed point is cut harmonically by the point, any circle, and the polar of the point with respect to the circle.

In a complete quadrilateral each diagonal is divided harmonically by the two other diagonals, and at the angular points through which it passes.

C.—ELEMENTARY ANALYTICAL GEOMETRY: Axes of co-ordinates. Position of a point in plane of reference.

Transformation of co-ordinates,—origin changed, or axes (rectangular) turned through a given angle.

$\pm 2 A = x_1 (y_2 - y_3) + \ldots + \ldots$

Co-ordinates of point dividing line joining $P_1 (x_1, y_1)$ and $P_2 (x_2, y_2)$ in ratio $m:n$ are $\quad x = \dfrac{m x_2 + n x_1}{m + n}, \quad y = \dfrac{m y_2 + n y_1}{m + n}$

$(P_1 P_2)^2 = (x_1 - x_2)^2 + (y_1 - y_2)^2$

Equations of straight lines.

$$\frac{x - x_1}{x_1 - x_2} = \frac{y - y_1}{y_1 - y_2}$$

$$\frac{x}{a} + \frac{y}{b} = 1.$$

Line defined by two points through which it passes.

$$\frac{x - a}{\cos \theta} = \frac{y - b}{\sin \theta} = r.$$

$$y = mx + b.$$

$$y = m(x - a).$$

$$x \cos a + y \sin a = p.$$

Line defined by one point through which it passes, and by its direction.

General equation of 1st degree, $Ax + By + C = 0$, represents a straight line.

Any line through (x_1, y_1) is $A(x - x_1) + B(y - y_1) = 0$.

If θ be angle between $Ax + By + C = 0$ and $A'x + B'y + C' = 0$, then

$$\tan \theta = \frac{A'B - AB'}{AA' + BB'}$$

Condition of $\perp$ rity, $AA' + BB' = 0$.

Condition of $\parallel$ ism, $\dfrac{A}{A'} = \dfrac{B}{B'}$.

Distance from (a,b) to $Ax + By + C = 0$, in direction whose direction cosines are (l, m) is $= \dfrac{Aa + Bb + C}{Al + Bm}$.

$\perp$ distance from (a, b) on $Ax + By + C = 0$.

$$= \pm \frac{Aa + Bb + C}{\sqrt{A^2 + B^2}}$$

THE CIRCLE—

Equations in forms:

$$x^2 + y^2 = r^2$$
$$(x - a)^2 + (y - b)^2 = r^2$$
$$x^2 + y^2 - 2rx = 0.$$

General equation $x^2 + y^2 + 2Ax + 2By + C = 0$,

or $(x + A)^2 + (y + B)^2 = A^2 + B^2 - C$,

represents a circle with centre $(-A, -B,)$ and radius $\sqrt{A^2 + B^2 - C}$

Tangent at (x', y') to $x^2 + y^2 = r^2$, is $xx' + yy' = r^2$.

Normal is $\dfrac{x}{x'} = \dfrac{y}{y'}$.

Tangent in form $y = mx \pm r\sqrt{1 + m^2}$.

Pole being (x', y'), polar is $xx' + yy' = r^2$.

If pole move along a line, polar turns about pole of that line.

Square of tangent from (x', y') to $x^2 + y^2 + 2Ax + 2By + C = 0$

is $x'^2 + y'^2 + 2Ax' + 2By' + C$.

Radical axis of $x^2 + y^2 + 2Ax + 2By + C = 0$,

$$x^2 + y^2 + 2A'x + 2B'y + C' = 0$$

Easy exercises on the preceding propositions.

One examination paper.

Physics.

A course defined as follows, the topics to be presented experimentally with mathematical applications simple and direct in character:

MECHANICS OF SOLIDS.—Metric and English units of length. Use of vernier calipers, screw-gauge, in measurement of wires, cylinders, spheres, plates, etc.

Unit of time.

Motion: velocity, uniform and variable; average velocity; velocity at a point.

Newton's first law of motion, force, inertia, and mass; metric and English units of mass.

Acceleration, measurement of uniform acceleration, acceleration due to gravity, value of gravity.

Momentum; Newton's second law; measurement of force; metric and English absolute and gravitational units of force.

Newton's third law; conservation of momentum; centripetal and centrifugal force with illustrations, centrifuge, cream separator, form of earth, etc.

Composition and resolution of forces; parallelogram of forces; triangle of forces; moments; couples; centre of gravity.

Friction: laws of friction; co-efficient of friction.

Gravitation: Newton's law of gravitation; Cavendish's experiment.

Work: measurement of work in metric and English absolute and gravitational units; energy; measurement of energy; kinetic and potential energy; conservation of energy.

Power: measurement of power; horse power; the watt.

Machines: mechanical advantage; lever; wheel and axle; pulley; inclined plane; screw; wedge; simple combinations of the foregoing.

MECHANICS OF FLUIDS.—Pressure: pressure at a point; Pascal's law; pressure due to gravity; equilibrium of fluids at rest; Archimedes' principle; buoyancy; hydraulic pressure; specific gravity; determination of specific gravity of solids and liquids.

Atmospheric pressure: barometers; weight of air; pressure due to molecular motion; lift and force pumps, siphon; the use of compressed air, airbrakes, air tools.

Velocity due to pressure: Torricelli's theorem; pressure in moving column of fluid varies with the velocity; application to explain the principle of the atomizer, the Bunsen burner, the Bunsen filter pump, forced draught, the curved flight of a ball.

Surface tension: surface force; surface energy; capillarity; practical applications.

TRANSFORMATIONS OF ENERGY.—Mechanical equivalent of heat, measured mechanically and electrically; measurement of electrical energy; the kilowatt hour.

Chemistry.

An experimental course defined as follows: Chemistry of the Middle School reviewed and continued. Reversible reactions. Chemical equilibrium. Rate of reaction and conditions that affect it (including catalysis). A study of the following elements and their most characteristic compounds, having regard to Mendelejeff's classification and to their most important economic and industrial applications, hydrogen, sodium, potassium, magnesium, zinc, calcium, strontium, barium, aluminium, carbon, silicon, tin, lead, nitrogen, phosphorus, arsenic, antimony, bismuth, oxygen, sulphur, fluorine, chlorine, bromine, iodine, iron, copper.

Biology.

ZOOLOGY.—Practical study of the external form of all types, and the dissection or the study of prepared specimens (or models), as specified below. Observational drawings are essential. An elementary knowledge of the chief functions of the body—nutrition, irritability, motility, excretion, reproduction—and of the mode of life and the life history of the various types. Study of the principles of classification in any one group, and recognition of the commonest forms in all.

THE FROG.—Practical study of the external features; skeleton; visceral dissection; central nervous system; action of a typical muscle. Practical study of a cross-section for arrangement of organ systems. Observation of external features of development.

THE FISH.—Practical study of the external form; chief visceral organs; circulation and respiration; comparison with frog as to organs of locomotion, circulation, and respiration.

THE REPTILE.—Practical study of the external form of a snake and a turtle. Comparison with a lizard.

THE BIRD.—Practical study of the external form, plumage, and skeleton of some common bird. Adaptations to flight. Modification of bill and foot, in so far as they are of value in distinguishing the different chief types.

THE MAMMAL.—Practical study of the chief features of the skeleton, the visceral organs, and the chief divisions of the brain of a rabbit or a cat. Major characteristics of mammalian dentition and foot structure, as illustrated by the pig, horse, sheep, rabbit, dog, mole, and bat.

THE WORM.—Practical study of the external features, and dissection of the earth-worm. Study of cross-section for arrangement of chief organ systems only.

THE ARTHROPOD.—Practical study of the external form of the crayfish, including segmentation and appendages. Comparison of the external form of the crayfish, grasshopper (or cricket), millipede, and spider.

THE MOLLUSC.—Practical study of the external form, and mode of locomotion and respiration, of the fresh-water clam; comparison in these respects with the snail.

THE PROTOZOAN.—A practical study of the living amœba or paramœ·cium.

NOTE.—Dissection of at least the frog and the earth-worm by the pupil will be required. In other cases, prepared specimens or models may be used. Cross-sections will be studied with the low power microscope.

BOTANY.—General types of the great natural groups of plants; classification.

MORPHOLOGY.—Morphology of seed, root, stem, leaf, flower, and fruit. A study of the cellular structure of the leaf and of the relative arrangement of the more important tissues and tissue-systems of the stem and root (as shown by sections) of bean and maize, or of any other typical dicotyledon and monocotyledon.

PHYSIOLOGY.—Practical studies of absorption (osmosis), plasmolysis, transpiration, photosynthesis, respiration, irritability (*e.g.*, heliotropism), growth and movement. An elementary knowledge of the phenomena of fertilization and reproduction.

ECOLOGY.—Modifications of organs for special functions. Seed dispersal. Light relations, Pollination and adaptations for cross-pollination. Plant associations, *e.g.*, mesophytes, hydrophytes, xerophytes.

CRYPTOGAMS.—The practical study of representatives of the chief subdivisions of the cryptogams; spirogyra, chara, a mushroom, a lichen, a liverwort, a moss, a horsetail, a clubmoss, and a fern. Distribution and economic importance of yeasts and bacteria. Microscopic structure of the yeast cell; reproduction by budding. Macroscopic observation of a bacterial colony.

PHANEROGAMS.—The practical study of representatives of the seed plants of the locality, including at least one member of each of the following orders: Coniferae, Carophyllaceae, Ranunculaceae, Cruciferae, Rosac ae, Leguminosae, Sapindaceae, Umbelliferae, Ericaceae, Labiatae, Scrophulariaceae, Borraginaceae, Compositae, Gramineae (so far as the structure of the flower and stem is concerned), Liliaceae.

NOTE.—As form becomes intelligible only in the light of a knowledge of function and adaptation, it is advisable that the physiological and ecological studies should be taken up in appropriate connection with the morphological. It is also to be emphasized that the making of faithful and neat records of observations is a most important adjunct. In many cases these should be expressed as drawings, but it should be borne in mind that drawing loses much of its value as an educative factor unless there be an insistence on absolute accuracy and the careful naming of all the features represented. Judgment should, therefore, be exercised in requiring no more than can be done well.

—8

FACULTY OF ARTS.

DEGREE OF BACHELOR OF ARTS.

I. ENTRANCE.

1. There are two ways of entering the Faculty of Arts, by passing either (*a*) the Junior Matriculation·Examination, with or without Honours, or (*b*) the Senior Matriculation Examination.

(A)—By Junior Matriculation.

2. The subjects of Pass Junior Matriculation are:—Latin, English, History, Mathematics, and any two of the following—Greek, German, French, Spanish, Experimental Science. In each subject two papers are set. A candidate who has passed Junior Matriculation without Honours can be admitted only to the Pass Course of the First Year. A candidate preparing to enter an undergraduate Honour Course should select his options so as to meet the requirements of that course. See Sections 24, 57 and 59.

3. The pass standard is forty per cent. of the marks assigned to a paper with an average of sixty per cent. and with such modification or exceptions as may be deemed proper in consideration of the total number of marks and the reports of the staff of the school.

4. A candidate who has obtained the average of sixty per cent. on the required twelve papers but has failed to obtain forty per cent. in at most three of the papers may complete Junior Matriculation by obtaining forty per cent. on each of these papers at any one subsequent examination.

5. A candidate who has obtained forty per cent. on each of at least eight papers, with an average of sixty per cent. on the same, will be credited with these papers. In order to complete his matriculation he must obtain, at one subsequent examination, forty per cent. on each of the remaining papers, with an average of sixty per cent.

6. The annual examinations for Junior Matriculation are held in June and September by the Department of Education, under the direction of the University Matriculation Board.

7. Certificates of examinations recognized as equivalent in value may be accepted *pro tanto* for Pass Junior Matriculation.

8. In view of recent advances in the standards for Junior Matriculation, only those certificates which meet the requirements of this University as to subjects and percentages will be accepted for matriculation.

9. The regulations respecting Junior Matriculation with the schedule of examinations which may be accepted are to be found in the Curriculum for Junior Matriculation.

(B)—By Senior Matriculation.

10. The Senior Matriculation examination is the same as that of the First Year, and a successful candidate ranks thereafter as an undergraduate in the Faculty of Arts.

11. The subjects and standards for Senior Matriculation are those prescribed for the Pass Course or for an Honour Course of the First Year.

12. A student (a) who is entitled to complete his Junior Matriculation by passing in at most two papers (see Sections 4 and 5), or (b) who is over twenty-one years of age and has no qualifying certificate, when writing on the examination of the First Year, is held to be a candidate for Senior Matriculation. Such a student, when in attendance on lectures, is known as a NON-MATRICULATED STUDENT. See Sections 22 (b) and (c).

13. The Senior Matriculation examination may be taken without attendance on lectures in the University, except in the case of those HONOUR COURSES in which laboratory work is required.

14. A candidate for Senior Matriculation without attendance on lectures at the University must have completed the sixteenth year of his age on or before the first of October preceding the examination at which he presents himself.

15. The annual examinations for Senior Matriculation are held in May June, and September. Examinations in Pass subjects only are held in June and September.

16. Certificates of examinations recognized as equivalent in value to the examination of the First Year may be accepted *pro tanto* for Senior Matriculation. See Section 63.

17. The acceptance of certificates of equivalent examinations makes it possible under definite conditions for MATRICULATED and NON-MATRICULATED students to enter the Pass Course or certain Honour Courses at the Second Year. See Sections 28 to 32.

II. PROCEDURE FOR ADMISSION.

(a) General Conditions.

18. A student on applying for permission to enter upon a course of study in any Year is required to present to the Registrar of the University (a) any certificates on which he may be granted (1) Junior Matriculation in whole or in part, (2) Senior Matriculation in whole or in part, or (3) exemption from instruction and examination in pass subjects of the First Year, or (b) any other evidence of ability to take the work proposed.

19. An applicant holding a certificate from the Department of Education of a Province of the Dominion other than Ontario must submit an official statement of marks with his application for admission.

20. An applicant should secure the necessary blank forms of application for admission from the Registrar of the University, return them to him properly filled out, **at as early a date as possible and await the decision of the Committee on Admissions before leaving for Toronto.**

21. Every applicant for admission must produce satisfactory certificates of good character.

(b) Entrance at the First Year.

22. Applications for admission to the First Year will be considered from the following classes of students:—

(a) The student who has complete Pass Junior Matriculation. This includes those students who possess certificates accepted by the University as equivalent to Junior Matriculation. Such a student when admitted becomes an UNDERGRADUATE in the Faculty of Arts. For the list of equivalent certificates see the Junior Matriculation Curriculum.

(b) The student who is entitled to complete his Junior Matriculation by passing in at most two papers. Such a candidate, when admitted, is known as a NON-MATRICULATED STUDENT and is required to fulfil such matriculation conditions as the Council may determine in order that he may be eligible for registration in the Second Year.

(c) The student without qualifying certificates who is over twenty-one years of age. Such a candidate, when admitted, is known as a NON-MATRICULATED STUDENT and is required to complete Senior Matriculation in order that he may be eligible for registration in the Second Year.

(d) The student who is not proceeding to a degree in Arts, i.e., an OCCASIONAL STUDENT. Such a student is admitted only on special petition and the continuance of registration will depend upon the satisfactory report of his instructors.

23. On or before the first of October of the session in which he applies for registration, a matriculated student or undergraduate must have completed the sixteenth year of his age, a non-matriculated student or candidate for Senior Matriculation should have completed the nineteenth year of his age, and an occasional student must have completed the nineteenth year of his age.

24. A student (undergraduate, non-matriculated, or occasional) who seeks admission to the classes of the First Year in any of the languages, Latin, French, German, in which he has not passed the Matriculation examination, must first satisfy the College in which he seeks enrolment, of his ability to undertake the work of these classes. The colleges do not undertake to provide instruction in elementary Latin, French, and German.

25.·On or before the first day of September the student who wishes to attend the University as a non-matriculated or occasional student should submit to the Registrar of the University an application for permission to attend lectures in the University or its Colleges. The applicant must satisfy the authorities of the University and of his College, by certificate or otherwise, before registration, of his ability to undertake the work of the class or classes he proposes to attend.

26. A candidate who has Junior Matriculation without Honours can be admitted only to the Pass Course of the First Year.

27. Unless special permission is granted by the Council, every student seeking to enter an Honour Course of the First Year must present a certificate on which he would receive credit in Pass Latin and in Pass Mathematics (Algebra and Geometry) of the First Year as well as in at least two other pass subjects. For the details see Section 59.

(c) Entrance at the Second Year.

28. A candidate holding a certificate on which he may be granted standing for all or all but one of the subjects of the First Year may enter the Second Year on payment of the fee of Fifteen Dollars. A candidate who lacks one subject will be required to pass in that subject at a subsequent examination, prior to admission to the Third Year.

29. The only courses open to a student entering on such certificates at the Second Year are the Pass Course, and on conditions to be determined by the Council, the Honour Courses in Political Science and in Philosophy.

30. A matriculated student entering the Second Year must have completed the seventeenth year of his age on or before the first of October of the session in which he proposes to enter.

31. A non-matriculated student wishing to enter the Second Year should be not less than twenty years of age.

32. A non-matriculated student in attendance upon lectures, proceeding regularly to.the degree, must complete either Junior Matriculation or Senior Matriculation, before he is eligible for registration in the Second Year.

(d) Admission Ad Eundem Statum.

33. An undergraduate of another University may be admitted *ad eundem statum* on such conditions as the Senate on the recommendation of the Council of the Faculty may prescribe.

34. An applicant for admission *ad eundem statum* must submit with his petition (1) a calendar of his University giving a full statement of the courses of instruction, (2) an official certificate of character and academic standing.

35. Such an applicant may not compete for scholarships at his first examination if admitted to a standing lower than that held in his own University, but, if he obtain honours at this first examination he shall subsequently enjoy all the rights and privileges of an undergraduate of this University.

III. REGISTRATION AND ENROLMENT.

36. Every student in attendance proceeding to the degree of Bachelor of Arts is required to register in the University and to enrol in either University College, or Victoria College, or Trinity College, or St. Michael's College.

37. Registration in the University, whether by mail or in person, should take place at as early a date as possible, and must be completed on or before the twenty-seventh of September, 1921. See Section 20.

Neglect of early registration will result in delay and inconvenience to the student.

38. Enrolment with the instructors of the University and of the Colleges will begin at 9 a.m. on the twenty-sixth of September and must be completed by the student in person by 5 p.m. on the twenty-seventh of September, 1921.

39. After the twenty-seventh of September no student, matriculated, non-matriculated, or occasional, will be allowed registration for the whole or part of the session 1921-1922, without the consent of the Council.

40. Every petition for registration subsequent to the twenty-seventh of September and prior to the first of November, must be accompanied by a sum of money reckoned at one dollar per diem for each day after the twenty-seventh of September. For sufficient cause the whole or part of such a sum may be refunded.

41. A student who has not enrolled in a subject or subjects on or before the twenty-seventh of September, may, at the discretion of the head of the department concerned, be refused admission to the classes or laboratories, until he shall have satisfied the head of the department that he is competent to proceed with the class. In order to qualify himself for admission such a student may be required to obtain tuition at his own expense.

42. A non-matriculated student, or a student who, having failed to obtain standing, is repeating a year, will be admitted on probation only, and will be allowed to register for the Easter Term, only on the recommendation of his College and with the consent of the Council.

IV. REGULATIONS RELATING TO STUDENTS IN ATTENDANCE.

43. No student will be enrolled in any year, or be allowed to continue in attendance, whose presence for any cause is deemed by the Council of the Faculty to be prejudicial to the interests of the University.

44. Students proceeding regularly to the degree are required to attend the courses of instruction and the examinations in all subjects prescribed for students of their respective standing, and no student will be permitted to remain in the University who persistently neglects academic work.

45. Unless special permission is granted by the Council, a student who, at the close of two sessions, has failed to secure standing in his year, will not be permitted further registration in the Faculty of Arts.

46. All interference on the part of any student with the personal liberty of another by arresting him, or summoning him to appear before any unauthorized tribunal of students, or otherwise subjecting him to any indignity or personal violence, is forbidden by the Council of the Faculty. In particular, students are warned against the practices known as the "hustling" of freshmen and against inter-year or inter-faculty "hustles". Any student convicted of participation in such proceedings will render himself liable to expulsion from the University.

47. A student who is under suspension, or who has been expelled from a College or from the University, will not be admitted to the University buildings or grounds.

48. The constitution of every University society or association of students in the Faculty of Arts and all amendments to any such constitution must be submitted for approval to the Council of the Faculty. All programmes of such societies or associations must, before publication, receive the sanction of the Council of the Faculty through the President. Permission to invite any person not a member of the Faculty of Arts to preside at or address a meeting of any society or association must be similarly obtained.

49. The name of the University is not to be used in connection with a publication of any kind without the permission of the Caput.

V. FEES.

For the schedule of fees see page 63.

VI. PHYSICAL TRAINING.

50. By order of the Board of Governors each male student proceeding to a degree must take Physical Training in the first and second years of his attendance. He must first undergo a medical examination by the Physical Director of the University in order to determine the character of his training.

VII. COURSES LEADING TO THE DEGREE.

51. A candidate for the degree of Bachelor of Arts must take one of the courses prescribed by the University.

52. The courses for the degree of Bachelor of Arts extend over a period of four academic years.

53. Unless specially exempted by the Council, every undergraduate proceeding to the degree must be in attendance on lectures at the University and at one of the Colleges throughout the session in all the subjects of his academic year.

54. Unless in exceptional cases and by special petition to the Council, no student will be allowed registration in more than two Courses in the First Year, and in not more than one in any subsequent year.

55. The courses leading to the degree of Bachelor of Arts are:

(a) THE PASS COURSE.

(b) The following Honour Courses:

CLASSICS.	MATHEMATICS AND PHYSICS.
GREEK AND HEBREW.	PHYSICS.
ORIENTAL LANGUAGES.	BIOLOGY.
ORIENTAL LANGUAGES (GK. OPT.).	PHYSIOLOGY AND BIOCHEMISTRY.
FRENCH, GREEK AND LATIN	PHYSIOLOGICAL AND BIOCHEMICAL
MODERN LANGUAGES.	SCIENCES.
ENGLISH AND HISTORY.	BIOLOGICAL AND MEDICAL
MODERN HISTORY.	SCIENCES.
POLITICAL SCIENCE.	CHEMISTRY AND MINERALOGY.
COMMERCE AND FINANCE.	CHEMISTRY.
PHILOSOPHY.	GEOLOGY AND MINERALOGY.
PHILOSOPHY, ENGLISH AND HIS-	HOUSEHOLD SCIENCE.
TORY.	HOUSEHOLD ECONOMICS.
PSYCHOLOGY.	SCIENCE FOR TEACHERS.

(c) THE ARTS AND FORESTRY COURSE.

56. A candidate who has Junior Matriculation without Honours can be admitted only to the Pass Course of the First Year.

Honour Course Entrance Requirements.

57. Unless special permission is granted by the Council, every student entering an Honour Course of the First Year must present, in addition to Pass Matriculation standing, a certificate based upon the work of Honour Matriculation or of an equivalent Examination in at least four subjects (two of which, Latin and Mathematics, i.e., Algebra and Geometry, are compulsory) with Honour or equivalent standing in the subjects specified under the requirements of the Honour Courses in Section 59. A student who has not met the above requirements in full, is advised to attempt to complete them at the Supplemental Pass and Honour Matriculation examinations which are held throughout the province in September.

58. In the following section "Honours" shall be interpreted as at least fifty per cent. of the marks assigned to a subject of Honour Matriculation or of an equivalent Examination.

59. The requirements for entrance to the Honour Courses, in addition to Pass Matriculation, are as follows:

CLASSICS:—Honours in Greek, Latin, Mathematics (Algebra and Geometry) and one of French, German, Physics, Biology, preferably French or German.

GREEK AND HEBREW:—Honours in Greek, Latin, Mathematics (Algebra and Geometry) and one of English, French, German.

FRENCH, GREEK AND LATIN:—Honours in Latin, Mathematics (Algebra and Geometry) and two of Greek, English, French.

MODERN LANGUAGES:—Honours in Latin, French, Mathematics (Algebra and Geometry) and one of English, German, History.

ENGLISH AND HISTORY:—Honours in Latin, Mathematics (Algebra and Geometry), and two of Greek, English, French, German.

MODERN HISTORY:
POLITICAL SCIENCE: Honours in Latin, Mathematics (Algebra and Geometry), History *or* English, and French *or* German.

COMMERCE AND FINANCE:—Honours in Latin, English, Mathematics (Algebra, Geometry and Trigonometry) and French or German.

PHILOSOPHY:—Honours in Latin, English, Mathematics (Algebra and Geometry) and one of History, Greek, French, German, Physics.

PHILOSOPHY, ENGLISH AND HISTORY:—Honours in Latin, Mathematics (Algebra and Geometry), one of History, English, Physics, and one of Greek, French, German.

PSYCHOLOGY:—Honours in Latin, Mathematics (Algebra, Geometry and Trigonometry), French *or* German, and one of Physics, Biology, Chemistry.

MATHEMATICS AND PHYSICS:—Honours in Latin, Mathematics (Algebra, Geometry and Trigonometry), Physics, and French or German.

PHYSICS:
BIOLOGY:
PHYSIOLOGY AND BIOCHEMISTRY:
BIOLOGICAL AND MEDICAL SCIENCES:
CHEMISTRY AND MINERALOGY:
CHEMISTRY:
GEOLOGY AND MINERALOGY:
HOUSEHOLD SCIENCE:
SCIENCE FOR TEACHERS: Honours in Latin, Mathematics (Algebra, Geometry and Trigonometry), French *or* German, and one of Physics, Biology, Chemistry.

HOUSEHOLD ECONOMICS:—Honours in Latin, Mathematics (Algebra and Geometry) and two of English, French or German, Physics, Biology, Chemistry; preferably French or German and a science.

60. A student admitted to an Honour Course of the First Year by special permission of the Council will be admitted on probation only, and will be allowed to enroll in the Honour Course for the Easter Term, only on the recommendation of his College and of the Department in which he is enrolled on probation.

61. Unless specially exempted by the Council, a student admitted on probation to an Honour Course of the First Year, before proceeding in the Honour Course in the Second Year, must fulfil the conditions of the Pass Course of the First Year in addition to those of the Honour Course.

62. A student admitted on probation to an Honour Course of the First Year will not be allowed by the Council to enroll in any subject beyond the requirements of his course except on the recommendation of his College and of the Department in which he is enrolled on probation.

Equivalent Examinations—First Year.

63. Certificates of having passed the whole or a part of the following examinations *may* be accepted *pro tanto* for Pass Course subjects but not for the individual papers of a subject at the examination of the First Year or Senior Matriculation. Before exemption is granted on any of the certificates mentioned in this Section, a candidate may be required to satisfy the authorities of the University, and of his College, as to the equivalence of the examinations for which exemption is sought.

Province of Ontario.

The Honour Junior Matriculation Examination and the Entrance to the Faculties of Education Examination or examinations of the same standard under other titles.

Province of Nova Scotia.

Grade XII Examination.

Province of Manitoba.

Grade XII Examination.

Province of British Columbia.

Senior Grade Examination.

Province of Alberta.

Grade XII Examination.

Province of Saskatchewan.

First Class Diploma or Senior Matriculation.

Newfoundland.

Associate in Arts (Senior) Examination.

Great Britain.

The local Examinations for Senior students, conducted by the Universities of Oxford and Cambridge.

64. A candidate submitting any of the certificates mentioned in the preceding section must submit an official statement of the marks on which the certificate was obtained.

65. In view of the recent change in the standard for passing in the Pass Course only those certificates which meet these conditions as to subjects and percentages will be accepted. Exemption will not be given in part of a subject of the First Year, *e.g.*, a pass percentage in Geometry will not be accepted; a student must pass in each of Algebra and Geometry at one examination to receive credit in Mathematics.

66. The Council will consider applications for the recognition of certificates other than those mentioned.

67. A candidate presenting *pro tanto* certificates is eligible for scholarships and for ranking in Honour Courses but not for standing in the Pass Course.

THE DEGREE OF BACHELOR OF ARTS UNDER SPECIAL CONDITIONS.

68. In order to assist teachers and others who desire to proceed to the degree of Bachelor of Arts, provision has been made for their instruction by 1, Teachers' Classes during the regular session, 2, (*a*) supervision during the academic year, and (*b*) the Summer Session.

69. The Pass Course according to the following scheme will be the basis of instruction:

First Year....English, Latin, French, Elementary Science, Mathematics (Algebra and Geometry), Trigonometry.

Second Year...⎧ English, French, Science, Two of
Third Year...⎨ History, Political Economy,
Fourth·Year...⎩ Psychology.

For those who have already entered upon the work of the Third Year, the course in the Third and Fourth Years will be as follows:

Third Year...English, History, Political Economy. One of (1) Latin, Greek and Roman History, French or German. (2) Chemistry, Geology and Mineralogy.

Fourth Year...English, History, Political Economy. One of (1) Latin, Greek and Roman History, French or German. (2) Chemistry, Geology and Mineralogy.

70. The subjects of the Second Year are divided into two groups, which are given in alternate years. The subjects for 1921-22 are English, French, and Science.

71. The subjects of the Third Year are divided into two groups which will be given in alternate years. The subjects for 1921-22 are English, Psychology, Political Economy, and Science for students taking the Teachers' Classes and for students taking the Summer Session.

72. These courses are open to persons actually engaged in teaching and to such others as have been approved by the Council. In all cases application for admission must be made to the Registrar of the University through the Director of University Extension.

73. Only under exceptional circumstances will a candidate be allowed to attend classes in more than three subjects during one session of the Teachers' Course.

74. A student holding an Upper School certificate or its equivalent, may enter the Second Year on payment of the fee of $15.00, provided he has credit for at least five of the six subjects of the First year.

75. A student proceeding to the degree shall on or before the *first of October* of each year submit a statement of the work which he proposes to take (*a*) in the Teachers' Classes or (*b*) under supervision preparatory to the Summer Session, and on or before the *fifteenth of May* of each year, a similar statement of the work he desires to take during the Summer Session.

76. A student will receive credit for each subject in which he secures fifty per cent.

77. A candidate will not receive credit for a subject of a higher year until he has passed the examination of the lower year in the same subject. He may, however, be a candidate for examination in the work of two successive years in the same subject.

78. A candidate who has not been granted complete First Year standing may not enter upon the work of the Third Year, nor a candidate who has not been granted complete Second Year standing, upon the work of the Fourth Year.

79. Pursuant to Section 124 of the Revised Statutes of Ontario 1913, in the case of a candidate for the degree of Bachelor of Arts, registered in the Teachers' Course, enrolment in one of the Arts Colleges shall not be necessary.

80. Instruction during the regular session will be given as far as possible to meet the convenience of the members of the classes residing in Toronto and its immediate vicinity.

81. The Summer Session is held during July and a part of August, and is open (*a*) to persons engaged in teaching, (*b*) to such others as have been approved by the Council of the Faculty of Arts, and (*c*) to regular students who have failed to receive credit in one or at most two subjects of the Pass Course, provided always that instruction in such subjects has been arranged for that Summer Session.

82. The work of the Second, Third, and Fourth Years of the Teachers' Course may be covered in five years and will involve (*a*) attendance on Teachers' Classes during four regular sessions or (*b*) attendance for four Summer Sessions and supervision during four regular sessions.

83. Instead of completing his course under this plan a candidate proceeding to the degree is advised to attend the regular courses of instruction in the Fourth Year, in which case the fourth Summer Session is not compulsory. Students are advised to acquaint themselves with the regulations of the Department of Education respecting High School Assistants' certificates. See page 94.

84. A candidate will not be allowed to present himself for examination in any subject until he has attended one Summer Session and has had supervision of his work during one academic year, or until he has attended Teachers' Classes in that subject during one regular session or until he has completed the necessary minimum of attendance (See 82, above).

85. Supervision of work should precede the Summer Session, but as such supervision may follow class instruction, assistance in the work of either group of the Second Year or of the Third Year will be provided.

VIII. CONDITIONS FOR ACADEMIC STANDING.

Credit in Pass Subjects.

86. To receive credit in a Pass Subject, a candidate must obtain at least fifty per cent. of the examination marks, as well as fifty per cent. of the aggregate of the term and examination marks in that subject; but where he has at one examination obtained an average of fifty per cent. of all the marks assigned to the Pass subjects of his annual examination, forty per cent. will (subject to the provisions of Section 120) be accepted in lieu of the fifty per cent. required above.

87. Except for candidates writing on the whole examination, fifty per cent. in each subject will be required at supplemental examinations.

88. If a candidate, who is exempt from examination in Greek or Latin or French or German, pass subjects attached to Honour Courses of the First Year, obtains a minimum of fifty per cent. on any one or more of these subjects as an Honour subject of the First Year, he shall be exempt in the Second Year from examination in such pass subject or subjects. A student shall not be granted credit a second time for a Pass or Honour subject for which he has already received credit.

89. In the First and Second Years a candidate who has failed to receive credit in one of a group of optional subjects may with the approval of the Council present himself at the supplemental examinations in any other of the alternative subjects, except in the case of those subjects in which term work is an integral part of the subject. In such a substitution, however, the candidate must, unless exempted by the Council, comply with all the conditions respecting term work, *i.e.*, there can be no transfer of term marks from the subject originally chosen to that substituted.

90. A successful candidate in a subject is graded as "A" or "B" or "C" or "Below the Line (B.L.)" according to the precentage obtained in the subject. For grade "A", a candidate must obtain at least seventy-five per cent., for grade "B", at least sixty per cent., for grade "C", at least fifty per cent. of the marks assigned to a subject, provided he has obtained at least fifty per cent. of the examination marks in the subject. For grade "B.L" he must obtain at least forty per cent. of the marks assigned to a subject.

91. A candidate in an Honour Course who has failed to secure standing in his year will receive credit in any pass subject in which he has obtained seventy-five per cent. of the examination marks as well as seventy-five per cent. of the aggregate of the term and examination marks in that subject. A candidate who has received credit under this section shall not, in repeating the year, be eligible for scholarships or relative ranking in an Honour Course.

Standing in the Pass Course.

92. A candidate in May, June or September will be granted standing, provided he obtains credit under Section 86, (1) in all of the subjects of the year and in the one subject of the previous year in which he may have failed, or (2) in all but one of these subjects, or (3) in all but two of these subjects.

93. A candidate who has been granted standing in the First Year, but who has failed in two subjects, must obtain credit in at least one of these subjects before he can register in the Second Year.

94. A candidate who has been granted standing in the Second or Third Years, but who has failed in two subjects, must obtain credit for **both** these subjects before he can register in the higher year.

95. A candidate for the examination of the First Year who has been granted exemption from examination in one or more subjects will be granted standing provided he obtains credit in the subjects necessary to complete his year, under the conditions laid down in Sections 86 and 92.

96. A candidate who has failed to secure complete First Year standing may not enter upon the work of the Third Year, nor may a candidate who has failed to secure complete Second Year standing enter upon the work of the Fourth Year.

97. A candidate who obtains an average of seventy-five per cent. of all the marks assigned to the subjects of his annual examination will be awarded Grade A standing in his course, provided that he has not failed in more than one subject either of his academic year or of the previous year.

98. A candidate who obtains under like conditions an average of sixty per cent. will be awarded Grade B standing.

99. A candidate who obtains under like conditions an average of fifty per cent. will be awarded Grade C standing.

Credit in Honour Subjects.

100. A candidate who obtains at least seventy-five per cent. of the marks assigned to an Honour subject will be awarded First Class Honours.

101. A candidate who obtains at least sixty-six per cent. but less than seventy-five per cent. of the marks assigned to an Honour subject will be awarded Second Class Honours.

102. A candidate who obtains at least sixty per cent. but less than sixty-six per cent. of the marks assigned to an Honour subject will be awarded Third Class Honours.

103. A candidate who obtains at least fifty per cent. but less than sixty per cent. of the marks assigned to an Honour subject will be ranked as "Below the Line".

104. No candidate will be granted Honours or Below the Line in an Honour subject where term work is taken into account, unless he obtain at least fifty per cent. of the marks at the May examination, as well as fifty per cent. of the aggregate of the term work and examination marks in that subject.

105. A candidate who fails to obtain fifty per cent. in an Honour subject, may be granted pass standing therein.

Standing in Honour Courses.

106. In order to obtain standing in an Honour Course, a candidate must have obtained (a) at least fifty per cent. in each Honour subject of the course as well as (b) credit as defined in Section 86 in all, or all but one of the Pass subjects attached thereto.

107. A candidate in the Fourth Year who fails to obtain standing in his Honour Course may on recommendation of the examiners be awarded a Pass degree. Such a candidate may accept the award or may repeat the year and again compete for Honours.

108. A candidate will be awarded First Class Honours in order of merit who has obtained an average of seventy-five per cent. of all the marks assigned to the Honour subjects of his course, and has also fulfilled the conditions regarding Pass subjects attached thereto. (See Section 106.)

—9

109. A candidate will be awarded Second Class Honours in order of merit who has obtained an average of at least sixty-six per cent. but less than seventy-five per cent. of all the marks assigned to the Honour subjects of his course, and has also fulfilled the conditions regarding Pass subjects attached thereto. (See Section 106.)

110. A candidate will be awarded Third Class Honours who has obtained an average of at least sixty per cent. but less than sixty-six per cent. of all the marks assigned to the Honour subjects of his course, and has also fulfilled the conditions regarding Pass subjects attached thereto. (See Section 106).

111. A candidate will be ranked as "Below the Line" who has obtained less than sixty per cent. of all the marks assigned to the Honour subjects of his course, and has also fulfilled the conditions regarding Pass subjects attached thereto. (See Section 106.)

112. A candidate in an Honour Course, who has failed in two Pass subjects, will have his standing deferred both in the Honour Course and in the individual subjects thereof, and will be debarred from registration and enrolment until he has passed in both of these Pass subjects.

113. A candidate in an Honour Course will not be granted standing in his year if he fail in more than two Pass subjects.

114. A candidate of the First or Second Year who fails to secure standing in an Honour Course may be transferred to the Pass Course on such conditions as the Council may impose. Such a candidate may accept the award or may repeat the year and again compete for Honours.

115. A candidate in an Honour Course of the Third Year who fails to secure standing must repeat the Year, unless he be transferred to the Pass Course by the Council on the special report of the Board of Examiners.

116. A candidate who has not been granted complete First Year standing, may not enter upon the work of the Third Year, nor a candidate who has not been granted complete Second Year standing upon the work of the Fourth Year.

Term Work.

117. In the Pass Course, reports on the term work of every student proceeding to a degree will be made in all the subjects of each year, except in purely lecture courses where the Council, on the recommendation of the teaching staff, may have approved the omission of such reports.

118. The marks for term work in a subject of the Pass Course will be determined in the manner considered most suitable by the teaching staff in that subject.

119. In all subjects of the Pass Course, the ratio of term marks to examination marks will be as fifty to one hundred, except in English where the ratio is as one hundred to one hundred.

120. Term work in English is an integral part of this subject; a candidate whose term work is reported as unsatisfactory must repeat it.

121. Term work in the Pass Sciences of the Second, Third and Fourth Years is an integral part of each of these subjects. A candidate who obtains less than 50 per cent. of the marks assigned to the term work in any one of these subjects must repeat such term work.

122. When a student fails to secure credit in a Pass subject because of a deficiency in term marks he must either (1) earn a new term mark under conditions to be determined by the staff in the subject, and repeat the examination or (2) make up the deficiency of term marks by securing a corresponding increase in his examination marks. In the case of English and of the Pass Sciences of the Second, Third and Fourth Years, see Sections 120 and 121.

123. In the Honour Courses, reports in term work will be made wherever such work is specified as an integral part of the course.

124. In an Honour Course, the ratio of term marks to examination marks in a subject will be determined by the staff in that subject.

125. A term examination shall not, unless it be so specified in the calendar, take the place of the Annual Examination in May on any portion of the prescribed work of an Honour Course.

Conditions of Entrance to the Various Years.

126. Unless in exceptional cases and by special petition to the Council of the Faculty, a non-matriculated student who desires to enter an Honour Course of the First Year must, in addition to evidence respecting other subjects, submit proof that his knowledge of Latin is at least equivalent to that required for Junior Matriculation.

127. Unless special permission is granted by the Council, every student entering an Honour Course of the First Year must present a certificate on which he would receive credit in Pass Latin, and in Pass Mathematics (Algebra and Geometry) of the First Year as well as in at least two other subjects as specified in Section 59.

128. Unless special permission is granted by the Council, a student of the Pass Course in the Second Year is not permitted to attempt the work of an Honour Course in addition to his Pass Course.

129. In order to proceed in an Honour Course in the Second Year a candidate at the examination of the First Year (1) must have fulfilled the conditions of Section 106, (2) must, if his standing is deferred, have fulfilled the conditions of Section 112, and (3) in the case of non-matriculated students must have fulfilled the conditions of Section 32.

130. In order to proceed in an Honour Course in the Third Year, a candidate at the examination of the Second Year (1) must have fulfilled the conditions of Section 106, (2) must have complete First Year standing, and (3) must, if his standing is deferred, have fulfilled the conditions of Section 112. A candidate who fails to comply with these conditions must either

repeat the Second Year of his Honour Course or, if transferred, proceed in the Pass Course of the Third Year, *i.e.*, he cannot in the Third Year take both the Pass Course and an Honour Course without the consent of the Council.

131. In order to proceed in a Honour Course in the Fourth Year, a candidate at the examination of the Third Year, (1) must have fulfilled the conditions of Section 106, (2) must have complete Second Year standing, and (3) must, if his standing is deferred, have fulfilled the conditions of Section 112. A candidate who fails to comply with these conditions must repeat the Third Year of the Honour Course unless transferred to the Pass Course by the Council on the special report of the Board of Examiners.

Repeating the Year.

132. A student who has been granted standing in any year of the Pass Course may on conditions to be determined by the Council repeat that year in an Honour Course, and on obtaining standing, may proceed therein.

133. A candidate in any course who for any cause is debarred from the higher year, may repeat the whole examination in the following May, but is not eligible for scholarships, medals, or prizes.

IX. EXAMINATIONS.

134. No candidate will be admitted to examination unless the Head of the College in which he is enrolled certifies that he has complied with all the requirements of that College affecting his admission to such examination.

135. A candidate will not be admitted to an examination unless he has paid all the fees due from him. A candidate who fails to pay his examination fees on or before the fifteenth of March—the last day for receiving fees prior to the May examination—must pay an additional fee of one dollar.

136. A candidate who fails to send his "application for examination" by the day appointed for receiving such applications must pay an additional fee of one dollar.

137. No candidate in a course involving practical work in a laboratory will be admitted to examination if the Professor under whom his work is carried on reports that he has neglected his laboratory work or signally failed in the practical examinations.

138. Representations on the part of candidates with regard to the examination must be made in writing to the President. Applications for aegrotat standing must be made to the Registrar BEFORE THE CLOSE OF THE EXAMINATION."

The May Examination.

139. The May examination is held at the University and is open to candidates of all the Years in the Pass Course and in all the Honour Courses.

140. Arrangements will be made, whenever possible, to allow a graduate, who is engaged in teaching in Ontario and who desires to receive credit in subjects not taken during his undergraduate course, to take such examinations in his own locality.

141. If the time-table permits, a candidate may present himself for examination in subjects in which he has previously failed to receive credit.

142. In the case of Fourth Year candidates, where there is a conflict in the time-table, a special supplemental examination may be arranged.

143. A candidate for examination is required to send an application according to a printed form, to the Registrar not later than the 15th of March.

The June Examination.

144. The June Examination, which is held at the University, and may be held at local centres as well, is exclusively for candidates for Senior Matriculation in the Pass Course.

145. A candidate for this examination is required to send an application, according to a printed form, tó the Registrar not later than the 1st of May.

The September Supplemental Examination.

146. The September Supplemental examination is held at the University, and is open (1) to candidates who failed in subjects of the Pass Course at a previous examination, and (2) to candidates in any year of the Pass Course, who were prevented by sickness, domestic affliction or other causes beyond their control, from attending the May Examination. The latter candidates must prove to the satisfaction of the Council the sufficiency of the alleged cause of absence.

147. If feasible this supplemental examination will be held at Winnipeg, Regina, Saskatoon, Edmonton, Calgary and Vancouver. The candidate for whom such an examination is held must meet the expenses incurred and should make early application for the privilege.

148. A candidate for this examination is required to send an application, according to a printed form, to the Registrar not later than the 1st of August.

The January Supplemental Examination.

149. The January examination is held at the University and is open to candidates who were awarded standing in the subjects of their course at the May or June examination and were prevented by sickness, domestic affliction or other causes beyond their control from attending the September examination. Such candidates must prove to the satisfaction of the Council the sufficiency of the alleged cause of absence.

150. A candidate for this examination is required to send an application, according to a printed form, to the Registrar not later than the 1st of December.

Local Senior Matriculation Examinations.

151. Local Senior Matriculation examinations will be held in June at such centres as may from time to time be authorized by the Council of the Faculty.

152. Applications for the establishment of such an examination in June must be made through the Registrar not later than the 1st of May.

153. The presiding examiner or examiners at a local Senior Matriculation examination will be appointed by the Council of the Faculty, and should, if necessary, be competent to conduct an examination in French or German Dictation.

154. The expenses in connection with such local Senior Matriculation examination must be met by the candidates at the centre or by the authorities of the school or college on whose application the examination is held.

155. The fee for the presiding examiner will be $5 per diem during the whole examination period.

THE LIBRARY.

The University Library is contained in a building of its own, situated on the east side of the campus that lies to the south of the Main Building. All students who have paid a library fee to the Bursar of the University are entitled to the privileges of the Library. Besides Reading Rooms the building contains Departmental Studies, which may be used as study-rooms by honour students in the various branches in which the Professors hold seminary courses, and private studies, intended for members of the Faculty or advanced students engaged in research work. The Library is opened at 8.45 every morning and remains open until 5.15 in the afternoon (6 p.m. during the second term). Books in ordinary use may not be taken out of the building during the daytime, but are lent for the night shortly before the hour of closing, to be returned the following morning before 10 o'clock. Books not in general demand may, on special application, be borrowed for a longer period. Failure to return a borrowed book at the proper time and other breaches of the regulations are punishable by fine or suspension from the privileges of the Library.

ROYAL ONTARIO MUSEUM.

ARCHAEOLOGY, GEOLOGY, MINERALOGY, PALAEONTOLOGY, ZOOLOGY.

Students of the University in all departments are recommended to avail themselves of the privileges of the Museum, which, although under separate control, is intimately connected with the work of the University.

The Museum is open on all week days from 10 a.m. to 5 p.m., Sundays 2 to 5 p.m. The Admission is free to the public on Tuesday, Thursday, Saturday and Sunday. On other days an admission fee of fifteen cents is charged.

By a resolution of the Board of Trustees all regular students of the University may be admitted free on all days of the week by presenting their card of registration.

HART HOUSE.

Hart House, the gift of the Massey Foundation, is the Undergraduates Union of the University of Toronto.

Hart House contains completely equipped Club rooms, including common rooms; reading room; music room; lecture room; sketch room; photographic dark rooms; the Great Hall, used as a dining hall; a small chapel; the offices and class rooms of the Y.M.C.A.; gymnasia and swimming pool; rifle range; billiard room; and the Hart House Theatre.

All male students proceeding to a degree in the University are members of Hart House. An annual fee imposed by the University covers the fee of the Students' Administrative Council, all club fees in connection with Hart House, and membership in the Athletic Association, including the medical examination.

Other male students in the University, or students in the affiliated or federated institutions receiving instruction in the University, may become members of Hart House on payment of the required fee.

Graduates are entitled to the full privileges of membership on payment of the annual fee of $10. Out-of-town Graduates may become members on payment of an annual fee of $2.50.

A group of rooms is set apart for the use of the Faculty Union. There is also a common room for the use of Graduates. Five guests rooms are available for the use of guests, for periods of a week or less, at a reasonable rental.

The Theatre is under the management of the Players' Club of the University of Toronto, and is available for productions by any of the Dramatic Clubs within the University.

For further information, apply to the Warden of Hart House.

UNIVERSITY COLLEGE WOMEN'S UNION.

85 St. George Street.

Resident Head, Miss M. M. Waddington, Ph.D.

The Union contains a common room, library, dining rooms, and guest room for the use of members.

MEMBERSHIP—All women undergraduates of University College are members of the Union. Graduates may also belong. (For membership fee see Fees).

MEALS are by flat rate or ticket.

Flat rate per week................................	$5.00
Breakfast (7 tickets)............................	2.00
Luncheon (5 tickets)............................	1.25
Dinner (7 tickets)...............................	3.50

REGISTRATION—All women undergraduates in University College are required to register with the Resident Head at the beginning of term.

BOARDING HOUSES—Women undergraduates who are away from home and not living in Queen's Hall or a College residence must have their boarding houses approved by the Resident Head. Students who need boarding houses are asked to communicate with her by letter after August, 1st.

VICTORIA COLLEGE WOMEN'S STUDENT UNION

The Women's Student Union, situated in the South end of Annesley Hall, with entrance by the south-west gate, comprises a common-room, library, committee room, guest room, tea room, kitchen and cloak rooms. These serve as common rooms for the women graduates and undergraduates of the College, and are the centre of their social activities. The rooms are available for committee meetings, discussion groups, Bible study classes, larger meetings, and class receptions. The Women's Undergraduate Association, under the supervision of the Dean's council, makes the rules and regulations for the use of the rooms.

Luncheon and dinner for a limited number may be had in the Annesley Hall dining-room.

For graduates living in Toronto the annual fee is $3.00; for those living out of the city $1.00; for women undergratuates $4.00; all to be paid to the fees clerk of the College. The money so derived will be applied to the maintenance of the common rooms.

For further information please apply to the Dean of Women Students, Victoria College.

RESIDENCES

UNIVERSITY OF TORONTO.

Residence for Men.

By the generosity of Mr. and Mrs. E. C. Whitney and other friends, the University can now offer to some hundred and fifty men the peculiar advantages of residential life and excellent accommodation within its own grounds. The Residence, opened in November, 1908, consists of three Houses situated on the north side of Hoskin Avenue, opening upon a quadrangle, the fourth side of which is formed by Devonshire Place. They stand about two hundred yards to the north of University College and close to Hart House to which is attached the University Dining Hall. The buildings are known as the South, East and North Houses.

Each House contains twenty-four single rooms, one single suite, one double room and eleven suites, a suite comprising a study and two bedrooms. A large room in each building, with an open hearth and a library, has been set aside as a common room. A lavatory with hot and cold shower baths is provided for every eight men. The buildings are heated by steam and lighted by electricity.

The University supplies the table, chairs, book-case, chiffonier, bed, mattress, pillows, linen and window shades for each room; it is prepared to furnish a desk-lamp for a nominal rental.

Each occupant is charged $4.00 room-rent per week, payable to the Bursar four weeks in advance. The charge for each single suite is $5.00 per week. These charges cover heat, light, house-service, house-laundry, and the use of the telephone. There is no separate dining hall connected with the Residence, but board may be obtained at the adjacent University Dining Hall.

Applications for rooms must be made in writing to the Secretary of the Residence Committee (address the Registrar's Office) and must be accompanied by a deposit of $5.00. This deposit will be returned if the application is not granted, but will be forfeited if a room is assigned to the applicant and not taken by him, unless notice of his refusal of the room is received by the Secretary in writing before September 22nd. It will be returned in full at the end of the College year if the room key is given back and the room and furniture left in a satisfactory condition. The following principles govern the allotment of rooms: (i) No student, who as a result of the annual Spring examinations is not assured of being able to proceed to a subsequent year, will be admitted into the Residence. Exception to this rule will be made in the case of a student in the Faculty of Medicine who has obtained standing at the May examination, but is debarred by the rules of that Faculty from proceeding to the subsequent year until he a s passed his Supplemental examinations. Such a student will be assigned a room provisionally, but cannot occupy it unless he passes his Supplemental examinations in September. (ii) The rooms in each house will be distributed among the various Faculties and Years. (iii) A limited number of rooms will be reserved for members of the incoming First Year until September 12th. (iv) Applications will be considered in order of priority.

The University lays down three general rules, designed to prevent hazing, the use of intoxicants and gambling. The students in each House shall elect a House Committee, which is entrusted by the University with the making and enforcing of any other needed rules and with the maintenance of order. A member of the Faculty resides in each House to act as friend and adviser to the men in residence.

Queen's Hall, Residence for Women, Nos. 4, 7, 9 Queen's Park.

Superintendent, Miss Louise I. Livingstone, B.A.

Accommodation is provided for 97 students. The rate for room and board is $9.50 per week and these dues must be paid to the Bursar four weeks in advance.

Applications for rooms must be made in writing and a deposit fee of $5.00 must accompany each application. The fee will be returned if the application is not granted or if it is withdrawn before the 15th of September. It will be returned in full at the end of the college course if the room is left in good condition and there are no breakages.

Applications from First Year Students will be considered first, the other years in order of priority. Applications of those only who have completed matriculation will be considered. Those undergraduates who have supplemental examinations to write must be successful before they can be enrolled.

The students elect a House Committee to assist the superintendent in the maintenance of order and for the general welfare of the household.

UNIVERSITY COLLEGE.

Residence for Women, 94 St. George Street.

94 St. George Street was opened in the autumn of 1919 in connection with the University College Women's Union. Accommodation is provided for thirty-six students. The rate for rooms is $4.00 to $5.00 a week, payable in advance by the month or term to the Bursar. Meals are taken at the Union. The rate for meals is $5.00 a week. Applications for residence are to be made to Miss Wrong, 85 St. George Street, Toronto, and are to be accompanied by a deposit of $5.00, which will be refunded if the application is withdrawn before September 15th. The deposit will be returned in full at the end of the College Course if the room is left in good condition.

VICTORIA COLLEGE.

The Residence for Men.

There is accommodation in the four houses of the Residence for 132 undergraduates of Victoria College. Each room is completely furnished as a combined study and bed room. About 15 rooms have fire places. There is a Common Room in each House. The weekly charge to men in Residence for room and meals is from $9.00 to $10.00. The Dining Hall, known as Burwash Hall, is mainly for the use of students of Victoria College, but there is accommodation for a limited number of men from other Colleges and Faculties. Applications for rooms and all inquiries should be addressed to the Dean of Residence, Victoria College.

Residences for Women.

The women students of Victoria College are housed in four buildings—Annesley Hall, South Hall, the Annex, Oaklawn, accommodating sixty-one, twenty-five, fourteen, and twenty-six students respectively. The houses are all near the College.

Applications for rooms must be accompanied by a deposit fee of $10.00, which will be refunded if the application is withdrawn before September the first. Fees for the year range from $265 to $400, according to the location of the room, and are payable half on the first of October and half on the first of February.

Additional fees are:—medical examination $2.00; nurse's fee $5.00; use of laundry $2.00. These charges are subject to change.

For further information kindly write to the Dean of Women Students, Victoria College, Queen's Park, Toronto.

TRINITY COLLEGE.

Trinity College provides residences for both men and women students. The men reside in Trinity College, in which there is accommodation for about seventy students. The women reside in St. Hilda's College and St. Hilda's Lodge, in which together accommodation for about fifty is provided.

Residence for Men.

Excellent accommodation for men is to be found in the residence set apart for their use. Several members of the staff are resident in the building. The students' living rooms are so arranged that two students may room together, or a student may have a room to himself, as may be preferred. Details as to fees for room and board, which are maintained at the lowest rate consistent with first class service, will be sent on request. There is a students' common room, gymnasium—which is used also for basket-ball and boxing—a hockey rink, tennis courts, a large field for sports, and ample grounds surrounding the College buildings. College affairs affecting student life are arranged by the students themselves in the "College Meeting", which is formally organized and embraces all the students of the College under the chairmanship of the senior student, known as "Head of College".

Applications for rooms in College are to be made on a printed form provided for this purpose, and are received at any time after the 1st of January for the succeeding Michaelmas Term, being subject to withdrawal on written notice up to the 1st September. Most of the rooms, being furnished partly by the College and partly by the occupants, may be fitted up to suit the taste of the individual student. Further information, with blank forms of application, will be supplied on request being made to "The Provost, Trinity College, Toronto".

Residence for Women.

Exceedingly comfortable accommodation is provided for the Women Students of Trinity in St. Hilda's College and St. Hilda's Lodge, which are situated in the grounds of Trinity College, less than four minutes' walk from the lecture rooms. The buildings are well planned, with ample common rooms and very attractive living rooms for the students. The young ladies have their own tennis courts, and provision is made for basketball in the gymnasium of Trinity College. The rooms are furnished. The houses are in charge of experienced ladies.

For information as to rates and the academic qualifications for admission, with blank form of application, address: "The Provost, Trinity College, Toronto". For other particulars regarding the residence, address: "The Principal, St. Hilda's College, Toronto".

ST. MICHAEL'S COLLEGE.

For Catholic students St. Michael's now offers all the advantages peculiar to a Catholic College.

Residence for Men.

There is accommodation for the men at St. Michael's College. Parents are most careful of the dangers and temptations to which students, away from home for the first time, are subjected. This is a point that St. Michael's chiefly considers, and she is in a position almost to guarantee that the student will be as safe in every way as if he were in his own home, in addition to receiving all the advantages of the University.

The residents are subjected to a reasonable rule with a view to careful supervision, and a solid moral and religious training. Constant and intimate intercourse between staff and student is a feature.

The health and development of body and mind is promoted by regulated hours of study and recreation. Opportunity is given for all kinds of athletic exercise. For terms and application, address "The Superior".

Residence for Women.

For women students, St. Joseph's Convent, St. Alban's Street, and Loretto Abbey College, 385 Brunswick Avenue, are providing residences to meet in every way the wishes of all. Address "The Superior".

ARGYLL HOUSE, 100 Queen's Park.

Accommodation for thirty women students is afforded by Argyll House. Applications should be made to the Secretary of the Argyll House Committee, 85 St. George Street, Toronto, from whom terms of residence may be obtained.

STUDENTS' ADMINISTRATIVE COUNCIL.

The Students' Administrative Council has been entrusted by the Caput with supervision of the conduct of the students, and has disciplinary powers to deal with violation of the regulations governing conduct.

Any student who may be convicted of having taken part in a parade or procession through the city which has not been authorized by the police authorities after application by the Executive of the Students' Administrative Council, will be severely disciplined.

WOMEN STUDENTS' ADMINISTRATIVE COUNCIL.

The Women Students' Administrative Council is the representative organ of the women students of the University of Toronto and aims to coördinate all intercollegiate activities. It consists of representatives from all colleges and faculties. A fee of $3 is paid for the council by each woman student proceeding to the Bachelor's degree. The council assumes joint financial responsibility with the men's council for the publication of *Varsity*, *Torontonensis*, and *the Directory*.

CANADIAN OFFICERS' TRAINING CORPS

The Toronto Contingent of the Canadian Officers Training Corps was organized in 1914, with a strength of 12 Companies. Its primary object is to provide students at Universities with a standardized measure of military training with a view to their qualifying for commissions in the country's auxiliary forces. C.O.T.C. certificates of qualification exempt their holders from examination for commissioned rank on joining a Militia unit. The facilities which are offered by the contingent for obtaining a qualification while at the University, are intended to enable gentlemen to give personal service to their country with the least possible interference with their civil careers, to ensure that units have their establishments complete in the junior commissioned ranks, and to build up an adequate reserve of scientifically trained officers who have completed a period of consecutive and systematic military training, on academic lines, of a nature calculated to produce good officers.

The contingent provides the practical work for students taking the Military Studies option for the Arts degree, as also physical exercise for students who may choose this as the form in which they will take their compulsory Physical Training. In addition to service in the corps for a University credit, students of any year or faculty are trained in it to qualify for the Militia Department's officers' certificates. As the corps develops, after the set-back subsequent to its continuous activities during the war, it is hoped that it may be possible to form companies according to faculties and so to arrange the training of each that on leaving the University students will be qualified for commissions in that branch of the Militia to which their University course particularly applied.

The C.O.T.C. is a unit of the non-permanent Active Militia but forms no part of the organization for war and cannot be called out for active service as such. It is a training centre for the educated youth of the country from whom, as from all its sons, the Empire requires hard service, but the hardest from those to whom most has been given.

The present Headquarters are at 184 College Street, and include armouries, members' reading room, library, and lecture room.

The Contingent's Staff is,
Officer Commanding, COLONEL W. R. LANG, Late Gen. Staff, C.E.F.
Second in Command, MAJOR T. R. LOUDON, late Can. Eng., C.E.F.
Adjutant, MAJOR H. H. MADILL, late C.E.F.
Quartermaster, LIEUT. V. C. KERRISON, late C.A.S.C., C.E.F.
Paymaster, LIEUT. T. A. REED.
Musketry Officer,
Contingent Sergeant-Major, S.M. W. HUNT, late Royal Welch Fusiliers.

THE ROLL OF SERVICE.

The final edition of the Roll of Service of the University is now being published. In it the records of all the members of the University who were on active service in the war are given in an abbreviated form similar to that used in the previous editions, but with more details, in so far as the facts have been ascertained in each case. The records of those who died while on service are given more fully.

FEES

All University fees, as also the fees of students enrolled in University College, are payable at the Bursar's Office in the Main University Building, between the hours of ten and one o'clock, except on Saturday.

The College fees of students enrolled in Victoria College are payable to the Fees Clerk of that College.

The College fees of students enrolled in Trinity College or St. Michael's College are payable to the Bursar of the College.

I. UNIVERSITY FEES.

Matriculated and non-matriculated students, proceeding to the degree of Bachelor of Arts and enrolled in University College, or Victoria College, or Trinity College, or St. Michael's College, may attend the lectures of University professors and lecturers in the Faculty of Arts without payment of fees, except those imposed for laboratory supplies, but such students must register in the University.

Ad Eundem Statum Fees.

For admission, by certificate, to Second Year..........$15.00
For admission ad eundem statum..................... 10.00

Library Fees.

The annual fee....................................... $2.00

Every matriculated and non-matriculated student in attendance, proceeding to the degree of Bachelor of Arts, is required to pay at the time of the entry of his name with the Registrar the annual library fee.

No occasional or graduate student shall be admitted to the library save upon the payment of the annual fee.

Charges for Laboratory Supplies.

Charges for supplies shall include laboratory materials and instruments used by or for the student, and ordinary wear and tear of instruments, but not charges for waste, neglect and breakage, which are to be met out of a deposit to be fixed by the Professor.

The annual supply charges for a student shall be according to the following table in which for convenient reference, the college fees for each year of the various courses are also included, reference being made to the annual fee if paid in October, and not by instalments, for the details of which see pages 66-67.

COURSES.

Courses	College Regist.	Labor. Suppli.	College Registration	Laboratory Supplies	C ⟍F				Laboratory Supplies
1 Pass Course	45	:	40	:	40	:	40	40	5
2 Philosophy	45	:	40	:	40	:	40	40	3
3 Psychology	45	5	40	5	40	8	40	35	10
4 Ae and ... fee	45	3	40	3	40	3	40	40	3
5 Mathematics and Physics	45	5	40	5	40	5	40	35	:
6 Physics	45	:	40	:	40	8	40	35	10
7 Astronomy and Physics	:	:	40	:	:	:	:	30	10
8 Biology	45	5	40	5	40	9	35	30	22
9 Physiology and Bi...mary	45	5	40	5	40	6	35	30	20
10 Biological and Medical Sciences	45	5	40	5	40	6	35	30	20
11 Physiological and ...tal Sci	:	:	40	:	40	5	35	35	10
12 Chemistry and Mineralogy I and Chemistry	45	5	40	5	40	5	35	40	3
13 Chemistry and Mineralogy II	45	5	40	5	40	9	40	40	3
14 Geology and Mineralogy	45	5	40	5	40	11	35	30	20
15 Household Science and ...hold Emics	45	5	40	5	40	9	35	30	20
16 Science for Teachers	45	:	40	:	40	:	40	40	:
17 Any other ...G.									

1 The Laboratory ... ... fee in the Third ... ad ... ... oly ... m those students who are taking the
...d Science ... in.

2 The ... ry Supply fee is not ... qui ed from st... ... s of St. Michael's College or from those who do not take the
Psychological ... in.

3 The ... ry Supply fee is ... ... d ... ... s taking a Sci... ... e as a Pass subject.

4 The fees for ... he Faculty of ... Me ... ae ... ot ... ld.

5 The fees for Drawing ... ad Assaying ... ae ... ot ... ld.

6 At ... ... the ... es ... ae ... G, ... Gr. ad ... W, Oriental Languages, Oriental Languages (Greek Option),
French Greek ... ad Latin, ... Mn Languages, English ... ad History, Modern History, Political Science, Philosophy
... gh ... ad Hist ... ov.

—10

Hart House and the Students' Administrative Council.

The annual fee.....................................$11.00

Every male student in attendance, proceeding to the degree of Bachelor of Arts, is required to pay to the Bursar at the time of the entry of his name with the Registrar the annual fee of eleven dollars for the maintenance of Hart House and the Students' Administrative Council.

Women Students' Administrative Council Fee.

Every woman student proceeding to the degree of Bachelor of Arts is required to pay to the Bursar at the time of the entry of her name with the Registrar the annual fee of three dollars for the maintenance of the Women Students' Administrative Council.

Examination Fees.

Students proceeding regularly to the B.A. degree.

For the June Senior Matriculation or January Supplemental Examination..............................$15.00
For each examination other than June and January...... 10.00
For each Supplemental examination.................... 10.00
Teachers' Course, Occasional and Summer Session Students.
For examination in one subject of any year, each........ 5.00
Maximum fee...................................... 10.00

A candidate who fails to pay his University fees on or before the fifteenth of March—the last day for receiving fees prior to the May examination— must pay an additional fee of one dollar.

A candidate who fails to send his application for examination by the day appointed for the receipt of such applications must pay an additional fee of one dollar.

Degree Fees.

For the degree of B.A..............................$10.00
For admission ad eundem gradum (B.A.)............... 20.00

Miscellaneous Fees.

For certificate of honour $1.00

The fee for admission *ad eundem statum,* or for dispensation from attendance upon lectures, or for certificates of honour, must be paid at the time of application.

A candidate who fails to pay his University fees on or before the fifteenth of March—the last day for receiving fees prior to the May examination— must pay an additional fee of one dollar.

II. COLLEGE FEES.

A graduate in Arts, who during his undergraduate course, was enrolled in either University College, or Victoria College, or Trinity College, or St. Michael's College, may attend lectures free in the college in which he was so enrolled.

Every matriculated and non-matriculated student proceeding to the degree of Bachelor of Arts shall, on each year's enrolment in University College, or Victoria College, or Trinity College, or St. Michael's College, pay an enrolment fee according to the following table, which fee shall include all instruction for which fees are chargeable except laboratory supply charges and library fees:—

Table of Fees.

FIRST YEAR.

MATRICULATED STUDENTS—Any course, if paid in full in
October..$40.00
By instalments:—
First instalment, if paid in October.................... 20.00
Second instalment, if paid in January................. 21.00
NON-MATRICULATED STUDENTS—Any course, if paid in full in
October.. 45.00
By instalments:—
First instalment, if paid in October.................... 23.00
Second instalment, if paid in January................. 23.00

SECOND YEAR.

MATRICULATED STUDENTS—Any course, if paid in full in
October.. 40.00
By instalments:—
First instalment, if paid in October.................... 20.00
Second instalment, if paid in January................. 21.00
NON-MATRICULATED STUDENTS—Any course, if paid in full in
October.. 45.00
By instalments:—
First instalment, if paid in October.................... 23.00
Second instalment, if paid in January................. 23.00

THIRD YEAR.

Biology, *or* Physiology and Biochemistry, *or* Biological and Medical Sciences, *or* Chemistry and Mineralogy I, *or* Chemistry, *or* Household Science, *or* Household Economics, *or* Science for Teachers.
If paid in full in October............................ 35.00
By instalments:—
First instalment, if paid in October.................... 18.00
Second instalment, if paid in January................. 18.00

Any other course, if paid in full in October.................. 40.00
   By instalments:—
     First instalment, if paid in October.................... 20.00
     Second instalment, if paid in January.................. 21.00

FOURTH YEAR.

Psychology, *or* Physics, *or* Astronomy and Physics, *or* Chemistry and
    Mineralogy I, *or* Chemistry.
    If paid in full in October............................. 35.00
   By instalments:—
     First instalment, if paid in October....................$18.00
     Second instalment, if paid in January.................. 18.00
Biology, *or* Biological and Medical Sciences, *or* Physiological and
    Biochemical Sciences, *or* Household Science, *or* Household
    Economics, *or* Science for Teachers.
    If paid in full in October............................. 30.00
   By instalments:—
     First instalment, if paid in October.................... 15.00
     Second instalment, if paid in January.................. 16.00
Any other course, if paid in full in October.................. 40.00
   By instalments:—
     First instalment, if paid in October.................... 20.00
     Second instalment, if paid in January.................. 21.00
Arts and Forestry—First, second, third, fourth, fifth, and
    sixth years. Annual fee, including tuition, library,
    laboratory supply, and one annual examination, (the
    College fee in each of the first, second, and third years
    is $30.):—
    If paid in full in October............................. 70.00
   By instalments:—
     First instalment, if paid in October.................... 35.00
     Second instalment, if paid in January.................. 36.00
Course in Commerce—First, second, third and fourth years.
    Annual fee, including tuition, library and one annual
    examination, (the College fee in each of the first, second,
    third and fourth years is $30.):—
    If paid in full in October............................. 80.00
   By instalments:—
     First instalment, if paid in October.................... 40.00
     Second instalment, if paid in January.................. 41.00

All the above fees are payable in advance. After October 31st, a penalty
of $1.00 per month will be imposed until the whole amount is paid. In the
case of payment by instalments the same rule as to penalty will apply.
A student will not be admitted to any of the University lectures or laboratories who is in arrears for his fees.

The annual enrolment fee of a matriculated student taking under the regulations more than one honour course shall be $40 only.

The enrolment fee of a matriculated student attending lectures for one term shall be $20.

The enrolment fee for students receiving dispensation from attendance upon lectures in University College, or Victoria College, or Trinity College, or St. Michael's College, shall be $5 for each term, in addition to the University fee of $5. The payment of these fees entitles the student to supervision of "term work" prescribed in connection with his course.

UNIVERSITY COLLEGE WOMEN'S UNION.

The Annual Fee... $4.00

Every woman student registered in University College as proceeding to the degree of Bachelor of Arts, is required to pay to the Bursar at the time of the entry of her name with the Registrar, the annual fee of four dollars for the maintenance of the Women's Union. A reduction will be made (a) in the case of those University College students who have paid four dollars for instruction in Athletics, and (b) in the case of graduates, and in these two cases the fee for the privileges of the Union will be reduced to three dollars.

III. FEES FOR OCCASIONAL STUDENTS, TEACHERS' COURSE.

"A course in laboratory work" means the continuous course of instruction in laboratory or practical work offered to students in any one year in any of the subjects in which laboratory work is or may be prescribed.

"A course of lectures" means the continuous course of instruction offered in any one year in any of the subjects in which instruction is or may be given.

Laboratory fees are divided into (a) Fees for practical instruction in the laboratory, (b) Charges for supplies, which are the same as for students proceeding to the degree. (See page 64).

The payment of fees shall not entitle any occasional student to be admitted to the laboratory work of a later year without having taken that of the earlier year or years, unless this requirement is dispensed with by the Council of the Faculty on the recommendation of the Professor.

The annual fee for an occasional student attending a course, or partial course, of lectures shall be as follows—

	For the Session	For the Term
Tuition Fees.		
For a course in any one subject.....................$10.00		$5.00
For a course in more than one subject, each subject...... 9.00		5.00
Maximum Fee...................................... 45.00		23.00

Examination Fees.

For examination in one subject of any year, each................ $5.00
Maximum examination fee.................................... 10.00

All instruction fees are payable strictly in advance.

PRIZES, MEDALS, SCHOLARSHIPS AND FELLOWSHIPS.

No candidate will be permitted to hold more than one scholarship; but any one who would, but for this provision, have been entitled to a second scholarship, will have his name published in the lists.

All undergraduate scholars must sign a declaration of intention to proceed to a degree in Arts in this University, and must attend lectures in one of the Colleges for the academic year immediately following such examination. The Senate, however, on the recommendation of the Faculty, may, upon satisfactory reasons being shown, permit such scholar to postpone attendance upon lectures for a year. If at the end of the year a further postponement is necessary, special application must again be made. In every such case the payment of the scholarship will likewise be postponed. The scholarships are paid in three instalments—on the fifteenth of November, the fifteenth of January and the fifteenth of March; and each scholar is required to send to the Registrar a certificate of attendance upon lectures at least three days before the date of each payment.

No scholarship or medal will be awarded to any candidate who has been placed lower than the first class in the department to which the scholarship or medal is attached.

When the letter "U" is prefixed, the award is made by the Senate of the University on the recommendation of the Council of the Faculty as the result of competition open to the students of all the Colleges. In all other cases the letter indicates the governing body by which the award is made:— the Council of University College by the letter "C", the Senate of Victoria College by the letter "V", the Corporation of Trinity College by the letter "T", and the Council of St. Michael's College by the letter "M".

With the exception of the Jean Balmer Scholarship in Science of the First Year, all honours awarded by the Senate on the recommendation of the Faculty are open to the students of all the Colleges.

The competition for a College scholarship, medal or prize is confined to the students registered in that College and shall be subject to such regulations as the College may from time to time determine.

PRIZES.
First Year.

ITALIAN.

U. The Italian Prize, the gift of the Minister of Foreign Affairs for the Kingdom of Italy.

ENGLISH.

V. The Class of 1902 Prize, the gift of Professor C. E. Auger, B.A., of the value of $10 to the student ranking highest in English of the Pass Course.

Awarded in 1920 to F. G. Ward.

M. A prize of the value of $10 to the student ranking highest in English of the Pass Course.

Awarded in 1920 to E. P. Butler.

Second Year.

ITALIAN.

U. The Italian Prize, the gift of the Minister of Foreign Affairs for the Kingdom of Italy.

ENGLISH.

C. The Alumnae Prize, the gift of the Toronto Alumnae, of the value of $10 in books, to the student ranking highest in English Composition.

Awarded in 1920 to Miss H. M. Cochrane.

M. A Prize of the value of $10, to the student ranking highest in English of the Pass Course.

Awarded in 1920 to R. J. Dobell.

V. The Webster Prize, the gift of the late J. G. Hodgins, Esq., M.A., LL.D., I.S.O., of the value of $10, to the student ranking highest in English of the Pass Course.

Awarded in 1920 to R. de la P. Stewart.

HEBREW.

V. The Robert Johnston Prize, the gift of the Rev. Professor J. F. Mc-. Laughlin, B.A., D.D., of the value of $15, to the student ranking highest in Hebrew of the Pass Course.

Awarded in 1920 to H. M. Wright.

PHILOSOPHY.

M. The Kernahan Prize of the value of $25, the gift of W. T. Kernahan, Esq., in memory of the late Rev. Gregory Kernahan, to the student ranking first in the examinations in Philosophy.

Awarded in 1920 to L. J. Stock.

First and Second Years.

ENGLISH.

V. Two prizes, of the value of $10 each, will be awarded for the two best essays on a subject to be assigned by the Staff in the Department of English. Neither of these prizes will be granted twice to the same student.

Awarded in 1920 to L. H. Miller and Miss M. V. Ray.

Third Year.

ITALIAN.

U. The Italian Prize, the gift of the Minister of Foreign Affairs for the Kingdom of Italy.

ENGLISH.

V. The Hodgins Prize, the gift of the late J. G. Hodgins, Esq., M.A., LL.D., I.S.O., of the value of $12, to the student ranking highest in English of the Pass Course.

No award in 1920.

M. The Dockeray Prize of the value of $25, to the student ranking highest in English of the Pass Course.
Awarded in 1920 to T. S. Melady.

ENGLISH BIBLE.

V. The Massey Bursaries, established by the late Hart A. Massey, Esq., one of $25 and one of $15, to the students ranking first and second at the examination in the English Bible.
Awarded in 1920 to Miss G. L. Rutherford and E. M. Cook.

PHILOSOPHY.

M. The Hanrahan Prize of the value of $25, the gift of W. T. Kernahan, Esq., in memory of the late John Hanrahan, Esq., to the student ranking first in the examinations in Philosophy.
No award in 1920.

HOUSEHOLD SCIENCE.

U. The Anna Howe Reeve Prize of the value of $25, the gift of Dr. R. A. Reeve, "in memory of a true helpmate, whose unselfishness enabled the donor the better to discharge his duty to his Alma Mater". The Committee of Award consists of the President of the University, Professor Laird and Professor Benson.
Awarded in 1920 to Miss M. G. Webster.

Fourth Year.

ITALIAN.

U. The Italian Prize, the gift of the Minister of Foreign Affairs for the Kingdom of Italy.

ENGLISH.

M. The Dockeray Prize, of the value of $25, to the student ranking highest in English of the Pass Course.
Awarded in 1920 to Miss F. T. Ronan.

FRENCH.

U. The Quebec Bonne Entente Prize, the proceeds from $1,000, the gift of the delegates from the Province of Quebec to the Bonne Entente Movement.
The Prize shall be awarded on the results of (a) an essay in French written on one of a number of subjects in the Examination Hall, (b) translation from English into French, (c) an oral test in which regard shall be had especially to facility in speaking, understanding and pronouncing French. The Prize shall be in money, and it is suggested that it be expended in acquiring a more perfect knowledge of French.
Awarded in 1920 to Miss H. M. McCrimmon.

CANADIAN CONSTITUTIONAL HISTORY.

V. The Robertson Prize, the gift of W. J. Robertson, Esq., B.A., LL.B., of the value of $10, to the student ranking highest in Canadian Constitutional History.
Awarded in 1920 to H. D. Lang.

CLASSICS.

T. The Prince of Wales' Prize, $18, for the highest first class honours in Classics.
Awarded in 1920 to J. B. West.

T. MATHEMATICS.
The Prince of Wales' Prize, $18, for the highest first class honours in Mathematics.
Awarded in 1920 to P. Lowe.

NATURAL SCIENCE.

T. A prize of $15 for the highest first class honours in any graduating department of the Natural and Physical Sciences.
No award in 1920.

M. A prize of the value of $10 to the student ranking highest in Science (Natural and Physical).
No award in 1920.

MODERN LANGUAGES.

T. A prize of $15 for the highest first class honours in Modern Languages.
No award in 1920.

ENGLISH AND HISTORY.

T. A prize of $15 for the highest first class honours in English and History.
No award in 1920.

MODERN HISTORY.

T. A Prize of $15 for the highest first class honours in Modern History.
No award in 1920.

PHILOSOPHY.

T. A Prize of $15 for the highest first class honours in Philosophy.
No award in 1920.

M. The M. J. O'Brien Prize, of the value of $100, to the student ranking highest in the Department of Philosophy (St. Michael's College).
Awarded in 1920 to J. L. G. Keogh.

POLITICAL SCIENCE.

T. A Prize of $15 for the highest first class honours in Political Science.
Awarded in 1920 to D. A. C. Martin.

T. A Prize of $15 for the highest first class honours in Commerce and Finance.
Awarded in 1920 to T. Oakley

PASS COURSE.

T. A Prize of $15 for the highest ranking in Grade A Standing in the Pass Course.
No award in 1920.

Third and Fourth Years.

BIBLICAL GREEK.

V. The Wallbridge Prize, the gift of the late A. F. Wallbridge, Esq., of the value of $10, to the student ranking first in New Testament Study III.
Awarded in 1920 to H. C. Wolfraim.

NEW TESTAMENT INTRODUCTION.

V. The Joy Wallace Prize, established by the Rev. Professor F. H. Wallace, M.A., D.D., of the value on $15, to the student ranking first in New Testament Study IV.
Awarded in 1920 to J. H. Garden.

All the Years.

ENGLISH.

V. The Lily Denton Keys Prize, of the annual value of $25, endowed by Mr. Norman A. Keys, B.A., as a memorial for his wife, Lily Denton, B.A., is open for competition among all the Arts undergraduates of Victoria College. The subject of the essay shall be "The Present Day Novel".
Awarded in 1920 to H. D. Langford.

FRENCH COMPOSITION.

C. The Squair French Prose Prize, of the annual value of $10, endowed by Professor Squair, is open for competition among students in attendance upon lectures in University College. The award shall be made annually by the Council of University College on the recommendation of the teaching staff in French. The books awarded are to be chosen by the winner after consultation with the staff in French.
Awarded in 1920 to Miss K. M. Asman and Miss H. C. Kirkwood, *aeq.*

NEW TESTAMENT HISTORY.

V. The Ryerson Prize, the gift of the late J. G. Hodgins, Esq., M.A., LL.D., I.S.O., of the value of $12, to the student ranking first in New Testament Study II.
Awarded in 1920 to J. E. Mitchell.

ORATORY.

V. The Michael Fawcett Prize of $40 is awarded annually for "the best extempore oration" on a subject to be assigned at the commencement of each college year by the trustees of the fund. This prize is open to all candidates on probation for the ministry of the Methodist Church.
No award in 1920.

GREEK.

T. A Prize of $20 for Greek Prose.
No award in 1920.

LATIN.

T. A Prize of $20 for Latin Verse.
No award in 1920.

T. A Prize of $20 for Latin Essay.
No award in 1920.

GREEK OR LATIN.

T. A Prize of $20 for an essay in English on some subject of classical study.
No award in 1920.

FRENCH.

T. A Prize of $20 for a French Essay.

ENGLISH.

. T. A Prize of $20 for an English Essay.
No award in 1920.

T. A Prize of $20 for an English Poem.
No award in 1920.
The subjects of these Trinity College Prizes will be posted on the
College notice board.

HELLENISTIC GREEK.

V. The Driver Prize of $10 is awarded annually on the result of an examina-
tion held in September on the Septuagint and allied versions. The prize
is to be open to undergraduate and graduate students.
No award in 1920.

MEDALS.
Second Year.

THE PASS COURSE.

U. The Governor-General's Silver Medal will be awarded to that candidate
who, taking not less than seventy-five per cent. in this examination,
takes also the highest aggregate of marks when the results of the First
and Second Year examinations in this course are added together, such
examinations having been taken in two consecutive calendar years.
The discretion of the examiners, as in the examination for the Governor-
General's Gold Medal, shall apply also to this examination.
No award in 1920.

Fourth Year.

GENERAL PROFICIENCY.

U. The Governor-General's Gold Medal is intended for the encouragement
of the study of English in those departments in which English is not
an integral portion of the work of the third and fourth years and will
be awarded to that candidate who, taking not less than sixty-six per
cent. in English (as defined below), and not less than seventy-five per
cent. in some one of the following honour departments:—(a) Classics,
(b) Greek and Hebrew, (c) Oriental Languages, (d) Modern History,
(e) Political Science, (f) Commerce and Finance, (g) Philosophy,

(*h*) Mathematics, (*i*) Physics, (*j*) Biology, (*k*) Biological and Medical Sciences, (*l*) Physiological and Biochemical Sciences, (*m*) Chemistry and Mineralogy, (*n*) Chemistry, (*o*) Geology and Mineralogy, (*p*) Household Science, (*q*) Household Economics—shall also take the best aggregate mark in English and the Honour Department.

English shall be understood to mean only the papers based on English Courses 4*a*, 4*b* and 4*e*. The essays prescribed for Honour students are not taken into account in this award.

In order to obviate any unfairness arising from a different system of marking in different departments, the principle shall always be adopted of raising the marks of the best candidate in the first class of each department to the maximum, and those of the others in proportion, unless the examiners of any department report that the marks of the best candidate in their department are not of sufficient merit to be so raised.

The Registrar shall publish not only the name of the successful candidate, but also the names of all candidates who, by satisfying the above conditions, are eligible for the award.

Awarded in 1920 to J. N. D. Bush, Miss M. A. Dickinson *proxime accessit.*

V. The Prince of Wales' Gold Medal, endowed by His late Majesty King Edward VII, will be awarded to the student who ranks first in Grade A Standing in the Pass Course.

No award in 1920.

V. The Prince of Wales' Silver Medal, endowed by His late Majesty King Edward VII, will be awarded to the student who ranks second in Grade A Standing in the Pass Course.

No award in 1920.

V. The Governor-General's Silver Medal will be awarded to the candidate standing highest in Honour Modern English of the Fourth Year examination, provided he has taken First or Second Class in his Honour Department or Grade A Standing in the Pass Course at graduation, First Class Honour Men having the preference and provided that this English is not an integral portion of his course. In case such a candidate has already received the Governor-General's Gold Medal, the next in rank shall be eligible.

Honour Modern English shall be understood to mean only the papers based on English Courses 4*a*, 4*b* and 4*e*. The essays prescribed for Honour students are not taken into account in this award.

No award in 1920; J. N. D. Bush (mention).

T. The Governor-General's Silver Medal will be awarded to the student taking the best degree, provided that First Class Honours shall have been obtained in an Honour Course or Grade A Standing in the Pass Course.

Awarded in 1920 to P. Lowe.

CLASSICS.

C. The McCaul Medal (Gold), established in 1886 by the late W. H. C. Kerr, M.A., Gold Medallist in Classics of 1859, in memory of the Rev. John McCaul, LL.D., First Professor of Classics, and First President of University College. It was presented by Mr. Kerr from 1886 up to his death, and from 1891 to 1894, after his death, by his widow. Since then the donors have been in 1895 John Hoskin, K.C., LL.D., Chairman of the Board of Trustees 1906-1910; in 1896 Nicol Kingsmill, M.A., K.C., Classical Medallist of 1856; in 1897, A. M. Crombie, Esq., of Montreal, in memory of his brothers Ernestus Crombie, M.A., Gold Medallist in Classics of 1854, and Marcellus Crombie, M.A., LL.B., Gold Medallist in Classics of 1857; in 1898 and 1899 William Dale, M.A., Gold Medallist in Classics of 1871; in 1900 the late John Fletcher, M.A., LL.D., Gold Medallist in Classics of 1872, and Maurice Hutton, M.A., LL.D.; in 1901 Adam Carruthers, M.A., Gold Medallist in Classics of 1880; in 1902 W. S. Milner, M.A., Gold Medallist in Classics of 1881; in 1903 the late G. W. Johnston, Ph.D.; in 1904-1921 the Hon. Sir J. M. Gibson, M.A., LL.D., by whom it will be presented in 1922.

The winners of the McCaul Medal have been as follows:—
1886, W. P. Mustard, Ph.D.; 1887, E. O. Sliter; 1888, H. J. Crawford; 1889, H. J. Cody, D.D., LL.D.; 1890, James Colling; 1891, C. A. Stuart; 1892, F. W. Shipley, Ph.D.; 1893, F. B. R. Hellems, Ph.D.; 1894, J. H. Brown (*ob.*); 1895, W. T. F. Tamblyn, Ph.D.; 1896, Donald McFayden; 1897, R. O. Joliffe; 1898, Miss Florence E. Kirkwood; 1899, W. H. Alexander, Ph.D.; 1900, Miss Landon Wright; 1901, E. J. Kylie (*ob.*); 1902, E. H. Oliver, Ph.D.; 1903, A. G. Brown; 1904, W. H. Tackaberry (*ob.*); 1905, S. A. Cudmore; 1906, R. W. Hart; 1907, W. A. Rae; 1908, Miss C. M. Knight; 1909, A. G. Hooper; 1910, no award; 1911, C. N. Cochrane; 1912, C. H. Carruthers; 1913, H. V. Wrong (*ob.*); 1914, D. Breslove; 1915, H. R. Kemp; 1916, W. M. Hugill; 1917, Miss E. A. Sinclair; 1918, no award, 1919, Miss E. Harris; 1920, Miss M. A. Dickinson.

V. The Edward Wilson Gold Medal, founded by the late Bishop Edward Wilson in memory of his son Edward Wilson.
Awarded in 1920 to J. N. D. Bush.

V. The S. H. Janes Silver Medal.
No award in 1920.

MODERN LANGUAGES.

C. The Governor-General's Silver Medal.
Awarded in 1920 to G. H. Unwin.

V. The J. J. Maclaren Gold Medal.
Awarded in 1920 to Miss E. M. Thornton.

V. The S. H. Janes Silver Medal.
No award in 1920.

POLITICAL SCIENCE.

V. The J. Reginald Adams Gold Medal, established by Rev. and Mrs.
G. K. B. Adams as a memorial of their son Lieut. J. Reginald Adams
who died of wounds at Etaples, France, November 26th, 1917.
Awarded in 1920 to E. H. McKinney.

V. The J. Reginald Adams Silver Medal.
No award in 1920.

PHILOSOPHY.

V. The E. J. Sanford Gold Medal.
Awarded in 1920 to W. H. Moss.

V. The S. H. Janes Silver Medal.
No award in 1920

MATHEMATICS AND PHYSICS.

V. The S. H. Janes Silver Medal.
Awarded in 1920 to G. M. Shrum.

PHYSICS.

U. The James Loudon Gold Medal, the gift of the local Committee for
The Toronto Meeting of the American Association for the Advancement of Science. Awarded to the candidate ranking highest in first
class honours.
Awarded in 1920 to J. A. Sonley.

ASTRONOMY AND PHYSICS.

U. The Royal Astronomical Society of Canada Gold Medal, awarded
to the candidate obtaining the first place in first class honours.
No award in 1920.

NATURAL SCIENCE.

V. The G. A. Cox Gold Medal, the gift of Mr. Herbert C. Cox.
Awarded in 1920 to Miss E. V. Eastcott.

V. The S. H. Janes Silver Medal.
No award in 1920.

All the Years.

NATURAL SCIENCE.

U. The Cawthorne Medal, the gift of F. T. Shutt, M.A., awarded on the
recommendation of the Natural Science Association.
No award in 1920.

SCHOLARSHIPS AND FELLOWSHIPS.
First Year.

CLASSICS.

C. The Moss Scholarship, of the value of $60, founded by subscription in
honour of the late Hon. Chief Justice Thomas Moss.
Awarded in 1920 to L. A. MacKay.

V. The Robertson Scholarship, of the value of $50, the gift of Professor J. C. Robertson, M.A.
Awarded in 1920 to Miss R. V. Kendrick.

SEMITIC LANGUAGES *or* GREEK AND HEBREW.

T. The Pettit Scholarship, of the value of $40, with free tuition for three years, provided the scholar obtains first class honours at subsequent examinations.
Awarded in 1920 to J. Lowe.

ORIENTAL LANGUAGES.

V. The A. P. Misener Scholarship of the value of $25, the gift of the Rev. W. A. Potter, M.A., B.D., in memory of the late Rev. Professor Misener.
Awarded in 1920 to F. G. Ward.

MODERN LANGUAGES.

C. The Edward Blake Scholarship, of the value of $60, the gift of the late Hon. Edward Blake, formerly Chancellor of the University.
Awarded in 1920 to Miss K. R. Manson.

POLITICAL SCIENCE.

U. The Bankers' Scholarship, of the value of $70, the gift of the Bank of Toronto, the Canadian Bank of Commerce, the Dominion, Imperial, Standard, and Traders Banks, and the Union Bank of Lower Canada. Only such candidates are eligible as have passed the examination of the First Year and as may undertake to proceed to graduation in the Department of Political Science. A special examination on some special text-book of history or finance will be held at the time of the Supplemental examination in September. This scholarship is not tenable with any other.
The prescribed text-books are as follows:—
1921: CLAY, *Economics for the General Reader.*
1922: LAYTON, *An Introduction to the Study of Prices.*
Awarded in 1920 to Miss H. M. Dean.

MATHEMATICS AND PHYSICS.

U. The Alexander T. Fulton Scholarship, of the value of $60, the gift of the late Alexander T. Fulton, Esq.
Awarded in 1920 to M. S. Bell.

NATURAL AND PHYSICAL SCIENCES.

U. The First Alexander T. Fulton Scholarship, of the value of $50, the gift of the late Alexander T. Fulton, Esq.
Awarded in 1920 to W. J. Clapson.

U. The Second Alexander T. Fulton Scholarship, of the value of $40, the gift of the late Alexander T. Fulton, Esq.

U. The Third Alexander T. Fulton Scholarship, of the value of $30, the gift of the late Alexander T. Fulton, Esq.
The Second and Third Scholarships were awarded in 1920 to G. C. Kelly and C. W. Sweitzer, *aeq.*

U. The Jean Balmer Scholarship in Science, of the value of $50, the gift of Mrs. Jane Balmer in memory of her daughter Miss Jean Balmer, B.A. and in fulfilment of the wish expressed in the will of another daughter Miss Eliza M. Balmer, B.A.
This Scholarship is open for competition only to students registered in University College.
Awarded in 1920 to W. J. Clapson.

PASS COURSE.

M. The Knights of Columbus Scholarships, of the value of $25 each, with free tuition for one year, to the four students ranking highest at the examination of the First Year, on condition that such students in the following session enter Honour Courses of either the First or Second Year.

Second Year.

CLASSICS.

C. The William Mulock Scholarship, of the value of $60, the gift of the Hon. Sir William Mulock, M.A., LL.D., for many years Vice-Chancellor of the University.
Awarded in 1920 to J. E. A. Johnstone.

V. A Scholarship of the value of $50.
No award in 1920.

T. The Hart-Moorhouse, of the value of $40, the gift of Alumni, commemorating Messrs. W. Hart and A. C. Moorhouse, who were drowned in their graduating year, 1906, to the student ranking highest in first class honours in Classics, or, failing these, in English and History with the classical option.
Awarded in 1920 to J. Lowe.

MODERN LANGUAGES.

C. The George Brown Scholarship, of the value of $60, founded in honour of the late Hon. George Brown.
Awarded in 1920 to Miss E. A. J. Shaw.

FRENCH.

V. The Essa Van Dusen Dafoe Scholarship, of the value of $50, the gift of Dr. W. A. Dafoe, in memory of his wife, Essa Van Dusen, to be awarded annually to the student standing highest in a special examination in both oral and written French to be held in the Easter Term.
Awarded in 1920 to L. H. Miller.

ORIENTAL LANGUAGES.

V. A Scholarship of $50, the gift of the Rev. Professor J. F. McLaughlin, B.A., D.D., and others.
No award in 1920.

PHILOSOPHY.

U. The John Macdonald Scholarship, of the value of $50, the gift of the late Hon. John Macdonald.
Awarded in 1920 to W. M. Mustard.

T. A Scholarship in Mental and Moral Philosophy, which entitles the holder to free tuition in the Third Year and in the Fourth Year, if he obtains first class honours in the Second and Third Year.
No award in 1920.

POLITICAL SCIENCE.

U. The First Alexander Mackenzie Scholarship, of the value of $75, the gift of the friends of the late Hon. Alexander Mackenzie.
Awarded in 1920 to R. Wood.

U. The Second Alexander Mackenzie Scholarship, of the value of $50, the gift of the friends of the late Hon. Alexander Mackenzie.
Awarded in 1920 to G. G. Brown and R. de la P. Stewart, *aeq.*

T. A Scholarship in Political Science which entitles the holder to free tuition in the Third Year and in the Fourth Year, if he obtains first class honours in his Second and Third Year.
No award in 1920.

MATHEMATICS AND PHYSICS.

U. The William Mulock Scholarship, of the value of $60, the gift of the Hon. Sir William Mulock, M.A., LL.D., for many years Vice-Chancellor of the University.
Awarded in 1920 to Miss F. F. Halliday.

PHYSICS.

U. The Edward Blake Scholarship, of the value of $45, the gift of the late Hon. Edward Blake, M.A., LL.D., ex-Chancellor of the University.
No award in 1920.

BIOLOGICAL AND MEDICAL SCIENCES.

U. The Edward Blake Scholarship, of the value of $45, the gift of the late Hon. Edward Blake, M.A., LL.D., ex-Chancellor of the University.
Awarded in 1920 to J. H. Couch.

(1) BIOLOGY AND (2) GEOLOGY AND MINERALOGY.

U. The Edward Blake Scholarship, of the value of $45, the gift of the late Hon. Edward Blake, M.A., LL.D., ex-Chancellor of the University.
No award in 1920.

CHEMISTRY AND MINERALOGY.

U. The Edward Blake Scholarship, of the value of $45, the gift of the late Hon. Edward Blake, M.A., LL.D., ex-Chancellor of the University.
Awarded in 1920 to F. L. Hutchison.

In case one or more of the four foregoing scholarships is not awarded, the amount rendered available will be divided among the other scholars, but no award shall exceed $60.

—11

CHEMISTRY AND MINERALOGY.

V. The James G. Burns Scholarship, of the value of $50, the gift of the Rev. Dr. and Mrs. R. N. Burns as a memorial of their son Major James G. Burns, D.S.O., B.A., killed in action at Cambrai, France, September 28th, 1918.

Third Year.

CLASSICS.

C. The Moss Scholarship, of the value of $60, founded by subscription in honour of the late Hon. Chief Justice Thomas Moss.
Awarded in 1920 to M.D.C. Tait.

MODERN LANGUAGES. .

C. The Julius Rossin Scholarship, of the value of $60, the gift of the late Julius Rossin, M.A.
Awarded in 1920 to R. A. Allen.

PHILOSOPHY.

C. The John Macdonald Scholarship, of the value of $50, the gift of the late Hon. John Macdonald.
Awarded in 1920 to F. G. Lightbourne.

V. The George John Blewett Scholarship, of the value of $50, the gift of Mrs. G. J. Blewett in memory of the late Rev. Professor Blewett.
Awarded in 1920 to E. W. Jewitt.

POLITICAL SCIENCE.

U. The First Alexander Mackenzie Scholarship, of the value of $75, the gift of the friends of the late Hon. Alexander Mackenzie.
Awarded in 1920 to C. M. Vining.

U. The Second Alexander Mackenzie Scholarship, of the value of $50, the gift of the friends of the late Hon. Alexander Mackenzie.
Awarded in 1920 to A. F. Annis.

MATHEMATICS AND PHYSICS.

U. A Scholarship of the value of $60, the gift of the Local Committee for the Toronto meeting of the American Association for the Advancement of Science. In awarding this scholarship, the theoretical and practical work in this department will be estimated in the proportion of three to one.
Awarded in 1920 to H. G. Smith.

MATHEMATICS AND PHYSICS, PHYSICS.

U. The Ramsay Scholarship, of the value of $50, the gift of the late Mr. William Ramsay, of Bowland, Scotland. The scholarship is open for competition to all students in the Third Year in the courses of (1) Physics and (2) Mathematics and Physics. The award is made to the student who obtains the highest aggregate standing in experimental physics during the first three years of his course and who elects to proceed to the B.A. Degree in Physics in his final year.
No award in 1920.

PHYSICS.

U. A scholarship of the value of $55, the gift of the Local Committee for the Toronto meeting of the American Association for the Advancement of Science.

Awarded in 1920 to Miss M. F. Cale and W. C. H. McQuarrie, *aeq.*

BIOLOGICAL AND MEDICAL SCIENCES.

U. The Daniel Wilson Scholarship, of the value of $30, the gift of the late William Christie, Esq.

Awarded in 1920 to Miss E. H. Chant.

BIOLOGY.

U. The Daniel Wilson Scholarship, of the value of $30, the gift of the late William Christie, Esq.

Awarded in 1920 to N. B. Laughton.

In case either of the two foregoing scholarships is not awarded, the amount rendered available will be given to the scholar in the other department.

CHEMISTRY AND MINERALOGY.

U. The Daniel Wilson Scholarship, of the value of $30, the gift of the late William Christie, Esq.

Awarded in 1920 to W. G. Noble.

GEOLOGY AND MINERALOGY.

U. The Daniel Wilson Scholarship, of the value of $30, the gift of the late William Christie, Esq.

Awarded in 1920 to H. F. Swann.

In case either of the two foregoing scholarships is not awarded, the amount rendered available will be given to the scholar in the other department.

Fourth Year.

HONOUR COURSE.

T. The Jubilee Scholarship, of the value of $120, tenable for two years, was founded by the Society for the Propagation of the Gospel, and is awarded yearly to the most deserving Bachelor of the Year who has obtained at least second class honours. On admission to the scholarship a declaration must be signed by the holder that it is his purpose to complete the Divinity Course in Trinity College and to present himself as a candidate for Holy Orders. Should he fail to do so, he will be held bound to refund to the College such proceeds of the scholarship as he shall have received.

Awarded in 1920 to P. W. Dawson.

First and Third Years.

The McClure Scholarship of $45 will be awarded to the student of the First or Third Year Arts who takes the highest standing in First Year Hebrew at the University, and who is preparing for the study of Theology in Knox College.

In order to hold this scholarship a student must give attendance on the lectures of the session in which the scholarship is won, and must sign a declaration that it is his intention to enter the ministry of the Presbyterian Church in Canada, and to prosecute theological study in Knox College.

All the Years.

V. An endowment of $13,500, provided by a bequest of the late W. E. H. Massey, Esq., will furnish a number of additional scholarships which are awarded under the terms of the will in aid of deserving students.

T. The late Ven. Archdeacon Nelles, of Brantford, left $2,000 to Trinity College to be used for the assistance of students in Arts or Theology during their course in the College. Loans will be made from this fund to be repaid by the students after the completion of their College course. There are also other funds from which similar loans will be made.

V. The Rowell Scholarships, one of $30 and one of $20, the gift of the Hon. Mr. N. W. Rowell, K.C., M.P., LL.D., and Mrs. Rowell, open to all students of Victoria College, will be awarded annually to the students ranking first and second in Church History.
Awarded in 1920 to C. L. Wood and J. E. Mitchell.

V. The Hamilton Fisk Biggar Scholarships, of the value of $50 each, awarded on the results of the May examinations to the students standing first in the University in those courses, Pass or Honour, where no prizes or scholarships are now offered. Preference will be given to the students of the third year.
Awarded in 1920 to R. W. Hardy, T. R. S. Broughton, N. S. Clark, W. L. Swanson, A. E. R. Westman, Miss M. V. Ray, Miss N. A. Yeomans and L. V. Smith.

V. The Lincoln G. Hutton Scholarship of the value of $50, the gift of Mr. and the late Mrs. F. Hutton in memory of their son Lieutenant Lincoln G. Hutton who fell in action in France on December 18th, 1916.
Awarded in 1920 to J. N. D. Bush.

"Industrial Canada" Prizes.

During the years 1912-1918, "Industrial Canada", the official publication of the Canadian Manufacturers Association, offered two prizes of the value of $60 and $30, respectively, for the two best essays submitted on specified economic subjects. The awards were as follows: 1912. I.—W. J. Little; II.—R. Forsyth. 1913. C. S. McKee and R. S. Rodd, aeq. 1914. I.—No award; II.—W. McL. Clarke. 1915. I.—No award; II.—A. W. Kennedy. 1916, 1917, 1918, no awards.

These prizes are no longer offered.

UNDERGRADUATE AND GRADUATE.

HISTORY.

U. The All Souls' Historical Essay Prize.

1. The Prize shall be called The All Souls' Historical Essay Prize.
2. It shall be of the value of one hundred and fifty dollars.
3. It shall be open to all undergraduate members of the University of Toronto, and to graduates who at the time of the awarding of the prize shall not have exceeded one year from the time of graduation.
4. It shall be awarded in every second year, beginning in 1910, and the subject shall be announced two years before the time of the award.
5. There shall be a choice of two subjects for the Essay—one to be taken from Ancient European History, and one from Mediæval or Modern European History.
6. The choice of subjects and the awarding of the prize shall be in the hands of an examining board—to consist of the President of the University of Toronto, the Professor of History in the University, and the Professor of Ancient History in University College; should any of these be unable to act, the remaining members of the Board shall be empowered to name a substitute.
7. The Essay shall involve research work of an original nature, and no particular books or courses shall be prescribed.
8. If the examiners judge any essay to be worthy, it shall be published at the expense of the University.
9. The examining board shall have power to prescribe limits as to the length of the essay, and to draw up additional regulations for the administration of the prize, provided always that sections 3, 5 and 7 of these regulations remain unchanged.
10. If no essay of sufficient merit be forthcoming it shall be in the power of the examiners to withhold the prize for that term, and to recommend that the money be devoted to whatever purpose they judge most fit to encourage historical research.

Essays must be sent to the Registrar of the University on or before April 1, 1922; they must be accompanied by a motto or pseudonym, and by another and separate envelope containing the name of the candidate, the name of his college, and the month and year of his matriculation. Candidates are advised to have their essays typed, and to confine them to (approximately) 30,000 words.

The subject for 1922 is:—Greek Criticism of Democracy *or* The Irish Question since 1869; Home Rule and the Land.

The awards have been as follows:—

1912—G. L. B. Mackenzie (*ob.*).

1914—W. F. Wallace.

1918—Miss M. G. Reid.

ENGLISH VERSE.

U. The Jardine Memorial Prize for English Verse, of the value of $100.

1. It shall be open to any regular undergraduate student who has been in actual attendance at the University during the academic year preceding the date of submission (November 1) or who graduated in the previous academic year.

2. The subject and metre of the poem shall be left to the choice of the competitor.

3. It is suggested that the length of the poem should be not less than 100 or more than 300 lines.

4. The poems shall be in the hands of the Registrar of the University by November 1st.

5. Each poem shall be signed with a pseudonym and the competitor's name shall be submitted to the Registrar in a sealed envelope on which the pseudonym shall be written.

6. With his or her name the competitor shall enclose a signed statement that the poem is absolutely his or her original work.

7. The competition shall be judged by a board of five examiners, consisting of the head of the Department of English in each of the four colleges, and of a fifth examiner to be chosen by these four.

8. The examiners shall have the power to withhold the award in any year if no poem which has been submitted for that year be found worthy of the prize.

Awarded in 1920 to H. D. Langford.

POLITICAL SCIENCE.

U. The Ramsay Scholarship in Political Economy of the value of $60, the gift of Mr. William Ramsay. The scholarship is open for competition to all graduates or undergraduates who have been placed in the first class in one of the Economic subjects of the Fourth Year in the honour department of Political Science; but not more than two years must have elapsed since the competitor passed the examination above specified. The award is made upon an essay, the subject of which must be some question in Economics or Finance, of interest to the commercial community in Canada, to be announced in May of each year and the competition closes on the 15th of September thereafter, by which date the essays must be in the hands of the Registrar of the University.

1921. The Effect on the Trade of Canada with the United States of Exchange Fluctuations, Embargoes, and Tariff Changes During Recent Years.

Authorities must be carefully stated in every case.

1922. The Restoration of the Gold Standard.

No award in 1920.

PHILOSOPHY.

U. The George Paxton Young Memorial Fellowship in Philosophy, of the value of $300, will be awarded in June, 1923. The holder must be a Bachelor of Arts who has taken an honour course in Philosophy. This scholarship is tenable for one year, and the holder must devote his whole time to the study of some topic falling under the general term Philosophy. He may pursue his studies either in the University of Toronto, or in some other University approved by the Council of the Faculty; but in either case he shall furnish to the Council of the Faculty such evidence as may from time to time be required that he is faithfully observing the conditions under which the scholarship was awarded. Applications must be in the hands of the Registrar on or before June 15th, 1923. Further particulars may be obtained from the Registrar.

Those who have held the Young Fellowship are:—1897, M. A. Shaw, B.A., Ph.D.; 1899, G. J. Blewett, B.A., Ph.D. (*ob.*); 1899, R. J. Richardson, B.A.; 1901, F. S. Wrinch, B.A., Ph.D.; 1903, Miss M. A. Downing, B.A.; 1905, J. I. Hughes, B.A.; 1907, W. T. Brown, B.A., Ph.D.; 1911, J. S. Sanderson, M.A., Ph.D.; 1913, E. A. Bott, B.A.; 1915, C. A. Gowans, B.A.; 1917, no award; 1919, L. C. Harvey, B.A.

FLAVELLE TRAVELLING FELLOWSHIP.

During the years 1901-1919, through the liberality of Sir Joseph Flavelle, Bart., of Toronto, a Travelling Fellowship was offered of the value of $750 per annum, tenable for two years in the Modern History School of the University of Oxford.

The Fellowship, which is now discontinued, was awarded to the following:—1901, E. J. Kylie, M.A. (*ob.*); 1903, A. G. Brown, M.A.; 1905, S. A. Cudmore, B.A.; 1907, W. S. Wallace, B.A.; 1910, D. P. Wagner, B.A.; 1911, F. H. Underhill, B.A.; 1913, H. V. Wrong, B.A. (*ob.*); 1919, H. H. Wrong, B.A.

SCIENCE.

U. The 1851 Exhibition Science Research Scholarship, of an annual value of £200, is awarded in alternate years by His Majesty's Commissioners for the Exhibition of 1851, on the recommendation of the Senate, to a student who has given evidence of capacity for advancing Science or its application by original research.

This Scholarship will be awarded in 1921.

The regulations of His Majesty's Commissioners are as follows:—

1. The Scholarships are intended, not to facilitate attendance on ordinary collegiate studies, but to enable students who have passed through a College curriculum and have given distinct evidence of capacity for original research, to continue the prosecution of Science with the view of aiding its advance or its application to the industries of the country.

2. The Scholarships are of £200 a year, and are ordinarily tenable for two years, the continuation for the second year being dependent on the work done in the first year being satisfactory to the Scholarships Committee.

3. A limited number of the Scholarships are renewed for a third year where it appears that the renewal is likely to result in work of scientific importance.

4. Candidates are recommended by the governing bodies of the Universities and Colleges to which Scholarships are allotted, and the recom-

mendations are considered and decided upon by the Scholarships Committee.

5. The candidate must be a British subject.

6. The candidate must have been a *bona fide* student of Science in a University or College in which special attention is given to scientific study for a term of three years.

7. The candidate shall be eligible for a Scholarship, provided (1) that he has spent the last full academic year immediately prior to the time of nomination as a student in any faculty or scientific department of that institution by which he is nominated, or (2) that he has been a student of such institution for a full academic year ending within twelve months prior to the time of nomination and since ceasing to be a student of that institution has been engaged solely in scientific study.

The word "student" in the preceding regulation must be understood as comprehending one engaged in undergraduate or post-graduate work.

8. The candidate must indicate high promise of capacity for advancing Science or its applications by original research. Evidence of this capacity is strictly required, this being the main qualification for a Scholarship. The most suitable evidence is a satisfactory account of a research already performed, and the Commissioners will decline to confirm the nomination of a candidate unless such an account is furnished, or there is other equally distinct evidence that he possesses the required qualification.

9. A candidate whose age exceeds thirty will only be accepted under very special circumstances.

10. A Scholarship may be held at any University in England or abroad, or in some other institution to be approved of by the Commissioners. Every scholar is, in the absence of special circumstances, required to proceed to an institution other than that by which he is nominated.

11. The principal work of a scholar must be research in some branch of Science, the extension of which is important to the national industries.

12. Scholars are required to devote themselves wholly to the objects of the Scholarships, and are forbidden to hold any position of emolument.

13. Scholars are required to furnish reports of their work at the end of each year of the tenure of their Scholarships. At the expiration of each Scholarship the reports of the scholar are referred to an eminent authority on the subject treated of, who furnishes an opinion thereon to the Commissioners.

14. The Scholarship stipend is payable half-yearly in advance, but £25 is reserved from the fourth payment until the scholar has made a satisfactory final report.

The regulations adopted by the Senate are as follows:—

The departments, students of which shall be eligible to be candidates, are:—1. Bacteriology; 2. Biology; 3. Chemistry; 4. Chemistry (applied); 5. Engineering (chemical); 6. Engineering (electrical); 7. Engineering (mechanical); 8. Engineering (civil); 9. Engineering (mining); 10. Forestry; 11. Geology; 12. Mineralogy; 13. Pathology; 14. Physics; 15. Physiology.

A student shall not be deemed to be ineligible because of his being on the teaching staff of the University, if he has not been in receipt of a salary of more than $500 per annum and, has not been on the teaching staff for more than two years from graduation.

A student shall be deemed to be eligible in the year in which he intends to graduate, but if nominated for the Scholarship his nomination shall be subject to his being successful in passing his examination for his degree.

The nomination of the candidate shall be made by a Board composed of seven members appointed by the Senate, and the Board shall consist of the Chancellor, the President, the Reverend Dr. Bowles, Mr. Feather-stone Osler, the Honourable Mr. Justice Maclaren, the Honourable Mr. Justice Riddell and Mr. J. A Worrell, and the Board shall have power to call to its aid as assessor any member of the teaching staff.

In the event of there being no suitable candidate, the Senate may recommend that a probationary bursary of £70 be awarded to a student who is not immediately qualified for a scholarship, but who gives promise of becoming so, after a year's experience of research work.

The regulations of His Majesty's Commissioners respecting probationary Bursaries are as follows:—

1. A Bursary is intended for the maintenance for one year of a student who proposes to become a Science Research Scholar under the scheme of the Commissioners at the expiration of the period covered by the Bursary, in order to afford him an opportunity of proving his power to carry on independent research. The authorities of an institution recommending a student for a Bursary will be presumed to have satisfied themselves that he *bona fide* intends to accept a Scholarship if subsequently appointed to one.

2. An applicant for a Bursary must, except as to evidence of capacity for original research, fulfil all the conditions for the time being laid down for appointment to a Science Research Scholarship. He must have passed a B.Sc. examination (or its equivalent) with honours before the commencement of the period covered by the Bursary. His age must not exceed twenty-five, except under very special circumstances.

3. A Bursary is tenable for one year, and is of the value of £70, payable by half yearly instalments in advance, the second instalment being payable on the receipt of a certificate from the Professor under whom the holder has been working that he has faithfully performed his duties.

4. A Bursary will be awarded on condition that the nominating institution undertakes to provide for the holder facilities for conducting research, and the requisite supervision, free from charge and incidental expenses.

5. The holder of a Bursary shall devote himself exclusively to research and work preparatory to research, and none of his time shall be spent in assisting a teacher in his duties. The holder of a Bursary must not hold any other Bursary, Scholarship, or position of emolument.

6. The holder of a Bursary shall on or before 1st May in the year of tenure send to the office of the Commissioners an account of the research work performed by him, together with an application for appointment to a Science Research Scholarship. The Commissioners will expect to

receive from the Professor under whom the holder of the Bursary shall have worked, a confidential opinion as to his capacity and qualifications.

7. The Commissioners may either appoint the holder of a Bursary to a Science Research Scholarship, or at their absolute discretion decline to appoint him, and in the latter case, shall not be called upon to state any ground for their decision.

8. A Science Research Scholarship, if granted, shall be held on the usual conditions attached to the Scholarships or on any special conditions which the Commissioners may impose. But a scholar who previous to appointment has held a Bursary shall not be eligible for exceptional renewal of his Scholarship for a third year.

The 1851 Exhibition Science Research scholars:—

F. J. Smale, B.A., Ph.D., 1892-93, 1893-94, 1894-95.

F. B. Kenrick, M.A., Ph.D., 1894-95, 1895-96, 1896-97.

A. M. Scott, B.A., Ph.D., 1896-97, 1897-98.

W. G. Smeaton, B.A., Ph.D., 1898-99, 1899-1900.

J. Patterson, B.A., 1900-01, 1901-02.

W. C. Bray, B.A., 1902-03, 1903-04.

E. F. Burton, Ph.D., 1904-05, 1905-06.

R. H. Clark, M.A., 1906-07, 1907-08.

C. S. Wright, M.A., 1908-09, 1909-1910.

W. P. Thompson, B.A., 1910-11, 1911-12.

A. J. Dempster, M.A., 1912-13, 1913-14.

A. R. McLeod, M.A., 1914-1915 (Bursary).

1916, 1918, 1919, no awards.

A. L. Marshall, M.A., 1920-21.

HOUSEHOLD SCIENCE.

U. The Marion Dickenson Scholarship in Household Science.

1. This Scholarship, which has been founded from a bequest of the late Miss Marion Dickenson, shall be called the Marion Dickenson Scholarship, and is of the annual value of $200.

2. The Scholarship shall be awarded either to an undergraduate of the University of Toronto, or to a graduate student who holds a Degree from this University.

3. The scholar shall undertake studies in Household Economics in Teachers College, Columbia University, New York, within three years after the award is made, but the Scholarship shall not be paid until after the scholar shall have regularly entered upon the course in Columbia University.

4. A candidate for the Scholarship shall have obtained First Class Honour standing in Household Science at least in her term work on graduation.

5. A candidate who proposes to enter upon an academic career shall have preference.

6. In the event of an award not being made in any year the Scholarship may in exceptional cases be granted for the second year to a previous holder.

7. The award shall be made by the Council of the Faculty of Arts on the recommendation of the President and the heads of the Departments of Household Science and Food Chemistry in the Faculty of Household Science.

These conditions are subject to change by the Senate and the Board of Governors.

The Rhodes Scholarship.

The trustees of the late Mr. C. J. Rhodes have assigned one of the Rhodes Scholarships to the Province of Ontario.

This scholarship will hereafter be thrown into open competition in the Province, subject to the following conditions:—

1. Candidates must be British subjects, with at least five years' domicile in Canada, and unmarried. They must have passed their nineteenth, but not have passed their twenty-fifth birthday, on October 1st of the year for which they are elected.

2. Candidates must be at least in their Sophomore Year at some recognized degree-granting University or College of Canada, and (if elected) complete the work of that year before coming into residence at Oxford.

3. Candidates must elect whether they will apply for the Scholarship of the Province in which they have acquired any considerable part of their educational qualification, or for that of the Province in which they have their ordinary private domicile, home or residence. They must be prepared to appear before the Committee of Selection for the Province they select.

In each Province there will be a Committee of Selection, appointed by the Trustees, in whose hands the nomination will rest. The Secretary of the Committee of Selection for Ontario is J. M. Macdonnell, Esq., National Trust Company, Limited, 18-22 King Street East, Toronto.

The Committees of Selection will be instructed to bear in mind the suggestions of Mr. Rhodes, who wished that, in the choice of his Scholars, regard should be had to literary and scholastic attainments, fondness for and success in outdoor sports, qualities of manhood, moral force of character, and leadership in school and college life.

Every candidate for a Scholarship is required to furnish to the Committee of Selection for his Province the following:—

(a) A certificate of age.

(b) A written statement from the President or Acting President of his College or University to the effect that his application as a suitable candidate is approved.

(c) Certified evidence as to the courses of study pursued by the Scholar at his University, and as to his gradings in those courses. This evidence should be signed by the Registrar, or other responsible official, of his University.

(d) A brief statement by himself of his athletic and general activities and interests at College, and of his proposed line of study at Oxford.

(*e*) Not more than four testimonials from persons well acquainted with him.

(*f*) References to four other responsible persons, whose addresses must be given in full, and of whom two at least must be professors under whom he has studied.

It is in the power of the Committee of Selection to summon to a personal interview such of the candidates as they find desirable to see, and, save under exceptional circumstances, no Scholar will be elected without such an interview. Where such an interview is dispensed with, a written statement of the reasons will be submitted to the Trustees.

The next appointment will be made for 1922; applications for this Scholarship with all required material must reach the Secretary of the Committee of Selection not later than October 11th, 1921.

The Scholarships are of the value of £300 a year, and are tenable for three years, subject to the continued approval of the College at Oxford of which the Scholar is a member. They will be paid quarterly. The first payment (£75) will be made at the beginning of the Scholar's first term at Oxford. No request for any earlier payment can be considered.

The Rhodes Scholars elected by this University previous to 1919 are as follows:—

1904: E. R. Paterson, B.A., University College. (*ob.*)

1906: R. C. Reade, B.A., University College.

1908: W. K. Fraser, B.A., University College.

1910: A. L. Burt, B.A., Victoria College.

1913: C. H. Carruthers, B.A., University College.

1915: A. K. Griffin, B.A., Trinity College.

The following Rhodes Scholars, undergraduates of this University, have been nominated by the Committee of Selection for Ontario:—

1919: M. D. C. Tait, University College.

1920: J. R. Stirrett, University College.

U. Tutorial Fellowships in Mathematics, Chemistry and Biology, of the annual value of $500 each, are awarded annually. The selection is made from among graduates of the University. Each Fellow is appointed annually; but he may be reappointed for a period not exceeding, in all, three years.

Each Fellow is required to assist in the teaching and practical work of his department, under the direction of the professor or lecturer. The Fellows are selected with a special view to their aptitude for teaching and their attainments in the department in which the appointment is to be made. Every Fellow on accepting his appointment comes under an obligation to fulfil the duties of his Fellowship during the academic year in which he is appointed, unless specially exempted.

In the Departments of Psychology, Physics, Biology, Physiology, Chemistry and Mineralogy a number of Assistant Demonstrators and Class Assistants are appointed annually, whose appointments are made subject to the same conditions as those governing the Tutorial

Fellowships. The annual remuneration attached to these positions varies according to the extent of the duties assigned to the appointees.

Candidates for the Fellowships must send their applications annually to the Registrar, not later than the first day of June.

THE McCHARLES PRIZE.

This prize was established in connection with the bequest of the late Æneas McCharles of Provincial Government bonds of the value of $10,000, and is awarded on the following terms and conditions, namely, that the interest therefrom shall be given from time to time, but not necessarily every year, like the Nobel prizes in a small way: (1) To any Canadian from one end of the country to the other, and whether student or not, who invents or discovers any new and improved process for the treatment of Canadian ores or minerals of any kind, after such process has been proved to be of special merit on a practical scale; (2) Or for any important discovery, invention or device by any Canadian that will lessen the dangers and loss of life in connection with the use of electricity in supplying power and light; (3) Or for any marked public distinction achieved by any Canadian in scientific research in any useful practical line. The following conditions, as passed by the Board of Governors, determine the method of award:—

(1) The title shall be the McCharles Prize.

(2) The value of the prize shall be One Thousand Dollars ($1,000.00) in money.

(3) The term "Canadian" for the purpose of this award shall mean any person Canadian born who has not renounced British alliance; and for the purpose of the award in the first of the three cases provided for by the bequest, domicile in Canada shall be an essential condition.

(4) Every candidate for the prize shall be proposed as such in writing by some duly qualified person. A direct application for a prize shall not be considered.

(5) No prize shall be awarded to any discovery or invention unless the same shall have been proved to the satisfaction of the awarding body, to possess the special practical merit indicated by the terms of the bequest.

(6) The order of priority in which the three cases stand in the wording of the bequest shall be observed in making the award; that is, the award shall go *caeteris paribus* to the inventor of methods of smelting Canadian ores; and, failing such inventions, to the inventor of methods for lessening the dangers attendant upon the use of electricity; and only in the third event, if no inventors of sufficient merit in the field of metallurgy and electricity present themselves, to the inventor distinguished in the general field of useful scientific research.

(7) The first award was made in 1910.

(8) The composition of the awarding body shall be as follows:—

An expert in Mineralogy,

An expert in Electricity,

An expert in Physics,

and four other persons. All of the members of this body shall be nominated by the Board of Governors of the University of Toronto.

THE PEARSON KIRKMAN MARFLEET LECTURESHIP.

In November 1910, Mrs. Lydia A. Marfleet, of Prophetstown, Illinois gave the sum of $5,000 to found a lectureship in the University of Toronto, to be called, in memory of her late husband, the Pearson Kirkman Marfleet Lectureship.

The Governors accepted the trust, and have established and agreed to maintain the lectureship in perpetuity.

The Governors have undertaken to appoint at least once in every four years some person or persons to deliver a course of lectures in the University of Toronto on this foundation; and as the late Pearson Kirkman Marfleet, an American citizen, devoted constant thought to the public welfare of his own country, and also watched the growth of the Dominion of Canada with profound interest, the Governors have further undertaken that such person or persons as may from time to time be appointed shall, as far as possible, be chosen with regard to their special ability to set forth some phase or phases of the national movements of each or both countries.

The first course of lectures under this foundation was delivered on February 10th, 11th and 12th, 1915, by the Honourable William Howard Taft, Ex-President of the United States.

UNIVERSITY OF OXFORD.

A student of this University who has completed two years of the course in Arts may be admitted to the status of a Junior Colonial Student at the University of Oxford, while a student who has completed three years, and has taken honours in the final examination or who has obtained second class honours in the Third or Fourth Year, may be admitted as a Senior Colonial Student. In each of these cases, on complying with certain conditions, a student may obtain his degree at Oxford in two years.

A student of this University, who has passed the examination in Greek of the Second or the Third or the Fourth Year is exempt from the examination in Greek, which is compulsory for all candidates for degrees in Arts in the University of Oxford.

UNIVERSITY OF CAMBRIDGE.

The University of Toronto is affiliated to the University of Cambridge and matriculated students who have passed the examinations of the First and Second Years are entitled to admission to the privileges of affiliation, which enable a student to take his degree at Cambridge without completing the full period of residence.

ACADEMIC STANDING FOR HIGH SCHOOL CERTIFICATES.

I. ORDINARY CERTIFICATES.

The academic standing for admission to the course leading to an Ordinary High School Assistant's certificate is a degree in Arts from a British University based upon courses approved by the Minister of Education.

II. SPECIALISTS' CERTIFICATES.

Subject to the conditions specified below, the academic standing for admission to the courses leading to High School Specialists' certificates in Classics, English and French, English and German or Spanish, French and German or Spanish, English and History, Mathematics and Physics, Science, and Household Science is an Honour degree in Arts from any one of:—the University of Toronto, Queen's University, McMaster University, and the Western University.

1. The courses in the departments specified above shall be the Honour courses as defined in the calendars of the respective Universities for the year 1920-21. After due notice from any one of the four Universities, the Minister may accept modifications of its courses for Specialist standing.

2. Honour degrees in Arts from other British Universities on courses which are deemed to be the equivalent of those prescribed in the calendars of the four Ontario Universities may be accepted for Specialist.

3. The courses shall extend over at least five years from Pass Matriculation or, as may be determined under the regulations of the University concerned, over four years from Honour Matriculation.

4. Candidates shall attend for at least two full academic years. Under the direction of the University they may substitute for one of those years, at least two Summer Sessions.

5. The standard for each year shall be that prescribed by the University for candidates taking Honour courses, with the additional provision that in the final Honour work of the department in which specialist standing is sought, the standard shall be at least Second Class Honours (66 per cent.).

6. The Minister shall have authority to deal with any case not covered under the above. Each University shall submit to the Minister a recommendation on any case whose merits justify special consideration.

COURSES OF INSTRUCTION.

The members of the staff indicated under the headings "The Classics" etc., in the following pages, are those of the Session 1920-1921.

THE CLASSICS.

The University of Toronto:
　　A. I. Bell, M.A., Ph.D........*Professor of Comparative Philology.*

University College:
　　Maurice Hutton, M.A., LL.D................*Professor of Greek.*
　　J. Macnaughton, M.A., LL.D................*Professor of Latin.*
　　A. Carruthers, M.A...*Professor of Greek Literature and Archaeology.*
　　W. S. Milner, M.A.........*Professor of Greek and Roman History.*
　　G. Oswald Smith, M.A..............*Assistant Professor of Latin.*
　　E. A. Dale, M.A....................*Assistant Professor of Latin.*
　　A. Grant Brown, M.A.....*Assistant Professor of Ancient History.*
　　C. N. Cochrane, M.A......*Assistant Professor of Ancient History.*
　　W. D. Woodhead, M.A., Ph.D........*Assistant Professor of Greek.*
　　D. Duff, M.A., B.D................*Assistant Professor of Latin.*
　　J. B. West, B.A..............................*Instructor in Latin.*

Victoria College:
　　A. J. Bell, M.A., Ph.D......................*Professor of Latin.*
　　J. C. Robertson, M.A.......................*Professor of Greek.*
　　A. L. Langford, M.A........................*Professor of Greek.*
　　N. W. DeWitt, B.A., Ph.D...................*Professor of Latin.*
　　C. B. Sissons, B.A.................*Professor of Ancient History.*
　　H. Grant Robertson, B.A............................*Lecturer.*

Trinity College:
　　Rev. H. T. F. Duckworth, M.A......*Professor of Ancient History.*
　　E. T. Owen, M.A............................*Professor of Greek.*
　　G. S. Brett, M.A.......*Professor of Ethics and Ancient Philosophy*
　　W. A. Kirkwood, M.A., Ph.D................*Professor of Latin.*
　　J. N. Woodcock, M.A....................*Professor of Latin.*
　　S. M. Adams, M.A...............................*Lecturer.*
　　Miss S. G. Morley, M.A.............................*Lecturer.*

St. Michael's College:
　　Rev. Henry Carr, B.A......................*Professor of Greek.*
　　Rev. R. McBrady...........................*Professor of Latin.*
　　Rev. F. G. Powell..................*Associate Professor of Latin.*
　　Rev. V. J. Murphy..................*Associate Professor of Latin.*
　　Rev. J. B. Walsh, M.A.....................*Lecturer in Latin.*
　　M. M. St. Clare, B.A.......................*Lecturer in Latin.*

N.B.—The following books are recommended for the use of all students taking work in the Classical Department: Dictionaries: Greek—LIDDELL AND SCOTT, *Greek-English Lexicon* (unabridged or intermediate size); Latin—LEWIS AND SHORT, *A Latin Dictionary* (unabridged or intermediate size); Grammars: Greek—GOODWIN, *Greek Grammar;* Latin—ALLEN AND GREENOUGH or GILDERSLEEVE AND LODGE, *Latin Grammar*, Histories of Literature; Greek—GILBERT MURRAY or WRIGHT; Latin—MACKAIL, *Latin Literature;* Atlases: MURRAY, *Classical Atlas* or *The Atlas of Ancient and Classical Geography* in Everyman's Library.

GREEK.

PASS COURSES.

1*a*. Translation at sight of passages of ordinary difficulty from Xenophon's historical works; Greek Grammar (including sentences to test accidence and syntax); NORTH AND HILLARD, *Greek Prose Composition*, Exercises A, pages 1-85; BELL, *Second Greek Reader*. Four hours a week.

1*b*. WHITE, *First Greek Book*.

(This course may be taken only by those specially recommended by their College, and the course must be continued through all four years.)

2*a*. Translation at sight of easy passages of Greek; Greek Grammar; translation from English into Greek of sentences based on NORTH AND HILLARD, *Greek Prose Composition*, pages 1-155 inclusive; EURIPIDES, *Medea;* THUCYDIDES, I. Chap., 89-117, 128-138 both inclusive. Three hours a week.

2*b*. EDWARDS, *Salamis;* FREEMAN AND LOWE, *Greek Reader;* Translation at sight. (This course is for those who have completed 1*b*.)

3*a*. PURVES, *Selections from Plato;* Translation at Sight. To be read in English: additional prescribed portions of Plato; THUCYDIDES, *Pericles' Funeral Speech;* DEMOSTHENES, *Philippic I.;* DICKINSON, *Greek View of Life;* GRANT, *Age of Pericles*. Three hours a week.

4*a*. Translation at sight of easy passages of Greek; Greek Grammar; PLATO, *Phaedo;* BUTCHER, *Aspects of Greek Genius*, Chaps. 1 and 2, and *Harvard Lectures*, Chaps. 1, 2, and 3. Three hours a week.

4*b*. HOMER, *Iliad* I., 1-350, VI., 237 to end, XXII.; *Odyssey*, VI. and IX.; SOPHOCLES, *Œdipus Rex;* Translation at sight. To be read in English: SOPHOCLES, *Antigone;* EURIPIDES, *Medea;* ARISTOPHANES, *Birds*. BUTCHER, *Aspects of Greek Genius*, Chaps. 1 and 2, and *Harvard Lectures*, Chaps. 1, 2 and 3; LIVINGSTONE, *Greek Genius;* JEBB, *Classical Greek Poetry*. (This course will not be given until the Session 1922-23.)

—12

HONOUR COURSES.

1c. *Classics:* Greek Grammar; translation at sight; Greek prose composition; PLATO, *Apology;* HOMER, *Iliad* XVIII., XXII.-XXIV.; THUCYDIDES, I, 89-117, 128-138, and IV, 1-41, 76-108. Five hours a week.

1d. *English and History:* The same as 1c, omitting THUCYDIDES IV.

1e. *Greek and Hebrew:* The same as 1c.

1f. *Philosophy, English and History:* Greek Prose Composition, PLATO and THUCYDIDES, as in 1d.

2c. *Classics:* Greek Grammar; translation at sight; Greek prose composition; SOPHOCLES, *Antigone;* DEMOSTHENES, *Philippic* I, *Olynthiacs* I., II., III.; THEOCRITUS, *Idylls* I., VII., VIII., XIII., XV., XXI., ARISTOPHANES, *Birds;* THUCYDIDES, I. Five hours a week.

2d. *English and History:* The same as 2c, omitting Greek Grammar, DEMOSTHENES, *Olynthiacs* II., III., and THUCYDIDES. Three hours a week.

2e. *Greek and Hebrew:* Translation at sight, SOPHOCLES and THUCYDIDES, as in 2c. Two hours and a half a week.

2f. Hellenistic Greek: CONYBEARE AND STOCK, *Selections from the Septuagint.* One hour a week.

3b. *Classics:* Greek Grammar; Greek prose composition; translation at sight; EURIPIDES, *Bacchae;* SOPHOCLES, *Œdipus Rex;* ARISTOPHANES, *Clouds;* HERODOTUS, VII.; VIII., IX.; THUCYDIDES, II., and III.; PLATO, *Republic* I. to IV.; ARISTOTLE, *Ethics* I. to IV.. and X., Chaps. 5 to 9; Ancient Philosophy including (a) Greek speculative theories before Socrates; (b) Socrates and his contemporaries; (c) the doctrines of Plato and Aristotle; elementary course with special reference to prescribed texts. In addition to the Greek texts here prescribed, the student should read GROTE, *History of Greece,* Chaps. LXVII. and LXVIII.; and CUSHMAN, *Beginner's History of Philosophy,* or ROGERS, *Students' History of Philosophy.* Nine hours a week.

3c. *English and History:* PLATO, as in 3c.

3d. *English and History (Special Option):* ARISTOTLE, as in 3c.

3e. *Greek and Hebrew:* PLATO, ARISTOTLE, and History of Greek Philosophy, as in 3c

3f. Hellenistic Greek; Grammar and Philology; The Septuagint, *Judges;* New Testament, *Acts, 13-28.*

3g. Essays on prescribed topics.

4c. *Classics:* Greek Grammar and Philology; Greek prose composition; translation at sight; THUCYDIDES, V. to VIII.; PLATO, *Republic;* ARISTOTLE, *Ethics,* Book X., Chaps. 6 to 9; ARISTOTLE, *Politics* I., Chaps 1 to 7, II, Chaps. 5, 7, 8, 9; V.; a survey of Greek Philosophy from Socrates to Aristotle (WINDELBAND, *History of Ancient Philosophy);* ÆSCHYLUS, *Agamemnon;* ARISTOPHANES, *Frogs;* ARISTOTLE, *Poetics,* with the history of the Greek genius and Greek poetry so far as covered by the following books: BUTCHER, *Aspects of Greek Genius* (2nd edition); *Harvard Lectures;* MATTHEW ARNOLD, *On Translating Homer;* BUTCHER, Essays in his edition of the Poetics; JEBB, *Classical Greek Poetry;* MOULTON, *Ancient Classical Drama.* Seven hours a week.

4d. English and History: ARISTOTLE, *Poetics* (with books) as in 4c. A knowledge of Greek is not essential for this course.

4e. English and History (Special Option): PLATO, *Republic* as in 4c.

4f. Greek and Hebrew: PLATO, *Republic;* History of Philosophy with special reference to Philo, Neo-Platonism, and the Stoicism of the Empire.

4g. Hellenistic Greek: Grammar and Philology; Selections from *Wisdom Literature;* New Testament, *Hebrews.*

4h. A course of reading to be approved by the Department, with essays on prescribed topics.

LATIN.

PASS COURSES.

1a. Translation at sight of an easy prose passage; translation into Latin of sentences based on the prescribed Cicero; questions on grammar and prosody, and on the subject-matter of the texts; CAESAR, *Bellum Gallicum* V., chap. 24 to end; CICERO, *In Catilinam* I., III.; OVID, Selections (Gleason, omitting No. IV). Four hours a week.

2a. Translation at sight; translation into Latin of sentences to illustrate Latin syntax; translation into Latin of simple narrative based on the prescribed Livy; LIVY, Selections from Books I.-X; (Dennison, 60 pages); CATULLUS (Simpson); questions on grammar and prosody and on the subject matter of the texts. Three hours a week.

3a. Course for 1921-1922: Latin Grammar; Latin Prose Composition; Sight Translation; TACITUS, *Agricola;* HORACE, *Epistles,* Book I.; selections from GILLIES AND CUMMING, *Latin of the Empire;* JUVENAL, *Satires* I, III., X.; PLINY, *The Death of the Elder Pliny, The Eruption of Vesuvius, The Treatment of the Christians.* WARDE FOWLER, *Social Life at Rome in the Age of Cicero.* Three hours a week.

3a. Course for 1922-1923: Latin Grammar; Latin Prose Composition; Sight Translation; CICERO, *Pro Archia;* VIRGIL, *Eclogues* I. and IV., *Aeneid* VI.; selections from GILLIES and CUMMING, *Latin of the Empire;* QUINTILIAN, *Estimate of Latin Writers;* SENECA, *The Choice of Books, The God Within Us;* LUCAN, *The Causes of the Civil War;* MARTIAL, *Country Life, To his Book, To Quintilian, The Day in Rome, A Suburban Villa, The Schoolmaster's Neighbour, The Happy Life, Bilbilis and Rome, To His Townsmen, To Juvenal;* STATIUS, *To Sleep;* AUSONIUS, *The Moselle;* CLAUDIAN, *Imperial Rome, The Old Man of Verona;* RUTILIUS NAMATIANUS, *Farewell to Rome;* TIBERIANUS, *A Country Scene;* MACKAIL, *Latin Literature.* Three hours a week.

4a. Course for 1921-1922.   The same as *3a.*   Three hours a week.

NOTE 1.   Students of the Fourth Year who have not passed in the Latin of their Third Year, will be required at the B.A. examination of 1922 to take an additional paper on the work of the alternative course.

NOTE 2.   Students of the Fourth Year, who through absence from the University, have not taken the two Latin courses in consecutive years, will, at their Final Examination, be required to take the paper on the authors prescribed in *3a*, which they did not take in their Third Year.

HONOUR COURSES.

1b. Classics: Latin Grammar, including prosody; Latin Prose Composition; Sight Translation; VIRGIL, *Georgics* IV., *Aeneid* VI. (Sidgwick or Page); CATULLUS (Simpson); HORACE, The Odes not read for the Honour Matriculation Examination of 1921; CICERO, *Pro Murena, Pro Archia, Philippic* II.   The paper on grammar will be based largely on the prescribed authors; the papers on the texts will include questions on the contents, style, and literary history of the books.   Four to five hours a week.

1c. English and History: The same as *1b*, omitting VIRGIL, *Georgics* IV., and CICERO, *Pro Murena.*   Four hours a week.

2b. Classics: Latin Grammar; Latin Prose Composition; Sight Translation; TACITUS, *Annals,* Books I. and II.; LIVY, Books I. and VI.; VIRGIL, *Eclogues;* PLAUTUS, *Rudens;* TERENCE, *Phormio;* MARTIAL, *Select Epigrams;* HORACE, *Epistles;* SELLAR, *The Roman Poets of the Republic.*   Five to six hours a week.

2c. English and History: The same as *2b*, omitting Latin Grammar, LIVY and TACITUS.   Three hours a week.

3b. Classics: Latin Grammar; Latin Prose Composition; Sight Translation; HORACE, *Satires;* PERSIUS, *Satire* V.; JUVENAL, *Satires* I., III., V., VII., VIII., X., XIII.; the history of Roman Satire.

TIBULLUS, I., 1 and 3, II., 1 and 5; PROPERTIUS, I., 1, 2, 8, II., 13*b*, 31, 34, III., 1, 3, 7, 9, IV., 2, 6, 11; CARTER, *Latin Elegiac Poets;* VIRGIL, *Aeneid,* Books I-VI.; LUCRETIUS, Book V.

CICERO, *Letters* (Watson), Books I. and II.; CAESAR, *Civil War,* Book I.

TACITUS, *Annals,* Books III. to VI. (Furneaux, large edition); Monumentum Ancyranum (Mommsen); reign of Tiberius and introduction to the history of the principate (MERIVALE, *The Romans under the Empire,* Vols. III., IV., and V.; BOISSIER, *Tacitus*).   Six hours a week.

3c. English and History: HORACE, *Satires;* PERSIUS, *Satire* V.; JUVENAL, *Satires* I., III., V., VII., VIII., X., XIII.; the history of Roman Satire; TIBULLUS, I., 1 and 3, II., 1 and 5; PROPERTIUS, I., 1, 2, 8, 11, 13*b*, 31, 34, III. 1,, 3, 7, 9, IV., 2, 6, 11; CARTER, *Latin Elegiac Poets;* LUCRETIUS, Book V.   Two hours a week.

3*d.* *English and History (Special Option):* CICERO, *Letters* (Watson), Books I. and II.; CAESAR, *Civil War*, Book I.

3*e.* Essays on prescribed topics.

3*f.* The same as 3*b*, omitting CICERO and TACITUS and adding PLAUTUS and TERENCE as in 2*b*.

4*b.* *Classics:* Latin Grammar and Philology; Latin Prose Composition; Sight Translation; VIRGIL, *Aeneid*, with questions in Virgilian criticism.

HORACE, *Ars Poetica*, and QUINTILIAN, Book X., with questions on the history of Roman literature.

LUCRETIUS, Books I. and III.; CICERO, *De Finibus*, Books I. and II.; Stoic and Epicurean Philosophy.

·CICERO, *Letters* (Watson), Books III. to V.; SALLUST, *Catiline*; CAESAR, *Civil War;* Roman constitutional history from the death of Sulla to the death of Cicero (Mommsen, Book V.; Ferrero). Five hours.

4*c.* *English and History;* CICERO, *Letters* (Watson), Books III. to V.; SALLUST, *Catiline;* CAESAR, *Civil War.* Two hours.

4*d.* A course of reading to be approved by the Department, with essays on prescribed topics.

GREEK AND ROMAN HISTORY.
PASS AND HONOUR COURSE.

1. General History of Greece to 146 B.C. General History of Rome to A.D. 476. GOODSPEED, *History of the Ancient World;* BURY, *Student's History of Greece* (Kimball); PELHAM, *Outlines of Roman History.* The course aims at a simple outline of the general historical movement in the Græco-Roman world and at an appreciation of the most characteristic features of this Mediterranean civilization.

PASS COURSES.

3*a.* A more mature study of Greek History, based upon Thucydides, Herodotus and Plutarch (Everyman's Library); and an examination of the influence of Greece on Rome.

4*a.* The causes, social, economic and political, of the fall of the Roman Republic; and the history of the Roman Empire to the death of Justinian.

HONOUR COURSES.

2*a.* Greek History to 454 B.C.; GROTE (Mitchell and Caspari), Chaps. I. to XV.

2*b.* Roman constitutional and political history to B.C. 264: the city state, criticism of the regal period, the revolution of 509, the struggle between the orders, the conquest and organization of Italy. MOMMSEN, Books I. and II.; TAYLOR, *Constitutional and Political History of Rome;* WARDE FOWLER, *The City State*; FUSTEL DE COULANGES, *La Cité antique*, omitting those portions of the book which deal with Greek history. Classical students are recommended to purchase Mommsen complete early in their course, but HOW AND LEIGH, *History of Rome* (cc. i-xvii.) covers this period satisfactorily.

3*b*. Greek History from B.C. 454 to B.C. 399; GROTE (Mitchell and Caspari), Chaps. XVI. to XXI.; ZIMMERN, *The Greek Commonwealth;* historical questions on the prescribed Thucydides.

3*c*. Roman History from B.C. 264 to B.C. 78, *i.e.*, the period of foreign conquest and the beginning of the Revolution; MOMMSEN, Books III. and IV.; TAYLOR, *Constitutional and Political History of Rome.*

4*b*. General questions on Greek History.

4*c*. Roman Constitutional and Political History from the death of Sulla to the death of Cicero; MOMMSEN, Book VI., FERRERO.

4*d*. Roman Institutions: GREENIDGE, *Roman Public Life;* WARDE FOWLER, *The Religious Experience of the Roman People;* DELOUME, *Les Manieurs d'argent à Rome.*

PHILOLOGY.

Greek and Roman Phonetics, Inflections and Conjugations.

ORIENTAL LANGUAGES.

UNIVERSITY COLLEGE:

J. F. McCURDY, PH.D., LL.D..................*Professor Emeritus.*
W. R. TAYLOR, PH.D...........................*Professor.*
J. A. CRAIG, M.A., B.D., PH.D......................*Professor.*
W. A. IRWIN, M.A., D.B............................*Lecturer.*

VICTORIA COLLEGE:

REV. J. F. McLAUGHLIN, B.A., D.D....................*Professor.*
S. H. HOOKE, M.A., B.D............................*Professor.*
REV. W. A. POTTER, M.A., B.D...............*Associate Professor.*

TRINITY COLLEGE:

REV. F. H. COSGRAVE, M.A., B.D.....................*Professor.*
REV. W. ROLLO, M.A................................*Lecturer.*

PASS COURSES.

1*a*. *Pass Course.* A course in the history of the Hebrew people from the Exodus to 586 B.C.; a literary study of the books of Amos, Hosea, Isaiah and Micah. One hour a week.

1*b*. *Pass Course.* Hebrew Grammar; translation from Hebrew into English of Gen. 1-4, 18; Pss. 1, 8, 24; translation from English into Hebrew. Introduction to Oriental History. DAVIDSON, *Hebrew Grammar;* KITTEL, *Biblia Hebraica.* Four hours a week

2*a*. *Pass Course.* A course in the history of the Hebrew people from 586 to 4 B.C.; a study of the Prophetic, Legal and Historical ·Literature of the Old Testament. Two hours a week.

2b. *Pass Course.* Hebrew Grammar with special attention to syntax; translation from English into Hebrew; translation into English of *Genesis* 37, 40-45; *Ex.* 3, 4, 15; *Ruth; II. Samuel* 14-19; history of the Massoretic Text and the Versions; outlines of the geography of Palestine. DAVIDSON, *Hebrew Grammar;* KITTEL, *Biblia Hebraica;* BROWN, DRIVER, AND BRIGGS, *Lexicon;* KENT, *History of the Hebrew People,* Vol. I. Three hours a week.

3a. *Pass Course.* A literary study of the Poetical books of the Old Testament and of the Synoptic Gospels. Three hours a week.

3b. *Pass Course: Greek and Hebrew.* Translation from English into Hebrew; Hebrew history from the settlement in Canaan to the end of the Kingdom (586 B.C.). Translation into English of *Amos; Isaiah* 1-6, 40-45 and 52-55; *II. Kings* 15-25; *Deuteronomy* 5-11; KITTEL, *Biblia Hebraica;* DAVIDSON, *Hebrew Grammar* (20th edition); DAVIDSON, *Hebrew Syntax;* BROWN, DRIVER AND BRIGGS, *Lexicon.* KENT, *A History of the Hebrew People,* Vols. II. and III. Three hours a week.

4a. *Pass Course.* A study of the Early Literature of Christianity. Three hours a week.

4b. *Pass Course: Greek and Hebrew.* Translation from English into Hebrew: characteristics of Hebrew poetry; Jewish history from the fall of Jerusalem 586 B.C. to the end of the Maccabaean period. Translation into English of selected *Psalms,* 100, 95, 24, 15, 48, 87, 114, 81, 147, 148, 150, 46, 47, 93, 97, 8, 19, 29, 103, 104, 65, 67, 118, 21, 116, 30, 74, 89, 90, 20, 72, 42, 43, 22, 51, 137, 84, 122, 110, 107, 23, 78, 127, 133, 45; *Zechariah* 1-8; *Jonah; II. Chronicles* 1-9; KITTEL, *Biblia Hebraica;* DAVIDSON, *Hebrew Syntax;* GESENIUS-KAUTZSCH, *Hebrew Grammar;* KENT, *History of the Jewish People,* Vols. III. and IV. Three hours a week.

HONOUR COURSES.

2c. *Orientals: Greek and Hebrew.* Hebrew Grammar with special attention to syntax. Translation into English, the same as 2b. Hebrew prose exercises. DAVIDSON, *Hebrew Grammar* (20th edition); DAVIDSON, *Hebrew Syntax.* Three hours a week.

2d. *Orientals: Greek and Hebrew.* Translation into English of the *Book of Judges* 1-12; *I Sam.* 9-19; *II Kings* 17-23. Two hours a week.

2e. *Orientals.* Translation into English of *Exodus* 8-20; *Deuteronomy* 17. Two hours a week.

2f. *Orientals.* Grammar of Palestinian Aramaic with translation of extracts from BAER AND DELITZSCH, *Text of Daniel and Ezra;* MARTI, *Biblisch-Armaeische Grammatik.* Michaelmas Term. Two hours a week.— Syriac Grammar with translation of easy prose into English; BROCKELMANN, *Syrische Grammatik;* ROEDIGER, *Chrestomathia Syriaca.* Easter term. Two hours a week.

2g. Orientals: Greek and Hebrew. History of the Western Orient until 722 B.C. H. R. HALL, *The Ancient History of the Near East.* One hour a week.

3c. Orientals. Translation into English, the same as *3b.* One hour a week.

3d. Orientals: Greek and Hebrew. Translation into English of selections from *Isaiah* 1-39. Two hours a week.

3e. Orientals. Translation into English of selections from *Jeremiah, Ezekiel,* and the Minor Prophets. Two hours a week.

3f. Orientals. Hebrew prose composition and sight translation. GESE-NIUS-KAUTZSCH, *Hebrew Grammar.* One hour a week.

3g. Orientals: Greek and Hebrew. History of the Western Orient from 722 B.C. to 330 B.C., with special attention to the history, literature and institutions of the Hebrews. One hour a week.

3h. Orientals. Arabaic First Course: THATCHER, *Arabic Grammar* with exercises in translating easy prose into English. Two hours a week.

3i. Orientals. Advanced course in Aramaic or Syriac. Two hours a week.

3j. Orientals. Elements of Assyrian; FR. DELITZSCH, *Assyrische Leses-tücke.* Outlines of Comparative Grammar of the Semitic Languages; BROCKELMANN, *Vergleichende Grammatik.* Two hours a week.

4c. Orientals. Translation into English, the same as *4b.* One hour a week.

4d. Orientals: Greek and Hebrew. Translation into English of selections from *Job, Proverbs* and *Ecclesiastes.* One hour a week.

4e. Orientals. Selections from Late Biblical or Post-Biblical Hebrew. One hour a week.

4f. Orientals. Hebrew prose composition and sight translation. DAVIDSON, *Hebrew Syntax.* One hour a week.

4g. Orientals: Greek and Hebrew. History of the Western Orient from 330 B.C. to 135 A.D. with special attention to the history and literature of the Jews, and the History of Mahomet and the Caliphate. One hour a week.

4h. Orientals. Arabic Second Course; THATCHER, *Arabic Grammar* (continued); BRÜNNOW, *Chrestomathy of Arabic Prose Selections;* HARDER, *Arabic Chrestomathy.* Two hours a week.

4i. Orientals. Advanced course in Aramaic or Syriac. Two hours a week.

4j. Orientals. Advanced course in Assyrian. Inscriptions of Senna-cherib, Sargon, Asurbanipal. Two hours a week.

MODERN LANGUAGES.
ENGLISH.

UNIVERSITY COLLEGE:

W. J. ALEXANDER, PH.D., LL.D......................*Professor.*
D. R. KEYS, M.A.....................*Professor of Anglo-Saxon.*
M. W. WALLACE, B.A., PH.D.........................*Professor.*
R. S. KNOX, M.A...........................*Associate Professor.*
W. H. CLAWSON, M.A., PH.D.................*Assistant Professor.*
MISS M. M. WADDINGTON, PH.D.........................*Lecturer.*
MISS G. E. WOOKEY, B.A.............................*Assistant.*
A. S. P. WOODHOUSE, B.A...........................*Assistant.*

VICTORIA COLLEGE:

A. H. REYNAR, M.A., LL.D...................*Professor Emeritus.*
O. P. EDGAR, B.A., PH.D.............................*Professor.*
L. E. HORNING, B.A., PH.D...........................*Professor.*
C. E. AUGER, B.A...........................*Associate Professor.*
E. J. PRATT, PH.D....................................*Lecturer.*
J. N. D. BUSH, B.A......................................*Fellow.*

TRINITY COLLEGE:

H. C. SIMPSON, M.A.................................*Professor.*
MISS MABEL CARTWRIGHT, B.A........................*Lecturer.*
L. C. A. HODGINS, M.A................................*Lecturer.*

ST. MICHAEL'S COLLEGE:

W. P. M. KENNEDY, M.A., LITT.D....................*Professor.*
REV. E. J. McCORKELL, M.A.................*Associate Professor.*
M. M. MARGARITA, B.A................................*Lecturer.*
MISS RUTH AGNEW, B.A..............................*Lecturer.*

Composition: In the first two years of the undergraduate course original essays are required during the session from students taking the Pass and Honour Courses in English, even from those who have received dispensation from attendance upon lectures. These essays, after being carefully examined, are returned with suggestions and criticisms, and the marks assigned are reckoned in determining standing in the May examinations.

Throughout the course Composition shall be regarded as a subject distinct from literature, and candidates failing to secure the necessary standing in these essays are required to repeat the work of the year in English Composition.

Provision will be made by a special paper in English composition for the examination of those candidates for Senior Matriculation who are not in attendance, and who have not presented the essays required.

PASS COURSES.

1a. Composition: The writing of at least four original compositions during the session.

1b. Familiarity with and intelligent appreciation of the following texts: *Sir Patrick Spens, Edward, The Braes o' Yarrow, Waly Waly;* DRYDEN, *A Song for St. Cecilia's Day, Alexander's Feast;* THOMSON, extracts from *Summer* and *Winter;* GRAY, *Spring, Eton College, Elegy, The Fatal Sisters;* GOLDSMITH, *Deserted Village;* BURNS, *Address to the De'il, To John Lapraik,. To a Mouse, Last May a Braw Wooer, A Man's a Man for a' that;* WORDS-WORTH, *Sonnets* (omitting *Personal Talk, Scorn not the Sonnet, A Poet —he hath put his heart to school);* SCOTT, *Rosabelle, Brignall Banks, Lochinvar, The Antiquary;* KEATS, *On Chapman's Homer, "Bright Star! would I", The Eve of St. Agnes, On a Grecian Urn, To a Nightingale, To Autumn;* GEORGE ELIOT, *Silas Marner;* BROWNING, *Fra Lippo Lippi, Andrea del Sarto, The Bishop orders his Tomb, An Epistle;* TENNYSON, *The Palace of Art;* RUSKIN, *Crown of Wild Olive.* The selections from Canadian Poets in *Representative Poetry.* [The poetical selections in this paragraph are contained in *Representative Poetry,* third edition, Students' Book Department, University of Toronto.]

Two hours a week.

2a. Composition: The writing of at least four original compositions during the session.

2b. SHAKESPEARE, *Romeo and Juliet, Henry IV., Parts I. and II., Twelfth Night, Hamlet.*

Two hours a week.

3a. The writing of essays on subjects connected with one of the Third Year courses in literature.

3b. Transition and earlier nineteenth-century literature: The selections from COLLINS to SCOTT inclusive in *Representative Poetry;* GOLDSMITH, *The Vicar of Wakefield;* BURKE, *American Taxation, Conciliation with America;* SCOTT, *Marmion* (with introductory epistles); the essays by WORDSWORTH, COLERIDGE, LAMB and HAZLITT in *English Critical Essays of the Nineteenth Century* (World's Classics); JANE AUSTEN, *Pride and Prejudice;* LAMB, *Poor Relations, Detached Thoughts on Books and Reading, Christ's Hospital;* NEWMAN, *Idea of a University (Knowledge its own end* and *Knowledge in relation to learning);* CARLYLE, *Signs of the Times, Characteristics.*

Three or two hours a week.

4a. The writing of essays on subjects connected with one of the Fourth Year courses in literature.

4b. Later nineteenth-century literature: selections from BYRON to MORRIS in *Representative Poetry;* essays by SHELLEY, ARNOLD, RUSKIN, MILL and BAGEHOT in *English Critical Essays of the Nineteenth Century* (World's Classics); CARLYLE, *Sartor Resartus* (Books I. and II.);

THACKERAY, *Vanity Fair;* RUSKIN, *A Joy Forever;* ARNOLD, *The Function of Criticism, The Literary Influence of Academies.*
Three or two hours a week.

HONOUR COURSES.

1*a*. Composition: The writing of at least four original compositions during the session.

1*c*. (i) CHAUCER, *Prologue, Nun's Priest's Tale,* with some outline of the history of the English language.
One hour a week.

(ii) SHAKESPEARE, *Much Ado About Nothing, Antony and Cleopatra;* CARLYLE, *The Hero as Prophet, The Hero as Poet;* NEWMAN, *Idea of a University (Knowledge its own end, Knowledge in relation to Learning);* RUSKIN, *Crown of Wild Olive;* ARNOLD, *The Study of Poetry (Essays in Criticism,* second series); SCOTT, *The Antiquary;* GEORGE ELIOT, *Silas Marner;* BROWNING, *Fra Lippo Lippi, Andrea del Sarto, The Bishop orders his Tomb, An Epistle.*
Two hours a week.

2*a*. Composition: The writing of at least four original compositions during the session.

2*c*. (i) SHAKESPEARE, *Romeo and Juliet, Henry IV.,* Parts I. and II. *Twelfth Night, Hamlet.*

(ii) An outline of later seventeenth· and earlier eighteenth century literature, with special study of the following texts: DRYDEN, *Essay of Dramatic Poesy, Preface to the Fables;* BUNYAN, *Grace Abounding;* SWIFT, *Gulliver's Travels,* Books I. and II.; ADDISON and STEELE, *Sir Roger de Coverley* ((Cassell's National Library); DEFOE, *Robinson Crusoe;* JOHNSON, *Preface to Shakespeare, Lives of the Poets (Dryden, Addison* and *Pope);* BOSWELL, *Life of Johnson* (May 16, 1763—end of 1764; April 3, 1773—end of May, 1773; March 21, 1775—May 21, 1775); selections from DRYDEN to GRAY inclusive in *Representative Poetry.*
Four hours a week.

3*a*. The writing of essays on subjects connected with one of the Third Year courses in literature.

3*b*. Transition and earlier nineteenth-century literature: The selections from COLLINS to SCOTT inclusive in *Representative Poetry;* GOLDSMITH, *Vicar of Wakefield;* BURKE, *American Taxation, Conciliation with America;* SCOTT, *Marmion* (with introductory epistles); the essays by WORDSWORTH, COLERIDGE, LAMB and HAZLITT in *English Critical Essays of the Nineteenth Century* (World's Classics); JANE AUSTEN, *Pride and Prejudice;* LAMB, *Poor Relations, Detached Thoughts on Books and Reading, Christ's Hospital;* NEWMAN, *Idea of a University (Knowledge its own end,* and *Knowledge in relation to learning);* CARLYLE, *Signs of the Times, Characteristics.*
Three or two hours a week.

3c. BRIGHT, *Old English Grammar* and selections from the *Reader;* Outlines of Old English literature. Two hours a week.

3d. Seventeenth-century literature with special study of: MILTON, *L'Allegro, Il Penseroso, Arcades, Comus, Lycidas, Sonnets, Paradise Lost, Paradise Regained, Samson Agonistes;* selections from JONSON to BUTLER inclusive in *Representative Poetry;* MILTON, *Of Reformation, The Reason of Church Government, Of Education, Areopagitica;* BROWNE, *Religio Medici;* HALIFAX, *Character of a Trimmer.*

.Two hours a week.

4a. The writing of essays on subjects connected with one of the Fourth Year courses in literature.

4b. Later nineteenth-century literature: selections from BYRON to MORRIS in *Representative Poetry;* essays by SHELLEY, ARNOLD, RUSKIN, MILL and BAGEHOT in *English Critical Essays of the Nineteenth Century* (World's Classics); CARLYLE, *Sartor Resartus* (Books I. and II.); THACKERAY, *Vanity Fair;* RUSKIN, *A Joy Forever;* ARNOLD, *The Function of Criticism, The Literary Influence of Academies.*

Three or two hours a week.

4c. (i) Historical English grammar.

(ii) A course on CHAUCER and his age with special study of the following selections: *The Prologue to the Canterbury Tales, The Knightes Tale, Sir Thopas, The Nonne Preestes Tale, Compleynte unto Pite, Parlement of Fowls, Wordes unto Adam, The Former Age, Fortune, Truth, Proverbs, Prologue to Legend of Good Women.* [Chaucer (Oxford Press) or the Globe Chaucer (Macmillan) or MacCracken's Chaucer (Yale University Press); *The Chaucer Epoch,* by J. C. Stobart (Arnold).]

Two hours a week.

4d. NEWMAN, *Apologia, The Idea of a University, Preface and Discourses V.-VIII.;* J. S. MILL, *Essays on Bentham, Coleridge, Civilization, Utilitarianism, Liberty;* CARLYLE, *Past and Present, Book III., Shooting Niagara —and After?;* RUSKIN, *Unto this Last;* ARNOLD, *Culture and Anarchy, Democracy, Equality;* MORLEY, *Compromise.*

Two hours a week.

4e. The Development of the English Drama to 1642. Reading of the following texts: *Noah's Flood, The Sacrifice of Isaac, Secunda Pastorum, Everyman* (Pollard's *Miracle Plays*); UDALL, *Ralph Roister Doister;* LYLY, *Endymion;* GREENE, *Friar Bacon;* MARLOWE, *Tamburlaine,* Part I. *Edward II.;* KYD, *Spanish Tragedy;* SHAKESPEARE, *Othello, King Lear, Antony and Cleopatra, The Tempest;* BEN JONSON, *Every Man in his Humour;* BEAUMONT AND FLETCHER, *Philaster;* WEBSTER, *Duchess of Malfi.*

Two hours a week.

GERMAN.

UNIVERSITY COLLEGE:

W. H. VAN DER SMISSEN, M.A., PH.D..........*Professor Emeritus.*

G. H. NEEDLER, B.A., PH.D............................*Professor.*

B. FAIRLEY, M.A., PH.D....................*Associate Professor.*

T. J. HEDMAN, PH.B........................*Assistant Professor.*

G. E. HOLT, M.A., MUS.BAC.............................*Lecturer.*

VICTORIA COLLEGE:

L. E. HORNING, B.A., PH.D.............................*Professor.*

A. E. LANG, M.A.......................................*Professor.*

MISS M. E. T. ADDISON, B.A.............................*Lecturer.*

J. D. ROBINS, B.A.......................................*Lecturer.*

TRINITY COLLEGE:

A. H. YOUNG, M.A., D.C.L..............................*Professor.*

MISS L. C. SCOTT, M.A.................................*Lecturer.*

ST. MICHAEL'S COLLEGE:

REV. M. J. OLIVER, B.A., PH.M...............*Associate Professor.*

S. M. PERPETUA, B.A..................................*Lecturer.*

PASS COURSES.

1*a.* Grammar; dictation; pronunciation; translation from modern German; translation from English into German. Four hours a week.

1*b.* Reading of easy prescribed texts in scientific German; translation of similar passages at sight. Two hours a week.

2*a.* Grammar; dictation; pronunciation; translation from modern German; translation from English into German. Three hours a week.

2*b.* Reading of prescribed texts in scientific German; translation of scientific German at sight. Two hours a week.

3*a.* Grammar; dictation; pronunciation; translation from English into German; translation at sight from modern German; outlines of the history of German literature to 1740; life and works of LESSING and SCHILLER, with special attention to LESSING, *Minna von Barnhelm;* SCHILLER, *Poems* (ed. Nollen), *Wilhelm Tell.* Three hours a week.

4*a.* Grammar; dictation; pronunciation; translation from English into German; translation at sight from modern German; outlines of the history of German literature from 1740; life and works of GOETHE with special attention to *Poems* (ed. Schutze), *Faust*, Part I. Supplementary reading. Three hours a week.

HONOUR COURSES.

1*c.* Translation at sight from modern German; FIEDLER, *Book of German Verse* (pages 1-143 inc.); KELLER, *Die drei gerechten Kammacher;* ERNST, *Flachsmann als Erzieher.* Supplementary reading. Two hours a week.

1*d*. Oral term work; composition. One hour a week.

1*e*. Political and social history of Germany to 1500. One hour a week.

1*f*. Reading of selected texts in German. Two hours a week.

1*g*. Composition; writing of business letters; practice in reading and writing German script; oral exercises. One hour a week.

2*c*. Translation at sight from modern German; history of German literature in the eighteenth century with special attention to LESSING and SCHILLER; LESSING, *Minna von Barnhelm, Emilia Galotti;* SCHILLER, *Wallensteins Tod, Die Braut von Messina.* Supplementary reading. Two hours a week.

2*d*. Oral term work; composition. One hour a week.

2*e*. Political and social history of Germany from 1500 to 1713.

2*f*. Practice in business correspondence and conversation in German. Reading of German texts. Three hours a week.

3*b*. Life and works of GOETHE with special attention to *Lyrical Poems* (ed. Schütze), *Götz von Berlichingen, Torquato Tasso, Dichtung und Wahrheit* (ed. von Jagemann), *Faust,* Part I. Supplementary reading. Three hours a week.

3*c*. Oral term work; composition. One hour a week.

3*d*. Political and social history of Germany from 1713 to 1815. One hour a week.

3*e*. Essays on prescribed topics.

4*b*. A general acquaintance with the development of German literature of the nineteenth century, with special attention to KLEIST, *Der zerbrochene Krug;* GRILLPARZER, *Die Jüdin von Toledo;* HEBBEL, *Herodes und Mariamne;* HEINE, *Harzreise* (ed. Gregor); LUDWIG, *Zwischen Himmel und Erde;* KELLER, *Romeo und Julia auf dem Dorfe.* Supplementary reading. Two hours a week.

4*c*. Oral term work; composition. One hour a week.

4*d*. Middle High German Grammar; history of the German language; history of Middle High German literature; *Middle High German Primer* (WRIGHT). One hour a week.

4*e*. Political and social history of Germany from 1815 to the present.

4*f*. Essays on prescribed topics.

FRENCH.

UNIVERSITY COLLEGE:

JOHN SQUAIR, B.A..........................*Professor Emeritus.*
J. H. CAMERON, M.A...............................*Professor.*
J. S. WILL, B.A....................................*Professor.*
ST. E. DE CHAMP, B. ÈS L., O.I.P.............*Associate Professor.*
F. C. A. JEANNERET, B.A...................*Assistant Professor.*
M. MORAUD, L. ÈS L., AGRÉGÉ DE L'UNIVERSITÉ...*Assistant Professor.*

H. S. McKELLAR, B.A.................................*Lecturer.*
W. D. EVANS, B.A....................................*Lecturer.*
MISS A. CHALUFOUR, B. ÈS L..........................*Lecturer.*
L. A. BIBET ....*Instructor (Part time).*
W. J. McANDREW, M.A..................*Instructor (Part time).*

VICTORIA COLLEGE:
  H. E. FORD, M.A...................................*Professor.*
  VICTOR DE BEAUMONT, A.M..................*Associate Professor.*
  Miss M. C. ROWELL, B.A.............................*Lecturer.*
  A. LACEY, M.A......................................*Lecturer.*

TRINITY COLLEGE:
  R. E. L. KITTREDGE, M.A............................*Professor.*
  A. A. NORTON, B.A..................................*Lecturer.*
  VICTOR DE BEAUMONT, A.M....................*Special Lecturer.*
  L. A. BIBET......................................*Instructor.*
  A. LACEY, M.A....................................*Instructor.*
  MISS L. C. SCOTT, M.A...............................*Reader.*

ST. MICHAEL'S COLLEGE:
  REV. R. McBRADY...................................*Professor.*
  REV. W. H. MURRAY, B.A.............................*Lecturer.*
  REV. J. E. PAGEAU..................................*Lecturer.*
  S. M. AGNES, B.A...................................*Lecturer.*
  MISS ELIZABETH O'DRISCOLL, M.A. ....*Lecturer.*

NOTE.—In order to be a member of any class in French, a student must satisfy the instructor as to his ability to profit by the instruction given. Supplementary reading under the direction of the staff will be required of all students in all years.

Students taking the full honour French course must make satisfactory progress in the oral use of the language. Opportunity for this work will be provided in each of the four years.

PASS COURSES.

1*a*. Grammar; dictation; translation from English into French; translation at sight from modern French. The following texts are prescribed for critical study: BAZIN, *Les Oberlé;* SANDEAU, *Mademoiselle de la Seiglière;* FEUILLET, *Le Village;* DAUDET, *Lettres de mon moulin.* Four hours a week.

1*b*. Course for Science Students. Two hours a week.

2*a*. Grammar; dictation; translation from English into French; translation at sight from modern French. The following texts are prescribed for critical study: BARRÈS, *Colette Baudoche;* PAILLERON, *Le Monde où l'on s'ennuie;* COPPÉE, *Pour la couronne; French Short Stories* (ed. Buffum), or GEORGES DURUY, *Histoire sommaire de la France, classe de septième.* Three hours a week.

2*b*. Course for Science Students. Two hours a week.

3*a*. Standards of the classical age and the main ideas of the eighteenth century, studied in French literature from Malherbe to the *philosophes*. PELLISSIER, *Précis de l'histoire de la littérature française*, pp. 139-364; *French Prose of the XVIIth Century* (ed. Warren); CORNEILLE, *Le Cid;* MOLIÈRE, *Le Misanthrope;* RACINE, *Andromaque;* LA FONTAINE, *Fables;* VOLTAIRE'S *Prose* (ed. Cohn and Woodward); Supplementary reading. Translation from English into French; translation at sight from modern French. Three hours a week.

4*a*. Forces and movements in French literature since 1750. PELLISSIER: *Précis de l'histoire de la littérature française*, pp. 365-544; *Pages choisies de J.-J. Rousseau* (ed. Rocheblave); *French Lyrics of the XIXth Century* (ed. Henning); HUGO, *Hernani;* BALZAC, *Gobseck;* AUGIER, *Les Effrontés; Quelques Contes des romanciers naturalistes* (ed. Dow and Skinner); ROSTAND, *Cyrano de Bergerac;* BAZIN, *Le Blé qui lève;* Supplementary Reading. Translation from English into French; translation at sight from modern French. Three hours a week.

HONOUR COURSES.

1*c*. Grammar; dictation; pronunciation; translation from English into French; translation at sight from modern French.

Survey of French literature with special reference to the mediæval period. The following texts are prescribed for critical study: AUGIER, *Le Gendre de Monsieur Poirier;* FRANCE, *Le Crime de Sylvestre Bonnard; Quelques Contes des romanciers naturalistes* (ed. Dow and Skinner); *French Lyrics* (ed. Canfield). Four hours a week.

1*d*. Outlines of Mediæval History.

1*e*. Course for Commerce Students. Three hours a week.

2*c*. History of French literature from the middle of the sixteenth century to the end of the seventeenth century, illustrated by the reading of texts from which the following are prescribed for critical study: *French Verse of the XVIth Century* (Wright); BOSSUET, *Oraison funèbre de Louis de Bourbon;* LA BRUYÈRE, *Caractères* (De la société et de la conversation); CORNEILLE, *le Cid;* RACINE, *Andromaque;* MOLIÈRE, *Tartuffe, le Misanthrope;* BOILEAU, *l'Art poétique;* LA FONTAINE, *Fables* (ed. Clément). Two hours a week.

2*d*. History of France in the sixteenth and seventeenth centuries.

2*e*. Simple narrative composition; translation from English into French; translation at sight. One hour a week.

2*f*. Course for Commerce Students.

3*b*. History of French literature during the eighteenth century, illustrated by texts from which the following are prescribed for critical study: LESAGE, *Turcaret;* MARIVAUX, *Le Jeu de l'amour et du hasard;* MONTESQUIEU, *Esprit des lois* (Books I, II, III); VOLTAIRE, *Zaïre, Zadig, Prose* (ed.

Cohn and Woodward, pp. 1-73, 118-162, 294-347); ROUSSEAU, *Pages choisies* (ed. Rocheblave); BEAUMARCHAIS, *Le Mariage de Figaro* or *Le Barbier de Séville;* ANDRÉ CHÉNIER (ed. Becq de Fouquières), *Bucoliques I and XV, Hymnes et Odes III and VII;* CHATEAUBRIAND, *Atala.*

3c. The Class·c ideal as represented in critical writings from the Pléiade to the beginnings of Romanticism. The following texts will be used: DU BELLAY, *Défense et illustration de la langue française;* BOILEAU, *Selections from the Satires, Epistles, and the Art poétique;* VOLTAIRE, *Essai sur la poésie épique;* DIDEROT, *De la poésie dramatique;* ROUSSEAU, *Lettre à M. d'Alembert;* MME DE STAËL, *De la littérature.*

3d. History of France in the eighteenth century.

3e. Composition; translation from English into French; translation at sight.

3f. Essays on prescribed topics.

4b. History of French literature during the nineteenth century, illustrated by the reading of texts from which the following are prescribed for critical study: LAMARTINE, *Œuvres choisies, Poésie* (ed. René Waltz); HUGO, *Poems* (ed. Canfield), *Notre-Dame de Paris* (ed. Léon Delbos) or *Quatre-vingt-treize, Hernani;* BALZAC, *Eugénie Grandet, le Curé de Tours;* AUGIER, *Les Effrontés;* MICHELET and TAINE in *Extraits des historiens français du XIXᵉ siècle* (ed. Jullian); LECONTE DE LISLE, *Poèmes barbares;* ALPHONSE DAUDET, *Fromont jeune et Risler aîné.*

4c. A course in contemporary literature: FRANCE, LOTI, BRIEUX, MARGUERITTE, MAETERLINCK, BARRÈS, ROSTAND.

4d. History of France from the beginning of the nineteenth century to the present.

4e. Composition; translation from English into French; translation at sight from French authors of any period.

4f. Elementary course in Old French.

4g. Essays on prescribed topics.

ITALIAN AND SPANISH.

M. A. BUCHANAN, B.A., PH.D. . . . . *Professor.*
J. E. SHAW, A.B., PH.D. . . . . *Professor.*
E. GOGGIO, M.A., PH.D. . . . . *Assistant Professor.*
G. C. PATTERSON, B.A. . . . . *Lecturer.*
J. PIJOAN, L.LITT . . . . *Instructor.*

Italian.

1. Grammar; pronunciation and dictation; translation; oral exercises. Text-books: WILKINS AND ALTROCCHI, *Italian Short Stories;* WILKINS, *First Italian Book.* Three hours a week.

2. Grammar; dictation; translation; composition; oral exercises. Text-books: GRANDGENT, *Italian Grammar;* FOGAZZARO, *Pereat Rochus;* GIACOSA *Tristi amori* (Altrocchi and Woodbridge). Three hours a week.

—13

3*a*. Grammar; translation. Text-book: CARDUCCI, *Antologia* (ed. Mazzoni e Picciola). One hour a week.

3*b*. History of Italian literature: the later Renaissance. Text-books: CASTIGLIONE, *Il Cortegiano* (ed. Cian); CELLINI, *Vita* (ed. Bianchi); ARIOSTO, *Orlando Furioso* (ed. Papini); ROSSI, *Storia della Letteratura Italiana*. Two hours a week.

3*c*. Composition in Italian and oral exercises; lectures in Italian on the art, history, and literature of Italy. Two hours a week.

3*d*. Essays on prescribed topics.

4*a*. History of Italian literature: the early Renaissance. Text-books: DANTE, *Divina Commedia* (ed. Grandgent); *Vita Nuova* (ed. Scherillo); PETRARCH, *Rime* (ed. Carducci e Ferrari); ROSSI, *Storia della Letteratura Italiana*. Three hours a week.

4*b*. Composition and oral exercises; lectures in Italian on the art, history, and literature of Italy. Two hours a week.

4*c*. Essays on prescribed topics.

Spanish.

1*a*. Grammar; pronunciation and dictation; translation; oral exercises. Text-books: HILLS AND FORD, *First Spanish Course;* HILLS, *Spanish Tales.* Three hours a week.

1*b*. Elementary Spanish for students in the Faculty of Applied Science.

1*c*. (For students who have matriculated in Spanish.) The same as 2*a*.

2*a*. Grammar; dictation; translation; composition; oral exercises. Text-books: PÉREZ GALDÓS, *Marianela;* COOL, *Spanish Composition;* ESPINOSA, *Composition.* Three hours a week.

2*b*. (For students who have matriculated in Spanish.) The same as 3*a*.

3*a*. History of Spanish literature in the nineteenth century. Text-books: MORATÍN, *El sí de las Niñas;* ESPRONCEDA, *El Estudiante de Salamanca* (ed. Northup); VALERA, *Pepita Jiménez* (ed. Lincoln); PÉREZ GALDÓS, *Trafalgar;* ECHEGARAY, *El gran Galeoto* (ed. Espinosa); BENAVENTE *Los Intereses creados* (ed. Van Horne); FITZMAURICE-KELLY, *Historia de la Literatura española.* Three hours a week.

3*b*. Composition in Spanish and oral exercises; lectures in Spanish on the art, history, and literature of Spain and Spanish America. Two hours a week.

3*c*. Essays on prescribed topics.

4*a*. History of Spanish literature: the Golden Age. Text-books: CERVANTES, *Don Quijote;* VÉLEZ DE GUEVARA, *El Diablo cojuelo* (ed. Rodríguez Marín); LOPE DE VEGA, *Amar sin saber a quién;* CALDERÓN, *La Vida es Sueño; Spanish Ballads* (ed. Morley); FITZMAURICE-KELLY, *Historia de la Literatura española.* Three hours a week.

4*b*. Composition and oral exercises; lectures in Spanish on the art, history, and literature of Spain and Spanish America. Two hours a week.

4*c*. Essays on prescribed topics.

Phonetics.

Elementary physiological phonetics, with practical exercises in the sounds of the modern languages studied. One hour a week in the Second Year of the Modern Language Course.

HISTORY.

G. M. WRONG, M.A.......................................*Professor.*
R. HODDER WILLIAMS, M.A......................*Associate Professor.*
G. M. SMITH, M.A..............................*Associate Professor.*
R. FLENLEY, M.A., B.LITT....................*Associate Professor.*
W. P. M. KENNEDY, M.A., LITT.D.................*Assistant Professor.*
W. S. WALLACE, M.A..............................*Special Lecturer.*
S. H. HOOKE, M.A., B.D.........................*Special Lecturer.*
MISS M. C. WRONG, M.A...............................*Instructor.*
E. H. BLAKE, M.A....................................*Instructor.*

First Year.

1*a*. The History of Canada to 1763.
1*b*. An introduction to Mediaeval History.
1*c*. An introduction to Constitutional History.
1*d*. An introduction to Historical Geography.

Second Year.

2*a*. (i) The History of the British Empire from 1763 to the present time, with special reference to Canada.

(ii) The American Revolution and the framing of the Constitution of the United States.

2*b*. The History of England from 1485 to 1558 with an outline of the chief features of the Continental Renaissance.

2*c*. The History of England from 1558 to 1660.

2*d*. The Constitutional History of England to 1603.

2*e*. The Middle Ages: a general study of mediaeval society and an outline of the principal movements of the period.

2*f*. Selected texts in Modern History.

Third Year.

3*a*. Eighteenth Century Europe, the French Revolution and the Age of Napoleon.

3*b*. The History of England from 1660 to 1815.

3*c*. The Constitutional History of England since 1603. The working of modern British Institutions.

3*d*. The British Constitution and its development.

Fourth Year.

4a. British and European History from 1815 to the present time.

(i) British Domestic History and Foreign Policy.

(ii) Modern France, *or* Modern Germany *or* Modern Italy.

(iii) The History of the United States in the 19th Century with special reference to the Civil War.

4b. The History of England since 1815.

4c. The Constitutional History of Canada with references to Australia and South Africa and to other federal systems.

Third and Fourth Years.

5. A special subject studied with reference to original authorities. The following subjects, of which one shall be chosen, are offered for the year 1920-21:

(a) The American Revolution, 1775-1781, with special reference to Loyalist opinion.

(b) The Revolutions of 1848.

(c) Modern Egypt—from the British occupation to the British Protectorate.

(d) The Peace Treaties of 1919.

(e) The Theory and Practice of Representative Government.

6. A Course in Political Theory based on the study of Aristotle: Politics. Students will be required to show a knowledge of the history of political thought and to read from the works of Machiavelli, Hobbes, Rousseau, Burke, J. S. Mill, and Maine.

All Years.

Students are examined in Historical Geography in connection with the periods prescribed for Political History in each year.

Essays are required from Honours students in tutorial classes and from students of the Pass Course.

General Statement.

The Honour Course in Modern History includes the following historical subjects: (1) The Social and Political History of England since 1485, (2) the continuous Constitutional History of England (on a documentary basis) and the working of modern British Institutions, (3) an introductory study of European History in the Middle Ages and during the Renaissance Period, (4) the general History of Europe since the French Revolution, (5) the continuous History of Canada (including Constitutional History and the working of present day Canadian Institutions), (6) the continuous History of the American Colonies and the United States (with special stress on the Revolutionary Period and the Civil War), (7) a special historical subject, studied with reference to original authorities.

It also includes: (1) Periods of English Literature connected in each year with the periods of English Social and Political History, (2) Political Theory, (3) Economic History with Economic Theory, (4) One Modern Language (French *or* German) for reading purposes, (5) Political and Descriptive Geography.

The historical prescription in the Honour Course of Political Science lays stress upon the Political and Constitutional History of Canada and England and upon General History since 1763.

In the English and History Course, the stress is laid upon the Social and Political History of England but students may take additional options of General History in the Third and Fourth Years.

The Pass Course in Modern History includes: (1) the Mediaeval Period, (2) the general History of Europe (including Great Britain) since the French Revolution, (3) the History of Canada since 1763 (including Constitutional History), (4) the History of the American Colonies and the United States since 1763, (5) the working of modern British Institutions.

POLITICAL ECONOMY.

JAMES MAVOR, PH.D.....................................*Professor.*
R. M. MACIVER, M.A., D.PHIL...................*Associate Professor.*
W. JACKMAN, M.A.............................*Assistant Professor.*
G. E. JACKSON, B.A...........................*Assistant Professor.*
H. A. INNES, M.A., PH.D.............................*Lecturer.*
H. MARSHALL, B.A....................................*Lecturer.*
H. R. KEMP, M.A......................................*Lecturer.*

1. (*a*) Term essays (*b*) January examinations may be held in certain subjects concluded in the first term.

Second Year: The first essay in the Second Year shall be a topographical and economic account of the student's home town, city, county or district. A printed outline indicating the plan to be followed may be obtained from the Registrar. This essay shall be due on the second Wednesday in November. The other essays are on subjects to be prescribed during the session.

Third Year: The subjects are to be selected after consultation with the Professor on topics connected with Economic Theory.

Fourth Year: The subjects are to be selected after consultation with the staff, on topics connected with the work of the year.

First Year.

2. Economic Geography. The course consists of an account of Physical Geography in its economic aspects, the natural resources of the chief countries, ways and communications, ancient and modern trade routes together with an account of the more important economic changes of

modern times. Books recommended: NEWBIGIN, *Modern Geography;* LYDE, *Short Commercial Geography;* GREGORY, KELLER AND BISHOP, *Physical and Commercial Geography;* ADAM, *Commercial Geography;* CHISHOLM, *Commercial Geography; Consular Reports,* Great Britain and United States. Twenty-five hours.

3. Elements of Economics. An introduction to the study of economic theory. The following text-book is recommended, JOHNSON's *Introduction to Economics.* Twenty-five hours.

4. Elements of Commerce. A general account of commercial practice, movements of prices and their causes. The following books are recommended: CLAY, *Economics for the General Reader;* MARSHALL's *Reading in Industrial Society.*

Second Year.

5. General introduction to the study of Political Economy. The following works will' be found useful: CLAY, *Economics for the General Reader;* MARSHALL, *Economics of Industry;* CHAPMAN, *Political Economy;* TAUSSIG, *Principles of Economics;* ADAM SMITH, *Wealth of Nations;* JOHN STUART MILL, *Principles of Political Economy;* BLAND, BROWN AND TAWNEY, *English Economic History, Select Documents;* HOBSON, *Evolution of Modern Capitalism;* MANTOUX, *La Revolution Industrielle;* BEVERIDGE, *Unemployment;* LAYTON, *Introduction to the Study of Prices; Wholesale Prices,* Canada; *Labour Gazette* (Ottawa); and *Census of Canada.* Fifty hours.

6. Canadian Economic History and Descriptive Economics. (a) An account of the economic organization of Society under the French régime. The development of agriculture, transportation, industry and commerce since 1763. Books recommended: MUNRO, *The Seigneurial System in Canada;* MUNRO, *Documents relating to Seigneurial Tenure in Canada;* PORRITT, *Sixty Years of Protection in Canada;* MAVOR, *Economic History of Canada; Census of Canada; Archives of Canada and of Ontario; Canada and its Provinces,* Vols. 2, 4, 5, 9, 10; county histories. (b) An account of the exploitation of the natural resources and of the principal industries and industrial centres of Canada. Books recommended: *British Association Handbook of Canada,* 1897; MAVOR, *Report on North-West of Canada;* GÉRIN, *L'habitant de Saint-Justin;* MÈTIN, *La Colombie Britannique;* HOPKINS, *Canada, an Encyclopædia;* HOPKINS, *Canadian Annual Review;* PORRITT, *The Revolt against the New Feudalism;* ALEXANDER HAMILTON INSTITUTE, *Modern Business,* 12 volumes; *Canada Year Book.* Twenty-five hours.

7. Economic History and Theory with special reference to the eighteenth and nineteenth centuries. Books recommended for study: CLAY, *Economics for the General Reader;* GIBBINS, *Industry in England;* RAND, *Economic History since 1763;* TOYNBEE, *Industrial Revolution;* WEBB, *History of Trade Unionism in England;* HOBSON, *Evolution of Modern Capitalism.* Twenty-five hours.

8. General Introduction to the Study of Economics. For Pass students. Elements of Economic Theory, Sketch of Economic History, and of important social changes and movements. GIDE, *Political Economy*. Fifty hours.

9. Rural Economics. (For Honour students). Fundamental economic principles as applied to rural conditions. Problems of production, marketing, financing, rural organization. Books recommended: Publications of the International Institute of Agriculture; NOURSE, *Agricultural Economics; Reports of the National Conference on Marketing and Farm Credits;* Reports and other publications of the British Board of Agriculture; reports and investigations of the departments of agriculture in the United States and Canada. Fifty hours.

Third Year.

10a. History of Economic Theory. The following books are recommended. MUN, *England's Treasure by Foreign Trade;* TURGOT, *Reflections on the Formation and the Distribution of Riches;* ADAM SMITH, *Wealth of Nations,* ed. Nicholson; RICARDO's *Works,* ed. Gonner; INGRAM, *History of Political Economy;* HANEY, *History of Economic Thought;* ASHLEY, *Economic History,* Part I. Chap. 3, Part II. Chap. 6; SEWALL, *Theory of Value before Adam Smith* (Publications of American Economic Association, 1901); BONAR, *Philosophy and Political Economy;* NYS, *Researches in the History of Economics;* GIDE AND RIST, *History of Economic Doctrines* (tr. Richards). Thirty-seven hours.

10b. History of Economic Theory. An introductory course for Honour students in Philosophy, with the same subject matter as course 10a.

11a. Criticism of current economic theories of value, interest, rent and wages. The following books are recommended: TAUSSIG, *Principles of Economics;* J. S. MILL, *Principles of Political Economy;* MARSHALL, *Principles of Economics* and *Industry and Trade;* BÖHM-BAWERK, *Capital and Interest,* and the *Positive Theory of Capital* (trans. Smart); WIESER, *Natural Value;* SMART, *Introduction to the Theory of Value;* NICHOLSON, *Principles of Economics;* HOBSON, *Economics of Distribution;* J. B. CLARK, *Distribution of Wealth;* PIERSON, *Principles of Economics.* Thirty-seven hours.

11b. An introductory course for Honour students in Philosophy on the subject matter of course 11a.

12. International Trade: The history and theory of international trade description of current methods in international commerce. Books recommended: BASTABLE, *Theory of International Trade* and· *Commerce of Nations;* TAUSSIG, *Tariff History of the U.S.;* McLEAN, *Tariff History of Canada;* PORRITT, *Sixty Years of Protection in Canada;* RABBENO, *American Commercial Policy;* FUCHS, *The Trade Policy of Great Britain;* ASHLEY, *Modern Tariff History.* Twenty-five hours.

13. Foreign Exchange: The principles and practice of foreign exchange; the movements of credits. Books recommended: GOSCHEN, *Theory of Foreign Exchanges;* CLARE, *A, B, C of the Foreign Exchange.* Five hours.

14. Money: Functions of money, standard money, legal tender, Gresham's law, quantity theory, bimetallism, monetary systems and policies of the leading countries. Books recommended: BAGEHOT, *Lombard Street;* JEVONS, *Money and the Mechanism of Exchange;* NICHOLSON, *Banker's Money;* L. L. PRICE, *Money and Prices;* NICHOLSON, *Money and Monetary Problems;* WITHERS, *The Meaning of Money;* NELSON, *A, B, C of Wall Street;* KINLEY, *Money;* HULL (edit.), *Practical Problems in Banking and Currency;* NOYES, *Forty Years of American Finance;* LAYTON, *Introduction to the Study of Prices.* Twenty-five hours.

15. Money: Advanced course (primarily intended for students in the graduating departments of Commerce and of Commerce and Finance). Books recommended: LAUGHLIN, *Principles of Money;* IRVING FISHER, *Purchasing Power of Money.* Twelve hours.

16. Statistics: An outline of the history of statistics, methods of statistical analysis and study of statistical problems. Text-books and works of reference are: KING, *Elements of Statistical Method;* BOWLEY, *Introductory Manual of Statistics;* MEITZEN, *History, Theory and Technique of Statistics* (supp. vol. to Annals of American Academy of Political and Social Science, Philadelphia, 1891); *Census Reports,* Canada, Great Britain, and U.S.; *Canada Year Book.* Thirteen hours.

17. Statistics: Advanced course (primarily intended for students in the graduating departments of Commerce and of Commerce and Finance). BOWLEY, *Elements of Statistics.* See also article, "Statistics", in *Encyclopædia Britannica; the Statesman's Year Book;* BLOCK, *Traité théorique et pratique de Statistique;* GEORG VON MAYR, *Statistik und Gesellschaftslehre;* publications of Royal Statistical Society; publications of the American Statistical Association; reports of Ontario Bureau of Industries; *Statistical Abstract for the United Kingdom; Labour Gazette* (Ottawa). Thirteen hours.

18. Economic history from the early Middle Ages down to 1776. Books recommended: ASHLEY, *Economic History,* Parts I., II.; SEEBOHM, *English Village Community;* MEREDITH, *Economic History of England;* UNWIN, *Industrial Organization in the Sixteenth and Seventeenth Centuries;* MAVOR, *Economic History of Russia;* VINOGRADOFF, *The Growth of the Manor;* VINOGRADOFF, *Villenage in England;* GOMME, *The Village Community;* GROSS, *Gild Merchant,* Chaps. 1-4; ROGERS, *Six Centuries of Work and Wages,* Chaps. 1-6, 8-10; CUNNINGHAM, *Growth of English Industry and Commerce;* LIPSON, *The Economic History of England—Middle Ages;* BLAND, BROWN AND TAWNEY, *English Economic History, Select Documents.* Twenty-five hours.

19. Economic Theory. Books recommended: CLAY, *Economics for the General Reader;* MARSHALL, *Economics of Industry;* CHAPMAN, *Outlines of Political Economy;* GIDE AND RIST, *History of Economic Doctrines;* TAUSSIG,

Principles of Economics; ADAM SMITH, *Wealth of Nations;* MALTHUS on *Population;* MILL, *Principles of Political Economy;* SPARGO, *Socialism.* Seventy-five hours.

Fourth Year.

20. Economic history from 1776 till the present time. Books recommended: CUNNINGHAM, *Growth of English Industry and Commerce in Modern Times,* Part II.; SMITH, *The Free Trade Movement;* SMART, *The Return to Protection;* JEVONS, *The State in Relation to Labour;* BAINES, URE, and other histories of special industries; MANTOUX, *La Révolution Industrielle;* TOYNBEE, *Industrial Revolution;* PROTHERO, *English Farming, Past and Present;* WEBB, *History of Trade ·Unionism;* BLAND, BROWN AND TAWNEY, *English Economic History, Select Documents; Poor Law Commission Reports;* PORTER, *Progress of the Nation;* JACKMAN, *Transportation in Modern England.* Thirty-seven hours.

21. Recent Economic Development. Books recommended: HOBSON, *Evolution of Modern Capitalism;* LAYTON, *Introduction to the Study of Prices;* WELLS, *Recent Economic Changes.* The following official reports should also be consulted: *Canada, Census of 1911; U.S. Census Reports; Great Britain, Reports of Royal Commissions on Labour, Depression of Trade and Industry, Shipping Rings* and the *Poor Laws;* also reports of various committees on reconstruction. Thirteen hours.

22. Labour Problems: An account of the rise of trade unionism in England and America and a comparison of the labour legislation of leading countries. Books recommended: WEBB, *Industrial Democracy;* ELY, *The Labour Movement in America;* CLARK, *The Labour Movement in Australasia;* SEAGER, *Social Insurance;* COMMONS, *Principles of Labour Legislation;* COMMONS, *History of Labour in the United States;* HOXIE, *Trade Unionism in the United States; Bulletins of the U.S. Bureau of Labour; Labour Gazette* (English); *The Labour Gazette* (Canadian). Thirteen hours.

23. Transportation: An account of ocean and land transportation and its bearing upon commercial and industrial development. Railway policy, its history in Europe and America, railway rates, etc. Books recommended: HADLEY, *Railway Transportation;* MAVOR, *English Railway Rates;* BROWN, *Transportation Rates and their Regulation;* ACWORTH, *Elements of Railway Economics;* MACGIBBON, *Railway Rates and the Canadian Railway Commission;* KNOOP, *Outlines of Railway Economics;* H. R. MEYER, *Government Regulation of Railway Rates;* JOHNSON AND VAN METRE, *Principles of Railroad Transportation;* McLEAN, *Governmental Regulation of Railways in the United States;* McLEAN *The St. Lawrence Route* (Railway Age). Thirteen hours.

24. Transportation: Advanced course (primarily intended for students in the graduating department of Commerce and Finance); the technique of railway rate making, the finances and administration of railways, marine transportation, docks. Books recommended as in preceding section, together with JOHNSON, *Ocean and Inland Transportation.* Twelve hours.

25. Banking: Nature and functions of a bank, management of the reserve, commercial banks and saving banks, clearing house system, trust companies, comparative study of banking policy. Books recommended: DUNBAR, *Theory and History of Banking;* BAGEHOT, *Lombard Street;* CONANT, *Modern Banks of Issue;* HOLDSWORTH, *Money and Banking;* SCOTT, *Money and Banking;* JOHNSON, *Report on the Canadian Banking System;* HAGERTY, *Mercantile Credit;* CANNON, *Clearing Houses;* KIRKBRIDE AND STERRETT, *The Modern Trust Company.* Thirteen hours.

26. Banking: Advanced course (primarily intended for students in the graduating department of Commerce and Finance). Books recommended: *Publications of the National Monetary Commission* (U.S.). Twelve-hours.

27. Corporation Finance: Economic services of corporations, capitalization, stocks and bonds, problems of financial management, corporation reports, method of control, public policy in regard to corporations, speculation on the stock exchange. Books recommended: H. WITHERS, *Stocks and Shares;* DUGUID, *The Stock Exchange;* RIPLEY, *Trusts, Pools and Corporations* (assigned portions); GERSTENBERG, *Materials of Corporation Finance;* PRATT, *The Work of Wall Street;* MEADE, *Corporation Finance.* Thirteen hours.

28. Public Finance: National and local finance, history of financial science, public debts and the policy of national and local governments in relation to their issue, administration and redemption; administration of the public domain—lands, forests, minerals. Books recommended: BASTABLE, *Public Finance;* LEROY-BEAULIEU, *Science des Finances*, Livre II., Chaps. 4, 5, 9, 10; PLEHN, *Public Finance;* COHN, *The Science of Finance;* SELIGMAN, *Essays on Taxation.* Twenty-five hours.

29. Theory of Taxation: Principles of taxation; incidence of taxation; progressive taxation. Books recommended: SELIGMAN, *The Incidence of Taxation;* SELIGMAN, *Progressive Taxation* (American Econ. Assn., 1909). Five hours.

30. Revenue systems of Modern States: Revenue systems of Great Britain, Germany, France, United States and Canada. Federal, provincial and municipal revenues. Methods of taxation of land, and of individuals and corporations. Books recommended: Official reports of taxing authorities in the various countries; J. W. GRICE, *National and Local Finance;* SELIGMAN, *The Income Tax;* KENNAN, *Income Taxation;* PLEHN, *The Property Tax in California;* MAVOR, *Taxation of Banks in Canada, Taxation of Corporations in Canada* (State and Local Taxation Conference, 1908). Thirteen hours.

31. History and Criticism of Political Theories. Books recommended: HOBBES, *Leviathan;* LOCKE, *On Civil Government;* ROUSSEAU, *Social Contract;* SIDGWICK, *Elements of Politics;* POLLOCK, *History of the Science of Politics;* BONAR, *Philosophy and Political Economy;* RITCHIE, *Principles of State Interference;* SEELEY, *Introduction to Political Science;* MACKENZIE, *Introduction to Social Philosophy;* BARKER, *Political Thought of Plato and*

Aristotle; and *Political Thought 'from Spencer to the Present Day;* LASKI, *Studies in the Problems of Sovereignty,* and *Authority in the Modern State;* DUGUIT, *The Law and the State.* Twenty-five hours.

32. Comparative Politics: An account of the contemporary political systems of modern nations, especially Great Britain, the self-governing Dominions, and the Dependencies; Germany, France and the United States. The political institutions, methods of election of representatives and political parties of these countries, contemporary projects of change— direct legislation, the referendum, proportional representation, etc. Literature: LOWELL, *The Government of England;* LOWELL, *Governments and Parties in Continental Europe;* BODLEY, *France;* HOWARD, *The German Empire;* BRYCE, *American Commonwealth;* CROMER, *Ancient and Modern Imperialism;* JEBB, *Colonial Nationalism.* Twelve hours.

33. Public Administration: A comparative account of methods of central and local administration, professional and non-professional methods, departmental administration. "Good government" movements in various countries. Books recommended: LOWELL, *The Government of England;* REDLICH AND HURST, *Local Government in England; English Citizen Series,* (Macmillan); *Reports of conferences on Good City Government.* Thirteen hours.

34. A General Sketch of Economic History. Books recommended: SELIGMAN, *The Economic Interpretation of History;* BLAND, BROWN AND TAWNEY, *English Economic History;* BOGART AND THOMPSON, *Readings in the Economic History of the United States;* GIBBINS, *Industry in England;* DAY, *A History of Commerce;* LIPSON, *Economic History of England;* PERRIS, *Industrial History of Modern England;* PROTHERO, *English Farming;* HAMMOND, *The Village Labourer, The Town Labourer, The Skilled Labourer;* WEBB, *Trade Unionism;* COMMONS, *Principles of Labour Legislation;* COLE, *The World of Labour;* FAIRCHILD, *Immigration;* LEVY, *Monopoly and Competition;* LAYTON, *Introduction to the Study of Prices.* Fifty hours.

(35. Social Problems: A post-graduate class held by Professor Mavor for candidates for the degree of M.A. and Ph.D. in subjects selected by them.

36. Business Administration. Special lectures by experts on aspects and methods of business administration, *e.g.,* employment management, buying and selling, advertising, etc. About twenty hours.

LAW.

T. H. BLACK, M.A., B.Sc., LL.B.......*Professor of Roman Law and Jurisprudence.*
A. R. CLUTE, B.A., LL.B.............*Lecturer in Constitutional Law.*
H. W. A. FOSTER, LL.B...*Lecturer in Commercial and International Law.*

1. History of English Law. Anglo-Saxon Customs and Dooms. The Norman century: feudal tenures and Church Courts. Foundation of the Common Law: writs and jury-trial. Legislation of Edward I. Expansion of the Common Law: entails; contracts and torts. Equity. Development

by legislation and decisions. Struggle between Chancery and Common Law Courts in the reign of James I. Reform by Equity. Legislation and Common Law before the Reform Bill period. Rigidity of the Equity system. Progress by legislation in England and Ontario. For reference: MAITLAND AND MONTAGUE, *A Sketch of English Legal History* (Putnam, 1915); POLLOCK AND MAITLAND, *History of English Law* (Book I.); STORRY DEANS, *Student's Legal History;* JENKS, *Short History of English Law.*

2. Roman Law. 1. History: The early legal system and procedure by *legis actiones*. The Twelve Tables statute. Republican law: development by *jus civile* of the jurisconsults and by the praetor's edict; procedure by *formula*. The Principate: equity, *jus gentium* or *jus naturale;* development of rigidity in the law. Absolute Monarchy: codification by imperial legislation; Justinian's system. 2. Elements of Private Law: law of persons, family, and slaves. Law of inheritance, legacies and trust-bequests. Law of property. *Obligationes:* contract and delict. Text-books: SOHM, *Institutes of Roman Law* (Ledlie's translation); SANDARS or MOYLE, *Justinian's Institutes*. For general reading and reference: GAIUS, *Institutes*. GIRARD, *Manuel*, or ROBY, *Roman Private Law;* chapter 44, of GIBBON, *Decline and Fall;* and the Article on "*Roman Law*" in last edition of Encyclopædia Britannica, *or* MUIRHEAD,*Historical Introduction to the Private Law of Rome.*

3. Jurisprudence. Scope of the science; definition and analysis of *law* and of *rights;* solution of disputes by inflexible rules or by juridical determination. Classification of legal rights and the departments of law. Sources of law and the juridical development of law. Jurisprudence of legal personality; family; succession; trusts; property; contract; delict or tort; evidence and procedure; public rights. Application of the methods of Jurisprudence to International Law. Text-books: T. E. HOLLAND, *Elements of Jurisprudence;* SIR H. MAINE, *Ancient Law* with Pollock's notes. For general reading and reference: SALMOND, *Jurisprudence;* MAINE, Lectures XII., XIII., in *Early History of Institutions;* SIR F. POLLOCK, *First Book of Jurisprudence;* SIR H. MAINE'S works so far as not above specified; and BRYCE, *Lectures on History and Jurisprudence.*

4. A course in Federal Constitutional Law. The lectures deal with the essential features of federal government in a comparative view of the leading federal States. Special attention is given to the constitutions of Canada, Australia, South Africa, and the United States. Text-books: LEFROY, *Short Treatise on Canadian Constitutional Law, Leading Cases in Canadian Constitutional Law;* KENNEDY, *Canadian Constitutional Documents;* BRYCE, *American Commonwealth* (Vol. I.); WOODROW WILSON, *Congressional Government;* POLEY, *Federal Systems of the United States and the British Empire.*

5. A course in English Constitutional Law, in which the distinctive features of the English Constitution, the Rule of Law and the Sovereignty of Parliament, the two Houses of Parliament, the Cabinet and the relation to the Crown and Parliament, the prerogative, the conventions, the Courts, and the position of the subject under English law, are the principal topics.

Students are recommended to read: Dicey, *Law of the Constitution;* Anson, *Law and Custom of the Constitution;* Thomas, *Leading Constitutional Cases;* Low, *Governance of England;* Marriott, *English Political Institutions;* Ridge, *Constitutional Law.*

6. A course in Colonial Constitutional Law, in which the lectures deal with the various forms of colonial government with special reference to the self-governing colonies and to current problems. Students are recommended to read: Todd, *Parliamentary Government in the Colonies* (to page 318); and either Tarring, *Law in Relation to the Colonies;* Jenkyns, *British Rule and Jurisprudence beyond the Seas;* or the section on Colonies and Dependencies in Halsbury, *Laws of England.*

7. International Law: 1. The nature, history and sources of international law. 2. The subjects of international law: the notion of sovereignty and the classification of states; the origin, continuity and extinction of states; the independence of states, self-preservation and intervention; the equality of states, the system of Europe and the Monroe Doctrine. 3. The objects of international law: territorial sovereignty and state territory; modes of acquiring territory; territorial, boundary and international waters; the open sea; jurisdiction; nationality and alienage. 4. International intercourse; international agents; treaties; negotiation, mediation and arbitration; forcible measures short of war. 5. War: general notions; immediate legal effect; enemy character of persons; rule of non-intercourse; laws of war with regard to enemy persons; enemy character of property and laws of war with regard to property; military occupation; enemy merchantmen, their crews and cargoes; prize courts; instruments and methods of naval warfare; non-hostile intercourse of belligerents. 6. Neutrality: nature and history; violation and cessation; neutralization; the obligations of a neutral state; the duties of prevention, abstention and impartiality; the rights of a neutral state; inviolability of territory, right of asylum, right of commerce; nationals of neutral state subject to state law and to rights of belligerent states; visit and search; contraband of war; blockade; unneutral service. 7. For reference: (1) general treatises: Hall, Westlake, Lawrence, Oppenheim; (2) cases and documents: Moore, Cobbett, Scott, Whittuck, Lawrence, Evans; (3) prize court decisions, official documents relating to the late war and covenant of the League of Nations.

8. Commercial Law: General principles of the law of contracts. Rules relating to parties to contract; agency, partnership and companies. General view of the following: sale of goods, negotiable instruments, powers of banks, relation of banker and customer, insurance, carriage of goods, suretyship and guarantee, bills of sale and chattel mortgages, bankruptcy and insolvency. Text-book: Stephen, *Elements of Mercantile Law* (5 ed. 1911 by H. Jacobs). A larger book of a general character is Smith, *Mercantile Law.* The lecturer will if desired refer students to special works on any of the foregoing topics.

9. Commercial Law: A second course, an extension of Course 8.

PHILOSOPHY.

UNIVERSITY OF TORONTO:

J. G. HUME, A.M., PH.D......*Professor of History of Philosophy.*
G. S. BRETT, M.A.....................*Professor of Philosophy.*
T. R. ROBINSON, PH.D..........*Assistant Professor of Philosophy.*

UNIVERSITY COLLEGE:

F. TRACY, B.A., PH.D...,....................*Professor of Ethics.*

VICTORIA COLLEGE:

W. B. LANE, M.A., PH.D.....................*Professor of Ethics.*
W. T. BROWN, M.A., PH.D..........*Associate Professor of Ethics.*

TRINITY COLLEGE:

G. S. BRETT, M.A........*Professor of Ethics and Ancient Philosophy.*

ST. MICHAEL'S COLLEGE:

REV. D. CUSHING, LL.D............*Professor Emeritus of Cosmology.*
REV. H. CARR, B.A............*Professor of History of Philosophy.*
REV. F. G. POWELL................`.`.......*Professor of Philosophy.*
M. DEWULF, M.A., PH.D., LL.D., *Professor of Mediæval ·Philosophy.*
SIR BERTRAM C. A. WINDLE, M.A., M.D., SC.D., LL.D., F.R.S.,
Professor of Anthropology.
REV. E. J. McCORKELL, M.A........ *Professor of Social Ethics.*
REV. H. S. BELLISLE, M.A.....................*Professor of Logic.*
REV. M. J. OLIVER, B.A., PH.M.........*Professor of Psychology.*
REV. C. P. DONOVAN, B.A.................*Lecturer in Ethics.*

PASS COURSES.

2a. An Introductory Course in Philosophy. Two hours a week. The course will deal with the general problems of Philosophy.

3a. Social Ethics. Three hours a week. (1) Study of primitive morality, character of early societies, and lines of progress. (2) Greek morality as represented in Plato and Aristotle, with especial reference to (a) the intellectual ideals of Greece; (b) the development of democracy; (c) social conditions; (d) the expansion of Greek thought (Stoic and Epicurean systems), and the comparative study of Greek and Christian ideals. (3) Modern thought from Hobbes to Mill with special reference to (a) the transition from mediæval to modern thought; (b) the progress of individualism; (c) modern economic and social conditions in their ethical significance; (d) comparison of ancient and modern views of the state with reference to democracy. Prescribed texts: PLATO, *Republic*, Books I.-IV.; ARISTOTLE, *Politics*, Books I., VII., VIII.; HOBBES, *Leviathan*, Book I.; J. S. MILL, *Utilitarianism*. References: DARWIN, *Descent of Man;* MAINE, *Ancient Law;* ARISTOTLE, *Ethics;* ROGERS, *Short History of Ethics;* SIDGWICK, *History of Ethics;* Brett, *The Government of Man;* J. G. Hume, *Political Economy and Ethics;* Dewey and Tufts, *Ethics;* James Seth, *A Study of Ethical Principles.*

3*b.* History of Philosophy. History of the Problems of Ancient and Mediæval Philosophy. Three hours a week. Texts: Plato *Republic;* Aristotle *Ethics;* works of reference as prescribed in the course of instruction.

4*a.* Modern Ethics. Three hours a week. The lectures will be (*a*) Historical, tracing the rise and development of the leading problems of ethics, and the formation of the chief schools and systems, Hedonist, Intuitionist, etc.; (*b*) Expository and critical. The following texts will be studied in the class, and their doctrines examined. Hume, *Enquiry concerning the Principles of Morals,* with Appendices; Spencer, *Data of Ethics;* J. G. Hume, *Young's Ethics of Freedom;* Green, *Prolegomena to Ethics.*

4*b.* History of Philosophy. History of the problems of Modern Philosophy with special reference to British Philosophy. Three hours a week. References: Seth, *English Philosophers and Philosophical Schools;* Calkins, *The Persistent Problems of Philosophy;* Cushman, *History of Philosophy,* Vol. II.; Rand, *Classical Philosophers;* A. D. Lindsay, *Kant;* M. M. Waddington, *The Development of British Thought.*

HONOUR COURSES.

1*a.* Introductory Course in Philosophy—Ethics. Two hours a week. Prescribed text: Johnston, *An Introduction to Ethics.*

2*b.* Ethics. Elementary Course. Two hours a week. Outline study of the subject matter and method of Ethics, with its leading problems and schools. Ethical development among the Hebrews, Greeks and Romans.

Prescribed texts: MacKenzie, *Manual of Ethics;* Selections from the Old Testament; Plato, *Republic;* Aristotle, *Nicomachean Ethics;* Cicero, *De Finibus,* and from other Greek and Roman writers, as given in Bakewell, *Source Book in Ancient Philosophy.*

References: Rogers, *Short History of Ethics;* Muirhead, *Elements of Ethics;* Seth, *Ethical Principles;* Dewey and Tufts, *Ethics;* Watson, *Hedonistic Theories;* Mitchell, *Ethics of the Old Testament.*

2*c.* Logic. One hour a week. Introductory Course. Development of Logic among the Greeks. Texts: Plato, *Theaetetus, Republic;* Aristotle, *Organon* (Selections); Creighton, *Introductory Logic.*

2*d.* History of Philosophy. Two hours a week. Texts: Locke, *Essay on the Human Understanding.* Berkeley, *Principles of Knowledge.*

3*c.* Ethics. Two hours a week. Modern Ethics from Hobbes to Spencer, with special attention to the Ethics of Naturalism. Exposition and criticism of Hedonism, Utilitarianism, and Evolutionism.

Prescribed texts: HOBBES, *Leviathan;* HUME, *Enquiry concerning the Principles of Morals;* MILL, *Utilitarianism;* SPENCER, *Data of Ethics;* together with other selections, from RAND, *Classical Moralists,* or SELBY-BIGGE, *British moralists.*

References: ALBEE, *History of English Utilitarianism;* WATSON, *Hedonistic Theories;* SORLEY, *The Ethics of Naturalism;* MARTINEAU, *Types of Ethical Theory;* RASHDALL, *Theory of Good and Evil.*

3d. History of Philosophy. Modern Philosophy. (a) The rationalistic school; selections from Des-Cartes, Spinoza, Leibnitz. Two hours a week; (b) The empirical school; selections from Hume, Mill, Spencer, James. One hour a week.

3e. Logic. Fifty hours. (a) Development of Logic from Aristotle to Bacon. (b) Empirical Logic and Scientific Methods.* Texts: BACON, *Novum Organum and Advancement of Learning;* J. S. MILL, *A System of Logic;* HOBHOUSE, *Theory of Knowledge.*

4c. Ethics. Two hours a week. Rationalism and Idealism. Exposition and Criticism of the Ethics of Kant and T. H. Green. Discussion of selected problems in Ethics.

Prescribed texts: KANT, *Groundwork of the Metaphysic of Ethics,* and *Critique of Practical Reason;* GREEN, *Prolegomena to Ethics.*

References: CAIRD, *The Critical Philosophy of Kant;* WATSON, *The Philosophy of Kant Explained.*

4d. Social Ethics. Two hours a week. (1) The evolution of society; philosophy of social progress, its nature and the forces directing it. (2) Theories of the mutual relation of the state and the individual; grounds of political obligation. (3) Modern social conditions and problems. Texts: FAIRBANKS, *Introduction to Sociology;* GREEN, *Theory of Political Obligation;* ELWOOD, *Sociology and Modern Social Problems.*

4e. History of Philosophy. (a) KANT, *Critique of Pure Reason* (Michaelmas Term). (b) Modern Systems after Kant (Easter Term). Three hours a week.

4f. Logic. (a) Michaelmas Term. Development of Modern Logic: historical and critical. (b) Easter Term. Students will be required to make independent studies of selected theories or works in the sphere of general logic (nature of knowledge, principles of investigation, method of philosophical criticism). Two hours a week.

St. Michael's College.

PASS COURSES.

2e. Introduction to Philosophy. A presentation of the leading problems of philosophy with something of their historical setting. Two hours a week during the Michaelmas term. Prescribed texts: M. DE WULF, *History of Mediæval Philosophy;* PLATO, *Republic;* ARISTOTLE, *Politics;* CICERO, *De Finibus;* Encyclopedia articles.

2f. An outline of Greek philosophic thought.   Two hours a week during the Easter term.

3f. General Philosophy.   Modern physical and chemical views in relation to the conception of matter and form; the uniformity of the Universe and the orderliness of Nature; proofs of the existence of God; the argument from design.   Two hours a week.

3g. Logic.   The standpoint and problem of Logic; important stages in the development of Logic; the syllogism; the problem of induction; assumptions of induction; the laws of thought; types of judgment; nature of inference; science and philosophy; philosophy as the interpretation of the sciences.   Prescribed texts: BOSANQUET, *Essentails of Logic;* JOYCE, *Principles of Logic;* MILL, *Logic;* COFFEY, *Science of Logic;* BUTCHER, *Aspects of Greek Genius, Essay on the Unity of Learning.*

3h. Psychology.   An introductory course.   A study of common human experiences presenting the main problems of Psychology; various fields of consciousness and methods of study: normal, human, adult psychology. Prescribed texts: MAHER, *Psychology,* Part I.; Manuals by BREESE, DUBRAY and MERCIER.

3i. General Ethics.   An analysis of the idea of the Good with a criticism of the various theories; the problem of Duty; the Virtues.   Two hours a week.   Prescribed texts: CRONIN, *Science of Ethics,* Vol. I.; MACDONALD. *Principles of Morality;* RICKABY, *Moral Philosophy;* MING, *Data of Ethics,*

4g. General Philosophy.   The cell and cellular life; Bio- and Abiogenesis; development, vegetable and animal kingdoms; vitalism, Geology and early man; races of mankind; transformism; the origin of man.   Two hours a week.

4h. Metaphysics.   The nature and need of Metaphysics; the notion of Being; essence and existence; unity, truth, and goodness of Being; the possibilities of Being; the finite and infinite in Being; substance and accident; personality; causality; relation, space, and time.   Two hours a week.

4i. Psychology.   A study of the nature of the human mind; the mind-body relation; psychical research.   Two hours a week.   Text: MAHER, *Psychology,* Part II.; BARRET, *Psychical Research;* McDOUGALL, *Mind and Body.*

4j. Social Ethics.   The origin of rights; natural law; rights of the individual, of the family, of the state; the origin and role of authority; the problem of state-interference.   Prescribed texts: CRONIN, *Science of Ethics,* Vol. II.; MERCIER, *Manual of Modern Scholastic Philosophy;* RICKABY, *Aquinas Ethicus.*

HONOUR COURSES.

1b. A course of lectures on the elements of moral science.   Two hours a week.

—14

2g. Introduction to Philosophy. A presentation of the leading problems of philosophy with something of their historical setting. Two hours a week during the Michaelmas term. Prescribed texts: M. DE WULF, *History of Mediæval Philosophy;* PLATO, *Republic;* ARISTOTLE, *Politics;* CICERO, *De Finibus;* Encyclopedia articles.

2h. An outline of Greek philosophic thought. Two hours a week during the Easter term.

2i. Logic. The standpoint and problem of Logic; important stages in the development of Logic; the syllogism; the problem of induction; assumptions of induction; the laws of thought; types of judgment; nature of inference; science and philosophy; philosophy as the interpretation of the sciences. Prescribed texts: BOSANQUET, *Essentials of Logic;* JOYCE, *Principles of Logic;* MILL, *Logic;* COFFEY, *Science of Logic;* BUTCHER, *Aspects of Greek Genius, Essay on the unity of Learning.*

2j. Seminar in Logic. Special problems arising from the reading of DESCARTES' *Method* and NEWMAN's *Grammar of Assent.* One hour.

2k. Psychology. An introductory course. A study of common human experiences presenting the main problems of Psychology; various fields of consciousness and methods of study; normal, human, adult psychology. Two hours a week. Prescribed texts: MAHER, *Psychology,* Part I.; Manuals by BREESE, DUBRAY and MERCIER.

2l. Social Psychology. Behaviour and action; theories of action. One hour a week. Reference: W. McDOUGALL, *Social Psychology.*

2m. General Ethics. An analysis of the idea of the Good, with a criticism of the various theories; the problem of Duty; the Virtues. Two hours a week. Prescribed texts: CRONIN, *Science of Ethics,* Vol. I.; McDONALD, *Principles of Morality;* RICKABY, *Aquinas Ethicus;* MING, *Data of Ethics.*

3j. General Philosophy. Modern chemical and physical views in relation to the conception of Matter and Form, the uniformity of the Universe and the orderliness of Nature; proofs of the existence of God; the argument from design. Two hours a week.

3k. Logic. The problems of Epistemology, scepticism, positivism, dogmatism; exposition and criticism of each; knowledge and the external world; critical study of DESCARTES, LOCKE and HUME from this viewpoint; the criteria of valid knowledge. One hour.

3l. Seminar in Logic. Discussion of the problems arising from the reading of BERKELEY, *Principles of Knowledge; Essay on the Human Understanding;* HUME, *Inquiry Concerning the Human Understanding.* One hour.

3m. Metaphysics. The nature and need of Metaphysics; the notion of Being; essence and existence; unity, truth, and goodness of Being; the possibilities of Being; the finite and infinite in Being; substance and accident; personality; causality; relation, space and time. Two hours a week.

3*n*. Social Ethics. The origin of rights; natural law; rights of the individual, of the family, of the state; the origin and role of authority; the problem of state interference. Two hours. Prescribed texts: CRONON, *Science of Ethics*, Vol. II.; MERCIER, *Manual of Modern Scholastic Philosophy;* RICKABY, *Aquinas Ethicus.*

3*o*. Seminar in Social Ethics. Selected readings from PLATO, ARISTOTLE and ST. THOMAS.

3*p*. History of Mediæval Philosophy. Two hours a week.

4*l*. General Philosophy. The cell and cellular life; Bio- and Abiogenesis; development; vegetable and animal kingdoms; vitalism; Geology and early man; races of mankind; transfromism; the origin of man. Two hours a week.

4*m*. Epistemology. An investigation of the grounds of Certitude with special reference to HUME, KANT and J. S. MILL. One hour a week during the Michaelmas term.

4*n* Contemporary Thought. Bergson and British and American realists. One hour a week during the Easter term.

4*o*. Psychology. A study of the nature of the human mind; the mind-body relation; psychical research. Two hours a week. Prescribed texts: MAHER, *Psychology*, Part II.; Readings: BARRETT, *Psychical Research;* MCDOUGALL, *Mind and Body.*

4*p*. Seminar in Psychology. The History of Psychology. References: MERCIER, *The Origin of Modern Psychology;* BRETT, *History of Psychology.*

4*q*. Social Ethics. A course of lectures on the problem of distributive justice; the moral aspect of private property in land, profits, interest, wages. Three hours a week. Prescribed text: RYAN, *Distributive Justice.* Readings: RYAN, *Living Wage;* HILLQUIT-RYAN, *Socialism-Promise or Menace?;* SKELTON, *A Critical Analysis of Socialism,* HENRY GEORGE, *Progress and Poverty;* LEO XIII., *Aeterne Deus.*

4*r*. History of Modern Philosophy. Two hours a week.

4*s*. A dissertation on some selected topic in Philosophy to be chosen by the student and approved by the department on or before November 1.

PSYCHOLOGY DEPARTMENT.

1. Abnormal Psychology. Problem of the feebleminded, school life, adult life; intelligence tests as applied to children and their results; feebleminded and their relation to society; relation of Psychiatry to Psychology; drugs and their effect; heredity as a factor in insanity; general outline of diseases of the mind; treatment of mental diseases in general, results; duty of the state as a factor; cause of the increase of mental diseases.

PSYCHOLOGY

UNIVERSITY OF TORONTO:

    C. K. CLARKE, M.D., LL.D...............*Professor of Psychiatry.*
                    Director of the Psychological Department.
    W. G. SMITH, B.A.........................*Associate Professor.*
    E. A. BOTT, B.A..........................*Assistant Professor.*
    W. A. COOK, M.A.....................................*Lecturer.*

ST MICHAEL'S COLLEGE:

    REV. M. J. OLIVER, B.A., PH.M.......................*Professor.*
    V. A. McDONOUGH, M.B........................*Lecturer.*

Lectures.

A—COURSES IN THE FACULTY OF ARTS.
PASS COURSES.

2*a*. Elementary Psychology. Analysis of Sense Perception and more complex processes.

3*a*. The application of psychology to social conditions.

3*b*. Learning processes and educational measurements.

4*a*. Psychology as a factor in the history of human culture.

4*b*. Psychological aspects of educational theories from 17th century onwards.

HONOUR COURSES.

2*b*. Introduction to Psychology.

2*c*. History of Psychology with special reference to views bearing directly on seventeenth century thought.

3*c*. Psychology in its social applications. Intelligence tests with their history, methods and results. Seminary.

3*d*. General outline of psycho-physical measurement and methods of correlation.

3*e*. Instinct and motivation.

4*c*. Critical discussion of psychology in its outstanding definitions.

4*d*. Sight and hearing in relation to higher processes.

4*e*. Relation of psychiatry to psychology. History of the treatment of mental disease with special reference to State aid.

4*f*. Methods of social psychology in relation to allied sciences.

B—COURSES IN THE FACULTY OF MEDICINE.

2*d*. Introductory psychology for medical students (psychiatrical option).

3*f*. Special psychology for medical students. Short lecture course.

3*g*. Advanced course for medical students (psychiatrical option).

C—COURSES IN THE DEPARTMENT OF SOCIAL SERVICE.

1a. Introduction to psychological investigation. Behaviour of normals and abnormals in social life. Personal and family history.

2e. Mental Testing. History and standardisation of tests. The Binet-Simon scale with revisions. Application of methods to social problems.

Laboratory Work.

2f. Quantitative and qualitative analysis of sense-perception.

3h. Psycho-physical measurements.

3i. Learning processes and acquisition of skill (m).

3j. Experimental work in mental tests (e).

3k. Short course for medical students (psychiatrical option).

4g. Analysis of the higher processes.

4h. Selected laboratory problems for graduates and advanced students.

MATHEMATICS.

ALFRED BAKER, M.A., LL.D.....................*Professor Emeritus.*
A. T. DeLURY, M.A..*Professor.*
M. A. MACKENZIE, M.A...................................*Professor.*
J. C. FIELDS, B.A., PH.D., F.R.S..........................*Professor.*
S. BEATTY, PH.D...............................*Associate Professor.*
I. R. POUNDER, M.A...........................*Assistant Professor.*
J. L. SYNGE, B.A..............................*Assistant Professor.*
N. E. SHEPPARD, M.A......................................*Lecturer.*
A. B. STEVENSON, B.A..*Fellow.*
MISS M. E. G. WADDELL, M.A...............................*Fellow.*

A.—COURSES IN THE FACULTY OF ARTS.

PASS COURSES.

1a. Algebra: Simple equations of one, two and three unknown quantities; quadratic equations of one and two unknown quantities; elementary treatment of variation, proportion and progressions; interest forms and annuities. Text-book: DELURY, *Intermediate Algebra.* Twenty-five hours.

1b. Analytical Geometry: A course in elementary analytical geometry of two dimensions, establishing the more important properties of the conic sections. Text-book: BAKER, *Analytical Geometry for Beginners.* Twenty-five hours.

1c. Plane Trigonometry: Trigonometrical ratios with their relations to one another: sines, etc., of the sum and difference of angles, with deduced formulas; solution of triangles, expressions for the area of triangles; radii of circumscribed, inscribed and escribed circles. HALL AND KNIGHT, *Elementary Trigonometry.* Twenty-five hours.

2a. Algebra: A course in limits and infinite series, serving as an introduction to the calculus. Thirty-seven hours.

2*b*. Analytical Geometry: A review and extension of the earlier course in two dimensions, with special attention to the graphs of functions, and an elementary course in three dimensions treating of the plane, the line, the sphere and the conicoids. Thirty-seven hours.

3*a*. Differential and Integral Calculus. The elementary theory and applications. Seventy-five hours.

4*a*. Calculus and Differential Equations. A continuation of the course in the Third Year, with an elementary course in differential equations. Twenty-five hours.

4*b*. Geometry: A course in the modern methods of treating pure geometry. Fifty hours.

HONOUR COURSES.

1*d*. Algebra: Limits, infinite series with a special study of the binomial, exponential and logarithmic series, continued fractions, elementary number-theorems and determinants. Text-books: HALL AND KNIGHT, *Higher Algebra;* C. SMITH, *Treatise on Algebra;* CHRYSTAL, *Algebra.* Fifty hours.

1*e*. Analytical Geometry. An advanced course. Text-book: C. SMITH, *Conic Sections.* Fifty hours.

1*f*. Spherical Trigonometry. Text-book: TODHUNTER AND LEATHAM, *Spherical Trigonometry.* Ten hours.

1*g*. Analytical Trigonometry. De Moivre's Theorem and a study of the more important trigonometrical infinite series and infinite products. Text-books: TODHUNTER AND HOGG, *Plane Trigonometry;* HOBSON, *Trigonometry.* Fifteen hours.

2*c*. Differential and Integral Calculus: The elementary theory and applications. Text-book: OSGOOD, *Differential and Integral Calculus.* Fifty hours.

2*d*. Differential Calculus. An advanced course. Text-books: WILLIAM; SON, *Differential Calculus;* SERRET, *Differential-und Integral-Rechnung,* DE LA VALLEE POUSSIN, *Cours d'Analyse Infinitésimale.* Fifty hours.

2*e*. Integral Calculus: An advanced course. Text-books: WILLIAMSON-*Integral Calculus;* SERRET, *Differential-und Integral-Rechnung;* DE LA VALLEE POUSSIN, *Cours d'Analyse Infinitésimale.* Fifty hours.

2*f*. Solid Geometry: An advanced course. Text-books: C. SMITH, *Solid Geometry;* SNYDER AND SISAM, *Analytic Geometry of Space.* Fifty hours.

2*g*. Newton's Principia. Section I. Text-books: MAIN's EVANS' *Principia;* FROST's *Principia.* Fifteen hours.

3*b*. Differential Equations: An elementary course. Text-books: COHEN, *Differential Equations;* CAMPBELL, *Differential Equations.* Ten hours.

3*c*. Theory of Equations: An elementary course including applications to number-theory and geometry. Text-books: DICKSON, *Elementary Theory of Equations;* BURNSIDE AND PANTON, *Theory of Equations.* Fifteen hours.

4c. Differential Equations: The advanced course. Text-book: JOHNSON, *Differential Equations;* FORSYTH, *Differential Equations.* Fifty hours.

4d. Higher Plane Curves: With Introductory course in Modern Geometry. Text-books: SALMON, *Higher Plane Curves;* CLEBSCH, *Vorlesungen über Geometrie.* Twenty-five hours.

4e. Quaternions with outlines of other Space Analyses. Text-books: KELLAND AND TAIT, *Quaternions;* JOLY, *Manual of Quaternions;* TAIT, *Quaternions.* Fifty hours.

4f. Invariant Theory. Text-books: SALMON, *Higher Algebra;* ELLIOTT, *Algebra of Quantics;* GORDAN, *Invariantentheorie;* GRACE AND YOUNG, *Algebra of Invariants.* Fifty hours.

4g. Theory of Numbers. Text-books: MATHEWS, *Theory of Numbers;* DIRICHLET, *Zahlentheorie* (fourth edition). Fifty hours.

4h. Theory of Substitutions. Text-books: NETTO, *Theory of Substitutions;* WEBER, *Lehrbuch der Algebra.* Fifty hours.

4i. Elementary Theory of Functions. Text-books: HARKNESS AND MORLEY, *Introduction to Analytic Functions;* FORSYTH, *Theory of Functions.* Fifty hours.

4j. Elliptic Functions. Text-books: APPELL AND LACOUR, *Fonctions Elliptiques.* Fifty hours.

4k. Tangential Co-ordinates or Trilinear Co-ordinates. Text-books, PAPELIER, *Coordonnées Tangentielles;* FERRERS, *Trilinear Co-ordinates* Fifty hours.

4l. Modern Synthetic Geometry. Text-books: REYE, *Geometry of Position* (translated by Holgate); CREMONA, *Projective Geometry;* LACHLAN, *Modern Pure Geometry;* DURELL, *Plane Geometry for Advanced Students,* VEBLEN AND YOUNG, *Projective Geometry.* Fifty hours.

4m. Theory of Probability. Text-books: Article on "*Probability*" in the eleventh edition of the Encyclopædia Britannica. Twenty-five hours.

Course 4m. is an alternative course for Course 9, Actuarial Science, offered for those students of the Fourth Year who have not taken Actuarial Science in the earlier years.

B.—COURSES IN THE FACULTIES OF ARTS AND MEDICINE.

1h. Elementary Analysis. A course in limits and infinite series, with a special study of the Binomial, Exponential and Logarithmic Series.

1i. Elementary Analytical geometry.

2h. Differential and Integral Calculus. An elementary course with special attention to applications.

3d. Finite Differences: Methods and use of formulae. Elementary Mathematical statistics.

C.—COURSES IN THE FACULTY OF APPLIED SCIENCE.

1*j*. Algebra: Equations, variation, progressions, permutations and combinations, limits, convergency and divergency of series, the binomial, exponential and logarithmic series. Fifty hours.

1*k*. Analytical Geometry: An elementary course emphasizing the general method in this subject. Fifty hours.

1*l*. Plane Trigonometry: Solution of triangles and other practical problems. Twenty-five hours.

2*j*. Differential and Integral Calculus: An elementary course with applications. Fifty hours.

MECHANICS.

W. J. LOUDON, B.A. . . . .*Professor.*
N. E. SHEPPARD . . . .*Lecturer.*

1. Elementary Mechanics: A course of fifteen lectures, twice a week during Michaelmas term.

2. Elementary Statics and Dynamics: A course of forty lectures, three times a week during the Easter term.

3. Advanced Statics: A course of thirty-five lectures, three times a week during Easter term.

4. Particle Dynamics: A course of twelve lectures, twice a week during Michaelmas term.

5. Rigid Dynamics: A course of twenty-five lectures, twice a week.

6. Celestial Mechanics: A course of twenty-five lectures, twice a week.

7. Method of Least Squares: Once a week during the Easter term.

8. Dynamics of Rotation: A course of forty lectures, once a week.

9. Principles of Mechanics: For students taking the Second Year of the course in Commerce and Finance. Fifteen lectures.

10. Elementary Mechanics: A course of lectures for Third Year Pass Course.

ACTUARIAL SCIENCE.

M. A. MACKENZIE, M.A., F.I.A. . . . .*Professor.*
W. S. FERGUSON . . . .*Lecturer in Accounting.*

1. Arithmetic: Decimals, interest and discount, annuities certain, bond values, etc. Twenty-five hours.

2. Elementary Mathematics of Statistics. Twelve hours.

3. Accounting: An introductory course in general principles. Twenty-five hours.

4. Accounting, advanced: A critical examination of the Theory and Practice of Accounting and the preparation of financial statements. Fifty hours.

5. The Elements of the Theory of Life Annuities and Life Assurances. Twenty-five hours.

6. Finite Differences: Elementary methods and formulæ. Twenty-five hours.

7. The Theory of Interest: An advanced course. Twelve hours.

8. The Theory of Life Contingencies: An advanced course, Part I. Fifty hours.

9. The Theory of Life Contingencies: An advanced course, Part II. Fifty hours.

ASTRONOMY.

C. A. CHANT, M.A., PH.D. . . . . *Professor of Astrophysics.*
F. L. BLAKE. . . . .*Assistant.*
J. A. PEARCE, B.A. . . . .*Assistant.*
W. S. VAUGHAN. . . . .*Assistant.*
J. B. RUSSELL. . . . .*Assistant.*

PASS COURSE.

1. Descriptive Astronomy: A course of fifty lectures, intended specially for students in the Pass Course. Twice a week. Text-book: TODD, *New Astronomy.*

PASS AND HONOUR COURSES.

2. Elementary Practical Astronomy: Intended to accompany 1. Consisting of observation (including photography) of the heavenly bodies; together with exercises in simple astronomical measurements and in the use of almanacs, globes, star-maps, photographs, etc. Two hours a week, in afternoon or evening as arranged. Text-book: WHITING, *Exercises in Astronomy.*

3. Elementary Astronomy: A course intended specially for students in the Science courses. Fifty lectures, twice a week. Text-book: YOUNG, *Manual of Astronomy.*

HONOUR COURSES.

4. Astronomy: A more advanced course. Text-books: ANDOYER, *Cours d'Astronomie*, tome i; *The Nautical Almanac.* For reference: GODFRAY, *Astronomy;* CHAUVENET, *Spherical Astronomy.* Forty hours, twice a week.

5. Practical Astronomy: Observations with the equatorial telescope, the transit instrument and the sextant. Two evenings a week. By courtesy of the director of the Meteorological Observatory the astronomical instruments there are used by the students of the University. Text-book: CAMPBELL, *Practical Astronomy.*

6. Computation Course: A course for the discussion of astronomical observations and for computation, associated with Course 5. Two hours a week.

7. Introduction to Astrophysics: A course of fifty lectures, twice a week. Text-books: Scheiner, *Astronomical Spectroscopy;* Baly, *Spectroscopy;* Salet, *Spectroscopie Astronomique.*

8. Practical Astrophysics: A laboratory course to accompany Course 7. One afternoon a week in the Michaelmas and two in the Easter term.

9. Celestial Mechanics (see under Mechanics, p. 135).

10. Method of Least Squares (see under Mechanics, p. 135).

PHYSICS.

J. C. McLennan, O.B.E., Ph.D., D.Sc., LL.D., F.R.S.,
Professor and Director of the Physical Laboratory.
E. F. Burton, B.A. Ph.D.........................*Associate Professor.*
Lachlan Gilchrist, M.A., Ph.D..................*Assistant Professor.*
John Satterly, M.A., D.Sc.....................*Assistant Professor and Assistant Director of Undergraduate Laboratory Work.*
H. A. McTaggart, M.A.........................*Assistant Professor.*
Miss K. M. Crossley, B.A............................*Demonstrator.*
Miss I. B. Giles, M.A.............................*Demonstrator.*
Miss M. I. Mackey, M.A...........................*Demonstrator.*
Miss H. C. Millar, M.A.............................*Demonstrator.*
Miss F. M. Quinlan, M.A.........................*Demonstrator.*
V. P. Lubovich......................................*Demonstrator.*
E. D. MacInnes, B.A.......................*Assistant Demonstrator.*
W. C. McQuarrie, B.A......................*Assistant Demonstrator.*
P. Lowe, B.A..............................*Assistant Demonstrator.*
Miss H. I. Eadie, B.A...........................*Class Assistant.*
F. W. Kemp, M.A....................*Class and Research Assistant.*
Miss A. T. Reed, B.A...........................*Class Assistant.*
P. A. Petrie..............................*Research Assistant.*

The work of instruction in Physics consists of a series of courses of lectures and of practical work in the laboratories, which are embodied in the following schedule:

1. A course of fifty lectures on Properties of Matter, Mechanics, Hydrostatics and Heat. These lectures are illustrated by experiments. Text-books: Eggar, *Mechanics;* Wagstaff, *Properties of Matter;* Stewart and Satterly, *Text-book of Heat.*

2. Properties of Matter, Mechanics, Hydrostatics and Heat: A laboratory course of seventy-five hours, one afternoon a week, throughout the year, designed to illustrate the lectures in Course 1 in Physics, and Course 1 in Mechanics. Text-books: As for Course 1, also Allen and Moore, *Text-book of Practical Physics,* Parts I and IV: Clark, *Mathematical and Physical Tables.*

3. Elementary Magnetism and Electricity: A course of thirty-five lectures, given in two divisions 3a and 3b. Text-books: HADLEY, *Magnetism and Electricity for Students;* SYLVANUS THOMPSON, *Electricity and Magnetism;* BROOKS AND POYSER, *Electricity and Magnetism;* WATSON, *A Text-book of Physics;* STEWART, *Electricity and Magnetism;* HUTCHINSON, *Advanced Magnetism and Electricity.*

4. Elementary Light: A course of twenty-five lectures, one a week beginning in the Michaelmas term. Text-books: STEWART AND SATTERLY, *Text-book of Light;* EDSER, *Light for Students;* WATSON, *A Text-book of Physics.*

5. Elementary Acoustics: A course of fifteen lectures, one a week. Text-books: CATCHPOOL, *Text-book of Sound;* POYNTING AND THOMSON, *Sound;* WATSON, *A Text-book of Physics;* D. C. MILLER, *The Science of Musical Sounds.*

The lectures in Courses 1, 3a, 3b 4 and 5 are illustrated by experiments.

6. Magnetism, Electricity, Light and Acoustics: A laboratory course of one hundred and fifty hours, two afternoons a week throughout the year, designed to illustrate the lectures in Courses 3a, 3b, 4 and 5. Text-books: ALLEN AND MOORE, *Text-book of Practical Physics;* CARHART AND PATTERSON, *Electrical Measurements;* C. M. SMITH, *Electric and Magnetic Measurements;* EDSER, *Light for Students;* CLAY, *Treatise on Practical Light;* CATCHPOOL, *Sound.*

7. A course of lectures one hour a week on Mathematics as applied to the solution of Physical Problems including the simple use of the Calculus. Text-book: STERN AND TOPHAM, *Practical Mathematics;* S. P. THOMPSON, *Calculus Made Easy;* PERRY, *Calculus for Engineers;* TUTTLE, *The Theory of Measurements.*

8. A series of lectures, being a portion of the first year Pass Course, on the principles and application of Science.

9. A course of lectures and laboratory work, four hours a week, for second year pass students. This course includes Properties of Matter, Mechanics, Hydrostatics, and Heat. The lectures will deal with simple measurements, energy, gravitation and the pendulum, the general properties of solids, liquids and gases such as elasticity, viscosity and capillarity, the determination of fluid pressures, specific gravity and the theory and use of common forms of pumps, barometers, etc.; the thermal characteristics of various substances, including expansion, various thermometers, specific and latent heat and calorimetry; the phenomena observable during the change of state of substances from one form to the other; conduction, radiation, heat and energy, the first and second laws of thermodynamics, engines; the liquefaction of gases and liquid air, the kinetic theory of matter.

10. A course of lectures and laboratory work, four hours a week, for third year pass students. This course includes work in light and acoustics, and consists of a general explanation of wave motion, the reflection, refrac-

tion and diffraction and interference phenomena connected with wave motion; the production, propagation, and detection of sound waves; tuning forks, organ pipes and vibrating strings; various musical scales; analysis of complex sounds, the ear and voice; a study of mirrors, prisms and lenses; the eye, microscope, telescope and other optical instruments; dispersion, colour and spectroscopy; interference and diffraction; double refraction and polarisation; theories of light.

11. A course of lectures and laboratory work, four hours a week, for fourth year pass students. This course will consist of lectures and laboratory work in electricity and magnetism, including recent developments, such as radioactivity and radiology; laws of magnetism, static electricity, condensers, electrical conduction in solids, liquids and gases, voltaic cell, chemical, magnetic and heating effect of the electrical current, potential; Ohm's law and its application, laws of electrical resistance, electromotive forces, induced currents, the induction-coil, alternating and high frequency currents, electrical waves, X-rays and radioactivity.

12. Applications of the theory of Potential to Physics: A course of forty lectures.

13. Properties of Matter: A course of lectures, two a week beginning in the Michaelmas term. Text-books: POYNTING AND THOMSON, *Properties of Matter;* TAIT, *Properties of Matter;* EDSER, *General Physics.*

14. Geometrical Optics: A course of thirty lectures. Text-book: HOUSTON, *A Treatise on Light;* HEATH, *Geometrical Optics;* SOUTHALL, *Mirrors, Prisms, and Lenses.*

15. Advanced Heat and Elementary Thermodynamics: A course of thirty lectures. Text-books: EDSER, *Heat for Advanced Students;* HART, *A Student's Heat;* PRESTON, *Heat;* E. H. GRIFFITHS, *Thermal Measurement of Energy;* E. GRIFFITHS, *Methods of measuring Temperature.*

16. Thermodynamics: A course of twelve lectures on thermometry and pyrometry, gas and vapour equations and the fundamental principles of thermodynamics. Text-books as for Course 15.

17. A laboratory course on the accurate determination of physical constants, together with practice in laboratory arts. This course involves about one hundred and fifty hours' laboratory work. Text-books: ALLEN AND MOORE, *Text-book of Practical Physics;* WATSON, *A Text-book of Practical Physics;* SEARLE, *Simple Harmonic Motion;* SEARLE, *Experimental Elasticity;* TUTTLE, *Theory of Measurements.*

18. Calculations for Science Students: A course of practical instruction in mathematical drawing, graphs and their applications, calculations and their accuracy, elementary calculus and statistics. Text-books: TUTTLE, *Theory of Measurements;* S. P. THOMPSON, *Calculus Made Easy.*

19. A short course of lectures and laboratory work on Radiation, including atomic structure and radioactivity.

20. Theory of Optics:. A course of lectures twice a week throughout the year. Text-books: DRUDE, *Theory of Optics;* MANN, *Manual of Advanced, Optics;* BALY, *Spectroscopy;* WOOD, *Physical Optics;* SCHUSTER, *Theory of Optics;* HOUSTON, *A Treatise on Light.*

21. Elasticity: A course of lectures, two a week throughout the year dealing with the mathematical theory of elasticity with application to the theory of double refraction and polarisation of light. Text-books: POYNT-ING AND THOMSON, *Properties of Matter;* CHRISTIANSEN, *Elements of Theoretical Physics;* PELLAT, *Polarisation et Optique Crystalline.*

22. Fourier's Series: A course of fifteen lectures on Fourier's Series and its applications to Physics. Text-books: DONKIN, *Acoustics;* BYERLY, *Fourier's Series and Spherical Harmonics;* BARTON, *A Text-book on Sound;* CARSE AND SHEARER, *Fourier and Periodogram Analysis;* LAMB, *Dynamical Theory of Sound;* CARSLAW, *Fourier's Series and Integrals.*

23. Thermodynamics: A course of lectures one a week throughout the year. Text-books: POYNTING AND THOMSON, *Heat;* PARTINGTON, *Thermodynamics;* MAXWELL, *Heat;* LEWIS, *System of Physical Chemistry;* WHET-HAM, *Solution and Electrolysis.*

24. Hydromechanics: A course of lectures during the Easter term. Text-books: MINCHIN, *Hydrostatics;* BESANT, *Hydro-mechanics;* LAMB, *Hydrodynamics;* BARTON, *Mechanics of Fluids;* RAMSEY, *Hydrodynamics.*

25. Colloidal Solutions: A course of lectures on the physical properties of colloidal solutions. Text-book: BURTON, *The Physical Properties of Colloidal Solutions.*

26. A course of lectures on Electricity and Magnetism including the Electromagnetic Theory of Light, Electron Theory of Matter, Dispersion, Absorption, Polarisation, Magneto-Optics, Electrical Oscillations, Conduction of Electricity in Gases, and Radioactivity. Text-books: J. J. THOMSON, *Elements of Electricity and Magnetism, Recent Researches in Electricity and Magnetism, Conduction of Electricity through Gases;* ABRA-HAM AND LANGEVIN, *Ions, Electrons, Corpuscles;* DRUDE, *Theory of Optics;* LORENTZ, *The Theory of Electrons;* N. R. CAMPBELL, *Modern Electrical Theory;* RUTHERFORD, *Radioactive Substances and their Radiations;* STAR-LING, *Electricity and Magnetism;* MILLIKAN, *The Electron; Radio Instruments and Measurements* (ed. by Bureau of Standards).

27. A laboratory course designed as an extension of Course 17, and as an introduction to research work. A seminar is held once a fortnight in connection with this course, under the supervision of the Director of the Laboratory, at which reports on papers in the current physical journals are presented and discussed.

28. A course of lectures and laboratory work, specially designed for students taking a one-year course in Physics.

29. History of Physics. Cajori, *History of Physics;* Whittaker, *History of the Theories of Aether and Matter.*

30. High Frequency Alternating Currents: A course of twenty-five lectures,

31. Vector Analysis: A course of twenty-five lectures: Coffin, *Vector Analysis.*

Regulations.—*Deposit Fee:* Each student taking laboratory course 2, 6, 10, 11, 17, or 28 is required to make a deposit of three dollars ($3.00) before beginning work. All supplies, apparatus broken or destroyed and all fines will be charged against this deposit, which must be renewed when exhausted. At the close of the session cash balances will be returned on a day appointed for the purpose.

Additional Text-books.

General Physics: White, Watson, Ganot, Kimball, Hastings and Beach, Deschanel (ed. Everett), Jamin, Violle, Nichols and Franklin, Barlow, Thomson and Tait, Lehfeldt, Millikan and Gale, Mann and Twiss, Daniell, H. A. Wilson, Houston (An Introduction to Mathematical Physics), Duncan and Starling.

Elementary Mechanics: Ashford, Lock, Glazebrook, Briggs and Bryan, Magnus, Loney, Garnet; Satterly (*Measurements and Mechanics*).

Elementary Hydrostatics: Glazebrook, Briggs and Bryan, Loney.

Elementary Mechanics and Heat: Gregory and Hadley.

Elementary Heat: Glazebrook, Stewart, Tyndall, Balfour Stewart, Tait, Draper, Darling, Scarlett, Stewart and Satterly. (*Heat for Engineers*).

Elementary Light: Stewart and Satterly, Jones, Tyndall, Tait, Wright, Glazebrook, Emtage.

Elementary Electricity and Magnetism: Poyser, Glazebrook, Lehfeldt, Cumming, Day, Ashford, Wagstaff, Hutchinson, Ashford and Kempson.

Sound: Tyndall, Taylor, Capstick, Zahm.

Geometrical Optics: Herman, Aldis, Heath, Parkinson, Percival, Whittaker, Leathem, Searle, Southall (*Geometrical Optics and Elementary Optics*), S. P. Thompson (*Optical Tables and Data*); Von Rohr, *Theory of Optical Instruments*, trans. by R. Kantchack, and A. Gleichen, *Theory of Modern Optical Instruments*, trans. by Elmsly and Swain.

Household Science: Hale, Lynde.

Mechanics: Perry (*Applied Mechanics*), Barton, Cox, Thomson and Tait, Lamb.

Hydromechanics: Greenhill, Basset.

Sound (or Acoustics): DONKIN, RAYLEIGH, HELMHOLTZ, AIRY, KOENIG, LAMB.

Elasticity: WILLIAMSON, LAMB, IBBETSON, LOVE, TODHUNTER, SEARLE.

Physical Optics: DRUDE, JAMIN, VERDET, BASSET, GLAZEBROOK, MACLAURIN, MASCART, SCHUSTER, WOOD, PRESTON, POYNTING (*Pressure of Light*), GEHRCKE, MALLIK, KAYSER.

Heat and Thermodynamics: CLAUSIUS, BUCKINGHAM, PARKER, WHET-HAM, PLANCK, PRESTON, MAXWELL, TAIT, PARTINGTON, DONNAN, LEWIS (*Physical Chemistry*), GIBBS, EWING (*The Production of Cold*); EWING (*The Steam Engine*); HOBBS (*The Thermo-dynamics of engine design*); CLAUDE. (*Liquid Air, Oxygen, Nitrogen*); DARLING (*Pyrometry*), LE CHATELIER, GRIFFITH (*Method of measuring temperatures*); R. BLONDLOT, *Introduction a l'étude de la Thermodynamique.*

Properties of Matter: MEYER, *Kinetic Theory;* JEANS, *Dynamical Theory of Gases;* DARLING, *Liquid Drops and Globules;* TAIT, *Properties of Matter;* EDSER, *General Physics;* FINDLAY, *Osmotic Pressure;* PHILIP, *Physical Chemistry;* BOYS, *Soap Bubbles;* WILLOWS AND HATCHEK, *Surface Tension.*

Electricity and Magnetism: POYNTING AND THOMSON, EMTAGE, MAX-WELL, MASCART AND JOUBERT, GRAY, HEAVISIDE, DuBOIS, FOSTER AND PORTER, WEBSTER, STRUTT, SODDY, FOURNIER D'ALBÉ, ECCLES, BARLOW (*Mathematical Physics*, Vol. 1); KNAPP; JAMES (*Alternating Currents*); DRYSDALE (*Alternating Currents*), LIVEN, HUTCHINSON.

Relativity: CONWAY, CUNNINGHAM, ROBB, SILBERSTEIN, TOLMAN, EDDINGTON, CARMICHAEL, LAWSON, FREUNDLICH, CARR.

Modern Theories: COMSTOCK AND TROLAND, DUNCAN, BRAGG (*X-rays and Crystal Structure*), SODDY, KAYE (*X-rays*); J. J. THOMSON, RUTHER-FORD.

Practical Physics: LOUDON AND McLENNAN, BOWER AND SATTERLY. STEWART AND GEE, BARNES, GLAZEBROOK AND SHAW, KOHLRAUSCH. AYRTON, NICHOLS, FINDLAY, WATSON, SCHUSTER AND LEES, SEARLE, CLAY (*Light*), TUTTLE (*An Introduction to Laboratory Physics*).

Practical Mathematics (and Mechanics): CLARKE, SAXELBY, CASTLE, CARSE AND SHEARER (*Pediorogram analysis*); GIBSON (*Graphs*); MINCHIN AND DALE, STERN AND TOPHAM, PERRY; GIBSON (*Graphs*).

Calculus (suitable for Physics students): EDWARDS, EDSER, LODGE, PROCTOR, BLAINE, MERCER, PERRY (for Engineers), GIBSON, MELLOR (*Higher Mathematics for students of Physics and Chemistry*), GRAHAM. ORMSBY, GODFREY AND SIDDONS, LOVE, LAMB.

Theory of Measurements and Errors: LUPTON, STEVENS, MACGREGOR, GOODWIN, TUTTLE, HOLMAN, MERRIMAN, JOHNSON.

Mathematical and Physical Tables: BOTTOMLEY, CASTLE, CLARKE, CHAMBERS, DALE, HALL, KAYE AND LABY, MACFARLANE, McAULAY, the Smithsonian, LONGLEY, WOODWARD, CHAPPELL.

The Slide Rule: BLAINE, DUNLOP AND JACKSON.

BIOLOGY.

R. R. WRIGHT, M.A., D.Sc., LL.D.................*Professor Emeritus.*
B. A. BENSLEY, B.A., PH.D......................*Professor of Zoology.*
W. H. PIERSOL, B.A., M.B., *Associate Professor of Histology and Embryology.*
E. M. WALKER, B.A., M.B................*Associate Professor of Biology.*
A. G. HUNTSMAN, B.A., M.B.......*Associate Professor of Marine Biology.*
A. F. COVENTRY, B.A.....*Assistant Professor of Vertebrate Embryology.*
W. A. CLEMENS, M.A., PH.D...*Assistant Professor of Elementary Biology.*
E. H. CRAIGIE, PH.D......`........*Lecturer in Comparative Anatomy.*
J. W. MACARTHUR, M.A..............*Lecturer in Experimental Biology.*
W. H. T. BAILLIE, M.A., M.B........*Lecturer in Mammalian Anatomy.*
J. R. DYMOND, M.A............*Lecturer in Systematic Vertebrate Zoology.*
H. G. ARMSTRONG, M.B......,.........................*Demonstrator.*
N. K. BIGELOW, B.Sc..............*Assistant in Systematic Biology.*
MISS N. H. C. FORD, B.A................*Special Assistant in Biology.*
N. FOUND, B.A., M.B..............................*Class Assistant.*
A. E. McCULLOCH, B.A., M.B......................*Class Assistant.*
J. M. MACDONALD, M.D., C.M......................*Class Assistant.*
A. G. McPHEDRAN, B.A., M.B......................*Class Assistant.*
P. D. SPOHN, M.B.,.............................*Class Assistant.*
W. V. JOHNSTON, B.A..............................*Class Assistant.*
L. M. MURRAY, B.A................................*Class Assistant.*
H. DeW. BALL, M.B................................*Class Assistant.*
P. J. F. HOUSTON, M.B.............................*Class Assistant.*
L. A. PEQUEGNAT, M.B................'.......*Class Assistant.*
O. C. J. WITHROW, M.B.............................*Class Assistant.*
N. B. LAUGHTON.................................*Class Assistant.*
H. W. PRICE.................`.................*Class Assistant.*

Courses extending over only the Michaelmas or the Easter term are indicated as (m) *and* (e) *respectively.*

With the exception of Course I, the lectures and practical instruction in this department are given in the University Biological Building. The instruction includes courses in General Biology, Zoology, Comparative Anatomy, Histology and Embryology, these courses being indicated in the various prescriptions as Zoology 2, 3, 4, etc.

For supplementary reading, except as specified below, the General Reading List of the Department may be consulted.

The following courses are provided:

A.—COURSES IN THE FACULTY OF ARTS.

PASS COURSES.

1. Elementary Science: A course of seventy-five lectures on the general principles and applications of science. This is a co-operative course, given by members of the departments of Physics, Chemistry, Geology, Botany and Zoology.

2. Elementary Biology: (*a*) A general educational course of two hours a week on the principles of science as applied to living organisms. The instruction is chiefly zoological, emphasis being placed upon the history of animal types and upon the biological aspects of the nature and social development of mankind. (*b*) A practical course of fifty hours in illustration of the principles and laboratory methods of Biology.

3. Invertebrate Zoology: A course of one hundred hours lectures and laboratory work on the elements of the principal branches of zoology as applied to the lower animals.

4. Vertebrate Zoology: A course of one hundred hours lectures and laboratory work on the principal branches of zoology as applied to vertebrates, with special reference to those of human application.

HONOUR COURSES.

5. Elementary Zoology: A course of two lectures a week throughout the Easter term on the nature, structure and classification of animals. For Honour Science students.

6. Elementary Zoology: A laboratory course of seventy-five hours on the general structure of the animal body, its organs and tissues and their functions; principles of adaptation, specialisation, and homology, based on selected types. Text-book: HEGNER, *College Zoology.* For reference: PARKER AND HASWELL, *Text-book of Zoology* (e).

7. Comparative Anatomy: A laboratory course of one hundred and fifty hours, comprising dissection and comparative study of selected vertebrate types: Part 1, Mammalian Anatomy (m); Text-book: BENSLEY, *Anatomy of the Rabbit;* Part 2, Anatomy of Lower Chordates (e). For reference: PARKER, *Zootomy;* KINGSLEY, *Vertebrate Zoology;* PARKER AND HASWELL, Text-book, Vol. 2; WIEDERSHEIM, *Comparative Anatomy;* REYNOLDS, *Vertebrate Skeleton;* KINGSLEY, *Comparative Anatomy.*

8. Vertebrate Zoology: A course of twenty-five lectures on the system, structure and history of the vertebrates. For reference, as above (7); GADOW, *Classification of Vertebrata;* SMITH WOODWARD, *Vertebrate Palæontology.*

9. Invertebrate Zoology: A course of twenty-five lectures and seventy-five hours laboratory work on the system and morphology of the invertebrates. Text-book: PARKER AND HASWELL, Vol. I. (m).

10. A course on mammalian anatomy and histology and on the natural history of animal foods. For Household Science students (m).

11. A special course in Invertebrate Zoology, dealing chiefly with those groups which include parasitic forms. For reference: PARKER AND HASWELL, *Text-book of Zoology*, Vol. I.; FANTHAM, STEPHENS AND THEOBALD, *Animal Parasites of Man;* RILEY AND JOHANNSEN, *Medical Entomology;* DOANE, *Insects and Disease;* CHANDLER, *Animal Parasites and Human Disease.* Seventy-five hours (m).

—15

12. Zoological Collection: Students entering the Third Year in the special course of Biology are required to submit, as evidence of field proficiency, a collection of invertebrate animals from a prescribed group, together with an essay on the character and habits of the forms collected. Special directions may be had on application to the Biological Department.

13. Vertebrate Embryology: (a) A course of twenty-five lectures and (b) forty hours laboratory work on the embryology of the vertebrates.

14. A lecture and laboratory course of one hundred hours on vertebrate histology and cytology, including histological technique.

Text-books: PIERSOL, *Norman Histology*, 8th edition; BÖHM, v. DAVIDOFF AND HUBER, *Text-book of Histology*, 2nd edition. For reference: PRENANT, BOUIN, MAILLARD, *Traité d'Histologie;* SCHÄFER, *Text-book of Microscopic Anatomy.*

15. History and Theory of Biology: An opportunity is afforded to advanced students to become acquainted with the main problems of biology and with the history of the subject. The instruction includes fifty lectures and conferences conducted by different members of the staff, and a course of prescribed reading from advanced texts and current literature. The library is provided with the various works for consultation, a partial statement of which will be found in the departmental reading list.

16. Vertebrate Embryology: A laboratory course of one hundred hours on the general embryology of the vertebrates and on the special embryology of the mammalia. For reference: JENKINSON, *Vertebrate Embryology;* HERTWIG, *Lehrbuch der Entwickelungsgeschichte;* LILLIE, *Development of the Chick;* BAILEY AND MILLER, *Embryology;* KELLICOTT, *Embryology;* PRENTISS, *Text-book of Embryology.*

17. Special Embryology of the Mammalia: A laboratory course of fifty hours on human embryology. For reference: MINOT, MCMURRICH, KOLL-MANN, KEIBEL AND MALL (e).

18. Structural Neurology: A short course of lectures and laboratory work on the structure and development of the vertebrate nervous system. For reference: EDINGER, *Anatomy of the Nervous System;* HERRICK, *Introduction to Neurology.*

19. Zoological Collection: Students entering the Fourth Year in any one of the subdivisions of Biology are required to submit a collection of vertebrate animals from specified groups, together with an essay on the characters and habits of the forms collected. For reference: JORDAN, *Manual of Vertebrates.*

20. A lecture and laboratory course of one hundred hours on general invertebrate and vertebrate histology and cytology, including histological technique.

Text-book: DAHLGREN AND KEPNER, *Principles of Animal Histology.* For reference: WILSON, *The Cell in Development and Inheritance;* GURWITSCH, *Morphologie und Biologie der Zelle;* SCHNEIDER, *Histologie der Thiere;* PRENANT, BOUIN, MAILLARD, *Traité d'Histologie* (Vol. I., Cytologie).

21. Vertebrate Zoology: A practical course of one hundred hours of laboratory and museum work on the morphology, classification and distribution of the vertebrates. For reference: GADOW, *Classification of Vertebrates;* FLOWER AND LYDEKKER, *Mammals Living and Extinct;* LYDEKKER, *Geographical History of Mammals; Cambridge Natural History,* Vols. vii-x; REYNOLDS, *The Vertebrate Skeleton;* FLOWER, *Osteology of the Mammalia;* SMITH WOODWARD, *Outlines of Vertebrate Palæontology;* PARKER AND HASWELL, Vol. 2; WILLEY, *Amphioxus;* WIEDERSHEIM, *Comparative Anatomy.*

22. Advanced Invertebrate Zoology: A course of one hundred hours of lectures, laboratory and museum work on the morphology, embryology, classification and distribution of the invertebrates. This course is also designed to give training in laboratory methods and microscopic technique. For reference: PARKER AND HASWELL, Vol. I.; HERTWIG'S *Zoology,* edited by Kingsley; *Cambridge Natural History,* Vols. I.-VI.; KORSCHELT AND HEIDER, *Embryology;* SCHNEIDER, *Histologie der Thiere;* selected papers; LEE, *Microtomist's Vade Mecum;* GUYER, *Animal Micrology.*

23. A special course of one hundred hours on the system and natural history of animals, with special reference to those of Ontario or of Canada.

Research: The members of the staff in this department are prepared to suggest problems for investigation in certain branches and to provide materials and laboratory facilities for properly qualified students. See "Announcement of Graduate Courses".

B.—COURSES IN THE FACULTY OF MEDICINE.

24. A course of ninety lectures serving as an introduction to the biological fields in relation to medicine. The topics include (1) the general nature of living organisms and of cell processes, (2) the types of lower organisms of interest to students in Medicine, (3) the elements of comparative anatomy, and (4) biological principles as applied to man.

25. A laboratory course of one hundred and eighty hours, including microscope practice, elementary experimental studies on the nature of cell processes, types of lower organisms, and a selected list of vertebrates.

The entire course of two hundred and forty hours in the second year of the Six Year Medical Course consists of:

26. A course of ten lectures and twenty hours laboratory work introductory to embryology and histology.

27. A course of fifteen lectures and sixty hours laboratory work on histogenesis and general histology.

28. A course of twenty lectures and forty hours laboratory work on the development of the human body.

29. A course of fifteen lectures and sixty hours laboratory work on human microscopic anatomy.

30. An introductory course of fifty lectures on the principles of evolution, heredity and eugenics.

D. P. H., *Parasitology*. See course 11.

C.—COURSE IN THE FACULTY OF APPLIED SCIENCE.

31. A practical course in experimental biology including microscope practice with the lower organisms.

D.—COURSES IN THE FACULTY OF FORESTRY.

In addition to Course 5 and 6, which are taken by students in Forestry, the following special courses are provided:

32. Economic Entomology; twenty-five lectures and fifty hours laboratory work (e). Text-book: SANDERSON AND JACKSON, *Elementary Entomology*.

33. A short course on the principles of conservation as applied to animals.

E.—UNIVERSITY EXTENSION.

34. An elementary course on the general structure and functions of the animal body. The instruction is primarily for teachers, emphasis is being placed upon method, classification and natural history of animals, and the materials of nature study.

BOTANY.

J. H. FAULL, B.A., PH.D..................................*Professor.*
R. B. THOMSON, B.A.......................*Associate Professor.*
H. B. SIFTON, M.A...................*Assistant Professor (Research).*
G. H. DUFF, M.A.. *Lecturer.*
MISS J. G. WRIGHT, M.A..................................*Lecturer.*
MISS M. V. McCULLOCH, B.A....................*Technical Assistant.*
MISS M. E. CURRIE, M.A.......................*Technical Assistant.*
E. H. MOSS, M.A. ....*Assistant.*
A. R. WALKER, B.A ....*Assistant.*
MISS J. McGUGAN, B.A......................................*Fellow.*
H. D. BROWN..*Assistant.*
F. B. ADAMSTONE..*Assistant.*
MISS L. M. HUNTER...*Assistant.*
MISS C. W. FRITZ, B.A., M.Sc......................*Research Assistant.*

Courses extending over only the Michaelmas or the Easter term are indicated as (m) and (e) respectively.

The lectures and practical instruction in this subject are given in the Botany and Forestry Building.

The following courses are provided:

A.—IN THE FACULTY OF ARTS.

PASS COURSES.

1. Composite Science Course. See p. 143.

2a. Introductory Course in Botany: An introductory course of two hours a week on the general principles of Biology based mainly on the seed plants. Text-book: BERGEN AND CALDWELL, *Introduction to Botany* (N. & Cent. U.S. Edition). For reference: KERNER AND OLIVER, *Natural History of Plants.*

2b. A laboratory course of two hours a week in connection with Course 2a.

3. A lecture and laboratory course dealing with the general characteristics of each of the great primary divisions of the vegetable kingdom, with the general course of evolution within these divisions, and their relationships one to the other, with the typical habits and distribution of the plants of each group and their place in the economy of nature and of man. Four hours a week. Text-book: CURTIS, *Nature and Development of Plants.*

4. A lecture and laboratory course on the physiology and the adaptive relationships of plants; and on the general principles of heredity and plant breeding. Four hours a week.

HONOUR COURSES.

5. Elementary Botany: A course of twenty-five lectures on the life, structure and classification of plants. Text-book: CURTIS, *Nature and Development of Plants.* For reference: COULTER, BARNES AND COWLES, *Text-book of Botany;* GANONG, *A Text-book of Botany for Colleges;* KERNER AND OLIVER, *Natural History of Plants* (m).

6. A laboratory course of fifty hours in connection with Course 5 (m).

7. Phanerogamic Botany: A course of twenty-five lectures and fifty hours laboratory work on the anatomy and morphology of the flowering plants. Text-book: STRASBURGER, JOST, SCHENCK AND KARSTEN, *Text-book of Botany,* 4th English Edition (1912), and GRAY, *New Manual of Botany.* For reference: COULTER, *Seed-Plants;* BRITTON AND BROWN, *An Illustrated Flora* (e).

8. Classification of Flowering Plants: A lecture and laboratory course of fifty hours in which representatives of the main divisions of the flowering plants are studied in illustration of the fundamental principles of classification. Reference is also made to distribution, especially of the local flora, and to the food plants and other economic plants of the group (m).

9. Botanical Collection: Students entering the Second Year in Biology are required to submit a collection of at least 100 species of flowering plants, properly pressed, classified, mounted and labelled. For reference: GRAY, *New Manual of Botany;* BRITTON AND BROWN, *An Illustrated Flora of the Northern United States and Canada.*

10. A course of 100 hours dealing with the lower seed-plants, living and fossil. Text-book: COULTER AND CHAMBERLAIN, *Morphology of Gymnosperms.* For reference: SCOTT, *Fossil Botany;* PENHALLOW, *North American Gymnosperms;* DEBARY, *Comparative Anatomy of the Phanerogams and the Ferns;* JEFFREY, *Anatomy of Woody Plants.*

11. A course of 100 hours dealing with the higher seed-plants. Text-book: COULTER AND CHAMBERLAIN, *Morphology of Angiosperms.* For reference: DEBARY, *Comparative Anatomy of the Phanerogams and the Ferns;* JEFFREY, *Anatomy of Woody Plants.*

12. Cryptogamic Botany: A lecture and laboratory course of one hundred and twenty-five hours on the system and morphology of the cryptogams. For reference: COULTER, BARNES AND COWLES, *Text-book of Botany,* Vol. I.; CAMPBELL, *Mosses and Ferns;* BOWER, *Origin of a Land Flora* (m).

13. An elementary course on the morphology and physiology of Bacteria, Yeasts and Molds for Household Science students. For reference: BUCHANAN, *Household Bacteriology;* MARSHALL, *Microbiology;* SAVAGE, *Bacteriological Examination of Food and Water;* CONN, *Bacteria, Yeasts and Molds in the Home;* COULTER, BARNES AND COWLES, *Text-book of Botany* (e).

14. A lecture and laboratory course of one hundred hours on the system and morphology of the algae, fungi, bacteria, and slime molds. For reference: LISTER, *Mycetozoa;* JORDAN, *General Bacteriology;* STRASBURGER, JOST, SCHENK AND KARSTEN, *Text-book of Botany;* DEBARY, *Comparative Morphology and Biology of the Fungi, Mycetozoa and Bacteria;* DUGGAR, *Fungous Diseases of Plants.*

15. Classification of cryptogams: A lecture and laboratory course of fifty hours in which representatives of selected groups of cryptogams are studied from the taxonomic standpoint. Reference is also made to distribution, especially of the local flora (e).

16. Botanical Collection: Students entering the Fourth Year in Biology are required to submit a collection of cryptogamic plants from prescribed groups.

17. Plant Physiology: A course of twenty-five lectures and seventy-five hours laboratory work on the physiology of plants. For reference: JOST, *Plant Physiology;* GANONG, *The Living Plant;* PFEFFER, *Physiology of Plants;* PALLADIN (Livingston), *Plant Physiology* (e).

18. Oecology and Plant Geography: A course on factors of habitat and the adaptations of plants to them; plant associations and their geographical distribution. For reference: WARMING, *Ecology of Plants;* SCHIMPER, *Plant Geography.* One hundred hours.

19. An advanced course of one hundred hours on the physiology of plants.

20. A lecture and seminar course on the history of Botany and on the general principles of Biology as related to botanical problems. Text-book: WALTER, *Genetics*. A list of other assigned literature is obtainable on application to the Department. Students proposing to take this course should secure this list at the close of their third year.

21. Students in the Third and Fourth Years of the Special Course in Biology will be expected to show a reading knowledge of French and German.

22. Palaeobotany: A course of fifty hours on fossil plants.

23. Research studies on selected topics for advanced students. One hundred and fifty hours.

Research: The members of the staff in this department are prepared to suggest problems for investigation in certain branches and to provide materials and laboratory facilities for properly qualified students.

B.—COURSES IN THE FACULTY OF APPLIED SCIENCE.

24. A lecture and laboratory course of seventy-five hours on fundamental biological principles.

C.—COURSES IN THE FACULTY OF FORESTRY.

25. Plant Pathology: A lecture and laboratory course of fifty hours on the lower Cryptogams, and on the diseases of plants, especially of trees.

D.—COURSES IN THE DEPARTMENT OF VETERINARY SCIENCE.

26. Elementary Botany and Poisonous Plants: A course of fifty hours. Text-book: BERGEN AND CALDWELL, *Introduction to Botany*. For reference: PAMMEL, *Manual of Poisonous Plants*.

27. Special course on poisonous plants for second year students in Veterinary Science.

ANATOMY.

J. PLAYFAIR McMURRICH, M.A., PH.D., LL.D.............*Professor.*
J. C. WATT, M.A., M.D.........................*Assistant Professor.*
W. A. SCOTT, B.A., M.B., F.R.C.S.......................*Assistant.*
R. E. GABY, B.A., M.D..*Assistant.*
F. W. WESTON, B.A., M.B...............................*Assistant.*
H. L. ROWNTREE, M.B.....................................*Assistant.*
R. O. FISHER, M.B...*Assistant.*
H. B. VANWYCK, B.A., M.B..............................*Assistant.*
A. S. LAWSON, M.B...*Assistant.*
E. E. SHOULDICE, M.B......................................*Assistant.*
K. G. McKENZIE, M.B.......................................*Assistant.*
G. W. D. CARLETON, M.B. ....*Assistant.*
I. R. SMITH, M.B...*Assistant.*
H. A. CATES, M.B...*Assistant.*

L. B. ROBERTSON, B.A., M.B...........................*Assistant.*
R. M. JANES, M.B...*Assistant.*
P. D. SPOHN, M.B...*Assistant.*
L. C. PALMER, M.B..*Assistant.*
E. A. McCULLOCH, B.A., M.B............................*Assistant.*
J. C. MAYNARD, M.B......................................*Assistant.*
L. A. PEQUEGNAT, M.B...................................*Assistant.*

1. Practical Anatomy.—A laboratory course extending throughout the year.

2. Anatomy of the Nervous System.—A course of three lectures a week, with demonstrations twice a week, throughout the Michaelmas term.

3. Anatomical Research.—Opportunities will be afforded to properly qualified students for carrying on investigation in anatomical problems.

Text-books: PIERSOL, *Human Anatomy;* MORRIS, *Human Anatomy;* CUNNINGHAM, *Text-book of Anatomy;* GRAY, *Anatomy; Guide to the Dissection of the Human Body;* SOBOTTA-McMURRICH, *Atlas and Text-book of Human Anatomy;* SPALTEHOLZ, *Hand Atlas of Human Anatomy;* TOLDT, *Atlas of Human Anatomy;* McMURRICH, *The Development of the Human Body;* HERRICK, *Introduction to Neurólogy;* VILLIGER, *Brain and Spinal Cord;* BARKER, *The Nervous System;* RANSON, *The Anatomy of the Nervous System.*

BIOCHEMISTRY.

A. HUNTER, M.A., B.SC., M.B., CH.B.....................*Professor.*
H. WASTENEYS, PH.D...............................*Associate Professor.*
MISS C. C. BENSON, B.A., PH.D....*Associate Professor of Physiological Chemistry in the Faculty of Household Science.*
H. B. SPEAKMAN, M.SC.......*Associate Professor of Zymology (Research).*
MISS C. M. HARWOOD, B.A., *Instructor in Food Chemistry in the Faculty of Household Science.*
MISS J. McFARLANE, M.A..........................*Demonstrator.*
R. W. I. URQUHART, B.A............................*Fellow.*
N. S. Clark, B.A......................................*Fellow.*
A. M. WYNNE, M.A....................*Fellow and Research Assistant.*
H. BORSOOK...*Fellow.*

The following courses of instruction, each extending throughout the session, are offered:

1. A course of lectures in General Biochemistry; two a week.

2. A course of lectures and conferences in Advanced Biochemistry; two a week.

3. A laboratory course in General Biochemistry; four to six hours a week.

4. An advanced laboratory course in Biochemistry; six or more hours a week.

5. A course of lectures on the Principles of Nutrition; one hour a week during the Easter term. Open only to students who have taken Course 1.

6. An introductory course consisting of 60 hours of lectures and laboratory work; intended mainly for veterinary students.

7. Research in Biochemistry.

Text-books and Works of Reference:

(a) Elementary or General: HAMMARSTEN, *Text Book of Physiological Chemistry;* ABDERHALDEN-HALL, *Text Book of Physiological Chemistry;* MATHEWS, *Text Book of Physiological Chemistry;* ROBERTSON, *Principles of Biochemistry.*

(b) Advanced or Special: *Monographs on Biochemistry,* edited by Plimmer and Hopkins; ROBERTSON, *Physical Chemistry of the Proteins;* TAYLOR, *Digestion and Metabolism;* LUSK, *Science of Nutrition;* EFFRONT, *Biochemical Catalysts in Life and Industry;* EULER, *General Chemistry of the Enzymes;* ABDERHALDEN, *Biochemisches Handlexikon;* NEUBERG, *Der Harn.*

Laboratory Handbooks:

(a) Elementary: PLIMMER, *Practical Organic and Biochemistry;* HAWK, *Practical Physiological Chemistry;* FOLIN, *Laboratory Manual of Biological Chemistry;* HALLIBURTON, *Essentials of Chemical Physiology;* COLE, *Practical Physiological Chemistry.*

(b) Advanced: ABDERHALDEN, *Handbuch der biochemischen Arbeitsmethoden;* ELLINGER, *Analyse des Harns.*

FOOD CHEMISTRY.

MISS C. C. BENSON, PH.D.........................*Associate Professor.*
MISS C. M. HARWOOD. B.A.............................*Instructor.*
MISS E. F. D. MARTIN, B.A..............................*Assistant.*

HONOUR COURSES.

1. A course of lectures, two a week, on the Chemistry of Foods and Nutrition.

2. A laboratory course on the Chemistry of Foods. Six hours a week.

3. An advanced laboratory course on the Chemistry of Foods and on problems of Nutrition, with discussion of supplementary reading.

4. Research work in Food Chemistry and Metabolism.

PASS COURSES.

5. Chemistry of Food Constituents. Laboratory work for pass students of the Third Year. One afternoon a week.

6. Composition of Foods. Lectures and laboratory work for pass students of the Fourth Year. Four hours a week.

Text-books and works of reference include: WINTON, *Food Analysis;* LEACH, *Food Inspection and Analysis;* LUSK, *Science of Nutrition;* PAVLOV, *The Work of the Digestive Glands;* ALLYN, *Elementary Applied Chemistry;* SNELL, *Household Chemistry;* SNYDER, *Human Foods;* HALLIBURTON, *Essentials of Chemical Physiology;* Canadian and American bulletins on the chemistry of foods.

PHYSIOLOGY.

J. J. R. MACLEOD, M.B., CH.B., D.P.H......*Professor of Physiology.*
J. M. D. OLMSTED, M.A., PH.D.....*Assistant Professor of Physiology.*
N. B. TAYLOR, M.B. ....*Lecturer.*
S. U PAGE, B.A..*Fellow.*
MISS J. M. LANG, B.A...*Fellow.*
J. W. MAC ARTHUR, M.A.............................*Demonstrator.*
MISS C. J. FRASER, M.A.........................*Fellow (part time).*
E. C. NOBLE.....................*Fellow and Research Assistant.*
C. H. BEST.........................*Fellow and Research Assistant.*
C. F. KNIGHT, M.B.............................*Fellow (part time).*
E. FIDLAR, B.A., M.B.............................*Research Assistant.*

The following courses of instruction each extending throughout the Session are offered:

1. Systematic lectures and demonstrations in human physiology. Four a week.

2. Lectures in general physiology.

3. Advanced lectures. Two a week.

4. General laboratory courses. (Total of 135 hours).
   (*a*) Neuro-muscular Physiology.
   (*b*) Circulation, respiration and digestion.
   (*c*) Nervous system and special senses.

5. Laboratory course in general physiology.

6. Advanced laboratory courses.

7. Research in physiology.

8. Journal Club. One hour a week.

9. Elementary lectures on the principles of human physiology.

Text-books and works of reference: G. N. STEWART, *Manual of Physiology;* J. J. R. MACLEOD, *Physiology and Biochemistry in Modern Medicine;* STARLING'S or HOWELL'S *Physiologies;* BAYLISS, *General Physiology;* LUCIANI, *Physiology* (trans. by F. Welby); *Monographs in Physiology* (ed. by E. H. Starling). *Monographs in Experimental Biology* (ed. by J. Loeb and W. J. V. Osterhout). Other works important for consultation are MARSHALL, *Physiology of Reproduction;* SCHAFER, *Endocrine Organs; Text-book of Physiology* (ed. by E. A. Schäfer); *Recent and Further Advances in Physiology* (ed. by Leonard Hill); C. S. SHERRINGTON, *Mammalian Physiology.*

CHEMISTRY.

W. L. MILLER, B.A., PH.D.............*Professor of Physical Chemistry.*
F. B. ALLAN, PH.D....................*Professor of Organic Chemistry.*
Secretary of the Department of Chemistry.
F. B. KENRICK, M.A., PH.D.............................*Professor.*
J. B. FERGUSON, B.A....................*Associate Professor (Research).*
J. T. BURT-GERRANS, PHM.B., M.A., *Assistant Professor of Electrochemistry.*
L. J. ROGERS, B.A.Sc.......*Assistant Professor of Analytical Chemistry.*
W. S. FUNNELL, M.A...................................*Lecturer.*
W. H. MARTIN, M.A....................................*Lecturer.*
J. KELLEHER, B.A.Sc............................*Research Assistant.*
J. E. CLARK, B.A.Sc....................................*Assistant.*
N. A. CLARK, B.S.A., M.A.....................................*Assistant.*
C. S. GILBERT, B.S....................................*Assistant.*
E. HAAS, B.S....................................*Assistant.*
W. B. LEAF, B.S....................................*Assistant.*
G. H. W. LUCAS....................................*Assistant.*
T. C. McMULLEN, B.A....................................*Assistant.*
J. W. REBBECK, B.Sc....................................*Assistant.*
MISS I. L. ROBERTS, B.A....................................*Assistant.*
M. E. SMITH, M.A.....................................*Assistant.*
G. WILLIAMS, B.S....................................*Assistant.*

This subject forms part of the courses of study prescribed for students proceeding to degrees in Arts, Applied Science, Forestry, Medicine, and Veterinary Science.

In the Honour Course "Chemistry and Mineralogy" in the Faculty of Arts, provision is made by suitable options for students who wish to qualify as Specialists in Science under the Department of Education; in the Honour Course "Chemistry" no such provision is made. In both these courses the laboratory work of the fourth year consists of research in one of the branches of chemistry; and arrangements have been made under which this work may be carried out by students of the "Chemistry" course either in the Chemical Laboratory or in the laboratories of the department of Chemical Engineering or of Biochemistry, and in the case of students in the "Chemistry and Mineralogy" course either in the Chemical Laboratory or in the laboratories of the department of Chemical Engineering.

Lectures.

The following courses are provided:

1. Elementary Chemistry: An introductory course in general chemistry with experimental illustrations. Two lectures a week during session.

2. A course of lectures on the influence of chemistry on the progress of civilization. Two lectures a week during session. Note—These lectures are intended for fourth year Pass students but if the class is too small to justify the giving of this course, Course 7 will be substituted.

3. Elementary Organic Chemistry: A course of experimental lectures on the systematic classification of the aliphatic compounds and some of the more common aromatic compounds. Two lectures a week during session.

4. Organic Chemistry: The work in Course 3 is reviewed and extended, fuller consideration being given to the isocyclic compounds. Two lectures a week during session.

5. Advanced Organic Chemistry: A course on heterocyclic compounds, synthetic methods and stereochemistry. Two lectures a week during session.

6a. History of Chemistry: A short course of lectures, commencing in January, on the development of chemistry and chemical theory.

6b. Essays on Prescribed Topics.

7. Elementary Physical Chemistry: An experimental course on the elements of chemical mechanics and electrochemistry. Fifty lectures.

8. Elementary Electrochemistry: Twenty-five lectures illustrated by experiments.

9. A course on the application of geometry and the calculus to physico-chemical problems. Fifty lectures.

10. Chemical equilibrium in two-component systems, based on the theory of chemical potential. Fifty lectures.

11. Advanced Physical Chemistry. The phase rule, chemical thermodynamics, and chemical kinetics. Fifty lectures.

12a. Applied Chemistry.

12b. Applied Organic Chemistry.

Laboratory Work.

13. Elementary quantitative chemistry.

14. Elementary quantitative chemistry (shorter course).

15. Analysis, chemical mechanics and organic preparations. Four hours a week.

16. Quantitative and qualitative analysis.

17. Analysis of minerals and rocks.

18. Analysis, organic preparations and physico-chemical measurements.

19. Practical organic chemistry.

20. Physico-chemical measurements, and electro-chemistry.

21. Research work for advanced students.

24. A short course of physico-chemical measurements, including electrical conductivity, migration, and freezing point of solutions.

25. Electrochemistry, to accompany lecture Course 8.

26. A laboratory course to accompany course 2.

27. Analysis, including electroanalysis.

28. Chemical equilibrium between salts and their aqueous solutions.

29. Chemical equilibrium, including silicates.

Laboratory Regulations.

Each student proposing to attend lectures or practical work in the chemical laboratory must apply for a card which will have marked on it the number of his seat in the lecture room, of his working place in the laboratory and of his locker. These cards will be given only to students presenting their registration cards, and no working place in the laboratory will be allotted until a deposit of four dollars (for some classes three dollars) has been made. Each student will be held responsible for the seat, etc., allotted him, and no change may be made without permission. At the close of the Easter term this card must be presented for certificate of attendance.

Each student is provided with a suitable note-book in which to keep an account of the work done by him during the year. These books will be examined from time to time, and marks will be assigned. The student's standing in practical chemistry is based upon these marks, together with those assigned for the practical examinations of the term, and for written examinations on the work.

An account will be kept with each student; all apparatus broken or destroyed and all fines will be charged against his deposit, which must be renewed when exhausted.

The apparatus provided is intended for use in the laboratory only, and may not be removed from the building. At the close of the term's work it must be returned clean and dry.

GEOLOGY AND PALÆONTOLOGY.

A. P. COLEMAN, M.A., PH.D., F.R.S............*Professor of Geology.*
W. A. PARKS, PH.D.......................*Professor of Palaeontology.*
A. MacLEAN, B.A..............................*Assistant Professor.*
W. S. DYER, B.A..............................*Research Assistant.*

PASS COURSES.

1. Elementary Geology and Physiography: A course of twenty-five lectures is given weekly throughout the session. Works of reference: SCOTT, *Introduction to Geology;* DAVIS, *Physical Geography.*

2. (a) A course of fifty lectures and (b) fifty hours' practical work, designed to cover the whole field in a general way. Works of reference: As in course No. 1.

3. Dynamic and Structural Geology. A shorter course for students of the pass course. Twenty-five lectures.

4. Palaeontology: (a) A course of twenty-five lectures on Invertebrate and Vertebrate Palaeontology; (b) a laboratory course of fifty hours.

5. Historical Geology. A course of fifty lectures and fifty hours laboratory work on historical geology and palaeontology with special reference to Canada.

HONOUR COURSES.

6. Historical and Stratigraphical Geology and Palæontology. A course of fifty lectures is given throughout the session. Works of reference: SCOTT, *Introduction to Geology;* GEIKIE, *Text-book of Geology;* PIRRSON AND SCHUCHERT, *Text-book of Geology.*

7. Illustrative practical course to accompany No. 6. A course of thirty hours in the use of maps and sections, and the study of fossils typical of the different formations.

8. Dynamical and Structural Geology: A course of fifty lectures. Works of reference: GEIKIE, *Geology;* CHAMBERLIN and SALISBURY, *Geology.*

9. Invertebrate Palæontology: A course of fifty lectures throughout the session. Works of reference: Eastman's translation of ZITTEL's *Text-book of Palæontology;* NICHOLSON, *Manual of Palæontology;* STEINMANN-DÖDERLEIN, *Elemente der Palæontologie;* GRABAU, *North American Index Fossils.*

10. Invertebrate Palæontology: A laboratory course of seventy-five hours. Works of reference: As in course No. 9; Palæontological publications of the Geological Survey of Canada, and of the different State surveys; Bulletins and Monographs of the Geological Survey of the United States.

11. Drawing and Cartography: A practical course of fifty hours in the Faculty of Applied Science.

12. Archæan Geology: A course of twenty-five hours throughout the session. Works of reference: VAN HISE, *Precambrian Geology;* GEIKIE, *Text-book of Geology;* Reports of the Geological Survey of Canada and of the Ontario Department of Mines.

13. Glacial Geology and Physiography: A course of twenty-five lectures throughout the session. Works of reference: GEIKIE, *Great Ice Age;* PENCK, *Morphologie der Erdoberfläche;* DE LAPPARENT, *Géographie Physique.*

14. Geological Surveying and Cartography: A course of field work and practical work in drafting. Three hours per week throughout the year.

15. Economic Geology: A course of fifty lectures throughout the session. Works of reference: KEMP, *The Ore Deposits of the United States and Canada;* TARR, *Economic Geology of the United States;* RIES, *Economic Geology of the United States;* BECK, *The Nature of Ore Deposits;* PHILLIPS, *Ore Deposits;* Reports of the Geological Survey of Canada and of the Ontario Department of Mines.

16. Practical Economic Geology: A course of fifty hours' laboratory work to illustrate course No. 15.

17. Meteorology: A course of twenty-five lectures. Works of reference: DAVIS, *Elementary Meteorology;* HANN, *Klimatologie.*

18. Vertebrate Palæontology: A course of twenty-five lectures. Works of reference: WOODWARD, *Vertebrate Palæontology;* NICHOLSON AND LYDEKKER, *Manual of Palæontology;* ZITTELL, *Text Book of Palæontology,* Vol. II. (translation by Eastman).

19. Stratigraphic Palæontology: A course of seventy-five hours lectures and laboratory work. Works of reference: The publications in the Library of the Department, including various monographs on special subjects and the palæontological reports of the different states and societies.

20. Mining Geology: A course of twenty-five lectures on geological problems associated with mining, typical mining regions in Canada, the United States, and elsewhere being discussed from the geological side. Works of reference: As in courses Nos. 12 and 15.

21. Fifty hours laboratory work on the geology and palæontology of the Province of Ontario.

22. A shorter course of (*a*) fifty lectures and (*b*) seventy-five hours' laboratory work on palaeontology and stratigraphy.

23. A course of fifty lectures on the history of the sciences of geology and palaeontology.

24. Fifty hours of laboratory work on structural geology.

25. Twenty-five hours' laboratory work on vertebrate palaeontology.

26. Seventy-five hours' laboratory work to supplement course 16.

27. Seventy-five hours in field palaeontology.

MINERALOGY AND PETROGRAPHY.

T. L. WALKER, M.A., PH.D...............................*Professor.*
A. L. PARSONS, B.A.....................................*Associate Professor.*
J. E. THOMSON, B.A.SC....................................*Lecturer.*
E. W. TODD, B.A..*Research Assistant.*

For students in the Faculty of Arts of the University of Toronto the following courses of lectures and demonstrations have been arranged:

1. Elementary Mineralogy: A course of twenty-five lectures once a week throughout the year. Books of reference: DANA, *Text-book of Mineralogy;* ROGERS, *Mineralogy.*

2. A short practical course illustrative of the above, involving twenty hours' laboratory work. Books of reference: As for Course 1.

3. Morphological Crystallography: A course of twenty-five lectures once a week throughout the year. Books of reference: WALKER, *Crystallography*.

4. Blowpipe Analysis and Determinative Mineralogy: A laboratory course of three hours a week throughout the year (two hours a week for pass students). Books of reference: EAKLE, *Mineral Tables;* BRUSH-PENFIELD, *Blowpipe Analysis.*

5. Determinative Mineralogy: A laboratory course in continuation of Course 4. Two hours a week. Book of reference: BRUSH-PENFIELD, *Blowpipe Analysis.*

6. Physical Mineralogy: A course of fifty hours' lectures and laboratory work, introducing the student to optical and physical crystallography as a preparation for the study of microscopic petrography (seventy-five hours for pass students). Books of reference: DANA, *Text-book of Mineralogy;* WALKER, *Crystallography.*

7. Practical Crystallography, including goniometric measurements, crystal drawing, projection and calculation with experiments in physical mineralogy. One day a week during the Michaelmas term.

8. Systematic Mineralogy: A course of fifty hours' lectures and laboratory work, being a continuation of courses 1 and 2. Books of reference: DANA, *Text-book of Mineralogy;* EAKLE, *Mineral Tables.*

9. General Mineralogy: Twenty-five lectures on special subjects to be selected from year to year. Books of reference: KOBELL, *Geschicte der Mineralogie;* FOUQUÉ ET MICHEL-LÉVY, *Synthèse des Minéraux et des Roches.*

10. General Mineralogy: Practical course of seven hours a week throughout the year.

11. Petrography: One hour a week lectures and practical work throughout the session. Books of reference: KEMP, *Handbook of Rocks;* HARKER, *Petrology for students.*

12. Petrography: Two hours a week devoted to practical petrography, both macroscopic and microscopic. Books of reference: LUQUER, *Minerals in Rock Sections;* HARKER, *Petrology for Students.*

13. Assaying: Laboratory work in the different branches of the subject, occupying three hours a week throughout the session.

14. Advanced Petrography: Twenty-five lectures on the characteristics of the rock-forming minerals and on general petrography. Book of reference: IDDINGS, *Rock Minerals.*

15. Mineralography: Fifty hours laboratory work in the study of opaque minerals by microscopic methods in reflected light. Book of reference: DAVY AND FARNHAM, *Microscopic Examination of the Ore Minerals.*

16. A course in Mineral Analysis, seventy-five hours.

17. Metallurgy, an introductory course of twelve hours.

The work in Mineralogy is carried on in the Mineralogical Laboratories in the Chemistry and Mineralogy Building.

HOUSEHOLD SCIENCE.

Members of the Faculty of Household Science.

MISS A. L. LAIRD, M.S.........................*Associate Professor.*
MISS H. HILL, B.S...*Lecturer.*
MISS E. M. HICKMANS, M.Sc...............................*Lecturer.*
MISS F. GRAPER, B.S..................................*Instructor.*
MISS E. W. PARK, B.A.........................*Laboratory Assistant.*
MRS. F. J. NETHERCOTT, M.A.....................*Research Worker.*

A.—IN THE FACULTY OF ARTS.
PASS COURSES.

1*a*. History of Home Life: A course of lectures one~ hour a week throughout the session.

3*a*. Household Science for Third Year students. A course of lectures and laboratory work throughout the session.

4*a*. Household Science for Fourth Year students. A course of lectures and laboratory work throughout the session.

HONOUR COURSES.

1*b*. Household Science: One hour a week throughout the session.

2. Household Management: A course of six hours a week throughout the session. This includes (*a*) a study of metals, woods, textiles, etc., used in the home, and the principles underlying their care, (*b*) the house, (*c*) the home care of the sick.

3*b*. Foods and Food Values: A course of twelve hours a week throughout the session—lectures and laboratory work.

4*b*. Economics of the Household: A lecture course of two hours a week throughout the session. It includes the economics of spending, the division of the income, etc.

4*c*. Dietetics: A lecture course of two hours a week throughout the session and discussion periods, two hours a week. Methods of investigating the kind and amount of food required under varying conditions are discussed. Practical application of this knowledge is made in the construction of dietaries for different classes of people.

4*d*. An advanced laboratory course of six hours a week throughout the session. It includes practice in marketing and in preparing and serving meals and special diets. Each student is given the opportunity to investigate special problems bearing on her work.

B.—COURSE IN DEPARTMENT OF PUBLIC HEALTH NURSING.

5. A lecture course in nutrition and dietetics, family budgets are also discussed.

Occasional Work: Under certain conditions, occasional students may be admitted to Courses 3*a* and 4*a*.

—16

Graduate Work: Opportunities are offered in the laboratories to graduate students who desire to engage in research work.

Laboratory deposit fee: a deposit of three dollars ($3.00) is required of each student taking laboratory courses. This amount, minus the cost of equipment and apparatus destroyed, will be returned at the end of the year.

Books of reference: HUTCHISON, *Food and Dietetics;* WATSON, *Food and Feeding;* LUSK, *Science of Nutrition;* CARTER, HOWE AND MASON, *Nutrition and Clinical Dietetics;* SHERMAN, *Chemistry of Food and Nutrition;* HESS, *Principles and Practice of Infant Feeding;* BAILEY, *Source, Chemistry and Use of Food Products;* SHERMAN, *Food Products;* VULTÉ AND VANDERBILT, *Food Industries;* LEACH, *Food Inspection and Analysis;* WILEY, *Foods and Their Adulteration;* WELD, *Marketing of Farm Products;* McKILLOP AND ATKINSON, *Economics, American Academy of Political and Social Science, Cost of Living;* HASKINS, *How to Keep Household Accounts;* SHEAFFER, *Household Accounting;* CAMPBELL, *Household Economics;* RICHARDS, *Cost of Living, Cost of Shelter;* RICHARDS AND ELLIOTT, *Chemistry of Cooking and Cleaning;* RAVENHILL, *Household Administration;* TINKLER AND MASTERS, *Applied Chemistry,* Vol. I.; CLARK, *The Care of a House;* BALDERSTON, *Laundering;* MARSH, *Laundry Work;* BALDERSTON, *Housewifery;* VAN RENSSELAER, ROSE AND CANON, *Manual of Home Making;* HAMPTON-ROBB, *Nursing, Its Principles and Practice;* MAXWELL AND POPE, *Practical Nursing;* KINNE AND COOLEY, *Shelter and Clothing;* WOOLMAN AND McGOWAN, *Textiles;* McGOWAN AND WAITE, *Textiles;* DOOLEY, *Textiles;* KINNE, *Equipment for Teaching Domestic Science;* Government Bulletins; *Journal of Biological Chemistry, Journal of Home Economics.*

RELIGIOUS KNOWLEDGE.

REV. W. R. R. ARMITAGE, M.A.......................Wycliffe College.
REV. JAMES BALLANTYNE, B.A., D.D...................Knox College.
REV. H. S. BELLISLE, M.A......................:.....St. Michael's College.
W. T. BROWN, M.A., PH.D..........................Victoria College.
REV. F. H. COSGRAVE, B.A., B.D....................Trinity College.
REV. R. DAVIDSON, PH.D............................Knox College.
REV. H. T. F. DUCKWORTH, M.A....................Trinity College.
REV. ALFRED GANDIER, M.A., D.D., LL.D.............Knox College.
REV. W. T. HALLAM, B.A., D.D.....................Wycliffe College.
S. H. HOOKE, M.A., B.D............................Victoria College.
REV. A. J. JOHNSTON, B.A..........................Victoria College.
REV. T. C. S. MACKLEM, M.A., D.D., LL.D., D.C.L..... Trinity College.
REV. E. A. McINTYRE, M.A., B.D...................Wycliffe College.
REV. J. F. McLAUGHLIN, B.A., D.D.................Victoria College.
REV. WILLIAM MANSON, M.A........................Knox College.
REV. J. H. MICHAEL, M.A..........................Victoria College.
REV. H. W. K. MOWLL, M.A........................Wycliffe College.

Rev. M. J. Oliver, Ph.M......................St. Michael's College.
Rev. T. R. O'Meara, B.A., LL.D...................Wycliffe College.
E. T. Owen, M.A.....................................Trinity College.
Rev. C. Venn Pilcher, M.A., B.D.................Wycliffe College.
Rev. W. A. Potter, M.A., B.D.....................Victoria College.
Rev. D. M. Ramsay, D.D.............................Knox College.
Rev. J. D. Robertson, M.A., D.Sc....................Knox College.
Rev. F. H. Wallace, M.A., D.D....................Victoria College.
Rev. J. B. Walsh, M.A........................St. Michael's College.

First Year—

1a. A first course in the English Bible. One hour.
1b. A first course in Natural and Revealed Religion. One hour.
1c. A first course in the language of the Greek New Testament. Three hours.
1d. Oriental Languages 1a, p. 101. One hour.

Second Year—

2a. A second course in the English Bible. Two hours.
2b. A second course in Natural and Revealed Religion. Two hours.
2c. A second course in the language of the Greek New Testament. Not less than two hours.
2d. A course in Church History (Victoria). Two hours.
2e. Oriental Languages 2a, p. 101. Two hours.

Third Year—

3a. A third course in the English Bible. Three hours.
3b. A third course in Natural and Revealed Religion. Three hours.
3c. A first course in the Literature and Language of Greek Testament. Three hours.
3d. A course in Church History. Three hours.
3e. A first course in the History and Philosophy of Religion. Three hours.
3f. Oriental Languages 3a, p. 102. Three hours.

Fourth Year—

4a. A fourth course in the English Bible. Three hours.
4b. A fourth course in Natural and Revealed Religion. Three hours.
4c. A second course in the Literature and Language of Greek Testament. Three hours.
4d. A course in Church History. Three hours.
4e. A second course in the History and Philosophy of Religion. Three hours.
4f. Oriental Languages 4a, p. 102. Three hours.

WORLD HISTORY.

C. T. CURRELLY, M.A.........*Professor of the History of Industrial Art.*

Students of the Third and Fourth Years will attend the same lectures and will take course 3 and either course 1 or course 2.

A.—ART AND ARCHAEOLOGY.

1. A course on the History of Art.
2. A course on the Development of the Mechanical Industries.

These courses are to be taken in alternate sessions.

B.—HISTORY OF SCIENTIFIC THOUGHT.

3. A course on the Progress of Ideas with special reference to the evolution of the sciences, scientific discoveries, and the relation of science to problems of life and thought.

MILITARY STUDIES.

W. R. LANG, D.Sc., COLONEL, (late General Staff, C.E.F.)......*Director.*

These courses are options in all Arts courses of the second, third and fourth years respectively. Students who have had some military training— C.E.F., Militia, or Cadet Corps—are admitted.

1. This course comprises elementary tactics, topography, musketry, organization and administration, and in addition to these professional subjects lectures on citizenship, the relations between the various parts of the Empire with regard to defence, trade-routes, coal and fuel stations, naval power, and the distribution of the Empire's armed forces.

2. The professional subjects of course 1 are continued.

In addition to the educative nature of the subjects considered in these two courses, they comprise the work necessary for C.O.T.C. certificate "A" which qualifies for substantative commissions as Lieutenants of Infantry. Candidates completing these and passing the examination conducted by the Militia Department will be recommended for this certificate.

3. This course will cover the work required for the higher Certificate and will involve the study of the Science of War, Strategy, and some portion of Military History. Those who complete this course successfully and have had defined military experience will be recommended to the Militia Department for the certificate.

For particulars of the C.O.T.C., in which the practical portion of these courses is done, see page 60.

TIME-TABLE.

	MONDAY.	TUESDAY.	WEDNESDAY.
8			
9	1 Latin 2 German 3 Ethics 4 English	1 English 2 Latin 3 Hebrew, Rel. Know. 4 Ethics	1 Latin 2 Rel. Know., Mil. Stud. 3 Ethics 4 English
10	1 German 2 French 3 Latin 4 Latin	1 French 2 German 3 English 4 Math. I, Chem.	1 French 2 English. 3 Phys., G. & M., H.S. 4 French
11	1 Mathematics 2 Zool. or Bot., Math. II 3 Anc. & Mod. Hist. 4 Rel. Know., Mil. Stud.	1 Trig., Rel. Know. 2 Greek 3 Math. I, Chem. 4 Hist. Phil.	1 Heb., Ital., Span. 2 Chem., Math. I 3 Economics 4 Anc. & Mod. Hist.
12	1 Science 2 Greek 3 Hist. Phil. 4 Math. II, Zool., Bot.	2 History 3 Math. II, Bot., Zool. 4 Greek	1 Science 2 Phys., G. & M. 3 Anc. & Mod. Hist. 4 Hebrew, Phys., G. & M., H. S.
1			
2	1 French 2 †Chemistry 3 †Phys., †G. & M., †H.S. 4 Economics	1 Greek 2†Phys., †G. & M. 3 Ital., Span. 4 Ital., Span.	1 Greek 2 †Zool., †Bot. 3 French 4 German
3	1 Greek 2 †Chemistry 3 †Phys., †G. & M., †H.S.	1 Heb., Ital., Span. 2†Phys., †G. & M. 3 Economics 4 †Zool., †Bot..	2 †Zool., †Bot., G. & M. 3 German 4†Phys., †G. & M., †H.S.
4	2 Philosophy	2 Economics 3 Psychol. 4 †Zool., †Bot.	2 Heb., Ital., Span. 3 Greek 4†Phys., †H. S.
5			

The third and fourth year hours of instruction in the Sciences are subject to change of which due notice will be given to the students concerned.

TIME-TABLE.

	THURSDAY.	FRIDAY.	SATURDAY.
8			
9	1 English 2 Latin, G. & M. 3 Ethics 4 Rel. Know., Mil. Stud.	1 Latin 2 Greek 3 Rel. Know. 4 English	2 Rel. Know., Mil. Stud. 3 English 4 French
10	1 Greek 2 French 3 English 4 Anc. & Mod. Hist.	1 German 2 Latin 3 French 4 Ethics	1 Latin 2 English 3 Greek, French 4 German
11	1 Heb., Ital., Span. 2 Chem. or Math. I 3 Phys., G. & M., H.S. 4 Math. II, Zool., Bot.	1 Mathematics 2 French 3 Latin 4 Latin, Math. I., Chem.	1 French 2 Heb., Ital., Span. 3 German 4 Hebrew, Phys., G. & M., H.S.
12	1 Anc. History 2 Zool., Bot., Math. II 3 Hist. Phil., Zool., Bot., Math. II 4 Ital., Span.	1 Science 2 Phys. 3 Math. I, Chem. 4 Hist. Phil.	1 German 3 Hebrew, Mil. Stud.
1			
2	1 German 2 Economics 3 †Chemistry 4 †Chemistry	1 Heb., Ital., Span. 2 German 3 Ital., Span., Heb. 4 Economics	
3	2 Heb., Ital., Span. 3 †Chem. 4 †Chemistry	2 Philosophy 3 †Zool., †Bot. 4 Greek	
4	2 History 3 Psychol.	3 †Zool., †Bot.	
5			

† Laboratory periods.

PRESCRIPTION FOR COURSES.

The courses leading to the degree of Bachelor of Arts are

(a) THE PASS COURSE.

(b) The following Honour Courses:—

CLASSICS.	PSYCHOLOGY.
GREEK AND HEBREW.	MATHEMATICS AND PHYSICS.
ORIENTAL LANGUAGES.	PHYSICS.
ORIENTAL LANGUAGES, (GK. OPT.)	BIOLOGY.
	PHYSIOLOGY AND BIOCHEMISTRY.
FRENCH, GREEK AND LATIN.	PHYSIOLOGICAL AND BIOCHEMICAL
MODERN LANGUAGES.	SCIENCES.
ENGLISH AND HISTORY.	BIOLOGICAL AND MEDICAL SCIENCES.
MODERN HISTORY.	CHEMISTRY AND MINERALOGY.
POLITICAL SCIENCE.	CHEMISTRY.
COMMERCE AND FINANCE.	GEOLOGY AND MINERALOGY.
PHILOSOPHY.	HOUSEHOLD SCIENCE.
PHILOSOPHY, ENGLISH AND HISTORY.	HOUSEHOLD ECONOMICS.
	SCIENCE FOR TEACHERS.

(c) THE ARTS AND FORESTRY COURSE.

The requirements for each of these courses are detailed in the following schedules, where the numerals refer to the corresponding numbers of the courses on the pages indicated.

PASS COURSE.

First Year.

1. English 1a, 1b, p. 105	2 hours
2. Latin 1a, p. 98	4 "
3. One of Greek 1a *or* 1b, p. 96	4 "
Hebrew 1b, p. 101	4 "
German 1a, p. 108	4 "
French 1a, p. 110	4 '
Italian 1, p. 112 *or* Spanish 1a *or* 1c, p. 113	3 '
4. One of a second language from 3	4 "
Elementary Science 1, p. 143	3 '
5. Mathematics 1a, 1b, p. 132	2 "
6. One of Greek and Roman History 1, p. 100	1 '
Mathematics 1c, p. 132	1 '
Religious Knowledge 1a *or* 1b *or* 1c *or* 1d, p. 162	1 "

A student of Chinese birth and education is permitted to substitute Chinese for Latin in the First and Second Years. For such students a special curriculum in Chinese will be prepared.

Second Year.

In selecting the subjects of study in the Second Year the student should have in mind the subjects intended to be taken in the Third and Fourth Years.

1. A subject chosen in the Second Year should be continued through the Third and Fourth Years; foreign languages continued from the First Year, viz., Greek, Latin, Hebrew, German, French, Italian, Spanish, as well as English, History and Philosophy, may be taken in the Second Year without obligation to continue them in the Third and Fourth Years.

2. Political Economy, Psychology, Mathematics I, Mathematics II, Physics, Zoology, Botany, Chemistry, Geology and Mineralogy, Military Studies, if taken in the Second Year, must be continued throughout the Course.

3. Ethics, History of Philosophy and Ancient History may be begun in the Third Year, but if chosen must be continued in the Fourth Year.

4. English, Modern History and Religious Knowledge may be taken in the Third and Fourth Years without having been taken in the Second Year.

5. A student who proposes to take Household Science in the Third and Fourth Years is required to take Chemistry in the Second Year and Food Chemistry in the Third and Fourth Years.

6. A student who has no credit in Science in the First Year must take in the Second Year either Elementary Science of the First Year or one of the Sciences (including Mathematics I and Mathematics II) beginning in the Second Year. In the latter case the subject chosen must be continued through the Third and Fourth Years.

7. No student may take three foreign languages or three Sciences except by special permission of the Council on the recommendation of his College, but this permission does not carry with it the right to continue the three subjects in the Third and Fourth Years.

8. A student of the Second Year who has not previously taken Hebrew may, with the consent of his College and of the Council of the Faculty of Arts, substitute Hebrew of the First Year for a language of the Second Year, on condition that he substitute Hebrew of the Second and Third Years for a language of the Third and Fourth Years respectively.

9. The choice of subjects made in the Second Year cannot be varied except on joint action of the College and University authorities.

Prescription for the Second Year Pass Course.

(Five subjects).

1. One of Greek 2a *or* 2b, p. 96	3 hours
Latin 2a, p. 98	3 "
Hebrew 2b, p. 102	3 "
Mathematics I: Mathematics 2a, 2b, pp. 132, 133	3 "
Mathematics II: Actuarial Science 1, p. 135	3 '

Second Year—*Continued.*

Physics 9, p. 138	4 hours
Zoology 2, p. 144	4 "
Botany 2a, 2b, p. 148	4 "
Chemistry 1, 14, pp. 154, 155	4 '
Geology and Mineralogy: Mineralogy 1, 4, 11, pp. 158, 159	4 '

2. One of Greek 2a *or* 2b, p. 96 .... 3 '
   Latin 2a, p. 98 .... 3 ''
   Hebrew 2b, p. 102 .... 3 '
   German 2a, p. 108 .... 3 '
   French 2a, p. 110 .... 3 '
   Italian 2, p. 112 *or* Spanish 2a *or* 2b, p. 113 .... 3 '

3. Three of
   An additional language from 2 .... 3 '
   English 2a, 2b, p. 105 .... 2 '
   History 2a, 2e, p. 114 .... 2 '
   Political Economy 8, p. 118 .... 2 '
   Philosophy 2a, p. 125 *or* †2e, 2f, pp. 127, 128 .... 2 ''
   Religious Knowledge 2a *or* 2b *or* 2c *or* 2d *or* 2e, p. 162 .... 2 "
   Military Studies 1, p. 163 .... 2 '
   Not more than two of

   Psychology 2a, p. 131 .... 2 ''
   Mathematics I: Mathematics 2a, 2b, pp. 132, 133 3 "
   Mathematics II: Actuarial Science 1, p. 135 .... 3 "
   Physics 9, p. 138 .... 4 '
   Zoology 2, p. 144 .... 4 "
   Botany 2a, 2b, p. 148 .... 4 "
   Chemistry 1, 14, pp. 154, 155 .... 4 '
   Geology and Mineralogy: Mineralogy 1, 4, 11, pp. 158, 159, ... 4 '
   Elementary Science 1, p. 143 .... 3 "

Third and Fourth Years.

The plan upon which the work of the Third and Fourth Years is arranged is indicated so that students of the Second Year may make their choice of subjects of that year in such a way as to be able to enter the particular group desired in the higher years with the least possible adjustment.

The subjects of the Third and Fourth Years are arranged as follows:

(*a*) Greek, Latin, Hebrew .... 3 hours
(*b*) German, French, Italian *or* Spanish .... 3 "
(*c*) English .... 3 "
(*d*) Religious Knowledge *or* Military Studies 3
    †*St. Michael's College.*

(e) Ancient History *or* Modern History, Ethics, History of Philo-
     sophy, Political Economy, Psychology   3 hours
(f) Mathematics (3 hours), Physics, Zoology, Botany, Chemistry,
     Geology and Mineralogy   4
(g) Household Science   4

Notes—(a) Five subjects are to be chosen, not more than two from any
one group.

(b) Not more than three subjects may be chosen from groups (a), (b),
(c) and Religious Knowledge 3c, 4c, of (d).

(c) A student of the Third Year who has not previously taken Hebrew
may, with the consent of his College and of the Council of the Faculty of
Arts, substitute Hebrew of the First Year for a language of the Third Year,
on condition that he substitute Hebrew of the Second Year for a language
of the Fourth Year.

Based upon the arrangement of subjects the following groups are announced in this calendar as affording opportunities for wide choice of subjects and for the aptitudes of individual students.

A student in the Pass Course who is entitled to register in the Third
Year is required to submit to the authorities of his College, his selection
of subjects for each of the Third and Fourth Years. Registration cannot
be completed until the College has formally approved of his selection.

GROUP I.

1. Greek *or* Latin *or* Hebrew
2. A second language from 1
3. English *or* Religious Knowledge
4. Ancient History *or* Modern History *or* Political Economy *or* Ethics
     or History of Philosophy *or* Psychology *or* Physics *or* Zoology *or*
     Botany *or* Chemistry *or* Geology and Mineralogy *or* Religious
     Knowledge courses b, d, e, f (if not already chosen).
5. A second subject from 4.

GROUP II.

1. Greek *or* Latin
2. Ancient History
3. Political Economy *or* Ethics *or* History of Philosophy *or* Psychology *or*
     Religious Knowledge
4. English *or* a second foreign language *or* Religious Knowledge
5. An additional subject from 3 *or* 4 *or* Physics *or* Zoology *or* Botany *or*
     Chemistry *or* Geology and Mineralogy.

GROUP III.

1. Hebrew
2. Ethics
3. Ancient History *or* Modern History *or* Political Economy *or* History of
     Philosophy *or* Psychology *or* Religious Knowledge
4. English *or* a second foreign language *or* Religious Knowledge
5. An additional subject from 3 *or* 4 *or* Physics *or* Zoology *or* Botany *or*
     Chemistry *or* Geology and Mineralogy.

GROUP IV.

1. Latin
2. French
3. English
4. Modern History *or* Ethics *or* History of Philosophy *or* Psychology *or* Religious Knowledge
5. A second subject from 4.

GROUP V.

1. French *or* German *or* Italian *or* Spanish
2. A second language from 1
3. English *or* Modern History *or* History of Philosophy
4. A second subject from 3
5. Political Economy *or* Physics *or* Zoology *or* Botany *or* Chemistry *or* Geology and Mineralogy *or* Religious Knowledge.

GROUP VI.

1. English
2. Latin *or* French *or* History of Philosophy
3. A second subject from 2
4. A third subject from 2 *or* Modern History
5. Religious Knowledge *or* any subject possible under the timetable and consistent with the arrangement of subjects as found in the paragraph under the heading Third and Fourth Years.

GROUP VII.

1. Modern History
2. English
3. Latin *or* French
4. Zoology *or* Botany *or* Geology and Mineralogy
5. History of Philosophy *or* Political Economy *or* Religious Knowledge.

GROUP VIII.

1. Modern History
2. Ethics *or* History of Philosophy *or* Psychology
3. Greek *or* Latin *or* Hebrew
4. French *or* German
5. English *or* Religious Knowledge.

GROUP IX.

1. Ethics *or* History of Philosophy
2. Political Economy
3. Greek *or* Latin *or* Hebrew *or* French *or* German *or* Italian *or* Spanish
4. English *or* Physics *or* Zoology *or* Botany *or* Chemistry *or* Geology and Mineralogy
5. Religious Knowledge *or* any subject possible under the timetable and consistent with the arrangement of subjects as found in the paragraph under the heading Third or Fourth Years.

GROUP X.

1. Mathematics I
2. Mathematics II
3. German *or* French *or* Italian *or* Spanish
4 Ethics *or* History of Philosophy *or* Psychology *or* Political Economy
5. English *or* Modern History *or* Religious Knowledge.

GROUP XI.

1. Physics *or* Zoology *or* Botany *or* Chemistry *or* Geology and Mineralogy
2. A second Science from 1 *or* Mathematics I *or* Mathematics II
3. English
4. French
5. Religious Knowledge *or* any subject possible under the timetable and consistent with the arrangement of subjects as found in the paragraph under the heading Third and Fourth Years.

GROUP XII.

1. Household Science
2. Chemistry
3. English *or* Modern History
4. Ethics *or* Economics
5. Religious Knowledge *or* any subject possible under the timetable and consistent with the arrangement of subjects as found in the paragraph under the heading Third and Fourth Years.

Prescription for the Third Year Pass Course.

Greek 3a, p. 96	3 hours
Latin 3a, p. 98	3 "
Hebrew 3b, p. 102	3 "
English 3a, 3b, p. 105	3 '
German 3a, p. 108	3 '
French 3a, p. 111	3 '
Italian 3a, 3b, p. 113	3 "
Spanish 3a, p. 113	3 "
Greek and Roman History 3a, p. 100	3 '
Modern History 3a, 3d, p. 114	3 '
Political Economy 19, p. 119	3 '
Philosophy 3a, p. 125 *or* †3i, p. 128	3 '
Philosophy 3b, p. 126 *or* †3f, 3g, 3h, p. 128	3 '
Psychology 3a, 3h, pp. 131, 132 *or*	3 '
Psychology 3b, 3i, pp. 131, 132	3 '
Mathematics I: Mathematics 3a, p. 133	3 '
Mathematics II: Mechanics 10, p. 135	3 '
Physics 10, pp. 138, 139	4 '
Zoology 3, p. 144	4 '
Botany 3, p. 148	4 "
Chemistry 3, 18, p. 155	4 '

† *St. Michael's College.*

Third Year—*Continued.*

Chemistry 3, p. 155 *and* Food Chemistry 5, p. 152	4 hours
Geology and Mineralogy: Geology 3, p. 157, *and* Geology 4, p. 157 *or* Mineralogy 6, p. 159	4 "
Household Science 3a, p. 160	4 '
Religious Knowledge 3a *or* 3b *or* 3c *or* 3d *or* 3e *or* 3f, p. 162	3 "
Military Studies 2, p. 163	3 '

Prescription for the Fourth Year Pass Course.

Greek 4a, p. 96	3 hours
Latin 4a, p. 99	3 "
Hebrew 4b, p. 102	3 "
English 4a, 4b, pp. 105, 106	3 '
German 4a, p. 108	3 ''
French 4a, p. 111	3 "
Italian 4a, p. 113	3 "
Spanish 4a, p. 113	3 '
Greek and Roman History 4a, p. 100	3 '
Modern History 4a, 4c, p. 115	3 '
Political Economy 34, p. 122	3 '
Philosophy 4a, p. 126 *or* †4j, p. 128	3 '
Philosophy 4b, p. 126 *or* †4g, 4h, 4i, p. 128	3 '
Psychology 4a, 4g, pp. 131, 132 *or*	3 '
Psychology 4b, 4h, pp. 131, 132	3 '
Mathematics I: Mathematics 4a, 4b, p. 133	3 '
Mathematics II: Astronomy 1, 2, p. 136	3 ''
Physics 11, p. 139	4 "
Zoology 4, p. 144	4 "
Botany 4, p. 148	4 '
Chemistry 2, 26, pp. 155, 156	4 "
Food Chemistry 6, p. 152	4 "
Geology and Mineralogy: Geology 13, 5 *or* 15 *and* 16, pp. 157, 158	4 "
Household Science 4a, p 160	4 "
Religious Knowledge 4a *or* 4b *or* 4c *or* 4d *or* 4e *or* 4f, p. 162	3 "
Military Studies 3, p. 163	3 '

CLASSICS.

Entrance Conditions.

Every student applying to enter the First Year of the Honour Course in Classics, must present, in addition to Pass Matriculation standing, a certificate of having obtained at Honour Matriculation or at an equivalent examination, at least 50% in Greek, Latin, Mathematics (Algebra and Geometry) as well as in at least one of French, German, Physics, Biology, preferably French or German.

† *St. Michael's College.*

A student who, on admission to this course, has not fulfilled all the entrance conditions, must do so at the examination of the First Year. Vide Secs. 57-62, pp. 41-43.

First Year.

English 1a, 1b, p. 105	2 hours
One of German 1a, p. 108	4 "
French 1a, p. 110	4 "
One of Mathematics 1c, p. 132	1 '
Religious Knowledge 1a *or* 1b *or* 1c *or* 1d, p. 162	1 "

(Candidates who are exempt from Science or German as a Pass subject of the First Year may offer this subject in lieu of Religious Knowledge.)

*Greek 1c, p. 97	5 hours
*Latin 1b, p. 99	4½"
*Greek and Roman History 1, p. 100	1 "

Second Year.

One of English 2a, 2b, p. 105	2 hours
German 2a, p. 108	3 "
French 2a, p. 110	3 "
One of English 2a, 2b, p. 105 (if not already chosen)	2 '
History 2a, 2e, p. 114	2 '
Religious Knowledge 2a *or* 2b *or* 2c *or* 2d *or* 2e, p. 162	2 "
Military Studies 1, p. 163	2 "
*Greek 2c, p. 97	5 "
*Latin 2b, p. 99	5½"
*Greek and Roman History 2a, 2b, p. 100	2 "

Third Year.

One of Greek 3g, p. 97 *and* Latin 3e, p. 100	1 hour
Religious Knowledge 3a *or* 3b *or* 3c *or* 3d *or* 3e *or* 3f, p. 162	3 hours
Military Studies 2, p. 163	3 "
*Greek 3b, p. 97	9 "
*Latin 3b, p. 99	6 '
*Greek and Roman History 3b, 3c, p. 101	1 '

Fourth Year.

One of Greek 4h, p. 98 *and* Latin 4d, p. 100	1 hour
Religious Knowledge 4a *or* 4b *or* 4c *or* 4d *or* 4e *or* 4f, p. 162	3 hours
Military Studies 3, p. 163	3 "
*Greek 4c, p. 97	7 "
*Latin 4b, p. 100	5 '
*Greek and Roman History 4b, 4c, 4d, p. 101	2 "
*Philology p. 101	1 "

* *Honours.*

GREEK AND HEBREW.

Entrance Conditions.

Every student applying to enter the First Year of the Honour Course in Greek and Hebrew, must present, in addition to Pass Matriculation standing, a certificate of having obtained at Honour Matriculation or at an equivalent examination, at least 50% in Greek, Latin, Mathematics (Algebra and Geometry) as well as in at least one of English, French, German.

A student who, on admission to this course, has not fulfilled all the entrance conditions, must do so at the examination of the First Year. Vide Secs. 57-62, pp. 41-43.

First Year.

English 1a, 1b, p. 105	2	hours
One of Mathematics 1c, p. 132	1	"
Religious Knowledge 1a *or* 1b *or* 1c *or* 1d, p. 162	1	"
*Greek 1e, p. 97	5	"
*Greek and Roman History 1, p. 100	1	
*Oriental Languages 1b, p. 101	4	

Second Year.

One of English 2a, 2b, p. 105	2	hours
Philosophy 2a, p. 125 *or* †2e, 2f, pp. 127, 128	2	"
Religious Knowledge 2a *or* 2b *or* 2c *or* 2d *or* 2e, p. 162	2	"
Military Studies 1, p. 163	2	"
One of Latin 2a, p. 98	3	
German 2a, p. 108	3	
French 2a, p. 110	3	"
*Greek 2e, 2f, p. 97	3½	"
*Greek and Roman History 2a, p. 100	½	"
*Oriental Languages 2c, 2d, 2g, pp. 102, 103	6	'

Third Year.

Greek and Roman History 3a, p. 100	3	hours
One of English 3a, 3b, p. 105	3	"
Philosophy 3a, p. 125 *or* †3i; p. 128	3	"
Philosophy 3b, p. 126 *or* †3f, 3g, 3h, p. 128	3	'
Religious Knowledge 3a *or* 3b *or* 3c *or* 3d *or* 3e *or* 3f, p. 162	3	"
Military Studies 2, p. 163	3	
*Greek 3e, 3f, p. 97	5	
*Oriental Languages 3b, 3d, 3g, pp. 102, 103	6	

† *St. Michael's College.*
* *Honours.*

Fourth Year.

Greek and Roman History 4a, p. 100	3	hours
One of English 4a, 4b, pp. 105, 106	3	"
Philosophy 4a, p. 126 *or* †4j, p. 128	3	"
Philosophy 4b, p. 126 *or* †4g, 4h, 4i, p. 128	3	"
Religious Knowledge 4a *or* 4b *or* 4c *or* 4d *or* 4e *or* 4f, p. 162	3	"
Military Studies 3, p. 163	3	"
*Greek 4f, 4g, p. 98	5	"
*Oriental Languages 4b, 4d, 4g, pp. 102, 103	5	

ORIENTAL LANGUAGES.

Entrance Conditions.

Every student applying to enter the Honour Course in Oriental Languages at the beginning of the Second Year is required to obtain at the examination of the First Year, at least Grade B Standing in the Pass Course with not less than 66 per cent. in Hebrew. It is recommended that the optional language should be either Greek or German.

It is possible however to transfer from any other Honour Course at the beginning of the Second Year, provided the candidate has obtained not less than 66 per cent. in Hebrew.

First Year.

English 1a, 1b, p. 105	2	hours
Latin 1a, p. 98	4	"
One of Greek 1a *or* 1b, p. 96	4	"
German 1a, p. 108	4	'
French 1a, p. 110	4	'
Mathematics 1a, 1b, p. 132	2	'
One of Mathematics 1c, p. 132	1	"
Greek and Roman History 1, p. 100	1	'
§Religious Knowledge 1a *or* 1b *or* 1c *or* 1d, p. 162	1	"
Oriental Languages 1b, p. 101	4	"

§*Students in this Course, who have not taken Greek previously, and who do not take Greek 1b, 2b, etc., are advised to take Religious Knowledge 1c, and the similar Courses in the subsequent years.*

Second Year.

English 2a, 2b, p. 105	2	hours
One of Greek 2a *or* 2b, p. 96	3	"
Latin 2a, p. 98	3	"
German 2a, p. 108	3	"
French 2a, p. 110	3	"

†*St. Michael's College.*

Honours.

Second Year—*Continued*.

One of History 2a, 2e, p. 114	2 hours
Philosophy 2a, p. 125 *or* †2e, 2f, pp. 127, 128	2 "
Religious Knowledge 2a *or* 2b *or* 2c *or* 2d *or* 2e, p. 162	2 "
Military Studies 1, p. 163	2 '
*Oriental Languages 2c, 2d, 2e, 2f, 2g, pp. 102, 103	10 "

Third Year.

Two of English 3a, 3b, p. 105	3 hours
Greek and Roman History 3a, p. 100	3 ".
History, 3a, 3d, p. 114	3 "
Philosophy 3a, p. 125 *or* †3i, p. 128; *or*	3 '
Philosophy 3b, p. 126 *or* †3f, 3g, 3h, p. 128	3 '
Religious Knowledge 3a *or* 3b *or* 3c *or* 3d *or* 3e *or* 3f, p.162	3 "
Military Studies 2, p. 163	3 '
One of Greek 3a, p. 96	3 '
Latin 3a, p. 98	3 '
German 3a, p. 108	3 '
French 3a, p. 111	3 '
*Oriental Languages 3c, 3d, 3e, 3f, 3g, p. 103	9 '
*Oriental Languages, one of 3h, 3i, 3j, p. 103	2 '

Fourth Year.

Two of English 4a, 4b, pp. 105, 106	3 hours
Greek and Roman History 4a, p. 100	3 "
History 4a, 4c, p. 115	3 "
Philosophy 4a, p. 126 *or* †4j, p. 128; *or*	3 '
Philosophy 4b, p. 126 *or* †4g, 4h, 4i, p. 128	3 '
Religious Knowledge 4a *or* 4b *or* 4c *or* 4d *or* 4e *or* 4f, p. 162	3 "
Military Studies 3, p. 163	3 '
One of Greek 4a, p. 96	3 '
Latin 4a, p. 99	3 '
German 4a, p. 108	3 '
French 4a, p. 111	3 '
*Oriental Languages 4c, 4d, 4e, 4f, 4g, p. 103	7 '
§*Oriental Languages, one of 4h, 4i, 4j, p. 103	2 "

§Students must continue the course selected in the Third Year.

Every candidate in this course shall, during the Fourth Year, present a dissertation on some subject connected with Oriental Languages or Literature, such subject to be previously approved by his instructors in the department. The essay will, on or before the 1st of April in each year, be laid before the instructors in Oriental Languages in University

†*St. Michael's College.*
*Honours.
—17

College, Victoria College and Trinity College, who will examine it and·
assign to it marks according to their judgment of its merit. Such marks
will be reported to the Registrar and be taken into account by the examiners in determining the standing of the candidate at the examination of
the Fourth Year.

ORIENTAL LANGUAGES.
Greek Option.
Entrance Conditions. .   ·

Every student applying to enter the Honour Course in Oriental Languages with Greek Option, at the beginning of the Second Year, is required
to obtain at the examination of the First Year, at least Grade B Standing
in the Pass Course with not less than 66% in Greek and Hebrew.

First Year.

English 1a, 1b, p. 105	2 hours
Latin 1a, p. 98	4 "
Mathematics 1a, 1b, p. 132	2 "
One of Mathematics 1c, p. 132	1 '
Religious Knowledge 1a or 1b or 1c or 1d, p. 162	1 '
Greek and Roman History 1, p. 100	1 '
Greek 1a, p. 96	4 '
Oriental Languages 1b, p. 101	4 '

Second Year.

English 2a, 2b, p. 105	2 hours
Latin 2a, p. 98	3 "
One of History 2a, 2e, p. 114	2 "
Philosophy 2a, p. 125 or †2e, 2f, pp. 127, 128	2 '
Religious Knowledge 2a or 2b or 2c or 2d or 2e, p. 162	2 "
Military Studies 1, p. 163	2 '
Greek 2a, 2f, pp. 96, 97	4 '
*Oriental Languages 2c, 2d, 2g, pp. 102, 103	6 '
Not less than 66% must be obtained in Greek.	

Third Year.

Greek and Roman History 3a, p. 100	3 hours
One of English 3a, 3b, p. 105	3 "
Philosophy 3a, p. 125 or †3i, p. 128	3 "
Philosophy 3b, p. 126 or †3f, 3g, 3h, p. 128	3
Religious Knowledge 3a or 3b or 3c or 3d or 3e or 3f, p. 162	3 "
Military Studies 2, p. 163	3
*Greek 3e, 3f, p. 97	5
*Oriental Languages 3b, 3d, 3g, pp. 102, 103	6

†*St. Michael's College.*
*Honours.

Fourth Year.

Greek and Roman History 4a, p. 100	3 hours
One of English 4a, 4b, pp. 105, 106	3 "
Philosophy 4a, p. 126 *or* †4j, p. 128	3 "
Philosophy 4b, p. 126 *or* †4g, 4h, 4i, p. 128	3 '
Religious Knowledge 4a *or* 4b *or* 4c *or* 4d *or* 4e *or* 4f, p. 162	3 "
Military Studies 3, p. 163	3
*Greek 4f, 4g, p. 98	5
*Oriental Languages 4b, 4d, 4g, pp. 102, 103	5

FRENCH, GREEK AND LATIN.
Entrance- Conditions.

Every student applying to enter the First Year of the Honour Course in French, Greek and Latin, must present, in addition to Pass Matriculation standing, a certificate of having obtained at Honour Matriculation or at an equivalent examination, at least 50% in Latin, Mathematics (Algebra and Geometry), and two of Greek, English, French.

A student who, on admission to this course, has not fulfilled all the entrance conditions, must do so at the examination of the First Year. Vide Secs. 57-62, pp. 41-43.

In each year of the Course, French, Greek and Latin are to be taken, two as honour subjects, the third as a pass subject. Candidates taking Greek as their pass subject, may begin the study of Greek in their First Year under the recently instituted course, Greek 1b, 2b, etc.

First Year.

One of Mathematics 1c, p. 132	1 hour
Religious Knowledge 1a *or* 1b *or* 1c *or* 1d, p. 162	1 "

(Candidates who are exempt from Science or German as a Pass subject of the First Year may offer this subject in lieu of Religious Knowledge.)

One of Greek 1a *or* 1b, p. 96	4 hours
Latin 1a, p. 98	4 "
French 1a, p. 110	4 "
Two of *Greek 1d, p. 97	5
*Latin 1b, p. 99	5
*French 1c, 1d, p. 111	5
*English 1a, 1c (ii), p. 106	2
*Greek and Roman History 1, p. 100	1

Second Year.

One of English 2a, 2b, p. 105	2 hours
Religious Knowledge 2a *or* 2b *or* 2c *or* 2d *or* 2e, p. 162	2 "
Military Studies 1, p. 163	2 "

† *St. Michael's College.*
* *Honours.*

Second Year—*Continued.*

One of Greek 2a *or* 2b, p. 96	3 hours
Latin 2a, p. 98	3 "
French 2a, p. 110	3 "
Two of *Greek 2c (omitting Thucydides), p. 97	4 "
*Latin 2b (omitting Livy, Bk. VI), p. 99	4½ "
*French 2c, 2d, 2e, p. 111	4½ "
Two of *Greek and Roman History 2a, p. 100	1 "
*Greek and Roman History 2b, p. 100	1
*Phonetics, p. 114	1 "

Third Year.

One of English 3a, 3b, p. 105	3 hours
French 3f, p. 112	2 „
Religious Knowledge 3a *or* 3b *or* 3c *or* 3d *or* 3e *or* 3f, p. 162	3 "
Military Studies 2, p. 163	3 "
One of Greek 3a, p. 96	3 '
Latin 3a, p. 98	3 '
French 3a, p. 111	3 '
Two of *Greek (to be prescribed later)	
*Latin 3f, p. 100	5 "
*French 3b, 3c, 3d, 3e, pp. 111, 112	5 "

Fourth Year.

(Available 1922-23.)

One of English
    Religious Knowledge
    Military Studies
One of Greek 4a *or* 4b
    Latin 4a
    French 4a
Two of *Greek
    *Latin
    *French

MODERN LANGUAGES.

Entrance Conditions.

Every student applying to enter the First Year of the Honour Course in Modern Languages, must present, in addition to Pass Matriculation standing, a certificate of having obtained at Honour Matriculation or at an equivalent examination, at least 50% in Latin, French, Mathematics (Algebra and Geometry), and in one of English, German, History.

Honours.

A student who, on admission to this course, has not fulfilled all the entrance conditions, must do so at the examination of the First Year. Vide Secs. 57-62, pp. 41-43.

In determining the standing of candidates in English, French, German, Italian and Spanish, examiners will take into account the report of the instructors in the University and Colleges in these subjects.

First Year.

One of	Mathematics 1c, p. 132	1 hour
	Elementary Science 1, p. 143	3 "
	Religious Knowledge 1a or 1b or 1c or 1d, p. 162	1 "
Three of	*English 1a, 1c, p. 106	3
	*German 1c, 1d, 1e, pp. 108, 109	4
	*French 1c, 1d, p. 111	4 "
	*Italian 1, p. 112	3 "
	*Spanish 1a, p. 113	3 "

Note—Not more than one new language may be begun in this First Year.

Second Year.

One of	Philosophy 2a, p. 125 or †2e, 2f, pp. 127, 128	2 hours
	Religious Knowledge 2a or 2b or 2c or 2d or 2e, p. 162	2 "
	Military Studies 1, p. 163	2 "
Three of	*English 2a, 2c, p. 106	4
	*German 2c, 2d, 2e, p. 109	4
	*French 2c, 2d, 2e, p. 111	4
	*Italian 2, p. 112	3 ..
	*Spanish 2a, p. 113	3 "
*Phonetics p. 114		1 "

Third Year.

§One of	German 3e, p. 109	2 hours
	French 3f, p. 112	2 "
	Italian 3d, p. 113	2 "
	Spanish 3c, p. 113	2 '
	Philosophy 3b, p. 126 or †3f, 3g, 3h, p. 128	3 '
	Religious Knowledge 3a or 3b or 3c or 3d or 3e or 3f, p. 162	3 '
	Military Studies 2, p. 163	3 "
Two of	*English 3a, 3b, 3c, pp. 106, 107	5 "
	*German 3b, 3c, 3d, p. 109	5 "
	*French 3b, 3c, 3d, 3e, pp. 111, 112	5 '
	*Italian 3a, 3b, 3c, p. 113	5 '
	*Spanish 3a, 3b, p. 113	5 "

†*St. Michael's College.*
**Honours.*

Fourth Year.

§One of German 4f, p. 109	2 hours
French 4g, p. 112	2 "
Italian 4c, p. 113	2 "
Spanish 4c, p. 113	2 '
Philosophy 4b, p. 126 or †4g, 4h, 4i, p. 128	3 '
Religious Knowledge 4a or 4b or 4c or 4d or 4e or 4f, p. 162	3 "
Military Studies 3, p. 163	3 '
Two of *English 4a, 4c, 4b or 4e, p. 107	5 '
*German 4b, 4c, 4d, 4e, p. 109	5 '
*French 4b, 4c, 4d, 4e, 4f, p. 112	5 "
*Italian 4a, 4b, p. 113	5 "
*Spanish 4a, 4b, p. 113	5 "

§Students in the *Third Year* selecting German 3e or French 3f or Italian 3d or Spanish 3c, and students in the *Fourth Year* selecting German 4f or French 4g or Italian 4c or Spanish 4c, must choose one of the languages in which they are taking honours.

ENGLISH AND HISTORY.

Entrance Conditions.

Every student applying to enter the First Year of the Honour course in English and History, must present, in addition to Pass Matriculation standing, a certificate of having obtained at Honour Matriculation or at an equivalent examination, at least 50% in Latin, Mathematics (Algebra and Geometry), and in any two of Greek, English, French, German.

A student who, on admission to this course, has not fulfilled all the entrance conditions, must do so at the examination of the First Year. Vide Secs. 57-62, pp. 41-43.

First Year.

§One of Greek 1a, p. 96	4 hours
Latin 1a, p. 98	4 "
German 1a, p. 108	4 "
French 1a, p. 110	4
§A language not selected for honours must be chosen.	
One of History 1a, p. 114	1
Mathematics 1c, p. 132	1
Elementary Science 1, p. 143	3
Religious Knowledge 1a or 1b or 1c or 1d, p. 162	1
*English 1a, 1c, p. 106	3

†*St. Michael's College.*
**Honours.*

First Year—*Continued.*

*Greek and Roman History 1, p. 100	. 1 hour
Two of*Greek 1d, p. 97	4 "
*Latin 1c, p. 99	4 "
*German 1c, 1d, 1e, pp. 108, 109	4 "
*French 1c, 1d, p. 111	4

Second Year.

One of Political Economy 7, p. 117	1 hour
Religious Knowledge 2a *or* 2b *or* 2c *or* 2d *or* 2e, p. 162	2 "
Military Studies 1, p. 163	2 "
*English 2a, 2c, p. 106	4
*History 2a, 2b *or* 2c, p. 114	3
Two of *Greek 2d, p. 97	3
*Latin 2c, p. 99	3 ‘
*German 2c, 2e, p. 109	3 ‘
*French 2c, 2d, p. 111	3 ‘

Third Year.

One of Philosophy 3b, p. 126 *or* †3f, 3g, 3h, p. 128	3 hours
Religious Knowledge 3a *or* 3b *or* 3c *or* 3d *or* 3e *or* 3f, p. 162	3 "
Military Studies, 2, p. 163	3 "
*English 3a, 3b, 3d, pp. 106, 107	5 "
*History 3b, p. 114	1 "
One of *Greek 3c, p. 97	3 "
*Latin 3c, p. 99	2
*German 3b, p. 109	3
*French 3b, p. 111	2
One of *English 3c, p. 107	2
*History 3a, p. 114	2
*Greek 3d, p. 97 *and* History 6, p. 115	2
*Latin 3d, p. 100 *and* History 6, p. 115	2

Fourth Year.

One of Philosophy 4b, p. 126 *or* †4g, 4h, 4i, p. 128	3 hours
Religious Knowledge 4a *or* 4b *or* 4c *or* 4d *or* 4e *or* 4f, p. 162	3 "
Military Studies 3, p. 163	3 "
*Greek 4d, p. 98	1
*English 4a, 4b, 4d, 4e, p. 107	7
*History 4b, p. 115	1
One of *English 4c, p. 107	2
*History 4a, p. 115	2
*Greek 4e, p. 98 *and* History 6, p. 115	2
*Latin 4c, p. 100 *and* History 6, . 115	2 "

†*St. Michael's College.*
Honours.

MODERN HISTORY.

Entrance Conditions.

Every student applying to enter the First Year of the Honour Course in Modern History, must present, in addition to Pass Matriculation standing, a certificate of having obtained at Honour Matriculation or at an equivalent examination, at least 50% in Latin and Mathematics (Algebra and Geometry), and in History *or* English, and in French *or* German.

A student who, on admission to this course, has not fulfilled all the entrance conditions, must do so at the examination of the First Year. Vide Secs. 57-62, pp. 41-43.

First Year.

Elementary Science 1, p. 143	3 hours
One of Mathematics 1c, p. 132	1 "
Religious Knowledge 1a *or* 1b *or* 1c *or* 1d, p. 162	1 "
*Greek and Roman History 1, p. 100	1 '
*English 1a, 1c (ii), p. 106	2 '
*French 1c, p. 111 (see Note)	4 '
'History 1a, 1b, 1c, 1d, p. 114	3 "

A student who offers Honours in German at Matriculation may by special arrangement continue the study of German (instead of French) in the first two years of the Course.

Second Year.

One of History 2f, p. 114	1 hour
Religious Knowledge 2a *or* 2b *or* 2c *or* 2d *or* 2e, p. 162	2 "
Military Studies 1, p. 163	2 "
*English 2a, 2c (i), p. 106	2
*French 2a, p. 110	3
*History 2a, 2b *or* 2c, 2d, p. 114	4
*Political Economy 1b, 5, pp. 116, 117	2

Third Year.

One of English 3b, p. 105	3 hours
Religious Knowledge 3a *or* 3b *or* 3c *or* 3d *or* 3e *or* 3f, p. 162	3 "
Military Studies 2, p. 163	3 "
*English 3d, p. 107	2
*History 3a, 3b, 3c, 5, 6, pp. 114, 115	6
*Political Economy 1b, 10a, 11a, pp. 116, 118	3 '

   Honours.

Fourth Year.

One of English 4b, pp. 105, 106	3 hours
Religious Knowledge 4a *or* 4b *or* 4c *or* 4d *or* 4e *or* 4f, p. 162	3 "
Military Studies 3, p. 163	3 "
*English 4d, p. 107	2
*History 4a, 4b, 4c, 5, 6, pp. 115	7
*Political Economy 1b, 31, 32, pp. 116, 121, 122	2

POLITICAL SCIENCE.
Entrance Conditions.

Every student applying to enter the First Year of the Honour Course in Political Science, must present, in addition to Pass Matriculation standing, a certificate of having obtained at Honour Matriculation or at an equivalent examination, at least 50% in Latin, Mathematics (Algebra and Geometry) and in History *or* English and in French *or* German.

A student who, on admission to this course, has not fulfilled all the entrance conditions, must do so at the examination of the First Year. Vide Secs. 57-62, pp. 41-43.

A candidate who is awarded Grade B Standing, *i.e.*, an average of sixty per cent, in the Pass Course of the First Year may in the Second Year proceed in the Honour Course in Political Science.

First Year.
COURSE A.

1. English 1a, 1b, p. 105	2 hours
2. Latin 1a, p. 98 ′	4 "
3. One of Greek 1a, p. 96	4 "
Hebrew 1b, p. 101	4
German 1a, p. 108	4
French 1a, p. 110	4
4. One of a second language from 3	4
Elementary Science 1, p. 143	3
5. Mathematics 1a, 1b, p. 132	2
6. One of Greek and Roman History 1, p. 100	1 "
Mathematics 1c, p. 132	1 '
Religious Knowledge 1a *or* 1b *or* 1c *or* 1d, p. 162	1

COURSE B.

One of Greek 1a, p. 96	4 hours
German 1a, p. 108	4 "
French 1a, p. 110	4 "
One of Greek and Roman History 1, p. 100	1
Mathematics 1c, p. 132	1
Religious Knowledge 1a *or* 1b *or* 1c *or* 1d, p. 162	1
One of *Greek 1d, p. 97	4
*Latin 1c, p. 99	4

Honours.

COURSE B—*Continued*.

One of *German 1c, 1d, 1e, pp. 108, 109	4 hours
*French 1c, p. 111	4 "
*English 1a, 1c (ii), p. 106	2 "
*History 1a, 1b, p. 114	2 "
*Political Economy 2, p. 116	1 "

Honour standing in Greek or Latin or German or French will relieve a candidate of the corresponding language of the General Course subjects.

Second Year.

English 2a, 2b, p. 105	2 hours
One of Philosophy 2a, p. 125 or †2e, 2f, pp. 127, 128	2 "
Religious Knowledge 2a or 2b or 2c or 2d or 2e, p. 162	2 "
Military Studies 1, p. 163	2 "
*Greek and Roman History 2b, p. 100	1 "
*History 2a, 2d, p. 114	3 "
*Political Economy 1a, 1b, 5, 6, pp. 116, 117	3
*Actuarial Science 1, p. 135	1

Third Year.

English 3a, 3b, p. 105	3 hours
One of Philosophy 3a, p. 125 or †3i, p. 128	3 "
Religious Knowledge 3a or 3b or 3c or 3d or 3e or 3f, p. 162	3 "
World History 1 or 2, 3, p. 163	2
Military Studies 2, p. 163	3 "
*History 3a, 3c, p. 114	3 "
*Political Economy 10a, 11a, 22 enlarged, pp. 118, 120	5 "
*Law 1, 5, 6, pp. 122, 123	2 "
One of *Political Economy 12, 13, 14, 15, 25, 26, pp. 118, 119, 121, or 16, 17 enlarged, p. 119 or *Law 2, p. 123	2 "
	16 or 17 "

Fourth Year.

English 4a, 4b, pp. 105, 106	3 hours
One of Religious Knowledge 4a or 4b or 4c or 4d or 4e or 4f, p. 162	3 "
World History 1 or 2, 3, p. 163	2 "
Military Studies 3, p. 163	3 "
*History 4a, 4c, p. 115	3 "
*Political Economy 18, 20, pp. 119, 120	2 "
*Law 4, 7, pp. 123, 124	2 "
Two of *Political Economy 23, 24 enlarged, p. 120; 21, 27 enlarged, pp. 120, 121; 28, 29, 30, 33, pp. 121, 122: 31, 32 enlarged, pp. 121, 122; Rural Economics; *Law 3, p 123	4 "
	16 or 17 "

†*St. Michael's College.*
Honours.

COMMERCE AND FINANCE.
Entrance Conditions.

Every student applying to enter the First Year of the Honour Course in Commerce and Finance, must present, in addition to Pass Matriculation standing, a certificate of having obtained at Honour Matriculation or at an equivalent examination, at least 50% in Latin, English, Mathematics (Algebra, Geometry, Trigonometry) and in either French or German.

A student who, on admission to this course, has not fulfilled all the entrance conditions, must do so at the examination of the First Year. Vide Secs. 57-62, pp. 41-43.

First Year.

One of German 1a, p. 108	4 hours
French 1a, p. 110	4 "
One of Greek and Roman History 1, p. 100	1 "
Mathematics 1c, p. 132	1
Religious Knowledge 1a or 1b or 1c or 1d, p. 162	1 "
*English 1a, 1c (ii), p. 106	2 "
*History 1a, p. 114	1
*Political Economy 2, p. 116	1
*Actuarial Science 1, 3, p. 135	2

Second Year.

English 2a, 2b, p. 105	2 hours
Two of Latin 2a, p. 98	3 "
German 2a, p. 108	3 "
French 2a, p. 110	3 "
Mathematics 2c, p. 133	2 '
Physics 9, pp. 138	4 '
Chemistry 1, 14, pp. 154, 155	4
Geology and Mineralogy: Mineralogy 1, 4, 11, pp. 158, 159	4 "
One of History 2a, p. 114	1 '
Mechanics 9, p. 135	½
Geology and Palaeontology 1, p. 156	1
Religious Knowledge 2a or 2b or 2c or 2d or 2e, p. 162	2 "
Military Studies 1, p. 163	2 '
*Political Economy 1a, 1b, 5, 6, pp. 116, 117	3
*Actuarial Science 2, 4, 5, 6, pp. 135, 136	4

One of the languages of the First Year must be continued in the Second Year

Third Year.

English 3a, 3b, p. 105	3 hours
One of Latin 3a, p. 98	3 "
German 3a, p. 108	3 "
French 3a, p. 111	3
Physics 10, pp. 138, 139	4

*Honours

Third Year.—*Continued*

Chemistry 3, 15, p. 155	6 hours
Geology and Mineralogy: Geology 3, p. 157, *and*	
Geology 4, p. 157 *or* Mineralogy 6, p. 159	4
One of History 3a, 3d, p. 114	3 '
Philosophy 3a, p, *or* †3i, p. 128	3 '
Religious Knowledge 3a *or* 3b *or* 3c *or* 3d *or* 3e *or* 3f, p. 162	3 "
World History 1 *or* 2, 3, p. 163 ·	2 "
Military Studies 2, p. 163	3
*Political Economy 10a, 11, 22 enlarged, pp. 118, 120	4
One of *Political Economy 12, 13, 14, 15, 25, 26, pp. 118, 119, 121	
or 16, 17 enlarged, p. 119 *or* *Actuarial Science 7, 8, p. 136	2 "

14 or 18 "

Fourth Year.

English 4a, 4b, pp. 105, 106	3 hours
One of Latin 4a, p. 99	3 "
German 4a, p. 108	3 "
French 4a, p. 111	3 '
Physics 11, p. 139	4
Chemistry 7, 8, 25, pp. 155, 156	6
Geology 13, 5 *or* 15 and 16, pp. 157, 158	4 "
One of History 4a, 4c, p. 115	3
Religious Knowledge 4a *or* 4b *or* 4c *or* 4d *or* 4e *or* 4f, p. 162	3 "
World History 1 *or* 2, 3, p. 163	2 "
Military Studies 3, p. 163	3 "
*Political Economy 18, 20, p. 119, 120	2 "
*Law 8, 9, p. 124	1
Lwo of *Political Economy 23, 24 enlarged, p. 120; 21, 27 enlarged,	
pp. 120, 121; 28, 29, 30, 33, pp. 121, 122; 31, 32	
enlarged, pp. 121, 122; Rural Economics; *Actuarial	
Science 9, p. 136	4 "

13 or 17 "

PHILOSOPHY.
Entrance Conditions.

Every student applying to enter the First Year of the Honour Course in Philosophy, must present, in addition to Pass Matriculation standing, a certificate of having obtained at Honour Matriculation or at an equivalent examination, at least 50% in Latin, English, Mathematics (Algebra and Geometry) and in one of History, Greek, French, German, Physics.

A student who, on admission to this course, has not fulfilled all the entrance requirements must do so at the examination of the First Year. Vide Secs. 57-62, pp. 41-43.

Honours.

A candidate who obtains an average of 60% in the Pass Course or in any of the Honour courses at the examination of the First Year may in the Second Year proceed in the Honour Course in Philosophy.

First Year.

COURSE A.

1. English 1a, 1b, p. 105	2 hours
2. Latin 1a, p. 98	4 "
3. One of Greek 1a *or* 1b, p. 96	4 "
Hebrew 1b, p. 101	4
German 1a, p. 108	4
French 1a, p. 110	4
Italian 1, p. 112 *or* Spanish 1a *or* 1c, p. 113	3
4. One of a second language from 3	4
Elementary Science 1, p. 143	3
5. Mathematics 1a, 1b, p. 132	2
6. One of Greek and Roman History 1, p. 100	1
Mathematics 1c, p. 132	1
Religious Knowledge 1a *or* 1b *or* 1c *or* 1d, p. 162	1

COURSE B.

Elementary Science 1, p. 143	3 hours
One of Mathematics 1c, p. 132	1 "
Religious Knowledge 1a *or* 1b *or* 1c *or* 1d, p. 162	1 "
One of *Greek 1c, p. 97	5
*Latin 1b, p. 99	5
*Hebrew 1b, p. 101	4
*German 1c, 1d, 1e, p. 108, 109	4
*French 1c, p. 111	4
*Greek and Roman History 1, p. 100	1
*English 1a, 1c (ii), p. 106	2
*Philosophy 1a, p. 126 *or* †1b, p. 128	2

Second Year.

English 2a, 2b, p. 105	2 hours
One of Greek 2a *or* 2b, p. 96	3 "
Hebrew 2b, p. 102	3 "
History 2a, p. 114	2
Foreign Philosophical Texts	2
Religious Knowledge 2a *or* 2b *or* 2c *or* 2d *or* 2e, p. 162	2 "
Military Studies 1, p. 163	2 "
*Philosophy 2b, 2c, 2d, p. 126 *or* †2g, 2h, 2i, 2j, 2l, 2m, p. 129	5 "
*Psychology 2b, p. 131 *or* †*Philosophy 2k, p. 129	2

†*St. Michael's College.*
*Honours.

Third Year.

One of English 3a, 3b, p. 105	3 hours	
Greek 3a, p. 96	3	"
Hebrew 3b, p. 102	3	"
Foreign Philosophical Texts	2	
Religious Knowledge 3a or 3b or 3c or 3d or 3e or 3f, p. 162	3	"
Military Studies 2, p. 163	3	
Political Economy 10b, 11b, p. 118	2	'
*Philosophy 3c, 3d, 3e, pp. 126, 127 and *Psychology 3c, p. 131; or	8	"
*†Philosophy 3j, 3k, 3l, 3m, 3n, 3o, 3p, pp. 129, 130 and	10	'
*†Psychology 1, p. 130	1	'

Fourth Year.

One of English 4a, 4b, pp. 105, 106	3 hours	
Greek 4a, p. 96	3	"
Hebrew 4b, p. 102	3	"
Foreign Philosophical Texts	2	'
Religious Knowledge 4a or 4b or 4c or 4d or 4e or 4f, p. 162	3	"
Military Studies 3, p. 163	3	"
*Philosophy 4c, 4d, 4e, 4f, p. 127 and *Psychology 4f, p. 131; or	11	"
*Philosophy 4d, 4e (b), 4f (a), p. 127 and *Psychology 4c, 4d, 4f,		
4g, 4h, pp. 131, 132; or	11	'
*†Philosophy 4l, 4m, 4n, 4o, 4p, 4q, 4r, 4s, p. 130	11	'

PHILOSOPHY, ENGLISH AND HISTORY.
Entrance Conditions.

Every student applying to enter the First Year of the Honour Course in Philosophy, English and History, must present, in addition to Pass Matriculation standing, a certificate of having obtained at Honour Matriculation or at an equivalent examination, at least 50% in Latin and Mathematics (Algebra and Geometry): in one of History, English, Physics: and in one of Greek, French, German.

A student who, on admission to this course, has not fulfilled all the entrance requirements, must do so at the examination of the First Year. Vide Secs. 57-62, pp. 41-43.

First Year.

Elementary Science 1, p. 143	3 hours	
One of Mathematics 1c, p. 132	1	"
Religious Knowledge 1a or 1b or 1c or 1d, p. 162	1	"
One of *Greek 1f, p. 97	4	
*Latin 1c, p. 99	4	
*German 1c, 1d, 1e, pp. 108, 109	4	
*French 1c, p. 111	4	
*Greek and Roman History 1, p. 100	1	

    †*St. Michael's College.*
    Honours.

First Year—*Continued*.

*English 1a, 1c, p. 106	3 hours
*History 1a, p. 114	1 "
*Philosophy 1a, p. 126 *or* †1b, p. 128	2 "

Second Year.

Political Economy 7, p. 117	1 hour
One of Selected Texts in History and Philosophy	
Religious Knowledge 2a *or* 2b *or* 2c *or* 2d *or* 2e, p. 162	2 "
Military Studies 1, p. 163	2 "
*English 2a, 2c, p. 106	4
*History 2a, 2c, p. 114	3
*Philosophy 2c, 2d, p. 126 *or* †2g, 2h, 2i, p. 129	3
*Psychology 2b, p. 131 *or* *†Philosophy 2k, p. 129	2

Third Year.

One of Selected Texts in History and Philosophy	
Religious Knowledge 3a *or* 3b *or* 3c *or* 3d *or* 3e *or* 3f, p. 162	3 hours
Military Studies 2, p. 163˙	3 "
*English 3b, 3d, pp. 106, 107	5 "
*History 3a, p. 114	2 '
*Philosophy 3b, 3c, 3e, pp. 126, 127 *or* †3j, 3k, 3n, 3p, pp. 129, 130	7 "

Fourth Year.

(Available 1922-1923).

One of Selected Texts in History and Philosophy	
Religious Knowledge 4a *or* 4b *or* 4c *or* 4d *or* 4e *or* 4f, p. 162	3 hours
Military Studies 3, p. 163	3 "
Political Economy 31, p. 121	1 "
*English 4b, 4d, p. 107	5
*History 4a, p. 115	2
*Philosophy 4b, 4c, 4f, pp. 126, 127 *or* †4l, 4m, 4n, 4q, 4r, p.130	8 "

PSYCHOLOGY.
Entrance Conditions.

Every student applying to enter the First Year of the Honour Course in Psychology, must present, in addition to Pass Matriculation standing, a certificate of having obtained at Honour Matriculation or at an equivalent examination, at least 50% in Latin and Mathematics (Algebra, Geometry and Trigonometry) as well as in either German or French, and in at least one of Physics, Biology and Chemistry.

A student who, on admission to this course, has not fulfilled all the entrance conditions, must do so at the examination of the First Year. Vide Secs. 57-62, pp. 41-43.

†*St. Michael's College.*
Honours.

First Year.

English 1a, 1b, p. 105	2 hours
German 1b, p. 108	2 "
French 1b, p. 110	2 "
One of Political Economy 2, pp. 116, 117	1
Mathematics 1c, p. 132	1
Religious Knowledge 1a *or* 1b *or* 1c *or* 1d, p. 162	1
*Mechanics 1, p. 135	1
*Physics 1, 2, 18, pp. 137, 139	5½
*Zoology 5, 6, p. 144	3¼
*Botany 5, 6, p. 148	3¼ "
*Chemistry 1, 13, pp. 154, 155	6½ "
*Geology and Palaeontology 1, p. 156	1

Second Year.

English 2a, 2b, p. 105	2 hours
One of German 2b, p. 108	2 "
French 2b, p. 111	2 "
One of Political Economy 7, p. 117	1
Religious Knowledge 2a *or* 2b *or* 2c *or* 2d *or* 2e, p. 162	2 "
Military Studies 1, p. 163	2 "
*Philosophy 2c, p. 126	1 "
*Psychology 2b, 2f, pp. 131, 132	4
*Mathematics 1h, 1i, p. 134	2
*Physics 4, 5, 6 part, p. 138	3½ "
*Zoology 7 part, p. 144	4
*Physiology 1, 4a, 4c, pp. 153	4

Third Year.

(Available 1922-1923).

A reading knowledge for French and German for scientific purposes.

Physics	2 hours
Two of History	3 "
Political Economy	3 "
Religious Knowledge	3 "
Military Studies	3 "
*Mathematics	3 "
*Philosophy	1 "
*Psychology	11
*Anatomy (m) and *Physiology (e)	2
60% in Physics, History and Political Economy.	

Honours.

Fourth Year.

(Available 1923-1924).

A reading knowledge of French and German for scientific purposes.

One of Political Economy	3 hours
Religious Knowledge	3 "
Military Studies	3 "
*History	2
*Philosophy	1
*Psychology	15
*Zoology	2

60% required in Political Economy.

MATHEMATICS AND PHYSICS.

Entrance Conditions.

Every student applying to enter the First Year of the Honour Course in Mathematics and Physics, must present, in addition to Pass Matriculation standing, a certificate of having obtained at Honour Matriculation or at an equivalent examination, at least 50% in Latin, Mathematics (Algebra, Geometry, Trigonometry), Physics, as well as in either French or German.

A student who, on admission to this course, has not fulfilled all the entrance conditions, must do so at the examination of the First Year. Vide Secs. 57-62, pp. 41-43.

First Year.

English 1a, 1b, p. 105	2 hours
One of German 1a, p. 108	4 "
French 1a, p. 110	4 "
One of Greek and Roman History 1, p. 100	1
Religious Knowledge 1a *or* 1b *or* 1c *or* 1d, p. 162	1
*Mathematics 1d, 1e, 1f, 1g, p. 133	5
*Mechanics 1, p. 135	1
*Actuarial Science 1, p. 135	1
*Physics 1, 2, 18 part, pp. 137, 139	6
*Chemistry 1, 14, pp. 154, 155	4

Second Year.

English 2a, 2b, p. 105	2 hours
One of German 2a, p. 108	3 "
French 2a, p. 110	3 "
One of History 2a, p. 114	2
Religious Knowledge 2a *or* 2b *or* 2c *or* 2d *or* 2e, p. 162	2 "
Military Studies 1, p. 163	2

*Honours.

—18

Second Year—*Continued*

*Mathematics 2d, 2e, 2f, p. 133	6 hours
One of *Mathematics 2g, p. 133	½ "
*Actuarial Science 2, 5, 6, pp. 135, 136	2 "
*Mechanics 2, p. 135	1½
*Physics 3a, 4, 5, 6, p. 138	9

Third Year.

One of History 3a, p. 114	2 hours
Religious Knowledge 3a *or* 3b *or* 3c *or* 3d *or* 3e *or* 3f, p. 162	3 "
World History 1 *or* 2, 3, p. 163	2 "
Military Studies 2, p. 163	3
*Mathematics 3b, 3c, p. 133	1
One of *Actuarial Science 7, 8, p. 136	2
*Physics 31, p. 141	1
*Mechanics 3, 4, 5, p. 135	2
*Astronomy 3, p. 136	2
*Physics 12, 13, 14, 15, 17, p. 139	11

Fourth Year.

One of History 4a, p. 115	2 hours
Religious Knowledge 4a *or* 4b *or* 4c *or* 4d *or* 4e *or* 4f, p. 162	2 "
World History 1 *or* 2, 3, p. 163	2 "
Military Studies 3, p. 163	3

One of the following divisions:

I. MATHEMATICS DIVISION.

Five of *Mathematics 4c, 4d, 4e, 4f, 4g, 4h, 4i, 4j, 4k, 4l, p. 134, *Astronomy 4, p. 136, the choice to be determined by the Department	12
One of *Mathematics 4m, p. 134	1
*Actuarial Science 9, p. 136	2

II. PHYSICS DIVISION.

One of *Mechanics 7, p. 135	½
*Mineralogy 6, p. 159	2
*Physics 20, 21, 22 *or* 24, 23, 25, 26, 27, p. 140	17

III. ASTRONOMY AND PHYSICS DIVISION.

*Mathematics 4c, p. 134	2
*Mechanics 6, 7, p. 135	2½
*Astronomy 4, 5, 6, 7, 8, pp. 136, 137	15½
*Physics 20, 27 (*Light*), p. 140	4 "

Candidates in the Astronomy and Physics Division are required to take the lectures of Course 20 during the Michaelmas Term and laboratory work in Optics of Course 27 for two afternoons a week during the Michaelmas Term.

*Honours

PHYSICS.

Entrance Conditions.

Every student applying to enter the First Year of the Honour Course in Physics, must present, in addition to Pass Matriculation standing, a certificate of having obtained at Honour Matriculation or at an equivalent examination, at least 50% in Latin and Mathematics (Algebra, Geometry and Trigonometry) as well as in either French or German, and in at least one of Physics, Biology, Chemistry.

A student who, on admission to this course, has not fulfilled all the entrance conditions, must do so at the examination of the First Year. Vide Secs. 57-62, pp. 41-43.

First Year.

English 1a, 1b, p. 105	2 hours
German 1b, p. 108	2 "
French 1b, p. 110	2 "
One of Mathematics 1c, p. 132	1
Religious Knowledge 1a or 1b or 1c or 1d, p. 162	1
*Mechanics 1, p. 135	1 "
*Physics 1, 2, 18, pp. 137, 139	5½ "
*Zoology 5, 6, p. 144	3¼ "
*Botany 5, 6, p. 148	3¼ "
*Chemistry 1, 13, pp. 154, 155	6½ "
*Geology and Palaeontology 1, p. 156	1 "

Second Year.

One of English 2a, 2b, p. 105	2 hours
German 2b, p. 108	2 "
French 2b, p. 111	2 "
Religious Knowledge 2a or 2b or 2c or 2d or 2e, p. 162	2 "
Military Studies 1, p. 163	2
A reading knowledge of French and German for scientific purposes.	
*Mathematics 1e, 2c, p. 133	4
*Physics 3a, 4, 5, 6, p. 138	9
*Chemistry 3, 7, 15, 24, pp. 155, 156	8

Third Year.

One of Physics 29, p. 141	1 hour
Religious Knowledge 3a or 3b or 3c or 3d or 3e or 3f, p. 162	3 "
Military Studies 2, p. 163	3 "
A reading knowledge of French and German for scientific purposes.	
*Mathematics 2f first half, 3b, p. 133	2
*Mechanics 3, 4, p. 135	3
*Physics 12, 13, 14, 15, 17, p. 139	11 "

Honours

Fourth Year.

One of Physics 29, p. 141   1 hour
    Religious Knowledge 4a *or* 4b *or* 4c *or* 4d *or* 4e *or* 4f, p. 162   3 "
    Military Studies 3, p. 163   3 "
*Mechanics 5, p. 135   1
One of *Mechanics 7, p. 135
    *Mineralogy 6, p. 159   2
*Physics 20, 21, 22 *or* 24, 23, 25, 26, 27, p. 140   17

BIOLOGY.

Entrance Conditions.

· Every student applying to enter the First Year of the Honour Course in Biology, must present, in addition to Pass Matriculation standing, a certificate of having obtained at Honour Matriculation or at an equivalent examination, at least 50% in Latin and Mathematics (Algebra, Geometry and Trigonometry) as well as in either French or German, and in at least one of Physics, Biology, Chemistry.

A student who, on admission to this course, has not fulfilled all the entrance conditions, must do so at the examination of the First Year. Vide Secs. 57-62, pp. 41-43.

First Year.

English 1a, 1b, p. 105   2 hours
German 1b, p. 108   2 "
French 1b, p. 110   2. "
One of Mathematics 1c, p. 132   1 '
    Religious Knowledge 1a *or* 1b *or* 1c *or* 1d, p. 162   1 ''
*Mechanics 1, p. 135   1 "
*Physics 1, 2, 18, pp. 137, 139 $5\frac{1}{2}$ "
*Zoology 5, 6, p. 144 $3\frac{1}{4}$ "
*Botany 5, 6, p. 148 $3\frac{1}{4}$ "
*Chemistry 1, 13, pp. 154, 155 $6\frac{1}{2}$ "
*Geology and Palaeontology 1, p. 156   1 "

Second Year.

English 2a, 2b, p. 105   2 hours
†One of German 2b, p. 108   2 "
    French 2b, p. 111   2 · "
    Religious Knowledge 2a *or* 2b *or* 2c *or* 2d *or* 2e, p. 162   2 "
    Military Studies 1, p. 163   2 '
*Physics 3b, 4, 5, 6, p. 138   7
*Zoology 9, p. 144   4
*Botany 7, 9, p. 148   4
*Chemistry 3, 7, 15, 24, pp. 155, 156   8
*Geology and Palaeontology 6, 7, p. 157   3

   *Honours
   †*The selection of the language must be approved by the Staff in Biology.*

Third Year.

One of English 3a, 3b, p. 105	3 hours
Astronomy 3, p. 136	2 "
Religious Knowledge 3a *or* 3b *or* 3c *or* 3d *or* 3e *or* 3f, p. 162	3 "
Military Studies 2, p. 163	3 "
*Zoology 7, 8, 12, 13 (a), pp. 144, 145	9 "
*Botany 12, 17, p. 149	9
*Biochemistry 1, p. 151	2
*Physiology 2, 5, p. 153	5 "

Fourth Year.

One of History of Science	2 hours
Religious Knowledge 4a *or* 4b *or* 4c *or* 4d *or* 4e *or* 4f, p. 162	3 "
Military Studies 3, p. 163	3 "
*Zoology 19, p. 145	
*Botany 16, p. 149	
*Zoology 15, p. 145 *or* *Botany 20, p. 150	

One of the following divisions:

Division I. Zoology, Histology, Embryology.

1.*Zoology 20 (Histology), p. 145	4 hours
2.*Zoology 16 (Embryology), p. 145	4 "
3. One of *Zoology 21 (Vert. Zool.), p. 146	4 "
*Zoology 22 (Invert. Zool.), p. 146	4
*Zoology 23 (System. Zool.), p. 146	4
4. The two remaining subjects of 3 *or* Special work in *any* one subject of the Division	8

Division II. Botany.

1.*Botany 18 (Œcology) *or* 19, p. 149	4 hours
2.*Botany 10 *or* 11 (Phan. Bot.), p. 149	4 "
3.*Botany 14 (Crypt. Bot.), p. 149	4 "
4. Special work in *any* one subject of the Division	8

Division III. General Biology (five subjects).

*Zoology 2 *or* 3 subjects of Division *I*	8 or 12 hours
*Botany 3 *or* 2 subjects of Division *II*	12 or 8 "

Note—Students proceeding to graduate or special work, in which an acquaintance with the original literature is required, are advised to seek proficiency in reading scientific French and German during their undergraduate course.

Honours.

PHYSIOLOGY AND BIOCHEMISTRY.

Entrance Conditions.

Every student applying to enter the First Year of the Honour Course in Physiology and Biochemistry, must present, in addition to Pass Matriculation standing, a certificate of having obtained at Honour Matriculation or at an equivalent examination, at least 50% in Latin and Mathematics (Algebra, Geometry and Trigonometry). as well as in either French or German, and in at least one of Physics, Biology, Chemistry.

A student who, on admission to this course, has not fulfilled all the entrance conditions, must do so at the examination of the First Year. Vide Secs. 57-62, pp. 41-43.

First Year.

English 1a, 1b, p. 105	2 hours
German 1b, p. 108	2 "
French 1b, p. 110	2 "
One of Mathematics 1c, p. 132	1
·Religious Knowledge 1a or 1b or 1c or 1d, p. 162	1
*Mechanics 1, p. 135	1 "
*Physics 1, 2, 18, pp. 137, 139	5½ "
*Zoology 5, 6, p. 144	3¾ "
*Botany 5, 6, p. 148	3¾ "
*Chemistry 1, 13, pp. 154, 155	6½ "
*Geology and Palaeontology 1, p. 156	1 "

Second Year.

English 2a, 2b, p. 105	2 hours
Mathematics 1h, 1i, p. 134	2 "
One of German 2b, p. 108	2 "
French 2b, p. 111	2
Religious Knowledge 2a or 2b or 2c or 2d or 2e, p. 162	2 "
Military Studies 1, p. 163	2
*Physics 3b, 4, 5, 6, p. 138	7 "
*Zoology 7, 8, p. 144	7
*Chemistry 3, 7, 15, 24, pp. 155, 156	8

The curriculum of this course in the First and Second Years is the same as that for Biological and Medical Sciences (the combined course in Arts and Medicine, see pp. 198, 199). During the Third and Fourth Years the curriculum will be arranged for specialization in Physiology and Biochemistry *without reference to Medicine.*

*Honours..

Third Year.

One of Religious Knowledge 3a *or* 3b *or* 3c *or* 3d *or* 3e *or* 3f, p. 162	3 hours
Military Studies 2, p. 163	3 "
Astronomy 3, p. 136	2 "
History of Science	2 '
Mathematics 2h, p. 134	2 '
A reading knowledge of scientific French and German.	
*Zoology 14 part, p. 145	2 '
*Biochemistry 1, 3, p. 151	7 '
*Physiology 1, 4, p. 153	9½ '
*Physics 25, p. 140	½ '
*Chemistry 4, 19 part, p. 155	8 '

PHYSIOLOGICAL AND BIOCHEMICAL SCIENCES.

Fourth Year.

One of Religious Knowledge 4a *or* 4b *or* 4c *or* 4d *or* 4e *or* 4f, p. 162	3 hours
World History 1 *or* 2, 3, p. 163	2 "
Military Studies 3, p. 163	3 "
*Physics 25, p. 140	½
*Anatomy 2, p. 151	3
*Biochemistry 2, 4, p. 151	8
*Physiology 3, 4, 6, 8, p. 153	11

BIOLOGICAL AND MEDICAL SCIENCES.

Entrance Conditions.

Every student applying to enter the First Year of the Honour Course in Biological and Medical Sciences, must present, in addition to Pass Matriculation standing, a certificate of having obtained at Honour Matriculation or at an equivalent examination, at least 50% in Latin and Mathematics (Algebra, Geometry and Trigonometry) as well as in either French or German, and in at least one of Physics, Biology, Chemistry.

A student who, on admission to this course, has not fulfilled all the entrance conditions, must do so at the examination of the First Year. Vide Secs. 57-62, pp. 41-43.

First Year.

English 1a, 1b, p. 105	2 hours
German 1b, p. 108	2 "
French 1b, p. 110	2 "
One of Mathematics 1c, p. 132	1
Religious Knowledge 1a *or* 1b *or* 1c *or* 1d, p. 162	1

Honours.

First Year—*Continued*.

*Mechanics 1, p. 135	1 hour
*Physics 1, 2, 18, pp. 137, 139	5½ "
*Zoology 5, 6, p. 144	3¼ "
*Botany 5, 6, p. 148	3¼ "
*Chemistry 1, 13, pp. 154, 155	6½ "
*Geology and Palaeontology 1, p. 156	1 "

Second Year.

English 2a, 2b, p. 105	2 hours
Mathematics 1h, 1i, p. 134	2 "
One of German 2b, p. 108	2 "
French 2b, p. 111	2 .
Religious Knowledge 2a *or* 2b *or* 2c *or* 2d *or* 2e, p. 162	2 "
Military Studies 1, p. 163	2
*Physics 3b, 4, 5, 6, p. 138	7
*Zoology 7, 8, p. 144	7 .
*Chemistry 3, 7, 15, 24, pp. 155, 156	8 .

Third Year.

One of Mathematics 2h, p. 134	2 hours
Religious Knowledge 3a *or* 3b *or* 3c *or* 3d *or* 3e *or* 3f, p.1 62	3 "
Military Studies 2, p. 163	3 "
*Zoology 13, 14, 29, pp. 145, 146	8
*Anatomy 1, p. 151	13
*Biochemistry 1, p. 151	2
*Physiology 1, 2, 5, p. 153	4

Fourth Year.

One of Mathematics 3d, p. 134	2 hours
History of Science	2. "
Religious Knowledge 4a *or* 4b *or* 4c *or* 4d *or* 4e *or* 4f, p. 162	3 "
Military Studies 3, p. 163	3 "
*Anatomy 2, p. 151	3
*Biochemistry 3, 5, pp. 151, 152	7
*Physiology 1, 3, 4, 6, 8; p. 153	10 "
*Bacteriology: Third Year course in the Faculty of Medicine	4½"
*Special work in one subject to be arranged with head of department	
of subject elected by student.	6 '

Honours.

CHEMISTRY AND MINERALOGY.
Entrance Conditions.

Every student applying to enter the First Year of the Honour Course in Chemistry and Mineralogy, must present, in addition to Pass Matriculation standing, a certificate of having obtained at Honour Matriculation or at an equivalent examination, at least 50% in Latin and Mathematics (Algebra, Geometry and Trigonometry) as well as in either French or German and in at least one of Physics, Biology, Chemistry.

A student who, on admission to this course, has not fulfilled all the entrance conditions, must do so at the examination of the First Year. Vide Secs. 57-62, pp. 41-43.

First Year.

English 1a, 1b, p. 105	2 hours
German 1b, p. 108	2 "
French 1b, p. 110	2 "
One of Mathematics 1c, p. 132	1
Religious Knowledge 1a or 1b or 1c or 1d, p. 162	1
*Mechanics 1, p. 135	1 "
*Physics 1, 2, 18, pp. 137, 139	5½ "
*Zoology 5, 6, p. 144	3¼ "
*Botany 5, 6, p. 148	3¼ "
*Chemistry 1, 13, pp. 154, 155	6½ "
*Geology and Palaeontology 1, p. 156	1 "

Second Year.

English 2a, 2b, p. 105	2 hours
A reading knowledge of French and German for scientific purposes.	
†One of German 2b, p. 108	2
French 2b, p. 111	2
One of Chemistry 6b, p. 155	
Religious Knowledge 2a or 2b or 2c or 2d or 2e, p. 162	2 "
Military Studies 1, p. 163	2
*Mathematics 2c, p. 133	2 "
*Physics 3a, 6 part, p. 138	3½ "
*Chemistry 3, 7, 9, 16, p. 155	
*Geology and Palaeontology 6, 7, p. 157	3
*Mineralogy and Petrography 1, 3, 4, pp. 158, 159	5

Division I.
Third Year.

A reading knowledge of French and German for scientific purposes.

One of History 3a, p. 114	2 hours
Chemistry 6b, p. 155	
Religious Knowledge 3a or 3b or 3c or 3d or 3e or 3f, p. 162	3 "
Military Studies 2, p. 163	3 "

*Honours.

†Selection to be approved by the Staff in Chemistry and Mineralogy.

Third Year—*Continued.*

*Mathematics 3b, p. 133	½ hours
*Physics 6, p. 138	6 "
*Chemistry 4, 8, 10, 12a, 19, 20, p. 155	
*Mineralogy and Petrography 6, p. 159	2

Fourth Year.

A reading knowledge of French and German for scientific purposes.

One of History 4a, p. 115	2 hours
Chemistry 6b, p. 155	
Religious Knowledge 4a *or* 4b *or* 4c *or* 4d *or* 4e *or* 4f, p. 162	3 "
Military Studies 3, p. 163	3 "
*Physics 16, p. 139	½ "
One of *Zoology 9, 12, pp. 144, 145, *and* *Botany 7, 9, p. 148	4 "
A defined part of *Chemistry 21, p. 155	
*Chemistry 5, 6a, 11, 21, p. 155	

Division II.
Third Year.

One of History 3a, p. 114	2 hours
Religious Knowledge 3a *or* 3b *or* 3c *or* 3d *or* 3e *or* 3f, p. 162	3 "
Military Studies 2, p. 163	3 "
A reading knowledge of French and German for scientific purposes.	
*Physics 6, p. 138	6 "
*Chemistry 8, p. 155	
*Geology and Palaeontology 8, 9, 10, 11, p. 157	9 "
*Mineralogy and Petrography 5, 6, 7, 8, 11, p. 159	10 "

Fourth Year.

One of History 4a, p. 115	2 hours
Religious Knowledge 4a *or* 4b *or* 4c *or* 4d *or* 4e *or* 4f, p. 162	3 . "
Military Studies, 3 p. 163	3 "
A reading knowledge of French and German for scientific purposes.	
One of *Zoology 9, 12, pp. 144, 145, *and* *Botany 7, 9, p. 148	4 "
*Geology and Palaeontology 14, 16, pp. 157, 158	5 "
*Geology and Palaeontology 12, 13, 15, 19, 20, pp. 157, 158	8 "
*Mineralogy and Petrography 9, 10, 12, 13, 14, p. 159	14 '

CHEMISTRY.
Entrance Conditions.

Every student applying to enter the First Year of the Honour Course in Chemistry, must present, in addition to Pass Matriculation standing, a certificate of having obtained at Honour Matriculation or at an equivalent examination, at least 50% in Latin and Mathematics (Algebra, Geometry and Trigonometry) as well as in either French or German and in at least one of Physics, Biology, Chemistry.

Honours.

A student who, on admission to this course, has not fulfilled all the entrance conditions, must do so at the examination of the First Year. Vide Secs. 57-62, pp. 41-43.

First Year.

English 1a, 1b, p. 105	2 hours
German 1b, p. 108	2 "
French 1b, p. 110	2 "
One of Mathematics 1c, p. 132	1
Religious Knowledge 1a *or* 1b *or* 1c *or* 1d, p. 162	1
*Mechanics 1, p. 135	1 "
*Physics 1, 2, 18, pp. 137, 139	5½ "
*Zoology 5, 6, p. 144	3¼ "
*Botany 5, 6, p. 148	3¼ "
*Chemistry 1, 13, pp. 154, 155	6½ "
*Geology and Palaeontology 1, p. 156	1 "

Second Year.

English 2a, 2b, p. 105	2 hours
†One of German 2b, p. 108	2 "
French 2b, p. 111	2 "
One of Chemistry 6b, p. 155	
Religious Knowledge 2a *or* 2b *or* 2c *or* 2d *or* 2e, p. 162	2 "
Military Studies 1, p. 163	2
*Mathematics 2c, p. 133	2
*Physics 3a, 4, 5, p. 138	3
*Chemistry 3, 7, 9, 16, 17, p. 155	
*Mineralogy and Petrography 1, 2, p. 158	2

Third Year.

A reading knowledge of French and German for scientific purposes.
One of Chemistry 6b, p. 155

Religious Knowledge 3a *or* 3b *or* 3c *or* 3d *or* 3e *or* 3f, p. 162	3 hours
Military Studies 2, p. 163	3 "
*Mathematics 3b, p. 133	½ "
*Chemistry 4, 8, 10, 12a, 12b, 19, 20, p. 155	
*Mineralogy and Petrography 3, p. 159	

Fourth Year.

A reading knowledge of French and German for scientific purposes.
One of Chemistry 6b, p. 155

Religious Knowledge 4a *or* 4b *or* 4c *or* 4d *or* 4e *or* 4f, p. 162	3 hours
Military Studies 3, p. 163	3 "
*Chemistry 5, 6a, 11, 21, p. 155	

Honours.

†*Selection to be approved by the Staff in Chemistry.*

GEOLOGY AND MINERALOGY.
Entrance Conditions.

Every student applying to enter the First Year of the Honour Course in Geology and Mineralogy, must present, in addition to Pass Matriculation standing, a certificate of having obtained at Honour Matriculation or at an equivalent examination, at least 50% in Latin and Mathematics (Algebra, Geometry, and Trigonometry) as well as in either French or German and in at least one of Physics, Biology, Chemistry.

A student who, on admission to this course, has not fulfilled all the entrance conditions, must do so at the examination of the First Year. Vide Secs. 57-62, pp. 41-43.

First Year.

English 1a, 1b, p. 105	2 hours
German 1b, p. 108	2 "
French 1b, p. 110	2 "
One of Mathematics 1c, p. 132	1 '
Religious Knowledge 1a or 1b or 1c or 1d, p. 162	1 '
*Mechanics 1, p. 135	1 "
*Physics 1, 2, 18, pp. 137, 139	5½ "
*Zoology 5, 6, p. 144	3¼ "
*Botany 5, 6, p. 148	3¼ "
*Chemistry 1, 13, pp. 154, 155	6½ "
*Geology and Palaeontology 1, p. 156	1 "

Second Year.

English 2a, 2b, p. 105	2 hours
†One of German 2b, p. 108	2 "
French 2b, p. 111	2 "
One of Geology and Palaeontology 17, p. 158	1
Mathematics 2c, p. 133	1
Religious Knowledge 2a or 2b or 2c or 2d or 2e, p. 162	2 "
Military Studies 1, p. 163	2
*Physics 3b, 4, 5, 6, p. 138	7
*Zoology 9, p. 144	4 "
*Botany 7, p. 148	3 "
*Chemistry 3, 7, 15, 24, pp. 155, 156	8 '
*Geology and Palaeontology 6, 7, p. 157	3 '
*Mineralogy and Petrography 1, 2, p. 158	2

Third Year.

One of English 3a, 3b, p. 105	3 hours
Religious Knowledge 3a or 3b or 3c or 3d or 3e or 3f, p. 162	3 "
Military Studies, 2, p. 163	3 "

*Honours.

†Selection to be approved by the Staff in Geology and Mineralogy.

Third Year—*Continued.*

A reading knowledge of French and German for scientific purposes.
*Chemistry 17, p. 155

*Geology and Palaeontology 8, 9, 10, 11, p. 157	9 hours
*Mineralogy and Petrography 3, 4, 6, 8, 11, p. 159	9 " .

Fourth Year.

One of English 4a, 4b, pp. 105, 106	3 hours
Religious Knowledge 4a *or* 4b *or* 4c *or* 4d *or* 4e *or* 4f, p. 162	3 "
Military Studies 3, p. 163	3 "

A reading knowledge of French and German for scientific purposes.

One of *Zoology 23 part, p. 146 *and* *Botany 8, 15, pp. 148, 149	3 "
*Geology and Palaeontology 14, p. 157 *and* *Mineralogy and Petrography 14, p. 159	3
*Geology and Palaeontology 12, 13, 15, 16, 18, 19, 20, 25, pp. 157 158	12
*Mineralogy and Petrography 5, 7, 9, 12, 13, p. 159	11

HOUSEHOLD SCIENCE.

Entrance Conditions.

Every student applying to enter the First Year of the Honour Course in Household Science, must present, in addition to Pass Matriculation standing, a certificate of having obtained at Honour Matriculation or at an equivalent examination, at least 50% in Latin and Mathematics (Algebra, Geometry and Trigonometry) as well as in either French or German and in at least one of Physics, Biology, Chemistry.

A student who, on admission to this course, has not fulfilled all the entrance conditions, must do so at the examination of the First Year. Vide Secs. 57-62, pp. 41-43.

First Year.

English 1a, 1b, p. 105	2 hours
German 1b, p. 108	2 "
French 1b, p. 110	2 "
One of Mathematics 1c, p. 132	1 '
Religious Knowledge 1a *or* 1b *or* 1c *or* 1d, p. 162	1
*Mechanics 1, p. 135	1 "
*Physics 1, 2, 18, pp. 137, 139	5½ "
*Zoology 5, 6, p. 144	3¼ "
*Botany 5, 6, p. 148	3¼ "
*Chemistry 1, 13, pp. 154, 155	6½ "
*Household Science 1b, p. 160	1 "

Honours.

Second Year.

English 2a, 2b, p. 105	2 hours
One of German 2b, p. 108	2 "
French 2b, p. 111	2 "
Religious Knowledge 2a *or* 2b *or* 2c *or* 2d *or* 2e, p. 162	2 "
*Physics 3b, 4, 5, 6, p. 138	7 '
*Zoology 10, p. 144	2 '
*Botany 13, p. 149	2 '
*Chemistry 3, 7, 15, 24, pp. 155, 156	8 '
*Household Science 2, p. 160	6 '

Third Year.

One of English 3a, 3b, p. 105	3 hours
History 3a, p. 114	2 "
Religious Knowledge 3a *or* 3b *or* 3c *or* 3d *or* 3e *or* 3f, p. 162	3 "
One of *Physiology 2, 5, p. 153	5 "
*Zoology 9, p. 144 *and* *Botany 7, 9, p. 148	8 "
*Biochemistry 1, 3, p. 151	7 "
*Household Science 3b, p. 160	12 "
*Hygiene and Sanitation	1 "

Fourth Year.

English 4a, 4b, pp. 105, 106	3 hours
One of History 4a, p. 115	2 "
Political Economy 34, p. 122	3 "
Religious Knowledge 4a *or* 4b *or* 4c *or* 4d *or* 4e *or* 4f, p. 162	3 "
*Food Chemistry 1, 3, p. 152	10
*Household Science 4b, 4c, 4d, p. 160	10

(Available 1922-1923).

English *or* History *or* Religious Knowledge
*Food Chemistry *and*
*Household Science

HOUSEHOLD ECONOMICS.

Entrance Conditions.

Every student applying to enter the First Year of the Honour Course in Household Economics, must present, in addition to Pass Matriculation standing, a certificate of having obtained at Honour Matriculation or at an equivalent examination, at least 50% in Latin and Mathematics (Algebra and Geometry) as well as in two of English, French or German, Physics, Biology, Chemistry; preferably in French or German and a Science.

Honours.

A student who, on admission to this course, has not fulfilled all the entrance conditions, must do so at the examination of the First Year. Vide Secs. 57-62, pp. 41-43.

First Year.

English 1a, 1b, p. 105	2 hours
One of German 1a, p. 108	4 "
French 1a, p. 110	4 "
One of Household Science 1a, p. 160	1
Religious Knowledge 1a or 1b or 1c or 1d, p. 162	1
*Physics 28, p. 140	4 "
*Zoology 5, 6, p. 144	3¼ "
*Botany 5, 6, p. 148	3¼ "
*Chemistry 1, 13, pp. 154, 155	6½ "
*Household Science 1b, p. 160	1 "

Second Year.

One of English 2a, 2b, p. 105	2 hours
Religious Knowledge 2a or 2b or 2c or 2d or 2e, p. 162	2 "
One of German 2a, p. 108	3 "
French 2a, p. 110	3
*Zoology 10, p. 144	2
*Botany 13, p. 149	2
*Chemistry 3, 15 part, p. 155	4
*Household Science 2, p. 160	6 "
*Physiology 9, p. 153	1

Third Year.

Philosophy 3a, p. 125 or †3i, p. 128	3 hours
One of English 3a, 3b, p. 105	3 "
History 3a, p. 114	2 "
Religious Knowledge 3a or 3b or 3c or 3d or 3e or 3f, p. 162	3 "
*Biochemistry 1, 3, p. 151	7
*Household Science 3b, p. 160	12
*Hygiene and Sanitation	1

Fourth Year.

Political Economy 34, p. 122	3 hours
One of English 4a, 4b, pp. 105, 106	3 "
History 4a, p. 115	3 "
Philosophy 4a, p. 126 or †4j, p. 128	3 '
Religious Knowledge 4a or 4b or 4c or 4d or 4e or 4f, p. 162	3 "
*Food Chemistry 1, 2, p. 152	8 '
*Household Science 4b, 4c, 4d, p. 160	10 '

†*St. Michael's College.*
*Honours.

SCIENCE FOR TEACHERS.

Entrance Conditions.

Every student applying to enter the First Year of the Honour Course in Science for Teachers, must present, in addition to Pass Matriculation standing, a certificate of having obtained at Honour Matriculation or at an equivalent examination, at least 50% in Latin and Mathematics (Algebra, Geometry and Trigonometry) as well as in either French or German and in at least one of Physics, Biology and Chemistry.

A student who, on admission to this course, has not fulfilled all the entrance conditions, must do so at the examination of the First Year. Vide Secs. 57-62, pp. 41-43.

First Year.

English 1a, 1b, p. 105	2 hours
German 1b, p. 108	2 "
French 1b, p. 110	2 "
One of Mathematics 1c, p. 132	1
Religious Knowledge 1a *or* 1b *or* 1c *or* 1d, p. 162	1
*Mechanics 1, p. 135	1 "
*Physics 1, 2, 18, pp. 137, 139	5½ "
*Zoology 5, 6, p. 144	3¼ "
*Botany 5, 6, p. 148	3¼ "
*Chemistry 1, 13, pp. 154, 155	6½ "
*Geology and Palaeontology 1, p. 156	1 "

Second Year.

English 2a, 2b, p. 105	2 hours
One of German 2b, p. 108	2 "
French 2b, p. 111	2 "
Religious Knowledge 2a *or* 2b *or* 2c *or* 2d *or* 2e, p. 162	2 "
Military Studies 1, p. 163	2 '
A reading knowledge of French and German for scientific purposes.	
*Mathematics 2c, p. 133	2
*Physics 3b, 6 part, p. 138	4
*Zoology 9, p. 144	4
*Botany 7, 9, p. 148	4
*Chemistry 7, 15, p. 155	6
*Geology and Palaeontology 6, 7, p. 157	3
*Mineralogy and Petrography 1, 2, p. 158	2

Honours.

Third Year.

One of History 3a, p. 114	2	hours
Religious Knowledge 3a *or* 3b *or* 3c *or* 3d *or* 3e *or* 3f, p. 162	3	"
Military Studies 2, p. 163	3	"
*Astronomy 3, p. 136	2	
*Physics 4, 5, 6 part, 13, pp. 138, 139	8	
*Zoology 7 part, 12, pp. 144, 145	3	
*Botany 17, p. 149	3	"
*Chemistry 3, p. 155	2	"
*Geology and Palaeontology 8, p. 157	2	
*Mineralogy and Petrography 3, 4, p. 159	4	

Fourth Year.

One of History 4a, p. 115	2	hours
Religious Knowledge 4a *or* 4b *or* 4c *or* 4d *or* 4e *or* 4f, p. 162	2	"
Military Studies 3, p. 163	3	"
*Astronomy 2, p. 136	2	
*Physics	4	
*Zoology 23, p. 146 *or* *Botany 12, p. 149	4	
*Chemistry 8, 25, pp. 155, 156	4	
*Geology and Palaeontology 13, 18, pp. 157, 158 }	4	
*Mineralogy and Petrography 6, 11 part, p. 159 }		
One of *Physics	4	
*Zoology 23, p. 146 *or* *Botany 10 *or* 14, 20, pp. 149, 150	4	"
*Chemistry	4	
*Geology and Palaeontology 15, 16, pp. 157, 158	4	"
*Mineralogy and Petrography 9, 12, 14, p. 159	4	

ARTS AND FORESTRY.
Six Year Course.

The following schedule shows the subjects and amount of time to be devoted to each. In order to meet the exigencies of the time-table their location in each year may be varied, with the concurrence of the Faculties concerned.

First Year.

Latin 1a, p. 98, *or* Greek 1a, p. 96	4	hours
English 1a, 1b, p. 105	2	"
One of German 1a, p. 108	4	"
French 1a, p. 110	4	
Mathematics 1a, 1b, 1c, p. 132 *or* 1j, 1k, 1l, p. 135	3	
Mechanics 1, p. 135	1	
Physics 1, 2, p. 137	5	
Zoology 5, 6, p. 144	3¼	

Honours.

—19

First Year—*Continued.*

One of Greek and Roman History 1, p. 100	1 hour
Religious Knowledge 1a *or* 1b *or* 1c *or* 1d, p. 162	1 "
†Forestry 1 (Synopsis)	1 "

Second Year.

English 2a, 2b, p. 105	2 hours
One of German 2a, p. 108	3 "
French 2a, p. 110	3 "
History 2a, p. 114	1
Botany 5, 6, 9, p. 148	3
Chemistry 1, 14, pp. 154, 155	4
One of Latin 2a, p. 98	3 "
Physics 3b, p. 138	1½ "
Military Studies 1, p. 163	2 ".
One of Religious Knowledge 2a *or* 2b *or* 2c *or* 2d *or* 2e, p. 162	2 "
Geology 1, p. 157	1
†Forestry 2a	3

Third Year.

English 3a, 3b, p. 105	3 hours
One of German 3a, p. 108	3 "
French 3a, p. 111	3 "
One of Mathematics 2j, p. 135	2
Actuarial Science 3, p. 136	1
Botany 7, 17, pp. 148, 149	7
Chemistry 3, p. 155	2 "
Geology, §Course 150	1 "
Mineralogy, §Course 160	2
One of Religious Knowledge 3a *or* 3b *or* 3c *or* 3d *or* 3e *or* 3f, p. 162	3 "
World History 1 *or* 2, 3, p. 163	2
Military Studies 2, p. 163	3 "
Surveying and Map Drawing, §Course 205	5
†Forestry 2b, 8	5

Fourth Year.

History 4a, p. 115	2 hours
Geology 13, p. 157	1 "
One of Philosophy 3b, p. 126	3 "
Physics 4, 5, p. 138	1½ "
Chemistry 4, p. 155	2 "
One of Religious Knowledge 4a *or* 4b *or* 4c *or* 4d *or* 4e *or* 4f, p. 162	3 "
World History 1 *or* 2, 3, p. 153	2 .
Military Studies 3, p. 163	3
Surveying and Map Drawing, §Courses 206, 207	7
†Forestry 6, 9	4 "
†Nursery work	2 weeks

§*See Calendar of the Faculty of Applied Science and Engineering.*
†*See Calendar of the Faculty of Forestry.*

Fifth Year.

English 4a, 4b, pp. 105, 106	2 hours
Political Economy 1a, 1b, 5, pp. 116, 117	2 "
Law 4, p. 123	2 "
One of Philosophy 4a, p. 126	3
Science, to be arranged	3
Zoology 32, p. 147	3
†Forestry 3, 4, 5, 7, 11	15 "
†Practice camp	6 weeks

Sixth Year.

Law 8, p. 124	1 hour
Botany 25, p. 150	2 "
Chemistry 12a, p. 155	1 "
Philosophy 4b, p. 126	3
Forest Engineering, to be arranged	
†Forestry 10, 12, 13, 14	5

Summary.

Latin	4 (+4) hours
Greek	(+4) "
English	9 "
German	11 "
French	11
Mathematics	5 (+1) "
History	4 (+4)
Political Economy	3
Law	2
Philosophy	3 (+6)
Physics	5 (+3)
Zoology	6¼
Botany	11 "
Chemistry	7 (+2) '
Geology	2 (+1) '
Mineralogy	2 '
Mechanics	1
Science	2 '
Religious Knowledge	(+8) '
Military Studies	(+8) '
Surveying and Map Drawing	12 '
Forest Engineering	
Forestry	31 "
Field Work	8 weeks

Hours in parenthesis are options exchangeable with other Departments.

†*See Calendar of the Faculty of Forestry.*

COURSE FOR THE DEGREE OF BACHELOR OF COMMERCE.

Students in Commerce have the choice of proceeding to a degree in Arts in the Department of Commerce and Finance or of proceeding to the degree of Bachelor of Commerce. The former offers the advantages in general education of an Arts degree; the latter is designed to provide instruction in those branches of education specially adapted to the study of business.

The intention of the course is to provide a training for business and commercial life in general and at the same time to prepare applicants for the consular service, trade commissionerships abroad, for the foreign representation of Canadian firms as well as for the statistical and employment departments of large business houses.

Entrance Requirements.

Part I.　Pass Matriculation: English, History, Mathematics and three of Greek, Latin; German, French, Spanish, Science, of which one at least must be a Modern Language.

Part II.　Honour Matriculation: English, Mathematics and one of German, French, Spanish.

A student who submits a Part I. Commercial Specialists' Certificate may substitute the same for Ancient History and a language of Pass Matriculation and for the Geometry and Trigonometry of Honour Matriculation.

General Regulations for the Course.

A candidate will not receive credit in a subject unless he obtains at least fifty per cent. of the Examination marks as well as fifty per cent. of the aggregate of the term and Examination marks in that subject.

A candidate will be granted Honour standing who, obtaining at least fifty per cent. in each of the subjects of a year, also secures an average of seventy-five per cent. of all the marks assigned to the subjects of the year.

A candidate for the Examination of any year will be granted Pass standing provided he passes in all, or all but one of the subjects of the year.

A candidate who has failed in two subjects at the Annual Examination will be debarred from registration and enrolment until he has completed the work of the year.

Before the completion of the course of four years a candidate must produce evidence of employment for a definite period in a commercial firm, in public service or in some business capacity.

By arrangement with the Department of Education graduates in this course who have obtained a Part I. Commercial Specialists' Certificate either prior to entering the University or during the course, will be recognized as having secured the academic standing required from candidates for the Commercial Specialists' Certificate.

First Year.

English 1a, 1c (ii), p. 106	2 hours
Mathematics (to be defined)	2 "
Actuarial Science 3, p. 135	1 "
Two of French 1e, p. 111	3 '
German 1f, 1g, p. 109	3 '
Italian 1, p. 112 *or* Spanish 1a, p. 113	3 '
Economics 1a, 1b, 2, 3, 4, pp. 116, 117	3 "
Elementary Science 1 part, p. 143 (Michaelmas Term)	1½ "

A student who selects Italian or Spanish must continue the language chosen in at least the second year.

Second Year.

English 2a, 2c (i), p. 106	2 hours
One of Mathematics 2c, p. 133	2 "
Philosophy 2a, p. 125 *or* †2e, 2f, pp. 127, 128	2 "
Two of French 2f, p. 111	3 "
German 2f, p. 109	3 '
Italian 2, p. 112 *or* Spanish 2a, p. 113	3 '
Actuarial Science 5, 6, p. 136	2 '
Actuarial Science 4, p. 136	2 '
Political Economy 1a, 1b, 5, 6, 9, pp. 116-118	

Third Year.
(Available 1922-23).

One of German
    French
    Italian
    Spanish

Economic Theory, International Trade, Foreign Exchange, Money, Statistics, Business Administration.

Commercial Law.

Theory of Interest, Life Contingencies.

Fourth Year.
(Available 1923-24).

One of German
    French
    Italian
    Spanish

Economic History, Labour Problems, Transportation, Finance, Political Theory, Public Administration, Business Administration.

Commercial Law.

Cost Accounting, etc., particulars to be announced later.

NOTE—The prescriptions for the Third and Fourth Years are subject to revision. As the course develops, changes may be considered necessary; these will appear in subsequent issues of this Calendar.

† *St. Michael's College.*

GRADUATE STUDIES

GENERAL REGULATIONS.

Admission.

1. Advanced courses of instruction and facilities for research are offered to students who are graduates of any University or College of recognized standing.

2. Admission to these advanced courses, or to the privileges of research, does not in itself imply admission to candidacy for a higher Degree.

Registration.

3. Application for registration as a graduate student must be made to the Secretary of the Board of Graduate Studies not later than the 5th of October in any year, and the application must be accompanied by statements of the applicant's degrees, of the courses pursued as an undergraduate and his standing therein, and of the courses he wishes to pursue.

Degrees.

4. The Degrees which the University of Toronto offers to graduate students are those of Master of Arts, Doctor of Philosophy, and Doctor of Medicine.

REGULATIONS FOR THE

DEGREE OF MASTER OF ARTS.

5. A candidate for the Degree of Master of Arts must have been regularly registered as a graduate student in this University in accordance with the provisions of Section 3. Should the course of study extend over more than one year registration must be repeated at the beginning of each year.

6. If not registered as a graduate student at the beginning of the academic year, as provided in the regulations given above, the candidate shall not be eligible for the degree in the following June.

7. A statement of the course of study or the subject of the thesis proposed, must be sent to the Secretary of the Board of Graduate Studies not later than the 1st of November, and must be accompanied by the approval of the department or departments concerned.

8. Attendance during at least one session is obligatory on candidates for the Master's Degree; but the Board of Graduate Studies may dispense with such attendance if the department or departments concerned recommend such dispensation on the ground of special facilities existing elsewhere.

9. A candidate will proceed to the Degree under one or the other of the following sets of regulations according as he is a Bachelor of Arts in an Honour Course or a Bachelor of Arts in the Pass Course. In accepting as a candidate a graduate of another University or a graduate of a faculty other than that of Arts, the Board of Graduate Studies shall, on the basis of his qualifications, assign him, for the purpose of this clause, to one or the other of these classes.

I. BACHELORS OF ARTS IN AN HONOUR COURSE.

(a) By the pursuit for at least one year of an approved course of study and the passing of a satisfactory examination therein. A course of study shall not be approved by the Board unless (1) it is a continuation of a course previously pursued for graduation, or (2) it has been recommended by the department concerned on account of other special qualifications possessed by the candidate. In this latter case the course will normally extend over at least two years *or*

(b) By presenting a thesis embodying the results of some special study or investigation and adjudged to be of sufficient merit. The thesis shall be accepted only on the approval of the department or departments concerned. The candidate shall be required to pass an examination, written or oral, or both written and oral, conducted by the department or departments concerned, on the subject of the thesis and on his general knowledge of the subject of the department or departments. This examination shall not be held earlier than six months after the date of registration, and a printed or typewritten copy of the thesis submitted must be presented to the Secretary of the Board of Graduate Studies at least two weeks before the Examination takes place. The thesis must be presented not later than the 1st of May, in order that the candidate may be eligible for the Degree in the following June.

II. BACHELORS OF ARTS IN THE PASS COURSE.

(a) By the pursuit for at least two years, under the direction of one department, of an approved course of study and the passing of a satisfactory examination therein. No course of study shall be approved by the Board unless it is based on courses which have been taken for at least three years in the undergraduate course.

(b) Under exceptional circumstances only, the Board of Graduate Studies may permit a Bachelor of Arts in the Pass Course to proceed to the Degree of Master of Arts by thesis, in accordance with the regulations in clause 9, I (b). The candidate must be of at least two years' standing as Bachelor of Arts.

Graduates in Arts of this University, who have fulfilled all the requirements for the Degree of Doctor of Philosophy, may, on payment of the fee for the Degree of Master of Arts, be admitted to that Degree without further examination. Graduates in Arts of another University, or graduates in other Faculties of this or another University, who have fulfilled all the requirements for the Degree of Doctor of Philosophy, may, on special recommendation to that effect by the departments concerned, also be admitted to the Master's Degree without further examination, on payment of the fee for that Degree.

REGULATIONS FOR THE
DEGREE OF DOCTOR OF PHILOSOPHY.

10. A candidate for the Degree of Doctor of Philosophy must have been regularly registered as a graduate student in this University in accordance with the provisions of Section 3. Registration must be repeated at the beginning of each year of the course.

11. The candidate shall, as a registered graduate student, have pursued in this University for at least three years, under the direction of some one department, an advanced course of study, which must be approved by the Board of Graduate Studies. Exemption from one of the three years required may be granted by the Board of Graduate Studies, on the report of the department concerned, to a candidate who has furnished satisfactory evidence of having pursued for at least one year a course of advanced study in his major subject at another University, or who, at graduation as Bachelor of Arts in this University, has obtained First Class Honours in a special course, covering one year of advanced study, approved by the Board of Graduate Studies.

It must be clearly understood, however, that the Degree is granted only to such students as give evidence of general proficiency, power of investigation and high attainments in the special field in which the major work is done.

12. A statement of the course of study proposed, must be sent to the Secretary of the Board of Graduate Studies not later than the 1st of November of the first year of registration and must be accompanied by the approval of the departments concerned.

13. The course shall include the study of a special subject, termed the major subject, and of two other subjects, termed the minor subjects, Only one minor subject shall be selected from the group of subjects of the department which includes the major subject. The time devoted to the two minor subjects should not exceed two-thirds of that required for the major subject.

14. The candidate must have an adequate knowledge of French and German. For special reasons the substitution of another foreign language for one of these will be permitted. In some departments a knowledge of Latin is also essential.

15. At a time to be determined by the Board of Graduate Studies on the advice of-the department or. departments concerned, the candidate shall undergo written and oral examinations both on his major subject and on his minor subjects, conducted by the departments in which the major and minor subjects are included. The examiners may dispense with written examinations in one or both minor subjects provided they are satisfied, from the candidate's record, that he has a competent knowledge of such subject or subjects. Such dispensation must be reported to the Board of Graduate Studies.

16. The candidate shall present, either during his course of study or at the completion of it, a thesis embodying the results of an original investigation, conducted by himself, on some approved topic selected from his major subject.

17. The acceptance of the thesis shall be determined by the Board of Graduate Studies on the report of the department which includes the major subject. This report shall state, in terms to be approved by the Board, whether the thesis complies with the conditions prescribed by this University, and, in the judgment of the department, is worthy of publication, and whether the department recommends that the thesis be accepted in conformity with the requirements for the Degree of Doctor of Philosophy.

18. On the acceptance by the Board of Graduate Studies of the thesis submitted by a candidate, and of favourable reports from the departments in which his major and minor subjects have been taken, he shall be deemed to have fulfilled the requirements for the Degree in so far as his knowledge of those subjects is concerned. The candidate shall then be required to undergo an oral examination before the Board of Graduate Studies in order to establish his general fitness for the Degree.

19. Before the Degree is conferred upon a candidate he must, subject to the approval of the Board of Graduate Studies, make such arrangements as will ensure the publication of the thesis, and the presentation within a specified time of such number of copies as the Board of Graduate Studies may direct. Each printed copy shall, on its title page, contain the words "A thesis submitted in conformity with the requirements for the Degree of Doctor of Philosophy in the University of Toronto".

20. On the report of the Board of Graduate Studies that all the requirements have been complied with, the Senate may, either at a Convocation or at any one of its regular meetings, confer on the candidate the Degree of Doctor of Philosophy.

REGULATIONS FOR THE
DEGREE OF DOCTOR OF MEDICINE.

21. A Bachelor of Medicine will be eligible for the Degree of Doctor of Medicine on the following conditions:

(i) At least one year must elapse between the date of conferring the degree of Bachelor of Medicine and that of conferring the degree of Doctor of Medicine.

(ii) He must present an approved thesis embodying the results of an original research conducted by the candidate in any department of Medicine.

(iii) The subject of the thesis must be submitted to the Secretary of the Board of Graduate Studies for the approval of the Board at least five months before the degree is conferred.

(iv) The degree may be conferred at a Convocation or at any regular meeting of the Senate.

FEES.

Master of Arts:—

Registration and tuition..................first year	$25.00
Each subsequent year...............................	5.00
Examination.......................................	10.00
Degree..	10.00

Doctor of Philosophy:—

Registration and tuition.................... first year	$25.00
Registration and tuition........(second and third years)	45.00
Examination.......................................	25.00
Degree..	25.00

If the course is extended over more than three years a registration fee of $5.00 only for each additional year is required.

If the candidate is required to repeat either examination an additional fee of $10.00 will be charged.

Graduate Students not proceeding to a degree—

	For the Session.	For the Term.
For a course in any one subject, including registration..	$10.00	$5.00
For a course in more than one subject, each subject including registration........................	9.00	5.00
Maximum Fee..................................	45.00	23.00

Doctor of Medicine:—

Examination of Thesis................................	$10.00
Degree...	10.00

The fee for registration shall be paid by the candidate immediately upon being notified of admission to the course.

The fee for tuition shall be paid by the 31st of October in each year. There will be a penalty of $1.00 per month for delay in payment after registration is complete.

If any or all of the courses taken by a Graduate student are later accepted by the Board of Graduate Studies as part of the student's course of instruction for the Degree of Master of Arts or Doctor of Philosophy, an additional fee shall be charged, if necessary, to bring the total fees paid for registration and tuition up to the amount paid by a candidate registered for the Degree of Master of Arts or Doctor of Philosophy.

Candidates for the Degree of Master of Arts shall pay $25.00 for registration and tuition for one year of the course. If the course is extended over more than one year a registration fee of $5.00 only must be paid for each additional year.

FELLOWSHIPS.

The University offers annually to qualified students intending to pursue advanced graduate study a number of fellowships, each amounting to at least $500, the holders of which will, for the year of their tenure, be entitled to free tuition.   The majority of these are confined to special Departments, but those specified in paragraph (1.) below are open to students in all Departments, who are proceeding to the degrees of M.A. and Ph.D. Others are called Tutorial Fellowships because the holders of them are required to give a certain amount of instruction in the class-room or laboratory in elementary subjects, but the time so devoted is small and, accordingly, the holders are given opportunity to pursue their special advanced courses of study.

These Fellowships are as follows:

1. Special open Fellowships.

There are four of these available to students who undertake to pursue graduate work in any of the courses offered by the Departments of this University for the degrees of M.A. and Ph.D. under the authority of the Board of Graduate Studies.   The value of each Fellowship is $500 for one year with free tuition.   If the holder of a Fellowship gives satisfactory evidence of progress in his work during the year, he may receive the renewal of it for a second year.   Preference will be given to candidates who are graduates of the Universities of Canada outside Ontario, in the first instance to those from the West.   Applications together with details of undergraduate courses taken and certificates therefor should be addressed to the President of the University not later than the 1st of June.

2. Special Departmental Fellowships.

(a) Alexander Mackenzie Research Fellowships, two in number, of $500 each for research in the Department of Political Science, and awarded to graduates of any university, on the recommendation of a committee. Applications for these Fellowships should be addressed to the Head of the Department not later than the 1st of June.

(b) James H. Richardson Fellowship, of $500, awarded in Anatomy by the Senate on the recommendation of the Professors of Anatomy, Biology and Surgery.   Applications for this Fellowship should be addressed to the Professor of Anatomy.

(c) The George Brown Memorial Fellowship, of $500, awarded in alternate years to the graduate in Medicine of the University of Toronto, who has distinguished himself most in the subjects of Anatomy, Physiology, Biochemistry, Pharmacology, Pathology and Pathological Chemistry, in the undergraduate course.   The holder of the

Fellowship is expected to devote himself to research in one of the laboratories of the University on some subject bearing on the advancement of medical science.

3. MEDICAL RESEARCH FELLOWSHIPS.

These were established in 1913 through the generosity of a number of the leading citizens of Toronto, for the promotion of Clinical and Laboratory Research in the Department of Medicine. Each is tenable for three years, providing that the progress in research made by the holder is satisfactory. The value of the Fellowships for the first year is $750, and in the senior years may be as much as $1,000 and $1,500. Applications for these Fellowships should be addressed to the Secretary of the Medical Research Fellowship Committee.

4. TUTORIAL FELLOWSHIPS.

There are eight of these Fellowships, the holders of which are required to give part of their time to elementary instruction in the classroom or laboratory, and are also to engage in advanced study and research.

These Fellowships are annually awarded in the following Departments: two in Mathematics, three in Physiology and Biochemistry, one in Pathology, and two in Botany.

These Fellowships are open to graduates of any university and the appointments to them are made, on the recommendation of the staffs in the respective Departments, by the Board of Governors.

DEMONSTRATORSHIPS, ASSISTANT DEMONSTRATORSHIPS, AND ASSISTANTSHIPS.

Certain of the Departments of Science offer annually to qualified graduates of any University positions as Demonstrators, Assistant Demonstrators, or Assistants, which involve instruction to elementary laboratory classes, but only a certain number of hours per week in each case is required, and the instructors are accordingly free to pursue advanced study and research with the object of qualifying for the degrees of M.A. and Ph.D.

The number of these posts varies from year to year, but for the session 1920-1921 they were, according to Departments, as follows:

Physics, nine Assistant Demonstratorships; Chemistry, eleven Assistantships; Botany, five Assistantships; Pathological Chemistry, four Assistantships; Biochemistry, one Demonstrator, four Fellows; Physiology, one Demonstrator, six Fellows.

Applications for these positions should be addressed to the Head of the Department in each case. The honorarium is $500 or more.

CLASSICS.

The departments included under the Classics are four in number: Greek, Latin, Greek and Roman History, Comparative Philology and Sanskrit.

Degree of Master of Arts.

A student who is proceeding to the degree of Master of Arts in accordance with the general regulations must consult the staff in Classics as to the selection of suitable courses of study.

Degree of Doctor of Philosophy.

A graduate student, proceeding to the degree of Doctor of Philosophy, may select any one of the following divisions as his Major:

> Greek Literature.
> Latin Literature.
> Greek and Roman History.
> Greek and Roman Philosophy.
> Comparative Philology and Sanskrit.

All candidates for the degree of Doctor of Philosophy whose major subject lies within the Classics shall give evidence of proficiency in Greek and Latin Prose Composition, or (with the consent of the staff in Classics) in one or other of them, and to this end shall take such courses as the staff may prescribe.

A graduate student will be required, before entering upon more advanced courses, to have taken such of the courses marked below by an asterisk as the staff in Classics may recommend, having regard to the range of work already completed and to the nature of the course of study he expects subsequently to pursue.

No absolute rule is laid down as to the selection of the Minors to be chosen by a candidate whose Major is in one of the classical departments, but one of them at least should be chosen from the remaining subjects in these departments, and the other, if chosen from some different department should have a definite relation to the candidate's major subject. Where both minor subjects are chosen from the departments included under the Classics, one half of the courses constituting the two minor subjects should consist of courses not marked by an asterisk.

Courses òf Instruction.

I. GREEK.

*1—Greek Prose Composition.

*2—Plato, Republic, Bks. I-IV.

*3—Plato, Republic, Bks. V-X.

*4—Greek Drama (Aeschylus, Agamemnon; Sophocles, Antigone, Oedipus Rex; Euripides, Bacchae; Aristophanes, Birds, Clouds, Frogs).

*5—Aristotle, Ethics, Bks. I-IV, X (6-9).

*6—Aristotle, Poetics.

*7—History of Greek Philosophy (Introductory Course). `

8—Plato, Phaedrus, Phaedo, Gorgias. Professor Hutton.

9—Plato, Laws. Professor Hutton.

10—Pindar. Mr. W. D. Woodhead.

11—Aeschylus. Professor Owen.

12—Sophocles and Euripides. Professor Macnaughton.

13—Aristophanes. Professor Langford.

14—Aristotle, Ethics, Bks. V, VI, VII. Professor Brett.

15—Demosthenes, De Falsa Legatione, and Aeschines, De Falsa Legatione with life and career of the orator. Professor Carruthers.

16—The Political and Ethical Thought of Plato. Professor Robertson.

17—The Influence of Greek Thought upon the New Testament. Professor Macnaughton

18—History of Greek Philosophy from Plato to Plotinus. Professor Brett.

19—The Relation between the Metaphysics of St. Augustine and Plato. Professor Carr.

20—Graeco-Roman Literary Criticism with special study of Longinus. Professor Dale.

21—The Greek Conception of the Function of Art in the State. Professor Milner.

22—Greek Archaeology. Professor Carruthers.

[See also Greek and Roman History, 1, 2, 4, 9, 10, 11].

II. LATIN.

*1—Latin Prose Composition.

*2—Roman Satire.

*3—Virgil, Eclogues, Georgics, Aeneid.

*4—Horace.

*5—Roman Elegy.

*6—Cicero, De Finibus, Bks. I, II; Lucretius, Bk. I.

7—The Interpretation of Virgil, with special reference to poetic diction. Professor Bell.

8—The Minor Poems of Virgil. Professor DeWitt.

9—Catullus, Tibullus, Propertius, Ovid. Professor Macnaughton.

10—Roman Public Life, with the study of selected -speeches of Cicero. Professor Smith.

—20

11—Roman Literary Criticism with special reference to Cicero's rhetorical writings.   Professor DeWitt.

12—Roman Stoicism, with special study of Cicero, De Finibus, Bks. III, IV.   Professor Robertson.

13—Cicero, Academica, and the Eclectic Philosophy.
                                              Professor Robertson.

14—Roman Archaeology.   Professor Kirkwood.

15—Latin Epigraphy.   Professor DeWitt.

16—Roman Religion.   ,   Professor DeWitt.

[See also Greek and Roman History, 5, 6, 15, 16, and Greek 17].

III. Greek and Roman History.

*1—Thucydides, Bks. I-III, VI, VII.

*2—Herodotus, Bks. VII, VIII, IX.

*3—Greek History, B.C. 454 to B.C. 399.

*4—Aristotle, Politics, Bks. I, II, III.

*5—Tacitus, Annals, Bks. I-VI, and the Principate.

*6—Cicero, Letters (Watson); Sallust, Catiline; Caesar, Civil War.

*7—Roman History (to death of Cicero).

*8—Roman Institutions.

9—Thucydides.   Professor Sissons.

10—Aristotle, Politics.   Professor Milner.

11—The Public Career of Demosthenes, with the study of De Corona and Aeschines' Contra Ctesiphontem.   Professor Carruthers.

12—The History of the Pentecontaëty.   Professor Sissons.

13—The Letters of Cicero.   Professor Milner.

14—The Geography of the Mediterranean World.
                                            Professor Cochrane.

15—The Second Punic War with a special study of Livy's Third Decade.   Professor Kirkwood.

16—Interpretation of Greek and Roman History to 476 A.D.
                                            Professor Milner.

[See also Latin 10].

IV. Comparative Philology and Sanskrit.

*1—Comparative Philology.

2—Comparative Greek and Latin Syntax.   Professor Bell.

3—Comparative Syntax continued, with special treatment of Moods and Tenses.   Professor Bell.

4—Introduction to the study of Sanskrit.   Professor Bell.

5—Advanced Course in Sanskrit.   Professor Bell.

6—Introduction to Oscan and Umbrian.   Professor Bell.

The following are the minor subjects offered in the Classics:*

A—Greek Literature: Greek, 2, 4, 6.

B—Latin Literature: Latin, 2, 3, 4, 5.

C—Greek History: Greek and Roman History, 1, 2, 3, 4.

D—Roman History: Greek and Roman History, 5, 6, 7, 8.

E—Greek Philosophy: Greek, 2, 3, 5, 7.

F—Comparative Philology and Sanskrit, 1, 2, 4.

G—Sanskrit: Comparative Philology and Sanskrit, 4, 5.

H—Greek and Roman Archaeology: Greek, 20; Latin, 14, 15, 16.

*For the courses constituting these minor subjects, equivalent courses may be substituted with the approval of the staff in Classics.

SEMITIC LANGUAGES.

Degree of Master of Arts.

Candidates for this degree are accepted under the general regulations.

Degree of Doctor of Philosophy.

A candidate proceeding to the degree of Doctor of Philosophy in the department of Semitic Languages must give proof of his fitness for advanced study in this department either as being an honour graduate of the University of Toronto or as possessing an equivalent standing in some field of Semitic Philology in a recognized University or College.

A course of study must be elected by the candidate in consultation with the members of the department under whom it is proposed to pursue the major and minor subjects and must be submitted to and approved by the department.

The department will not recommend a student for the degree merely on the ground of faithful study for a definite period but only because of high attainment in such study manifested in the examinations and by the thesis.

The following divisions are offered as Majors:

Hebrew Language and Literature.

Aramaic Language and Literature.

Syriac Language and Literature.

Assyrian and Babylonian Language and Literature.

Arabic Language and Literature.

The following Minors are recommended for candidates taking a Major in this department:

Language cognate to the major subject.

Greek (Classical).

Philosophy.

Hellenistic Greek (Biblical and Patristic).

These Minors shall be chosen in accordance with section (22) of the general regulations.   These recommendations do not prohibit other Minors being arranged between the candidate and the department.   When a minor subject is elected outside of the department, the candidate must obtain the consent of the department concerned to the choice of such Minor and he shall be subject to the regulations of that department in respect thereto. No student of this department shall be exempt from the written examination on more than one Minor.

Courses of Instruction.

1—Hebrew: Prophetical Literature of the Old Testament.   One hundred and twenty-five hours.

2—Hebrew: Hebrew Poetical Literature.   Seventy-five hours.

3—Assyrian: Elementary Course, Translation of inscriptions of Tiglathpileser I, Shalmaneser II, Sennacherib (1110—681 B.C.).   Fifty hours.
Professor Craig.

4—Assyrian: Advanced course, Translation of The Story of the Deluge, Ishtar's Descent to Hades, Hymns and Prayers.   Fifty hours.
Professor Craig.

5—Arabic: Elements of Arabic Language and Simple Texts.   Fifty hours.

6—Arabic: Reading of representative selections from Arabic Literature. Fifty hours.

7—Syriac: Introductory Grammar and the translation of easy Prose. Fifty hours.

8—Aramaic: Introductory Palestinian Aramaic with translations from Daniel and Ezra, and the Targums.   Fifty hours.

9—History of Israel.   Fifty hours.

10—History of Hebrew Literature.   Fifty hours.

11—History of Mohammedanism.   Twenty-five hours.

12—Semitic Archaeology and Art.   Twenty-five hours.

13—Hebrew Lyric Poetry.   One hundred hours.   Professor Cosgrave.

14—The Social Development of the Hebrews.   Fifty hours.
Professor Taylor.

15—The Hebrew Wisdom Literature.   Fifty hours.
Professor McLaughlin.

16—Hebrew Prophecy and Apocalypse.   Fifty hours.
Professor McLaughlin.

17—Semitic Philology.   Comparative studies in the development of Word-formation in Hebrew.   Twenty-five hours.   Professor Craig.

18—Studies in Arabic Literature.   Fifty hours.   Professor McLaughlin

19—Aramaic: The development of the Aramaic Dialects.   Twenty-five hours.   Professor Hooke.

20—Semitic Epigraphy.   Twenty-five hours.   Professor Hooke.

21—Syriac Patrology.   Professor Hooke.

22—Advanced Assyrian. Continuation of Course 4. Fifty hours.

Professor Craig.

23—Hellenistic Literature. Fifty hours. Professor Taylor.

NOTE.—Courses 9 to 12 do not require a knowledge of Semitic Languages.

The following Minors are offered in this department:

Semitic Languages A—Course 1.
" " B—Course 2.
" " C—Courses 3 and 4.
" " D—Courses 5 and 6.
" " E—Courses 7 and 8.
" " F—Any two of Courses 9 to 12.
" " G—Any selection from Courses 13 to 22 involving not less than seventy-five hours instruction.

ENGLISH.

Degree of Master of Arts.

Students admitted as candidates for this degree must have graduated with Honours in English at this University, or give evidence of possessing similar qualifications. They are required to be in actual attendance, to cover satisfactorily the work of three of the courses outlined below and to submit a dissertation on some subject connected with their work.

Degree of Doctor of Philosophy.

Students admitted as candidates for this degree in English are required to be in actual attendance, to cover satisfactorily the work of at least ten of the courses outlined below (or their equivalents), and to submit a thesis: this thesis must, in the opinion of the department, be worthy of publication. They shall further be required to take one Minor from each of the groups (a) and (b) enumerated below.

The selection of Minors, of courses, and of subjects for the thesis must in every case be approved by the department.

Courses of Instruction.

The annexed schedule is intended to indicate the general character and the extent of the work required, but equivalent courses may be substituted for those contained in the list. Those courses which are available for the session 1921-22 are marked by an asterisk:

*1—Old English: Grammar and reading of Selections. Fifty hours.

Professors Horning and Keys.

*2—Middle English and Historical Grammar. Fifty hours.

Professors Horning and Keys.

*3—Milton and Seventeenth Century Literature.   Fifty hours.
Professors Edgar and Wallace.

*4—The Development of the Drama.   Fifty hours.
Professors Edgar, Simpson, and Wallace.

*5—Nineteenth Century Thought: Newman, Carlyle, Mill, Arnold and Ruskin.   Fifty hours.   Professors Edgar, Simpson, and Wallace.

*6—Beowulf.   Fifty hours.   Professor Keys.

*7—Chaucer and his School. Fifty hours.   Professor Clawson.

*8—The English and Scottish Ballads   Professor Clawson.

. 9—The Arthurian Romances.   Professor Horning.

10—Shakespeare (Comedies or Tragedies)   Professor Alexander.

*11—Development of the Drama (Advanced Course).   Professor Knox.

*12—The English Novel in the Eighteenth and Nineteenth Centuries.
Fifty hours.   Professor Keys.

*13—Bibliography of English Literature.   Professor Wallace.

14 and 15—The study of two authors approved by the Department other than those mentioned in this list.

16 and 17—The study of two selected periods of literature other than those mentioned in this list.

18—Recent English Literature: George Meredith, Thomas Hardy, Joseph Conrad, H. G. Wells, Bernard Shaw, and the chief writers of poetry since 1901   Professor Edgar.

The following Minors are recommended for students taking their Major in this department:

Group (a)—Any one of the following courses:

*1—Gothic as an Introduction to the Study of Philology.   Fifty hours.
Professors Horning and Keys.

2—The History of Literary Criticism.

3—English Political Thought.   Fifty hours.   Professor Kennedy.

*4—The Connection of English and French Literature in the Eighteenth Century.   Professor Edgar.

5—The Connection of English and German Literatures in the Eighteenth Century.   Professor Horning.

Group (b)—Any of the Minors offered in Classics, French, German, Italian, Spanish, History, and Philosophy.

Minors in English for candidates who are not taking their Major in English will be arranged on application.

GERMAN.

The selection of courses and of theses for the degrees of Master of Arts and Doctor of Philosophy must in every case be approved by the department.

Degree of Master of Arts.

Students admitted as candidates for the degree of Master of Arts in German must cover satisfactorily the work of at least three of the major courses outlined below and must submit a thesis on some subject connected with the work.

Degree of Doctor of Philosophy.

Students admitted as candidates for the degree of Doctor of Philosophy in German must cover satisfactorily the work of at least ten major courses and must submit a thesis which, in the opinion of the department, is worthy of publication. They shall further be required to select two Minors in two approved departments other than German.

Candidates taking their Major in departments other than German may select as a Minor in German any three courses of fifty hours each.

Courses of Instruction.

Major courses (fifty hours each).

1—Gothic, and Introduction to the Study of Germanic Languages.
Professor Horning.

2—The Middle High German Popular Epic: The Nibelungenlied.
Professor Needler.

3—History of the German Drama from the Beginning to Lessing.
Professor Needler.

4—Middle High German Lyrical Poetry.   Professor Horning.

5—Lessing.   Professor Young.

6—Goethe's Autobiographical Prose Writings.   Professor Young.

7—Goethe's Faust.   Professor Lang.

8—Schiller's Philosophical Writings.   Professor Fairley.

9—The German Drama in the Nineteenth Century.   Professor Lang.

10—Schopenhauer in Relation to German literature. Professor Fairley.

Minor courses (fifty hours each).

11—A general acquaintance with the German Literature of the Nineteenth Century, with the reading of approved texts.
Professor Lang, Professor Young.

12—Middle High German Grammar and Literature.
Professor Horning, Professor Needler.

13—The Austrian Drama in the Nineteenth Century.
Professor Lang, Professor Young.

14—Goethe and his English contemporaries.   Professor Needler.

15—Goethe's political opinions.   Professor Needler.

16—Goethe's *Singspiele* and his relation to the art of music in general.
Professor Needler.

17—Swedish.   Professor Hedman.

18—Dano-Norwegian.   Professor Hedman.

19—The Dramas of Ibsen   Professor Hedman.

20—The Modern German Lyric   Professor Hedman.

Note—Other courses, major or minor, will be arranged to meet the individual needs of candidates.

ROMANCE LANGUAGES.

Degree of Master of Arts.

The general conditions of candidacy for the Master's degree will be found on page 7. Proposed courses of study and the subject of the thesis must receive the approval of the staff in French, or in Italian, or in Spanish, in one of which the candidate must do the major part of his work.

A knowledge of standard classic authors is presupposed.

Degree of Doctor of Philosophy.

A candidate for the degree of Doctor of Philosophy shall select his major and minor subjects under the direction of the staff in Romance Languages in accordance with the general regulations. The major subject shall be chosen from one of the following groups:

Romance Philology.   Italian Language and Literature.
French Language and Literature.   Spanish Language and Literature.

Both Minors may be selected within the department of Romance Languages. One Minor *must* be selected within the department. If the second minor is selected outside of this department it must be chosen from a department cognate with that of the major subject.

The department will not recommend the conferring of this degree merely because of the completion of a certain programme of studies. Evidence must be exhibited of special aptitude and of high attainment in the field chosen by the candidate. The thesis must be a distinct contribution to the literature of the subject discussed.

A student whose major subject is not in Romance Languages, but who requires a Minor in one of its groups, will be expected to make his choice of such Minor only after consultation with the staff in Romance Languages.

Courses of Instruction.

The following courses are offered for students proceeding to the degree of Master of Arts or Doctor of Philosophy. Courses 1, 2, 7, 8, and 9 are intended for candidates beginning graduate work.

1—Methods of Research, Bibliography. One hour a week.
                              Professor Buchanan.
2—Introduction to Romance Philology. Two hours a week.
                              Professor Ford.
3—Old French Epic and Romance.   Professor de Beaumont.
4—The French Renaissance. (Not given in 1921-1922). Professor Will.
5—The French Drama of the Seventeenth Century.
                              Professor Cameron.
6—History of French Criticism.   Professor de Beaumont.
7—The History of Prose Fiction in France, with special reference to the Eighteenth and Nineteenth Centuries. Two hours a week.
                              Professor Kittredge.

8—The Development of French Thought and Ideals from the Renaissance to Modern. Times. (Not given in 1921-1922). Professor Will.

9—French Romanticism, its origins and development.

Professor Moraud.

10—The Literary Relations between France and England in the Eighteenth century. Professor Moraud.

11—Types of Prose Fiction in the Romance Countries and in England.
  i. The novel of manners and its antecedents.
  ii. The historical novel and its antecedents.

Professor Kittredge.

12—Italian Lyric Verse in the Thirteenth Century. Professor Shaw.

13—Italian Renaissance. Professor Goggio.

14—Calderon. Seminar. Professor Buchanan.

15—Old Provençal. Prerequisite: course 2. Professor Ford.

HISTORY.

Degree of Master of Arts.

Candidates for this degree are accepted under the general regulations, but, before being admitted, must give evidence of having adequate training for advanced study in History. Subjects of Study may be taken from the list given below in respect to the degree of Ph.D., but other periods or subjects may be arranged as required.

Degree of Doctor of Philosophy.

Graduate work leading to this degree is offered in the subjects named below, from which a choice of major and minor courses may be made.

Instruction will be given in tutorial groups and candidates must present a thesis of such a character as to constitute an addition to the literature of the subject selected.

List of Periods and Subjects.

1. The History of Canada.
2. The American Revolution.
3. The Sixteenth Century.
4. The French Revolution and the Napoleonic Era.
5. Nineteenth Century Europe.
6. The American Civil War.
7. The Working of Modern Political Institutions.

POLITICAL SCIENCE.

Degree of Master of Arts.

Candidates for the degree of Master of Arts in the department of Political Science must present evidence of fitness for advanced study in the department, either by having taken special undergraduate courses in Political Science, Commerce and Finance, History, or Philosophy; or by giving such other proof of sufficient knowledge as will justify their acceptance as advanced students. Each candidate is required to submit, for the approval of the staff in Political Science, on or before the date prescribed in the general regulations in this connection, the title of the thesis proposed. The thesis must be submitted in complete form on or before the 30th April. An oral examination upon the subject of the thesis will be conducted by the staff of the department before the candidate is recommended to the Board of Graduate Studies for the degree.

Degree of Doctor of Philosophy.

Candidates may proceed to the Degree of Doctor of Philosophy in the manner prescribed in the general regulations. They may select their major course from the following list:

Economic History.
Economic Theory.
Public Finance.
Philosophy of Politics.
Constitutional History and Law.

Special subjects cognate to any or all of the above general courses are to be regarded as included under them.

Special postgraduate courses, varying in topics according to the needs of the students, are customarily given by the staff in the department. Importance is attached to individual assistance in the investigation of specific problems. The thesis offered by the candidate must present either the results of an original investigation into some problem and thus form a contribution to knowledge or a critical examination of the results of investigation by others and thus form a contribution to scholarship. One Minor subject must be selected from the lists given above and the other from the subjects offered by the departments of History and Philosophy. In exceptional circumstances candidates may submit for the approval of the department some other subject of study as a second Minor, even though not obviously related to the Major.

An oral examination will be conducted by the staff of the department in the major and in the first minor subject before the candidate is recommended to the Board of Graduate Studies for the degree.

PHILOSOPHY.
Degree of Master of Arts.

·Candidates for this degree will proceed under the general regulations, to be found on pages 7-9. Except in special cases, candidates will be expected to qualify by pursuing an approved course of study, and passing a satisfactory examination therein.

Candidates for this degree fall into two classes, viz., those who have, and those who have not taken the Honour work in Philosophy for their B.A. degree.

Those who have taken the B.A. degree with honours in Philosophy must select their subjects of study from Courses 8-20, given below. Four courses of study will be required for the degree. Not more than two courses may be selected from any one division of the department. In cases where permission is granted by this department, one subject may be taken from another department. Subject to the approval of this department a thesis may be substituted for one of the courses.

Those students who have not graduated with honours in Philosophy, will be required, before being admitted as candidates for the degree, to take such preliminary courses, or to furnish such other proof of sufficient knowledge as will justify their admission to graduate courses. They will select their subjects of study in consultation with the staff in Philosophy. The work may be expected to require two years in most cases.

Candidates who furnish evidence satisfactory to the staff of the department of their qualifications for original investigation may with the consent of the department qualify by writing an approved thesis, and taking special work in consultation with the staff in Philosophy (9, I. (b)).

The writer of a thesis will be required to report regularly to the head of the department, and also to the head of the division in which his thesis falls.

Degree of Doctor of Philosophy.

Candidates for this degree must present a thesis embodying the results of independent investigation, of such a character as to make a distinct contribution to the literature of the subject and to show capacity for original research on the part of the writer. The writer of a thesis must report regularly to the head of the department, and also to the head of the division in which his thesis falls.

Students are recommended to complete the work for the degree of Master of Arts as part of the work for this degree.

A candidate who has completed the work for the degree of Master of Arts must take in addition, one course of study in the division in which his first Minor falls, and for the second Minor, must fulfil the requirements of the department in which such Minor is taken. Both Minors must be selected after consultation with the staff in Philosophy.

Divisions of the department: History of Philosophy, Logic and Epistemology, Ethics.

Courses of Instruction.

The following courses are offered to graduate students. In each of these courses fifty hours will be required, including lectures and seminar work, and examinations will be held at the close of the course.

GENERAL.

1—History of Philosophy. Kant and modern systems.

Professor Hume.

2—History of Modern (chiefly British) Philosophy. Professor Hume.

3—History of Ancient Philosophy. Professor Brett.

·4—Logic, Deductive and Inductive. Theory of the Judgment.

Professor Brett.

5—Ethics, Kant and Green. Professors Tracy and Lane

6—Modern Ethics. Professors Tracy and Brown.

7—Social Ethics. Professors Robinson and Lane.

HISTORY OF PHILOSOPHY.

8—Proofs of God's Existance in Modern Philosophy. Professor Hume.

9—Modern Philosophy, with special reference to the Hegelian Movement. Professor Hume.

10—(In alternate years with 9) Modern Philosophy, with emphasis on the Anti-Rationalist, Empiricist, and Pragmatist Writers.

Professor Hume.

11—Problems of Modern Philosophy. Individuality and Value.

Professor Lane.

12—Ancient Philosophy from Thales to Plato. Professor Brett.

13—Ancient Philosophy from Plato to Augustine. Professor Brett.

LOGIC AND EPISTEMOLOGY.

14—Principles and Methods of Modern Thought—Special Subject for 1921-2: Realism. Professor Brett.

15—Recent discussions in the Theory of Knowledge and Being.

Professor Brown.

ETHICS.

16—Selected Problems in Ethics. Professor Tracy.

17—Idealism in Ethical Theory. Professor Tracy.

18—The Philosophy of Bergson, with emphasis on its Ethical Aspects.

Professor Lane.

19—The Evolution of Morals. Professor Robinson.

20—Social and Political Ethics. Professor Robinson.

The following Minors are offered in this department for candidates who se Majors lie in other departments:

Philosophy A—Courses 1 and 2.

Philosophy B—Courses 3 and 12 or 13.

Philosophy C—Courses 4 and either 13 or 14.

Philosophy E—Courses 6, and either 5 or 7.

PSYCHOLOGY AND PSYCHIATRY
Degree of Master of Arts.

Candidates for this degree are accepted under the general regulations.

Applicants who have not satisfied the staff as to their fitness for advanced work in this department must first take such preliminary work as the staff may recommend. In such cases the time required·for the degree will normally be two years.

Candidates may qualify by selecting a course of study comprising not less than three graduate courses of instruction; two of these must be selected from courses named below, and the remainder may be selected from other courses offered in the University. The selection of courses must be approved by the staff of this department.

Candidates who satisfy the department as having special qualifications for original work may be allowed to qualify for this degree by writing an approved thesis (regulation 16, 1-b) and by consulting regularly with those members of the staff who supervise the work undertaken.

Courses of Instruction.

A. *Psychology.*
1. A critical study of intelligence tests and their social utility.
2. Psychology as a factor in the historical development of science.
3. Psychological· doctrines of space and time.
4. Content and function in psychology.
5. Experimental studies in sense perception and associated processes.
6. Theories of emotion and their expression.
7. The doctrine of Association of Ideas and Memory investigations.
8. The background of the Deistic movement.
9. Psychology of religion.
10. Immigration and mental defectives.
11. Individual differences in relation to selected problems in Applied Psychology.
12. Studies in Perception.

> [For subjects 1-10 applicants should consult Prof. W. G. Smith: for subjects 11-12 applicants should consult Prof. E. A. Bott.]

B. *Psychiatry.*
1. History of public attitude toward mental disease.
2. Description of types of mental diseases.

> [Applicants will consult Dr. Clarke in respect of these courses].

Degree of Doctor of Philosophy.

Candidates for this degree must present a thesis containing the results of an original investigation and showing capacity for independent research.

The major subject and one minor may be selected from Psychology. The second minor may be selected from the minors offered by any other department in the University. The selection of the major and both minors must be made with the approval of the staff of this department.

The following minors are offered to candidates from other departments:

(a) Courses A 2 and A 5.
(b) Courses A 10 and B 1.
(c) Courses A 31 and A 12.
(d) Course A 9.
(e) Course A 11.

EDUCATIONAL THEORY.

Degree of Master of Arts.

Candidates for this degree are accepted under the general regulations.

Candidates may qualify for the degree by pursuing three approved courses of study. Of these three one must be selected from the M.A. courses specified below, one from the courses offered by another department of the University, and the third from the courses offered in this or any other department of the University. The selection of courses must be approved by the staff of this department.

Every candidate for the degree is required to present a thesis embodying the results of some special study or original investigation.

The time required to complete the requirements for the degree will normally be two years.

Degree of Doctor of Philosophy.

Courses leading to the degree of Doctor of Philosophy are offered to students qualified under the general regulations. Candidates may elect to take their major subjects in any of the sections A to D below. Of the minors one may be selected in the subjects offered below; one must, and both may, be chosen from minors offered in other departments of the University. The minors are also open to candidates whose major subject lies in another department.

The thesis submitted must be a distinct contribution to knowledge and show capacity for original research.

Courses of Instruction.

A. *Educational Administration:*

1. Educational Administration in Canada.   Dean Pakenham.
2. Educational Administration in other countries: England, France, Germany, Denmark and the United States.   Dean Pakenham.
*3. Educational Administration in Ontario.   Dean Pakenham.

B. *History of Education:*

4. History of Education in Great Britain during the nineteenth century.   Professor Macpherson.
5. History of Education in Ontario during the nineteenth century.
          Professor Macpherson.
*6. The Foundations of Modern Public Education.
          Professor Macpherson.

C. *Educational Psychology:*

    7. Physiological Psychology.   Professor Sandiford.

    8. The Learning Process.   Professor Sandiford.

    9. Fatigue—its nature and measurement.   Professor Sandiford.

  *10· The Original Nature of Man.   Professor Sandiford.

  *11· The Psychology of Elementary and High School Subjects.

                Professor Sandiford.

  *12· Statistics applied to Education and Psychology.

                Professor Sandiford.

D *The Principles of Education:*

    13. The Contributions made to Educational Theory by Philosophy.

                Professor Sandiford.

  *14· School and Society.   Professor Sandiford.

Note—Courses indicated * are M.A. courses and minors.

MATHEMATICS.

Degree of Master of Arts.

Candidates for this degree are accepted under the general regulations.

Degree of Doctor of Philosophy.

A candidate proceeding to the degree of Doctor of Philosophy in this department may select his major subject from any of the branches of Mathematics after consultation with the staff.

The thesis submitted for the degree must give evidence of original investigation and must constitute a distinct addition to the knowledge of the subject.

Courses of Instruction.

The following courses of instruction are open to graduate students:

    1—Differential Calculus. Fifty hours.   Professor Fields.

    2—Integral Calculus. Fifty hours.   Professor Pounder.

    3—Differential Equations. Fifty hours.   Professor Fields.

    4—Theory of Functions. Fifty hours.   Professor Beatty.

    5—Theory of Functions of a Real Variable. Fifty hours.

                Professor DeLury.

    6—Advanced Theory of Functions of a Complex Variable. One hundred hours.   Professor DeLury.

    7—Theory of Algebraic Functions and Abelian Integrals (Based on Riemann, Noether, etc.) Fifty hours.   Professor Fields.

8—Theory of Algebraic Functions and Abelian Integrals (Methods of the lecturer). Fifty hours. Professor Fields.

9—The Algebraic Theory of Algebraic Functions of one Variable. Twenty hours. Professor Beatty.

10—Theory of Elliptic Functions. Fifty hours. Professor Fields.

11—Calculus of Variations. Fifty hours. Professor Fields.

12—Determinants and Theory of Matrices. Fifty hours.
Professor Fields.

13—Theory of Rational Numbers. Fifty hours. Professor Fields.

14—Theory of Algebraic Numbers including the theory of the ideals. Fifty hours. Professor Fields.

15—Theory of Substitutions. With applications to Algebraic Equations. Fifty hours. Professor DeLury.

16—Theory of Continuous Groups. Fifty hours. Professor Beatty.

17—Theory of Sets and Transfinite numbers. One hundred hours.
Professor Beatty.

18—Infinite Series. Fifty hours. Professor Beatty.

19—Differential Geometry, one hundred hours.
Professors Beatty and Pounder.

20—Actuarial Science: Frequency Curves and Correlation, Measurement of Groups and Series. Fifty hours. Professor Mackenzie.

Candidates taking a Major in Mathematics may select as one Minor any of the above courses except Nos. 1 and 2. The second Minor may be selected from any of the Minors offered by departments of the University other than Mathematics.

Courses Nos. 1 and 2 constitute a Minor in Mathematics (Mathematics A) for departments other than Mathematics, Physics, and Astronomy. The department is prepared to offer other Minors which must be arranged by consultation with the staff in Mathematics and the staff of the department in which the major subject lies.

PHYSICS.

Degree of Master of Arts.

Candidates for this degree are accepted under the general regulations.

Degree of Doctor of Philosophy.

Candidates for admission to the Degree of Doctor of Philosophy must have a competent knowledge of Mathematics and Chemistry.

Candidates may proceed to the Degree of Doctor of Philosophy in this Department in either of the following major divisions:—

Experimental Physics.
Mathematical Physics.

Courses of Instruction.

1—Properties of Matter. Fifty lectures.

Professor Satterly.

2—Advanced Heat and Thermodynamics. Fifty lectures.

Professor Satterly.

3—Geometrical Optics. Thirty-five lectures.   Professor McTaggart.

4—Mathematical Theory of Electricity and Magnetism. Fifty lectures.

Professor Burton,

5—Theory of Optics. Fifty lectures.   Professor Gilchrist.

6—Elasticity Elastic Solid Theory of Light, Polarisation.   Fifty lectures.   Professor Burton.

7—Acoustics, Fourier's Series and its applications to Physics. Twenty-five lectures.   Professor Gilchrist.

8—Hydromechanics. Twenty-five lectures.   Professor Gilchrist.

9—The Physical Properties of Colloidal Solutions. Twenty-five lectures.   Professor Burton.

10—The Electromagnetic Theory of Light and the Electron Theory of Matter. Fifty lectures.   Professor McLennan.

11—Radioactivity. Twenty-five lectures.   Professor Satterly

12—Atomic Structure and the Origin and Characteristics of Spectra. Twenty-five lectures.   Professor McLennan.

13—Theories of Radiation, including Photoelectricity and other illustrations of the Quantum Theory. Twenty-five lectures.

Professor McLennan.

14—The Principle of Relativity with applications to Radiation and the Electron Theory. Twenty-five lectures.   Professor McLennan.

15—Osmotic Pressure and Related Phenomena. Twenty-five lectures.

Professor Satterly.

16—Vector Analysis. Twenty-five lectures.   Professor Burton.

17—Theory of Measurements. Twenty-five lectures.

Professor Satterly.

18—Experimental Physics. Courses of graduate laboratory work will be arranged to illustrate courses 1-13.

19—Physics Seminar. This organization consisting of all instructors, graduate students, and advanced students in the department meets fortnightly on Thursdays from 4.15 to 6 o'clock for the discussion of recent research.

· Candidates for the Degree of Doctor of Philosophy taking their major subject in either Experimental or Mathematical Physics may select but one Minor from the department of Physics. This Minor may be either one of Courses 1, 2, 4, 5, 6, 10, or two of Courses 3, 7, 8, 9, 11, 12, 13, 14, 15, 16, 17, together with one of the experimental courses 18. The second minor may be selected from Mathematics, Astronomy, Chemistry A, B, C, D, E, or Mineralogy A, B, C, Geophysics, Physical Botany.

—21

The following Minors are available in the Department:

Physics A—One of courses 1, 2, 4, 5, 6, 10, with one of the experimental Courses 18.

Physics B—Two of Courses 3, 7, 8, 9, 11, 12, 13, 14, 15, 16, 17, with one of the experimental Courses 18.

ASTRONOMY.

Degree of Master of Arts.

Candidates for this degree are accepted under the general regulations.

Degree of Doctor of Philosophy.

This department is not prepared at present to accept candidates for the degree of Doctor of Philosophy.

The following Minors are available for candidates taking their Major in other departments:

Astronomy A—The Application of Physical Methods to Astronomical Problems. Fifty lectures.   Professor Chant.

Astronomy B—Spherical Astronomy, including the use of the Nautical Almanac and exercises in computing. Forty lectures. Professor Chant.

BIOLOGY.

Degree of Master of Arts.

Graduate work leading to the degree of Master of Arts is offered in the various subjects enumerated below under "Courses of Instruction". Except in special cases, candidates will be expected to qualify in accordance with Section 16 (b) of the regulations.

Degree of Doctor of Philosophy.

Graduate work leading to the degree of Doctor of Philosophy is offered in the divisions indicated, subject to the following conditions:

1—Students electing major work must possess adequate qualifications for beginning work of a graduate character in the major subject, must be able to search the literature in the modern foreign languages, and must possess a competent though elementary knowledge of Physics and Chemistry. For the final examination a knowledge of the general field of Biology will be considered necessary. The thesis must include an original contribution to the knowledge of the subject.

2—Students electing major work must have their entire course of study approved by the instructor in charge of the major subject.

3—Students electing major work may not select more than one Minor out of the subjects separately listed as Minors for this Department.

4—Students electing minor work must have their selection approved by the instructor in charge of the subject.

5—The standing to be attained in a minor subject shall be understood to be in general equivalent to Honour standing in the four-hour course of a corresponding subject of the Fourth Year undergraduate course, except in special cases in which (a) exemption or part exemption from one Minor may be granted to students who already have competent knowledge of the subject, or (b) other requirements may be made depending on the previous training of the student.

Major work is offered in the following subjects:

Vertebrate Zoology.   Histology.
Invertebrate Zoology.   Embryology.
Limnobiology.   Animal Genetics.
Marine Biology.   Comparative Neurology.
Entomology.

Courses of Instruction.

1—†General Biology: A course of lectures and conferences on the general problems of Biology.   Professor Bensley.

2—*Vertebrate Zoology: A laboratory course of 100 hours on the system, morphology and distribution of the Vertebrates.
Professor Bensley.

3—*Invertebrate Zoology: A laboratory course of 100 hours on the system, morphology and distribution of the Invertebrates.
Professor Walker.

4—*Limnobiology: A course on the system, morphology and oecology of fresh-water organisms.   Professor Clemens.

5—‡Marine Biology: Special research on the oecology of marine organisms.   Professor Huntsman.

6—‡Entomology: A course on the morphology, classification and oecology of the Insects, with special research; in conjunction with Course 3.
Professor Walker.

7—†Animal Histology. A laboratory course of 100 hours on animal histology and cytology including histological technique.
Professor Piersol.

8—*Microscopic Anatomy of Vertebrates: A laboratory course of 100 hours including histological technique.   Professor Piersol.

9—*Vertebrate Embryology: A laboratory course of 100 hours on the general embryology of Vertebrates.   Professor Piersol.

11*—Animal Genetics. A course on the principles and problems of Animal breeding.   Mr. MacArthur.

12—*Comparative Neurology. A course on the composition of the nervous system in the mammalia and lower vertebrates.   Dr. Craigie.

Note—Courses indicated* are offered as Minors, or in conjunction with advanced work, literature, problems and research in a special division of the field as Majors.

Courses indicated † are offered as Minors only.

Courses indicated ‡ are available as Majors only, and must be taken in conjunction with the subjects specified.

Except for the conditions mentioned above (Sections 1-4), no restrictions are imposed with reference to the selection of major and minor subjects. Students are advised, in making a preliminary choice of subjects, to keep in view the possible requirements of their future fields of work.

BOTANY.

Degree of Master of Arts.

Graduate work leading to the degree of Master of Arts is offered in the various subjects enumerated below under "Courses of Instruction". Except in special cases, candidates will be expected to qualify in accordance with Section 15 (*d*) of the regulations.

Degree of Doctor of Philosophy.

Graduate work leading to the degree of Doctor of Philosophy is offered subject to the following conditions:

1—Students electing major work must possess adequate qualifications for beginning work of a graduate character in the major subject, and must possess a competent though elementary knowledge of Physics and Chemistry.   For the final examination a knowledge of the general field of Biology will be considered necessary.   The thesis must include an original contribution to the knowledge of the subject.

2—Students electing major work must have their entire course of study approved by the instructor in charge of the major subject.

3—Students electing major work may not select more than one Minor from the list enumerated below.

4—Students electing minor work must have their selection approved by the instructor in charge of the subject.

5—The standing to be attained in a minor subject shall be understood to be in general equivalent to Honour standing in the four-hour course of a corresponding subject of the Fourth Year undergraduate course, except in special cases in which (*a*) exemption or part exemption from one Minor may be granted to students who already have competent knowledge of the subject, or (*b*) other requirements may be made depending on the previous training of the student.

Major work is offered in the following subjects:
> Morphology of Cryptogams.
> Morphology of Phanerogams.
> Plant Anatomy.
> Plant Oecology.
> Plant Physiology.
> Plant Pathology

Courses of Instruction.

1—*Cryptogamic Botany I: A lecture and laboratory course of 100 hours on the system and morphology of the Liverworts, Mosses, Ferns and fern allies. Professor Faull.

2—*Cryptogamic Botany II: A lecture and laboratory course of 100 hours on the system and morphology of the Algae, Fungi, and Slime-moulds. Professor Faull.

3—*Mycology: A special course on the system, morphology, and biology of the Fungi. Professor Faull.

4—*Morphology of Phanerogams: A laboratory course of 100 hours on the morphology of Angi sperms, Gymnosperms and related fossil forms. Professor Thomson.

5—‡Anatomy of Gymnosperms: A special course on the comparative anatomy of the Gymnosperms; .n conjunction with Course 4. Professor Thomson.

6—*Plant Physiology: A lecture and laboratory course of 100 hours on the physiology of plants.

7—*Oecology and Plant Geography: A course of 100 hours on plant associations, the adaptations of plants to environmental factors, and geographical distribution.

8—*Palaeobotany: A special course on fossil plants. Research in conjunction with course 5. Professor Thomson.

9—†An experimental and seminar course on the principles of genetics. Professor Thomson.

10—*Plant Pathology Professor Faull.

11—*Structural Oecology. A lecture and laboratory course of fifty hours and research in conjunction with Courses 4 and 5. Professor Thomson.

12—*Poisonous Plants: 100 hour lecture and laboratory course.

Note—Courses indicated* are offered as Minors, or in conjunction with advanced work, literature, problems and research in a special division of the field as Majors.

Courses indicated ‡ are available as Majors only, and must be taken in conjunction with the subjects specified.

Courses indicated † are available as Minors only.

Except for the conditions mentioned above (Sections 1-4), no restrictions are imposed with reference to the selection of major and minor subjects. Students are advised, in making a preliminary choice of subjects, to keep in view the possible requirements of their future fields of work.

ZYMOLOGY.

Degree of Master of Arts.

Candidates for this degree will be required to show that they have reached the standard for the degree of B.A., or its equivalent, in at least two of the following subjects: Biochemistry, Organic Chemistry, Physiology, Plant Physiology or Plant Pathology. Courses of study for Major and Minor work are enumerated below. Students taking Zymology as their Major subject will be required to undertake some piece of research in the Department and to submit a thesis.

Degree of Doctor of Philosophy.

Candidates for this degree will be required to show that they possess a competent knowledge of Organic Chemistry and Animal or Plant Physiology. A knowledge of general Biochemistry is desirable before proceeding to undertake advanced research work in Zymology. Candidates are recommended to chose Minors in accordance with the Regulations from the following:

Biochemistry, 2, 4.
Plant Physiology, Botany, 6.
Physiology, 1, 3, 5.
Organic Chemistry, 1, 2.
Mycology, Botany 3.

Courses of Instruction.

1. *General Bacteriology:* A lecture and laboratory course in bacteriological theory and technique. Special attention will be given to the laboratory methods involved in the industrial applications of yeasts, moulds and bacteria. Facilities are provided for conducting some of these processes on a semi-commercial scale.

2. *Applied Zymology:* A lecture course on the practical methods obtaining in those industries dependent on the life processes of yeasts, moulds and bacteria.

3. *Enzyme Chemistry:* A lecture course dealing with recent advances in enzyme chemistry.

Course 1 is offered as a Minor.

ANATOMY.

Degree of Master of Arts.

Either of the minor courses described below may be taken as leading to the degree of Master of Arts. Course 5 is also open to those who have covered the ground represented by the Minors.

Degree of Doctor of Philosophy.

The work required of candidates for the degree of Doctor of Philosophy with a Major in Anatomy will be principally the preparation of a thesis based upon an investigation of some anatomical problem, together with the reading of the literature cognate to the research.

As a preliminary requirement it will be necessary that the candidate shall have taken a course in General Biology and courses in Vertebrate Anatomy (Biology Course 2), Histology (Biology Course 8) and Embryology (Biology Course 9). The last two may be taken as a Minor.

The following divisions lead to the degree of this department:

Anatomy.
Anatomy of the Nervous System.
Vertebrate Embryology.

Candidates taking Anatomy as a Major are recommended to select their Minors from the departments of Anatomy, Zoology, Physiology, Biochemistry, and Pathology.

Courses of Instruction.

The following courses of instruction are offered by the department:

1—Human Anatomy. Laboratory and lectures. Thirteen hours a week throughout the year. Professor McMurrich and Dr. Watt.

2—Anatomy of the Nervous System. Lectures and Demonstrations. Sixty-four hours. Professor McMurrich.

3—Advanced Human Anatomy and Embryology. Laboratory and reading. Open only to those who have taken Courses 1, and 2.
Professor McMurrich and Dr. Watt.

The following Minors are offered by the department:

Anatomy A—Course 1.
Anatomy B—Course 2.

BIOCHEMISTRY.

Degree of Master of Arts.

Candidates for this degree are accepted under the general regulations. All candidates who have not previously taken the course of lectures and laboratory work in advanced Biochemistry (Biochemistry 2 and 4) or its equivalent, will be required to take this course.

Degree of Doctor of Philosophy.

Candidates for the degree of Doctor of Philosophy are required to submit a thesis which constitutes a distinct addition to the knowledge of the subject, and of such value as to merit publication in one of the leading scientific journals.

Candidates for the degree of Doctor of Philosophy in this department who do not intend taking Physiology as a minor are reminded that the relationship between these two Sciences is so intimate as to render a knowledge of the elements of mammalian physiology extremely advisable. Candidates are furthermore reminded that mathematics is becoming of very great importance in the investigation of the chemical phenomena of life, and they are strongly urged to acquire a knowledge of elementary differential and integral calculus and of statistical methods.

Students taking their major in Biochemistry may select their minors from any other division of graduate study offered by the University. The following subjects of study are, however, suggested as appropriate adjuncts to the study of Biochemistry·

> Anatomy.
> Bacteriology.
> Biology.
> Botany.
> Chemistry.
> Histology.
> Household Science.
> Mathematics.
> Pathological Chemistry.
> Pathology.
> Pharmacology.
> Physics.
> Physiology.
> Psychology.
> Zymology.

Candidates for the degree of Doctor of Philosophy who desire to take a minor in Biochemistry will be required to pass an examination covering the field comprised in Courses 1, 2, 3 and 4.

Courses of Instruction.

1—General Biochemistry. Ninety Lectures.

. 2—Advanced Biochemistry. Sixty lectures.

3—A Laboratory Course in General Biochemistry. One hundred and twenty hours.

4—A Laboratory Course in Advanced Biochemistry.

PHYSIOLOGY.

Degree of Master of Arts.

Candidates for the degree are accepted under the general regulations. All candidates will be required to show credits for courses 1, 3 and 4 of this department or their equivalent. Courses 1 and 4 must be completed before entering upon the work for the M.A. degree, but Courses 2 and 5 may be taken simultaneously.

Courses of Instruction.

The following courses of instruction each extending throughout the session are offered:

1. Systematic lectures; two a week during second and third years.

(a) General and neuro-muscular physiology.

(b) Physiology of circulation, respiration, digestion and reproduction.

(c) Metabolism, the functions of the ductless glands and reproduction.

(d) Physiology of the central nervous system and special senses.

2. Lectures in General Physiology.

3. Advanced lectures; two a week (third year—optional).

4. General Laboratory courses (total 135 hours).

5. Laboratory course in General Physiology.

6. Advanced Laboratory courses (optional).

7. Research in Physiology.

8. Journal Club; one hour a week.

Degree of Doctor of Philosophy.

Candidates for the degree of Doctor of Philosophy are required to submit a thesis which constitutes a distinct addition to the knowledge of the subject, and of such value as to merit publication in one of the leading scientific journals.

Candidates for the degree of Doctor of Philosophy in this department who do not intend taking Biochemistry as a minor, or have not already taken the undergraduate courses in this subject are reminded that these two sciences are so intimate as to render a knowledge of general Biochemistry extremely advisable. They should at least take courses 1 (General Biochemistry) and 4 (a laboratory course in General Biochemistry) of the Department of Biochemistry. A general course in experimental Pharmacology is also almost essential. Certain courses in Biology, which should include vertebrate histology and cytology (12) vertebrate (14) and structural neurology (16) are of importance. A good training in Physics such as that mapped out for the honour degree in Physiology and Biochemistry is required. Similar courses in Mathematics are also required save in exceptional circumstances. Certain other courses in Physics are recommended.   Students taking their major in Physiology may select their minors from any other division of graduate study offered by the University. The following subjects are suggested as appropriate, their relative importance as adjunct to the study of Physiology being indicated in a general way by the order in which they stand:

> Biochemistry (1 and 4).
> Biochemistry (3 and 6).
> Pharmacology.
> Histology and Cytology (12 or 18 Biol.).
> Neurology (16 Biol. and 4 Anat.).

and one or more of the following:

> Embryology (14 Biol.).
> General Biology (13 Biol.)
> Mathematics.
> Pathological Chemistry.
> Physics 7, 19, 21, 25.
> Psychology.

When Physiology is taken as a minor, courses 1 and 4 are required as detailed above.

FOOD CHEMISTRY.

Degree of Master of Arts.

Candidates for this degree are accepted under the general regulations.

Courses of Instruction.

1—The Chemical Nature of the Constituents of Foods.   Lectures and laboratory work.

2—Fundamental Studies of Nutrition.   Lectures and laboratory work.

PATHOLOGY AND BACTERIOLOGY.

Degree of Master of Arts.

Candidates for this degree are accepted under the general regulations.

Degree of Doctor of Philosophy.

Candidates for the degree of Doctor of Philosophy are required to submit a thesis which constitutes a distinct addition to the knowledge of the subject, and of such value as to merit publication in one of the leading scientific journals.

Candidates in this department may proceed to the degree in either of the following major division:

> Experimental Pathology.
> Bacteriology, including Immunology.

As these two departments are closely inter-related candidates are reminded that either major division may necessarily include considerable work in the other and that consequently neither can be accepted as a minor.

Candidates taking Experimental Pathology are reminded that a prerequisite for the study of experimental pathology is a knowledge of Physiology and those who do not propose taking Physiology as a minor must show credits of undergraduate work of honour standing.

Candidates taking Bacteriology and Immunology must similarly take Biochemistry or Pathological Chemistry as a minor or show credits of Honour undergraduate standing in these subjects.

The following subjects are suggested as minors:

Physiology 1 and 4.
Biochemistry 1 and 4.
Pathological Chemistry 1, 3 and 4.
Chemistry 4 and 5.
Biology 1 and 8.
Physics 9 and 18.
Botany 2 or 3.

PATHOLOGY AND BACTERIOLOGY.

The following courses are offered as minors:
Bacteriology.

1—A laboratory course of ninety hours in the principles and technique of Bacteriology and the application of this subject to Medicine.

Professor J. J. Mackenzie.
Assistant-Professor H. B. Maitland.

2—A course of lectures, fifty hours, in Immunology.

Professor J. J. Mackenzie.
Assistant-Professor H. B. Maitland.

General Pathology.

1—A course of lectures. Fifty hours.   Professor J. J. Mackenzie.
2—A laboratory course. One hundred and twenty hours.

Professor J. J. Mackenzie.

PATHOLOGICAL CHEMISTRY.
Degree of Doctor of Philosophy.

Candidates proceeding to the degree of Doctor of Philosophy in this department must cover the field of Pathological Chemistry in addition to the investigation of some selected problem.

Students taking their Major in this department are recommended to select their Minors from the following:

Chemistry, A or C.
Biochemistry and Physiology, A or B.
Pathology.

Courses of Instruction.

1—General Pathological Chemistry.   Thirty lectures.
2—Special Pathological Chemistry.   Fifteen lectures.
3—Elementary Laboratory Course.   Sixty hours.
4—Advanced Laboratory Course. Sixty hours.
The following Minor is offered by the department:
    Pathological Chemistry A—Courses 1, 3 and 4.

CHEMISTRY.

Degree of Master of Arts.

A student who is proceeding to the degree of Master of Arts in accordance with the general regulations must consult the staff as to the selection
of suitable courses of study.

Degree of Doctor of Philosophy.

The thesis submitted for the degree of Doctor of Philosophy in this
department must constitute a distinct contribution to the knowledge of
the subject.
    The following major divisions leading to the degree are offered:
                    Organic Chemistry.
                    Physical Chemistry.

Candidates taking a Major in either of these divisions may not
select as Minors Chemistry A, C, or E.   The following Minors are
recommended:
Major subject—Organic Chemistry.
        Minors—Chemistry D.
                and
                    Bio-chemistry A, Pathological Chemistry A, or Botany 6.
Major subject—Physical Chemistry.
        Minors—Chemistry B and Mathematics A.

Courses of Instruction.

The following courses of instruction are open to graduate students.   The
selection of any of these courses presupposes an adequate knowledge of
elementary Chemistry.
    1—Systematic Organic Chemistry.   Fifty lectures.   (Open only to
students who have already attended a preliminary course).   Professor Allan.
    2—Practical Organic Chemistry.   Seventy-five hours.
    3—Advanced Organic Chemistry: Heterocyclic Compounds, Synthetic
Methods, Stereochemistry.   Fifty lectures.   Professor Allan.
    4—Physical Chemistry.   Fifty lectures.   (Open only to students who
have already taken a preliminary course and have had instruction in the
calculus.)   Professor Kenrick.

5—Practical Physical Chemistry. Seventy-five hours.

6—Advanced Physical Chemistry: The Phase Rule and Chemical Thermodynamics. Seventy-five lectures. Professor Miller.

7—Inorganic Chemistry: A course of reading on topics selected with reference to the major subject. The candidate must give evidence of proficiency in chemical analysis.

8—Chemical Theory. Sixty hours.

9—Mathematical Chemistry. Sixty hours.

The following Minors are offered by this department:
Chemistry A—Courses 1 and 2.
      "   B—Course 3.
      "   C—Courses 4 and 5.
      "   D—Course 6.
      "   E—Course 7.

GEOLOGY AND PALAEONTOLOGY.

Degree of Master of Arts.

Candidates for the degree of Master of Arts are accepted in this department under the general regulations.

Degree of Doctor of Philosophy.

Candidates for the degree of Doctor of Philosophy are required to submit a thesis which constitutes a distinct addition to the knowledge of the subject. In addition to the necessary preparation in Geology, a candidate must possess an adequate knowledge of the cognate sciences—Biology, Chemistry, Physics, and Mineralogy.

The following divisions constitute Majors in this department:
Geology.
Stratigraphical Geology and Palaeontology.
Economic Geology.

Courses of Instruction.

The courses of instruction open to graduate students are given below. None of these courses, as part of either a Major or a Minor, may be taken by a candidate without a preparatory knowledge of the subject:

1—Dynamical and Structural Geology. Fifty lectures.
Professor Coleman.

2—Invertebrate Palaeontology. Fifty lectures on Morphology and Classification. Professor Parks.

3—Practical Invertebrate Palaeontology. Seventy-five hours.
Professor Parks.

4—Archaean Geology. Twenty-five lectures. Professor Coleman.

5—Glacial Geology and Physiography. Twenty-five hours.

Professor Coleman.

6—Economic Geology. Fifty lectures.

Professors Coleman and MacLean.

7—Stratigraphical Geology. Seventy-five hours lectures and laboratory. Professor Parks.

8—Mining Geology. Twenty-five lectures. Professor Coleman.

9—Practical Economic Geology. Fifty hours. Professor MacLean.

10—Metamorphism. Twenty-five lectures. Professor Coleman.

11—Geological Climatology. Twenty-five lectures. Professor Coleman.

·12—Stratigraphy and Palaeontology of Canada. Fifty lectures.

Professor Parks.

13—Geological Seminar. One hour per week.

14—Field work. (a) Pleistocene Geology, two weeks; (b) Archaean
Geology, two weeks; (c) Palaeozoic Geology, two weeks.

Candidates pursuing a Major in any of the divisions of the department
may select one but not two Minors from the departments of Geology and
Mineralogy combined. The following Minors are recommended for
candidates taking a Major in this department:

MAJOR.	MINORS RECOMMENDED.
Geology.	Mineralogy A, B, or C, *and* Chemistry E or Biology 3.
Stratigraphical Geology and Palaeontology.	Geology A or C, or Mineralogy A *and* Chemistry E, or Biology 1' 3, or 11.
Economic Geology.	Geology A or B or Mineralogy A or C. *and* Chemistry C, or Physics A or B.

The following Minors are offered by the department:

Geology A—Courses 1, 4, and 5.

Geology B—Courses 2, 3, and 7.

Geology C—Courses 6, 8, and 9.

MINERALOGY.

Degree of Master of Arts.

Candidates for this degree are accepted under the general regulations.

Degree of Doctor of Philosophy.

In addition to the necessary preparation in Mineralogy proper, a candidate for admission to Mineralogy as a Major must possess an adequate
knowledge of the cognate sciences—Chemistry, Physics, and Geology.

The thesis submitted for the degree must indicate that the candidate has
made a distinct contribution to the knowledge of his subject.

Courses of Instruction.

1—Systematic Mineralogy. A course of twenty-five hours lectures and twenty-five hours laboratory. Professor Parsons.

2—Morphological Crystallography. A course of twenty-five lectures. Professor Walker.

3—Blowpipe Analysis and Determinative Mineralogy. Seventy-five hours laboratory. Mr. Thomson.

4—Determinative Mineralogy. Fifty hours laboratory in continuation of No. 3. Mr. Thomson.

5—Practical Crystallography. Seventy-five hours crystal measurement, drawing, projection, etc. Professor Parsons.

6—Physical Mineralogy. A course of twenty-five lectures and twenty-five hours laboratory. Professor Walker and Assistants.

7—Petrography. Twenty-five hours lectures and laboratory. Professor Walker.

8—Advanced Petrography. Twenty-five lectures. Professor Walker.

9—Petrography. Fifty hours laboratory. Professor Walker.

10—History of Mineralogy. Twenty-five lectures. Professor Walker.

11—Optical Mineralogy. One hundred hours. Professor Walker.

The Minors offered by this department are not available for candidates taking Mineralogy as a Major. For such candidates the following Minors are recommended:

Geology A, or Geology B, or Geology C.
and
Chemistry C, or Chemistry E.

The following groups of courses constitute Minors in this department:

Mineralogy A—Courses 1, 2, 3, 4 and 6.
Mineralogy B—Courses 1, 2, 5, 6 and 9.
Mineralogy C—Courses 1, 2, 6, 7, 8 and 9.

It is assumed that the candidate possesses a general acquaintance with the subject before entering on his studies as outlined above.

HYGIENE AND PREVENTIVE MEDICINE.

Degree of Doctor of Philosophy.

Candidates for the degree of Doctor of Philosophy in this Department are required to submit a thesis, which constitutes a distinct contribution to the knowledge of the subject. The work required will be that necessary for the preparation of the thesis and a study of literature cognate to the subject under investigation.

The following Major Divisions leading to the degree are offered:

Hygiene.
Preventive Medicine.

Candidates taking their Major in this department are recommended to select their minors from the Departments of:

Physiology.
Biochemistry.
Biology.
Chemistry.
Zymology.
Physics.

HOUSEHOLD SCIENCE.

Degree of Master of Arts.

Candidates for this degree are accepted under the general regulations.

SUMMER SESSION

UNIVERSITY OF TORONTO.

SUMMER SESSION 1921.

During the Summer Session of 1921 the University of Toronto offers:

(a) The Course leading to the Degree of Bachelor of Arts.

(b) Courses leading to the Degrees of Bachelor of Pedagogy and Doctor of Pedagogy.

General Information.

Session.

Enrolment with the instructors will begin at 10 a.m., Tuesday, July 5th, and should be completed by 12 o'clock the same day. The work of instruction will begin on the morning of Wednesday, July 6th, and continue through Friday, August 5th, including Saturday forenoons.

Registration.

Application for registration should be made on the form in this Calendar and should be forwarded to the Director of University Extension **before June 6th.**

Residences.

The University Residences will be open for the accommodation of students during the Summer Session. As rooms are assigned in the order in which applications are received, applications with the deposit fee of $5.00 should be sent as early as possible to Mr. A. T. Laidlaw, Registrar's Office, University of Toronto.

Library.

Students of the Summer Session will be admitted to the privileges of the University Library.

Excursions and Addresses.

Arrangements will be made, if students so desire, to visit a few places of interest under the personal direction of one who is able to give special instruction on the point of interest.

Evening lectures will be arranged during the session on subjects of general interest.

Admission.

As entrance qualifications to the Course leading to the degree of Bachelor of Arts, students should present the certificates in their possession. Holders of Faculty Entrance (Upper School) or equivalent certificates are eligible to enter upon the work of the Second Year.

Fees (B.A. Course).

TUITION—One subject $10.00; two subjects $18.00; three subjects $24.00.
For admission by certificate to the Second Year............... $15.00
For admission ad eundem statum.......................... 10.00
EXAMINATIONS—$2.00 each subject.

LABORATORY—For Practical Work in the laboratory, a deposit fee is required at the beginning of the Session to cover breakages. All, or part, of the fee is returned at the close of the term according to the number and value of the breakages.

Examinations (B.A. Course).

The examinations will be held, in Ontario, at the time of the regular University examinations in September and in May. In other Provinces examinations are held in September, at Winnipeg, Regina, Saskatoon, Edmonton, Calgary, and Vancouver.

The Course leading to the B.A. Degree.

The Pass Course according to the following scheme will be the basis of instruction:

First Year.....English, Latin, French, Elementary Science, Mathematics (Algebra and Geometry), Trigonometry.
Second Year... ⌠English, French, Science, Two of
Third Year....⌡History, Political Economy,
Fourth Year... ⌊Psychology.

Subjects Offered in Summer Session, 1921.

(For details of courses, see pages 8 and 9.)

First Year.....French.
Second Year...History, Psychology, Science, French.
Third Year....History, French, Science.
Fourth Year...(To be arranged.)

A student who wishes to take any subject not mentioned in this list must use the coupon on page 13 and state at once what other subject or subjects may be desired. Second Year French will not be given unless a reasonable number of applications are received for this subject before June 6th.

It is essential that requests for subjects should be sent in early so that the necessary arrangements for classes can be made. The time-table will not permit of a student taking, at the same time, other summer courses besides those offered by the University.

General Notes on the Teachers' Course.

1. The work of the First Year will ordinarily be taken in the Upper School courses conducted by the Department of Education. The Second Third, and Fourth Years will be taken under the Faculty of Arts.

2. A candidate holding an Upper School certificate, or an equivalent' certificate, may enter the Second Year, provided he has credit for not fewer than five of the six subjects of the First Year.

3. A candidate will not receive credit for a subject of a higher year until he has passed the examination of the lower year in the same subject. He may, however, be a candidate for examination in the work of two successive years in the same subject.

4. One year is allowed for active service in the Great War, 1914-1918. The Faculty of Arts has never allowed the First Year as military credit. Veterans are advised to graduate at the end of the Third Year. Those wishing to claim this credit must present a discharge certificate with their academic certificates.

5. For teachers who live sufficiently near the University, *Teachers' Classes* are available during the regular University Session. These lectures are given after 4 p.m. on certain afternoons of the week and on Saturday forenoons.

6. Other teachers are given correspondence work during the regular session in preparation for the Summer Session. This preparation is compulsory.

7. Only under exceptional circumstances is a student allowed to attend classes in more than three subjects during one session of the Teachers' Course.

8. The minimum attendance requirement for the work of the Second, Third, and Fourth Years is four Summer Sessions.

9. The pass standard in all subjects is 50 per cent.

10. A candidate will receive credit for each subject in which he secures the minimum percentage required for pass standing.

Information for Teachers in Upper School, Middle School, and Commercial Courses.

The Ontario Department of Education offers Summer Sessions each year in the subjects of the Upper School, Middle School, and Commercial Courses.

So short is the time for work during the Summer Session that it has been found to be in every way most desirable that every teacher who proposes taking a summer course should prepare the subjects during the winter. Teachers of experience will at once recognize that the necessity for some such preparation cannot be too strongly emphasized.

Because private study is difficult, usually unsatisfactory, and often spasmodic, the University offers correspondence work in the subjects of the Upper School, Middle School, and Commercial Courses. This assistance is given in the form of question bulletins which are prepared by competent instructors now engaged in teaching the work, are sent out monthly to candidates, are answered, sent to this office, corrected by the instructors, and returned to the writers. For this service a small fee is charged and such fees are paid over to the instructors concerned.

Teachers may write on any or all of the parts of the Upper and Middle School courses in June or in September.

Teachers who propose writing on any of the subjects of these courses in June or in September, 1922, should obtain from the Extension Office, University of Toronto, full information regarding the correspondence work which is carried on during the winter.

Courses of Instruction, Summer Session, 1921.

FACULTY OF ARTS.

First Year.

FRENCH.

Grammar; dictation; translation from English into French; translation at sight from modern French. The following texts are prescribed for critical study: BAZIN *Les Oberlé;* SANDEAU, *Mademoiselle de la Seiglière;* FEUILLET, *Le Village;* DAUDET, *Lettres de mon moulin.*

Second Year.

FRENCH.

Grammar; dictation; translation from English into French; translation at sight from modern French. The following texts are prescribed for critical study: BARRÈS, *Colette Baudoche;* PAILLERON, *Le Monde ou l'on s'ennuie;* COPPÉE, *Pour la couronne; French Short Stories* (ed. Buffum), *or* GEORGES DURUY, *Histoire sommaire de la France, classe de septième.*

HISTORY.

(i) The History of the British Empire from 1763 to the present time, with special reference to Canada.

(ii) The American Revolution and the framing of the Constitution of the United States.

(iii) The Middle Ages: a general study of mediaeval society and an outline of the principal movements of the period.

PSYCHOLOGY.

Elementary Psychology; Analysis of Sense Perception and more complex processes.

Zoology.

An elementary course on the general structure of the animal body, its organs and tissues and their functions, and the classification and natural history of the common animals of Ontario, with special attention to principles of specialization, adaptation, and distribution. The course is designed to give the student training in the scientific method and also to afford assistance in the teaching of Nature Study.

Third Year.

French.

Standards of the classical age and the main ideas of the eighteenth century, studied in French literature from Malherbe to the *philosophes*. Pelissier, *Précis de l'histoire de la littérature française*, pp. 139-364; *French Prose of the XVIIth Century* (ed. Warren); Corneille, *Le Cid;* Molière, *Le Misanthrope;* Racine, *Athalie;* La Fontaine, *Fables;* Voltaire's *Prose* (ed. Cohn and Woodward); Supplementary Reading. Translation from English into French; translation at sight from modern French.

History.

(i) Eighteenth Century Europe, the French Revolution and the Age of Napoleon.
(ii) The British Constitution and its development.

Zoology.

An elementary course on the general structure of the animal body, its organs and tissues and their functions, and the classification and natural history of the common animals of Ontario, with special attention to principles of specialization, adaptation, and distribution. The course is designed to give the student training in the scientific method and also to afford assistance in the teaching of Nature Study.

[Note:—In the Teachers' Course the sciences assigned are Botany for the Second Year, Zoology for the Third Year, and Geology for the Fourth Year. But these sciences are of equal value and may be taken in any order. This year Zoology is taken by both Second Year and Third Year students.]

SUMMER SESSION IN PEDAGOGY.
(Degrees of B.Paed. and D.Paed.).

Admission.

1. The candidate shall hold (*a*) a degree in Arts or Science, not being an honorary degree, from any university in the British Dominions; and (*b*) a first class or High School Assistant's certificate, granted by the Department of Education of Ontario, or a certificate of equal value.

3. Before he completes the examinations for the degree the candidate shall submit certificates of at least two years (in the case of the B.Paed. degree) or three years (in the case of the D.Paed. degree) of successful experience in teaching.

4. The candidate shall register in the Ontario College of Education at least six months before he presents himself for examination in May.

Fees.

Registration $10.00
  (This fee is paid only once for the complete course.)
Tuition 10.00
Examinations, each subject 3.00

SUBJECTS OFFERED IN SUMMER SESSION, 1921.

[Classes in the following subjects will be conducted in the buildings of the Ontario College of Education, 371 Bloor St. West.]

I. Educational Administration.

In this course the main emphasis will be placed on problems confronting Canadian educators. A comparative survey will also be made of the educational systems of England, France, Germany, and the United States.

II. History of Education (in Western Europe and in North America in modern times):

This course will consist of two parts. The first part will deal with the history of educational theory during the 19th century. The second will discuss the evolution of modern educational systems. In both parts the chief stress will be laid on the evolution of educational ideas in Canada, England, and the United States.

III. Educational Psychology.

In this subject six separate branches will be offered:

(a) The original nature of man—a discussion of man's heredity and native equipment for learning.

(b) The learning process—a discussion of the ways in which children learn, form habits, practise and become fatigued.

(c) Genetic psychology—the psychology of childhood and adolescence from the genetic standpoint.

(d) The psychology of elementary and high school subjects, including standard tests for the same.

(e) Intelligence, its nature and measurement. The various tests of intelligence will be discussed and demonstrations of their use made with individual children or with groups of children.

(*f*) Statistics applied to education—methods of presenting and interpreting educational data by statistical and graphical methods.

IV. Science of Education.

This subject comprises a study of the philosophical and sociological principles underlying the practice of education. The evolution of educational principles throughout the centuries will be included in this course.

V. Various review or "refresher" courses for inspectors and others are under consideration. Announcement of these will be given in a later bulletin.

SUGGESTIONS APPLICABLE TO ALL COURSES.

1. Fees are payable strictly in advance.

2. Remittance should be made by Money Order; if cheques are used, they must in every case be payable at par in Toronto to the University of Toronto.

3. The Library of the Department of Education, St. James Square, Toronto, is available for the use of all Ontario teachers and the Department is anxious that every teacher should make use of it. There are no fees— the teachers pay only return postage on books borrowed.

A NEW PRINCIPLE.

Attention is called to a recent pronouncement of the University Senate. This is not of particular interest to teachers except in so far as they may be able to make use of it when asked for advice by adults who are anxious to secure higher education. The new departure means simply the extension to the general public of arrangements which have for some years been in force for the special benefit of teachers.

At the March meeting of the Senate of the University of Toronto the following important principle was laid down. This was done on the recommendation of the Extension Committee and of the Council of the Faculty of Arts.

The University of Toronto is very anxious, up to the limit of its powers as determined by its finances and the size of its staff, to aid persons who are in employment during the day to secure education of university grade and will go a long way to provide credit for those proceeding to a degree, provided always, however, that the University retains full control of its own standards and of its staff. Therefore, the University is prepared to offer instruction and admission to examinations to students belonging to any organization in any locality in the Province under the following conditions: (1) the class must consist of not fewer than twenty members; (2) the fees paid by each student must be the same as those paid by students in the Teachers' Course; (3) the organization making application for such a class must collect the fees from every student and forward these fees to the University within the time limit stipulated in the case of students in the Teachers' Course; (4) the University will select and pay the members of its staff who give the tuition; (5) such class or classes may be held in classrooms supplied by the organization concerned, provided the equipment and library facilities are suitable, in the judgment of the University, for the work of such class, or classes; (6) the tuition given to such class or classes shall be of the same character as that given to students in the Teachers' Course; (7) the number of such classes shall be determined by the ability of the University to provide this instruction; (8) unless otherwise expressly stated in this section such class or classes shall be governed by the regulations at the time governing classes in the Teachers' Course.

UNIVERSITY COLLEGE.

UNIVERSITY COLLEGE.

University College is, since the Federation Act of 1887, the complement, in the system of higher education provided by the State, of the University of Toronto. The State furnishes through University College instruction in those departments of the Arts course in which it does not furnish instruction through the University. These departments are Greek, Latin, Ancient History, English, French, German, Oriental Languages and Ethics.

Principal..........................MAURICE HUTTON, M.A., LL.D.
Registrar..............................F. C. A. JEANNERET, B.A.

University College Council.

THE PRINCIPAL.

PROFESSOR ALEXANDER	PROFESSOR MILNER.
PROFESSOR CAMERON.	PROFESSOR NEEDLER.
PROFESSOR CARRUTHERS.	PROFESSOR TAYLOR.
PROFESSOR CRAIG.	PROFESSOR TRACY.
PROFESSOR KEYS.	PROFESSOR WALLACE.
PROFESSOR MACNAUGHTON.	PROFESSOR WILL.
ASSOCIATE PROFESSOR DE CHAMP.	ASSISTANT PROFESSOR COCHRANE.
ASSOCIATE PROFESSOR FAIRLEY.	ASSISTANT PROFESSOR DALE.
ASSOCIATE PROFESSOR KNOX	ASSISTANT PROFESSOR DUFF
ASSOCIATE PROFESSOR SMITH.	ASSISTANT PROFESSOR HEDMAN
ASSISTANT PROFESSOR BROWN.	ASSISTANT PROFESSOR JEANNERET.
ASSISTANT PROFESSOR CLAWSON.	ASSISTANT PROFESSOR MORAUD.

ASSISTANT PROFESSOR WOODHEAD.

Enrolment of Students.

All students of the University proceeding to a degree in Arts are required to enroll themselves in University College or in Victoria College or in Trinity College or in St. Michael's College.

The conditions precedent to enrolment in University College are determined by the Council of the College. Every student of the College must either be an undergraduate of the University, or, if he be an occasional student, must satisfy the College Council that he has a sufficient knowledge of the subject in which he proposes to attend College lectures to do so with advantage.

Discipline.

The College has full control of its students so far as concerns their attendance upon lectures in the courses provided by the College, and their admission to the University examinations. No student of the College will be received by the University for examination without a certificate from the College that he has complied with its regulations.

Religious Knowledge.

No student will be allowed to take a Religious Knowledge option in any other than University College without the consent of the College Council. Each student who wishes to take a course in Religious Knowledge outside University College must make formal application on or before October 25th, stating what course he desires to take, for what subject the course is an option, in which College the applicant proposes to take this course and for what reason he wishes to take it outside University College.

Student Societies.

Various societies and associations, both of young men and of young women, have been organized for the promotion of Christian effort, social intercourse, literary and scientific activity. The Young Men's Christian Association has a section of Hart House specially devoted to its purposes, in which a devotional meeting is held every Thursday, and a public meeting every Sunday, at which latter addresses are delivered by prominent Christian workers. There is also a Young Women's Christian Association, which meets weekly. The Literary and Scientific Society, whose membership is made up of male students, holds weekly meetings for discussion, the reading of essays, etc. The Women's Literary Society has similar aims and methods. Besides the above, there are several associations for the encouragement of special branches of study. These are the Classical Association, the Modern Language Club, the Oriental Association, etc. A paper devoted to literature and College news is published thrice weekly, its staff consisting of representatives from various sections of the undergraduate body. For lists of officers of the various societies, see Appendix.

Lodging and Board.

Lodging and board are readily obtainable in numerous private boarding-houses within convenient distance of the University at a cost of from nine dollars upwards for comfortable lodging with board; or rooms may be rented at a cost of from three dollars per week upwards, and board obtained separately. A list of accredited boarding-houses is kept by the Secretary of the Young Men's Christian Association and by the Resident Head of the University College Women's Union and students are recommended to consult them with reference to the selection of suitable accommodation. Board may also be obtained at moderate rates at Hart House.

Argyll House, 100 Queen's Park.

Accommodation for 30 women students in University College or in Medicine is afforded by Argyll House. Applications should be made to the Secretary of the Argyll House Committee, 85 St. George Street, Toronto, from whom terms of residence may be obtained.

Regulations Relating to Students, Terms and Examinations.

1. Students entering University College are required to produce satisfactory certificates of moral character and previous good conduct.

2. No student will be enrolled in any year, or be allowed to continue in attendance, whose presence for any cause is deemed by the Council to be prejudicial to the interests of the College.

3. Matriculated students are required to attend the courses of instruction and examinations in all subjects prescribed for students of their respective standing, and no student will be permitted to remain in the College who persistently neglects academic work.

4. The certificate required for admission to the University examinations will not be granted to students who have been reported to the Council for not conforming to the College regulations, or for improper conduct of any kind.

5. Matriculated students are required to reside, during the period of their attendance on lectures, in houses selected by their parents or guardians or approved by the College Council.

6. Men and women students, unless members of the same family, are not permitted to reside in the same lodging-houses.

7. All women undergraduates in University College are required to register with the Resident Head of the Union at the beginning of term. Her directions as to conduct are to be observed. Women undergraduates who are away from home and not in a College Residence must have their boarding-houses approved by her.

8. All interference on the part of any student with the personal liberty of another, by arresting him, or summoning him to appear before any unauthorized tribunal of students, or otherwise subjecting him to any indignity or personal violence, is forbidden by the Council. Any student convicted of participation in such proceedings will forfeit the certificate required for admission to the University examinations, and will render himself liable to expulsion from the College.

9. A student who is under suspension, or who has been expelled from the College or University, will not be admitted to the University buildings or grounds.

10. The constitution of every College society or association of students and all amendments to any such constitution, must be submitted for approval to the College Council. All programmes of such societies or associations must, before publication, receive the sanction of the Council. Permission to invite any person not a member of the Faculty of University College to preside at or address a meeting of any society or association must be similarly obtained. Societies and associations are required to confine themselves to the objects laid down in their constitution.

11. The name of the College is not to be used in connection with a publication of any kind without the permission of the College Council.

12. Certificates of attendance on lectures in any department during an

academic year may be given to occasional students who have been regular in their attendance, and who have also passed the examinations in such department.

13. All undergraduates are expected to wear the prescribed academic costume within the class-rooms and buildings. 🏰

14. All class receptions of the various years can be held on Saturday afternoons only. Class meetings held in the evenings are not to continue later than 11 p.m.

WINNERS OF PRIZES, MEDALS AND SCHOLARSHIPS IN THE COLLEGE IN 1920.

Prizes.

The Squair French Prose Prize............... $\left\{\begin{array}{l}\text{Miss K. M. Asman} \\ \text{Miss H. C. Kirkwood}\end{array}\right.$

The Toronto Alumnae Prize in English Composition of the
Second Year.............................Miss H. M. Cochrane

Medals.

Governor-General's Medal in Modern Languages (Fourth
Year)...G. H. Unwin
McCaul Medal in Classics....................Miss M. A. Dickinson

Scholarships.

The McCaul, for Classics (Junior Matriculation).........L. A. MacKay
The Moss, for Classics (First Year)....................L. A. MacKay
The Edward Blake, for Moderns (First Year).........Miss K. R. Manson
The William Mulock, for Classics (Second Year)....J. E. A. Johnstone
The George Brown, for Moderns (Second Year).......Miss E. A. J. Shaw
The Moss, for Classics (Third Year).....................M. D. C. Tait
The Julius Rossin, for Moderns (Third Year)................R. A. Allen
The John Macdonald, for Philosophy (Third Year)....F. G. Lightbourn

VICTORIA COLLEGE.

VICTORIA COLLEGE.

Victoria College was founded by resolution of the Conference of the Methodist Church in Canada, held in Kingston in August, 1830. The institution was opened for students at Cobourg on the 18th of June, 1836, with the Rev. Matthew Richey, M.A., as Principal. On the 12th of October, 1836, letters patent were issued by His Majesty King William IV, incorporating the institution as a seminary of learning for the Province of Upper Canada, under the name of "Upper Canada Academy".

In 1841 the Parliament of the United Provinces of Upper and Lower Canada, being now first constituted by Acts of the Imperial Parliament with power to grant such a charter, at its first session held in the city of Kingston, passed an Act extending the charter of the Academy under the name and style of "Victoria College," with power and authority to confer degrees of Bachelor, Master and Doctor of the various Arts and Faculties", which Act was assented to by the Governor-General on the 27th of August, 1841.

On the 21st of October, 1841, the Rev. Egerton Ryerson, having been appointed principal, opened the first college session under the enlarged charter.

In the year 1844 the Rev. A. McNabb, D.D., succeeded the Rev. Dr. Ryerson as Principal, and occupied the office until 1849. At the close of his term the number of students in the College was 140.

In 1850 the Rev. S. S. Nelles, M.A., was appointed Principal, and addressed himself to the task of organizing and enlarging the College to the status and work of a University. In the year 1854-55 the Faculty of Medicine was added and established in Toronto. In 1860 the Faculty of Law was added, and in 1871 the Faculty of Theology.

In the year 1883-84 a Commission, appointed by the General Conference of the Methodist Church, arranged for the consolidation of Albert College, Belleville, with Victoria College, Cobourg, and legal effect was given to this consolidation by Act of the Legislature of Ontario, 47 Vict., chap. 93.

The corporate name was by this Act changed to "Victoria University". The government of the University was vested in a Board of Regents, Chancellor, Vice-Chancellor and Senate. To these bodies was given power to affiliate outlying colleges, and full university powers in all faculties were continued. The Rev. S. S. Nelles, D.D., LL.D., as President, was *ex-officio* first Chancellor, and William Kerr, M.A., LL.D., K.C., Senator, was elected first Vice-Chancellor.

Under the provisions of the present charter the following colleges are affiliated in Arts with Victoria University:—Albert College, Belleville; the Ontario Ladies' College, Whitby; Alma College, St. Thomas.

In 1887, the Rev. S. S. Nelles, D.D., LL.D., died, and the Rev. N. Burwash, S.T.D., LL.D., was appointed President and Chancellor.

On the 12th of November, 1890, under the provisions of the Revised Statutes of Ontario, chap. 230, and the Acts amending the same, Victoria University was, by proclamation of the Lieutenant-Governor, federated with the University of Toronto.

On the first of October, 1892, the Faculty of Victoria College began work in the present Main Building in Queen's Park, Toeronto, and the federation of the Universities was practically consummated. The Faculty of Arts then assumed the work and relation of a College in the University of Toronto, providing instruction in all subjects assigned by the Federation Act to University College. In other subjects the students of Victoria College attend the lectures and laboratory practice of the University of Toronto, and receive their degrees under the statutory regulations of its Senate.

By the provisions of the Federation Act of 1887 the President of Victoria College, a representative of the Senate of Victoria College, and five representatives of the graduates in Arts, are members of the Senate of the University of Toronto, and the graduates and undergraduates of Victoria College are granted the same standing and privileges in the University of Toronto. By the provisions of the University Act of 1906, three members of the Arts Faculty of Victoria, chosen by that body, are sent as additional representatives to the Senate of the University of Toronto, and all the permanent members of the Arts Staff of Victoria as well as one member of the theological staff chosen by that Faculty are members of the Council of the Faculty of Arts of the University of Toronto.

At Federation five hundred and seventy-seven graduates of Victoria College were admitted to standing and privileges of the degree of B.A. in the University of Toronto; two hundred and thirty-one to those of M.A.; nine hundred and sixty-three to those of M.D.; one hundred and twenty-five to those of LL.B.; and forty to those of LL.D.

By the University Act of 1901 the electoral body in Convocation of Victoria College was made permanent, and was enlarged to include all graduates in Arts of the University of Toronto since 1892 who at graduation were enrolled in Victoria College.

The electoral body of Victoria College in the Convocation of the University of Toronto now consists of about 2047 graduates in Arts, besides the graduates in Law and Medicine, who form one body with those of the University of Toronto.

In 1913, the Rev. N. Burwash, S.T.D., LL.D., retired from the position of President and Chancellor and the Rev. R. P. Bowles, M.A., D.D., LL.D., was appointed in his stead.

The following Benefactions have been given to Victoria University for the endowment of chairs and erection of buildings:—

Mr. and Mrs. Edward Jackson for endowment of chair, $30,000.

Wm. Gooderham, Esq., for building and endowment, $200,000.

The Honourable Geo. A. Cox and Mrs. Cox, for endowment of two chairs, $100,000.

Hart A. Massey, Esq., for building and endowments, $960,000.

The Honourable John Macdonald, for building for federation purposes, $25,000.

W. E. H. Massey, Esq., for endowment, three hundred shares of Massey-Harris Stock.

Sir Joseph Flavelle, Bart., LL.D., for endowment, $30,000.

Andrew Carnegie, Esq., for library building, $50,000.

Cyrus A. Birge, Esq., for library endowment, $50,000.

From these and other sources the following Chairs have been endowed:—

The Edward Jackson Chair in Biblical and Systematic Theology.

The Ryerson Chair in Ethics and Evidences of Christianity.

The Nelles Chair in Ancient History.

The William Gooderham Chair in English Literature.

The Eliza Gooderham Chair in French Literature.

The H. A. Massey Chair in the English Bible.

The Eliza Phelps Massey Chair in Old Testament Exegesis.

The Geo. A. Cox Chair in New Testament Exegesis.

The Margaret Cox Chair in Homiletics and Pastoral Theology.

The W. E. H. Massey Chair in Greek Language and Philosophy.

The J. W. Flavelle Chair in Hebrew.

A special endowment for the Presidency of the College.

The John Macdonald Chair in Latin.

The buildings, library, furniture and grounds of Victoria College are now valued at $1,094,542.82; and the endowment is $1,080,319.18.

GOVERNMENT OF VICTORIA COLLEGE.

The Board of Regents.

Representatives of the General Conference:

Rev. S. D. Chown, D.D., *General Superintendent.*
Rev. J. W. Graham, B.A., D.D., LL.D., *Secretary of Education.*
Rev. J. S. Ross, M.A., D.D.
Rev. Thomas Manning, B.A., D.D.
Ret. R. N. Burns, B.A. D.D.
Rev. G. N. Hazen, B.A., D.D.
Rev. S. C. Moore, B.D.
Rev. T. W. Neal.
A. E. Ames, Esq.
C. D. Massey, Esq.
H. H. Fudger, Esq.
Hon. N. W. Rowell, LL.D., K.C., M.P.

Representatives of the Alumni:

Hon. J. J. Maclaren, M.A., LL.D., *Vice-Chancellor.*
Mrs. J. G. Blewett, B.A.
J. R. L. Starr, B.A., LL.D., K.C.
G. H. Locke, M.A.
F. N. G. Starr, C.B.E., M.D., C.M., F.A.C.S.
Rev. W. H. Graham, B.A.
Rev. A. P. Addison, B.D.
Professor C. T. Currelly, M.A.

Co-opted by the Representatives of the General Conference and Alumni:

Rev. R. P. Bowles, M.A., D.D,, LL.D., *Chancellor.*
E. R. Wood, Esq.
H. C. Cox, Esq.
W. E. Rundle, Esq.
G. H. Wood, Esq.
Rev. H. W. Crews, M.A., D.D.
Chas. Austin, Esq.
J. H. Gundy, Esq.

The Senate.

REV. R. P. BOWLES, M.A., D.D., LL.D., *Chancellor.*
HON. MR. JUSTICE MACLAREN, M.A., LL.D., *Vice-Chancellor.*
REV. S. D. CHOWN, D.D., *General Superintendent of the Methodist Church.*
A. P. COLEMAN, M.A., PH.D. (Bresl.) LL.D., F.R.S,. *Honorary Professor.*
PROFESSORS OF THE FACULTY OF ARTS.
PROFESSORS OF THE FACULTY OF THEOLOGY.
MEMBERS OF THE BOARD OF REGENTS.

Representative of Albert College:

F. W. MERCHANT, B.A., D.PAED.

Representative of the Ontario Ladies' College:

REV. F. S. FAREWELL, B.A.

Representative of Alma College:

REV. P. S. DOBSON, M.A.

Representatives of the Alumni:

G. G. MILLS, B.A.
H. W. AIKINS, B.A., M.D.
L. A. KENNEDY, M.A.
F. C. COLBECK, B.A.
REV. J. J. FERGUSON, M.A., D.D.
REV. W. B. CREIGHTON, B.A., D.D.
F. H. CLARKE, B.A.
H. W. GUNDY, B.A.

ADMINISTRATIVE OFFICIALS.

President....................REV. R. P. BOWLES, M.A., D.D., LL.D.
Dean of the Faculty of Arts....................J. C. ROBERTSON, M.A.
Dean of the Faculty of Theology............REV. J. F. MCLAUGHLIN, B.A.
Registrar....................................A. L. LANGFORD, M.A.
Librarian..A. E. LANG, M.A.
Bursar..............................REV. W. C. B. CASWELL, B.A.
Secretary of the Faculty....................N. W. DEWITT, B.A., PH.D.
Secretary of the Faculty of Theology......REV. W. A. POTTER, M.A., B.D.
Dean of Residence..............................C. V. MASSEY, M.A.
Senior Tutor in Residence........................G. M. SMITH, M.A.
Dean of Women Students..............MISS M. E. T. ADDISON, B.A.
Treasurer....................................W. E. RUNDLE, ESQ.

GENERAL REGULATIONS AND ANNOUNCEMENTS.
FOR STUDENTS IN ARTS.

Admission.

Students are admitted to registration in the Faculty of Arts on having passed the Matriculation examination prescribed by the University of Toronto, or on giving the Faculty satisfactory evidence of their ability to pursue the course of study proposed. They are required to observe the general regulations of the University of Toronto and of Victoria College in regard to attendance on lectures and examinations.

Examinations.

No student may present himself for any University examination subsequent to matriculation without having complied with all the requirements of his college affecting his admission to such examination.

Occasional Students.

Occasional students may be admitted to lectures on application.

Certificates of attendance on lectures in any department during an academic year may be given to occasional students who have been regular in their attendance and who have passed the examinations in such department.

Terms.

The term will not be allowed to students who have been reported to the President by any Professor as neglecting to attend the required lectures, or who have not conformed to the statutes and regulations of the College.

Instruction.

Instruction in the various subjects of the Arts course is given by the Arts Faculty of the University of Toronto and the Arts Faculty of Victoria College. Instruction in the Religious Knowledge options is given by the Theological Faculty of Victoria College.

College Examinations.

Students are required to attend all examinations prescribed by the Professors and Lecturers in their departments.

Prizes and honours are awarded on the recommendation of the Professors and Lecturers, in accordance with the requirements prescribed by them in their several departments.

Fees.

The fees required to be paid by students enrolled in Victoria College are those prescribed by the Governors of the University of Toronto. Enrolment fees are paid to the Fees Clerk of the College; all other fees are paid to the Bursar of the University of Toronto.

Discipline.

All students enrolled in Victoria College are subject to the regulations as to discipline prescribed by the Council of the Faculty of Arts of the University of Toronto.

Students are required to attend the lectures, as well as the examination s on all subjects necessary for students of their course and standing. Compliance with this rule will be required as a condition of admission to examination by the University unless dispensation has been obtained.

All interference with the personal liberty of the student, by arresting him, or summoning him to appear before any unauthorized tribunal of students, or otherwise subjecting him to any indignity or personal violence is forbidden by the Faculty. Any student convicted of participation in such proceedings will forfeit the certificate required for admission to the University examinations, and will render himself liable to expulsion from the College.

Religious Services.

Morning prayers are held daily except Saturday and Sunday in the Chapel, at which all students are expected to be present. Other religious services will be held at suitable times, to which all students are cordially invited.

Libraries, Museums, etc.

The students of Victoria College, besides having the use of the University of Toronto Library and the various Laboratories of the University, have free access to the Victoria University Library, which consists of a working collection of 30,000 bound volumes on the English, Latin, Greek. French and ' German languages and literatures, History, Philosophy and the various departments of Theology.

The College has loaned to the Royal Ontario Museum its mineralogical palaeontological and biological collections, as well as its collection of Egyptian and Indian relics.

Students not in Residence.

All students who do not reside in any one of the Residences or who do not reside with their parents or with such persons as their parents' or guardians direct, are recommended to board and lodge in such houses as are approved by the President of the College. A carefully selected list of boarding-houses, where board and rooms may be obtained, is prepared each year by the Young Men's Christian Association. Students will be expected to observe proper hours and to maintain the conduct of Christian ladies and gentlemen.

The Residence for Men Students

The Residence buildings comprise one hundred and sixteen bed-sitting rooms, and in each house there is a Common-Room with a fire-place on the ground floor, as well as a bedroom and sitting-room for the Tutor in Residence. About fifteen bedrooms have fire-places, and in one house there are two suites, each consisting of a bedroom and a study.

The Hall, known as Burwash Hall, is capable of seating 200 persons at meals. Used as a hall for lectures, it will seat about 700.

All inquiries should be addressed to the Dean of Residence, Victoria College, Toronto, from whom can be obtained further information.

The Residences for Women Students

The Residences for Women Students, Annesley Hall and other houses, furnish residence for one hundred and eleven women students of Victoria College.

Applications for rooms must be accompanied by a deposit fee of $10, which will be refunded if the application is withdrawn before September first. Fees are payable half on the first of October and half on the first of February.

Further information may be obtained by writing to the Dean of Women Students, Annesley Hall, Queen's Park, Toronto.

MEDALS, SCHOLARSHIPS AND PRIZES, 1920

FACULTY OF ARTS

The awards marked with an asterisk (*) are made by the University; the others (based also on University examinations) are College awards.

Fourth Year

*The Governor-General's Gold Medal....... J. N. D. Bush.

The Prince of Wales Gold Medal (1st in General Proficiency)....................... No award.

The Prince of Wales Silver Medal (2nd in General Proficiency)................... No award.

The Governor-General's Silver Medal (1st in Honour English)..................... J. N. D. Bush (mention).

The Edward Wilson Gold Medal (Classics)... J. N. D. Bush.

The S. H. Janes Silver Medal (Classics)...... No award.

The J. J. MacLaren Gold Medal (Eng. and Hist., Moderns)..................... Miss E. M. Thornton.

The Gold Medal (Modern History)......... H. M. Smith.

The J. Reginald Adams Gold Medal (Political Science)......................... E. H. McKinney.

The J. Reginald Adams Silver Medal (Political Science).......................... No award.

The E. J. Sanford Gold Medal (Philosophy).. W. H. Moss.

The S. H. Janes Silver Medal (Philosophy)... No award.

The Silver Medal (Mathematics and Physics). G. M. Shrum.

The Geo. A. Cox Gold Medal (Natural Science) Miss E. V. Eastcott.

The W. J. Robertson Prize (Can. Const. Hist.) H. D. Lang.

*J. F. Guenther received an award of $20 from the funds of The All Souls' Historical Prize in recognition of creditable work.

Third Year

*The Alexander Mackenzie Scholarships in Political Science....................... A. F. Annis.

*The Daniel Wilson Scholarship in Biology... N. B. Laughton.

*The Daniel Wilson Scholarship in Chemistry and Mineralogy...................... W. G. Noble.

*The Daniel Wilson Scholarship in Geology and Mineralogy........................... H. F. Swann.

The George John Blewett Scholarship (Philosophy).............................. E. W. Jewitt.

The Hamilton Fisk Biggar Scholarship (Classics)............................. T. R. S. Broughton.

The Hamilton Fisk Biggar Scholarship (Physiol. and Biochem. Sciences)........ N. S. Clark.

The Hamilton Fisk Biggar Scholarship (Chemistry and Mineralogy II).............. W. L. Swanson.

The Hamilton Fisk Biggar Scholarship (Chemistry)................................. A. E. R. Westman.

The Hamilton Fisk Biggar Scholarship (Eng. and Hist., Cl.)........................ R. W. Hardy.

The Hodgins Prize (1st in Pass English)...... No award.

Second Year

*The second Alexander Mackenzie Scholarship in Political Science.................... { G. G. Brown. / R. P. Stewart. }

*The Daniel Wilson Scholarship in Biological and Physical Sciences.................. J. H. Couch.

The Classical Scholarship.................. No award.

The Webster Prize (1st in Pass English)...... R. P. Stewart.

The Robert Johnston Prize (1st in Pass Hebrew)............................. H. M. Wright.

The Orientals Scholarship.................. No award.

The Hamilton Fisk Biggar Scholarship (Modern History).................... Miss M. V. Ray.

The Essa Van Dusen Dafoe Scholarship (French)........................... L. H. Miller.

First and Second Years

Regents' Prizes (1st and 2nd English Essays).. { 1. L. H. Miller. / 2. Miss M. V. Ray. }

First Year

*The Alexander T. Fulton Scholarship in Mathematics and Physics............. M. S. Bell.

*The second Alexander T. Fulton Scholarship in Natural Science.................... G. C. Kelly.

The Robertson Scholarship (Classics)........ Miss R. V. Kendrick.

The Austin Perley Misener Scholarship (Oriental Languages)..................... F. G. Ward.

The Class of 1902 Prize (1st in Pass English) . F. G. Ward.

The Hamilton Fisk Biggar Scholarship (Political Science and Modern History)........ { Miss N. A. Yeomans. / L. V. Smith. }

All the Years

The Lincoln G. Hutton Scholarship......... J. N. D. Bush.

The Lily Denton Keys Prize.............. H. D. Langford.

Junior Matriculation, 1919

The Flavelle Scholarship (1st in Classics)..... Miss R. V. Kendrick.

The W. E. H. Massey Scholarship (2nd in Classics)........................... No award.

AFFILIATED COLLEGES .

ALBERT COLLEGE
BELLEVILLE, ONT.
, FOUNDED, 1854.

Faculty

THE REV. E. N. BAKER, M.A., D.D., *President.*
ELLA GARDINER, B.A., *Lady Principal.*
R. J. F. STAPLES, B.A., *Secretary.*
D. H. BLATCHFORD, B.A.
S. F. MAINE, B.A., B.D.
ORY A. SHAW, M.A.
OLIVE RUSSELL.
MINNIE PARKS.
JEAN RAMSAY, B.A.
VICTORIA BURLEIGH.
V. P. HUNT, A.A.G.O.
S. M. ANGLIN, B.A.
ELIZABETH POTTER, MUS.BAC.
JESSIE TUITE.
BARBARA CRAWFORD.
MRS. JEAN BAKER.

Courses of Study

  I. Collegiate Course, embodying elective undergraduate studies.

 II. Junior and Senior Matriculation in Arts, Engineering, Law, Medicine and Theology.

III. Teachers' Course, to prepare for teachers' examinations.

IV. Preliminary Course, as prescribed by the General Conference of the Methodist Church.

 V. Depts. of Religious Education.

VI. Business College Course, comprising Theoretical and Practical Bookkeeping, Practical English, Shorthand and Typewriting.

VII. Musical Course in Musical Academy, comprising Pianoforte Course, Organ Course, Post Graduate Course and Voice Culture.

VIII. Courses in Elocution, Physical Culture and Deportment.

IX. Course in Fine Arts, embracing Painting, Drawing, etc.

X. Alexandra Ladies' College Course, leading to the M.L.A. and M.M.L.

ALMA COLLEGE

ST. THOMAS, ONT.

Opened, 1881.

Administrative Officers

Samuel Dwight Chown, M.A., D.D., LL.D.........*President of Board.*
W. H. Murch ....*Chairman of Executive.*
P. S. Dobson, M.A. (Oxon.) ....*Principal.*
Robert I. Warner, M.A., D.D. ....*Principal Emeritus.*
Margaret Shipley ....x................*Office Secretary.*
Mrs. Jean M. Holding...........................*Dean of Residence.*

Literary Department

P. S. Dobson, M.A................................*Bible and Latin.*
Robert I. Warner, M.A., D.D.........................*Psychology.*
Constance Kilborn, B.A........................*English; History.*
Ruth Woodworth, B.A.............................*French, Latin.*
Jean Wylie, B.A..............................*Mathematics, Science.*
Mary Vallentyne.............................*Preparatory Studies.*
Ruth Hopkins................................*Preparatory Studies.*

Music

Thomas Martin, *Director*...................*Pianoforte, Concert Solos.*
Stanley Oliver.....................*Organ, Harmony, Choral, Vocal.*
Harriet A. Jolliffe, A.A.C.M.........................*Pianoforte.*
Isabel Stevens....................................*Pianoforte.*
Helene Allen..*Violin.*
Miriam Edmiston...................................*Pianoforte.*
Catherine Reekie...................................*Pianoforte.*

Fine Arts

Wm. St. Thomas Smith, A.R.C.A., Director......*Painting, Drawing and Sketching.*
Eva St. Thomas Smith..............*Painting, Modelling and Sketching.*
S. M. McKay.....................................*China Painting.*

Commercial Science

Elva Foreman..*Bookkeeping, Phonography, Typewriting and Penmanship.*

Elocution and Physical Culture.

MARIAN HENRY, A.T.C.M., *Reading, Expression, Physical Culture.*

Household Science.

MABEL BALKWILL, *Cookery, Dietaries, Sewing.*

Diploma Courses.

(*a*) M.L.A. and M.E.L., embracing University Junior and Senior Matriculation, with options and additional subjects in Bible Study, English, etc.

(*b*) Music (Piano, Organ, Voice or Violin).

(*c*) Fine Art.

(*d*) Elocution and Physical Culture.

(*e*) Commercial and Shorthand.

(*f*) Household Science.

TRINITY COLLEGE.

TRINITY COLLEGE.

I. Trinity College, with Residence for Men.

J. A. Worrell, K.C., M.A., D.C.L., *Chancellor.*
The Rev. T. C. Street Macklem, M.A., D.D., LL.D., D.C.L., *Vice-Chancellor and Provost.*
A. H. Young, M.A., D.C.L., *Dean of Residence.*
W. A. Kirkwood, M.A., Ph.D., *Registrar.*
Rev. H. T. F. Duckworth, M.A., *Dean of the Faculty of Arts.*
Rev. F. H. Cosgrave, M.A., B.D., *Dean of Divinity.*
R. E. L. Kittredge, M.A., *Librarian.*
Sydney H. Jones, Esq., *Bursar.*

II. St. Hilda's College—Residence for Women.

Miss M. Cartwright, B.A., *Principal and Dean of Women Students.*
Miss L. C. Scott, M.A., *Assistant.*
Miss Cotterill, *Assistant.*
Sydney H. Jones, Esq., *Bursar.*

Trinity College, which entered into federation with the University of Toronto on the first day of October, 1904, was founded by the Honourable and Right Reverend John Strachan, D.D., LL.D., first Bishop of Toronto, one of the founders, and at one time President, of King's College. It was established, after the secularisation of King's College in 1850, for the purpose of combining religious instruction with a liberal education.

In 1851 Trinity College was incorporated by the Legislature of Canada. In 1852 a Royal Charter conferred upon it University powers, which were exercised in all Faculties down to 1904, under the style of the University of Trinity College. Since 1904 Trinity College has conferred degrees only in the Faculty of Divinity.

For a certain period state aid was granted to it in common with the other Universities of the Province, but this was subsequently withdrawn. In 1874 the question of federation was mooted, but no serious attempt at a solution was made till about the year 1885; and it was not till nearly twenty years later that satisfactory terms of federation were finally concluded.

Under the Federation Agreement, the degrees in Arts are conferred by the University of Toronto, the instruction being given by Trinity College in all College subjects, and by the University in the remaining subjects of the Arts curriculum, and Trinity College students having access without extra fees to the University classes and laboratories. In the Faculty of Divinity, Trinity College continues to exercise the functions of an independent University, having no relation to the University of Toronto in respect of degrees in this Faculty.

St. Hilda's College was founded in 1888 by the Rev. Dr. Body, the second Provost of Trinity College, to provide a residence for the women students of Trinity College, together with instruction in certain subjects of the Arts course. Later such instruction was discontinued in favour of complete co-education, St. Hilda's continuing to be the residence for women students of Trinity College.

Religious instruction for all its students in Arts having been one of the chief reasons for the foundation of Trinity College, this still remains one of its distinguishing features, the federation agreement with the University of Toronto preserving this right in perpetuity to all students of Trinity College.

Residence is another advantage offered by the College, accommodation being provided for about 100 men students. Here they come into close contact daily with one another and with the members of the staff, both resident and non-resident. In this way one very important element in education is provided.

The women students attend lectures with the men, and reside in St Hilda's College, which is conveniently situated in the Trinity College grounds, and offers to women all the advantages which are offered to men by the residence of Trinity College. All the women students, resident and non-resident, come under the supervision of the Dean of Women Students, Miss M. Cartwright, B.A., who is also Principal of St. Hilda's College. St. Hilda's Lodge, which adjoins the main building, is under the immediate charge of Miss L. C. Scott, M.A. These two buildings provide residence accommodation for about fifty students.

On week days both men and women attend the morning and evening services of the Chapels of their respective colleges. On Sundays they attend the Trinity College Chapel together, this latter regulation applying to residents and non-residents alike.

Though the College belongs to the Church of England, it is open without religious tests to members of other communions. They are allowed to absent themselves from the Chapel services on Sundays on stating to the Provost their intention to attend a church of their own denomination, on the understanding that they will present a certificate of attendance, so as to satisfy the College regulations in this respect.

Members of other communions are not required to take the courses of study prescribed in the Church Catechism and the Prayer Book, but are allowed to substitute for them courses in Church History, the Evidences of Christianity, or Christian Ethics.

All students are required to keep term in lectures and chapels, and upon enrolling are placed under promise to obey the rules and regulations of the College.

—24

Tuition (or registration) fees for regular and special students are the same as are paid in the other Colleges and are payable to the Bursar of Trinity College.

Particulars as to the amount of board fees, room rents, and the like may be obtained by applying to the Provost or the Dean of Residence.

Hazing.

Every student of Trinity College is required to sign the following declaration:—

"I do solemnly promise, that so long as I remain a student of this College—

1. I will discountenance all proceedings commonly known as hazing and will do my utmost to promote a healthy tone of feeling against them.

2. And, in particular, I will not interfere in any way with the personal liberty of any student, as, for example, by entering into, or remaining in, his room against his will; and I will not subject any student, or countenance his being subjected, to any indignity of any kind whatsoever.

These promises I make, fully understanding that any violation of them will render me liable to immediate expulsion from the College."

University Discipline.

Every regular student of Trinity College must conform to the regulations of the University when in attendance upon University lectures and examinations. He must also pay the Library fee and other University fees to the Bursar of the University.

Keeping Terms.

The College regulations require regular attendance at Lectures and at the services of the College Chapel, a minimum of 50 per cent in the case of Chapel services, and of 80 per cent. in the case of Lectures being necessary to the keeping of term.

Students in Arts who fail to keep their term, or are regarded as being otherwise unsatisfactory in respect of their work or conduct, will not be certified to the Registrar of the University for admission to the Annual Examination of the University in May.

Non-Matriculated Students.

Students may be admitted to College by the Provost without matriculation if he deems them to be sufficiently advanced in their studies to profit by the lectures.

GOVERNMENT OF THE COLLEGE.

By the provisions of the Royal Charter, the government of the University of Trinity College is vested in the Corporation, which body, by an Act of the Legislature of the Province of Canada (15 Vict. ch. 32), is composed of: 1. The Bishops of the six Dioceses into which the original Diocese of Toronto has been divided; 2. The Trustees; 3. The Council.

The Council is made up of the following classes of members:

Ex Officio Members.

The Chancellor and ex-Chancellors of the University of Trinity College, the Provost, the Deans of Residence, Arts, and Divinity, the Registrar of Trinity College, the Chairman of Convocation, and the Headmaster of Trinity College School, Port Hope.

Members Nominated.

By the Synod of each Diocese of the Province of Ontario, two clergymen and two laymen.

By the Bishops of Ottawa, Algoma, Ontario, Huron, Toronto and Niagara, four members each, representing their respective Dioceses, or two only, if the Synod of the Diocese elects members.

By each Medical, Musical, or Theological College affiliated with the University of Trinity College, one member.

Members Elected.

By the College Committee, one of the professors.

By the graduates in Arts and Divinity who are members of Convocation (see below) eight members, to hold office for four years, two retiring annually.

By the graduates in Law two members, to hold office for two years, one retiring annually.

By the graduates in Medicine who are members of Convocation two members, to hold office for two years, one retiring annually.

By the associate members of Convocation (see below) two members, to hold office for two years, one retiring annually.

By the sustaining members of Convocation, two members, to hold office for two years, one retiring annually.

By the whole Corporation ten members, elected for four years, of whom at least two shall be engaged in educational work in the High School system of the Province.

Chancellor.

J. A. WORRELL, K.C., M.A., D.C.L.

Nominated by the Archbishop of Algoma.

THE VENERABLE GOWAN GILLMOR, D.D., Sault Ste. Marie, *Archdeacon of Algoma.*

THE REVEREND CANON PIERCY, Sturgeon Falls.

THE REVEREND CANON HEDLEY, M.A., Toronto. .

THE REVEREND F. H. HINCKS, M.A., Haileybury.

Nominated by the Bishop of Huron.

THE REVEREND CANON FOTHERINGHAM, M.A., Brantford.

Elected by the Synod of Huron.

W. H. MOORHOUSE, M.B., London.

THE REVEREND CANON DAVIS, M.A., Sarnia.

Nominated by the Bishop of Toronto.

THE REVEREND CANON PLUMPTRE, M.A., Toronto.

THE REVEREND CANON RIGBY, M.A., LL.D., Port Hope.

THE HONOURABLE MR. JUSTICE ORDE, Toronto.

Nominated by the Bishop of Niagara.

THE VERY REVEREND D. T. OWEN, L.TH., D.D., Hamilton, *Dean of Niagara.*

W. M. LOGAN, M.A., Hamilton.

Elected by the Synod of Niagara.

THE REVEREND CANON SUTHERLAND, M.A., Hamilton, and E. T. LIGHT-BOURN, ESQ., Oakville, to hold office to 1921.

C. S. SCOTT, ESQ., Hamilton, and THE REVEREND CANON BROUGHALL, M.A., St. Catharines, to hold office to 1922.

Nominated by the Bishop of Ottawa.

No nomination.

Elected by the Synod of Ottawa.

THE REVEREND CANON ANDERSON, L.TH., Ottawa.

THE REVEREND CANON WHALLEY, Ottawa.

CAPT. A. F. MATHESON, M.A., Perth.

CHAS. MORSE, K.C., D.C.L., Ottawa.

Nominated by the Bishop of Ontario.

THE VERY REVEREND G. L. STARR, M.A., D.D., Kingston, *Dean of Ontario.*

THE VENERABLE G. R. BEAMISH, M.A., Belleville, *Archdeacon of Ontario.*

Elected by the Synod of Ontario.

W. B. CARROLL, K.C., M.A., Gananoque.
THE REVEREND GEORGE CODE, M.A., Smith's Falls.
THE REVEREND J. H. H. COLEMAN, M.A., Napanee.

Nominated by Trinity Medical College.

G. A. BINGHAM, M.D., C.M., Toronto.

Nominated by the Ontario Medical College for Women.

R. B. NEVITT, B.A., M.D., C.M., Toronto.

Nominated by the Toronto Conservatory of Music.

ALBERT HAM, MUS.DOC., F.R.C.O., Toronto.

Elected by Convocation.

(a) Graduates in Arts and Divinity.

THE REVEREND E. C. CAYLEY, M.A., D.D., Toronto, and R. J. READE, M.A., M.D., C.M., Toronto, to hold office to 1921.
R. B. BEAUMONT, M.A., Toronto, and THE REVEREND WALTER H. WHITE, M.A., Peterborough, to hold office to 1922.
COL. C. S. MacINNES, C.M.G., K.C., M.A., Toronto, and THE REVEREND CANON PLUMMER, L.Th., Toronto, to hold office to 1923.
THE REV. CANON J. S. BROUGHALL, M.A., Toronto, and G. C. HEWARD, M.A., Toronto, to hold office to 1924.

(b) Graduates in Law.

THE HONOURABLE MR. JUSTICE HODGINS, Toronto, to hold office to 1921.
D. T. SYMONS, K.C., B.C.L., Toronto, to hold office to 1922.

(c) Graduates in Medicine.

ARTHUR JUKES JOHNSON, M.B., to hold office to 1921.
HENRY CRAWFORD SCADDING, M.A., M.D., C.M., Toronto, to hold office to 1922.

(d) Elected by Associates of Convocation.

F. GORDON OSLER, ESQ., Toronto, to hold office to 1922.

(e) Elected by Sustaining Members of Convocation.

C. M. BALDWIN, M.A., Toronto, to hold office to 1921.
P. A. MANNINNG, ESQ., Toronto, to hold office to 1922.

Elected by the Alumnae Association of St. Hilda's College.

M. McLaughlin, Esq., to hold office to 1921.

Major G. B. Strathy, M.A., to hold office to 1922.

Secretary and Bursar.

Sydney H. Jones, Esq.

Honorary Treasurer.

Brig.-Gen. Sir H. M. Pellatt, C.V.O., D.C.L.

Auditors.

Rev. T. C. S. Macklem (*honorary*).

Messrs. Lawson, Welch and Campbell, *Chartered Accountants.*

Board of Endowment and Finances.

Sir Edmund Osler, M.P., *Chairman.*

Col. The Honourable Frederic Nicholls, *Vice-Chairman.*

Brig.-Gen. Sir H. M. Pellatt, C.V.O., D.C.L., *Treasurer.*

The Reverend T. C. S. Macklem, M.A., D.D., LL.D., D.C.L., *Secretary.*

Sir William Mackenzie.

Commission of Policy and Buildings

Col. H. C. Osborne, C.M.G., Ottawa, *Chairman.*

Capt. Gerald R. Larkin, Toronto, *Vice-Chairman.*

Capt. Vaughan Maclean Howard, Toronto, *Secretary*

The Chancellor.	F. Gordon Osler.
Chairman of Convocation.	R. H. Parmenter.
The Provost.	G. Larratt Smith.
Sir Henry Pellatt.	V. R. Smith.
Hon. Senator Nicholls.	Norman Sommerville.
Dr. A. H. Young.	W. A. Child (Hamilton).
Col. C. S. MacInnes, C.M.G.	Charles Bell (Hamilton).
Lt.-Col. Henry Brock.	Gordon Reid (Hamilton).
Major G. B. Strathy.	C. S. Scott (Hamilton).
Dr. R. J. Reade.	Archdeacon Snowdon (Ottawa).
D. T. Symonds, K.C.	Hamnet P. Hill, M.P.P. (Ottawa).
A. H. Campbell.	F. W. Fee (Ottawa).
Sydney H. Jones.	J. L. Bishop (Ottawa).
Angus Macdonald.	Major-General J. T. Fotheringham,
P. A. Manning.	C.M.G. (Ottawa).
Wilmot L. Matthews	Graham Campbell, Esq. (Toronto).
George W. Morley.	Dr. D. J. Goggin (Toronto).

Convocation.

Convocation, as at present organized, consists (in addition to the Chancellor, the Provost, the Vice-Provost, and the Professors of Trinity College) of all graduates who pay an annual fee of five dollars or upwards. It has been placed by the Corporation in the position of a Standing Committee of that body; and its members are in this way enabled, through their representatives, formally to lay their resolutions before the governing body of the University. Moreover, it is represented by fourteen members on the Corporation. (See above.) The Chairman is *ex officio* a member of the Corporation.

. An annual meeting for the transaction of business is held every year in the Michaelmas Term.

Friends of the University who are not graduates may become associate members of Convocation by the same annual payment of five dollars or upwards. Subscribers of a hundred dollars and upwards annually are known as sustaining members upon their election by the Executive Committee of Convocation.

Associate and Sustaining Members have the right of speaking and of voting at annual and other meetings of Convocation. They also elect annually a member of the Council.

The Chancellor of the University of Trinity College is elected for a period of five years by the graduate members of Convocation in good standing.

The Caput of Convocation, before which degrees are passed and conferred, consists of the Vice-Chancellor and four members of Convocation, to be elected by Convocation at the annual November meeting.

Since federation the only degrees conferred by the University of Trinity College are those in the Faculty of Divinity.

Chairman of Convocation.

W. H. PEPLER, M.D., C.M., L.R.C.P.

Clerk of Convocation.

PROFESSOR A. H. YOUNG, M.A., D.C.L.

Executive Committee.

(1) *Ex officio Members*—The Chancellor, the Chairman, the Clerk, the Provost, the Vice-Provost, The Dean of Residence, The Registrar of the University of Trinity College, the Dean of the Faculty of Arts, the Dean of the Faculty of Divinity, and former Chairmen of Convocation—J. A. Worrell, M.A., K.C., D.C.L.; D. T. Symonds, K.C., B.C.L.; R. B. Beaumont, M.A.; and D. J. Goggin, M.A., D.C.L.

(2) *Elected Members:*

C. M. Baldwin, M.A.,
The Rev. W. J. Brain, M.A.,
Miss M. Cartwright, B.A.,
Frank Darling, LL.D.,
Philip Dykes, Esq.,
G. C. Heward, M.A.,

Hon. F. E. Hodgins, B.C.L.,
Sydney H. Jones, Esq.,
A. Angus Macdonald, M.A.,
W. H. Pepler, M.D., C.M.,
The Rev. C. A. Seager, M.A., D.D.,
J. C. Wedd, Esq.

Scholars and Prizemen.
1920.
Arts.

FOURTH YEAR—

H.E. the Governor-General's Silver Medal for the Best Degree—
P. Lowe.

H.E. the Governor-General's Bronze Medal for Headship of St.
Hilda's College—Miss W. F. Scott.

The Jubilee Scholarship—P. W. Dawson.

The Prince of Wales Prize for the Highest First Class Honours in
Classics—J. B. West.

The Prince of Wales Prize for the Highest First Class Honours in
Mathematics—P. Lowe.

The Prize for the Highest First Class Honours in Political Science—
D. A. C. Martin.

The Prize for the Highest First Class Honours in Commerce and
Finance—T. Oakley.

THIRD YEAR—

The Wellington Scholarship in Classics—C. E. Phillips.

SECOND YEAR—

The Wellington Scholarship in Classics—J. Lowe.

The Hart-Moorhouse Scholarship in Classics—J. Lowe.

The Pettit Scholarship in Greek and Hebrew—J. Lowe.

The Dickson Scholarship in Modern Languages—Miss E. G. Gladman.

The Dickson Scholarship in Science—A. H. Gee.

FIRST YEAR AND SENIOR MATRICULATION—

The Dickson Scholarship in Science—R. H. M'Gonigle.

Junior Matriculation.
1920.

The Wellington Scholarship in Classics—T. C. B. DeLom, of Trinity
College School, Port Hope.

The Wellington Scholarship in Mathematics—C. F. Washington, of
Ottawa C.I.

The F. A. Bethune Scholarship (open to candidates from Trinity College
School)—T. C. B. DeLom.

Divinity Class Prize List.
1920.

FOURTH YEAR—
General Proficiency and Dogmatic Theology—A. N. Hoath.

THIRD YEAR—
General Proficiency—C. A. Bender.
Church History—J. S. Ditchburn.

BOTH YEARS—
Greek Testament
Patristics
Liturgics
Apologetics   A. N. Hoath.
Old Testament
New Testament
Sermon Prize

McDONALD PRIZES FOR BIBLE KNOWLEDGE—
A. N. Hoath and Miss S. G. Shore qualified for first and second prizes
respectively, but were ineligible.
Awarded by reversion to—1 and 2, C. F. Pashler and R. Booth (*aeq.*).

ESSAY PRIZE—
J. S. Ditchburn.

THE HAMILTON MEMORIAL PRIZE—
A. N. Hoath.

READING PRIZES—
College—H. P. Charters.
Doolittle (for improvement)—C. F. Pashler.
Osler—(1) H. P. Charters and C. F. Pashler (*aeq.*); (2) J. S. Ditchburn
and Rev. R. Melville (*aeq.*).

ST. MICHAEL'S COLLEGE

ST. MICHAEL'S COLLEGE.

St. Michael's College was founded in 1852, at the request of the Rt. Rev. Dr. de Charbonnel, then Bishop of Toronto. It was established for the purpose of combining religious instruction with a liberal education.

For a number of years it was granted state aid, in common with the other arts colleges of the Provinces. This came to an end when the Legislature of Ontario finally decided that no financial assistance should thereafter be given to denominational institutions.

In 1881, the College was affiliated with the University of Toronto; an arrangement having been entered into by which students proceeding to the degree of B.A. should attend lectures at University College in all subjects excepting Philosophy and History.

When in 1883-1884 a movement was on foot looking to the federation of every denominational college of the Province with the Provincial University, St. Michael's was the first to accept the terms proposed, and in 1890, federated upon the proclamation of the University Federation Act.

From the commencement it was understood that such arrangements could not be other than experimental, and meanwhile it became more and more apparent that the experiment must end in failure. After a quarter of a century of affiliation and federation, during which time the University population had been multiplied by five or six, there was scarcely any increase in the number of Catholic students attending University College. During those same years, the Catholic Colleges of the Province had been constantly increasing in the number of their students. It was evident that the plan in operation was not of the kind to secure the confidence of the Catholic population. That population evidently would not favour a purely secular education.

In 1905, St. Michael's found itself in a position to enter upon a scheme of providing instruction in all subjects known as "College Subjects", and made application to be admitted to federation on the same terms as Victoria and Trinity Colleges, claiming with them the privilege of free instruction for its students in University subjects. In response to this application, provision was made in the University Act of 1906 for the development of this scheme, upon the completion of which St. Michael's succeeds to the rank and privileges of a "College of the University". This plan has been worked out with the most satisfactory results.

The Catholic Church does not understand education without religious instruction. In St. Michael's, in every year of the student's course, a due proportion of time is reserved for this, and for the preservation of the religious spirit the greater number of the staff is chosen from the ranks of the clergy. It must be remembered, however, that St. Michael's is purely an Arts College, and has no theological faculty as such.

It is held as a fundamental principle, that the intimate association of students with one another, and with their teachers, contributes as much to true education as do the lecture room and library. In accordance with this, the majority of the students live in residence. The men students reside at St. Michael's College, the women students reside at St. Joseph's College, or Loretto Abbey College, and are subject from the point of view of discipline to the religious communities in charge of these institutions.

Administrative Officers

REV. H. CARR, B.A...*Superior.*

REV. F. G. POWELL.............................*Assistant Superior.*

REV. V. J. MURPHY...*Bursar.*

REV. E. J. McCORKELL, M.A.............................*Registrar.*

Scholarship and Prizes, 1920

FOURTH YEAR—

The M. J. O'Brien Prize for the highest first class honours in Phil-Philosophy—G. Keogh.

The Dockeray Prize to the student ranking highest in Pass English—Miss F. Ronan.

THIRD YEAR—

The Dockeray Prize to the student ranking highest in Pass English—T. Melady.

SECOND YEAR—

The Kernahan Prize for the highest first class honours in Philosophy—L. Stock.

The English Prize to the student ranking highest in Pass English—R. Dobell.

FIRST YEAR—

The English Prize to the student ranking highest in Pass English—E. Butler.

JUNIOR MATRICULATION—

The First Edward Blake Scholarship in Mathematics—Miss K. O'Neail.

The Silver Episcopal Jubilee Scholarship—Miss M. McCormick.

FACULTY OF MEDICINE

DEGREE OF BACHELOR OF MEDICINE.

1. The thirty-fifth session since the re-establishment of the Faculty of Medicine of the University of Toronto will commence on Tuesday, the 27th of September, 1921.

2. The Degrees in Medicine are Bachelor of Medicine—M.B., Bachelor of Science—B.Sc. (Med.), and Doctor of Medicine—M.D.

3. Candidates for the degree of Bachelor of Medicine are required to matriculate and to attend during six sessions of at least eight months each the courses of instruction presented, and to pass examinations taken at the end of each session.

ENTRANCE.

4. Details in individual cases as to entrance requirements to the University, may be obtained on application to the Registrar of the University.

Attention is drawn to the raising of the standard of entrance to the Faculty of Medicine which becomes effective in 1922.

ENTRANCE REQUIREMENTS FOR 1921.

The registration of students in the First Year will be greatly reduced from that of the session 1920-21.

Applications will be received until September 15th, after which date the selection of the students to be admitted, will be made. In this choice regard will be had

(a) to those returned soldiers who have then complied with the entrance requirements of October 1920,

(b) to those applicants whose certificates are of a higher standing than Pass Junior Matriculation.

Preference will be given in all cases to students from the Province of Ontario.

ENTRANCE REQUIREMENTS FOR 1922.

5. A student must have completed the seventeenth year of his age before the first of October of the year in which he proposes to enter. Only under exceptional circumstances will a candidate of thirty years or over be admitted.

The subjects for Matriculation in Medicine will be:

Part I—Pass Matriculation.

Latin (Authors, one paper; Composition, one paper).

English (Literature, one paper; Composition, one paper).

History (British and Canadian, one paper; Greek and Roman, one paper).

Mathematics (Algebra, one paper; Geometry, one paper).

Experimental Science (Physics, one paper; Chemistry, one paper).

Any one of

Greek (Authors, one paper; Composition, one paper).

French (Authors, one paper; Composition, one paper).

German (Authors, one paper; Composition, one paper).

Spanish (Authors one paper; Composition, one paper).

Part II—Honour Matriculation.

English (Literature, one paper; Composition, one paper); at least Third Class Honours.

Mathematics (Algebra, one paper; Geometry, one paper; Trigonometry, one paper); at least Third Class Honours.

One of:

Latin (Authors, one paper; Composition, one paper); at least Third Class Honours.

Greek (Authors, one paper; Composition, one paper); at least Third Class Honours.

French (Authors, one paper; Composition, one paper); at least Third Class Honours.

German (Authors, one paper; Composition, one paper); at least Third Class Honours.

Candidates for Matriculation in this Faculty are advised to take the complete Part I at one examination, and in a subsequent year, Part II.

6. A candidate possessing a degree in Arts from any recognized University may be considered as having fulfilled the entrance requirements.

7. A candidate coming from a Province of Canada other than Ontario must present certificates of a standard equivalent to that required from students of the Province of Ontario.

8. Students are required to complete matriculation before being admitted to the course in Medicine.

9. No fee will be charged for transferring from the Faculty of Arts to that of Medicine.

Application for Equivalent Standing.

10. Any student of another University or College who desires to be admitted to the Faculty of Medicine of this University with equivalent standing is required first to communicate with the Registrar of the University, forwarding to him a full statement of preliminary education with certificates. After receiving notice from the Registrar that the entrance requirements have been met, the student should send an application to the Secretary of the Faculty of Medicine together with—

(a) A calendar of the University in which he has studied, giving a full statement of the courses of study.

—25

(b) A complete official statement of the course he has followed and the standing obtained in percentage.

(c) A certificate of moral character and conduct.

After submission of this application to the Faculty Council the candidate will be notified as to the decision reached.

No student from a Medical Faculty of another University will be accepted unless his certificates show that he has completed the work and examinations in the subjects for which the certificates are presented.

REGISTRATION.

11. Students desiring to enter the course in Medicine are required to submit their application form in duplicate along with the certificates on which they claim entrance standing, to the Registrar of the University, in the Main Building, on or before September 15th. After this date each candidate will be notified as to whether his application has been accepted or not, a matriculation card being enclosed to those applicants who are accepted.

12. On presentation of this card on or before the day of registration (September 27th) to the Secretary of the Faculty of Medicine, candidates will be officially registered by him as students in Medicine.

13. Students in the Second and higher years will receive by mail from the Secretary, an application form for registration in the succeeding year. This form must be filled in and forwarded to the office of the Secretary of the Faculty of Medicine on or before September 15th.

14. On September 27th a student must present himself in person for his registration card which gives his number, section and class. No student shall be allowed to register in the Faculty of Medicine after the first day of term. No student shall be admitted to any laboratory or clinical class after its first meeting except at the discretion of the instructor concerned.

15. No student will be permitted to register in the second or any succeeding year until he has completed all the examinations of the preceding year.

16. Only under exceptional circumstances will a student be permitted to repeat his year more than once.

17. Subdivision into sections and clinical classes will be made by the Secretary. Students wishing to be placed in the same section or clinical class must apply conjointly in writing to the Secretary on or before June 1st.

It should be understood that the programme and regulations regarding courses of study and examinations contained in this Calendar, hold good for this calendar year only, and that the Faculty of Medicine, while fully sensible of its obligations towards the students, does not hold itself bound to adhere absolutely, for the whole six years of a student's course, to the conditions here laid down.

Attendance.

18. Students are required to attend lectures and receive practical instruction during each of the six years at this University.

19. A student who fails to do satisfactory term work in any subject is not permitted to present himself for examination until he is able to present satisfactory certificates of term work completed.

20. In cases of students applying for temporary positions in hospitals or for *locum tenens* to physicians, the permission of the Faculty Council must be obtained before they will be allowed to absent themselves from the lectures and laboratory work of the University.

No applications or petitions for exemptions from classes, laboratory work or examinations will be received or considered unless filed at the Secretary's office on or before October 15th of any year.

FEES FOR INSTRUCTION.

Regular Students in Medicine.

21. All University fees are payable at the Bursar's office in the Main University Building, between the hours of ten and one o'clock, except on Saturday.

22. *Regular Students.* First, Second, Third, Fourth, Fifth and Sixth Years—Annual Fee, including tuition, library, laboratory supply, hospital* and one annual examination—

If paid in full on or before November 10th $150.00
By instalments—
First instalment, if paid on or before November 10th 75.00
Second instalment, if paid on or before February 10th 78.00
Hart House and Students Administrative Council fee, to be paid
by all men students proceeding to the degree 11.00
Women Students' Administrative Council Fee, to be paid by all
women students proceeding to the degree $3.00

23. *Combined Courses in Arts and Medicine.*

Annual Fee, including college registration, library, laboratory supply, and one annual examination:

	Arts Fees.	Medical Fees.	Total.
First Year Arts............................	$57.00		$57.00
Second Year Arts...........................	58.00		58.00
Third Year Arts and Second Year Medicine...	57.00	$85.00	142.00
Fourth Year Arts and Third Year Medicine....	62.00	85.00	147.00

*The composite fee of $150.00 includes one session's clinical facilities at the Toronto General Hospital, St. Michael's Hospital, or Toronto Western Hospital, and the Hospital for Sick Children, but does not cover the midwifery ticket for the Burnside Lying-in Hospital, which must be obtained there.

The fees for the Fourth, Fifth and Sixth Years in the Faculty of Medicine are as for regular students.

Payment of the Medical portion of the fees—

If paid on or before November 10th..........................	**$85.00**
By instalments—	
First instalment, if paid on or before November 10th..........	43.00
Second instalment, if paid on or before February 10th..........	44.00

24. Fees for Graduate and Special Courses.

(1) Graduates attending undergraduate courses per month	$10.00
(2) D.P.H. Course.....................................	150.00
By instalments:	
1st instalment at the beginning of the Fall Session	75.00
2nd instalment at the beginning of the Winter Session....................................	75.00
Fee for the Diploma..........................	20.00
(3) Undergraduates taking Summer Course in clinical subjects, per course.............................	20.00
Three or more courses............................	50.00

25. All of the above fees are payable in advance. After November 10th, a penalty of $1.00 per month will be imposed until the whole amount is paid. In the case of payment by instalments the same rule as to penalty will apply. A student will not be admitted to any of the University lectures or laboratories who is in arrears for his fees.

26. *General Fees.*

Matriculation, or registration of Matriculation.................	**$5.00**
Supplemental examinations.................................	10.00
Admission *ad eundem statum*...............................	10.00
Degree of M.B...	20.00
Degree of M.D...	20.00
Admission *ad eundem gradum*..............................	20.00

In the case of candidates for the Final Examinations, the fee for the degree must be paid to the Bursar not later than the 20th of March.

Hart House and the Students' Administrative Council.

27. The annual fee...$11.00

Every male student in attendance, proceeding to the degree of Bachelor of Medicine, is required to pay to the Bursar at the time of the entry of his name with the Secretary, the annual fee of eleven dollars for the maintenance of Hart House and the Students' Administrative Council.

WOMEN STUDENTS' ADMINISTRATIVE COUNCIL FEE.

28. The Annual Fee...................................... $3.00

Every woman student in attendance, proceeding to the Degree of Bachelor of Medicine, is required to pay to the Bursar at the time of the entry of her name with the Secretary, the annual fee of three dollars for the maintenance of the Women Students' Administrative Council.

INSTRUCTION.

29. The course of instruction given by the Faculty of Medicine consists of six sessions of eight months each, preparing students for the degree of M.B.

30. The course is so framed that the requirements of the various Provincial Licensing bodies are fulfilled and it aims at giving the student such a training in the sciences as is now exacted of all those who desire to obtain any British Medical qualification in addition to a Canadian one.

The Senate of the University of Toronto determined that the increase in the length of the undergraduate course in medicine from five to six years should go into effect in the Autumn of 1919 (Session 1919-1920.) All students entering on or after this date will be required to proceed in the Six Years' Course. There will therefore be no Second Year of the Five Years' Course during Ssesion 1921-1922.

INSTRUCTION IN SIX YEARS' COURSE.

31. The student of Medicine is reminded that during his years of study he is preparing himself to enter a profession which presents manifold and diverse aspects. No prescribed course of study of practicable length can by any possibility fit the student for all of the special careers which the profession of medicine offers. The curriculum provided by the Faculty of Medicine is designed to furnish a framework of knowledge and technical skill which will adequately equip all students for the general practice of medicine and its branches, the time allotted for this purpose, in every subject of the course, being well in excess of that required as the minimum by examining boards and Universities in this and other countries. The six years' curriculum, however, also provides for the student filling in and amplifying his regular work with special studies that are designed either to broaden his general education, and therefore make him better fitted for the practice of medicine, or to enable him to undergo, in certain of the subjects of the curriculum, a somewhat more intensive training than is essential for all students, so as to prepare him for some particular type of medical career. To enable the student to accomplish these purposes a number of hours of optional study are prescribed, the precise subjects of study being largely left to the student's choice. It is, however, expected that this choice will not be aimless, but made of set purpose and designed to some particular end.

It will be of decided advantage to the student to form some conception of the general type of medical career which he desires to follow at an early period in his course. This is particularly so when a career in laboratory investigation (and teaching), hygiene or psychiatry is thought of. This choice should be made with great care, and only after a thorough investigation of the work involved. But it may be pointed out that it would not handicap a student if he should decide after trial of one type of course to change to another.

During the *first year* only a limited number of optional hours are available. The student who, upon entering the Faculty of Medicine is unfamiliar with scientific methods of work and thought is advised to utilize these hours in acquiring thorough familiarity with the prescribed subjects. The student who has some previous acquaintance with science and feels confident that he will not experience any exceptional difficulty in familiarizing himself with the prescribed subjects, is advised to devote a certain proportion of his optional hours to the study of such subjects of general knowledge as will assist in providing him with that breadth of outlook and catholicity of interests which will enable him to enter with intelligence into the life and interests of the communities with which he may find himself associated, and to speak and write in a clear, simple and convincing manner.

Among the various courses of this nature which are available to the first year student the following are especially recommended:—

English . . . . .2 hours
History . . . . .2 hours
Scientific French . . . . ,. . . . . . . .2 hours
    or
Scientific German . . . . .2 hours
Mathematics (recommended for students of Group B4).

It is at the beginning of his *second year* that it will be of decided advantage to the student who contemplates a career in laboratory investigation (and teaching) hygiene or psychiatry to make his choice. While the prescribed regular schedule for the second and third years adequately covers all the subjects necessary for a thorough grounding in the introductory medical sciences, there is a certain amount of extra time in which those students who may have decided that they wish to enter some special field, can take extra courses designed to fit them to that end, or in which other students may take courses in general knowledge which will be useful and valuable in whatever branch of medical science they may afterwards find their life work. It should be clearly understood that the regular and optional schedules are so arranged that it will ultimately be no hardship if a student, having mistakenly elected some special course, should decide to proceed in some other direction.

Broadly speaking the student should aim at preparing himself in one or other of the following directions:

(*a*) General Practice   Most students will naturally prepare themselves for the general practice of Medicine.

(*b*) There are certain students, however, who may desire to undergo a training which will qualify them for some special type of career. Such careers are as follows:

1. Medicine or Surgery.
2. Mental Diseases.
3. Public Health.
4. Laboratory investigation (and teaching).

Before entering upon one of the courses of Class (b) the student must have the sanction of the Faculty on the recommendation of his adviser.

(a) In preparing for *General Practice* the student should remember that shi profession will be at least as much a branch of social service as of technical scientific practice and that upon a number of occasions in his career he will likely be called upon for advice and guidance in matters in which not only his medical skill and knowledge will be involved, but also social, ethical and economic factors, a right understanding of which will often enable his services to be very much more effective. The student of this category is, therefore, urged to utilize a substantial proportion of his optional hours of study in acquiring some measure of knowledge of the leading principles of ethics and economics, including sociology. Optionals may be profitably chosen from among the following subjects:—

Second Year:—Any of the optionals of the first year also

*English.....................................2 hours.
*History......................................2 hours.
*Political Economy (Economics)...............2 hours
*Philosophy..................................2 hours.
*Psychology.
Chemistry (Physical Chem.).
Chemistry (Special course).
Physics.
Biology (Heredity and Eugenics).

Third Year:—Any of the optionals of the first two years also:

*Political Economy (Economics and Sociology)...2 hours.
Philosophy (Logic and Theory of Method)......2 hours.
History......................................3 hours.

Additional work in any of the Medical Sciences of the first three years.
Practical Dietetics (Household Science), 2 hours for 15 weeks.

(b) 1. In preparing himself for *Internal Medicine* or *Surgery* the student is recommended to equip himself as thoroughly as possible in the introductory Medical Sciences. He is, therefore, urged to choose the bulk of his optionals during his second and third years from subjects of this character. He must, however, also elect during both years, one of the asterisked subjects indicated above. Optionals may profitably be chosen from among the following subjects:—

---

*During each of these years every student must elect as one of his optionals at least one of the subjects marked with an asterisk.

Second Year:—Chemistry.
              Physics.
              Comparative Anatomy (Zoology).
              Additional Anatomy.
              Additional Histology and Embryology.
              Any of the subjects detailed under the second year of
                 Group (a).
Third Year: — Additional Biochemistry.
              Additional Physiology.
              Chemistry.
              Any of the subjects detailed under the second and third
                 years of Group (a).

(b) 2. The student who designs subsequently to devote himself to the study of *Mental Disease* is especially urged to equip himself with a knowledge of modern experimental psychology. He must elect one of the asterisked subjects under Group (a). Besides this the following subjects are recommended:—

Second Year:—Psychology.
              Chemistry.
              Physics (Electricity, etc.).
Third Year:—Psychology.
              Additional Physiology.
              Additional Biochemistry.

(b) 3. The student desiring to work in the field of *Public Health* should aim at acquiring some knowledge of economics in order to enable him to comprehend the political and social aspects of his work, and he should acquire a knowledge of Parasitology, of the structure, habits and control of disease-bearing insects, and especially of bacteriology immunology. He must elect one of the asterisked subjects of Group (a). Besides this the following subjects are recommended:—

Second Year:—Political Economy.
              Biology (Parasitology).
              Chemistry.
              Sanitary Engineering.
              Sanitary Chemistry.
Third Year: — Bacteriology.
              Protozoology.
              Additional Biochemistry.
              Statistics (Actuarial Science).

(b) 4. The student who aims at a career of *Laboratory Investigation* should be guided by the requirements of the field in which he desires to work, and should choose his subjects of optional study in conference with the adviser and the head of the department representing the subject in which he expects to be especially interested. The student is reminded, however, that in all fields of laboratory research, mathematics is becoming of rapidly increasing importance and he is strongly urged to acquire a knowledge of elementary calculus and of statistical methods. He must also elect one of the asterisked subjects of Group (a).

Student Adviser.

32. In order to assist the student in making a correct choice of optional subjects, a student-adviser has been appointed for each year. Every student is required to submit to the adviser a list of his proposed studies and his time table, and the written approval of the adviser and the consent of the Faculty Council will be required before the student's registration will be considered to have been completed. It is understood that any coherent plan of study designed by the student for a particular and intelligible purpose will be approved, but courses of study which appear to be manifestly unsuitable, and for his choice of which the student can furnish no adequate explanation or excuse, will not be approved by the adviser.

Student Adviser for Class of 1919............PROF. J. J. R. MACLEOD
Student Adviser for Class of 1920...............DR. E. S. RYERSON.
Student Adviser for Class of 1921............PROF. V. E. HENDERSON.

INSTRUCTION IN THE FIVE YEARS' COURSE.

33. During the Third Year of the Five Years' Course an attempt is made to bridge the gap which so commonly exists between the primary scientific and the final clinical subjects, by taking up Anatomy and Physiology at the same time as Surgery and Medicine throughout the year. Preliminary courses in Pathology and Pathological Chemistry are given during the Easter term. Instruction is also given in Pharmacology. A series of ten lectures upon Psychology is delivered in this year. Particular attention is paid during this year to teaching the student the methods of physical examination of both Medical and Surgical cases.

34. In the Fourth Year of the Five Years' Course the student devotes his mornings to clinical work at the various Hospitals. He spends the remainder of his afternoons at didactic lectures and at laboratory work in Pathological Histology and Gross Pathology. The clinical instruction is so directed as to prepare the student to undertake the complete physical examination of any patient, the greater part of his time being occupied with Medical and Surgical cases. In this year the student is introduced to the subjects of Obstetrics, Gynaecology, and the specialties of the Eye, Ear, Nose and Throat. Several weeks are spent in the study of Paediatrics and Orthopaedic Surgery at the Hospital for Sick Children. Lectures are also delivered during the year in Special Pathology, Therapeutics, Surgical Anatomy, Medical Jurisprudence, Toxicology and Hygiene.

35. During the Fifth Year of the Five Years' Course the student devotes one period of ten weeks to Clinical Medicine, one of ten weeks to Surgery and Surgical Pathology, and one period of five weeks to Obstetrics and

Gynaecology, and one of five weeks to Clinical Therapeutics, Opthal-mology, Oto-Laryngology, Dermatology, Paediatrics, Neurology and Psychiatry. Those students whose work and standing justify it, will be given special advanced courses of laboratory work in Pathology and Pathological Chemistry or some special instruction in one of the clinical departments. Clinical lectures in Medicine, Surgery and special subjects, Pathological Conferences, and short courses of lectures on Anaesthesia. Dentistry, Medical Ethics, History of Medicine, and Life Insurance are also given in the Fifth Year.

36. SUBJECTS OF INSTRUCTION.

Five Years' Course.   **Six Years' Course.**

FIRST YEAR.

1. Biology.
2 Chemistry.
3. Physics.
4. Science and Civilization.
5. English Expression.
6. Option.

SECOND YEAR.

1. Anatomy.
2. Histology.
3. Embryology.
4. Chemistry (Organic and Physical).
5. Option one.
6. Option two.

THIRD YEAR.

1. Anatomy.	1. Physiology including Psychology.
2. Physiology.	
3. Pharmacology.	2. Biochemistry.
4. Pathology.	3. Bacteriology.
5. Pathological Chemistry.	4. Anatomy.
6. Clinical Laboratory Methods.	5. Option one.
7. Medicine	6. Option two.
8. Surgery.	
9. Psychology.	

FOURTH YEAR.

1. Medicine including Paediatrics.
2. Surgery.
3. Obstetrics and Gynaecology.
4. Pathology
5. Pathological Chemistry.
6. Hygiene and Preventive Medicine.
7. Medical Jurisprudence.
8. Toxicology.
9. Psychiatry.
10. Ophthalmology.
11. Oto-Laryngology.
12. Therapeutics.

FIFTH YEAR.

1. Medicine including Paediatrics.
2. Surgery.
3. Obstetrics and Gynaecology.
4. Pathology.
5. Ophthalmology.
6. Oto-Laryngology.
7. Therapeutics.
8. Psychiatry

SUMMER COURSES IN CLINICAL SUBJECTS.

37. For students who have been conditioned in Clinical subjects, courses in the following subjects will be given during the summer months.

Clinical Medicine,
" Surgery,
" Obstetrics,
" Gynaecology,
" Ophthalmology,
" Oto-Laryngology,

These Courses will be held at the Toronto General Hospital, St. Michael's Hospital and the Hospital for Sick Children.

(For information regarding fees for these Courses, see page 31).

COMBINED COURSE IN ARTS AND MEDICINE.

38. It is possible for a student who takes this Biological and Medical Sciences Course, followed by the final years of the Medical Course, to obtain the degree of Bachelor of Arts at the end of four years and of Bachelor of Medicine after seven years study at the University. When entering the third year of the Arts course, these students register in the second year of Medicine and on entering their fourth year Arts, they register in the third year Medicine.

39. In the curricula of this Arts Course the Science subjects are treated more extensively than they are in the Medical curriculum.

40. The Biological and Medical Science Course completes the requirements of the first three years in Medicine with the exception of Bacteriology of the Second Year. First and Second Years in the Biological and Medical Science Course are equivalent to the First Year in Medicine. The first two years work is the same as that for the course in Physiology and Biochemistry. The students who proceed during the third and fourth years of the latter course take up the subjects of Physiology and Biochemistry *without reference to Medicine.*

41. These courses not only afford opportunities for a broader training and greater scientific attainment than is possible in the six years' course in Medicine, but they fit the student for a much wider field of usefulness after graduation. The graduate who has taken one of the Science Courses in Arts and subsequently the Course in Medicine is qualified to devote his life to one of the purely scientific lines of Medicine, if he should so elect, after leaving the University, and, moreover, he is, undoubtedly, better fitted to practise his profession should he desire to prepare himself for that alone.

42. Students who proceed to the Arts degree through other Science Courses may, on entering the Faculty of Medicine, be allowed exemption from such subjects in Medicine as they have taken in the curricula of the Faculty of Arts.

B.Sc. (MED.) COURSE.

43. The degree of B.Sc. (Med.) has been added to the curriculum in Medicine so as to encourage scholarship and give official recognition to students who have done exceptionally well in the introductory medical sciences.

1. Medical students of the Six Years' Course who have reached the end of the third year or subsequent years of their course, and who have maintained a standard to be subsequently determined in all of their classes, may become candidates for the degree provided: (a) They spend one year longer (a fourth year) in the introductory medical sciences in groups of courses which will be mapped out on the general basis that the greater proportion of time is spent in one department of the introductory medical sciences, and the lesser proportion in adjunct departments. These students would also, except in the case of those entering with senior or honour matriculation, be required to show facility in reading one modern language besides English, and to take sometime during the four years the two years optional course in Mathematics for medical students, or General Biology.

2. Graduates in Medicine irrespective of the standard of their entrance requirements, who have maintained a satisfactory standard throughout their entire medical course, may become candidates for the degree provided: (a) They spend one additional year in work in some laboratory department of this University (including those of the clinical years) and carry out a piece of research to the satisfaction of the head of the department. (b) They acquire facility in reading one modern language besides English. Medical graduates who return to laboratory departments as fellows or demonstrators will be eligible for the B.Sc. (Med.) degree, but the successful prosecution of a piece of research is essential.

ADMISSION TO EXAMINATIONS.

44. Every student who proposes to present himself at the Annual or Supplemental Examinations must see that the Secretary has in his possession the following:—

1. *An Application for Examination.* The form supplied must be filled in, signed, and left in the Secretary's Office on or before March 15th. Students presenting applications after this date must pay an additional fee of One Dollar.

2. *A Certificate of Attendance* indicating that he has complied with the regulations respecting attendance upon didactic, laboratory and clinical work in each of the subjects of instruction for the year in which he seeks examination. This Certificate is issued by the University and must be signed by the Head of each Department after completion of the course of instruction.

45. *Candidates for the Degree of Bachelor of Medicine* are required to have on their Certificates of Attendance the following additional particulars:—

(*a*) A certificate of having conducted at least twenty labours under the supervision of the Head of the Department of Obstetrics and Gynaecology.

(*b*) A certificate of proficiency in vaccination, from the Head of the Department of Hygiene.

(*c*) A certificate of having attended fifteen autopsies under the supervision of the Head of the Department of Pathology.

(*d*) A certificate of having administered anaesthetic on six occasions, under the supervision of the Head of the Department of Therapeutics.

46. No candidate will be admitted to the Annual or Supplemental Examinations unless he has paid all the fees due from him.

47. No candidate in a course involving practical work in a laboratory or clinic will be admitted to the Annual or Supplemental Examinations if the Professor under whom his work is carried on reports in writing to the Secretary that he has not done satisfactory laboratory or clinical work, or has signally failed in the practical examinations.

48. A candidate failing in Medicine, Surgery or other clinical subjects at the annual examinations, shall be required to take a course of additional instruction provided by the Faculty of Medicine in the subject or subjects in which he has failed, before again being admitted to examinations. The length of the term of additional instruction in each case of failure will be specified by the Board of Examiners in their returns at the Annual Examinations.

49. Undergraduates who have been prevented from attending the Annual Examinations by sickness, domestic affliction, or other causes beyond their control, may make application for permission to present themselves for examination at the Supplemental Examinations in September, and must give satisfactory evidence of the cause of absence.

EXAMINATIONS.

50. The Annual Examinations are held in May at the end of the First, Second, Third, Fourth, Fifth and Sixth academic years, and the Supplemental Examinations in September.

51. The minimum pass standard in each subject of examination is 50%.

SUBJECTS OF THE ANNUAL EXAMINATIONS.

SIX YEARS' COURSE.

52. First Examination.

Group A.
1. Biology.
2. Chemistry.
3. Physics.

Group B.
4. Science and Civilization and English Expression.
5. Option.

Candidates who have passed in all but one subject may present themselves at the Supplemental Examinations next ensuing.

Candidates who have passed in all but two subjects, provided that they are not both in Group A, may present themselves at the Supplemental Examinations next ensuing.

Candidates who have failed in three or more subjects or in any two subjects of Group A, must repeat the entire work of the year, including the examinations in every subject of that year.

(The students' attention is particularly drawn to paragraph 15 page 30).

53. Second Examination.

1. Anatomy.
2. Histology, Embryology.
3. Organic and Physical Chemistry.
4. Option one.
5. Option two.

54. Third Examination.

1. Physiology.
2. Biochemistry.
3. Anatomy.
4. Bacteriology.
5. Option one.
6. Option two.

55. Candidates at the Second and Third Examinations who have passed in all but two subjects may present themselves at the Supplemental Examinations next ensuing.

Candidates at the Second and Third Examinations failing in three or more subjects must repeat the entire work of the year including the examinations in every subject of the year.

56. Candidates at the Supplemental Examinations who succeed in passing in the one or the two subjects in which they were conditioned at the Annual Examinations shall be allowed their year.

57. Candidates at the Supplemental Examinations who fail in any subject in which they were conditioned, will be required to repeat the entire work of the year, including the examinations in every subject of the year.

58. It has been the regulation for some years that students be not informed of the marks they have obtained at the Annual or Supplemental Examinations. In future a statement will be sent to all students who have not completely passed in all examinations and to any other students who request the same *in writing*, from the Secretary indicating their approximate standing as follows:— A—75% to 100%.
B—50% to 74%.
C—40% to 49%.
D—below 40%.

59. SUBJECTS OF THE ANNUAL EXAMINATIONS

FIVE YEARS' COURSE.

THIRD EXAMINATION.

1. Anatomy.
2. Physiology.
3. Pharmacology.
4. Pathology and Pathological Chemistry.
5. Medicine.
6. Surgery.

NOTE.—The oral examination in General Anatomy will be held at the end of the Michaelmas term.

FOURTH EXAMINATION.

1. Medicine including Paediatrics.
2. Surgery.
3. Obstetrics and Gynaecology.
4. Pathology.
5. Pathological Chemistry.
6. Hygiene and Preventive Medicine.
7. Medical Jurisprudence and Toxicology.
8. Therapeutics.

Fifth Examination.

1. Medicine.
2. Surgery.
3. Obstetrics and Gynaecology
4. Pathology.
5. Paediatrics.
6. Clinical Ophthalmology.
7. Clinical Oto-Laryngology.
8. Clinical Therapeutics.

REGULATIONS FOR LICENCE TO PRACTISE.

The right to practise Medicine in Canada or its provinces is not conferred when a student receives his degree from the University. There is a licensing body for the Dominion and one for each of the provinces, each of which has formulated certain medical laws and a standard of general education with which the student must comply before he is entitled to practise. One of these requirements is that it is necessary to be registered in the province in which the student intends to practise, five years before he can obtain a license. Students are therefore advised to complete their registration for license to practise in the First or Second Year.

For official information of all matters relative to the regulations for licence to practise in the various Provinces in the Dominion, students should communicate with the Registrar. The following is a list of the names and addresses of the Registrars of the Medical Councils:

For official information regarding the Medical Council of Canada address: Dr. R. W. Powell, 180 Cooper Street, Ottawa, Canada.

Ontario—Dr. H. W. Aikins, 170 University Ave., Toronto.
Quebec—Dr. J. Gauvreau, 30 St. James Street, Montreal, and Dr. C. R. Paquin, Quebec, P.Q.
New Brunswick—Dr. John S. Bentley, St. John.
Nova Scotia—Dr. W. H. Hattie, Halifax, N.S.
Prince Edward Island—Dr. S. R. Jenkins, Charlottetown.
Newfoundland—Dr. H. Rendell, St. John's, Newfoundland.
Manitoba—Dr. J. S. Gray, 358 Hargrave Street, Winnipeg, or W. J. Spence, Registrar, University of Manitoba, Winnipeg.
Alberta—Dr. G. Macdonald, Calgary, Alta.
Saskatchewan—Dr. G. A. Charlton, Regina.
British Columbia—Dr. A. P. Proctor, Victoria, B.C.

HONOUR STANDING.

61. In the results of the examinations of each year, a list of those students who obtain an average of 75% in all subjects of the year and not less than 60% in any subject, shall be published as having obtained Honour Standing.

—26

The names of those students who have obtained Honour Standing in the last two years of the course, shall in the graduating list be marked so as to indicate the fact that they have graduated with Honours.

DOCTOR OF MEDICINE.

62. A Bachelor of Medicine will be eligible for the degree of M.D. on the following conditions—

(1) At least one year must elapse between the date of conferring the degree of M.B. and that of conferring the degree of M.D.

(2) He must present an approved thesis embodying the results of an original research conducted by the candidate in any department of Medicine.

(3) The subject of the thesis must be submitted to the Secretary of the Board of Graduate Studies at least five months before the degree is conferred.

(4) The degree may be conferred at Convocation or at any regular meeting of the Senate.

ADMISSION AD EUNDEM GRADUM.

63. A graduate of any of the universities in Great Britain or Ireland, if his degree be not an honorary one, may be admitted to the like degree in the University of Toronto. He must send in his certificate to the Registrar at least two weeks before the first meeting of the session of the Senate at which his application is to be brought forward.

The George Brown Memorial Scholarship in Medical Science.

64. Dr. A. H. F. Barbour, of Edinburgh, having placed one thousand pounds sterling at the disposal of the University of Toronto, for the purpose of founding a Scholarship in Medical Science in memory of the late Hon. George Brown, the following regulations have been adopted with regard thereto—

This scholarship shall be called the George Brown Memorial Scholarship in Medical Science and shall be awarded annually at the Convocation for conferring degrees in Medicine to the Bachelor of Medicine who shall have distinguished himself most in the subjects of Anatomy, Biology, Physiology, Biochemistry, Pharmacology, Pathology and Pathological Chemistry.

The award shall be made by a committee composed of the Professors in these subjects who shall report as to the successful candidates, after having given due attention to the results of the annual examinations, and to the character of the work done by the candidates in the University laboratories.

The holder of the scholarship during the year of tenure is required to engage in original research in any one of the laboratories of the University on some subject bearing on the advancement of medical science—the laboratory providing the material for the investigation.

The scholarship is to be paid in two portions, two-thirds at the time of award and one-third six months later, on the holder giving satisfactory report (to whomsoever the University may appoint) of the work he has already done.

A report of the research, when completed, is to be given to the University.

The value of the scholarship is five hundred dollars ($500.00).

The Starr Medals.

65. The late Richard Noble Starr, M.D., devised certain property for the encouragement of post-graduate study in Anatomy, Physiology and Pathology, and in fulfilment of this object one gold and two silver medals called the "Starr Medals", are awarded annually to three candidates for the degree of M.D., who have shown by the theses which they have presented for that degree, that they have successfully pursued such study in any one of these subjects. The theses for which these medals are given must attain a standard approved of by the Board of Examiners, and the relative value of the theses will determine the rank of the candidates for the medals.

George Armstrong Peters Scholarship.

66. The Scholarship will be awarded biennially to a graduate student of the University of Toronto on the recommendation of the Department of Surgery.

The first award was made in 1912. The holder of the Scholarship will be required to undertake work in one of the Departments of the University which will have some special bearing on Surgery.

This Scholarship will be available for any graduate who wishes to do special research work in connection with the Department of Surgery or in correlated subjects.

A graduate wishing to obtain the Scholarship must apply to the Department of Surgery and present his credentials, and the award will be made on the recommendation of the Department.

The value of the Scholarship is two hundred dollars ($200.00).

A Prize.

67. A portion of the fund of the Reeve Post-Graduate Scholarship will be devoted to establishing a prize of $50.00, to be awarded annually for the best published report of work done in the laboratories by a research Fellow or junior member of the staff in any department in Medicine.

The award shall be made in September by a Committee composed of the Professors of Anatomy, Physiology, Biochemistry, Pharmacology, Pathology and Pathological Chemistry.

The James H. Richardson Research Fellowship in Anatomy.

68. This Fellowship of the annual value of Five hundred dollars ($500.00) has been established in memory of the late Dr. James H. Richardson, for many years Professor of Anatomy in the University of Toronto. It is open to graduates in Medicine of the University of Toronto and of such other Universities and Medical Schools as may be approved by the Nominating Committee and to students in the University of Toronto who shall have completed the third year of the course in Medicine.

The fellowship is awarded on the nomination of a Committee consisting of the Professor of Anatomy, the Professor of Biology and the Professor of Surgery in the University of Toronto, and the holder of it is obliged, during its tenure, to devote his entire time to investigation in Anatomy under the direction of the Professor of Anatomy in the University of Toronto. The fellowship is tenable for one year, but the holder of it is eligible for re-appointment for not more than two additional years, at the discretion of the University Senate upon the recommendation of the Nominating Committee.

Applications for nomination to the Fellowship should be handed to the Professor of Anatomy not later than the first day of May of each year.

Research Medicine.

69. During the early months of 1913, on request, a number of business men subscribed to a fund for the promotion of Clinical and Laboratory Research work in the Department of Medicine. The fund has already reached upwards of $75,000.00; it is payable in five annual instalments.

The first aim is to establish one or more Fellowships annually, for the recent graduates. Each Fellowship is tenable for three years, and will be of the value of $750 the first year.

Ellen Mickle Fellowship.

70. A Fellowship, being the annual income from an endowment of Twenty Five Thousand Dollars ($25,000) has been established by the late Dr. W. J. Mickle, known as "The Ellen Mickle Fellowship", to be given to the student (or students) who in the examinations at the end of the fourth year of the Old Course or the fifth year of the New Course in Medicine, shall have taken honours of the first class in at least three fourths of the subjects of that year, and shall have obtained the highest marks in the examinations. The award will be made to the above referred to student (or students) provided he proceed to the degree of Bachelor of Medicine in this University and spend one year in post graduate study approved by the Council of the Faculty of Medicine.

Charles Mickle Fellowship.

71. This Fellowship, bequeathed by the late Dr. W. J. Mickle, being the annual income from an endowment of Twenty Five Thousand Dollars ($25,000) will be awarded annually to that member of the medical profession who is considered by the Council of the Faculty of Medicine of the University of Toronto to have done most during the preceding ten years to advance sound knowledge of a practical kind in medical art or science.

COURSES FOR GRADUATES IN MEDICINE.

72. The Faculty of Medicine of the University of Toronto recognizes that the practitioners of the Province are anxious to keep closely in touch with the advances in Medicine, and that they have a claim on the Provincial University to aid them in doing so. The Faculty considers this entails on it a duty second only to the instruction of the undergraduate.

At the present time the large amount of undergraduate teaching makes it impossible to offer during the academic session set courses of sufficient variety to meet all the needs of those who seek further study.

Those who have studied abroad know that the routine method is for the graduate to attend the instruction given to the students of the senior years in Medicine, to follow the ward rounds and to go to the out-patient department picking up what he can. The Faculty has opened the courses of instruction given to the higher years in Medicine to any one who cares to attend and refresh his knowledge in this way. A Standing Committee has been appointed whose duty it is to give any graduate interested, advice as to the clinics and lectures which should be taken and to confer with the heads of departments and individual teachers so as to arrange a course in advance for each applicant. Such a course may be modified by the committee if it does not prove suitable.

The Fifth Year student in Medicine is now receiving the most advanced type of clinical instruction, and his teachers often take advantage of the modern laboratory training given in the junior years and may thus make their instruction somewhat difficult to follow by those who have not had this preliminary training. The teacher will, however, be prepared to explain privately any difficulties or through the Committee to arrange for some special laboratory instruction. If special instruction is required in order to enable him to follow the clinical work, the Committee will attempt to arrange it.

During the past year 10 graduates attended undergraduate courses of this kind.

All the library facilities of the University will be open to any post graduate student under the usual conditions.

The staff fully realizes that every effort must be made to render the visit of each post-graduate student both pleasant and of real value. Instruction may be obtained as outlined above in the following:

Medicine.
Surgery.
Obstetrics and Gynaecology.
Paediatrics.
Otology, Rhinology, Laryngology.
Ophthalmology.
Preventive Medicine.
Pathology and Bacteriology.

The University will impose a minimum fee of $10.00 per month. This will be imposed for any course of less than a month as a registration fee. In such cases where extended work and attention is required, a special fee to cover the same will be arranged by the committee.

SPECIAL GRADUATE COURSES.

73. The Faculty has, during the past year, arranged several special graduate courses. A month's course in Paediatrics was given last July and a combined course in Medicine, Surgery and Obstetrics lasting one week in the Christmas holidays. These courses were attended by a large number of graduates. It is the intention of the Faculty to arrange courses of a similar character each year. Such courses deal exhaustively with a limited part of a subject, with the object of making it as useful as possible to the general practitioner.

EXTENSION LECTURES.

74. By an arrangement with the Ontario Medical Association the Medical Faculty of the University has offered to the profession some ninety lectures on the most important subjects in various fields of medical science. Application for these lectures may be made through the Secretary of the Ontario Medical Association, (from whom a copy of the titles of the lectures may be obtained), to the Faculty. Any society or group of physicians may apply for a course of lectures on any subject. Courses of this type on the Physiology of the Circulation and Respiration, the Chemistry of the Blood, as well as many clinical subjects, have been given this year in Hamilton, Ottawa and Brantford.

CURRICULUM FOR THE DIPLOMA OF PUBLIC HEALTH.

1. The University provides a Diploma of Public Health (D. P. H.) on the following conditions:—

2. Candidates for the Diploma must be graduates in Medicine of this University or some other University recognized for this purpose by the Senate.

3. The curriculum leading to the Diploma extends over one Winter Session of eight months and one Summer Session of three months.

4. The Winter Session is devoted to:—

Laboratory Courses and Lectures in :—

   (*a*) Bacteriology.
   (*b*) Sanitary Chemistry.
   (*c*) Parasitology.

and, to attendance at:—

   (*d*) Clinics for Communicable Diseases.
   (*e*) Psychopathic Clinics.
   (*f*) Venereal Diseases Clinics.
   (*g*) Tuberculosis Clinics.
   (*h*) Well-Baby Clinics.
   (*i*) Ante-Natal Clinics.

and, to Lectures or Practical Work in:—

   (*j*) General Hygiene.
   (*k*) Immunology.
   (*l*) Applied Physiology.
   (*m*) Sanitary Engineering.
   (*n*) Public Health Organization and Legislation, and Vital Statistics.
   (*o*) History of Preventive Medicine and Epidemiology.
   (*p*) Nutrition and Dietetics.
   (*q*) Industrial Hygiene.

The Provincial Board of Health of Ontario, the City Health Department of Toronto and the special Clinics at the Toronto General Hospital and the Hospital for Sick Children provide unusual facilities for instruction in the practice of Preventive Medicine.

5. The Summer Session is spent in Field Work in Public Health under the supervision of a recognized Department of Health and includes a study of the methods of dealing with communicable diseases, inspections of schools and other public buildings, factories and dairies, inspections of water supplies and sewage disposal plants; food and meat inspection and other forms of municipal sanitation, and medical inspection of school children.

6. When the required courses of study have been completed, written and practical examinations will be held on the subjects of the curriculum specified in paragraph 4.

7. Candidates who have passed the examinations and who have satisfactorily completed the work specified in paragraph 5 will be granted the Diploma in Public Health.

8. The fee for the course, as outlined in paragraphs 3, 4 and 5, is $150, payable in two instalments of $75.00 each, at the beginning of the Fall Session, and the Winter Session respectively. The fee for the Diploma is $20.00.

9. Candidates for the Diploma in Public Health are required to undertake the investigation of an assigned Public Health problem, complete the same and submit the results in the form of a report before being permitted to proceed to the examinations leading to the Diploma.

10. Graduates in Medicine, who for a period of two years have been engaged in full-time Public Health work, may, under the following conditions, take the examination specified in paragraph 6, when they have completed the courses required in paragraph 4.

The work required in the curriculum may be extended over a period of more than one academic year, and the examinations taken when all courses of study have been completed. A yearly fee of $75.00 payable at the beginning of the Fall Term, must be paid by candidates taking more than one year to complete the required courses. (If only one year is taken to complete the work the fee is $150.00).

11. Candidates who present satisfactory evidence of having completed work, the equivalent of that required in certain of the courses specified in paragraphs 4 and 5, may petition to be granted exemption from attendance on such courses. This will apply only in the cases of candidates who have been for at least two years engaged in full-time Public Health work, and who at the time of registration are so engaged.

12. The examination of those qualifying under clause 10 will be held in May and September, for others, in September only.

CHEMISTRY.

Professor of Organic Chemistry and Secretary of the Department of Chemistry:
F. B. ALLAN.
Professor: F. B. KENRICK.
Professor of Physical Chemistry: W. LASH MILLER
Associate Professor: J. B. FERGUSON.
Assistant Professor of Electrochemistry: J. T. BURT-GERRANS
Assistant Professor of Analytical Chemistry: L. J. ROGERS
Lecturers: W. S. FUNNELL, W. H. MARTIN
Assistants: J. E. CLARK, N. A. CLARK, C. S. GILBERT, E. HAAS, J. KELLE-
HER, W. B. LEAF, G. H. W. LUCAS, T. C. McMULLEN, J. W. REBBECK,
MISS I. L. ROBERTS, M. E. SMITH, G. WILLIAMS. .

All lectures and practical work will be given in the Chemistry Building.

First Year.

Lectures.—Students attend a course of experimental lectures delivered twice a week in the lecture theatre. This course embraces the study of the non-metallic and metallic elements and their principal compounds based on Mendelejeff's classification of the elements. These lectures are given by Professor W. R. Lang, Head of the Department from 1900 to 1919, when he took over the Department of Military Studies.

Practical Chemistry.—The laboratory work commences with quantitative and qualitative experiments illustrating the fundamental principles of chemistry; this is followed by work more intimately related to analytical chemistry. Instruction in quantitative methods of analysis is given.

Second Year.

Lectures.—A course of lectures on the systematic classification of organic compounds and on elementary physical chemistry, twice a week.

Practical Chemistry.—A special laboratory course to accompany the above lecture course will be given during the Easter Term.

Students working in the laboratory are provided with the necessary apparatus on making a deposit of four dollars at the commencement of the session, which will be returned at its close after the following charges have been deducted from it—

(1) The cost of all apparatus broken or destroyed.

(2) Any fines for breach of laboratory rules.

No certificate will be given for the practical work unless the student has passed the practical examinations conducted during the session.

There is an optional course in volumetric chemistry.

Text-books:—Modern Inorganic Chemistry, Mellor; Inorganic Chemistry, Newth; General Chemistry for Colleges, Alex. Smith; Organic

Chemistry, Norris; Physical Chemistry for Physicians and Biologists, Cohen and Fischer; An Elementary Laboratory Course in Chemistry, Kenrick and DeLury.

Books of reference recommended:—Inorganic Chemistry, Richter; Organic Chemistry, Richter.

PHYSICS.

Professor and Director of the Physical Laboratory: J. C. McLennan.

Associate Professor: E. F. Burton.

Assistant Professors; Lachlan Gilchrist, John Satterly, H. A. McTaggart.

Demonstrators: Miss K. M. Crossley, Miss I. B. Giles, Miss M. I. Mackey, Miss H. C. Millar, Miss F. M. Quinlan.

Assistant Demonstrators: E. D. MacInnes, W. C. McQuarrie.

Class Assistants: Miss H. I. Eadie, F. W. Kemp.

Secretarial Assistant: Miss A. T. Reed.

The work of instruction on Physics consists of a series of lectures and a course in practical work in the laboratories.

First Year.

Lectures.—The lectures on Physics will not only give a concise outline of the subject, but are intended to form a satisfactory foundation for future study in other branches of science.

A course of lectures on Practical Mathematics for students of Physics will be given one day a week during the whole year. Each lecture will be followed by one hour on the practical application of the principles dealt with in the lecture.

There will be three lectures in Physics per week during the year; one lecture each week bears directly on the practical work assigned to the student, while the other two lectures each week are part of a course dealing more particularly with the principles of Physics of special use to students of Medicine. The following is an outline of the work covered:

1. Applied Mathematics and Calculations.

Calculations of experimental results to show limits of accuracy: contracted methods: logarithms.

Trigonometrical ratios defined, and simple relations deduced; reading of tables of sines, cosines and tangents.

Graphical methods; equations to straight line and parabola; logarithmic curves; deduction of simple formulae from graphs; slope of curves from graphs.

Simple ideas involved in the calculus; illustration of velocity of a falling body from $s = \frac{1}{2} gt^2$.

2. MECHANICS.

Measuring instruments, length, volume; verniers, micrometers.

Forces: conditions of equilibrium; resolution of forces, moments; centre of gravity; levers and simple machines.

Velocity; acceleration, momentum, force, work and power; absolute and practical units in English and metric systems; mass and weight; value of 'g'.

Energy, kinetic and potential; transmutation of energy; law of conservation of energy.

Simple harmonic motion; the pendulum; combination of two motions perpendicular to each other; Lissajous figures; Blackburn's pendulum.

3. HYDROSTATICS AND HYDROMECHANICS.

Laws of pressure in fluids at rest; Pascal's Law and Archimedes' principle: specific gravity; the hydrostatic paradox; resultant vertical forces on walls manometers, barometers, mercury and aneroid; Bramah's press; pumps.

Archimedes' principle in air; weight of atmosphere.

Laws of pressure in fluids in motion; Bernouilli's principle; applications such as atomizer, Bunsen burner, filter pump; action of air in winds and curving of balls in flight.

4. PROPERTIES OF MATTER.

Principles of the kinetic theory of matter; structure of solids, liquids and gases; diffusion; molecules and molecular forces.

Elastic properties of solids; bulk modulus, torsion modulus or rigidity, Young's modulus; micro-photographic study of metals; crystallization.

Viscosity of fluids; velocity gradient; coefficient of viscosity; Poiseulle's law for tubes; experimental determination of coefficient; Ostwald viscosimeter; viscosity and temperature; relation to blood flow; capillaries.

Surface tension; experimental illustrations, definition of coefficient and determination of same; energy of surface; shapes of free surfaces.

Laws of gases; theoretical determination of pressure, $p = 1/3 \ mnV^2$; Boyle's Law; Charles' Law; laws of diffusion.

Change of state; solid to liquid, liquid to gas; vapour pressure, with measurement; relation to temperature; vapour density; liquefaction of gases; critical temperature and pressure; low temperatures.

Colloidal solutions; size of particles; physical properties; mobility; coagulation by electrolytes; Brownian movement and its molecular explanation; confirmation of the kinetic theory; dialysis; relation to body fluids and membranes.

5. HEAT.

Expansion of solids, liquids and gases; thermometers; Centigrade and Fahrenheit scales; absolute scale; maximum and minimum thermometers; clinical thermometer.

Capacity for heat; calorie; specific heats; latent heat of vaporization and fusion; calorimetry.

Heat as energy; mechanical equivalent of heat; Joule's law.

Vapour pressure; vapour density; dew point; various forms of hygrometers; relative humidity.

Radiation; laws of cooling; wave length of heat radiations; transmission of energy through space. Conduction.

6. ACOUSTICS.

Production, propagation and recording of sounds; characteristics of a note, pitch, intensity and quality; definition of wave length; determination of velocity; $V = n\lambda$; resonance; stationary waves; organ pipes; laws of strings; membranes; voice production and structure of ear; interference of sound waves; beats and beat tones; absorption and reflection of sound; musical scales.

7. ELECTRICITY AND MAGNETISM.

The fundamental phenomena associated with electrified bodies and the laws of the action of electrical charges. The methods of measurement of electrical charge, current, potential, capacity, resistance, conductance and the definition of the units of these quantities in the electrostatic, practical and electromagnetic systems.

The construction and action of the instruments used in measuring electrical quantities and the methods of calibrating them. These instruments include galvanometers, ammeters, voltmeters, electrometers, potentiometers and wattmeters.

The properties of liquid conductors, and the measurement of their conductivity. Faraday's laws of electrolysis and the method of determination of the electro-chemical equivalent.

The properties and laws of action of magnets and of the magnetic fields associated with a circuit having a current, the method of measuring magnetic mass and magnetic field intensity and the definition of the units of these quantities.

The method of production, the properties and the measurement of induced currents of varying frequencies and their application.

The discharge of electricity through gases, and the factors upon which their conductivity depends and the properties and uses of anode, cathode and X rays.

The methods of investigating and identifying radioactive substances. The properties of radioactive radiations and their uses.

8. LIGHT.

The electron as a source of light waves—nature of the waves—their velocity in free space, water and glass—their reception by the eye. Analogies in sound and wireless signalling.

Reflection of waves from plane and spherical mirrors—focal lengths of spherical mirrors—images—optical diagrams.

Refraction of waves at a plane surface—index of refraction—the critical angle—methods of finding the index. Refraction of waves at a spherical surface—foci and focal lengths—the dioptre—power of a lens—images—optical diagrams.

The eye.—Diagram of the eye—accommodation—the normal, myopia and hpyermetropia eye—the far point—lens necessary to correct myopia and hypermetropia—astigmatism.

Optical instruments.—The reading lens, compound microscope, telescope, prism binoculars.

Colour.—Variation of refractive index with colour—deviation of light by a prism—dispersion—kinds of optical glass manufactured—achromatic pair of prisms—direct vision spectroscope—colour blindness.

Spectroscopy.—Emission spectra of solids, liquids and vapours or gases—spectrum analysis—absorption spectra—range of ether waves from infra red to ultra violet waves and X-ray waves.

Polarised light.—Polarisation by reflection, by refraction, by natural crystals—the nicol prism—rotation of the plane of polarisation, the polarimeter.

Interference.—Interference of waves—colours in thin films.

Practical Work.—The Practical Work, consisting of a laboratory course of three hours each week designed to illustrate the principles dealt with in the lectures, will be conducted under the supervision of the Director of the Laboratory.

Tutorial Classes.—In addition to the above, each student is required to attend a tutorial class, one hour each week, in the general work covered by all the above courses.

Text-book: W. H. White, Hand-book of Physics.

Optional Courses in Physics.

In accordance with the plan outlined by the faculty optional courses in Physics are offered in years succeeding the first, as follows:

Second Year.

Advanced Electricity and Magnetism...............PROFESSOR BURTON.

This course of 60 hours is designed to follow on the work in electricity of the first year course.

Third Year.

Colloidal Solutions and Radioactivity.

I. *Colloidal Solutions*.........................PROFESSOR BURTON.

A course of thirty hours lectures and demonstrating on the preparation of colloidal solutions and the study of their properties.

II. *Radioactivity*.............................PROFESSOR SATTERLY.

A course of thirty hours lectures and practical demonstration on Radio-active Substances and their Radiations.

Fourth Year.

Acoustics and Optics.

I. *Acoustics*.................................PROFESSOR BURTON.

A course of thirty hours lecture and demonstrations in advanced acoustics.

II. *Optics*................................PROFESSOR McTAGGART.

A course of thirty hours lectures and demonstrations in advanced optics.

Fifth Year.

Radiation.................................PROFESSOR McLENNAN.

A course of sixty hours on radiations and their properties followed by practical work.

Sixth Year.

Radiology.................................PROFESSOR GILCHRIST.

A course of sixty hours lecture and laboratory work on Radiology.

REGULATIONS.—Deposit Fee: Each student taking the laboratory course is required to make a deposit of three dollars ($3.00) before beginning work. All supplies, apparatus broken or destroyed and all fines will be charged against this deposit, which must be renewed when exhausted. At the close of the session cash balances will be returned on a day appointed for the purpose.

Relation of Science to Civilization.

First Year.

Lectures.—The greater part of the assigned time of 60 hours will be devoted to a course of lectures designed to illustrate the influence which scientific thought and achievement have had on the development of modern civilization. The remaining time will be devoted to conferences and reviews. The lectures will be given jointly by several lecturers, but the course as a whole will be under the general direction of Professor Huntsman.

Attendance and examination requirements are the same for this as for other courses of the first year.

EXPRESSION.

First Year.

Tutorial Classes.—In this course instruction will be given in the correct use of written and spoken English, and opportunity will be afforded each student to acquire experience in public speaking.

In order that the instruction may be as thorough as possible, the class will be divided into several groups, each of which will meet twice a week.

BIOLOGY.

Professor of Zoology: B. A. BENSLEY.
Associate Professor of Histology and Embryology: W. H. PIERSOL.
Associate Professor of Zoology: E. M. WALKER.
Assistant Professor in Vertebrate Embryology: A. F. COVENTRY.
Assistant Professor in Biology: W. A. CLEMENS.
Lecturer in Comparative Anatomy: E. H. CRAIGIE.
Lecturer in Histology: W. H. T. BAILLIE.
Lecturer in Biology: J. C. MACARTHUR.
Class Assistants: H. D. BALL, N. FOUND, P. J. F. HOUSTON, W. V. JOHN-
STON, N. B. LAUGHTON, J. M. MACDONALD, E. MCCULLOCH, A.[G.
MCPHEDRAN, L. M. MURRAY, L. PEQUEGNAT, H. W. PRICE, P. D.
SPOHN, O. C. J. WITHROW.
Secretarial Assistant: MISS N. C. LAWLER.

First Year.

Lectures.—1. Students of the First Year will attend a course of ninety
lectures to be given three times a week during the session. The lectures
will serve as an introduction to the biological fields in relation to medicine.
The topics include (1) the general nature of living organisms and of cell
processes, (2) the types of lower organisms of interest to students of
Medicine, (3) the elements of comparative anatomy, and (4) biological
principles as applied to man.

Practical Work.—2. A course of one hundred and eighty hours, comprising two three-hour periods per week, the materials of which are based as
far as possible on Lecture course I. The work comprises microscope practice, elementary experimental studies on the nature of cell processes, types
of lower organisms, and a selected list of vertebrates, including the elements
of mammalian anatomy.

Second Year.

Lectures and Practical Work—

1. A course of ten lectures and twenty hours laboratory work introductory to Embryology and Histology.

2. A course of fifteen lectures and sixty hours laboratory work on
Histogenesis and General Histology.

3. A course of twenty lectures and forty hours laboratory work on the
development of the human body.

4. A course of fifteen lectures and sixty hours laboratory work on Human
Microscopic Anatomy.

OPTION.—A course on the principles of evolution, heredity and eugenics
in relation to medical and sociological problems (c.f. course 30, Arts
Calendar).

The student will have the opportunity of providing himself with a set of typical histological specimens.

Text-books: Biology: O'Donoghue, Shull, Borràdaile, McFarland, Bigelow, Parker.

Embryology: McMurrich, Manual of Embryology.

Mammalian Anatomy: Bensley, Practical Anatomy of the Rabbit.

Histology: Jordan, Text-book of Histology; Piersol, Normal Histology, 10th ed.; Bohm, v. Davidoff and Huber, Text-book of Histology, 2nd ed.; Bailey, Text-book of Histology.

Reference Text-books:—Embryology: Bailey and Miller, 3rd ed., Keibel and Mall, Prentiss and Arey. Histology: Schäfer, Text-book of Microscopic Anatomy (Quain's Anatomy, 11th edition; vol. II, pt. 1); Sobotta, Atlas of Human Histology.

Physiology (including General Physiology.)

Professor of Physiology: J. J. R. MACLEOD.

Assistant Professor of Physiology: J. M. D. OLMSTED.

Lecturer: N. B. TAYLOR.

Fellows: MISS J. LANG, S. U. PAGE.

Part Time Fellows: MISS C. FRASER, C. F. KNIGHT, E. C. NOBLE, C. H. BEST.

Librarian: MISS M. GRANGE.

Secretarial Assistant: MISS M. E. ARMOUR.

The following courses of instruction each extending throughout the session are offered.

1. Systematic lectures; two a week during 1st term and four a week during 2nd term of third year.

   a. General and neuro-muscular physiology.

   b. Physiology of circulation, respiration, digestion and secretion.

   c. Metabolism, the functions of the ductless glands and reproduction.

   d. Physiology of the central nervous system and special senses. /

2. Lectures in General Physiology.

3. Advanced lectures; two a week (third year—optional).

4. General laboratory courses (total of 180 hours).

   a. Neuromuscular Physiology (second year).

   b. Circulation, respiration and digestion (second and third years).

   c. Nervous system and special senses (third year).

   d. Reviews and Conferences.

5. Laboratory course in General Physiology.

6. Advanced laboratory courses (optional).

7. Research in Physiology.

8. Journal Club; one hour a week.

Every student must attain a certain standard in the laboratory exercises before he will be allowed to proceed to the University examinations in Physiology and Biochemistry.

Throughout the Session oral and, as may be necessary, written examinations will be held to ascertain the extent of the student's knowledge of Physiology, and the results of these, as well as his general work in the laboratory will be used to determine his position in the University Class Lists.

In the laboratory courses the students will be required to make good all loss through breakage or otherwise.

Text-books:—Manual of Physiology, G. N. Stewart; Physiology and Biochemistry in Modern Medicine, J. J. R. Macleod; Starling's or Howell's Physiologies; Bayliss' General Physiology; Luciani's Physiology (translated by F. Welby); Monographs in Physiology (edited by B. H. Starling). *Works of Reference:*—Other works important for consultation are Marshall's Physiology of Reproduction; Schäfer's Endocrine Organs; Text-Book of Physiology (edited by E. A. Schäfer); Recent and Further Advances in Physiology (edited by Leonard Hill); C. S. Sherrington, Mammalian Physiology.

Students are urged to become members of the Students' Medical Library from which they may borrow, for home reading, books and monographs bearing on the subject of Physiology.

BIOCHEMISTRY.

Professor of Biochemistry: ANDREW HUNTER.

Associate Professor of Biochemistry: HARDOLPH WASTENEYS.

Associate Professor of Zymology: H. B. SPEAKMAN.

Demonstrator in Biochemistry: MISS J. McFARLANE.

Fellows: R. W. I. URQUHART, N. S. CLARK, A. M. WYNNE, H. BORSOOK.

Secretarial Assistant: MISS M. DELAMERE.

The following are the Courses of Instruction in this department for students of Medicine.

Second Year.

1. A general course of lectures in Biochemistry; two a week.
2. A general laboratory course in Biochemistry; six hours a week.

—27

Third Year.

3. A course of advanced lectures on Biochemistry for Honour students; two a week.

4. An advanced laboratory course in Biochemistry for Honour students; six or more hours a week.

Every student must attain a certain standard in the laboratory exercises before he will be allowed to proceed to the University examinations in Biochemistry.

Throughout the Session oral and, as may be necessary, written examinations will be held to ascertain the extent of the student's knowledge of Biochemistry and the results of these as well as his general work in the laboratory, will be used to determine his position in the University Class Lists.

In the laboratory courses the students will be required to make good all loss through breakage or otherwise.

Text-Books and Works of Reference:

(a) *Elementary or General:*—Hammarsten, Text-book of Physiological Chemistry; Abderhalden-Hall, Text-book of Physiological Chemistry; Mathews, Text-book of Physiological Chemistry; Robertson, Principles of Biochemistry.

(b) *Advanced or Special:*—Monographs on Biochemistry, edited by Plimmer and Hopkins; Robertson, Physical Chemistry of the Proteins; Taylor, Digestion and Metabolism; Lusk, Science of Nutrition; Effront, Biochemical Catalysts in Life and Industry; Euler, General Chemistry of the Enzymes; Abderhalden, Biochemisches Handlexikon; Neuberg, Der Harn.

Laboratory Handbooks:

(a) *Elementary:*—Plimmer, Practical Organic and Biochemistry; Hawk, Practical Physiological Chemistry; Folin, Laboratory Manual of Biological Chemistry; Halliburton, Essentials of Chemical Physiology; Cole, Practical Physiological Chemistry.

(b) *Advanced:*—Abderhalden, Handbuch der biochemischen Arbeitsmethoden; Ellinger, Analyse des Harns.

ANATOMY.

Professor and Director of the Anatomical Department: J. PLAYFAIR McMURRICH.

Associate Professor of Clinical Anatomy: G. A. BINGHAM.

Assistant Professor in Anatomy: J. C. WATT.

Demonstrators: W. A. SCOTT, R. E. GABY, F. W. WESTON, R. L. ROWNTREE, R. O. FISHER, H. B. VAN WYCK, A. S. LAWSON, E. E. SHOULDICE, K. G. McKENZIE, G. W. CARLTON, I. R. SMITH, H. A. CATES, L. B. ROBERTSON, R. M. JANES, P. D. SPOHN, L. C. PALMER, E. A. McCULLOCH, J.C. MAYNARD, L. A. PEQUEGNAT, V. F. STOCK.

Secretarial Assistant—MISS G. H. DOWSLEY.

Second Year.

Practical Work.—During the Second Year each student is obliged to dissect thoroughly the various regions of the body, following the plan outlined in a "Guide to the Dissection of the Human Body". Demonstrators will be in attendance each day for the purpose of superintending the work and of giving instruction, and will hold frequent examinations with the object of testing the student's progress. Certificates of credit in Practical Anatomy will be granted only to those students whose work has been completed to the satisfaction of the instructors in charge.

The Laboratory will be open from 9 a.m. until 5 p.m. every week-day throughout the session, with the exception of Saturdays when it will be closed at 12 noon.

Lectures.—In connection with the laboratory work lectures will be given by members of the staff, reviewing the work that has been completed. The object of this course will be to supplement the work in the Laboratory by calling attention to the relations and significance of the parts that have been studied and by elucidating with the aid of diagrams and models the anatomy of difficult and important structures.

Third Year.

Lectures.—During the Michaelmas Term a course of lectures will be given on the Anatomy of the Central Nervous System.

Practical Work.—In connection with the above course of lectures the class will be divided into small sections, to each of which a Demonstrator will be assigned, for the purpose of a practical study of the Anatomy of the Brain.

In addition, when opportunity offers, lectures and demonstrations will
be given upon the anatomy of special regions and organs, special attention
being given to the correlation of the structure and functional activities of
the parts considered.

Opportunity will be afforded, when necessary, for the dissection of
parts that were uncompleted in the practical course of the Second Year,
or of which a further study seems advisable.

Text-books:—Piersol; Gray; Morris; Cunningham's Text-book; McMurrich's Development of the Human Body, Guide to the Dissection of the
Human Body for the use of Students in the Anatomical Laboratory of
the University of Toronto.

Reference Text-books:—Spalteholz, Hand-Atlas of Human Anatomy;
Toldt's Atlas of Human Anatomy; Sobotta's Atlas and Text-book of
Human Anatomy; Eycleshymer and Shoemaker, Cross-Section Anatomy;
Quain's Anatomy; Barker's The Nervous System; Johnston, Nervous
System of Vertebrates; Villiger, Brain and Spinal Cord; Herrick, Intro-
duction to Neurology; Ranson, Anatomy of the Nervous System; Von
Bardeleben's Handbuch der Anatomie; Rawlings, Landmarks; Treves,
Applied Anatomy.

PHARMACY AND PHARMACOLOGY; MATERIA MEDICA.

Professor: V. E. HENDERSON.

Assistant Professor—N. C. SHARPE.

Instructors in Pharmacy: J. A. MacDONALD, J. C. HALLAMORE, D. BIRKETT.

Secretarial Assistant: MISS JEAN DEAS.

Third Year.

Two courses of laboratory work accompanied by lectures and laboratory talks are given.

Practical Work.—LABORATORY COURSE I. Experimental pharmacology. In this course the student obtains an opportunity to become familiar with representatives of the drug-stuffs composing the various pharmacological groups. The chief object of the course is to get the student into the habit of accurate observation of the effects produced by drugs and to be able to describe them in accurate pharmacological language. In consequence a great deal of attention is given to the note books kept by each student. The course is accompanied by many mammalian demonstrations. The tracings of all demonstrations are analysed by each student.

LABORATORY COURSE II. Practical Pharmacy. This course is very brief, consisting only of a few hours' work on the chemical and physical incompatibles and in dispensing several mixtures, pills and ointments, in order that the student may obtain such insight into dispensing as is necessary to enable him to write prescriptions intelligently.

Total of these two courses, 90 hours.

Arrangements have also been made with the Toronto General Hospital the Hospital for Sick Children and the Western Hospital, by which the students of this year will be drafted in turn to act as Assistants in the Hospital Dispensaries for a period of a week.

Lectures.—A course of lectures on general pharmacology (35 in all). This course is designed to supplement and extend the knowledge gained in the laboratory and from the prescribed text-book.

Prescription Writing.—Each student is expected to hand in answers to the problems in prescription writing announced each week. These are corrected and returned, and opportunity is given for the discussion of any difficulties, with the staff during laboratory hours. Informal talks are also given from time to time as needed.

Text-books:—Pharmacy and Materia Medica, Henderson; Pharmacology, Dixon.

Reference Text-books:—Pharmacology, Cushny, Sollmann, Bastedo, Greene; Prescription Writing:—Bennett, Medical and Pharmaceutical Latin; Eggleston, Prescription Writing.

TOXICOLOGY.

Professor of Pharmacology: V. E. HENDERSON.

A course of ten lectures is given dealing with the pathology, pharmacology, symptomology and treatment of the more important poisons which are commonly the cause of either forensic or industrial cases of poisoning.

` MEDICINE

Emeritus Professor of Medicine: ALEXANDER McPHEDRAN.

Professor of Medicine: DUNCAN GRAHAM.

Associate Professor of Medicine: WILLIAM GOLDIE.

Clinicians in Medicine: R. G. ARMOUR, G. F. BOYER, W. R. CAMPBELL, A. H. CAULFEILD, F. A. CLARKSON, E. E. CLEAVER, H. K. DETWEILER, H. A. DIXON, J. H. ELLIOTT, A. A. FLETCHER, N. GWYN, G. W. HOWLAND, H. S. HUTCHISON, R. JAMIESON, J. D. LOUDON, A. G. McPHEDRAN, J. H. McPHEDRAN, W. F. McPHEDRAN, A. J. MAC-KENZIE, C. S. McVICAR, F. S. MINNS, L. MURRAY, W. OGDEN, J. A. OILLE, T. J. PAGE, H. C. PARSONS, C. A. RAE, F. W. ROLPH, D. KING SMITH, CHAS. SHEARD, Jr., G. S. STRATHY, E. J. TROW, G. S. YOUNG.

Clinical Microscopy, Demonstrator: G. W. LOUGHEED.

Assistant Demonstrator: A. B. MOFFAT.

Secretarial Assistant: MISS M. K. HARVIE.

THIRD YEAR.

Lectures:—During the Michaelmas term two lectures are given weekly on methods of physical examinations with the explanation and interpretation of physical signs. In the Easter term two lectures are given weekly on history taking, and methods of examination of the central nervous system, followed by an introduction to the study of Medicine dealing with the physiological aspects of disease.

Clinics:—Practical instruction in Clinical Medicine is given in the Hospital Wards and in the University Laboratories throughout the session. The Class is divided into small groups each of which is in charge of a clinician.

Instruction in the Clinics follows as closely as possible the work discussed in the lectures.

Clinical Microscopy.—Demonstrations and practical instruction are given in the microscopical examination of blood, urine, faeces, stomach contents, sputum, cerebrospinal fluid, transudates and exudates, together with the practical application of these examinations in the diagnosis of disease

Instruments:—Students beginning Clinical work are strongly advised to supply themselves with the following instruments: Stethoscope, Tape Measure, Dermograph, Haemocytometer (Levy-Neubauer), Haemoglobinometer (Dare or Sahli), Thermometer, Head-mirror, Ophthalmoscope, Laryngoscope, Microscope with Condenser and Oil Immersion Lens.

Special arrangements have been made for obtaining these instruments.

Text-books:—Pathological Physiology, Hewlett; Physical Diagnosis, Cabot; Clinical Methods, Hutchison and Rainy; Clinical Diagnosis, Emerson; Medicine, Osler, Taylor.

FOURTH YEAR.

Lectures:—In the Fourth Year a course of thirty lectures is given on the different types of disease dealing with the subject from the pathological physiological standpoint. This is supplemented by a course of sixteen lectures on Diseases of the Nervous System.

Clinics:—The students of the Fourth Year devote the greater part of their time available for Clinical Medicine to the Medical Wards, examining patients, taking histories and carrying out the Clinical Laboratory investigation of their cases under the direction of the Staff.

The Class is divided into small groups and Ward Clinics are given on the different types of disease.

Groups consisting of one-sixth of the Year attend clinical demonstrations of Infectious Diseases at the City Isolation Hospital and the Hospital for Sick Children once a week, for a period of ten weeks.

A weekly Clinic is held in the Hospital amphitheatre at which selected cases illustrating the different types of disease are presented.

Clinical and Pathological Conference:—Weekly Clinical and Pathological Conference will be held throughout the Easter session. Abstracts of the histories of the fatal cases of the week, with diagnosis made before the autopsy, are read. The specimens are then demonstrated, followed by a discussion of the case.

During the session, each student is required to prepare at least five complete records of medical cases. These records must be certified as satisfactory by the Clinician in Charge of the Clinic of which the student is a member.

FIFTH YEAR.

During a period of ten weeks one-third of the Class devotes its whole time to Clinical Medicine. Each student is required to take charge of a number of patients in the Wards personally, recording the results of his Clinical and Laboratory investigations on the cases under his care and attend to the General Medical Clinic of the Out Patient Department twice a week and assist in the examination of cases.

Each group has one Ward Clinic daily and attends in rotation Special Clinics in the Out Patient Department on Diseases of the Skin, Nervous System, Tuberculosis and Syphilis.

Two theatre Clinics a week are given in the Hospital amphitheatre at which selected cases are presented.

A weekly Clinical Pathological Conference is held at which students are required to report the results of their Clinical examination on fatal cases under their care. This is followed by a demonstration of the autopsy specimens and a discussion of the Clinical and Pathological findings.

The students of the Fifth Year will receive special instruction in Physio-therapy. The value of massage, gymnastics, electricity, hydropathy, etc., in the treatment of medical cases will be demonstrated.

Text Books—Diseases of the Chest, Norris and Landis; Diseases of the Heart, Mackenzie; Diseases of the Heart and Aorta, Hirschfelder; Clinical Disorders of the Heart-beat, Lewis; The Soldiers Heart and the Effort Syndrome, Lewis; Diseases of the Digestive Canal, Cohnheim; Diseases of the Nervous System; Purvis Stewart, Diseases of the Skin, Sequeira, Hartzell, Pussey; Pulmonary Tuberculosis, Fishberg; Diagnostics and Treatment of Tropical Diseases", Stitt.

Reference Books:—A System of Medicine, XI. Vols., Allbutt and Rolleston; Modern Medicine, V. Vols., Osler and McCrae; Monographic Medicine, VI. Vols., Barker; Oxford Loose Leaf Medicine, Christian and MacKenzie; Nelson's Loose Leaf Medicine; Internal Medicine", III. Vols., Wilson; Diseases of the Arteries and Angina Pectoris, II. Vols., Allbutt; Symptoms of Visceral Disease, Pottenger; Diseases of the Nervous System, Jeliffe and White.

PAEDIATRICS

Associate Professor of Medicine in Charge of Paediatrics: ALAN BROWN
Clinicians in Medicine in the Sub-department of Paediatrics: ALAN W. CANFIELD, ARTHUR M. GOULDING, BEVERLEY HANNAH, EDWARD A. MORGAN, GEORGE R. PIRIE, GEORGE E. SMITH.
Chemist to the Sub-department of Paediatrics: ANGELIA M. COURTNEY.
Assistant Chemist: IDA F. MacLACHLAN.

FOURTH YEAR.

Clinical Lectures:—The students of the Fourth Year will devote most of their time to learning the essential principles in paediatrics, and the difference in the manifestation of disease between adult and child. A series of thirty-two Clinical Lectures will be given, illustrated by Plates, Lantern Slides and Morbid Specimens; also by the presentation of patients when the nature of the subject under discussion makes it desirable. The subjects included in these Clinical Lectures are Physiology and Pathology of digestion in infants; percentage and caloric method of feeding; classification of · digestive disturbances; deficiency diseases of childhood; congenital and acquired cardiac disease; tuberculosis; syphilis; nephritis; acute conditions arising in the new born infant and child welfare.

FIFTH YEAR.

In the Fifth Year time will be devoted wholly to Clinics—Bedside and Out-patient.   In addition to this each student is required to spend seven hours in one of the child welfare clinics, conducted by the Department of Child Hygiene.   In these Clinics, he is given an idea of the normal feeding of infants and children.   During the Fifth Year Course three hours' practical work is required of each student in the milk modifying laboratory of the Children's Hospital, where he is taught the home modification of milk formulae.

Fellowships:—The Sub-Department of Paediatrics is prepared to offer two full-time Fellowships in Diseases of Children, to graduate students. These Fellowships will include a certain amount of clinical work as well as laboratory investigation, thus serving to keep the research worker in touch with clinical problems and further his interest in Clinical Paediatrics.

Text-books:—(1) Diseases of Infancy and Childhood, Holt; (2) Infant Feeding, Grulee; (3) Diseases of Nutrition and Infant Feeding, Morse and Talbot.

Reference Books:—(1) Diseases of Children, Garrod, Batten and Thursfield; (2) Common Disorders and Diseases of Childhood, Still; (3) System of Paediatrics (3 volumes), Dunn.

THERAPEUTICS.

Professor of Therapeutics: R. D. RUDOLF.

Demonstrator in Anaesthesia: S. JOHNSTON.

Demonstrators in Therapeutics: C. E. C. COLE.
S. R. D. HEWITT, W. V. WATSON,

Assistants in Anaesthesia: T. R. HANLEY, M. D. MCKICHAN, W. H. CARVETH, C. H. ROBSON, J. J. HURLEY, T. D. ARCHIBALD.

Therapeutics is taught in the two final years, and is made as practical as possible.

Fourth Year.

Lectures.—In the Fourth Year a course of lectures is given in which the general principles of the subject are considered in a systematic way, emphasis being laid upon the fact that Therapeutics includes far more than the employment of drugs.   The whole matter is considered more from the standpoint of disease than from that of drugs and other remedies.   Diet, specific therapy, hydrotherapy, the various forms of physio-therapy, and climate are also dealt with. Once a week one-third of the class are given a practical demonstration at the hospital of methods of therapy, patients being freely used to illustrate the points.

Fifth Year.

Clinical Work.—In the final year the students are taken in groups at the General Hospital and the different methods of dealing with diseased conditions are demonstrated, generally upon actual patients. Here also prescription writing is practised. These demonstrations are quite informal and are conducted thrice a week in the medical theatre at the hospital and in the wards.

Students of the Fourth and Fifth years will receive individual practical instruction in the administration of anaesthetics.

Text-book:—Hare's Practical Therapeutics; Rudolf's Medical Treatment.

Reference Text-books:—Hutchinson & Collier's Index of Treatment, Lauder Brunton, Action of Medicines; Friedenwald and Rührah, Diet in Health and Disease; Wood, Therapeutics, its principles and practice; Potter, Ortner's Treatment of Internal Diseases; Cushny, Pharmacology and Therapeutics; Shoemaker, Materia Medica and Therapeutics; Hare, System of Therapeutics; Forchheimer's General and Special Treatment of Diseases; Forchheimer's Therapeusis of Internal Diseases; Sajous, Cyclopaedia of Practical Medicine; Da Costa, Medical Treatment.

SURGERY AND CLINICAL SURGERY.

Professor of Surgery:

Professor of Clinical Surgery: A. PRIMROSE.

Associate Professor of Clinical Surgery and Clinical Anatomy: G. A. BINGHAM

Associate Professors of Clinical Surgery: H. A. BRUCE, F. N. G. STARR, P. W. H. MCKEOWN, S. M. HAY.

Associate Professor of Clinical Surgery and in Charge of Orthopaedics: C. L. STARR.

Associates in Surgery and Clinical Surgery: C. B. SHUTTLEWORTH, J. F. UREN, G. SILVERTHORN, E. S. RYERSON, W. A. SCOTT, W. W. JONES, W. E. GALLIE.

Demonstrators in Clinical Surgery: A. B. WRIGHT, M. H. V. CAMERON, N. S. SHENSTONE, G. E. WILSON, R. E. GABY, J. A. ROBERTS, A. S. MOORHEAD, A. H. PERFECT, D. E. ROBERTSON, OLIVER MABEE, F. A. CLELAND, J. A. MCCOLLUM.

Assistants in Clinical Surgery: ROBIN PEARSE, B. Z. MILNER, R. R. GRAHAM, L. B. ROBERTSON, C. H. HAIR, H. W. BAKER, C. B. PARKER, H. E. CLUTTERBUCK, G. M. DALE, G. C. MCINTYRE.

Temporary Assistants: H. HARRISON, J. S. SIMPSON, T. A. ROBINSON, C. H. GILMOUR, R. H. THOMAS F. E. WATTS, W. A. COSTAIN, A. S. LAWSON, A. B. LE MESURIER, E. C. BEER, J. H. WOOD, R. I. HARRIS, E. E. SHOULDICE, J. C. MCCLELLAND, R. A. MCCOMB.

THIRD YEAR SURGERY.

1. *Lectures.*—A course consisting of an introduction to the general principles of surgery.

2. *Clinical Work.*

(a) Clinical study in the Out-patient Department or the Ward. Each clinical class will be taught the surgical conditions following, with History Taking, Surgical Landmarks, and the methods of making physical examinations as applied to them: Inflammation; Suppuration and Abscess; Surgical conditions of the skin and subcutaneous tissues; Bursitis; Tenosynovitis; Surgical affections of the Lymph Glands; Wounds; Haemorrhage and Thrombosis; Sepsis, infection and infectious diseases; Ulceration; Gangrene; the general features of Fractures, Dislocations and Sprains; Hernia; Bandaging.

These conditions shall constitute the subjects of examination.

(b) A course of surgically applied clinical anatomy. This course will be conducted in the clinical theatre of the Toronto General Hospital. Regional anatomy will be studied on and illustrated by patients suffering from surgical conditions in different parts of the body. The anatomy of the different regions will be demonstrated by diagrams upon the blackboard, by frozen sections and by the use of the lantern.

(c) A series of demonstrations in surgical pathology. These demonstrations will be conducted conjointly by the clinicians and the pathologist and will consist of elementary demonstrations of the gross pathology, the histology, the bacteriology and the analyses of the blood, urine, etc., including not only microscopic findings, but the pathological chemistry necessary for complete clinical investigation. Individual types will thus be presented for the purpose of illustrating the steps necessary in the clinical study of surgical cases as indicated in the gross pathology together with the microscopic and chemical findings.

FOURTH YEAR SURGERY.

1. *Lectures.*—Thirty lectures are given throughout the session on some of the general principles of surgery. Short courses are included on the special surgery of certain regions of the body, *e.g.*, the abdomen; the head and neck; the extremities, etc., the courses varying from year to year.

2 *Clinical Work.*—(a) Clinical work in the wards will be conducted according to the time-table provided. During the year the student is taught to make a complete examination of surgical cases in order that he may be able to arrive at a diagnosis and to learn the appropriate scientific treatment. The following conditions will be studied and will be, as far as possible, the subjects of the clinics: (1) Injuries and diseases of the bones and joints; (2) the surgery of the neck, acute and chronic inflammation primary and secondary new growths, diseases of the thyroid gland; (3) surgery of the thorax, empyema, tumours of the breast; (4) surgery of the abdomen, appendicitis, cholecystitis, ulcer of the stomach and duodenum, cancer of the stomach, general peritonitis, tuberculous peritonitis, gall stones, acute and chronic intestinal obstruction, abdominal injuries, haemorrhoids, fistula in ano, anal fissure; (5) the surgery of the kidney, stone, pyonephrosis; (6) the surgery of the scrotum and testes, actue and chronic inflammation, tumours, hydrocele, varicocele; (7) the surgery of the mouth, ulcers, tumours of the lip, tongue and gum, tumours of the upper and lower jaw; (8) diseases and injuries of blood and lymph-vascular systems. ·

A special course in orthopaedic surgery will be given in the Hospital for Sick Children.

(b) Each student will be required to take three complete histories during the year. Each history is to be written in accordance with the standard of the American College of Surgeons. This work will be directed by the clinical clerk under the authority of the house-surgeon. One history is to be left at the secretary's office at the end of each trimester. Each history ·after being initialed by the clinician is to be examined by the Professor of Clinical Surgery.

(c) A course of surgically applied clinical anatomy.

This course will be conducted in the clinical theatre of the Toronto General Hospital. Regional anatomy will be studied on and illustrated by patients suffering from surgical conditions in different parts of the body. The anatomy of the different regions will be demonstrated by diagrams upon the blackboard, by frozen sections and by the use of the lantern.

(d) A series of demonstrations in surgical pathology.　•

These demonstrations will be conducted conjointly by the clinicians and the representatives of the Department of Pathology and will consist of demonstrations of the gross pathology, the histology, the bacteriology and the analyses of the blood, urine, etc., including not only microscopic findings, but the pathological chemistry necessary for complete clinical investigation. The demonstrations will illustrate the steps necessary in clinical study, and the appropriate treatment, based upon the gross pathology, together with the microscopic and chemical findings.

FIFTH YEAR SURGERY.

The work of the Fifth Year in Surgery is entirely clinical, including one weekly mid-day clinical lecture.

Clinical Work.

(a) Two clinics will be given in each week to the students of this year. The clinical classes in each Hospital will consist of the students assigned to the surgical services in the various Hospitals.

(b) The students in this year are assigned at the Secretary's Office to the surgical services at the Toronto General, St. Michael's, Western and Hospital for Sick Children, the number of men to each service depending on the number of students in the class. These men will be required to act as clinical clerks and to perform the two following groups of duties, the students alternating at the end of each five weeks.

GROUP 1.

(1) To act as assistants to the House Surgeon and to be prepared to carry out his instructions at all times.

(2) To take the history of each patient within twenty-four hours of his admission to the wards. To record the physical examination and to do and record the necessary laboratory work.

(3) To attend all the operations performed on his service, and to be prepared to act as assistant.

(4) To do whatever dressings are detailed to him by the House Surgeon.

(5) In the event of an autopsy on any patient who has been under his charge, to assist and make the necessary records.

GROUP 2.

(6) To work in the Out-patient Department and Emergency Departments.

(7) That he be required to attend the clinics given to the Third and Fourth Years on his service, and to be prepared to give a detailed account of the cases being presented, to the clinician, and if necessary, under the direction of the clinician, to act as demonstrator. Further, that he shall be required to provide and prepare the material for each clinic to the Third and Fourth Years.

(8) That during his term of service he shall be prepared when directed to do so, to assist in giving and to give anaesthetics to the patients on his service under the supervision of the anaesthetist.

(9) That he be responsible for keeping a record of the clinics given on his service and the passing of this record on to the next clinician when the classes change.

(c) Once a week a conference will be held in the Pathological Department, when the Professor of Pathology and the members of the Clinical teaching staff will meet to discuss the Pathological material which has been sent from the clinic to the Pathological Department during the preceding week. These conferences between the Pathologist and the Clinician will form a very important part of the tuition of the student in Surgery in the Fifth Year.

The students of the Fifth Year will receive special instruction in physiotherapy. The value of massage, gymnastics, electricity, hydropathy, etc., in the treatment of surgical cases will be demonstrated.

Text-books:—Rose & Carless; Spencer and Gask.; Da Costa; F. T. Stewart's "Manual"; Foote, Minor Surgery; Russell Howard; Surgical Diagnosis, Gould; A Synopsis of Surgery, Ernest W. Hey Groves; Surgical Materials and their Uses, Maclennan.

Reference Text-books:—

Surgery:—Principles of, Choyce, Thomson and Miles; Oxford Loose Leaf Surgery, Burghard and Kanavel; Surgical Treatment, Cheyne & Burghard; Binnie, Kocher, Alexis Thomson; Genito-Urinary Surgery, Thomas Walker; Bonney; Orthopædic Surgery, Bradford & Lovett, Whitman; Fractures and Dislocations, Stinson, Scudder; Diseases of the Rectum and Anus, Gant, 3rd ed.; Surgery of the Chest, Paget; Lungs, Fowler & Godlee; Preparatory and after treatment in Operative Cases, Haubold; Surgery of the Brain, Rawlings; Clinical Surgical Diagnosis, de Quervain (trans.).

OBSTETRICS AND GYNAECOLOGY.

Professor of Obstetrics and Gynaecology: B. P. WATSON.

Associate Professor of Obstetrics: K. C. McILWRAITH.

Associate Professor of Gynaecology: F. W. MARLOW.

Associate Professor of Obstetrics and Gynaecology: W. B. HENDRY.

Associate in Obstetrics: J. A. KINNEAR.

Demonstrators in Obstetrics and Gynaecology: J. G. GALLIE, W. A. SCOTT R. W. WESLEY, N. D. FRAWLEY, W. W. LAILEY.

Fourth Year.

Lectures.—Obstetrics:—A course of lectures illustrated by diagrams, lantern slides and models will be given. A syllabus indicating the scope of the work is provided. Stated generally, the course consists of two parts. The first part deals with the anatomy and physiology of the female organs of reproduction; the anatomy, physiology and management of normal pregnancy, labour and the puerperium, and the care of the infant. The second part is concerned with abnormal conditions arising during pregnancy, labour, and the puerperium, and with maladies of the infant.

Practical demonstrations on anatomy, the mechanism of labour, the use of obstetrical instruments, etc., will be given to small sections of students.

Gynaecology:—A course of lectures illustrated by pathological specimens, diagrams and lantern slides will be given. A syllabus is provided. The lesions of each organ are considered in detail and the methods of gynaecological diagnosis and treatment indicated.

Clinical Work.—Obstetrics:—The student attends clinics at the Toronto General Hospital or at St. Michael's Hospital. At these clinics practical instruction is given in the examination of patients, the diagnosis of pregnancy, the management of labour and the puerperium and the care of the infant.

Gynaecology:—Clinical instruction is given at the Toronto General Hospital, and the Western Hospital, in the method of case taking, the examination of patients, the use of instruments, and in the conduct of operations.

Pathological Demonstrations:—The naked eye and microscopic pathology, of the common obstetrical and gynaecological lesions will be demonstrated in the museum.

Fifth Year.

Obstetrics.—The student attends the Obstetrical Hospital for a period of five weeks during which time he is given an opportunity of seeing all the work of the hospital, and of assisting in the management and treatment of cases. He is also required to attend patients in their own homes and to perform other duties in connection with the Out-Patient Service. Clinical lectures are given once a week on interesting and abnormal cases

Gynaecology.—Clinical instruction in the examination and diagnosis of gynaecological cases is given to small sections of students. Each student is required to act as clinical clerk to the cases assigned him, to be present at any operations required, and to follow the after-treatment. Operations will be performed on stated days and at these the members of the clinic may be present.

Pathological Demonstrations:—A series of demonstrations in continuity with those held during the fourth year will be given in the museum.
Text-books:—

Obstetrics:—Eden; Berry Hart; Hirst; Edgar; Whitridge Williams; Jellett; Galabin; De Lee.

Gynaecology:—Barbour & Watson; Graves; Dudley; Gilliam; Crossen; Penrose; Eden & Lockyer; Ashton; Montgomery.

Reference Text-books:—

Obstetrics:—Bumm; Winckel; Munro Kerr, Operative Obstetrics; Davis, Operative Obstetrics; Lea, Puerperal Infection; Ballantyne, Antenatal Pathology.

Gynaecology.—Kelly, Operative Gynaecology; Berkeley & Bonney, Gynaecological Surgery; Winter & Ruge, Gynaecological Pathology, translated by Clark; Cullen, Cancer of the Uterus.

OPHTHALMOLOGY

Professor: J. M. MacCallum.

Demonstrators: D. N. Maclennan, W. H. Lowry, M. Lyon, W. W. Wright, F. A. Aylesworth, C. E. Hill.

Fourth Year.

Instruction will be given by quizzes, recitations or lectures. The class will be divided into small sections. In each section the applied anatomy of the eye, orbit and surrounding structures will be considered, followed by instruction in the use of the ophthalmoscope, retinoscope and other instruments of diagnosis. The methods of external examination of the eye, the use of the test type, test lenses and the principles of refraction will be thoroughly dealt with.

Fifth. Year.

Instruction will be wholly clinical and practical, and will include Ophthalmoscopy and its relations to general medicine, advanced refraction. Each student will be required to determine the refraction of patients in the Out-Patient Clinic and must, for this purpose, supply himself with an ophthalmoscope and a retinoscope. When possible the students will be shown the more usual operations on the eye.

There will be a short course of didactic lectures.

Ophthalmology:—

*Text-books:—*J. Edward Jackson; May; Mayou; Nettleship; Parker; Parsons; Swanzy; Veasey; Wood & Woodruff; Sym; Marshall.

*Works of Reference:—*de Schweinitz; Weeks; Fuchs; Posey & Wright; Theobald; Ball.

OTO-LARYNGOLOGY.

Professor: D. J. Gibb Wishart.

Assistant Professors: Gilbert Royce, P. G. Goldsmith.

Associate: George M. Biggs.

Clinicians: Edmund Boyd, J. C. Calhoun, C. W. L. Clark, Angus Cambpbell, W. G. MacKechnie, J. Sproule-Manson.

Pathologist:

Assistant: A. A. Halliday.

The course of instruction in oto-laryngology is carried on in the Toronto General Hospital, where the facilities placed at the disposal of the students are unusually complete. There is an indoor service of twenty beds, and in the outdoor, in addition to the large clinic, where the fifth year students receive instruction, there is a room set aside for the fourth year classes, with eight cubicles for examination purposes.

—28

Clinics will also be provided at the Hospital for Sick Children which presents unusual opportunities for study. There is an indoor service which varies from ten to fifteen beds. In the outdoor, the clinics are very largely attended, a feature of this being the establishment of separate clinics for ear cases.

This course is carried on during both the fourth and fifth years of the curriculum.

Fourth Year.

In the fourth year the students will receive instruction in:

(1) The normal anatomy of the ear, nose and throat.

(2) The methods of using the head mirror and the various instruments required in examining the ear, nose and throat.

(3) The ordinary tests for hearing.

(4) The recognition of the ear, nose and throat, in their normal conditions, as exemplified by clinical material.

At the close of the session a clinical examination will be held.

Fifth Year.

In the fifth year the students will be divided into small groups for the purpose of studying the commoner pathological conditions affecting the various organs, and as much clinical material as possible will be utilized for the purposes of personal observation.

A series of lectures will be delivered upon the various diseases of the ear, nose and throat, ordinarily met with by the general practitioner.

At the final (fifth year) examination the test will be clinical.

Text-books:—Porter, Diseases of the Throat, Nose and Ear, 3rd ed.; Lake, Diseases of the Ear; Parker, Throat and Nose; Gray, Ear; Coolidge, Diseases of the Nose and Throat.

For Reference:—McKenzie, Diseases of Throat, Nose and Ear; St. Clair Thompson, Throat and Nose; Milligan and Wingrave; Diseases of the Ear, Lambert Lack, Throat and Nose; Watson Williams, Throat and Nose; Phillips, Throat, Nose and Ear.

PSYCHIATRY.

Professor of Psychiatry: C. K. CLARKE.
Extra-Mural Professor of Psychiatry: N. H. BEEMER.
Associate of Psychiatry: HARVEY CLARE.
Special Lecturer in Psychology: E. A. BOTT.
Demonstrators F. S. VROOMAN, D. R. FLETCHER.

Fourth Year.

Lectures.—A series of didactic lectures is given, outlining some of the more important psychoses.

Fifth Year.

Clinical Work.—A clinical course will be given. The student will be afforded opportunity to obtain a practical knowledge of psychiatry, and to study the laboratory and clinical methods employed in the diagnosis and treatment of various forms of insanity.

Text-books:—Clinical Psychiatry, Diefendorf; Psychiatric Neurological Examination Methods, by Wimmer Hoisholt; Mental Diseases, by Walter Von Gulick; Dementia Praecox and Paraphrenia, by Emil Kraepelin.

PATHOLOGY.

Professor of Pathology and Bacteriology and Curator of the Museum and Laboratories: J. J. MACKENZIE.
Assistant Professor of Bacteriology: H. B. MAITLAND.
Demonstrator of Pathology and Assistant Curator of the Pathological Museum: W. L. ROBINSON.
Demonstrators of Pathology: I. H. ERB, A. B. LeMESURIER, G. F. LAUGHLIN, G. R. PHILP, A. McKAY.
Fellows in Pathology: G. C. CAMERON, W. P. WARNER.

The courses of instruction are as follows:—

Second Year.

Students receive a course of lectures and practical laboratory exercises during the Easter Term in general Bacteriology, including media making, staining and cultivation of pathogenic micro-organisms, the practical isolation and identification of the most important bacteria pathogenic to man.

Third Year.

Lectures.—1. A course of lectures in General Pathology is given during the Michaelmas and Easter Terms.

Practical Work.—2. A laboratory course in Pathological Histology is. held three afternoons a week during both terms, illustrating general pathological conditions, including inflammation (acute and chronic) repair, tumours, etc.

3. A practical laboratory class in hàematology and clinical microscopy.

Fourth Year.

Lectures.—1. A course of didactic lectures is delivered upon selected chapters of special pathology.

Practical Work.—2. A laboratory course in Pathological Histology takes place four afternoons a week during the Michaelmas Term. The work taken up in this class illustrates the special pathology of the organs. Alternating with this class are a series of Museum Demonstrations arranged to illustrate the course in Pathological Histology.

3. Throughout the Session autopsies are held at the three Hospitals which students are required to attend and take full notes. On the autopsies they have witnessed they are subsequently examined.

4. Once a week during the Easter Term a Clinical conference on autopsy material is held at the General Hospital.

Fifth Year.

1. The routine work for all students of the Fifth Year will consist of attendance and assistance at autopsies. Upon such cases as the students have studied in the wards full bacteriological and histological studies will be required.

2. A weekly conference in autopsy material will be held for the whole class.

3. Advanced classes will be held for students who have Honour standing, and for such other students whose work is of such a character as to permit them to do elective work.

An advanced laboratory class in surgical pathology may be arranged for similar students who can fulfil the same conditions.

Text-books:—

Pathology:—Adami, Pathology (General), vol. I.; (Special), vol. II.; Adami & McCrae, Text-book of Pathology; Delafield & Prudden, 11th ed.; MacCallum, A Text-book of Pathology; Mallory, Text-book of Pathological Histology; Pembrey & Ritchie, General Pathology.

Bacteriology:—Hiss and Zinsser; Muir and Ritchie; Park.

PATHOLOGICAL CHEMISTRY.

Professor of Pathological Chemistry: V. J. HARDING.
Lecturer in Pathological Chemistry:
Demonstrators of Pathological Chemistry: D. H. BODDINGTON, P. E. FAED.
Fellow: O. GAEBLER.

Third Year.

Practical Work.—Students receive practical instruction in the chemical methods employed in the examination of excreta, secretions, organs and body fluids, with special reference to the study and diagnosis of disease.

As occasion requires, the laboratory exercises are coordinated and supplemented by demonstrations and lectures.

The student will not be permitted to proceed to the University examination unless he has satisfactorily performed all the work of the class, and has paid for any apparatus he may have lost, damaged, or destroyed.

Fourth Year.

Lectures.—A course of lectures, extending throughout the year, is given on general disorders of the chemical processes of the body.

Clinical Laboratory.—To each student of the Fourth and Fifth years there is assigned, in the Department of Pathological Chemistry, a locker with apparatus and reagents, which he is expected to utilize in the conduct of all chemical examinations necessary to the proper study of the cases under his charge. Each Fourth Year student shall carry out in the laboratory at least six complete urine analyses, corresponding to the complete medical records demanded by the Clinician in charge of the Clinic of which he is a member. Such analyses shall be recorded both in the department of Pathological Chemistry and the department of Medicine. For the guidance of the student in such work an instructor is in regular attendance at a special hour each day. Occasional demonstrations will be given each trimester on the findings on ward cases representing different types of metabolic disturbance.

Fifth Year.

In addition to the routine clinical laboratory work, an advanced laboratory course is offered for students whose record is such as to permit them to do elective work. At the end of the Fifth year the student is required in surrendering his locker, to make good all loss of apparatus by breakage or otherwise. Until he has done so, he will not be permitted to sit for the final examinations.

Text-books:—Hawk, Practical Physiological Chemistry; Mathews, Physiological Chemistry; Wells, Chemical Pathology.

Reference Books:—Lusk, Science of Nutrition; Von Fürth (trans. Smith), Chemistry of Metabolism.

HYGIENE AND PREVENTIVE MEDICINE.

Professor: J. G. FITZGERALD.
Assistant Professor: R. D. DEFRIES.
Lecturer: D. T. FRASER.
Demonstrator in Industrial Hygiene: J. G. CUNNINGHAM.
Demonstrator in Sanitary Chemistry: H. M. LANCASTER.
Demonstrator in Hygiene: P. J. MOLONEY.

The Department of Hygiene and Preventive Medicine provides a course of lectures dealing with the problems of Preventive Medicine, Hygiene and Sanitation, for students in the Fourth Year in the Faculty of Medicine.

Lecture courses are provided also in Hygiene and Sanitation for students in the Faculties of Applied Science, Household Science and the Departments of Public Health Nursing and Social Service.

Laboratory and didactic courses of instruction are given to students in the Faculty of Applied Science who have elected the Sanitary and Highways option. In addition a series of lectures on Hygiene and Sanitation is delivered during the Winter Term to the Pupil Nurses of the Toronto Chapter of the Canadian Association of Nursing Education.

A course of instruction for graduates in Medicine leading to the Diploma in Public Health was instituted in 1904. Details of the curriculum leading to the Diploma in Public Health will be found on page 51.

Industrial Hygiene.

A course of instruction in Industrial Hygiene for graduates in Medicine is available for those wishing to undertake work in this Branch of Preventive Medicine.

Further details of the course may be obtained on application to the Head of the Department.

Facilities for Research in Preventive Medicine, Hygiene and Public Health (Immunity, Serology and Bacteriology) are provided in the Research Division of the Connaught Antitoxin Laboratories, for graduates in Medicine and other suitably qualified candidates desirous of prosecuting such studies.

Text-books:—Rosenau, Preventive Medicine and Hygiene; Park, Public Health and Hygiene; Overton & Denno, The Health Officer; Prescott & Winslow, Elements of Water Bacteriology; American Public Health Association, Standard Methods of Water Analysis; Egbert, Hygiene and Sanitation.

Reference Books:—Kolmer, Infection, Immunity and Specific Therapy; Ledingham & Arkwright, The Carrier Problem of Infectious Diseases; Whipple, Microscopy of Drinking Water; Chandler, Animal Parasites and Human Disease; Mock, Industrial Medicine and Surgery.

MEDICAL JURISPRUDENCE.
Professor: G. SILVERTHORN.
Fourth Year.

Lectures.—About eighteen lectures and class-room demonstrations will be given. These will be illustrated as required by lantern slides and by specimens from the Pathological Museum or from private collections.

The lecture course will embrace *inter alia* a discussion of:—Legal Criminal procedures and the relation of Medical men thereto. Medical evidence, documentary and oral, ordinary and expert. Personal identity of the living and of the dead. Thanatology: The reality of death; *post mortem* changes, autopsies and reports. Causes producing deaths by violence such as the various forms of asphyxia, heat, cold, electricity, etc. Wounds in their medico-legal relations. Blood stains and the examination of blood. Medico-legal aspects of the sexual functions, impotency, sterility and legitimacy. Pregnancy, abortion and infanticide. Rape and allied offences against chastity. Civil and criminal malpractice.

Text-books:—Glaister, Reese, Emerson, Draper; Buchanan's Text-book of Forensic Medicine and Toxicology.

Reference Text-books:—Taylor's Principles; Whitthaus and Becker; Peterson and Haines; Dixon Mann; Cattell's *Post Mortem Pathology*; Greene's Life Insurance; Atkinson's Law in Medical Practice; Cathell's The Physician Himself; Brother's Medical Jurisprudence; Wadsworth's Post Mortem Examinations.

RADIOLOGY.
Associate: G. E. RICHARDS.
Fourth Year.

A series of ten lectures will be given dealing with the principles underlying the use of X-rays and radium as therapeutic agents, and the practic application of these in the treatment of disease.

Fifth Year.

Twenty lectures and demonstrations are given. In this course the use of X-ray methods in the diagnosis of diseases of the Gastro-intestinal tract, the chest, and the skeletal system will be fully covered, and will be illustrated by plates and lantern slides. It is also proposed to make demonstrations to small groups in the use of the fluoroscope.

LECTURES IN DENTISTRY.

The Faculty have arranged for a course of lectures to be delivered during the Session, on the application of Dentistry to Medicine. The instruction will be given by a man properly qualified for the purpose and will be delivered to the students of the final year. The course will be obligatory.

THE MEDICAL BUILDING.

The Medical Building is situated between the University Library and the anatomical wing of the Biological Department.

It is three storeys in height in front, with an additional storey and sub-basement in the wings, which extend eastward. Two large lecture rooms are provided which flank the main building; the larger has accommodation for about three hundred and fifty students; the smaller for about two hundred students.

In the south wing, in what may be called the basement storey, are situated lavatories, recreation rooms and reading rooms for the students; in the same storey in the north wing is placed the Antitoxin laboratories.

The three main floors of the building are arranged upon what has been called the unit-system, a unit-room being thirty feet long by twenty-three feet deep, lighted on its long face by large windows.

These rooms may be united so as to form large laboratories or may be cut in two where it is necessary to have smaller rooms.

The south wing and the main portion of the building are occupied by the Department of Physiology and Biochemistry whilst the north wing accommodates the department of Hygiene.

On the ground floor in the main portion are situated in front the Secretary's office, a large faculty room, a lavatory, and a library.

In the north wing in this floor are placed a chart and preparation room behind the lecture theatre, and on the third floor units are occupied by the Department of Pharmacology.

As will be seen from the above description, a series of laboratories and lecture theatres is provided on the University grounds where the most ample facilities are afforded for both the practical and didactic instruction of students.

As heretofore, lectures and demonstrations will be given in the east wing of the Biological building in Biology and in the west wing in Anatomy; in the Chemical Laboratories in Chemistry and in the Physics building in Physics. It is impossible to provide more complete and efficient accommodation for the teaching of scientific medicine than that which exists in the University of Toronto to-day.

THE LIBRARY.

The University Library is contained in a building of its own, situated on the east side of the campus that lies to the south of the Main Building. All students who have paid a library fee to the Bursar of the University are entitled to the privileges of the Library. Besides Reading Rooms the building contains Departmental Studies, which may be used as study-rooms by honour students in the various branches in which the Professors hold seminary courses, and private studies, intended for members of the Faculty or advanced students engaged in research work.˙ The Library is opened at 8.45 every morning and remains open until 5.15 in the afternoon (6 p.m. during the second term). Books in ordinary use may not be taken out of the·building during·the daytime, but are lent for the night shortly before the hour of closing, to be returned the following morning before 10·o'clock. Books not in general demand may, on special application, be borrowed for a longer period. Failure to return a borrowed book at the proper time and other breaches of the regulations are punishable by fine or suspension from the privileges of the Library.

THE PATHOLOGICAL BUILDING.

This·building is situated on University Avenue and connected by a covered corridor with the Out-patient Department and so with the rest of the Toronto General Hospital. On the basement, or ground floor, are˙ the Pathological Museum, lecture room and autopsy room as well as students' coat room and lavatories. On the first floor are rooms for the Hospital Pathologist and the routine Hospital pathology and class rooms for pathological histology and bacteriology. On the second floor the Professor of Pathology and Lecturer in Bacteriology have their private laboratories, and there are rooms for the Departmental Library and special classes in Pathology, in addition to a set of laboratories for pathological chemistry for the use of students in the Fourth and Fifth Years. On the third floor are the class rooms for systematic instruction in pathological chemistry and the laboratories for the staff in this Department, including balance, polarimeter, combustion and experimental rooms. Above this in the roof is the accommodation for animals.

Connected with the autopsy room is a cold storage plant with accommodation for twelve cadavers, and by means of a brine circulation, refrigerators in the staff laboratories on the first, second and third floors are kept cold. For many of the laboratories too there is a compressed air service.

The lecture room has seats for about 150 students and is connected with˙ a room for preparing experimental demonstrations.

The museum is˙planned especially for the instruction of students: a small catalogue room and a preparation room are connected with it.

·The class rooms are divided into small units and are exceptionally ·well lighted.

Lockers are provided for more than 300 students in the laboratories for pathological chemistry so that every student working in the Hospital may have his own place and apparatus.

The building is of fire-proof construction throughout.

ROYAL ONTARIO MUSEUM.

Archaeology, Geology, Mineralogy, Palaeontology, Zoology.

Students of the University in all departments are recommended to avail themselves of the privileges of the Museum, which, although under separate control, is intimately connected with the work of the University.

The Museum is open on all week days from 10 a.m. to 5 p.m. Sundays 2 p.m. to 5 p.m. The admission is free to the public on Tuesday, Thursday, Saturday and Sunday. On other days an admission fee of fifteen cents is charged.

By a resolution of the Board of Trustees all regular students of the University may be admitted free on all days of the week by presenting their card of registration.

TORONTO GENERAL HOSPITAL.

The Hospital has more than seven hundred beds, and during the last year admitted to its wards 10,722 patients.

The Out-door Department, which has been elaborately equipped with especial attention to the requirements of teaching as well as treatment, is designed to receive and care for several hundred patients each day, if necessity demands. Last year 53,521 out-patients were treated.

The Hospital is for the treatment of acute medical and surgical diseases, and the members of the staff are, in nearly every instance, drawn from the University Medical Faculty.

The Hospital Block contains ten acres, and the group of buildings includes almost everything necessary to enable a student to acquire a practical knowledge of the profession of Medicine.

On the south-west corner is situated the large Pathological Building, which is also an integral part of the Hospital. In it are found the Pathological, Clinical and Chemico-Pathological Laboratories, as well as the Autopsy Room, Museums, etc. The Pathological Building is regarded as one of the most complete in America. There were 237 autopsies during the year.

North of the Pathological Unit is found the Out-Patients' Department already referred to; then follows the Emergency Hospital, fully equipped with every modern device necessary for the immediate care and treatment of emergency patients. In this building arrangements have been made for the teaching and demonstration of practical methods in minor surgery.

The Medical Wing, the Administrative Building and Surgical Wing face College Street. These groups embody every modern requirement in hospital equipment, and special facilities for the student are provided—such as lecture room, cloak room, etc.

Twelve Operating Rooms are to be found in the different Surgical sections. South of the Surgical Wing is located the Obstetrical Hospital with eighty beds. The number of births in this Department last year was 1,089.

The X-Ray Department is one of the most complete on the continent, and averages more than one hundred patients a day sent in for examination. Complete courses are given to the students, so that they can qualify themselves in X-ray work. A well equipped Hydro-Therapeutic Department exists in connection with the X-Ray Department.

HOSPITAL FOR SICK CHILDREN.

This large Hospital, with 250 beds, is entirely devoted to diseases in children, there having been 4,983 cases treated during the last year. In the Out-patient Department, 40,934 patients were attended. The old building has been remodelled and a large new wing has been built on the west side of the present building. These alterations and additions include new operating theatres, out-patient department, pathological laboratories and wards for infectious cases.

ST. MICHAEL'S HOSPITAL.

This institution is conducted as a General Hospital, where medical, surgical and obstetrical cases are admitted. The number of patients admitted last year was 5,283 while 28,562 cases were treated in the out-patient department. There were 434 births in the Obstetrical Department. The accommodation has been enlarged by the addition of a new wing, so that there are now 400 beds. An operating theatre has been provided constructed with all the necessary modern equipment for the practise of antiseptic surgery.

TORONTO WESTERN HOSPITAL.

This is a modern institution affording excellent opportunities for clinical study. During the past year 4,129 patients were admitted. There is an out-door service where dental, tubercular, surgical, medical, gynaecological and special clinics are held; the number of patients treated in the Out-patient Department last year was 7,378.

Two large operating theatres are provided and the operations performed last year numbered 2,622. There is also an Obstetrical Department.

There are four public wards specially adapted for clinical teaching each containing thirty beds; two of these wards are devoted to medical and two to surgical cases.

Resident Assistants in the Hospitals.

A number of resident assistants are appointed annually from the graduates in medicine of Universities, and hold their positions for one or two years.

They will have full opportunities for acquiring experience in the general and special wards of the Hospitals, and during the session they will have charge under the physicians and surgeons in the wards.

CONNAUGHT ANTITOXIN LABORATORIES.

Director: J. G. FITZGERALD.

Associate Director—R. D. DEFRIES.

Research Associate—A. H. CAULFEILD.

Research Chemist: P. J. MOLONEY.

Research Assistant: MISS L. HANNA.

The Connaught Antitoxin Laboratories, consisting of Research and Antitoxin Divisions, have a scope somewhat similar to that of the Lister Institute, London; The Pasteur Institute, Paris; and the Rockefeller Institute, New York, in the field of preventive Medicine, Bacteriology, Serology. and Immunity. . Primarily established for research in Preventive Medicine, these Laboratories are also engaged in the production and distribution of Public Health Biological Products. The distribution of diphtheria antitoxin was commenced in April, 1914, and since that date the production of other sera and vaccines has been undertaken and the distribution extended throughout Canada and Newfoundland, the British West Indies, and recently to New Zealand.

The products distributed include: diphtheria antitoxin, tetanus antitoxin, anti-meningitis serum, small-pox vaccine, anti-pneumococcus serum, typhoid vaccine and rabies vaccine.

Since February 1st, 1916, the Provincial Board of Health of Ontario has distributed, free of charge in Ontario, all of the above named products. The Secretaries of the Local Boards of Health need only make application to the Chief Officer of Health, Parliament Buildings, Toronto, and supplies are at once forwarded. Physicians and Hospitals are supplied by the Secretary of their Local Boards of Health.

Similarly in September, 1917, the Bureau of Public Health, Saskatchewan, began free distribution of diphtheria antitoxin in that Province. (The antitoxin so supplied is prepared by these Laboratories.)

The Department of Militia and Defence was supplied with tetanus antitoxin and other biological products used by the Canadian Expeditionary Force Overseas and in training in Canada.

In October, 1917, a farm of over fifty acres and completely equipped laboratories and stables were presented to the University by Colonel Albert Gooderham. These Laboratories were given to provide facilities for research in Preventive Medicine, especially along the lines of serum therapy, and also to provide for the production of serums and vaccines. In connection with these Laboratories there has been established the Connaught Laboratories Research Fund, the interest on which is to be utilized for the support of research work in Preventive Medicine.

GENERAL INFORMATION FOR STUDENTS.

PHYSICAL TRAINING.

By order of the Board of Governors each male student proceeding to a degree must take Physical Training in the First and Second Years of his attendance. He must first undergo a medical examination by the Physical Director of the University to determine the character of his training.

DISCIPLINE.

The Council of University College and the governing bodies of the federated universities and colleges, respectively, have disciplinary jurisdiction over and entire responsibility for the conduct of their students in respect of all matters arising or occurring in or upon their respective college buildings and grounds, including residences.

The councils of such of the faculties as have assigned for their separate use any building or buildings and grounds, including residences, have disciplinary jurisdiction over and entire responsibility for the conduct of all students in their respective faculties in respect of all matters arising or occurring in or upon such building or buildings and grounds.

In all such cases, and, save as aforesaid, as respects all students to whatsoever college or faculty they may belong, disciplinary jurisdiction is vested in the Caput, but the Caput may delegate its authority in any particular case or by any general regulation to the council or other governing body of the university or college or faculty to which the student belongs.

If there be any question as to the proper body to exercise jurisdiction in any matter of discipline which may arise, the same shall be determined by the Caput, whose decision shall be final.

Disciplinary jurisdiction includes the power to impose fines.

REGULATIONS RELATING TO STUDENTS.

1. No student will be registered in any year, or be allowed to continue in attendance, whose presence for any cause is deemed by the Faculty Council or Caput to be prejudicial to the interests of the University. Registration in any year does not entitle a student to registration in a subsequent year.

2. Students are required to attend the course of instruction and the examinations in all subjects prescribed for students of their respective standing, and no student will be permitted to remain in the University who persistently neglects academic work.

3. All interference on the part of any student with the personal liberty of another, by arresting him, or summoning him to appear before any tribunal of students, or otherwise subjecting him to any indignity or personal violence, is forbidden by the Council. Any student convicted of participation in such proceedings will render himself liable to expulsion from the University.

4. A student who is under suspension, or who has been expelled from a College or the University, will not be admitted to the University buildings or grounds.

. 5. The constitution of every University society or association of students and all amendments to any such constitution must be submitted for approval to the Caput. All programmes of such societies or associations must, before publication, receive the sanction of the Caput. Permission to invite any person not a member of the Faculty of the University to preside at or address a meeting of any society or association must be similarly obtained. Societies and associations are required to confine themselves to the objects laid down in their constitution.

6. The name of the University is not to be used in connection with a publication of any kind without permission of the Caput.

THE UNIVERSITY OF TORONTO MEDICAL SOCIETY.

This Society consists of the graduates and undergraduates enrolled in the Faculty of Medicine of the University of Toronto. It is under the patronage of the members of the Faculty of Medicine and its object is to deal with all matters pertaining to the general interest and welfare of the students, especially:—

(a) To encourage interest in general medical science and literature, and in pursuit of medical studies.

(b) To provide a supply of daily newspapers, periodicals, magazines and music for the reading rooms; also telephones for the convenience of students.

(c) To be a means of communication between the Student body and the Faculty or others, when such communication is desirable.

(d) To provide a series of entertainments for students at intervals during the Session.

(e) Each student will be required to pay the annual fee of two dollars to the Treasurer of the Society, to be divided as follows:—

Medical Society Fee	$1.00
Athletic Fee	.25
Class Fee	.75

FACULTY OF APPLIED SCIENCE
AND ENGINEERING.

MATRICULATION.

1. The matriculation requirements of this Faculty are based upon those given in the curriculum for Junior Matriculation, a copy of which may be obtained on application.

2. A candidate for matriculation must produce satisfactory certificates of good character.

3. The requirements for admission comprise two parts which are as follows:

Part I, Pass Matriculation standing in the following subjects: English, History, Mathematics and three of Greek, Latin, French, German, Spanish, Experimental Science. The candidate is recommended to choose French, German and Experimental Science as his optional subjects in Part I.

Part II, Honour Matriculation standing as follows: Honours (at least 50 per cent.) in Honour Mathematics, Pass standing (at least 40 per cent.) in Honour English, Pass standing (at least 40 per cent.) in one of the following Honour subjects—Greek, Latin, French, German, Spanish. The candidate is recommended to choose French as his option in Part II.

Notice is hereby given that it is the intention of the University to increase the requirements for admission for the Session 1922-23. The details of the changes will be announced as soon as possible.

4. The pass matriculation standard is forty per cent. of the marks, assigned to a paper, with an average of sixty per cent.

5. A candidate who has obtained an average of sixty per cent. on all the pass papers but has failed to obtain forty per cent. in not more than three papers may complete pass matriculation by passing on these papers at any one subsequent examination.

6. A candidate who has obtained forty per cent. on each of at least eight pass papers, with an average of sixty per cent. on the same, will be credited with these papers. In order to complete pass matriculation, he must obtain at one subsequent examination forty per cent. on each of the remaining papers, with an average of sixty per cent.

7. The examination for pass and honour Junior Matriculation is held annually in June at centres in Ontario, and, if application is made to the Senate, the examination may, with the co-operation of the Department of Education, be held at centres outside Ontario.

8. Applications for the June examinations must be sent not later than the 15th of May to the local Public School Inspector, or in the case of candidates intending to write at the University, to the Registrar.

9. A Supplemental Matriculation examination at which pass and honour papers will be set, will be held in September at the University and at such other centres as may from time to time be authorized. Candidates entitled to the privileges of supplemental examinations, as well as new candidates, may present themselves at this examination.

10. Applications to write on the September examination, together with the necessary fee, must be received at the Department of Education not later than September 1st, for those who wish to write at any centre established in Ontario, and not later than August 1st for any centre elsewhere in Canada.

11. Forms of application, the time-table of the September examination, and further particulars may be had upon application to the Department of Education.

ADMISSION.

A candidate for admission must have completed the seventeenth year of his age on or before the first of October of the year in which he seeks to enter.

Applications for admission must be made on blank forms supplied by the Registrar, and should be forwarded as early as possible to the Registrar of the University.

Applications will be considered from (a) those who have completed the pass and honour matriculation requirements, including those who hold certificates recognized as equivalent—see matriculation curriculum—, (b) those who have failed in not more than two papers of the pass matriculation examination. The latter must complete matriculation before being eligible to enter the second year.

Applications based upon other certificates than those mentioned will be considered as occasion may require. Such certificates must be accompanied by an official statement of the marks in the various subjects upon which the certificate was granted.

ADMISSION AD EUNDM STATUM.

An undergraduate of another University may be admitted *ad eundem statum* on such conditions as the Senate on the recommendation of the Council of the Faculty may prescribe.

An applicant for admission *ad eundem statum* must submit with his petition (1) a calendar of his University giving a full statement of the courses of instruction; (2) an official certificate of character and academic standing.

REGISTRATION.

Registration in the various years will begin Sept. 1st. Blank cards for the purpose will be supplied by the Secretary on request. (See "Dues and Deposits," next page.)

FEES.

All fees are payable at the Bursar's office between the hours 10 a.m. and 1 p.m. of each week day except Saturday.

The annual fees including tuition, library, laboratory supplies and one annual examination shall be as follows:

—29

First Year.

If paid in full on or before November 5th...................... $100.00
By instalments.
First instalment, if paid on or before November 5th............ 50.00
Second instalment, if paid on or before February 5th........... 55.00

Second Year.

If paid in full on or before November 5th...................... $110.00
By instalments:
First instalment, if paid on òr before November 5th............ 55.00
Second instalment, if paid on or before February 5th........... 60.00

Third and Fourth Years.

If paid in full on or before November 5th...................... $120.00
By instalments:
First instalment, if paid on or before November 5th........... 60.00
Second instalment, if paid on or before February 5th........... 65.00

Repeating the Year.

If paid in full on or before November 5th..................... $50.00

The above fees are payable in advance. After November 5th a penalty of $1.00 per month will be imposed until the whole amount is paid. In the case of payment by instalments the same rule as to penalty will apply.

Students desiring to pay in instalments must have paid the fees due in the first term before proceeding to the work of the second term.

General Fees.

Matriculation, or registration of Matriculation............... $5.00
Supplemental examination...................................... 10.00
Admission *ad eundem statum*.................................. 10.00
Hart House.. 11.00
Degree of B.A.Sc. (payable not later than April 1st)......... 10.00
Degree of M.A.Sc... 25.00

Dues and Deposits.

(Payable to the Secretary of the Faculty at the time of registration.)
Engineering Society membership............................... $2.00
Annual deposit, Departments 1, 3, 4, 7....................... 3.00
Departments 2, 6, 8.. 8.00

Charges for waste, neglect and breakage are to be met out of the deposit fee, the balance of which will be refunded to the student at the end of the session.

Hart House and the Students' Administrative Council.

The annual fee... $11.00

Every male student in attendance, proceeding to the degree of Bachelor of Applied Science, is required to pay to the Bursar at the time of the entry of his name with the Secretary the annual fee of eleven dollars for the maintenance of Hart House and the Students' Administrative Council.

Women Students' Administrative Council Fee.

Every woman student proceeding to the degree of Bachelor of Applied Science is required to pay to the Bursar at the time of the entry of her name with the Registrar the annual fee of three dollars for the maintenance of the Women Students' Administrative Council.

GENERAL INFORMATION FOR STUDENTS

The Council of University College and the governing bodies of the federated universities and colleges, respectively, have disciplinary jurisdiction over and entire responsibility for the conduct of their students in respect of all matters arising or occurring in or upon their respective college buildings and grounds, including residences.

The councils of such of the faculties as have assigned for their separate use any building or buildings and grounds, including residences; have disciplinary jurisdiction over and entire responsibility for the conduct of all students in their respective faculties in respect of all matters arising or occurring in or upon such building, or buildings and grounds.

In all such cases, and, save as aforesaid, as respects all students to whatsoever college or faculty they may belong, disciplinary jurisdiction is vested in the Caput, but the Caput may delegate its authority in any particular case or by any general regulation to the council or other governing body of the university or college or faculty to which the student belongs.

The Caput has also power and authority to determine by general regulations, or otherwise, to what college, faculty or other body the control of university associations belongs.

If there be any questions as to the proper body to exercise jurisdiction in any matter of discipline which may arise, the same shall be determined by the Caput, whose decision shall be final.

Disciplinary jurisdiction includes the power to impose fines.

HART HOUSE.

Hart House, the gift of the Massey Foundation, is the Undergraduates' Union of the University of Toronto.

Hart House contains completely equipped club rooms, including common rooms, reading room, music room, lecture room, sketch room, photographic dark rooms, the Great Hall, used as a dining hall, a small chapel, the offices and class rooms of the Students Christian Association, gymnasia and swimming pool, rifle range, billiard room and the Hart House theatre.

All male students proceeding to a degree in the University are members of Hart House. An annual fee imposed by the University, covers the fee of the Students' Administrative Council, all club fees in connection with Hart House, and membership in the Athletic Association, ncluding the medical examination.

Other male students in the University, or students in the affiliated or federated institutions receiving instruction in the University, may become members of Hart House on payment of the required fee.

Graduates are entitled to the full privileges of Hart House on payment of an annual fee of $10,00. Out-of-town graduates may become members on payment of an annual fee of $2.50.

A group of rooms is set apart for the use of the Faculty Union. There is also a common room for the use of graduates. Five guest rooms are available for the use of guests, for periods of a week or less, at a reasonable rental.

The Theatre is under the management of the Players' Club of the University of Toronto, and is available for productions by any of the Dramatic Clubs within the University.

For further information, apply to the Warden of Hart House.

REGULATIONS RESPECTING STUDENTS.

No student will be enrolled in any year, or be allowed to continue in attendance, whose presence for any cause is deemed by the Council to be prejudicial to the interests of the University.

All interference on the part of any student with the personal liberty of another, by arresting him, or summoning him to appear before any unauthorized tribunal of students, or otherwise subjecting him to any indignity or personal violence, is forbidden by the Council. In particular, students of all Faculties are warned agianst the practices known as the "hustling" of freshmen and against inter-year or inter-faculty "hustles". Any student convicted of participation in such proceedings will render himself liable to expulsion from the University.

All students shall be in attendance during the whole of each term. Those whose attendance of work is reported as unsatisfactory are liable to dismissal by the Council.

No student will be allowed to repeat the work of any year more than once.

Information as to the text-books, instruments and materials to be purchased by the students will be given on registration at the beginning of the session.

STUDENTS' ADMINISTRATIVE COUNCIL.

The Students' Administrative Council has been entrusted by the Caput with supervision of the conduct of the students, and has disciplinary powers to deal with violations of the regulations governing conduct.

Any student who may be convicted of having taken part in a parade or procession through the city which has not been authorized by the police authorities after application by the Executive of the Students' Administrative Council, will be severely disciplined.

WOMEN STUDENTS' ADMINISTRATIVE COUNCIL.

The Women Students' Administrative Council is the representative organ of the women students of the University of Toronto, and aims to co-ordinate all intercollegiate activities. It consists of representatives from all colleges and faculties. A fee of $3 is paid for the council by each woman student proceeding to the Bachelor's degree. The council assumes joint financial responsibility with the men's council for the publication of *Varsity, Toronto-nensis*, and the *Directory*.

PHYSICAL TRAINING.

By order of the Board of Governors each male student proceeding to a degree must take Physical Training in the first and second years of his attendance. He must first undergo a medical examination by the Physical Director of the University to determine the character of his training.

OPTIONS.

In the fourth year, optional courses are arranged in certain departments. Students are required to submit their selection to the Secretary in writing, not later than September 15th. The proposed selection must be approved by Council before adoption.

REGULATIONS RESPECTING EXAMINATIONS.

Regular Examinations.

Promotions from one year to another are made on the results of the annual examinations. Students proceeding to a degree must pass all the examinations in the subjects of his or her course and at the periods arranged from time to time by the Council.

Candidates who fail in passing the annual examinations will be required to take again the whole course of instruction, both theoretical and practical, of the year in which they fail before presenting themselves a second time for examination.

A student who in either term of the session fails to perform the work of his course in a manner satisfactory to the professors in charge, will not be allowed to present himself at the final examinations of the year.

In the second, third and fourth years annual examinations will be held at the beginning of the second term on all subjects completed during the first term.

No student will be allowed to write at the annual examinations who has not paid all fees and dues for which he is liable.

The minimum percentage of marks required to pass in the written examination will be fixed from time to time by the Council.

The minimum percentage of marks required to pass in the practical work connected with any subject shall be one and one-half times the minimum required in the case of a written examination.

In order to pass the practical examinations in the subjects of applied mechanics, descriptive geometry, electrical design, optics, surveying and architecture, the drawings set in these subjects must be made.

Term Examinations.

Term examinations may be held in any subject and at any time at the discretion of the instructor or by order of the Council, and the results of such examination may, if the Council so decides, be incorporated with those of the annual examinations in the same subjects.

Supplemental Examinations.

A candidate who fails in one or two subjects at the Annual Examinations will be required to take supplemental examinations in such subjects.

The supplemental written examinations will begin on the 23rd of September, 1921. Candidates are required to send to the Secretary of the Faculty not later than the 15th of September, notice in writing of their intention to take such examinations, and to remit to the Bursar the fee of $10.00. A penalty of $1.00 will be imposed upon all candidates who fail to give notice within the time stated.

In the case where a candidate fails to pass a supplemental examination it will count as one of the two supplemental examinations which may be allowed him after the next annual examination.

Vacation Work.

Vacation work must be handed in on or before the first day of the session.

Vacation notes must be on construction only, except in Department 2 (see p. 72), and contain not less than twenty, nor more than thirty pages of sketches. These sketches must be freehand pencil drawings with figured dimensions.

Notes must be made in standard note books approved of by the Faculty. Notes which have been taken during the session in connection with the work in drawing will not count as vacation work.

The minimum percentage of marks required for practical work must be made in the case of vacation notes.

Shop Work.

Students in Mechanical and in Electrical Engineering are not considered as having completed their course of study, nor are degrees granted until certificates have been submitted to the Council, and accepted as satisfactory, showing not less than eight months of mechanical experience in production of some kind under commercial conditions. Preferably the work undertaken should be in one of the manufacturing industries or trades with which the Course is related.

It is not desirable that any student in these Courses should enter sales or other non-production departments of the engineering industries without having acquired some personal experience in mechanical production. It is best to obtain this experience under commercial conditions. Otherwise one can not at all appreciate shop conditions and limitations.

Honours.

Honours will be granted in each department to the students who obtain at least 40 per cent. in each subject, and 66 per cent. of the total number of marks allotted to the department at the annual examinations.

Honour Graduate standing will be granted to those who obtain honours in the final and in one previous year.

REGULATIONS RESPECTING TERM WORK.

Students working in any laboratory must be governed by the regulations relating thereto as made known from time to time.

No laboratory reports or drawings may be removed from the laboratories without permission. The Council reserves the right to dispose of them as may be thought proper.

Field Work.

Field Work in Surveying of the First and Second Years will be taken on the University grounds, during the session.

The Field Work of the Third Year, for the session 1921-1922, will be taken previous to the session, during the months of August and September, 1921, on a tract of land lately purchased by the University, situated on the shore of Gull Lake, and about five miles from the Village of Minden, and being Lot No. 9 in 13th Concession of the Township of Lutterworth. The camp may be reached by taking the train leaving Lindsay for Haliburton, and getting off at Gelert.

Students of the Third Year, Department 1, are expected to reach Gelert in the afternoon of August 20th, and those of Department 2, on September 3rd, when conveyances will meet them to take them to the camp. Personal effects must be limited to sixty pounds in weight, which must include two pairs of blankets, or their equivalent; beds and mattresses only will be provided.

No field notes will be counted which have not been taken in the field and during the hours allotted to such work.

Students taking practical astronomy are required to take observations in the field for time, latitude, and azimuth.

Drafting Rooms.

Drawings and briefs for same, that are required to be finished the first term of the session will not be counted unless finished in that term.

The minimum number of drawings in first and second years shall be twenty-five, and the maximum number thirty-five.

No drawings or briefs for same will be counted which have not been made in the drafting rooms, and during the hours allotted to such work.

Theses.

In the Fourth Year each student is required to prepare a thesis on a subject approved by the Council. The title of the thesis must be sent to the Secretary of the Faculty for approval on or before November 1st, and the completed thesis must be handed in not later than the first day of the sccond term and shall become the property of the University. The rules governing size, form, etc., may be obtained on application to the Secretary.

EXEMPTIONS.

Applications for exemption from any of the regulations must be made to the Council in writing and the particulars of the case fully stated.

COURSES OF INSTRUCTION.

On the following pages the courses of instruction in the various departments are set forth in detail. The time devoted to the various subjects, both for lectures and practical work, is indicated as accurately as possible but is subject to modifications from time to time as occasion seems to require. In the First Year the course is common to all departments except Architecture and Chemical Engineering (courses 2 and 6). In the Second Year the courses in Mechanical and Electrical Engineering (courses 3 and 7) are identical.

1. DEPARTMENT OF CIVIL ENGINEERING.

The courses of study in Civil Engineering are designed to give the student a sound training in the fundamental scientific principles on which the practice of the profession is based. The instruction is given by means of lectures and practical work in the field, the drafting room and the laboratory. In this way the student is led to apply the principles developed in the class room.

First Year.

The same also for Mining, Mechanical, Electrical and Metallurgical Engineering.

Subject	No.	First Term Lect.	First Term Lab'y.	Second Term Lect.	Second Term Lab'y.
Algebra.................	187	2		2	
Plane Trigonometry........	189	2			
Analytical Geometry.......	188	1		2	
Descriptive Geometry......	115	1		1	
Surveying................	205, 206	1	5	1	
Statics...................	10	2		2	
Dynamics................	11	2		2	
Elementary Chemistry......	75	2		2	
Electricity................	135	2		2	
Engineering Problems......	193	1		1	
Drawing..................	117		11		20

Second Year.

Subject	No.	First Term Lect.	First Term Lab'y.	Second Term Lect.	Second Term Lab'y.
Vacation Work.............	220				
Calculus..................	190	2		2	
Spherical Trigonometry.....	191	1			
Elementary Astronomy.....	55	1		1	
Descriptive Geometry......	121	1		1	
Surveying................	207, 208	1	9	1	
Dynamics................	12	1		1	
Mechanics of Materials	13	2		2	
Optics....................	197	1	$1\frac{1}{2}$	1	$1\frac{1}{2}$
Hydrostatics..............	196			1	1
Engineering Chemistry......	85			1	
Organic Chemistry.........	87	1			
Mineralogy................	159, 161	2	1		2
Metallurgy................	183			1	
Finance..................	66	1		1	
Drawing..................	123		6		12
Chemical Laboratory	81		3		3

Civil Engineering—Third Year.

Subject	No.	First Term Lect.	First Term Lab'y.	Second Term Lect.	Second Term Lab'y
Least Squares.............	192		-	1	
Practical Astronomy and Geodesy.................	56, 57	2		2	
Surveying and Levelling.....	209, 210	1		1	
Descriptive Geometry......	127	1			
Hydraulics................	29, 30	2		2	3
Photography..............	199	1	1½		1½
Stress Graphics...........	19a	1		1	
Theory of Structures.......	18	2		2	
Cements and Concrete......	21			1	
Engineering Chemistry......	94	1		1	
Geology..................	150	1		1	
Commercial Law..........	67	1		1	
Heat....................	198	1	1½		
Mechanics of Materials.....	14		3		
Drawing.................	128		8		18

Fourth Year.

Subject	No.	First Term Lect.	First Term Lab'y.	Second Term Lect.	Second Term Lab'y
†Foundations..............	20	1	1	1	1
†Thermodynamics..........	34, 39a	1		1	2
Economic Geology........	151	1		1	
Contracts and Specifications	68			1	
Thesis...................	219				
And one of					
(a) Astronomy........	58, 59	2	23	2	
Geodesy..........	60	2		2	23
(b) Sanitary Engineering	213	1½	16	1½	16
Highway Engineering...	214	1	6	1	6
(c) Structural Engineering	215	6		7	
Mechanics of Materials Laboratory.......			3		6
Structural Design Drawing........	133		17		16
(d) Mechanics of Materials	16, 17, 22, 23	3½		3½	

Fourth Year (Continued).

Subject	No.	Hours per week			
		First Term		Second Term	
		Lect.	Lab'y.	Lect.	Lab'y.
Mechanics of Materials Laboratory...........			5		6
Structural Design Drawing...........	133a		6		5
with either:					
(1) Hydraulics...........	31, 31a, 32	3	10	3	10
or					
(2) Railway Engineering..	211, 212	2	11	2	11

† Not required of those taking the Astronomy option.

2. DEPARTMENT OF MINING ENGINEERING.

The course in Mining Engineering is intended to serve as a preliminary training for those who expect to practise the art of mining or metallurgy. In the second year it differs very little from the course in civil engineering, in the third year some subjects peculiar to mining and metallurgy are taken up.

In general this course is designed to first give the student a good training in the parts of engineering essential to all branches, such as surveying, drafting, etc., and then in the upper years to allow him to follow studies peculiar to mining engineering.

Candidates for the degree in this department will be required to present satisfactory evidence of having had at least six months' practical experience in work connected with mining, metallurgy or geology, for which they must have received regular wages. Certificate forms, giving full details as to acceptable classes of work, will be furnished on application, and should be obtained by all students before entering employment.

First Year.—*See page 457.*

Second Year.

Subject	No.	Hours per week			
		First Term		Second Term	
		Lect.	Lab'y.	Lect.	Lab'y.
Vacation Work...........	220				
Calculus..................	190	2		2	
Descriptive Geometry......	121	1		1	
Surveying................	207, 208	1	9	1	
Dynamics................	12	1		1	
Mechanics of Materials.....	13	2		2	
Optics.,..................	197	1	1½	1	1.
Hydrostatics..............	194			1	1
Inorganic Chemistry.......	79	1			
Organic Chemistry.........	87	1			
Engineering Chemistry......	85			1	
Mineralogy...............	157, 160	2	1		c
Geology..................	150	1		1	
Mining...................	170, 171	1	3		
Metallurgy...............	183			1	
Finance..................	66			1	
Drawing..................	123		3		12
Chemical Laboratory.......	81, 82		6		6

Mining Engineering—Third Year.

Subject	No.	First Term Lect.	First Term Lab'y.	Second Term Lect.	Second Term Lab'y.
Surveying and Levelling....	209, 210	1			
Theory of Structures.......	19	2			
Engineering Chemistry......	94	1		1	
Analytical Chemistry.......	80	1		1	3
Assaying..................	173	1	3		
Petrography..............	163	1		1	
Mineralogical Laboratory...	164		2		2
Economic Geology........	151, 156	1		2	2
Ore Deposits.............	155	1		1	
Mining...................	172			2	3
Hydraulics...............	29	2		2	
Ore Dressing.............	177	1		1	
Ferro-Metallurgy..........	181	1		1	
Metallurgy...............	184	1		1	
Commercial Law..........	67	1		1	
Drawing.................	129		7		2
Chemical Laboratory......	93				11
Analytical Chemistry.......	91				9

Fourth Year.

Subject	No.	First Term Lect.	First Term Lab'y.	Second Term Lect.	Second Term Lab'y.
Thermodynamics..........	34	1		1	
Electrochemistry..........	101	2			
Assaying.................	174			1	3
Petrography..............	165, 166	1	2	1	2
Geology, Archaean and Glacial..................	152, 154	2	1	2	
Geology, Mining..........	153	1		1	
Mining...................	175	1		1	
Ore Dressing.............	179	1		1	
Metallurgy...............	180, 182	1		1	
Mine and Plant Management	70	1		1	5
Milling..................	176				3
Power...................	32a, 39a, 141		3		2
Design...................	215		3		3
Chemical Laboratory......	112		10		
Thesis...................	219		4		2

3. DEPARTMENT OF MECHANICAL ENGINEERING.

The course in this Department is designed to meet the needs of those students who are intending to take up the work connected with Mechanical Engineering, such as the design of gas engines, steam engines, steam boilers, steam turbines, air compressors, etc.; the design and installation of the machinery connected with power plants and central stations, steam piping and other similar problems. The work is also so arranged that the student becomes somewhat familiar with the design of travelling cranes and mill buildings and similar problems connected with structural steel work.

Since the work of the mechanical engineer and of the electrical engineer is closely allied, the courses in these two departments in the first two years are identical and cover the subjects mentioned below.

In the third year the work becomes more specialized, the mechanical engineers paying more attention to heat engines of various types, and to mill building design and other work of similar nature. The study of electricity is continued and the student gets considerable practice in the mechanical and electrical laboratories.

In the fourth year the student devotes himself still more closely to his chosen work, placing the greater stress on thermodynamics and the theory and testing of heat engines, and problems in machine design. Much time is spent in the mechanical laboratories testing gas and steam engines and other machines.

Before receiving the degree in this department candidates are required to present satisfactory evidence of having had at least eight months' practical experience in one of the principal trades connected with Mechanical Engineering, the object being that graduates may have some practical knowledge of the duties of the workman in this branch of engineering, as distinguished from those of the purely technical man. Certificate forms will be furnished on application. These forms contain full details in regard to the work required and should be obtained by the candidate before he enters his employment.

Mechanical Engineering—First Year.—*See page 457.*

Second Year.

Subject	No.	First Term		Second Term	
		Lect.	Lab'y.	Lect.	Lab'y.
Vacation Work............	220				
Calculus.................	190	2		2	
Descriptive Geometry......	121	1		1	
Dynamics.................	12	1		1	
Theory of Mechanism......	25	2		2	
Steam Engines............	38			1	
Mechanics of Materials.....	13	2		2	
Optics...................	197	1	1½	1	1½
Hydrostatics..............	196			1	1
Electricity.................	138, 139	2	3	2	3
Engineering Chemistry......	85			1	
Organic Chemistry.........	87	1			
Finance...................	66	1		1	
Drawing..................	124		14		10
Chemical Laboratory.......	81		3		3
Machine Tools............	28*a*			1	

Third Year.

Subject	No.	First Term		Second Term	
Mechanics of Machinery....	26	1		1	
Machine Design...........	27	2	7	2	7
Thermodynamics...........	33, 35	2	2	2	2
Heat Engines..............	39	1		1	
Hydraulics................	29, 30	2		2	1
Theory of Structures........	19	2			
Stress Graphics.............	19*a*	1		1	
Magnetism and Electricity..	144, 142	2	4½	2	4½
Alternating Current........	143	1		1	
Engineering Chemistry.....	96	1		1	
Commercial Law..........	67	1		1	
Mechanics of Materials.....	14		2		
Drawing..................	132		8		2

Mechanical Engineering.—Fourth Year.

Subject	No.	Hours per week			
		First Term		Second Term	
		Lect.	Lab'y.	Lect.	Lab'y.
Structural and Mill Building Design.................	24, 24a, 134	2	3		3
Shop Management and Costs	69	1		1	3
Machine Design............	28	1	4	1	
Thesis...................	219			1	6
And two of					
(d) Mechanics of Materials	16, 17, 22, 23	3½		3	
(e) Hydraulics..........	31, 31a, 32	3	10		10
Mechanics of Materials Laboratory........			6	3½	
Structural Design Drawing..........	134a		4		3
(g) Thermodynamics......	36, 36a, 37	3	10	3	6
					10

4. DEPARTMENT OF ARCHITECTURE.

The instruction in this department is arranged to lay a broad foundation for the subsequent professional life of its graduates, and incidentally to prepare its students to be immediately useful in an architect's office. The curriculum has been arranged to meet the aesthetic and scientific needs of the profession, and includes History and Principles of Architecture, Free-hand Drawing in pencil, ink and colour, Modelling, Architectural Design, Analysis and Criticism of Buildings, Mathematics, Statics, Strength and Elasticity of Materials, Theory of Construction and Heating and Ventilation.

The equipment of the department includes a working library, a large file of periodicals, photographs, lantern slides, and a large collection of models and casts.

SUBJECTS OF INSTRUCTION.

First Year.

Subject	No.	Hours per week			
		First Term		Second Term	
		Lect.	Lab'y.	Lect.	Lab'y.
Analytical Geometry........	188	1		2	
Descriptive Geometry......	116	1		1	
Building Measurement......	52	1	9	1	
Statics...................	10	2		2	
Elementary Chemistry......	75	2		2	
Elements of Architecture....	45	1		1	
History and Principles of Architecture.............	40	1	3	1	
French....................	217	2		2	
Drawing..................	118		9		18
Freehand Drawing........	49		3		2
Modelling................	50		2		2

Second Year.

Subject	No.	First Term		Second Term	
		Lect.	Lab'y.	Lect.	Lab'y.
Vacation Work	220				
Calculus	190	1		2	
Descriptive Geometry	122	1		1	
Mechanics of Materials	13	2		2	
Illumination	200	1	1½	1	1½
Architectural Design	46	1		1	
History of Architecture	41	1		1	
History of Ornament	43	1		1	
French	217	1		1	
Finance	66			1	
Drawing Architectural Design }	125		17		17
Freehand Drawing	49a		3		3
Modelling	50a		2		2

Third Year.

Subject	No.	First Term		Second Term	
Descriptive Geometry	131	1			
Acoustics	195	1	1½	1	
History of Architecture	42	1		1	
History of Painting and Sculpture	44	1		1	
Architectural Design	47	1		1	
Building Materials	53	2		2	
Theory of Structures	19	2			
Cements and Concrete	21			1	
Commercial Law	67	1		1	
Mechanics of Materials	14				2
Photography	199	1	1½		1½
Modelling	50b		2		2
Water Colour Painting	49b		3		3
Drawing	130		7		
Architectural Design }			6		22

Fourth Year.

Subject	No.	Hours per week			
		First Term		Second Term	
		Lect.	Lab'y.	Lect.	Lab'y.
Mechanics of Materials......	22	1		1	6
Structural Design..........	26	1	1	1	1
Heating and Ventilating....	54*a*	1		1	
Sanitary Science...........	54	1		1	
Contracts and Specifications	68			1	
Thesis....................	219		3		3
Drawing from life..........	49*c*		3		3
Modelling from life.........	50*c*		2		2
And one of					
(*l*) Architectural Design..	48	2	17	2	17
(*m*) Architectural Engineering...........	216	4	19	3	23

6. DEPARTMENT OF CHEMICAL ENGINEERING.

In many industries there is a demand for a man who combines the technical knowledge of the mechanical engineer with a knowledge of chemistry. It is to fill this want that the course in Chemical Engineering is designed.

First Year.

Subject	No.	First Term Lect.	First Term Lab'y.	Second Term Lect.	Second Term Lab'y.
Algebra...................	187	2		2	
Plane Trigonometry........	189	2			
Analytical Geometry.......	188	1		2	
Descriptive Geometry......	115	1		1	
Statics...................	10	2		2	
Dynamics.................	11	2		2	
Elementary Chemistry......	75	2		2	
Mineralogy Laboratory.....	158				3
Electricity................	135	2		2	
Biological Laboratory.......	62		3		3
Engineering Problems......	193	1		1	
Drawing..................	119		4		4
Chemical Laboratory.......	78		10		10
German..................	218	1		1	

Second Year.

Subject	No.	First Term Lect.	First Term Lab'y.	Second Term Lect.	Second Term Lab'y.
Vacation Work............	220				
Calculus..................	190	2		2	
Strength of Materials.......	13	2		2	
Electricity................	138, 139	2	3	2	3
Engineering Chemistry.....	85			1	
Industrial Chemistry.......	86	1		1	
Organic Chemistry.........	88	2		2	
Organic Chemistry.........	89		7		
Physical Chemistry.........	90	2		2	
Inorganic Chemistry........	79	1			
Optics...................	197	1	1½	1	1½
Hydrostatics..............	196			1	1
German..................	218	1		1	
Finance..................	66	1		1	
Drawing.................	126		7		3
Chemical Laboratory.......	84		12		10
Metallurgy...............	183			1	
Machine Tools............	28a			1	

Third Year.

Subject	No.	Hours per week			
		First Term		Second Term	
		Lect.	Lab'y.	Lect.	Lab'y.
Theory of Structures.......	19	2			
Thermodynamics...........	33, 39a	2	2	2	
Electrochemistry...........	101, 102	2	3		
Engineering Chemistry......	96	1		1	
Organic Chemistry.........	97	2		2	
Industrial Chemistry........	95	1		1	
Analytical Chemistry.......	80	1		1	
Metallurgy................	186	1		1	
Ferro-Metallurgy..........	181	1		1	
Chemical Plant............	96	1		1	
Hydraulics................	29, 30	2		2	1
Commercial Law...........	67	1		1	
German...................	218	1		1	
Assaying..................	173				3
Drawing..................	132		3		3
Chemical Laboratory.......	92		8		11

Fourth Year.

Subject	No.	Lect.	Lab'y.	Lect.	Lab'y.
Machine Design............	27	2	4½		
Inorganic Chemistry........	103	1	3	2	
Organic Chemistry.........	106	1	13	1	
Shop Management and Costs	69	1		1	
Power.....................	141		2		2
German...................	218	1		1	
Thesis....................	219				
And one of					
(h) Electrochemistry......	108	2	9	2	24
(i) Industrial Chemistry..	106, 107	1	10	1	25
(j) Sanitary and Forensic Chemistry and Bacteriology...........	64, 110, 112	1	10	2	24
(k) Metallurgy..........	180	1	10	1	25

7. DEPARTMENT OF ELECTRICAL ENGINEERING.

The course in Electrical Engineering is arranged to provide preliminary training for those who would follow any of the various lines of activity connected with electrical industry.

The first two years of the course are devoted to fundamental scientific principles, and incidentally more or less of their application to engineering problems in mechanical, civil and electrical work. Many problems are solved in the drafting rooms by graphical methods. The third year includes further theoretical work, more particular attention being given to electrical and mechanical studies in theory, operation and design. The fourth year is devoted to advanced work in alternating current theory and practice combined with similar study in thermodynamics, hydraulics or electrochemistry.

A large amount of laboratory practice is provided, most of which belongs to the third and fourth years. In this last year most of the time is spent in laboratory investigations and studies resulting therefrom.

Candidates for the degree in this department will be required to present satisfactory evidence of having had at least eight months' experience in one of the principal trades connected with Electrical Engineering, the object being that graduates may have some practical knowledge of the technique of this branch of engineering. Certificate forms will be furnished on application. These forms contain full details in regard to the work required.

First Year.—*See page 457.*

Electrical Engineering.—Second Year.

Subject	No.	First Term		Second Term	
		Lect.	Lab'y.	Lect.	Lab'y.
Vacation Work.............	220				
Calculus.................	190	2		2	
Descriptive Geometry.......	121	1		1	
Optics....................	197	1	1½	1	1½
Hydrostatics..............	196			1	1
Dynamics.................	12	1		1	
Mechanics of Materials.....	13	2		2	
Theory of Mechanism.......	25	2		2	
Steam Engines.............	38			1	
Electricity................	138, 139	2	3	2	3
Engineering Chemistry......	85			1	
Organic Chemistry.........	87	1			
Finance..................	66	1		1	
Drawing..................	124		12	.	12
Chemical Laboratory.......	81		3		3
Machine Tools............	28a				1

Third Year.

Mechanics of Machinery....	26	1		1	
Machine Design...........	27	2	4½	2	4½
Hydraulics.......	29, 30	2		2	1
Thermodynamics..........	33, 35	2	2	2	1½
Heat Engines..............	39	1		1	
Electrochemistry..........	101, 102	2	3		
Magnetism and Electricity..	142	2		2	
Alternating Current........	143	1		1	
Electrical Design..........	145	1	3	1	3
Electrical Laboratory.......	144		6		6
Engineering Chemistry......	94	1		1	
Commercial Law..........	67	1		1	

Fourth Year.

Applied Electriciry.........	146, 147	3	20	3	20
Shop Management and Costs	69	1		1	
Thesis...................	219				
And one of:					
(e) Hydraulics...........	31, 31a, 32	3	10	3	10
(g) Thermodynamics......	36, 36a, 37	3	9	3	9
(h) Electrochemistry......	108, 109	2	9	2	9

8. DEPARTMENT OF METALLURGICAL ENGINEERING.

The object of this course is to provide instruction and preliminary training for those who intend to become metallurgical engineers. Candidates for the degree in this department will be required to present satisfactory evidence of having had at least eight months' experience in metallurgical work.

First Year.—*See page 457.*

Second Year.

Subject	No.	Hours per week			
		First Term		Second Term	
		Lect.	Lab'y.	Lect.	Lab'y.
Calculus.................	190	2		2	
Descriptive Geometry......	121	1		1	
Dynamics...............	12	1		1	
Mechanics of Materials.....	13	2		2	
Hydrostatics..............	196			1	1½
Steam Engines...........	38			1	
Inorganic Chemistry........	79	1			
Physical Chemistry.........	90	2		2	
Finance..................	66	1		1	
Chemical Laboratory.......	83		14		9
Mineralogy...............	169		1		1
Mining..................	170, 171	1	3	1	
Metallurgy...............	183, 185	1		2	
Spanish..................	218a	1		1	
Drawing.................	126		7		3
Engineering Chemistry......	85			1	

Metallurgical Engineering.—Third Year.

Subject	No.	Hours per week			
		First Term		Second Term	
		Lect.	Lab'y.	Lect.	Lab'y.
Theory of Mechanism......	25	2		2	
Theory of Structures.......	19	2			
Commercial Law..........	67	1		1	
Analytical Chemistry.......	80	1		1	
Electrochemistry..........	101, 102	2	3		
Ferro-Metallurgy...........	181	1		1	
Cement and Concrete.......	21			1	
Assaying..................	173	1	3		3
Metallurgy................	186		2		6
Mining...................	172			2	3
Ore Dressing..............	177	1		1	
Heat.....................	198	1	1½		
Chemical Laboratory.......	93		5		10
Drawing..................	132		3		

Fourth Year.

Subject	No.	First Term Lect.	Lab'y.	Second Term Lect.	Lab'y.
Thermodynamics..........	34	1		1	
Heat Engines.............	39	1		1	
Ore Dressing.............		2	2	2	4
Assaying.................	174			1	3
Mine and Plant Management	70	1		1	
Plant Design.............	186b	2		2	
Power...................	39a, 141		2		2
Metallurgy...............	186a	2	8	2	8
Thesis...................	219		6		6

OUTLINE OF COURSES OF INSTRUCTION.

APPLIED MECHANICS.

10. STATICS:—*T. R. Loudon.*

Departments 1, 2, 3, 4, 6, 7 and 8, I Year; 2 hours per week; both terms.

This course of lectures deals with forces in a single plane, and concerns chiefly the calculation of tension, compression and shearing stresses in frame structures and solid beams. It also deals with the consideration of problems relating to friction.

11. DYNAMICS:—*J. McGowan.*

Departments 1, 2, 3, 6, 7 and 8, I Year; 2 hours per week; both terms.

This course of lectures deals with bodies having motion of translation in one plane; also with relative motion, momentum, work and energy.

Text book:—Tutorial Dynamics—Briggs and Bryan.

12. DYNAMICS OF ROTATION:—*W. J. Loudon.*

Departments 1, 2, 3, 7 and 8, II Year; 1 hour per week; both terms.

This course covers angular motion, including moments of inertia, simple hramonic motion, the pendulum, centres of mass, suspension and percussion, the simple theory of the fly-wheel and the governor.

Text book:—Dynamics of Rotation—Worthington.

13. MECHANICS OF MATERIALS:—*P. Gillespie, C. R. Young.*

Departments 1, 2, 3, 4, 6, 7 and 8, II Year; 2 hours per week; both terms.

In this course the strength and elasticity of materials are mathematically treated. The stresses in such elements of structures as the tie rod, the beam, the strut and the member subjected to shear are investigated and the elementary principles of design established. In the lecture and drafting rooms through numerous problems involving the design of simple beams, columns, riveted connections, etc., these principles are exemplified. The work includes also the discussion of eccentric loading, suddenly applied loads and repeated stresses.

Reference Book:—Mechanics of Materials—Merriman.

14. MECHANICS OF MATERIALS:—*J. McGowan.*

Departments 1, 3 and 4, III Year; 3 hours per week; one term.

This course is intended to give the student an introduction to the experimental study of the strength and elasticity of materials. It is intended that he shall acquire some familiarity with the construction and operation of testing machines and with the properties of the ordinary building materials.   •

Reference Book:—Laboratory Instructions, Department of Applied Mechanics, U. of T., 1913.

16. THEORY OF STRUCTURES:—*J. McGowan.*

Departments 1 and 3, IV Year; 2 hours per week; both terms.

The work taken up in this course of lectures consists in swing bridges, arches, suspension bridges and some special features in column construction.

Reference Books:—Modern Framed Structures—Johnson.   Typical Steel Railway Bridges—Thomson.

17. MECHANICS OF MATERIALS:—*P. Gillespie.*

Departments 1, 3 and 4, IV Year; a laboratory course of about 4½ hours per week.

This course of experiments is intended to give the student practice in investigating the elastic and physical properties of iron, steel, concrete, timber and other building materials.

Reference book:—Materials of Construction—Johnson.

18. THEORY OF STRUCTURES:—*C. R. Young.*

Department 1, III Year; 2 hours per week; both terms.

The work of the first term comprises a thorough discussion of combined stresses, restrained, continuous and trussed beams, multiple beam and box girders, plate girders and certain practical aspects of column design.   A number of designs of girders and structural details are worked out in the class and drafting rooms.

The second term is given chiefly to the design of a riveted truss highway span and a riveted truss railway span, the complete designs being made in the lecture and drafting rooms.

19. THEORY OF STRUCTURES:—*C. R. Young.*

Departments 2, 3, 4, 6 and 8, III Year; 2 hours per week; first term.

The work is the same as that for Department 1 in the first term.

Text books:—Modern Framed Structures, Part III—Johnson, Bryan and Turneaure; Structural Problems—Young; Carnegie Pocket Companion; Cambria Steel.

19a. STRESS GRAPHICS:—*T. R. Loudon.*

Departments 1 and 3, III Year; one hour per week both terms.

This course of lectures deals mainly with graphic methods of solving
stresses in framed structures. The construction of Shearing
Force diagrams, Bending Moment diagrams and Influence Lines
is also dealt with.

20. FOUNDATIONS, RETAINING WALLS AND DAMS:—*P. Gillespie, W. J.
Smither.*

Department 1, IV Year; 1 hour per week; both terms.

This course of lectures is devoted to the design of the structures
mentioned. Preparatory to the discussion of the practical aspects
of the subjects, and in order to gain familiarity with the fundamental principles involved, a part of the first term is given over
to the consideration of the theory of compound stress. The most
approved forms of construction of retaining walls, footings, abut-
ments, piers and dams are then described, and typical designs are
worked out in the class and drafting rooms.

Text books and books of reference:—Retaining Walls for Earth—
M. A. Howe; Walls, Bins and Grain Elevators — M. S. Ketchum;
A Treatise on Masonry Construction—I .O. Baker; Design and
Construction of Dams—E. Wegmann.

21. CEMENTS AND CONCRETE:—*P. Gillespie.*

Departments 1, 4 and 8, III Year; 1 hour per week; second term.

The manufacture, testing and use of Portland cement and the funda-
mentals of the theory of reinforced concrete are discussed in this
course of lectures.

22. REINFORCED CONCRETE:—*P. Gillespie, W. J. Smither.*

Departments 1, 3 and 4, IV Year; 1 hour per week.

The theory of the strength of reinforced concrete elements including
the beam, the slab, the T-beam and the column, is continued in
this course.

The analysis of the monolithic arch by the elastic theory is discussed,
and the student is required in the drafting room to apply his knowledge to the design of simple structures.

Reference books:—Principles of Reinforced Concrete Construction—
Turneaure and Maurer; Reinforced Concrete Construction, Vol. I
—Hool.

23. IRON AND STEEL: —*G. A. Guess.*

Taken by students in IV Year, who select the options (c) Structural
Engineering, and (e) Strength and Elasticity of Materials.

Metallography—Mechanical Treatment, Heat Treatment; Metallurgy; Physical Properties; 1 lecture per week. Laboratory,
second term.

24. STRUCTURAL DESIGN:—*C. R. Young, W. J. Smither.*

Departments 1 (*Structural Engineering Option*) and 4, IV Year; 1 hour per week; both terms. Department 3, 1 hour per week; first term.

This course of lectures is devoted to the problems connected with the structural design of buildings of timber, steel and reinforced concrete. The various structural elements, such as the floors, columns, footings, walls and wind bracing, are fully discussed, and portions of typical buildings are designed in the class and drafting rooms.

Text books:—Handbook of Building Construction—Hool and Johnson; Architects' and Builders' Pocket Book—Kidder.

24a. MILL BUILDING DESIGN:—*C. R. Young, W. J. Smither.*

Departments 1 (*Structural Engineering Option*), 3 and 4 (*Architectural Engineering Option*), IV Year; 1 hour per week; first term.

Consideration is given in this course to the various types of mill buildings, to the conditions governing their choice and the details of construction in different materials. Designs of portions of mill buildings are worked out in the class and drafting rooms.

Text books:—Mill Buildings—Tyrrell; Steel Mill Buildings—Ketchum.

24b. MISCELLANEOUS STRUCTURES:—*W. J. Smither.*

Department 1 (*Structural Engineering Option* and *Sanitary and Highway Engineering Option*), IV Year; 1 hour per week, second term.

In this course of lectures the application of theoretical principles to the design of a variety of structures is made. Among those structures discussed are transmission line towers, elevated tanks and their supporting towers, standpipes, large pressure pipes, sewers, culverts, small highway bridges, sub-surface tanks and tall chimneys. Whenever possible the lecture work is followed up by designs in the drafting rooms.

MACHINERY.

25. THEORY OF MECHANISM:—*J. H. Parkin.*

Departments 3 and 7, II Year; Department 8, III Year; 2 hours per week; both terms.

This course of lectures treats of the motions of machines, the latter being assumed to be of sufficient strength to resist acting forces. The formation of machines is dealt with in a general way and the efficiency of machines considered. Investigations of the velocities of points and links are made. The design of cams is considered. The design of gear teeth and the application of trains of gears are taken up, also problems in static equilibrium.

Problems are worked out in the drafting room in which the methods given are employed.

Text book:—Theory of Machines—Angus.

26. MECHANICS OF MACHINERY:—*J. H. Parkin.*

Departments 3 and 7, III Year; 1 hour per week; both terms.

In this course the questions dealt with are the construction of acceleration diagrams, the determination of the accelerations of various parts of machines, the kinetic energy of machines, the effect of the weights and accelerations of parts on the velocity of the fly-wheel and the proper weight of the latter to fulfil given conditions. The theory of various forms of governors is taken up. The balancing of machines is fully studied and application is made to various machines.

Text book:—Theory of Machines—Angus.

27. MACHINE DESIGN—*J. H. Parkin.*

Department 3 and 7, III Year; lectures, 2 hours per week; both terms. Department 6, IV Year; first term only.

The design work occupies 7 hours per week for Department 3, 4½ hours per week, first term only, for Department 6 and 4½ hours per week for Department 7.

Using the previous work in mechanics and kinematics as a groundwork, the lectures in this course deal with the design of shafting, journal bearings, gearing, flywheels, belting, springs, clutches, ball and roller bearings, machine supports, framing, etc.

The problems worked out in the design room are planned to include the principal parts of some complete machine such as an engine or machine tool.

Text book:—Elements of Machine Design—Leutwiler.

28. ADVANCED MACHINE DESIGN— *J. H. Parkin.*

Department 3, IV Year; lectures, 1 hour per week; design, 4 hours per week; both terms.

The work of this course gives practice in the design of complete machines from specifications, having regard for durability, safety, cost of materials, and difficulties in casting, machining and assembling. Mechanisms are developed to give required motions and control.

The lectures deal also with compound stress, helical and worm gearing. Machine tools, jigs and fixtures and process machinery are discussed as far as time will allow.

28a. MACHINE TOOLS:—*J. H. Parkin.*

Departments 3, 6 and 7, II Year; 1 hour per week; second term.

This course of lectures is preparatory to those in Machine Design. It deals with casting, forging and the various machinery operations, together with the construction, operation and work of the principal machine tools.

The object of the course is to familiarize the student with the different shop methods and processes used in the production of machine parts to enable him to make proper provision in the design of such parts to facilitate their production.

Text book:—Text book of Advanced Machine Work—Smith.

HYDRAULICS.

29. HYDRAULICS:—*R. W. Angus.*

Departments 1, 2, 3, 6, and 7, III Year; 2 hours per week.

This is an introductory course of lectures in hydraulics, and is devoted to the development and discussion of fundamental formulas relating to the flow of water in pipes, the measurement of discharge by various methods, such as orifices and weirs, the conditions of flow obtaining in open channels, artificial and natural, and in pipes flowing partially full, together with other kindred subjects.

The object of this course is to provide the student with a good working knowledge of the fundamental principle of hydraulics, such as is useful in practical work, and is necessary to the intelligent investigation of more advanced problems, such as the design of water supply, sewerage and irrigation system, and water power plants.

30. HYDRAULIC LABORATORY:—*R. W. Angus.*

Department 1, III Year; 3 hours per week; second term. Departments 3, 6, and 7, III Year; 4 periods of 3 hours each.

The work in this course is intended to illustrate the lecture course given in Hydraulics and to give the student some working acquaintance with the formulas met with in practice. Experiments are made to determine the coefficients for an orifice and the coefficients of discharge for a weir. The results of these experiments are used in measuring the discharge in subsequent experiments on meters and for the determination of hydraulic resistances in various cases of flow in pipes.

31.⅝ HYDRAULICS—*H. K. Dutcher.*

Departments 1, 3 and 7, IV Year; 1 hour per week; both terms.

A study of the collection and application of stream flow data is followed by an investigation of precipitation and evaporation and their relation to run-off. Flow in pipes is taken up, special attention being paid to exponential formulas, flow in branched pipes, water-hammer and measurement of flow. Flow over weirs and in open channels is also studied.

31a. HYDRAULICS:—*R. W. Angus.*

Departments 1, 3, and 7, IV Year; 2 hours per week, both terms.

The most important question considered and to which most of the lectures are devoted is the theory of turbines and centrifugal pumps, the effect of the design on the speed, discharge power and efficiency being fully taken up.

Text books:—Centrifugal Pumps—Daugherty; Hydraulics—Merriman; Water Power Engineering—Mead.

32. HYDRAULICS:—*R. W. Angus.*

Departments 1, 3 and 7, IV Year; about 10 hours per week.

A laboratory course devoted to experimental work on turbines of various types and centrifugal and turbine pumps and other similar devices. This experimental work is arranged to illustrate the lectures on turbine and pump design. The experiments are made on two large turbine pumps used in the laboratory supply, as well as on apparatus specially designed for instruction. Various methods of measuring water-power and the efficiency of machines are also given.

32a. POWER.

Department 2, IV Year; 24 hours.

A laboratory course of experiments on orifices, weirs and meters.

32c. HYDRAULICS.

Department 1, IV Year.

A laboratory course of four hours per week, first term, on measurement of water, flow in open channels and pumps.

HEAT ENGINES.

33. THERMODYNAMICS:—*R. W. Angus.*

Departments 3, 6 and 7, III Year; 2 hours per week.

A lecture course in which the subject is treated in such a way as to make it of practical value and give a working acquaintance with the principles on which it is based. After the elemenatry ideas have been given and the proofs of the properties of Carnot's cycle, applications of the subject are made to the perfect gas air, saturated steam and to the various types of engines.

34. THERMODYNAMICS:—*N. P. F. Death.*

Departments 1, 2 and 8, IV Year; 1 hour per week; both terms.

This course is especially designed to give the student a working knowledge of thermodynamics as applied to the perfect gas and steam so that he will be able to understand clearly the action of air compressors, steam engines, etc. After deducing general principles, the efficiency of compressed air transmission and the relative merits of different types of compressors are discussed. The steam engine and boiler are also discussed.

35. THERMODYNAMICS AND MECHANICAL LABORATORY.

Department 3, III Year; 2 hours per week, first term; 3 hours per week, second term. Departments 7, III Year; 2 hours per week, first term; 1½ hours per week, second term.

This laboratory course is designed to assist in a clearer understanding of thermodynamics, machine design and mechanics of machinery. The work in thermodynamics consists in the setting of slide valves, indicating engines measuring the brake horse-power, simple engine and boiler tests and the testing of gas and gasoline engines under various conditions. The mechanical laboratory work deals with the efficiency of belts as well as of several machines of simple construction. An examination of lubricating oils is also made by means of well-known methods. Experiments are also made on the balancing of reciprocating and rotating masses.

36. THERMODYNAMICS:—*R. W. Angus.*

Departments 3 and 7, IV Year: 2 hours per week; both terms.

This is a continuation of the introductory course, the subject being here treated from a general standpoint and the idea of entropy and of the absolute scale of temperatures being introduced. The course includes the treatment of saturated and superheated vapours, gases, the flow of fluids, chimney and boiler efficiency and the theory of various engines and other appliances including air compressors, refrigerating machines, and injectors.

Text book:—Thermodynamics—Peabody.

36a. THERMODYNAMICS—*N. F. P. Death.*

Departments 3 and 7, IV Year; 1 hour per week, both terms.

Steam Power Plants. This course follows in logical order the courses on heat engines given in the second and third years. In it a study of the prime movers and auxiliary apparatus required in a power plant is made in such a manner as to indicate the proper choice of equipment under various conditions of operation.

—31

37. THERMODYNAMICS:—*R. W. Angus.*

Departments 3 and 7, IV Year; about 10 hours per week.

The work in this year is a continuation and extension of the work
covered in the third year laboratory course. Careful tests are
made of engines of various types, such as simple, tandem and
cross-compound steam engines; steam turbines; refrigerating
machines; injectors and steam pumps, etc.; and an application is
made of Hirn's analysis and the entropy diagram to the results
obtained. A complete set of experiments is made on each machine
and the result plotted so as to show clearly to the student the
effect of various alterations in the adjustment of the engine on
the resulting efficiency.

Several modern gas and gasoline engines and a gas producer give ample
opportunity for the study of this type of engine, and facilities are
provided for sampling the gas supply and exhaust.

Two experimental stacks and three boilers enable results to be obtained on boiler efficiency and chimney draft.

38. STEAM ENGINES:—*N. P. F. Death.*

Departments 3, 7 and 8, II Year; one hour per week; second term.

This course of lectures includes a discussion of the principles of action
of the steam engine; also the theory and design of various simple
forms of valve gears used in the operation of such engines.

39. HEAT ENGINES:—*N. P. F. Death.*

Departments 3 and 7, III Year; Department 8, IV Year; one hour per
week, both terms.

This course in heat engines is intended for students in Mechanical,
Electrical and Metallurgical Engineering, to be supplementary to
the general course of lectures in thermodynamics.

The principal commercial forms of heat engines are dealt with in a
more or less descriptive manner; special attention is given to con-
siderations affecting the design of the ordinary forms of steam
engines, gas engines and oil engines.

39*a*. POWER:—*R. W. Angus.*

Departments 1, 2 and 8, IV Year; Department 6, III Year; 21 hours.

A course of experiments with steam and gas engines, compressed
air, etc.

ARCHITECTURE.

40. HISTORY OF ARCHITECTURE:—*Adrian Berrington.*

Department 4, I Year; one hour per week; both terms.

In this course the development of architecture is treated very briefly
and in an elementary manner, from the Pyramids of Egypt to the

present, laying special emphasis on the Egyptain, Grecian and
Western Asiatic work. The antique Greek and Roman orders are
studied, and the students are required to make rendered drawings
in the studio of certain orders and elements. An attempt is made
to develop the student's sense of proportion, and in the latter part
of the second term he is required to study a simple problem in
design.

41. HISTORY OF ARCHITECTURE:—*Adrian Berrington.*
Department 4, II Year; one hour per week; both terms.
The Classical, Early Christian, Byzantine and Romanesque styles of
architecture are studied with the aid of the lantern. The student
is required to become acquainted with the best examples in these
styles in order that his sense of proportion and his taste may be
developed and his knowledge of the different elements extended.

42. HISTORY OF ARCHITECTURE:—*A. W. McConnell.*
Department 4, III Year; one hour per week, both terms.
In this course the work of the previous year is continued, with special
attention to the study of the masterpieces of the Renaissance and
modern buildings in planning and detail.

43. HISTORY OF ORNAMENT:—*H. H. Madill.*
Department 4, II Year; one hour per week, both terms.
In this course the development of Ornament is traced from the beginning through Egyptian, Assyrian, Grecian, Roman, Byzantine,
Romanesque, Gothic and Renaissance styles. An attempt is made
to analyze ornament of the best periods and to systematize the
principles followed in form and colour. The development and
types of mouldings are also studied.

44. HISTORY OF PAINTING:—*C. W. Jefferys.*
Department 4, III Year; one hour per week, first term.
The course will consist of an outline of the history and development
of painting and of the minor pictorial arts from the earliest time
until the present day.

44a. HISTORY OF SCULPTURE:—*J. L. Banks.*
Department 4, III Year; one hour per week, second term.
The course will consist of an outline of the history and development
of the different eras of sculpture ranging from the primitive to the
present day.

45. ELEMENTS OF ARCHITECTURE:—*H. H. Madill.*
Department 4, I Year; one hour per week, both terms.
Lectures on the Five Orders of Architecture, their affiliated forms and
the other elements used in design. Simple problems in elementary
design involving the use of the orders and other elements are set
from time to time.

46. Architectural Design:—*Adrian Berrington.*
Department 4, II Year; one hour per week, both terms.
This course is given by means of individual instruction in the class-
room by criticisms of the solutions of different problems set during
the year and by a series of lectures. It is in this course that the
student begins the serious study of design; continued practice in
architectural drawing and rendering affords the training necessary
to make the student a proficient draughtsman.

47. Architectural Design:—*A. W. McConnell.*
Department 4, III Year.
Theory and practice of Design.
This course is given by individual instruction in the studio and by
lectures. The greater part of the course is devoted to problems in
design, and forms a continuation of the course given in the preceding year.

8. Architectural Design:—*Adrian Berrington.*
Department 4, IV Year.
The entire course is devoted to advanced academic training in de-
signing the more monunmetal classes of buildings.

48a. Architectural Design:—*A. W. McConnell and Adrian Berrington.*
Department 4, IV Year; Architectural Engineering Option.
A short course of lectures and studio work referring especially to the
artistic side of the design of commercial buildings.

49. Freehand Drawing and Water Colour Painting:—*C. W. Jefferys.*
Department 4, I Year; 3 hours per week, both terms.
Drawing from still life objects. Primary free hand perspective.
Primary pencil charcoal and pen and ink rendering.

49a. Department 4, II Year; 3 hours per week, both terms.
Drawing and monochrome painting from still life.
Drawing from the cast.
Pencil, pen and ink, and monochrone rendering.
Primary water colour.
Drawing from landscape and natural objects.

49b. Department 4, III Year; 3 hours per week, both terms.
Drawing from the cast.
Water color from still life.   Water color rendering.
Drawing from landscape and natural objects.
Students who are sufficiently advanced are admitted to the Fourth
Year Life Drawing Class.

49c. Department 4, IV Year; 3 hours per week, both terms.
Water colour from still life and from landscape.
Drawing from life.
Water colour rendering.

50. MODELLING:—*J. L. Banks.*

Department 4; I Year; 2 hours per week, both terms.
The Orders.   Synopsis of styles.

50*a*. Department 4; II Year; 2 hours per week, both terms.
The styles elaborated.
Problems in figures and in relation to architecture.

50*b*. Department 4; III Year; 2 hours per week, both terms.
Styles continued.
Problems, combination of figure, ornament and architecture, and
their relative values.

50*c*. Department 4; IV Year; 2 hours per week, both terms.
Modelling from life.
Anatomy.
Composition of groups.

52. BUILDING MEASUREMENT:—*C. H. C. Wright.*

Depatrment 4, I Year; 1 hour per week, both terms.
In this course of lectures the principles of measurements and mensuration with special reference to buildings will be discussed.   With
this is combined practice in measurements of existing buildings,
quantities, etc.

53. BUILDING MATERIALS:—*C. H. C. Wright.*

Department 4, III Year; 2 hours per week, both terms.
The structural and aesthetic value of the various building materials.

54. SANITARY SCIENCE:—*C. H. C. Wright.*

Department 4, IV Year; 1 hour per week, both terms.
Modern pulmbing, its design and installation.

54*a*. HEATING AND VENTILATING:—*C. H. C. Wright.*

Department 4, IV Year; 1 hour per week, both terms.
The design of different systems, where they should be used, heating
specifications, etc.

ASTRONOMY AND GEODESY.

55. ASTRONOMY, ELEMENTARY:—*C. A. Chant.*

Department 1, II Year; 1 hour per week, both terms.
A course in descriptive Astronomy, explaining the ordinary astronomical terms, and describing the various celestial bodies and
their motions.   In the evenings opportunity will be given for
identifying the stars and for observing with telescopes.
Text book:—Manual of Astronomy—C. A. Young.

56. Astronomy and Geodesy:—*L. B. Stewart.*

Department 1, III Year; 2 hours per week.

The course of lectures deals with the determination of time, latitude, longitude and azimuth, by methods adapted to the use of the surveyor's transit and the sextant. It is designed to fulfil the requirements of the final examinations for Ontario and Dominion Land Surveyors.

In Geodesy an account is given of the principles and methods of a secondary triangulation survey, also of the principles involved in the North-West system of survey.

Text books:—Practical Astronomy as applied to Geodesy and Navigation—Doolittle; Nautical Almanac, 1922.

57. Field Work:—*L. B. Stewart, S. R. Crerar.*

Department 1, III Year; about 1 hour per week, first term.

The practical work in this subject comprises observations in the field with the transit and sextant for the determination of time, latitude and azimuth by the methods described in the lectures.

58. Astronomy (Advanced):—*L. B. Stewart.*

Department 1, IV Year; 2 hours per week.

The lecture course in this subject comprises the theory and adjustment of the instruments used in connection with a geodetic survey; the methods of taking and reducing observations for time, longitude, latitude, and azimuth, with the precision required on such a survey; and other matters relating to these subjects.

59. Geodesy and Metrology:—*L. B. Stewart.*

Department 1, IV Year; 2 hours per week.

The lecture course includes a description of the methods of measuring base lines and the angles of a triangulation; the geometry of the spheroid with applications to geodetic problems; the computation of geodetic positions; the solution of large triangles on the earth's surface, and the adjustment of a triangulation; trigonometric and precise spirit levelling; the determination of the figure of the earth by arc measurements, and by the pendulum; the theory of map projections, etc.

60. Astronomy, Geodesy and Metrology:—*L. B. Stewart.*

Department 1, IV Year; about 23 hours per week.

The practical work in the above subjects includes the observation of meridian transits for time and longitude determinations, and of prime vertical transits for latitude, with the astronomical transit instrument; the observation of meridian zenith distances of stars, and of azimuths at elongation for latitude, with the alt-azimuth; theodolite observations for azimuth; observations for latitude with the zenith telescope; the investigation of the constants of the instruments used, and the reduction of all observations; the measurement of a base line with the steel tape and with invar wires, and the determination of the constants of the tape; the measurement of the angles of a triangulation and the adjustment of the angles of network of triangles, etc.

BIOLOGY.

62. ELEMENTARY BIOLOGY:—*J. H. Faull.*

Department 6, I Year; 3 hours per week, each term.

An elementary laboratory course on the nature and identification of plant and animal tissues and products, with microscope practice.

63a. ELEMENTARY BIOLOGY:—*E. M. Walker.*

Department 1, IV Year.

A special Course of Laboratory work and demonstrations in General Biology, five hours per week, second term.

64. HYGIENE AND BACTERIOLOGY:—*J. G. Fitzgerald, R. D. Défries.*

Departments 1 and 6, IV Year.

(1) This is a course of twenty-five lectures, dealing with the principles of Hygiene and Sanitary Science and including a discussion of the facts in Bacteriology which are necessary for a proper understanding of Hygiene and Sanitary Science. The particular phases of the subject which are of importance from the standpoint of Sanitary Engineering are dealt with.

(2) This is a laboratory course of five hours per week, second term, dealing especially with the Bacteriology of water, milk and sewage.

ECONOMICS AND BUSINESS ADMINISTRATION.

66. FINANCE:—

All Departments, II Year; 1 hour per week, both terms.

Money and the instruments of credit; stocks and bonds.

67. COMMERCIAL LAW:—*A. R. Clute.*

All depatrments, III Year; 1 hour per week, both terms. General Principles of the Law of Contracts, Principal and Agent, Partnership and Limited Companies (with special reference to the Companies Acts). General view of the following:—Negotiable Instruments, Sale of Goods, Bills of Sale and Chattel Mortgages, Suretyship and Guarantee.

Text-Book:—Stephens' Elements of Mercantile La w (5th Ed., 1911.)

68. Contracts and Specifications:—*C. R. Young.*

Departments 1 and 4, IV Year; 1 hour per week, second term.

This course of lectures deals with the fundamental principles of contract and specification writing. The critical examination of typical specifications and agreements by the class forms an essential feature of the instruction.

Text books:—Engineering Contracts and Specifications—Johnson; Elements of Specification Writing—Kirby; Principles of Specification and Agreement Writing—Young.

69. Shop Management and Costs:—*H. W. Price.*

Departments 3, 5, 6 and 7, IV Year.

Works management, mechanical specifications, analysis of manufacturing costs, reports.

70. Mine and Plant Management.

Departments 2 and 8; IV Year; 1 hour per week, both terms.

First term:—*H. E. T. Haultain.*

Cost keeping in its relation to mining operations. The total cost of a ton of ore from the financier's point of view.

Second term:—*G. A. Guess.*

Lectures on labour, supplies and repairs as components of production costs. Plant organization, marketing of ores, smelter settlements, metallurgical economics, labour unions.

CHEMISTRY.

75. Elementary Chemistry:—*E. G. R. Ardagh.*

All Departments, I Year; 2 hours per week, both terms.

A lecture course in elementary chemistry dealing with the metals and non-metals, with experimental illustrations.

78. Inorganic Chemistry:—*L. J. Rogers.*

Department 6, I Year; 10 hours per week, both terms.

A laboratory course of quantitative experiments illustrating the use of the sensitive balance, and confirming the fundamental laws of chemistry; qualitative inorganic analysis; quantitative analysis of pure salts; inorganic preparations; molar weight determinations.

Text book:—Manual of Chemical Analysis, Qualitative and Quantitative—Newth.

79. Inorganic Chemistry:—*E. G. R. Ardagh.*

Departments 2, 6 and 8, II Year; 1 hour per week, first term.

A lecture course on the chemistry of the metals; a continuation of Course 75.

80. ANALYTICAL CHEMISTRY:—*L. J. Rogers.*

Departments 2, 6 and 8, III Year; 1 hour per week, both terms.

A lecture course on the principles of chemical analysis; select gravimetric and volumetric methods; technical analysis.

81. ANALYTICAL CHEMISTRY:—*E. G. R. Ardagh.*

Departments 1, 2, 3 and 7, II Year; 3 hours per week.

Laboratory practice in elementary qualitative and quantitative analysis.

Text book:—A Smaller Chemical Analysis—Newth.

82. ANALYTICAL CHEMISTRY:—*J. W. Bain.*

Department 2, II Year; 3 hours per week, both terms.

A laboratory course in the gravimetric determination of metals and acids, with elementary volumetric analysis.

Text book:—A Manual of Chemical Analysis, Qualitative and Quantitative—Newth.

83. ANALYTICAL CHEMISTRY:—*L. J. Rogers.*

Department 8, II Year; about 12 hours per week.

A laboratory course comprising gravimetric and volumetric methods, acidimetry and alkalimetry.

Text book:—A Manual of Chemical Analysis, Qualitative and Quantitative—Newth.

84. ANALYTICAL CHEMISTRY:—*L. J. Rogers.*

Eepartment 6, II Year; 11 hours per week, both terms.

A laboratory course in qualitative and elementary quantitative chemical analysis; inorganic preparations.

Text book:—A Manual of Chemical Analysis, Qualitative and Quantitative—Newth.

85. ENGINEERING CHEMISTRY:—*J. W. Bain.*

Departments 1, 2, 3, 6, 7, and 8 II Year; 1 hour per week, second term.

A lecture course consisting of a study of the industrial production and application of heat and light, and of the chemistry of fuel and the products of combustion.

86. INDUSTRIAL CHEMISTRY:—*J. W. Bain.*

Department 6, II Year; 1 hour per week, both terms.

A lecture course on the manufacture of salts, acids, alkalies and inorganic chemicals.

87. ORGANIC CHEMISTRY:—*M. C. Boswell.*

Departments 1, 2, 3 and 7, II Year; 1 hour per week, first term.

A lecture course in elementary organic chemistry.

Text book:—Theoretical Organic Chemistry—Cohen.

88. ORGANIC CHEMISTRY:—*M. C. Boswell.*
Department 6, II Year; 2 hours per week, both terms.
A lecture course dealing with the aplihatic compounds.
Text book:—Theoretical Organic Chemistry—Cohen.

89. ORGANIC CHEMISTRY:—*M. C. Boswell*
Department 6, II Year; 7 hours per week, 1st term.
A laboratory course in Organic preparations.

90. PHYSICAL CHEMISTRY:—*F. B. Kenrick.*
Departments 6 and 8, II Year; 2 hours per week, both terms.
A course of lectures on the elements of chemical mechanics, and the
theory of solutions.

91. ANALYTICAL CHEMISTRY:—*E. G. R. Ardagh.*
Department 2, III Year; 9 hours per week, for one term.
A laboratory course on the technical analysis of ores and furnace pro-
ducts.

92. INDUSTRIAL CHEMISTRY:—*E. G. R. Ardagh.*
Deaprtment 6, III Year; about 10 hours per week.
A laboratory course in industrial chemistry

93. ANALYTICAL CHEMISTRY:—*L. J. Rogers.*
Department 8, III Year; about 7 hours per week.
A laboratory course in metallurgical analysis.

94. ENGINEERING CHEMISTRY:—*J. W. Bain, E. G. R. Ardagh.*
Departments 1, 2, 3, 6 and 7, III Year; 1 hour per week, both terms.
A lecture course on the application of chemistry to engineering
problems; air, water, sewage, the materials of construction,
explosives, etc.

95. INDUSTRIAL CHEMISTRY:—*E. G. R. Ardagh.*
Department 6, III Year; 1 hour per week, both terms.
A lecture course on petroleum and its products, coal tar and its products; fats, oils, soap, sugar, starch, and gums; fermentation
industries, etc.

96. CHEMICAL PLANT:—*J. W. Bain.*
Department 6, III Year; 1 hour per week, both terms.
A lecture course on the machinery and plant used in chemical manu-
facturing.

97. ORGANIC CHEMISTRY:—*M. C. Boswell.*
Department 6, III Year; 2 hours per week, both terms.
A lecture course on the aromatic series.
Text book:—Theoretical Organic Chemistry—Cohen.

99. ORGANIC CHEMISTRY:—*M. C. Boswell.*
Department 6, III Year; 9 hours per week, 6 weeks.
A laboratory course in organic preparations in the aromatic series;
organic analysis.

101. Electrochemistry:—*W. L. Miller.*

Departments 6, 7 and 8, III Year; Department 2, IV Year; 2 hours per week, first term.

A lecture course on elementary electrochemistry, illustrated by experiments.

102. Electrochemistry:—*W. L. Miller and J. T. Burt-Gerrans.*

Departments 6, 7 and 8, III Year; 3 hours per week, first term.

A laboratory course in quantitative measurements to accompany Course 101.

103. Inorganic Chemistry:—*J. W. Bain.*

Departments 5 and 6, IV Year; 1 hour per week, first term; 2 hours per week; second term.

A lecture course on chemical theory.

104. Organic Chemistry:—*M. C. Boswell.*

Departments 5 and 6, IV Year; 1 hour per week, both terms.

A lecture course on advanced organic chemistry.

105. Organic Chemistry:—*M. C. Boswell.*

Departments 5 and 6, IV Year.

A laboratory course in advanced organic chemistry.

106. Industrial Chemistry:—*J. W. Bain.*

Departments 5 and 6, IV Year; 1 hour per week, both terms.

A lecture course on selected subjects in chemical technology.

107. Industrial Chemistry:—*J. W. Bain, E. G. R. Ardagh, M. C. Boswell.*

Departments 5 and 6, IV Year; about 28 hours per week, both terms.

A laboratory course in industrial problems.

108. Electrochemistry:—*J. T. Burt-Gerrans.*

Departments 5, 6, and 7, IV Year; 2 hours per week, both terms.

An advanced lecture course on the theory of solutions and electrolysis, and the application to the practice of electro-deposition and electrolytic refining of metals. The course also includes lectures on the electric furnace with special consideration of efficiency.

Text books:—Electrometallurgy—Borchers; Electrochemistry—Le Blanc; Electrochemistry—Luepke.

109. Electrochemistry:—*W. L. Miller and J. T. Burt-Gerrans.*

Departments 5, 6 and 7, IV Year; about 28 hours per week.

A laboratory course accompanying Course 108.

110. Sanitary and Forensic Chemistry:—*J. W. Bain.*

Department 5 and 6, IV Year; 1 hour per week, both terms.

A lecture course on the composition and examination of air, water and food; poisons and their detection.

111. Sanitary and Forensic Chemistry:—*J. W. Bain.*
Departments 5 and 6, IV Year
A laboratory course accompanying Course 110.

112. Analytical Chemistry:—*E. G. R. Ardagh.*
Department 2, IV Year, 12 hours per week, first term.
A laboratory course comprising analysis of ores and furnace products.

113. Sanitary Chemistry:—*E. G. R. Ardagh.*
Department 1, IV Year.
A lecture and laboratory course of about 6 hours per week on water
supply, sewage disposal, ventilation, etc.

DESCRIPTIVE GEOMETRY AND DRAWING.

115. Descriptive Geometry:—*J. R. Cockburn.*
Departments 1, 2, 3, 6, 7 and 8, I Year; 1 hour per week; both terms.
This course of lectures deals chiefly with the principles of orthographic
and oblique projections and the application of such principles to
the solutions of problems relating to straight lines and planes.

116. Descriptive Geometry:—*J. R. Cockburn.*
Department 4, I Year; 1 hour per week; both terms.
This course of lectures deals chiefly with the pricniples of orthographic
and oblique projections and the application of such principles to
the solution of problems relating to straight lines and planes,
special reference being made to the determination of shades and
shadows.

117. Drawing:—*J. R. Cockburn.*
Departments 1, 2, 3, 7 and 8, I Year; 11 hours per week, first term; 20
hours per week, second term.
Copying from the flat, lettering, topography; graphical solution of
problems in statics; problems in descriptive geometry, relating
to both orthographic and oblique projections; the plotting of
original surveys; measured drawings.

118. Drawing:—*J. R. Cockburn, H. H. Madill.*
Department 4, I Year; 9 hours per week first term; 18 hours per week,
second term.
Copying from the flat, lettering, rendering the graphical solution of
problems in statics; problems in descriptive geometry, relating
to both orthographic and oblique projections; measured drawings.
Elements and principles of Architecture.

119. Drawing:—*J. R. Cockburn.*
Department 6, I Year; 4 hours per week, both terms.
Copying from the flat, lettering, graphical solution of problems in,
statics, problems in descriptive geometry

121. DESCRIPTIVE GEOMETRY:—*J. R. Cockburn.*

Departments 1, 2, 3, 7 and 8, II Year; 1 hour per week, both terms.

This course of lectures is a continuation of the work taken in the first year with the following additions: Problems relating to curved surfaces, principles of shades, shadows and perspective.

122. DESCRIPTIVE GEOMETRY:—*J. R. Cockburn.*

Department 4, II Year; 1 hour per week, both terms.

This course of lectures is a continuation of the work taken in the First Year with the addition of problems relating to curved surfaces, shades, shadows and perspective.

123. DRAWING:—*J. R. Cockburn.*

Departments 1 and 2, II Year. Department 1, 6 hours per week, first term; 12 hours per week, second term. Department 2, 3 hours per week first term; 12 hours per week, second term.

Colouring and shading as applied to both topographical and construction drawings; problems in descriptive geometry relating to solids bounded by curved surfaces; principles of shades, shadows and perspective; solution of problems in optics and strength of materials; measured drawings; elementary design.

124. DRAWING:—*J. R. Cockburn.*

Departments 3 and 7, II Year; Department 3, 14 hours per week, first term; 10 hours per week second term; Department 7, 12 hours per week, both terms.

Coloring and shading as applied to construction drawings; problems in descriptive geometry relating to solids bounded by curved surfaces; principles of shades, shadows and perspective; solution of problems in optics, theory of mechanism and strength of materials; measured drawings; elementary design.

125. DRAWING:—*J. R. Cockburn, A. Wellesley McConnell, H. H. Madill.*

Department 4, II Year; 17 hours per week, both terms.

Exercises from the orders of architecture; principles of shades, shadows and perspective; elementary architectural design; problems in descriptive geometry relating to solids bound by curved surfaces; solution of problems in optics and strength of materials; measured drawings.

126. DRAWING:—*J. R. Cockburn.*

Departments 6 and 8, II Year; 7 hours per week first term; 3 hours per week, second term.

(Same as Department 3 with the exception that Dept. 6 has no descriptive geometry.

127. DESCRIPTIVE GEOMETRY:—*J. R. Cockburn, W. J. Smither.*

Department 1, III Year; 1 hour per week, first term.

This course of lectures deals with spherical projections, the principles of mapmaking, and the graphical solution of spherical triangles

128. DRAWING:—*J. R. Cockburn, C. R. Young.*

Department 1,III Year; 8 hours per week first term; 18 hours per week, second term.

Principles of mapmaking, spherical projection, plotting of original surveys relating to topographical and railway work; problems in theory of construction; original design of various structures; measured drawings.

129. DRAWING:—*J. R. Cockburn.*

Department 2, III Year; 7 hours per week first term; 2 hours per week, second term.

Plotting of original surveys, relating to topographical and railway work and mining; problems in theory of construction; original design; measured drawings.

130. DRAWING:—*J. R. Cockburn, A. Wellesley McConnell, H. H. Madill.*

Department 4, III Year; 13 hours per week, first term; 22 hours per week, second term.

Architectural design; advanced work in monochrome and colours; problems in shades, shadows and perspective; problems in theory of construction, including framed structures.

131. DESCRIPTIVE GEOMETRY:—*J. R. Cockburn.*

Depart 4, III Year; 1 hour per week, first term.
Advanced work in shades, shadows and perspective.

132. DRAWING:—J. *R. Cockburn.*

Department 4, III Year; 1 hour per week, first term.
Advanced work in shades, shadows and perspective.

132. DRAWING:—*J. R. Cockburn, C. R. Young.*

Departments 3, 6 and 8, III Year; Department 3, 8 hours per week, first term; 2 hours per week, second term; Department 6, 3 hours per week, both terms; Department 8, 3 hours per week, first term.
Problems in design dealing with hte theory of structures.

133. DRAWING:—*C. R. Young, W. J. Smither.*

Department, 1 IV Year; 17 hours per week, first term; 16 hours per week, second term.
Problems in structural design.

133a. DRAWING:—*C. R. Young, W. J. Smither.*

Department 1, IV Year; 6 hours per week, first term; 5 hours per week, second term.
Problems in structural design.

134. DRAWING:—*C. R. Young, W. J. Smither.*

Departments 3 and 4, IV Year; 3 hours per week, both terms.
Problems in mill building design.

134a. DRAWING:—*C. R. Young, W. J. Smither.*

Department 3, IV Year; 4 hours per week, first term; 6 hours per week, second term.

Problems in structural design.

ELECTRICITY.

135. ELECTRICITY:—*H. W. Price.*

Departments 1, 2, 3, 6, 7 and 8, I Year; 2 hours per week, both terms.

A course of lectures on basic principles relating to electric circuits, magnetic circuits, instruments and apparatus in general, distribution of electrical energy, etc., illustrated largely from commercial apparatus. ' The point of view of this work is quantitative rather than descriptive, for it is believed that men who can solve engineering problems are most likely to grasp underlying principles.

138. ELECTRICITY:—*W. S. Guest.*

Departments 3, 6 and 7, II Year; 2 hours per week, both terms.

Deals with the theory of electrical measurements, and detailed study of various methods applicable under different conditions in engineering practice to the measurement of resistance, current, potential difference, power and energy; calibration of commercial measuring instruments. The effect of choice of conditions of measurement on the accuracy of the result is considered.

139. ELECTRICAL LABORATORY:—*W. S. Guest.*

Departments 3, 6 and 7, II Year; 3 hours per week, both terms.

This laboratory course is closely associated with the lecture course 138 on electricity for the second year. The more important and useful methods of testing generators and circuits for electromotive force, resistance, current, grounds, etc., are practiced, often under conditions such as occur in practice. The work also includes methods of calibration of measuring instruments for voltage, current, power and energy, and certain studies of properties of incandescent lamps.

141. POWER:—*A. R. Zimmer.*

Departments 2, 6 and 8, IV Year; 21 hours.

Under the name "Power" a number of operating experiments are arranged to afford some familiarity with measuring instruments and direct and alternating current machinery.

142. MAGNETISM AND ELECTRICITY:—*T. R. Rosebrugh.*

Departments 3 and 7, III Year; 2 hours per week, both terms.

A course of lectures on theory of magnetism and magnetic circuits, theory of direct-current generators, motors, etc.

143. ALTERNATING CURRENT:—*T. R. Rosebrugh*.

Departments 3 and 7, III Year; 1 hour per week.

A first course of lectures on alternating current, covering principles of measurement and leading to the analytical and graphical treatment of the simpler problems relative to alternating-current circuits and machinery.

144. ELECTRICAL LABORATORY:—*A. R. Zimmer*.

Department 3, III Year; 4½ hours per week; Department 7, III Year; 6 hours per week.

This laboratory course is intended to afford the student an opportunity to become familiar with principles involved in continuous-current shunt, series and compound-wound generators and motors, and, to some extent, alternating-current circuits and machinery. Other sections of the work deal with the magnetic properties of iron and steel, and study of iron losses in transformers and generators.

The course is arranged to stand in close relation to the lecture courses in the subjects of magnetism and electricity and alternating current (142, 143) for III Year, and to certain design work (145).

145. ELECTRICAL DESIGN:—*H. W. Price*.

Department 7, III Year; 1 hour per week.

A course of lectures dealing with design of electrical apparatus and machinery, accompanied by designs to be worked out in the design room.

146. ELECTRICAL DESIGN:—*H. W. Price*.

Department 7, III Year; 3 hours per week

A design room is set apart for working out designs of electrical apparatus such as transformers, generators, motors, auxiliary apparatus, etc.

Special forms and notes are employed, arranged to suit the various studies. Certain models are provided to assist where necessary.

147. APPLIED ELECTRICITY:—*T. R. Rosebrugh*.;

Department 7, IV Year; 3 hours per week.

This course deals by analytical and vector methods with the theory of alternating-current circuits and machinery. Applications of theory are considered with regard to transformers, single and polyphase generators, synchronous motors and rotary converters, induction and commutating series motors, transmission lines, wave analysis, etc.

148. ELECTRICAL LABORATORY:—*A. R. Zimmer.*

Department 7, IV Year, in connection with 147; 20 hours per week.

This laboratory course involves a thorough study of principles and properties of single and polyphase circuits and apparatus. Both vector and analytical methods are applied to the solution of problems based on tests made on laboratory machines.

The work deals mainly with constant-voltage and constant-current transformers, single and polyphase alternators, synchronous motors, rotary converters, induction and single phase commutating motors, transmission line, etc. The work does not consist only of factory tests, but is designed to lead the student to apply theory to practice as illustrated in the apparatus under test, with a view to an exact understanding of methods and an appreciation of limitations under many conditions. Free use is made of the oscillograph as a necessary device for "seeing" conditions under investigation. The best commercial measuring instruments are available.

GEOLOGY.

150. GEOLOGY (Elementary):—*W. A. Parks.*

Department 2, II Year; Department 1, III Year; 1 hour per week, both terms.

This course deals chiefly with historical geology with special reference to Canadian formations.

Reference books:—Introduction to Geology—Scott; Text Book of Geology—Dana.

151. ECONOMIC GEOLOGY. (Including Dynamical and Structural Geology):—*A. P. Coleman.*

Department 2, III Year; 1 hour per week, first term; 2 hours per week, second term. Department 1, IV Year; 1 hour per week, both terms.

A study of the more important economic rocks, minerals and ores with their geological associations. Special attention paid to Canadian deposits.

152. ADVANCED GEOLOGY:—*A. P. Coleman.*

Department 2, IV Year; 2 hours per week, both terms.

(A) *Pre-Cambrian Geology.*—An account of the Keewatin, Huronian and Laurentian rocks of Canada, with their distribution, structural relations and economic features, and briefer accounts of similar formations in the United States and elsewhere.

Works of Reference:—Reports of the United States and Canadian Geological Surveys, of the Bureau of Mines of Ontario, etc.

—32

(B) *Pleistocene Geology.*—Lectures on the formation and distribution of the drift deposits of North America, with brief references to other regions. Glacial, Interglacial and Postglacial beds are described, changes of climate are discussed with their probable causes, and the economic features of the clays, sands and gravels are pointed out. A weekly excursion is made during October and November to points of interest near Toronto, which is the centre of the most important development of Pleistocene in America.

(C) *Physiography.*—A course of lectures on the surface forms of the earth, with the geological factors which have produced them. The broad features of the earth, its plains, tablelands, hills, valleys, mountains, oceans, rivers and lakes are discussed in a general way, methods of topographical surveys and mapping are referred to, and the chief physiographic areas of Canada are described.

153. MINING GEOLOGY:—*A. P. Coleman.*

Department 2, IV Year; 1 hour per week, both terms.
A course of lectures on geological problems associated with mining, typical mining regions in Canada, the United States and elsewhere being discussed from the geological side.
Works of reference:—Mineral Industry and the books mentione under (A).

154. GEOLOGICAL EXCURSIONS:—*A. P. Coleman.*

Department 2, IV Year.
Trips to points of interest in the vicinity of Toronto.

155. ORE DEPOSITS:—*A. P. Coleman.*

Department 2, III Year; 1 hour per week, both terms.
Discussion of the orgiin and classification of ore deposits in a general way, the mode of occurrence of the chief metals, and statistics of production, special attention being given to the metals mined in Canada.

156. ECONOMIC GEOLOGY:—*Alex. MacLean.*

Department 2, III Year; 2 hours per week, second term.
Laboratory work on ores, manner of occurrence, vien structure, etc Geological maps of typical mining regions.

MINERALOGY.

157. ELEMENTARY MINERALOGY:—*J. E. Thomson.*

Department 2, II Year; 2 lectures per week, first term.
After introducing the student to the chief chemical, physical, and crystallographic characteristics of minerals, the course becomes

descriptive and deals with about one hundred of the minerals most important from the industrial or scientific point of view.

Text Book:—Study of Minerals—Rogers.

158. MINERALOGY:—*J. E. Thomson.*

Department 6, I Year; 3 hours per week, one term.

Introduction to determination of minerals by inspection and physical tests.

Text Book:—Mineral Tables—Eakle.

159. PRIMARY MINERALOGY:—*A. L. Parsons.*

Department 1, II Year; 2 hours per week, first term.

A very brief introduction to the study of minerals and rocks.

Text books:—Study of Minerals—Rogers; Hand-Book of Rocks—Kemp.

160. MINERALOGY:—*A. L. Parsons, J. E. Thomson.*

Department 2, II Year; 1 hour per week, first term; 3 hours per week, second term.

Determination of minerals by inspection and by means of physical tests; introduction to blow-pipe practice.

Text books:—Mineral Tables—Eakle; Determinative Mineralogy—Lewis.

161. MINERALOGY:—*A. L. Parson, J. E. Thomson.*

Department 1, II Year; 1 hour per week, first term; 2 hours per week, second term.

Determination of minerals by inspection and by means of physical tests; study of common rock types and their identification.

Text books:—Mineral Tables—Eakle; Handbook of Rocks—Kemp.

163. ELEMENTARY PETROGRAPHY:—*T. L. Walker.*

Department 2, III Year; 1 hour per week.

A course of lectures and laboratory work introducing the student to the macroscopic study of rocks.

Text-books:—Handbook of Rocks—Kemp.

164. MINERALOGY:—*J. E. Thomson.*

Department 2, III Year; 2 hours per week.

Determination of minerals by means of the blow-pipe and physical properties.

Text books:—Mineral Tables—Eakle; Determinative Mineralogy—Lewis.

165. GENERAL PETROGRAPHY:—*A. L. Parsons.*

Department 2, IV Year; 1 hour per week.

Study of the chief rock-forming minerals and of some phases of petrography not covered in the course of the previous year.

Text Books:—Minerals in Rock-Sections—Luquer; Petrology for Students—Harker.

166. PETROGRAPHY:—*T. L. Walker.*

Department 2, IV Year; 2 hours per week, both terms.
Study of the chief rock-forming minerals, of rocks in thin sections
    and in hand specimens.
Text books:—Rocks and Rock Minerals—Pirsson; Minerals in Rock
    Sections—Luquer.

169. MINERALOGY:—*A. L. Parsons.*

Department 8, II Year; 1 hour per week.
Determination of minerals by physical properties.
Text Book:—Mineral Tables—Eakle.

MINING, ASSAYING AND ORE DRESSING.

170. MINING:—*H. E. T. Haultain.*

Department 2, II Year; 1 hour per week, first term. Department
    8, II Year; 1 hour per week; both terms.
An introduction to the study of mining and ore dressing methods.

171. MINING AND ORE DRESSING:—*H. E. T. Haultain, F. C. Dyer.*

Departments 2 and 8 II Year; 3 hours per week, first term.
Introductory work with rock-drills and various ore dressing appliances.

172. MINING:—*H. E. T. Haultain, F. C. Dyer.*

Departments 2 and 8, III Year; 2 hours' lectures per week, second
    term; 3 hours' laboartory work per week, second term.
General mining methods.

173. ASSAYING:—*H. E. T. Haultain, J. T. King.*

Departments 2 and 8, III Year; 1 hour lecture per week, first term;
    3 hours' laboratory work per week, both terms; Department 6,
    III Year; 3 hours' laboratory work per week, second term.
Assaying of various ores for gold, silver, lead and copper.

174. ASSAYING:—*H. E. T. Haultain, J. T. King.*

Departments 2 and 8, IV Year; 1 hour lecture per week, one term;
    3 hours laboratory work per week, one term.
Continuation of the work of III Year.

175. MINING:—*H. E. T. Haultain.*

Department 2, IV Year; 1 hour lecture per week, both terms.
Special mining methods, examinations, reports.

176. MILLING:—*H. E. T. Haultain, F. C. Dyer.*

Department 2, IV Year; 3 hours' laboratory work per week; both
    terms.
Advanced work with ore dressing appliances, complete mill tests.

177. ORE DRESSING:—*H. E. T. Haultain, F. C. Dyer.*
Departments 2 and 8, III Year; 1 hour per week; both terms.

179. ORE DRESSING:—*H. El T. Haultain, F. C. Dyer.*
Department 2, IV Year; 1 hour per week, both terms.

METALLURGY.

180. METALLURGY:—*G. A. Guess.*
Departments 2, 5 and 6, IV Year; 1 hour per week, both terms.
The metallurgy of gold, silver, copper, lead, nickel, and zinc, metallurgical problems.

181. FERRO-METALLURGY:—*G. A. Guess.*
Departments 2, 6, 7 and 8, III Year; 1 hour per week, both terms.
The physical properties of iron and steel and the circumstances that influence the strength, etc., of iron. The different modes of manufacture of iron and steel and the effect of different processes of making on the resulting products; explanations of specifications for iron and steel adopted by engineers.

182. METALLURGY:—*G. A. Guess.*
Department 2' IV Year; 6 hours' laboratory work per week, second term.
Calibration of pyrometers, blast furnace smelting and copper converting, cyanidation, acid leaching of copper ores, electrolytic refining of lead and copper, electrometallurgy.

183. METALLURGY:—*G. A. Guess.*
Departments 2, 6 and 8, II Year; 1 hour per week, second term.
An introduction to the study of metallurgy.

184. METALLURGY:—*G. A. Guess.*
Departments 2 and 6, III Year; 1 hour per week; both terms.
Fuels, temperatures of combustion, Specific heat, conductivity and problems thereon. Chimneys, furnaces, refractories, outlines of furnace metallurgy and hydro-metallurgy.

185. METALLURGY:—*G. A. Guess.*
Department 8, II Year; 1 hour per week, both terms.
A lecture course in the study of metallurgical fuels, their use, preparation, calorific value and temperature of combustion. Problems.

186. METALLURGY:—*G. A. Guess.*
Department 8, III Year; 1 hour per week, first term.
Lecture course preparatory to study of metallurgical processes and methods.
Two hours' laboratory per week, first term.
Four hours per week, second term.
Lecture and class room work, metallurgical processes and methods.
Six hours laboratory per week, second term.

186a. METALLURGY:—*G. A. Guess.*

   Department 8, IV Year; 2 hours per week, both terms, and 8 hours
      laboratory work, both terms.

   Design and arrangement of plants. Metallurgical book keeping,
      balance sheets, thermal balance sheets. Refining processes.
      The metallography of iron and steel and non-ferrous alloys.

186b. PLANT DESIGN:—*G. A. Guess.*

   Department 8, IV Year; 2 hours per week, both terms, during which
      is taken up a study of metallurgical flow sheets of typical plants.
      a critical reading and discussion of papers and articles describing
      metallurgical process or dealing with plant arrangement and con-
      struction; a consideration of some of the problems entering into
      general design of metallurgical plants.

MATHEMATICS.

187. ALGEBRA:—*A. T. DeLury.*

   . Departments 1, 2, 3, 6, 7, 8, 1 Year; 2 hours per week, both terms.

   Simple equations of one, two and three unknown quantities; quad-
      ratic equations of one and two unknown quantities; graphic
      representation of functions and the introduction of the gradient
      function; proportion and progressions; interest forms and annui-
      ties, permutations, combinations, limits, the general theory of
      infinite series, binomial theorem, exponential and logarithmic
      series.

   Text book:—Intermediate Algebra—DeLury.

188. ANALYTICAL GEOMETRY:—*I. R. Pounder.*

   All Departments, I Year; 1 hour per week, first term, 2 hours per week,
      second term.

   The course in Elementary Analytical Geometry covers the more
      familiar propositions in connection with the straight line, circle,
      parabola, ellipse and hyperbola. The subject is treated so as to
      illustrate the general methods of analytical geometry.

189. TRIGONOMETRY, PLANE:—*M. A. Mackenzie.*

   Departments 1, 2, 3, 6, 7, 8, I Year; 2 hours per week, first term.

   Solutions of triangles and practical problems.

   Text book:—Practical Trigonometry—Plane and Fawdry.

190. CALCULUS, DIFFERENTIAL AND INTEGRAL:—*S. Beatty.*

   Departments 1, 2, 3, 4, 6, 7, and 8 II Year; 2 hours per week, both
      terms.

   This is an elementary course in the infinitesimal calculus, but adequate
      to afford a knowledge of the character and methods of the subject
      and to enable students in chemistry, engineering, etc., to under-
      stand such of their text books as introduce the calculus.

191. TRIGONOMETRY, SPHERICAL:—*L. B. Stewart.*

Department 1, II Year; 1 hour per week, first term.

A course of lectures includes the derivation of formulæ and their application to the solution of triangles and to practical problems.

Text Book:—Spherical Trigonometry—Todhunter and Leatham.

192. LEAST SQUARES, METHOD OF:—*L. B. Stewart.*

Department 1, III Year; 1 hour per week, first term.

The course of lectures includes: The general principles of probability, the law of error, direct measurements of equal and different weights; mean square and probable errors; indirect measurements; conditioned observations; applications to empirical con stants and formulæ, etc.

Text book:—Least Squares—Merriman.

ENGINEERING PROBLEMS.

193. Departments 1, 2, 3, 6, 7, 8, I Year; 1 hour per week, both terms.

In this course the time is devoted to problem work involving an application of the theory and principles laid down in the lecture course of the various subjects of the First Year.

TECHNICAL PHYSICS.

195. ACOUSTICS:—*G. R. Anderson.*

Department 4, III Year.

Wave motion, propagation, reflection and transmission of sounds. Laws of vibrating strings, pipes and forks. Velocity of sounds. Musical scales. Absorption of sound by various substances, use of deadening material in buildings. Amount of reverberation permissible and desirable in public buildings. Lectures and laboratory work.

196. HYDROSTATICS:—*G. R. Anderson.*

All Departments, II Year.

Laws of fluid pressure and application to machines. Dentsiy of solids and fluids, theory of flotation.

Lectures and laboratory work. Spring term.

197. OPTICS:—*G. R. Anderson.*

Departments 1, 2, 3, 6 and 7, II Year.

Rectilinear propagation of light, illumination, photometry, light standards. Distribution of light by reflectors and diffusers, general and selective absorption, economic values of artificial lights.

Laws of reflection and refraction, theory of optical instruments.

Light considered as wave motion, dispersion, spectrum analysis, colour phenomena, polarization.

Lectures and laboratory work, both terms.

198. HEAT:—*G. R. Anderson.*

Departments 1, and 8, III Year.

Generation and propagation of heat. General and industrial ther-mometry, calorimetry and pyrometry. Linear and cubical ex-pansion, gas laws. Specific heat of solids, liquids and gases, latent heat of fusion and vaporization. Mechanical equivalent of heat. Carnot cycle.

Lecture and laboratory work, Fall term.

199. PHOTOGRAPHY:—*G. R. Anderson.*

Departments 1 and 4, III Year; Departments 3 and 7, IV Year.

The camera and its adjustments, lenses, shutters, screens. Plates for various purposes, films, prevention of halation. Lighting, ex-posure, development. Paper of various kinds, printing, enlarge-ment and reduction, blue printing and allied processes. Record photography, photogrammetry and photo-surveying. Photo-graphy in colour.

Lectures Fall term, and laboratory work both terms.

200. ILLUMINATION:—*G. R. Anderson.*

Department 4, II Year.

Principles of interior and street illumination. Artificial lighting of public and private buildings, etc.

SURVEYING.

205. SURVEYING:—*S. R. Crerar.*

Departments 1, 2, 3, 7 and 8, I Year; 1 hour per week, both terms.

The lecture course includes the general principles; surveying with the chain, the compass and chain and the transit and chain, and level, the applications of trigonometry to inaccessible heights and distances; mensuration of surfaces, co-ordinate surveying, division of land, etc.

Text books:—Plane Surveying—Tracy; Theory and Practice of Surveying—Johnston and Smith.

206. FIELD WORK:—*S. R. Crerar, E. W. Banting.*

Departments 1, 2, 3, 7 and 8, I Year; 5 hours per week, first term.

This course comprises testing chains; practice in chaining; a com-plete survey of a piece of land with the chain and transit; keeping of field notes; the use of the transit and compass in surveying closed figures and traverse lines and in ranging straight lines; plotting by latitudes and departures, and otherwise computing areas. Instrumental work with level.

207. SURVEYING:—*W. M. Treadgold, E. W. Banting.*

Departments 1 and 2, II Year; 1 hour per week, both terms.

This course of lectures takes up in detail, simple, reverse and compound curves as applied to railroad surveying. It also includes stadia, plane table and photographic surveying as applied to topographic work, and the main features of mine and hydrographic surveying.

Text books:—Henck, Searles, Allen (Field books for Engineers) Theory and Practice of Surveying—Johnston and Smith; Surveying—Breed and Hosner.

208. FIELD WORK:—*W. M. Treadgold, E. W. Banting, S. R. Crerar.*

Departments 1 and 2, II Year; 9 hours per week, first term.

This course of instruction embraces all adjustments of the transit and level, minor problems in triangulation and traversing—levelling and plane table practice.

209. SURVEYING AND LEVELLING:—*W. M. Treadgold, E. W. Banting.*

Department 1, III Year; 1 hour per week, both terms; Department 2, III Year; 1 hour per week, first term.

This course of lectures takes up the work of the railroad engineer on construction, including profiles, cross sectioning, computation of volume of earthwork, overhaul, transition curves, laying out turnouts, frogs and switches, etc.

Also a discussion of trigonometric and barometric levelling.

Text books:—Field Engineering—Searles; Railroad Curves and Earthworks—Allen.

210. FIELD WORK:—*W. M. Treadgold, E. W. Banting, S. R. Crerar.*

Departments 1 and 2, III Year.

This includes adjustments of levels and determination of profile, cross sectioning and computation of earthwork of located line on ground and plotting of same; also cross sectioning by use of hand level. A complete stadia topographic survey is made and plotted. Micrometer work and plane table traverse are also taken up.

This work is to be taken at Gull Lake Camp (see page 21.)

ADDITIONAL, FOURTH YEAR OPTIONS.

211. RAILWAY ENGINEERING:—*W. M. Treadgold.*

Department 1, IV Year; about 2 hours per week.

The object of this course is to make the student acquainted with the general principles of railroad and street railway engineering, and the subject will be studied from the standpoint of economic theory of location; train resistance; effect of grade, distance and curvature and rise and fall; maintenance of way; yards and terminals; tunnels, and street railway practice.

212. Field Work:—*W. M. Treadgold.*

' Department 1, IV Year; about 11 hours per week, first term.

The work consists of an original survey for a railroad some one or two miles in length, the work being conducted according to the most modern methods of location. Upon the completion of this work a contour map of the district surveyed is plotted in the drafting room and a line adjusted to it. This is staked out in the field, profiles taken and complete estimates of the cost of construction made.

213. Sanitary Engineering.

Sanitary Chemistry (113).

Biology (63a).

Hygiene and Bacteriology (64).

Re-inforced Concrete (22).

Hydraulics (32c).

Miscellaneous Structures (24b).

Sanitary Engineering:—A lecture course of 1 hour per week, both terms, in which consideration is given to the problems of water supply and sewage disposal as viewed by the engineer. Some practice in the design of works from assumed data is afforded.

Reference books:—Public Water Supplies—Turneaure & Russell; American Sewerage Practice—Metcalf & Eddy, 3 vols.

214. Highway Engineering:—

Department 1, IV Year.

A lecture and laboratory course of about 8 hours per week, dealing with materials, design and construction of highways and pavements and the testing of various materials used in such work.

215. Structural Engineering:—

Students in Civil Engineering who desire to specialize in the subjects best fitting them for designing or constructing engineers on bridge, building or other analogous work, may do so by selecting the Structural Engineering Option in the fourth year. In addition to the obligatory subjects, the following lecture and laboratory courses are provided for those selecting this option:

Theory of Structures (16).

Strength and Elasticity of Materials (17).

Iron and Steel (23).

Reinforced Concrete (22).

Structural Design (24).

Mill Building Design (24a).

Miscellaneous Structures (24b)

216. ARCHITECTURAL ENGINEERING—

Architectural students desiring to give special attention to the structural design of buildings may do so by electing to take the Architectural Engineering Option in the fourth year. The following subjects, in addition to those required of all students in the fourth year in Architecture, are required:

Mill Building Design (24a).

Architectural Design (48a).

MODERN LANGUAGES.

217. FRENCH:—*J. H. Cameron, Miss J. C. Laing.*

Required in Department 4, I Year; 2 hours per week, both terms; II year, 1 hour per week, both terms.

An elementary course intended to train the student in the translation of scientific journals and treatises.

218. GERMAN:—*G. H. Needler.*

Required in Department 6, all years; 1 hour per week, both terms.

An elementary course intended to train the student in the translation of scientific journals and treatises.

218a. SPANISH:—*M. A. Buchanan.*

Department 8, II Year; 1 hour per week, both terms.

An introduction to Spanish grammer, pronunciation and practice in reading Engineering Spanish.

THESIS.

219. THESIS.

Required in all Departments, IV Year, with the exception of Department 4, Architectural Design Option.

Each student is required to prepare a thesis of between six thousand and seven thousand words on a subject approved by Council. See circular of information.

OUTLINE OF VACATION WORK.

220. CONSTRUCTION NOTES.

II Year. See special circular of information.

The construction notes required consist of neat and complete dimensioned sketches in pencil of any structures, machines or plants which may be of interest. Any object chosen should be represented and dimensioned in such a manner that it could be completely constructed from the notes as the only available information.

From students in Department 2, who have been actually engaged during the summer with Government or other approved geological survey parties, geological field notes will be accepted in lieu of construction notes.

MASTER OF APPLIED SCIENCE DEGREE.

1. A candidate for the degree of Master of Applied Science (M.A.Sc.) shall hold the degree of Bachelor of Applied Science (B.A.Sc.) of this University.

2. He shall spend not less than one academic year in attendance as a student, in the Faculty of Applied Science, on a course of study approved by the Council.

3. He shall present a satisfactory thesis on a subject approved by the Council.

4. He shall pass such exaimnations as the Council may decide.

5. The candidate must register at the beginning of the academic year.

PROFESSIONAL DEGREES.

The attention of graduates is directed to the following regulations respecting professional degrees.

The following degrees have been established: Civil Engineer (C.E.), Mining Engineer (M.E.), Mechanical Engineer (M.E.), Electrical Engineer (E.E.), Chemical Engineer (Chem.E.), subject to the following regulations:

1. A candidate for one of the said degrees shall hold the diploma of the School of Practical Science or of the Faculty of Applied Science and Engineering or the degree of Bachelor of Applied Science.

2. He shall have spent at least three years after receiving the diploma or the degree in the actual practice of the branch of engineering wherein he is a candidate for a degree.

3. Intervals of non-employment or of employment in other branches of engineering shall not be included in the above three years. It shall not be necessary that the several periods requisite to make up the said three years be consecutive.

4. Satisfactory evidence shall be submitted to the University examiners as to the nature and length of the candidate's professional experience for the purpose of clauses 2 and 3.

The Examiners shall satisfy themselves by oral or written examinations in regard to the candidate's experience and competence.

5. The candidate shall prepare an original thesis on some engineering subject in the branch in which he wishes a degree, the said thesis to be accompanied by all necessary descriptions, details, drawings, bills of quantities, specifications and estimates.

The candidates may be required at the option of the Examiners to undergo an examination in the subject of this thesis.

6. Notice in writing shall be sent to the Secretary not later than the first day of February, informing him of the degree to which the candidate wishes to proceed and of the title of his proposed thesis for the approval of the Examiners.

7. The evidence under clause 4, and the thesis, with accompanying papers, described in clause 5, shall be sent to the Secretary not later than the first day of April.

8. The candidate shall be required to present himself for examination in the month of April at such time as may be arranged by the Examiners.

9. The fee for any one of the said degrees shall be twenty dollars, and shall be paid to the Bursar not later than the first day of April.

10. The thesis, drawings, and other papers submitted under clause 7 shall become the property of the University.

LABORATORY EQUIPMENT.

THERMODYNAMIC AND MECHANICAL LABORATORY.

The University in 1919 completed the erection of a large, well-equipped building for the accommodation of the steam, gas, mechanical and hydraulic laboratories. A more complete description of the laboratories has been published elsewhere, so that the present description is only intended to give the main features.

The part of the building set apart for thermodynamics and other mechanical work is the ground floor of a room 60 ft. x 155 ft. This room is lighted entirely from the roof in a very perfect way. A part of the space 40 ft. wide running the entire length of 155 feet is served by a 3 ton travelling crane and contains the following equipment:

50 h.p. Brown engine with separate jackets on both heads and barrel of cylinder.

Two-stage Rand air compresor having compound steam cylinders, each fitted with Meyer cut-off gear. The low pressure air cylinder has Corliss inlet gear.

30 h.p. high-speed Leonard tandem compound engine with shaft governor.

15 h.p. high-speed McEwan engine.

75 h.p. two-line compound Willans engine.

15 h.p. DeLaval turbine with special nozzles for condensing and non-condensing tests.

Two 15 h.p. Leonard engines with different types of valves, which are used for valve setting.

There are also two surface condensers with air pumps so arranged that any engine in the laboratory may be made to exhaust into the atmosphere through an open heater or into one of the condensers, the change from one arrangement to the other being accomplished in a few minutes without the aid of valves.

The laboratory further contains:

A 3 ton York refrigerating machine with tanks.

An Amsler transmission dynamometer.

Apparatus for testing injectors and steam pumps.

Numerous other pieces of apparatus and instruments.

The work on internal combustion engines and producers is performed on the following:

18 h.p. Canada suction gas producer.

14 h.p. National gas engine arranged for various compressions and points of ignition.

10 h.p. Fielding and Platt engine for city gas or coal oil, having various adjustments.

8 h.p. Otto gas engine.

6 h.p. marine gasoline engine.

Various accessories to above machines.

Steam for the laboratory is supplied by two 50 h.p. and one 100 h.p. Babcock and Wilcox boilers, the latter having an internal superheater. These boilers are located in a separate boiler room. They are used for experimental work only and are fitted up for testing. The gases pass up through two independent chimneys, and these have been arranged so that the draft and other conditions in the chimney at any point of its height may be examined.

In smaller work-rooms off the main laboratory are placed belt and oil testing machines, apparatus for testing the efficiency of gears and machines, and for experiments in the balancing of machinery.

HYDRAULIC LABORATORY.

The hydraulic laboratory occupies two floors each 40 feet x 112 feet, which are well lighted by large windows on the side and end.

The water for the experimental work is pumped through the various pieces of apparatus from a well by means of two turbine pumping units, both of which are driven by a Belliss and Morcom compound engine of 125 h.p. running at a speed of 525 revs. per minute. Both engine and pumps have been installed with a view to using them in experimental work as well as for supply of water for other apparatus used in the laboratory.

The pumping units are capable of delivering one cubic foot of water per second against heads of 250 feet and 300 feet respectively. These units are designed and connected up so that they may be run in series giving the above discharge at 550 feet head, or they may be run in parallel giving double the discharge at a lower head. Each pumping unit consists of two two-stage pumps mounted on a common base and driven by a single pulley, and the construction and piping are such that each two-stage pump may be driven separately or that all may be driven at once, discharging separately one cubic foot per second at about 125 feet head through each of four independent pipes, or else the pumps may be run in series or in parallel. The scheme is thus well adapted to laboratory work, and under the heads used on reaction turbines about six cubic feet per second may be obtained.

The laboratory further contains a large vertical steel tank 5½ feet diameter by 34 feet with arrangements for the attachment of nozzles and other mouthpicees, etc. Connections are also arranged for reaction turbines, the tank acting as a reservoir.

The discharge from the turbines or nozzles is measured in a weir tank nearly 6 feet wide and 21 feet long, containing a contracted weir 4½ feet wide. This weir may be calibrated by two weighing tanks, each having a capacity of about 240 cubic feet.

There are three reaction turbines and two impulse wheels all ready for experiment, the power being measured by brakes and the water by weir or orifices. Amongst the reaction turbines may be mentioned the one designed and built by Escher Wyss & Co., specially for the laboratory.

Smaller orifice and weir tanks, each about 3 x 3 x 12 feet with necessary measuring tanks, are arranged for instruction in coeficients of various kinds and practice with weirs and orifices.

A Venturi meter and other meters, also an hydraulic ram and similar devices are available for testing, and good facilities have been arranged for investigating friction and other properties of pipes and fire hose.

For special investigations on turbine and centrifugal pumps, other pumps in addition to those already described have been arranged.

The basement of the laboratory contains an open trough 5 feet wide, about 110 feet long, with a large weir at one end. It is intended to use this trough for experiments on the flow in open channels, for measurements of large discharges by means of the weir, and for experiments with current meters and Pitot tubes.

Numerous pieces of smaller apparatus, together with all instruments required, have also been provided, and the laboratory equipment is believed to be very complete.

AERONAUTIC EQUIPMENT.

For the purpose of the scientific study of problems connected with aviation and the best design of aeroplanes, and also of all problems connected with the effect of wind pressure, a wind tunnel 4 ft. square has been installed in the Hydraulic Laboratory and equipped with the latest form of balance and all the necessary instruments.

There are available for laboratory demonstration and instruction purposes the following aeroplanes:—one S.E. 5A, one Avro Training and two J.N. 4 Curtis Training, all the gift of the Royal Air Force.

The laboratory also contains a number of aeroplane engines of most modern type, both rotary and stationary, and a number of models; and also a complete Hispano Suiza aeroplane. These machines are available for inspection, and are of much help in studying the trend of development and design in the power plant of lightest weight.

DONATIONS TO THE THERMODYNAMIC AND HYDRAULIC LABORATORIES.

The following donations to the equipment of the laboratories have been made through the kindness of those mentioned:

50 h.p. Wheeler Surface Condenser, presented by Mr. F. M. Wheeler, New York.

Blake Feed Pump, presented by the manufacturers.

6-inch New American Turbine, presented by Wm. Kennedy & Sons, Owen Sound, Ont.

Two Crown Water Meters, presented by the National Meter Co., New York, through Mr. M. Warnock, Toronto.

Rock Drill, presented by Sullivan Machinery Co., New York, through Mr. A. E. Blackwood, '95·

Marine Gasoline Engine, presented by Canadian Fairbanks Co., Montreal.

Two engines with different types of valve, presented by Messrs. E. Leonard & Sons, London, Ont.

Bundy trap from American Radiator Co., through Messrs. Russell & Gifford.

Dunham steam trap from C. A. Dunham Co.

Sectional models of valves from American Radiator Co.

Sectional model Mason Reducing Valve by Russell & Gifford.

Tanks, etc., by John Inglis Co.

Pressure Fan from Sheldons Ltd., Galt.

Model water turbine test runner from Wellman, Seaver Morgan Co., Cleveland, O.

In addition to the above, other firms have materially assisted by offering apparatus at or below cost price, among whom·may be specially mentioned, The Canadian Rand Drill Co., Sherbrooke, Quebec.

The following machines are gifts from the Royal Air Force:
Liberty Aeroplane Motor 400 h.p.
200 B. h.p. Siddeley Deasey Aero Engine.
120 h.p. Beardmore Aero Engine.
Curtis Engine (Sectional).
Hispano Suiza Aero Engine.
80 h.p. Le Rhone Rotary Engine.
Clerget Rotary Engine.
Gnome Monosoupape Engine.
Admiralty Rotary Engine 150 h.p.
Hispano Suiza Aeroplane.
Models of Engines, etc., and numerous spare parts.

—33

PHYSICAL LABORATORIES.

The optical laboratory is equipped with Weinhold optical benches and accessories for determining the constants of mirrors and lenses and for demonstrating the construction and use of telescopes, field glasses, microscopes, etc.   There is also an equipment consisting of one or more of the following optical instruments:—field glasses, microscopes, reading telescope, small comparators, spectrometer, various types of photometer, small focometer, cathetometer, polariscope, illuminometer, standard gas light testing bench, precision electric light, photometry bench, projecting lanterns, etc.

The photographic laboratory is supplied with a number of hand cameras for the use of students.   There are also larger cameras for Departmental work, copying cameras, englaring lanterns and a kinematograph camera, printer and projector, electric blue-printing machine and the necessary dark rooms, complete equipment for photographic survey.

The hydrostatic laboratory contains a supply of various forms of hydrometers, hydrostatic balance, Jolly balance, Mohr's balance, hydrostatic press, vacuum pumps.

The heat laboratory is equipped with a full supply of calorimeters and accessories for determinations of latent and specific heat, expansion apparatus, air thermometer, apparatus for verification of Boyle's law and pressure and boiling point curve, and for determination of the absolute expansion of mercury, Callendar's apparatus for determination of the mechanical equivalent of heat.   Calorimeter for the determination of the value of solid, liquid, and gaseous fuels.

The acoustical laboratory is provided with sonometer, siren, forks ordinary and electric, Lissajous' and Melde's apparatus, organ pipes of various forms, manometric flame apparatus and a special equipment for work in architectural acoustics consisting of torsion chronograph, electropneumatic wind chest and standardized organ pipes and other accessories.

ELECTRICAL LABORATORIES.

New building.—At present the electrical laboratories are as described below. By October, 1921, however, the laboratory equipment will have been moved into the new building now ready for occupation. The new quarters will be found to be much more commodious and better lighted, as well as fireproof. There will be study rooms, a room for electrical design, three large main laboratories, and several rooms for special purposes such as high tension work, magnetic testing and electrical properties of conductors and insulators. There will be a shop, also excellent elevator facilities for moving equipment.

Instrument laboratory.—The equipment of this laboratory is, in part, as follows: A set of D'Arsonval galvanometers conveniently located at tables about the laboratory, a set of resistance boxes for use with the same; measuring instruments, including ammeters, voltmeters, wattmeters, potentiometers and standard cells. Apparatus for the measurement of low resistance, including a ductor, and for high resistance, including a megger; several Carey Foster outfits and a Roller bond tester. There are also experimental lines for practice in locating faults, photometer outfits with rotating devices and various types of arc lamps.

Another room is fitted more especially for calibration of electrical instruments for alternating and direct currents. About one hundred and twenty portable measuring instruments are available for students' use, also standard instruments, including Weston laboratory standards, and a Wolff potentiometer, with which the portable instruments may be compared.

Machine laboratory.—This laboratory, occupying two large rooms, contains twenty-five dynamos and motors varying in capacity from two to twenty kilowatts, adapted for experiments illustrating the properties of compound, shunt and series dynamos and motors, arc machines, as well as the use of interpoles. Switch-boards, numerous rheostats, lamp racks, starting boxes, circuit breakers, flexible cables, brakes, torsion dynamometers, tachometers, etc., are available for use with the machines.

This laboratory also contains two 15 kw., 25 cycle and two special 15 kw., 60 cycle General Electric polyphase revolving field alternators direct driven by motors, two 7½ kw. alternators, two rotary converters of 10 kw. and 5 kw. capacity, a 7½ kw. General Electric polyphase induction motor with slip ring rotor, Westinghouse three-phase squirrel cage induction motors, Wagner single phase motor and unity power factor motor, Swedish General Electric variable speed motor, Westinghouse single phase series motor, Westinghouse alternator, and several three phase and single phase induction motors; also transformers, reactive coils, and other details, as in the direct current sections of the laboratory described above, for experiments on the properties of alternating currents and alternating current apparatus in general. A constant-current transformer with its load of six series arc lamps, a three-element oscillograph, for studying wave forms, a high potential transformer and a mercury arc rectifier may also be mentioned. The students are supplied with Weston, Westinghouse and Thomson portable instruments for measuring purposes.

A motor generator set has been installed, comprising a 65 h.p. motor driving on the same shaft a 30 kw. 110 volt d.c. generator and a 30 kw. 60 cycle 110 volt alternator with direct connected exciter.

Appliances are also provided for the study of saturation and hysteretic properties of samples of iron and steel, and models for exercise in winding armatures.

High tension room. In a separate room with proper automatic devices for safety to the operator, there is installed a 20 kv-a. transformer with a range of voltages up to 200,000 volts. Studies of insulators may be carried out.

CHEMICAL LABORATORIES.

The Chemical laboratories are situated in the western half of the Chemistry and Mining building, on the first and second floors. The rooms are large and well lighted, and are supplied with the usual modern equipment.

The first and second year laboratory for qualitative work has accommodation for 112 students, each working space being supplied with water, gas and fume cupboard. The laboratory for quantitative analysis will accommodate 48 students; and is supplied with commodious fume cupboards and all necessary apparatus. A laboratory with working places for 36 is provided for the students engaged in the study of technical chemistry; it is equipped with appliances for the preparation and testing of chemical products. A laboratory for fourth year students with accommodation for eight workers has been fitted up. Each of these laboratories has its own balance room adjoining furnished with instruments from the best makers and adapted to the particular objects in view.

In addition there are rooms set apart for gas analysis, electrolytic analysis and a specially constructed fireproof laboratory for combustion, crucible and bomb furnaces. A calorimeter room has been equipped in the basement. Each of these laboratories is supplied with apparatus of the most approved design, providing excellent facilities for the prosecution of work in analytical and technical chemistry.

ELECTROCHEMICAL LABORATORIES.

The Electrochemical laboratories, which are situated in the Chemistry and Mining building, are priovded with special facilities for electrolytic work, including a large storage battery and electroplating dynamo with tanks as well as a good set of apparatus and electrical measuring instruments. The experimental work on electric furnaces is performed in two rooms specially equipped for this purpose with rheostats and switchboard connections to a 120 kw. d.c. generator which supplies the current required

ASSAYING LABORATORIES.

Two Assaying laboratories are situated in the basement of the Chemistry and Mining building. One has a floor space of 17 feet x 47 feet, and the other 28 feet x 37 feet. Adjoining each is a room 15 feet x 11 feet, with the necessary equipment for the wet work in connection with assaying. Common to both laboratories is a balance room furnished with gold balances set on a concrete pier. Each of the laboratories contains a number of melting holes for crucible fusions, various gas and oil furnaces both for crucibles and muffles, and two large brick muffle furnaces.

The furniture comprises lockers for the students, tables for the pulp balances and the necessary cabinets and shelving.

Adjoining the assay laboratories is a preparation room (19 feet x 13 feet) which is equipped with a motor, crusher, pulverizer, sample grinder and all the necessary hand pulverizers, screens, etc., for preparing ores for assay.

METALLURGICAL LABORATORY.

This laboratory is on the basement floor of the Chemistry and Mining Building. The main room has a floor space of 1,600 square feet.

Among the larger furnaces included in the equipment of the laboratory are a six hearth Wedge mechanical roasting furnace, the gases from which pass through Cottrell precipitating pipes 12 inches in diameter, and which are served with rectified current at 50,000 volts. There is also a gas fired muffle roasting furnace, a Steele-Harvey tilting furnace, a large resistance furnace for high temperature work, two water jacketed blast furnaces and a copper converter.

The laboratory has several small furnaces of various types. Facilities are provided for pyrometric work, for zinc retorting, for furnace gas analysis, for leaching of ores and for the electrolytic refining and precipitation of metals.

There is a laboratory for the testing of clays equipped with grinding pan, ball mill, presses, gas fired and oil fired kilns.

The metallographic laboratory is equipped with power driven polishing tables and microscope with metallographic camera.

MILLING AND CONCENTRATING LABORATORY.

A detached building, 72 feet x 70 feet in area, contains the milling and concentrating equipment. It is heated, lighted and supplied with electric power from the central plant, and is divided into two parts. The greater part, with 72 feet x 53 feet floor space, and 22 feet high, contains the milling and concentrating equipment. The machinery for the former operations consists of a five-stamp battery erected on concrete foundations, Challenge ore feeder, amalgamating plates, Wilfley table, a clean-up pan, steel settling tanks, a steel tank suspended from the roof girders to furnish a constant supply of water, and a track with travelling crawl to transport ore. This is driven by a 15-horsepower motor.

The concentrating part consists of a set of five revolving trommels for wet screenings, four three-compartment jigs, a trough classifier delivering three products, and two revolving buddles, Wilfley Slimer, Deister Slimer, Richard's Pulsating Classifier, Richard's Pulsating Jig, a dry sizer, besides experimental apparatus of various kinds for experimenting on the falling rates of ore particles, the settling of slimes, surface tension action in oil and flotation methods, etc. The waste products run to the same settling tanks as the tailings from the stamp battery. The ore is handled by a travelling crawl. All the machinery in this part is driven by electric motors.

The lower floor has been fitted up for lixiviation work with apparatus for the treatment of sands and slimes, different types of filter press, vacuum plant agitators, etc.

The plant throughout is intended mainly for teaching and experimental purposes and is made of such a size that numerous experiments can be carried out on small quantities of ore. Tests can also be made on lots of one to ten tons.

The other part of the milling building with 72 feet x 17 feet floor space and 15 feet high is divided into four separate rooms. The largest of the four rooms has an area of 476 square feet and is devoted to the crushing and pulverizing of the ores preparatory to their treatment in the milling and concentrating room. It is isolated in order to confine the dusty operations as far as possible to this one room, and is equipped with a gyrating crusher of Hadfield's make, a set of Hamilton rolls 16 inches by 12 inches, platform scales for weighing ore, a jib crane, pulleys, buckets, etc., for handling the rock. An adjoining room contains a 30 h.p. motor for driving the machinery of the crushing department, and storage bins for ore, work bench, etc. Another room with 17 feet x 15 feet floor space is furnished with a magnetic separator of the Rowan-Wetherill type, driven by its own motor.

MECHANICS OF MATERIALS LABORATORY.

This laboratory is intended for the scientific and commercial testing of materials of construction such as iron, steel, timber, concrete and masonry.

It is supplied with the following:

An Emery 50-ton hydraulic machine, built by Wm. Sellers & Co., of Philadelphia, for making tests in tension and compression.

A 100-ton screw power machine, built by Riehle Bros., Philadelphia. It is designed for making tests in tension, compression, shearing and cross-breaking, and will take in posts 12 feet long and beams up to 18 feet in length.

A Riehle 10-ton screw power universal testing machine.

A Riehle 50-ton screw power universal testing machine.

A 15-ton single lever-machine, built by J. Buckton & Co., Leeds, England.

A torsion machine, built by Tinius Olsen & Co., Philadelphia, for testing the strength and elasticity of shafting. This machine will twist shafts up to 16 feet in length and 2 inches in diameter.

A hand power torsion machine of simple mechanical construction, specially designed for the testing of short shafts of a maximum diameter of one inch.

A Riehle transverse testing machine of 5,000 pounds capacity, adapted to specimens up to 48 inches in length.

A Riehle compressometer, with spherical seat attachment for the adjustment of specimens having slightly non-parallel faces. This compressometer will receive specimens up to 10 inches in length.

An Olsen compression micrometer of standard type.

A 20,000 pound Olsen, hand power, wire testing machine, specially fitted for testing wooden columns with both fixed and pivoted ends.

A Riehle abrasion cylinder, built to the standard required by the National Brickmaker's Association, adopted in 1901.

A Berry strain-gauge for spans of 3 inches and 8 inches.

A Nalder dividing engine. This may be used either for the precise division of scales or for the calibration of instruments intended for refined measurements.

A Brinell hardness testing machine.

A Shore scleroscope for testing hardness.

A large number of extensometers of the usual degree of precision. These include the Bauschinger, Martens, Unwin, Ames, Riehle, Johnson, Henning (recording) and other types. In addition there are the usual scales, micrometers, telescopes and reflectors, voltmeters for the determination of metallic contact, and such other appliances as are necessary in the making of precise measurements.

The shop is equipped with a number of high-class machine tools specially fitted for reducing the specimens to the requisite shapes and dimensions with a minimum of hand labour. It is also supplied with the necessary appliances for making ordinary repairs and for making apparatus for special experiment and original investigation.

HIGHWAY LABORATORY.

This laboratory is equipped for carrying out investigations in the various materials employed in highway construction and maintenance, and comprises the following:

Page impact machine for testing the toughness of road materials.

Diamond core drill for preparing specimens for the toughness test.

Deval abrasion machine for testing the resistance to wear of road materials.

Cementation testing apparatus (Page type) for determining cementing properties of road materials.

Jaw crusher (Mitchell type) for crushing rock for various tests.

Power driven agitator with sieves for the mechanical analysis of sand, gravel and crushed rock.

The laboratory is also equipped with the appliances necessary for examining physical properties:—volatilization, specific gravity, viscosity, melting point, penetration, ductility, etc., of oils, asphalts, tars and other bituminous mixtures used in road construction and maintenance.

LABORATORY OF ONTARIO BOARD OF HEALTH.

Through the courtesy of the Secretary of the Provincial Board of Health for Ontario the facilities of the excellently equipped laboratory which the Board maintains at Stanley Park have, with certain conditions, been placed at the service of the University for the investigation of problems of interest to the sanitarian and the sanitary engineer. The equipment consists of various types of sewage sedimentation tank, sewage filter, sewage measuring devices, aerators, sterilizing appliances and a complete and representative plant intended for the filtration and sterilization of water by practically all known methods.

CEMENT TESTING LABORATORY.

This laboratory is fitted with all the ordinary moulds, sieves, balances burettes, steaming and drying tanks, tables, and other appliances necessary in making the usual physical tests of a Portland cement. It is also supplied with completely equipped cabinets·for individual work. In addition there are the following:

A 2,000 lb. Riehle machine fitted for either tension or compression.

A 2,000 lb. Riehle shot machine for tension.

A 2,000 lb. Fairbanks shot machine for tension.

A 1,000 lb. Olsen automatic shot machine fitted for tests in either tension or cross breaking.

An Olsen soapstone moist closet of modern design.

METROLOGICAL LABORATORY.

The department of surveying and geodesy is provided with all the ordinary field instruments, such as transits, levels, compasses, micrometers, sextants, planimeters,·plane tables, tapes, chains, etc., with which is carried on the instruction in practical field operations as detailed elsewhere.

A small laboratory is also established in the basement of the observatory described below, containing the necessary instruments for the refined measurements of geodetic surveying; as, a standard yard and metre, a Rogers 10-foot comparator, an invar base measuring apparatus, a Kater's pendulum with vacuum chamber, a level trier, micrometer microscopes, etc.

The geodetic observatory in connection with this department is used for the instruction of students of the Fourth Year in taking observations for time, latitude, longitude, and azimuth by the precise methods used in connection with a geodetic survey. It contains a 10-inch theodolite and zenith telescope by Troughton & Simms; an astronomical transit instrument and an 8-inch theodolite by Cooke; two electro-chronographs; a Howard astronomical clock; a Dent sidereal clock; a Dent sidereal break-circuit chronometer; a wireless receiving instrument; arithmometers, etc.

GEOLOGICAL AND MINERALOGICAL LABORATORIES.

In the Chemistry and Mining building on College Street the University possesses a modern laboratory for Geology and Mineralogy.

Courses are given in laboratory work, especially in personal examination of type sets of rocks, fossils, minerals and crystal models. These laboratory exercises serve to illustrate the introductory didactic instruction.

For the encouragement of pure crystallography the laboratories are supplied with goniometers of the various types, crystal models, appliances for the cutting of oriental crystal sections and for the physical examination of the same. Practical petrography is carried on in rooms provided with type sets of rocks, both macroscopic and microscopic. Advanced students are taught to make thin sections of rocks and fossils and to study them microscopically. For students in Mining a laboratory course in the interpretation of geological maps and section is provided. Typical mining regions are studied in detail and an opportunity is afforded for the examination of specimens illustrating economic geology.

The laboratory for the preparation of thin sections of rocks, minerals and fossils is provided with electric diamond saws and grinding appliances for the various types of work incidental to the preparation of thin sections and museum material.

A room is also provided for advanced work in cartography and geological surveying.

The departments possess 28 petrological microscopes and 5 of other types, so that it is now possible to provide advanced students with instruments and sets of thin sections for their own especial use. The blowpipe laboratory contains 156 lockers, especially designed for apparatus for students.

School of Engineering Research.

A School of Engineering Research, within the Faculty of Applied Science and Engineering was established in the Spring of 1917 at the suggestion of the late Dean Ellis.

The School is under the direct supervision of a Committee of Management composed of fifteen Members of the Faculty Council. To this Committee is entrusted the selection of researches to be undertaken under the auspices of the School, and the disposition of funds conducting them.

The School was organized chiefly for the training of graduates in methods of research, and for the carrying out of investigations. These latter may be problems relating to specific industries or raw materials and having a specific end in view, or general problems having to do with fundamental principles.

A number of research assistants are appointed annually in the various departments of the Faculty to carry on the work of research under direction of members of the staff. The facilities of the School are also open to graduates who desire to penetrate more deeply into particular phases of experimental work, or to undertake investigations either suggested by members of the staff or arising from their own work since graduation.

Address communications to the Secretary—Professor Maitland Boswell.

LIBRARY.

The University Library is contained in a building of its own, situated on the east side of the campus, that lies to the south of the Main Building. All students who have paid a library fee to the Bursar of the University are entitled to the privileges of the Library. Besides Reading Rooms the Building contains Departmental Studies, which may be used as study-rooms by honour students in the various branches and in which the Professors hold seminary courses, and private studies, intended for members of the Faculty or advanced students engaged in research work. The Library is opened at 8.45 every morning and remains open until 5.15 in the afternoon (6 p.m. during the second term). Books in ordinary use may not be taken out of the building during the daytime, but are lent for the night shortly before the hour of closing, to be returned the following morning before 10 o'clock. Books not in general demand may, on special application, be borrowed for a longer period. Failure to return a borrowed book at the proper time and other breaches of the regulations are punishable by fine or suspension from the privileges of the Library.

Rooms have been set apart in the Engineering and the Chemistry and Mining buildings for the housing of such periodicals and other literature of the University Library as is of special interest to the students of this faculty.

ROYAL ONTARIO MUSEUM.

Archaeology, Geology, Mineralogy, Palaeontology, Zoology.

Students of the University in all departments are recommended to avail themselves of the privileges of the Museum, which, although under separate control, is intimately connected with the work of the University.

The Museum is open on all week days from 10 a.m. to 5 p.m., and on Sundays from 2 p.m. to 5 p.m. The admission is free to the public on Tuesday, Thursday, Saturday and Sunday. On other days an admission fee of fifteen cents is charged.

By a resolution of the Board of Trustees all regular students of the University may be admitted free on all days of the week by presenting their card of registration.

UNIVERSITY OF TORONTO C.O.T.C.

The Toronto Contingent of the Canadian Officers Training Corps was organized in 1914, with a strength of 12 Companies. Its primary object is to provide students at Universities with a standardized measure of military training with a view to their qualifying for commissions in the country's auxiliary forces. C.O.T.C. Certificates of qualification exempt their holders from examination for commissioned rank on joining a militia unit. The facilities which are offered by the contingent for obtaining a qualification while at the University, are intended to enable gentlemen to give personal service to their country with the least possible interference with their civil careers, to ensure that units have their establishments complete in the junior commissioned ranks, and to build up an adequate reserve of scientifically trained officers who have completed a period of consecutive and systematic military training, on academic lines, of a nature calculated to produce good officers.

The contingent provides the practical work for students taking the Military Studies option for the B.A.Sc. degree, (see p. 19) as also physical exercise for students who may choose this as the form in which they will take their compulsory Physical Training. In addition to service in the corps for a University credit, students of any year or Faculty are trained in it to qualify for the Militia Department's officers' certificates. As the corps develops, after the set-back subsequent to its continuous activities during the war, it is hoped that it may be possible to form companies according to faculties and to so arrange the training of each that on leaving the University students will be qualified for commissions in that branch of the Militia to which their University course particularly applied.

The C.O.T.C. is a unit of the non-permanent Active Militia but forms no part of the organization for war and cannot be called out for active service as such. It is a training centre for the educated youth of the country from whom, as from all its sons, the Empire requires hard service but the hardest from those to whom most has been given.

The present Headquarters are at 184 College Street, and include armouries, members' reading room, library, and lecture room.

The Contingent's Staff is:

Officer Commanding.........Colonel W. R. Lang, late Gen. Staff, C.E.F.

Second in Command.........Major T. R. Loudon, late Can. Eng., C.E.F

Adjutant.................Major H. H. Madill, late C.E.F.

Quartermaster.............Lieut. V. C. Kerrison, late C.A.S.C., C.E.F.

Paymaster.................Lieut. T. A. Reed

Musketry Officer...........

Contingent Sergeant-Major...S.-M. W. Hunt, late Royal Welsh Fusiliers.

THE ONTARIO COLLEGE OF EDUCATION

THE ONTARIO COLLEGE OF EDUCATION.

GENERAL INFORMATION.

The Ontario College of Education is the University's professional school of education.   It trains candidates for diplomas and certificates as teachers and in particular for Provincial certificates as teachers-of Art, Household Science, and Physical Culture, as High School Assistants and Specialists and as First Class Public School teachers.   It also offers courses for the B.Paed., and D.Paed. degrees.

The buildings of the Ontario College of Education on Bloor Street contain well-equipped and well-ventilated lecture-rooms, laboratories, and reading-rooms for the accommodation of the students, and model class-rooms for observation and practice-teaching.   So far as necessary the observation and practice-teaching are supplemented by observation and practice-teaching in city schools in the neighbourhood.

While the chief exercises of the Ontario College of Education will be conducted in the buildings on Bloor Street, the students may use the University's library, gymnasium, athletic fields, etc., under such conditions as obtain with other students.   They will also be admitted free to the Royal Ontario Museum, Bloor Street, from 9 a.m. to 5 p.m., on presentation of their registration cards.   Thus, while they are subject to the same regulations, they enjoy all the privileges of the other University students.

BOARD AND LODGING.

Lodging and board are readily obtained in private boarding-houses within convenient distance of the University at a cost of from six dollars per week upwards for lodging with board; or, rooms may be rented at a cost of from one dollar and one-half per week upwards, and board obtained separately at reasonable rates.

The Secretary of the Ontario College of Education and the Secretary of the Christian Association of the University will forward accredited lists of boarding-houses on request.

COURSES.

The following courses are offered:

I. Courses for (1) Interim Ordinary High School Assistants' and High School Specialists' certificates with Interim First Class Public School certificates or Elementary certificates in Physical Culture and Art, (2) Ordinary certificates as teachers of Household Science.

II. Courses for the B.Paed. and D.Paed. degrees.

III. Courses under the Board of Graduate Studies for the degrees of M.A. and Ph.D.

I.

COURSES FOR INTERIM ORDINARY HIGH SCHOOL ASSIS-
TANTS' AND HIGH SCHOOL SPECIALISTS' CERTIFICATES
WITH INTERIM FIRST CLASS PUBLIC SCHOOL CERTIFI-
CATES OR ELEMENTARY CERTIFICATES IN PHYSICAL
CULTURE AND ART, AND FOR ORDINARY CERTIFICATES
AS TEACHERS OF HOUSEHOLD SCIENCE.

SESSIONS.

1. Enrolment in classes of the regular session will begin Monday,
September 26th, at 10 a.m., and the instruction will begin September 27th
at 10 a.m. The Autumn Term will end Friday, December 16th, at 12
noon, and the Winter Term will begin Tuesday, January 3rd, at 9 a.m.
The Spring Term will begin March 27th and end June 16th.

DUTIES OF STUDENTS.

2. (1) Regular attendance on the part of candidates for Provincial
certificates is indispensable, except for such as are exempt from attendance
under the regulations of the Department of Education, and for such as
are experienced teachers and are permitted by the Dean to act, after
Christmas, for not more than a total of one fortnight, as substitute teachers
in the schools of Ontario. A return of the attendance of each student will
be made to the Minister of Education at the close of the session.

(2) Students whose class-work shows them to be unduly deficient in
scholarship, or whose conduct or progress is unsatisfactory, may be dis-
missed from attendance by the Dean at any time during the session.

(3) On the Dean's report to the Minister of Education as to the
physical unfitness of a student for training for a Provincial certificate as a
teacher, the Minister may require a special medical examination of such
student, and, as a result thereof, may direct that his registration for such
training be cancelled.

STUDENT SOCIETIES.

3. Various religious, athletic, literary and dramatic associations are
formed each session. For professional improvement all students are
required to share in the activities of the literary and dramatic associations.

APPEALS.

4. The answer papers of the final examinations of all unsuccessful
candidates for Provincial certificates are re-read by the examiners, and
the results of the first reading reconsidered before a decision to reject is

reached. Despite this fact any unsuccessful candidate may have his case considered a third time if within two weeks after the announcement of the results he lodges with the Minister of Education his appeal, with a statement of the grounds on which it is based, and with a fee of $2.00. If made within the two weeks following, the fee will be $5, and no appeal will be entertained thereafter. The fee will be refunded if the appeal is sustained.

COURSE FOR INTERIM ORDINARY HIGH SCHOOL
CERTIFICATES.

PURPOSE.

5. The Course for Interim Ordinary High School certificates prepares candidates therefor in the theory and art of organizing, governing, and instructing pupils in the Continuation Schools, Grades A and B, and in High Schools.

CONDITIONS OF ADMISSION.

6. (1) Except as provided in (2) below, an applicant for admission to the course for an Interim Ordinary High School Assistant's certificate should make application not later than September 26th, to the Secretary of the Ontario College of Education on a form to be obtained from him and should submit with this application, on official forms also to be supplied by the Secretary:

(a) A certificate from the Deputy Registrar-General of Births, Parliament Buildings, Toronto, or an affidavit by one of the parents or other relative, or other person cognizant of the fact, that the applicant will be at least 20 years of age before October 1st, 1921.

(b) A certificate from a clergyman or other competent authority that he is of good moral character.

(c) A certificate from a duly qualified medical practitioner that for the purposes of this certificate he has made a careful examination of the applicant, and certifies as follows: (i) that he is free from heart disease or any other serious organic affection; (ii) that he is free from pulmonary affection, defective hearing, or seriously defective eyesight, or abnormal conditions of appearance which would interfere with his work as a teacher; and (iii) that in other respects also he is physically able for the work of a teacher as prescribed in the courses of study of the Ontario College of Education and of the Provincial Schools represented in the certificate for which he is a candidate. (See also Section 2 (3), p. 10.)

(d) An agreement, if successful in obtaining a teacher's certificate, to teach thereon in Ontario, for at least the first year of his subsequent teaching experience.

NOTICE.—*A violation of this agreement will render the certificate invalid.*

(e) A certificate from a competent authority that he is a British subject.

(f) His certificate of graduation as Bachelor or Master of Arts, Bachelor or Master of Science, Bachelor of Commerce, Bachelor of Agriculture, or Bachelor of Applied Science, from a British university, after a regular

—34

COURSE FOR INTERIM ORDINARY HIGH SCHOOL—*Cont.*

university course approved by the Minister of Education as to entrance requirements and as to content of the undergraduate courses. Each applicant must have Upper School or Honour Matriculation standing in English and History and Mathematics or the equivalent of such standing.

(2) An applicant for admission to this course who is not a candidate for the certificate of the Ontario Department of Education must comply with such conditions of admission as the Council of the Ontario College of Education may determine.

(3) Applications, by students not in attendance, for admission to the examinations should be made, at least one month before the examinations begin, to the Secretary of the Ontario College of Education, University of Toronto, on an official form to be obtained from the Secretary.

7. The annual fee for the Course for Interim Ordinary High School Assistants' certificates, which includes the library and examination fees, is $25.00. The fee for the examination in the Course for Interim High School Assistants' certificates when the examination is taken by students not in attendance, will be $15.00, or $10.00 for Part I and $5.00 for Part II, or in the case of partial examination, $2.00 per subject. The fee for the University diploma will be $2.00. A library deposit of $1.00 will be required of all students, and a fee of $8.00 for membership in Hart House of all male students. All male students will also be required to become members of the Students' Administrative Council.

TEXT-BOOKS.

8. The text-books for the academic work are those prescribed for the Lower and Middle Schools of the High Schools of Ontario in each subject of the student's course.

For Observation and Practice-teaching students should supply themselves with copies of the text-books authorized for use in the above-named grades of schools. They should also supply themselves with the professional text-books whose titles appear in italics in the lists given below under each subject.

PROGRAMME OF STUDIES.

9. (1) The course of training for Interim Ordinary High School Assistants' certificates consists of two parts as follows:

Part I: The Science of Education, School Management and Law, English, History, Geography, *and* (*a*) Latin, and French or German or Greek *or* (*b*) Mathematics and Science.

Part II: Observation and Practice-teaching.

COURSE FOR INTERIM ORDINARY HIGH SCHOOL—*Cont.*

(2) Students in attendance in the Interim Ordinary High School Assistants' course *may* also take the course in Vocal Music, and, if they possess the required academic qualifications, a Specialist's course, and *must* also take *either* the course for the First Class Public School certificate *or* the course for the Elementary certificate in Physical Culture *or* the course for the Elementary certificate in Art.

ORGANIZATION OF COURSE.

10. (1) The following introductory work will be taken up at the beginning of the session.

(*a*) About 20 lectures upon the General Method of the Recitation in the Science of Education.

(*b*) Supervised Observation and Practice lessons (about 10 of each) in the different grades or forms of the High Schools.

(2) The instruction in the special methodology of the subjects of the High School courses will be accompanied by a review from the academic standpoint of such portions of each subject as may be necessary to determine the scholarship of the students and to illustrate the methods of instruction in that subject, dealing in particular with those parts of the course that are difficult of presentation.

(3) In the order and grouping of the courses due regard will be had to the character of each subject, to its correlations with other subjects, and to the logical development of the courses.

(4) So far as the conditions permit the programme of instruction will be organized on the basis of intensive study of a few subjects at a time.

(5) (*a*) The lectures will be distributed among the various prescribed subjects approximately as follows: The Science of Education 100, School Management and Law 50, English 90, History 20, Geography 15, Mathematics 90, Latin 40, French or German or Greek 40, Science 40, Vocal Music 30.

(*b*) The courses in Mathematics, English, and Vocal Music will begin at the opening of the session and will continue until the close; those in the other subjects will be given, as far as practicable, in correlation with the Observation and Practice-teaching and will continue until completed.

(*c*) The Observation work will begin in the third week of the session, and the Practice-teaching in the fifth week. Exclusive of the introductory work, the programme of instruction will include for each student at least 50 Observation lessons and 30 Practice-teaching lessons. These numbers may be increased to meet the needs of individual students.

COURSE FOR INTERIM ORDINARY HIGH SCHOOL—*Cont.*

OBSERVATION AND PRACTICE-TEACHING.

11. (1) The introductory course defined herein will be followed by systematic Observation and Practice-teaching, under the general supervision of the lecturers in the Ontario College of Education.

(2) (*a*) The Observation and Practice-teaching lessons for each student will be arranged to represent as far as practicable the work in all forms and grades of the Lower and Middle Schools of the High Schools. There will also be Observation in the Upper School of the High School.

(*b*) So far as practicable continuous Practice-teaching for several periods will be required, the students being wholly responsible for the management of the classes.

(3) Students will be notified of the subject and scope of the Observation lesson, and should prepare the lesson beforehand. After observing the lesson they will discuss it with the teacher or lecturer concerned.

(4) Students will be notified of the subject and the scope of the practice-teaching lesson by the teacher concerned, and will prepare a plan of each Practice-teaching lesson for submission to the teacher.

(5) (*a*) Model lessons will be taught by the teachers of the Practice-schools in accordance with the regular programme of said schools.

(*b*) The lecturers of the Ontario College of Education will develop the details of their subjects in the teaching order, and after each suitable step, will also themselves teach model lessons in special classes and in the practice schools.

(6) (*a*) The necessary applications of the Science of Education and of Special Methods will be made systematically in connection with the Observation lessons and the Practice-teaching; so that the course may be taken up in terms of the pupil's mind and growth. Throughout the course the instructor in the Science of Education will himself illustrate by actual teaching the principles he has discussed in class.

(*b*) As far as practicable, the lecturers of the Ontario College of Education will be present at the Observation lessons and Practice-teaching of the students and will make jointly the criticism and valuation of their work.

EXAMINATIONS.

12. (1) For the purpose of determining the final standing of students the courses are classified into the following subjects:

Part I: Science of Education, School Management and Law, English, History, Mathematics, Geography, Latin, French, German, Greek, Science, Vocal Music.

Part II: Observation, Practice-teaching.

COURSE FOR INTERIM ORDINARY HIGH SCHOOL—*Cont.*

(2) (*a*) The final standing of students in attendance will be determined by the combined results of the sessional records and the records of the final examinations in the subjects of Part I, and by the results of the records of the Observations and Practice-teaching of Part II.

(*b*) The sessional records represent oral and written exercises, practical work, practice in making examination papers, and in valuing the answer-papers of pupils, and such other tests as the staff may prescribe.

(*c*) At the close of each term there will be final examinations in such courses of Part I as have been completed in the term.

(*d*) At the examinations in Part I, each paper will contain questions in methodology, based upon the academic subjects, which will test the candidate's academic knowledge and, if his sessional records and his answers to these questions show that his academic knowledge is defective, he will be rejected on this ground alone.

(*e*) The maximum marks assigned to each subject in Part I will be 100. In all subjects except Vocal Music, a maximum of 40% of the marks will be assigned to the sessional records and 60% to the final written examinations. In Vocal Music a maximum of 50% of the marks will be assigned to the sessional records and 50% to the final written examinations.

(*f*) A maximum of 800 marks will be assigned to Practice-teaching and of 400 to Observation. The standing of the student in Observation and in Practice-teaching will be based upon his sessional records in the lessons following those which form part of the introductory courses.

CERTIFICATES.

13. (1) A student who obtains 50% of the marks in each of the required subjects of Part I and 60% of the aggregate of the marks in each of the divisions of Part II, may, on the recommendation of the examiners, be awarded by the Minister of Education, an Interim Ordinary High School Assistant's certificate.

(2) A student who passes in Part II and fails in not more than two of the obligatory subjects of Part I will be exempted from further attendance.

(3) All other students who have failed to obtain the necessary final standing will be required to attend another session, beginning after the Christmas vacation.

(4) (*a*) (i) Candidates who are exempted from attendance at the Ontario College of Education, as provided in (2) above, may complete their standing for a certificate by re-writing, at one annual examina ion, or, separately, at different annual examinations, the examination in the subject or subjects in which they failed.

COURSE FOR INTERIM ORDINARY HIGH SCHOOL—*Cont.*

(ii) Candidates who failed at an examination under former Regulations and who were exempted from subsequent attendance at the Ontario College of Education will take, not later than a date determined in each case by the Minister of Education, the final examination papers as prescribed herein but their standing will be determined in the subjects as constituted under the Regulations in force when they first wrote.

(iii) Candidates who have been exempted by the Minister of Education from attendance at the Ontario College of Education on account of equivalent training in other provinces or countries, and who are required to write on the final examinations of the Ontario College of Education will take the prescribed final examinations in the subjects of Part I, and will also satisfy the examiners by teaching and other tests that they are competent for the work in the subjects covered by the certificate for which they are candidates.

(b) (i) The pass standard for candidates exempt from attendance will be the same as that for candidates in attendance but no allowance will be made for sessional work, if any, in the case of candidates not in attendance.

(ii) The final examinations in Vocal Music for students exempt from attendance, will include both a practical and a written test, 50 marks being assigned to the written test and 50 to the practical test.

(c) (i) Candidates exempt from attendance shall take their practical tests in Part II at such times during the session as may be agreed upon with the examiners. They shall take their examinations in the subjects of Part I in June on dates to be determined by the examiners or, in part, in June and, in part, at such times during the session as are set apart for the examination of students in attendance.

(ii) Students exempt from attendance may take their written examinations in Part I at Toronto, or at such local centres and under such conditions as may be determined by the Senate. They must, however, take their practical tests in Vocal Music, and in Teaching at Toronto.

(5) (a) Candidates who hold First Class Public School certificates, with the academic standing required for admission to the High School Assistants' Course and who submit certificates of at least one year's successful experience in a Continuation School from the Inspector or Inspectors under whom they have taught will be exempted from the attendance, excepting for the Spring Term, but will take the final examinations prescribed for Part I, and must also satisfy the examiners by practical tests that they are able to teach the subjects of the High School courses.

(b) Other candidates who hold a First or a Second Class certificate with the academic standing required for admission to the High School

COURSE FOR INTERIM ORDINARY HIGH SCHOOL—*Cont.*

Assistants'. Course will be exempted from attendance during the Autumn Term, but will take the final examinations prescribed for Part I and must also satisfy the examiners by practical tests that they are able to teach the subjects of the High School courses.

DIPLOMAS.

14. Successful candidates who are awarded Ordinary High School certificates by the Minister of Education and such other successful candidates as may be admitted to the course under section 6 (2), p. 13, may be awarded University diplomas.

COURSES FOR HIGH SCHOOL SPECIALISTS' CERTIFICATES.

PURPOSE.

15. The courses for Interim High School Specialists' certificates prepare candidates therefor in the theory and art of organizing and instructing the pupils of the High Schools and Collegiate Institutes, in certain departments or subjects of the courses of said Schools.

CONDITIONS OF ADMISSION.

16. (1) Applicants for admission to the courses for Interim High School Specialists' certificates, or to the final examinations for said certificates, must also be applicants for admission to the courses for Interim Ordinary High School Assistant's certificates, or must be applicants for admission to the examinations therefor without attendance throughout the session, or must already hold Ordinary High School Assistant's certificates. No candidate will be awarded an Interim High School Specialist's certificate or receive credit towards said certificate *before* he has been awarded an Interim Ordinary High School certificate.

(2) (*a*) A candidate for an Interim High School Specialist's certificate who is also a candidate for admission to the course for an Interim Ordinary High School Assistant's certificate, must comply with the conditions for admission prescribed for candidates for Interim Ordinary High School Assistants' certificates, and must also have his academic standing as a specialist approved by the Minister of Education before he will be admitted to said specialist course or to the examinations for the specialist certificate.

(*b*) A candidate for an Interim High School Specialist's certificate who holds an Ordinary High School Assistant's certificate, must have his academic standing as a specialist approved by the Minister of Education before he will be admitted to the examinations for the specialist certificate.

FEES.

17. When an Interim High School Specialist Course is taken concurrently with the Course for an Interim Ordinary High School certificate, or when an Interim High School Specialist examination is taken concurrently with the examination for an Interim Ordinary High School certificate, there is no additional fee. The fee for a specialist course or examination, one or both, taken apart from the course or examination for an Interim Ordinary High School certificate, will be $5.00 per course or per examination, one or both, as the case may be.

COURSES FOR HIGH SCHOOL SPECIALISTS—*Cont.*

COURSES.

18. (1) Courses will be offered for Interim High School Specialists' certificates in Agriculture Classics, Commerce, English and French, English and History, French and German, French and Spanish, Mathematics, Mathematics and Physics, Moderns and History, Science, and Household Science.

(2) Each specialist course will consist of at least two seminar-periods per week throughout the session, and of special Observation and Practice-teaching in the specialist department in which the candidate is an applicant for a certificate.

TEXT-BOOKS.

19. Students in the courses for High School Specialists' certificates will supply themselves with such special professional text-books as may be recommended by the instructors from the lists given under the details of each course. The other books and journals, whose names appear in these lists, may be consulted in the library of the Ontario College of Education.

EXAMINATIONS.

Subjects and Standards.

20. (1) Subject to the condition that no student may be awarded an Interim High School Specialist's certificate who does not already hold or is not also awarded an Interim Ordinary High School Assistant's certificate, the final standing of students in attendance in a specialist course will be determined by the records of the Observation and Practice-teaching in the department or subject concerned, and by the combined results of the sessional records and the records of the final examinations in the same department or subject. The sessional records represent oral and written exercises, practical work, practice in preparing examination papers, and in valuing the answer-papers of pupils, and such term work as the instructors may prescribe. The records of the final examinations will be based upon two examination papers taken in each department at the close of the session. The maximum marks represented in the Observation and Practice-teaching will be 100; in the sessional records 40; and in the final written examinations of the department or subject 60.

(2) The final standing of students not in attendance will be determined by the final written examinations and by teaching in the department concerned. For this purpose the maximum of marks in each case will be 100.

COURSES FOR HIGH SCHOOL SPECIALISTS—*Cont.*

CERTIFICATES.

21. (1) On the recommendation of the examiners the Minister of Education may grant Interim High School Specialists' certificates to students in attendance who have fulfilled the conditions of the course for Interim Ordinary High School certificates, who in their specialist department have obtained (a) 60% of the aggregate of marks represented in the sessional records and the records of the final examinations and (b) 60% of the marks assigned to the Observation and the Practice-teaching.

(2) On the recommendation of the examiners the Minister of Education may grant Interim High School Specialists' certificates to students exempt from attendance who hold or are awarded Ordinary High School certificates, who hold also the necessary academic certificates as specialists, and who obtain 60% of the marks assigned to the written examinations and to the Practice-teaching, respectively, in the specialist course concerned.

(3) (a) For students not in attendance the written examinations in the courses for Interim High School Specialists' certificates will be held at the end of the session at Toronto or at such local centres and under such conditions as may be determined by the Senate.

(b) For students not in attendance the practical examinations will be held at Toronto, except in the case of those to whose competency the visiting Provincial Inspector certifies, after due notification to such Inspector by the candidate of the latter's intention to become an applicant for a specialist's certificate.

COURSES FOR FIRST CLASS PUBLIC SCHOOL CERTIFICATES.

PURPOSE.

22. The course for First Class Public School certificates prepares candidates therefor in the theory and art of organizing, governing, and instructing the pupils of the Public, Separate, and Continuation Schools.

CONDITIONS OF ADMISSION.

23. Applicants for admission to the course for Interim First Class Public School certificates or to the final examinations for said certificates must comply with the conditions of admission prescribed for candidates for Interim Ordinary High School Assistants' certificates. No candidate will be awarded an Interim First Class Public School certificate or receive credit towards said certificate *before* he has been awarded an Interim Ordinary High School Assistant's certificate.

FEES.

24. When an Interim First Class Public School course is taken concurrently with the course for an Interim Ordinary High School certificate, or when the examination for an Interim First Class Public School certificate is taken concurrently with the examinations for an Interim Ordinary High School Assistant's certificate, there is no additional fee. The fee for a First Class Public School course or for the examinations of said course taken by one who already holds an Interim Ordinary High School Assistant's certificate will be $5.00 for the course or for the examinations, one or both, as the case may be, or $2.00 for each examination paper.

TEXT-BOOKS.

25. The text-books for the academic work of the course for Interim First Class Public School certificates shall be those prescribed in each subject for the High, Public and Separate Schools. The text-books for the professional work shall be those whose titles are printed below in italics.

PROGRAMME OF STUDIES.

26. (1) The course of training, which is supplementary to the course of training for Interim Ordinary High School certificates, consists of the following:

Part I: Reading, Spelling, Composition (including stories and biographies from History), Arithmetic, Algebra, Geometry, Latin, Science,

COURSES FOR FIRST CLASS PUBLIC SCHOOL—*Cont.*

Nature Study (including Geography), Writing, Music, Art, Hygiene, Physical Culture, Manual Training, and Household Science (for women), as defined in the Ontario Normal School courses for Interim First Class Public School certificates.

Part II: Observation and Practice-teaching—at least thirty observations and fifteen practice lessons—to be conducted under conditions defined in Ontario Normal School courses for Interim First Class Public School certificates.

(2) To the instruction in the subjects of the course will be allotted a maximum of two hundred lecture periods.

MODIFICATIONS OF COURSES.

27. (1) Students who take the Latin, Mathematics, Science, or Music of the Interim Ordinary High School Assistant's course will be exempted from the Latin, Algebra, Geometry, Science, or Music of the Interim First Class Public School course, but will be required to take the Arithmetic of said course.

(2) Students who hold Provincial professional certificates in Physical Culture, Writing, Music, Art, Manual Training, or Household Science will be exempted from the examinations thereon but will take the Observations and Practice-teaching therefor.

(3) Candidates who hold Provincial Second Class Public School certificates and who take Latin and a second language as the option o f the Interim Ordinary High School Assistants' course will be exempted from the instruction and examinations in all subjects of the Interim First Class Public School course except Mathematics and Science, while those who hold Provincial Second Class Public School certificates and take Mathematics and Science as the option will be exempted from the instruction and examinations in all subjects of the Interim First Class Public School course except Latin.

EXAMINATIONS.

28. (1) Subject to the condition that no student may be awarded an Interim First Class Public School certificate who does not already hold, or is not also awarded an Interim Ordinary High School Assistant's certificate, the final standing of the students in attendance in the course for Interim First Class Public School certificates will be determined by the records of the Observation and Practice-teaching and by the combined results of the sessional records and the records of the final examinations in said course. Subject to the same condition, the final standing of candidates not in attendance will be determined by the records of the final written examinations and of practice-teaching.

COURSES FOR FIRST CLASS PUBLIC SCHOOL—*Cont.*

(2) The examinations in the subjects of the course for Interim First Class Public School certificates shall be conducted, *pari passu*, in the terms and under the conditions set out in the Calendar of the course for Interim First Class Public School certificates of the Provincial Normal Schools.

CERTIFICATES.

29. (1) (*a*) Subject to the conditions of Sec. 28 (1), a candidate who obtains 50% of the marks in each subject of the course for Interim First Class Public School certificates and 60% of the aggregate of the marks in each of Observation and Practice Teaching may, on the recommendation of the examiners, be awarded by the Minister of Education, an Interim First Class Public School certificate.

(*b*) Subject to the same conditions, a candidate who passes in Observation and Practice Teaching and fails in not more than three subjects and who does not receive less than 45% in any subject, may, on the recommendation of the examiners, be granted by the Minister an Interim Second Class Public School certificate.

(*c*) Subject to the same conditions, a candidate who passes in the Observation and Practice-teaching and fails in not more than three subjects may be exempted from further attendance and may complete his course for an Interim First Class Public School certificate by rewriting at one annual examination, or, separately, at different annual examinations, the examinations in the subject or subjects in which he failed.

(2) All candidates other than those referred to in (*b*) and (*c*) who have failed to obtain the necessary final standing will be required to attend another session, beginning after the Christmas vacation.

(3) Regulations 13, (4) (*a*) (i), (ii), (iii), (*b*) (i), (*c*) (i), (ii), which apply to candidates for Interim Ordinary High School Assistant's certificates who are exempt from attendance apply also, *pari passu*, to candidates for Interim First Class Public School certificates who are exempt from attendance.

COURSES FOR ELEMENTARY CERTIFICATES IN PHYSICAL CULTURE AND IN ART.

PURPOSE.

30. The courses for the Elementary certificates in Physical Culture and Art prepare candidates therefor in the theory and art of organizing, governing, and instructing in Physical Culture and Art the pupils of Continuation and High Schools.

CONDITIONS OF ADMISSION.

31. Students who have been admitted to the course for Interim Ordinary High School certificates will take also either the course for an Interim First Class Public School certificate or the course for the Elementary certificate in Physical Culture or the course for the Elementary certificate in Art.

FEES.

32. As the course for the Elementary certificate in Physical Culture or in Art may be an obligatory part of the course for the Interim Ordinary High School Assistant's certificate, no additional fee is required.

TEXT-BOOKS.

33. Students in the courses for Elementary certificates in Physical Culture or Art will supply themselves with such text-books as may be recommended by the instructors from the lists given under the details of those subjects.

PROGRAMME OF STUDIES.

34. (1) The subjects of the course for Elementary certificates in Physical Culture or in Art are to be found on pages 42-45.

(2) To the instruction in the subjects of the course in Physical Culture or in Art will be allotted a maximum of one hundred and twenty lecture periods.

EXAMINATIONS.

35. (1) The final standing of candidates for the Elementary certificate in Physical Culture or in Art will be determined by the results of the sessional work, final practical tests, and final written examinations.

(2) (a) The following is the scheme of examinations and tests in Physical Culture:

COURSES FOR ELEMENTARY CERTIFICATES IN PHYSICAL CULTURE AND ART--*Continued.*

Written Examinations:

Anatomy 100, Physiology and First Aid 100.

Sessional and Final Practical Tests:

FOR WOMEN: Calisthenics 200, Apparatus 50, Games and Military Drill 200, Swimming 50.

FOR MEN: Calisthenics 100, Apparatus 200, Indoor Games and Athletics 100, Swimming 50.

Fifty per cent. of the marks in eaćh of the practical examinations will be assigned to the sessional and fifty per cent. to the final tests.

(*b*) The following is the scheme of examinations and tests in Art:

Sessional Work:

All sessional work must be completed satisfactorily before the other tests may be taken.

Practical Time Tests:

Drawing from common objects, in pencil, and in charcoal.
Drawing from nature.
Composition, simple illustration of a given subject.
Modelling of simple forms.
Design of conventionalized naturál forms, lettering.
Colour, painting still life in colour harmony.
Blackboard and memory drawing.

Written Tests:

Outlines of the history of art.
Theory of colour.
Design and applied art.
Elementary perspective.
Methods of teaching art in High and Continuation Schools.

Each subject and each paper shall be valued at 100.

CERTIFICATES.

36. (1) On the recommendation of the examiners the Minister of Éducation may grant an Elementary certificate in Physical Culture or Art, as the case may be, to the student in the course for an Interim Ordinary High School certificate, provided that said student is awarded an Interim Ordinary High School certificate and obtains (*a*) in Physical Culture a minimum of 50% of the marks assigned to each subject, (i) the written and (ii) the sessional and final practical tests, respectively, or (*b*)

COURSES FOR ELEMENTARY CERTIFICATES IN PHYSICAL
CULTURE AND ART—*Continued*.

in Art a minimum of 50% of the marks assigned to each subject or paper
of the practical and written tests, respectively.

(2) (*a*) No student will be awarded an Elementary certificate in
Physical Culture or Art whose attendance or progress in any part of the
course has been reported as unsatisfactory.

(*b*) The Dean will investigate the claims of the candidates who report
themselves as unable for physical reasons to take the course in swimming,
provided that such claims are presented to the instructor at the beginning
of the session on a form and after a manner defined by the Minister of
Education. If any candidate is exempted from the instruction in swimming by the Minister of Education that fact will be stated in his certificate.

(3) On the recommendation of the examiners, the Minister of Education may permit candidates in these courses who have completed the
sessional work and taken all practical tests successfully but who have
failed in one or more subjects of the written tests, to take the written tests
without attending again or repeating their practical work or tests.

DETAILS OF COURSES.

FOR ORDINARY HIGH SCHOOL ASSISTANTS', HIGH SCHOOL SPECIALISTS', AND FIRST CLASS PUBLIC SCHOOL CERTIFICATES AND FOR ELEMENTARY CERTIFICATES IN PHYSICAL CULTURE AND ART.

. 37. The topics of the subjects of the courses for Interim Ordinary High School Assistants' and High School Specialists' certificates and for Elementary certificates in Physical Culture or Art are given below. For the courses for Interim First Class Public School certificates these topics and subjects must be supplemented by the topics and subjects set out in the Normal School courses for First Class Public School certificates.

THE SCIENCE OF EDUCATION.

38. *Introduction.*—Democracy and education; the special need for education in a democracy; teaching as a vocation; teacher-training in a modern educational system.

General Method.—The meaning of method and its psychological foundations; procedures common to various branches of teaching; types of lessons; notes of lessons.

Principles of Education.—The nature and aims of education; the function in education of the state, home, church, vocation, etc.; the curriculum, its nature, purpose, and selection; modern movements for the reform of education.

Educational Classics.—The study in class of selected portions of a few educational classics.

Educational Psychology.—The original nature of man, including a study of heredity, instinct, and capacities.

The Psychology of the learning process, including the study of such topics as habit, rates of learning, practice, fatigue, memory, reasoning.

The Psychology of typical high school branches; standard scales for their measurement.

The measurement of general intelligence; an examination of the Binet-Simon and other tests.

Child Study, its aims, methods, and results.
—35

DETAILS OF COURSES.

Books of Reference:

   Ontario Normal School Manuals: Science of Education, History of Education.

   Adams (Ed.): The New Teaching.

   Dewey: Democracy and Education.

   Raymont: Principles of Education.

   Ruediger: Principles of Education.

   Sandiford: Mental and Physical Life of School Children.

   Starch: Educational Psychology.

   Waddle: Introduction to Child Psychology.

   Woodrow: Brightness and Dullness in Children.

SCHOOL MANAGEMENT AND LAW.

39. School Management, School Organization, School Administration; aims and scope of each; relation of each to the teaching process.

Forms of educational control; Department of Education and its functions; school boards and their functions; relation of inspectors and principals to teachers; teachers to caretakers, trustees; finance of education; business administration.

Types of schools; functions of each type, primary, secondary, and higher schools; consolidated schools; day and evening schools; training schools; commercial, industrial, agricultural, and technical schools; schools for subnormal children, defectives, and delinquents.

School sites and surroundings; school buildings; construction, caretaking, heating, ventilation, lighting, sanitation, decoration, and equipment; apparatus; libraries, selection, cataloguing, use; text-books, authorization, use and abuse; free text-books; visual aids; medical and dental inspection; the detection of communicable diseases.

The teacher: characteristics, qualifications, appointment, tenure of office, promotion, improvement of status; superannuation of the teacher; duties of the teacher in relation to pupils, parents, and other citizens; qualifications and characteristics of the successful teacher; his code of ethics.

The pupil: privileges and duties; the health of the pupil; the formation of his habits; the teacher's responsibility; fatigue; moral training.

The first day in school; the importance of the teacher's work and attitude.

Organization: grading and classification; promotion; retardation; elimination; care of individual and of abnormal.

The recitation: assignment of home and seat work; oral and written exercises; how to study; questioning; treatment of answers.

Discipline: its scope; relation to methods of teaching; incentives; causes of disorder and inattention; methods of dealing with weaknesses and offences; penalties.

DETAILS OF COURSES.

Time-tables: purpose; principles involved in construction; typical daily programmes for various kinds of schools.

Records and reports: keeping registers; value and kinds of school records; forms of reports.

Examinations and other tests of progress.

School Law and Regulations and Public Health Acts and Regulations in so far as they refer to the duties of school boards, teachers and pupils.

Books of Reference:

> *Regulations and Courses of Study for the Public, High and Continuation Schools of Ontario.*
> *Ontario Schools Acts, and Public Health Act.*
> *Ontario Normal School Manuals: School Organization and Management, History of Education.*
> Bennett: School Efficiency.
> Bagley: Class Management.
> Landon: Principles and Practice of Teaching and School Management.
> White: School Management.

ENGLISH.

40. (1) *Reading:* The importance of training in reading and in the principles of vocal expression to the pupil's ordinary speech and general culture.

The Reading Process: The factors involved in the process; the work of the eye in reading; word-recognition; the reading process as a specialized mode of the thought process; the relation of ideas to symbols; constant necessity for associating the printed symbol directly with the idea; the ideal conditions for the formation of this association.

The nature and function of silent reading; methods of conducting lessons in silent reading; the basis of expressive reading; the principles of vocal expression; the criticism of the pupil's reading; the place and limitations of imitative reading.

Practice; voice training; a class course in expressive reading; this work to be supplemented by practice in connection with the course in literature and with the activities of the Literary Society and the Dramatic Club.

Tests: Reading tests, *e.g.*, "The Courtis Standard Test in Reading".

(2) *Literature.*—The place of literature in school courses; the principles followed in Ontario and elsewhere in arranging literature courses for schools; books suitable for intensive study in the various forms or grades of the schools; class treatment of such types of literature as the

DETAILS OF COURSES.

short poem, the long narrative poem, the play, the short story, and the novel; examinations in literature; supplementary reading, its importance, selection of books, testing of reading.

The course in literature includes a consideration of the problems connected with the teaching of silent and expressive reading and voice training.

(3) *Grammar.*—Introductory: The meaning of English grammar; its relation to speech; reasons for and against retaining it in elementary schools; reasons for deferring the formal study till Form IV; introductory work of Form III in connection with composition.

Consideration of the content and value of the course in grammar in Continuation and High Schools; the work to be covered in each of the Forms of the Lower School; use of a text-book in grammar; terminology; the use of definitions; treatment of false syntax; methods of conducting instruction in grammar discussed and illustrated in lessons upon subjects selected from topics difficult of presentation.

(4) *Composition.*—Introductory: The value of language training; present-day tendencies in the teaching of composition.

Methods: How habits of speaking and writing good English are formed; expression as a stage in the development of every lesson; the forms of expression that aid most the development of language powers; the effect of the teacher's example upon the pupils' language; relative value of reading and telling stories; the story method; value of reading and memorizing good literature; incidental work in language training.

The relation of oral and written composition; purpose and value of oral exercises; criticism of oral work, the dangers connected therewith and the means of avoiding them.

The principles to be kept in view in conducting exercises in written composition; the method of gathering, selecting, and arranging material; value of topical outlines; supervision and aid during writing; the place of home work in written composition; the value of formal linguistic exercises; correction of common errors; letter-writing and business-forms.

The mechanics of written composition: Sentence and paragraph structure; paragraph compositions; the use of capitals, punctuation marks, quotation marks, abbreviations, etc.

The principles to be followed in arranging a course in composition; work suited to the age and experience of the student; use of a text-book in composition; amount of written work to be demanded; criticism of essays; standards of marking; place of rhetoric in the school course; importance of oral composition; sources of material; class procedure.

DETAILS OF COURSES.

Books of Reference:

> *Ontario High School Grammar.*
> *Ontario High School Composition.*
> *Ontario High School Reader.*
> *Public School Manual in Composition.*
> *High School Manual in Composition.*
> Bolenius: The Teaching of Literature in Grammar Grades and the High School.
> Carpenter, Baker and Scott: The Teaching of English.
> Chubb: The Teaching of English.
> Clark: How to Teach Reading in the Public School.
> Fairchild: The Teaching of Poetry.
> Huey: Psychology and Pedagogy of Reading.

HISTORY.

41. Stages in the study of history; the reflective stage; the tools of the history teacher; the High School course in history and civics; importance, content, methods of teaching. Illustration of methods in lessons on topics selected from the history prescribed for the Lower and Middle Schools. Students will be required to show their ability to gather historical material, and to present it in acceptable forms.

Books of Reference:

> *Public School Manual: History.*
> Bourne: The Teaching of History and Civics.
> Dunn: Social Studies in Secondary Education.
> Jarvis: The Teaching of History.
> Johnson: The Teaching of History.
> Macpherson: Visual Aids in the Teaching of History.
> The Committee of Seven: The Study of History in Schools.

SEMINAR IN ENGLISH AND HISTORY.

42. *English:*

(*a*) A study of topics difficult of presentation in the English grammar, composition, and literature prescribed in the High School courses of study.

(*b*) A discussion of the organization of the course in English throughout the various Forms of the High School.

(*c*) A study of the methods of class-room procedure in the teaching of English, and of problems arising therefrom.

DETAILS OF COURSES.

Books of Reference:

> Bolenius: *Teaching Literature in the Grammar Grades and High Schools.*
> Carpenter, Baker and Scott: The Teaching of English.
> Chubb: The Teaching of English.
> Hosic: Reorganization of English in Secondary Schools (Bulletin No. 2, 1917, Bureau of Education).
> Tomkinson: The Teaching of English.
> Lamborn: The Rudiments of Criticism.
> Articles in "The English Journal" and other journals.

HISTORY:

(*a*) A study of topics difficult of presentation in the prescribed history.

(*b*) A discussion of the courses in history that are adapted for pupils of various ages, and of the corresponding methods of teaching.

·(*c*) A study of the method of research in history. The preparation of short monographs on assigned topics.

Books of Reference:

> (*Johnson: The Teaching of History.*)
> Allen: The Place of History in Education.
> Dunn: Social Studies in Secondary Education (Bulletin No. 26, 1916, Bureau of Education).
> Keatinge: Studies in the Teaching of History.
> Articles in "The Historical Outlook" and other journals.
> Simpson: Supervised Study in History.

MATHEMATICS.

43. *Arithmetic.*—A brief study of present-day movements in Arithmetic; the fundamental changes in the purpose and method of teaching arithmetic; the content selected for teaching; and the relation of arithmetic to the life of the child.

The origin of number ; the various steps involved in the development of the number idea; the unit, its nature and use; the necessity for standard units; number, a ratio.

Methods: Analysis and synthesis, induction and deduction, illustrated and applied; the use of concrete material and apparatus; use of graphic methods; drill and devices to secure neatness, accuracy and rapidity of computation; importance, place, and treatment of mental arithmetic. Checking and verifying of results in arithmetic.

The value of problems; selection of problems; interest in problems for which the pupils themselves furnish the materials; where and how to assist pupils; type solutions; the unitary method, its merits and limitations; solutions by full analysis and by performing only necessary operations.

DETAILS OF COURSES.

Fractions: (*a*) vulgar, different interpretations; numeration and notation; operations; conditions under which these operations can be performed; measures and multiples; (*b*) decimal; as special fractions and as complements of common notation; correspondence of methods with those of integers. Approximations.

Compound rules; tables of weights and measures; reduction; operations. The metric system, when and how it should be taught.

Square root by factoring and by the formal method, illustrated geometrically and algebraically.

Commercial arithmetic: how to make topics like discount, stocks, exchange, etc., concrete to the pupil; use of tables in calculating interest, discount, taxes, etc.; commercial and business forms.

Mensuration; the application of arithmetic to space relations; theoretical and practical methods of obtaining formulae; practical problems to show the use of these formulae; the necessity of models in teaching mensuration.

Algebra.—Arithmetical algebra; transition from arithmetic to algebra; generalization of language and of method; the introduction and defining of symbols; the negative quantity; the simple rules; the distributive law, commutative law, index law, sign rule; the equation and its place in algebra; factoring; highest common factor and lowest common multiple; use of detached co-efficients; classes of simple equations; symmetry and its applications in elementary algebra; square root; method of dealing with problems and the object to be kept in view in their solution; verifyi ng and checking results; correlation of algebra and geometry; graphical methods of illustrating formulae and of interpreting the roots of equations.

The theory of fractional and negative indices; surds and surd equations; quadratic equations of one and two unknowns; theory of quadratics; simple ratio and proportion.

Geometry.—Practical geometry to precede the theoretical; use of instruments; paper.folding; necessity for accuracy; distinction between practical geometry and geometrical drawing; practical problems in the solution of triangles and in measuring heights and distances; limitations of appeals to the concrete; value of experimental proofs; need of clear and definite conceptions of the fundamental truths; the place of the definitions and axioms; when and how they should be introduced; the proposition; home-work and class-work; the analytic-synthetic method of dealing with propositions and deductions; the comparative values of propositions and deductions; the comparative values of propositions and exercises; how to get pupils to work original exercises; necessity of original work from the beginning of theoretical geometry; the indirect method of demonstration; methods of class teaching; importance of note-books for pupils' exercises; the grouping and relating of propositions; practical applications; algebraic solutions; Euclid's method compared with modern methods; method of

DETAILS OF COURSES. .

teaching the more important propositions and exercises in Book I of the authorized text.

Books of Reference:
  Public School Manual in Arithmetic.
  McMurry: Special Method in Arithmetic.
  Schultze: The Teaching of Secondary Mathematics.
  Smith: The Teaching of Elementary Mathematics.
  Suzzallo: The Teaching of Primary Arithmetic.
  Young: The Teaching of Mathematics.

SEMINAR IN MATHEMATICS.

44. The seminar in Mathematics will discuss methods in Trigonometry and the more advanced parts of Algebra and Geometry; the order of presenting the parts of these subjects so as to secure the most logical and impressive relation among the parts; the relations of the subjects themselves; the place of the teacher in dealing with more mature minds; the history and development of such special topics as the algebraic equation, the vulgar and decimal fraction, loci, maxima and minima, theory of parallel lines, etc.; examinations in mathematics, their purpose, when they should be held, the character of the paper, methods of marking, etc.

Books of Reference:
  Howell: A Foundation Study in the Pedagogy of Arithmetic.
  Fink: A Brief History of Mathematics.
  Schultze: The Teaching of Secondary Mathematics.
  Articles in "School Science and Mathematics".

GEOGRAPHY.

45. Scope and Method of Geography: Relationship to other subjects of the courses of study; general methods of presentation with advantages and disadvantages of each method.

Regional geography: Maps; different kinds, importance of each; map drawing; use of pictures, globes and other visual aids; use of text-books, readers, reference books; methods of treatment of typical regions.

Commercial Geography: Factors determining commerce; chief commercial commodities; geographical factors determining their production and distribution; relation of physical features to commerce; commercial geography of selected regions; methods of treatment of typical problems.

Physical Geography; Relation of physical to commercial and regional geography; importance of experimental work; use of such aids as contour, isobar, isotherm, and weather maps; interpretation of the physical geography of Ontario. A discussion of the method of treatment of topics difficult of presentation from the physical geography prescribed for the High Schools of Ontario.

' DETAILS OF COURSES.

Books of Reference:
   Public School Manual: Geography.
   Wallis: The Teaching of Geography.
   Chisholm: Handbook of Commercial Geography.
   Lake: Physical Geography.
   Andrew: A Text-book of Geography.

SCIENCE.

46. The following are the main topics of the course:

A: Scope and value of the natural sciences; meaning of science and scientific method; educational value of science; inductive and deductive methods of investigation.

Experimental work; how conducted, how recorded; manipulation of apparatus; glass-working; making of simple apparatus; classroom discussion, its purpose, method, and relation to the experimental work; the use of text-books; note-books, method of inspection, drawing; reference books, most suitable books in each subject for the library; supplementary reading; methods in biology, physics, and chemistry of the Lower School, illustrated in lessons upon subjects difficult of presentation.

. B. Laboratory equipment for the teaching of Elementary Science, and of Physics, Chemistry, and Biology; methods of demonstration; use of technical terms; theories, facts, scientific laws; text-books and reference books.

Chemistry: Order of treatment; introductory work. Methods of conducting instruction in Chemistry will be discussed, and illustrated in lessons upon subjects selected from such topics as the following: chemical laws and theories; valency; formulae and equations; nomenclature; qualitative and quantitative experiments; chemical arithmetic; the elements, with sodium and chlorine as types.

Physics: Methods of conducting instruction in the more difficult parts of the courses in heat, light, sound, magnetism, electricity, and mechanics will be discussed and illustrated in lessons upon subjects selected from such topics as the following: specific gravity, properties of liquids and gases, machines, temperature, specific heat, laws of reflection, images in mirrors and lenses, laws of vibrating strings with problems, interference of sounds, lines of magnetic force, relation between statical and current electricity, practical applications of electricity.

Biology: Dissection; experiments with plants; the microscope; aquaria and terraria; school museums; plant and animal ecology. Methods of

DETAILS OF COURSES.

conducting instruction in biology will be discussed and illustrated in lessons upon subjects selected from such topics as the following: relation of structure to function, animal and plant types as the grasshopper, frog, hepatica, fern. This discussion will assume a practical acquaintance on the part of the student with the common plants and animals of Ontario.

Books of Reference:

High School Manual: Suggestions for Teachers of Science.
Burlend: First Course in Biology.
Gregory and Simmons: Lessons in Science.
Twiss: Principles of Science Teaching.
Lloyd and Bigelow: The Teaching of Biology.
Smith and Hall: The Teaching of Chemistry and Physics.
Woodhead: The Study of Plants.

SEMINAR IN SCIENCE.

47. Manipulation: Practice with apparatus used in High School demonstrations; preparation of illustrative charts; the projection lantern; photography; preparation of lantern slides; care of aquaria and vivaria; growth of plants for experiments in vegetable physiology; collection and preservation of botanical and zoological material for Upper School work.

Equipment: Laboratory accommodation; arrangement of laboratories; lighting and ventilation; arrangement and structure of benches and other furniture; care and purchase of apparatus; chemicals and minerals, most suitable kinds, method of preparation and storage; reference works and periodicals in science for the High School library.

Methods of treating topics difficult of presentation in physical geography, physics, chemistry, biology, mineralogy and geology discussed, and illustrated in lessons selected from the following topics: geological history of the Great Lakes in its relation to the physical features of Ontario; geographical significance of minerals and rocks; protection and colour of animals; Mendelism; plants in relation to insects; form and colour of flowers; parasitic and saprophytic plants; insectivorous plants; laws of combination in chemistry; symbols, formulae, and equations; valency; atomic and molecular theories; Boyle's Law; Charles' Law; electron theory of matter; absolute temperature; relation of acceleration, momentum, force, and energy; surface tension; flow of liquids.

Books of Reference:

Davis: Natural History of Animals.
Ganong: The Teaching Botanist.
Ganot: Text-book in Physics.
Kerner: Natural History of Plants.

DETAILS OF COURSES.

Books of Reference:—Continued.

Laboratory Accommodation, Pamphlet No. 9 of Department of Education of Ontario.

Mann: The Teaching of Physics.

Mellor: Modern Inorganic Chemistry.

SEMINAR IN AGRICULTURE.

48. The history of agricultural education, especially in Denmark, the United States and Canada; methods of conducting laboratory and plot work; relation of the course in agriculture to vocational education; laboratory work.

Books of Reference:

Burkett, Stevens and Hill: Agriculture for Beginners.

Manual of Elementary Agriculture and Horticulture.

Marshall: Microbiology.

Plumb: Types and Breeds of Farm Animals.

Sanderson: Insects of Farm, Garden and Orchard.

Warren: Elements of Agriculture.

Waters: The Essentials of Agriculture.

CLASSICS (LATIN AND GREEK).

49. The relation of method in teaching Latin or Greek to linguistic method in general; the effect of the object of teaching Latin or Greek upon the method in various departments, such as oral reading, grammar, translation, sight reading, and the literary or historical content; illustration of methods in typical lessons.

Pronunciation; oral reading, sight reading, and English translation as prescribed for Normal Entrance or Pass Matriculation; general principles of word-structure and sentence-structure; word order; methods of teaching the parts of a lesson; the direct method; topics of inflection and syntax as found in the Latin and Greek Books; special emphasis on difficult topics.

Books of Reference:

Bennett: The Teaching of Latin.

Chickering and Hoadley: Beginner's Latin by the Direct Method.

Crawford: On Pronouncing Latin.

Hale: The Art of Reading Latin.

Westaway: Quantity and Accent in the Pronunciation of Latin.

Bristol: The Teaching of Greek.

Thompson: Homeric Grammar.

Goodwin: Greek Grammar.

Goodell: Greek Grammar.

Arnold: On Translating Homer.

DETAILS OF COURSES.

SEMINAR IN CLASSICS.

50. In the seminar in Classics, topics are chosen germane to the teaching of Horace, Vergil, Cicero, Caesar, Xenophon, and continuous Latin prose composition. The following list will show the nature of the topics for discussion:

The teaching of Horatian metres; the poetic art of Horace; the translating of Horace into English prose; the use of metrical versions; certain Asclepiadean odes; the national odes; Horace's treatment of religion, death, friendship, and fortune; the selection of "fine lines"; the complete teaching of an ode of Horace; the appropriate commentary.

The teaching of Vergil in an honour class; the difficulties in translating Cicero; what T. Rice Holmes has done for the teaching of Caesar; the sequence of tenses in Caesar's indirect discourse; the teaching of Latin prose composition; the teaching of Xenophon in an honour class; the classical library.

The direct method in Latin and Greek.

Books of Reference:

    Bennett and Bristol: The Teaching of Latin and Greek.
    Johnson: Pamphlets on the Teaching of Caesar and Vergil.
    Hale: Pamphlets on the Art of Reading Latin.
    Articles in the "Classical Journal".

FRENCH AND GERMAN.

51. Introductory: Importance of the study of a modern language; aims of the study.

Study of Methods: A comparison of methods in view of the present conditions in the schools, *e.g.*, the age and attainments of pupils, the size of classes, allotment of time, text-books in use, regulations governing the teacher; illustrative lessons.

Pronunciation: Study of phonetics; theory and practice.

Elementary Classes: Classes conducted without a text-book; conversation lessons; how to make use of the objects of the classroom, pictures and drawings; unison work; variety and interest; dictation; note-books and their correction; picture lessons; necessity for thorough drill.

Grammar: Inductive and deductive teaching; grammatical rules and their value; special illustrative lessons on essentials.

Translation into English: Importance; aims; methods of conducting the recitation. Special consideration of selected passages from the Reader and the Authors prescribed for Junior Matriculation.

Composition to be based on models; free reproduction; original essays; writing of letters; methods of correction; training in the use of the dictionary.

DETAILS OF COURSES.

Books of Reference:
  Bagster-Collins: The Teaching of German.
  Bahlsen: Teaching of Foreign Languages.
  Dumville: French Pronunciation.
  Heath: Report of the Committee of Twelve.
  Jespersen: How to Teach a Foreign Language.
  Palmer: Scientific Study and Teaching of Languages.
  Savory and Jones: Sounds of the French Language.
  Vietor: German Pronunciation.

SEMINAR IN FRENCH AND GERMAN.

52. The seminar will lay stress upon the consideration of the value, aims, and methods of linguistic training; the relation of linguistic training to literary culture; history of methods formerly employed in the teaching of modern languages in the secondary schools of France, Germany, Great Britain, and the United States; the necessity for better methods in Ontario; the Direct Method illustrated in the class-room; a study of French life, manners, and institutions; the importance of pronunciation; the value and use of phonetic symbols, use of phonetic charts and wall-pictures; typical lessons in advanced grammar, conversation, translation, sight reading, prose composition; free reproduction exercises, dictation, and audition; writing and correction of passages in French composition; consideration of books helpful to the teacher; the extent of the courses in the Upper School; writing essays on allotted subjects.

Books of Reference:
  Bagster-Collins: German in Secondary Schools.
  Bahlsen: Teaching of Modern Languages.
  Brebner: Method of Teaching Modern Languages in Germany.
  Breul: Teaching of Modern Languages.
  Dumville: French Pronunciation.
  Geddes: French Pronunciation.
  Gouin: The Teaching and Studying of Languages.
  Gouris: Teaching by the Direct Method.
  Jespersen: How to Teach a Foreign Language.
  Kittson: Theory and Practice of Language Teaching.
  Rippmann: Elements of Phonetics.
  Savory and Jones: Sounds of the French Language.
  Sweet: Practical Study of Languages.
  Walter: Zur Methodik des neusprachlichen Unterrichts.

VOCAL MUSIC.

53. Tune: All intervals of the Major Diatonic Scale, both from the Tonic Sol-fa and staff; the relative minor; transition.

DETAILS OF COURSES.

Time: Whole pulse, continued pulse, silent pulse, and pulse divided into halves, quarters, and thirds with the various combinations of these in simple and compound duple, quadruple, and triple times.   All the above in both the Tonic Sol-fa and staff notations.

Ear-training in Time and Tune: Recognition of rhythm and tone, of short musical phrases when played or sung, and their expression in either notation.

Voice-culture: Breath-control, tone production, vowel-formation, enunciation of consonants, correct intonation, blending of registers, and general training for quality, range, and flexibility.

Sight-singing: Singing from pointing on modulator or staff. Singing at sight easy passages containing the varieties of time and tune mentioned above.

Songs: The study of songs, in one or two parts, suited to the requirements of pupils in various school grades; with special attention to accent, enunciation, phrasing, quality of tone and expression.

Notation: Elements of notation, both Tonic Sol-fa and staff; the formation of the major and minor diatonic scales; elements of modulation and transposition.

Vocal Physiology: Anatomy of lungs, larynx, and resonating cavities; comparison of abdominal, intercostal and clavicular methods of breathing; action of vocal chords in production of tone and of the various vocal registers; influence of resonating cavities upon quality of tone and vowel; care of voice in speaking and singing.

Methods: The grading of school music to suit the development of the pupils and the methods of teaching both systems.

Books of Reference:

    Cringan: The Educational Music Course.
    Cringan : Teacher's Handbook of Tonic Sol-fa System.
    Curwen: The Standard Course.
    Curwen: The Teacher's Manual.
    Hardy: How to Train Children's Voices.
    Hulbert: Breathing for Voice Production.
    Mason: How to Teach the Staff Notation.

SEMINAR IN HOUSEHOLD SCIENCE.

54. The development of Household Science; the relation of household science to the other subjects of the curriculum; its value and aims; household science in the Public School, in the High and Technical Schools and in the University; accommodations and equipment for household science work in the various types of schools: courses of study; methods of instruction; use of equipment and note-books; use of text-books; discussion of selected parts of the High School course of study.

DETAILS OF COURSES.

Books of Reference:

Ontario Public School Manuals: *Household Science for Rural Schools, Household Management, Sewing.*

Balderston: Housewifery.

Baldt: Clothing for Women.

Cooley, Winthell, Spohr, Marshall: Teaching Home Economics.

Kinne: Equipment for Teaching Domestic Science.

PHYSICAL CULTURE.

55. PRINCIPLES: (For men and women):

Anatomy: Bone, composition, classification; bones of upper extremity; bones of the vertebral column; bones of the head; bones of the abdomen and thorax; bones of the lower extremity. Joints: Classification and description of movable joints; importance of joints. Muscle: Varieties, origin, insertion and action. Digestive system, stomach, liver, etc. Circulatory system: heart, arteries, veins, etc. Respiratory system. Nervous system.

Physiology: Oxidation and waste; metabolism; blood, composition, quality, the heart beat; respiration, mechanism, changes in the lungs, in the tissues; nervous mechanism of respiration; physiology of muscle. Digestion; digestive juices; function of saliva; gastric juice, pancreatic juice, and bile; succus entericus; changes in the food in the alimentary canal; lymph, movements; absorption. Nutrition; comparison of income and output of material, animal heat; diet.

First Aid to the Injured: Shock, wounds, bleeding, burns, exposure to cold, frostbite, fractures, sprains and dislocations, restoration of the apparently drowned, choking, foreign bodies in eye or ear, unconsciousness, fainting, apoplexy, heatstroke, poisons, bandaging.

Personal Hygiene.

PRACTICE: (For men only):

Calisthenics. Dumb-bells—Roberts, Barton, combinations; wands— elementary, Barton, miscellaneous; clubs—class club-swinging.

Elementary Exercises on Apparatus: Horse: vaults, flank, front, rear, screw, squat, straddle, wolf; mats: jumps and hops, jumps and hops with turns, underswings, underswings with turns, buck, vaults, same as on horse and vaulting bar.

Indoor Games: Course to enable teachers to coach and referee the following games: basketball, indoor baseball, volleyball.

Outdoor Athletics: Field and track sports. Course to enable teachers to coach athletics and to direct athletic meets, starting, sprinting, running, broad jump, high jump, shot put, hurdles.

Boxing and single sticks, bayonet exercises; squad and company drill; rifle and musketry practice and skirmishing; saluting ; signalling; instruction in use of subtarget.

DETAILS OF COURSES.

Swimming: Elementary.

Mutual instruction in the various exercises.

PRACTICE: (For women only):

Squad drill, marching tactics, wheeling, turnings.

Freehand exercises, including Strathcona Trust exercises; dumb-bell drills, elementary, advanced; wand drills, Barton; Anderson's twist drill; clubs, classified exercises.

Elementary exercises on the following apparatus: horse, mats, vaulting bar, buck, rings, Swedish stall bars, suspended ladder.

Indoor Athletic Sports: Running races, gymnasium games, including basket-ball; schoolroom and playground games.

Dancing: Technique of dancing; simplified athletic dances; folk dances and singing games; old English country dances.

Swimming: Elementary.

Mutual instruction in the various exercises.

Books of Reference:

The Syllabus of Physical Exercises for Schools.

Barton: Physical Training.

Bancroft: Games for Playground, Home, School and Gymnasium.

Burchenal: Dances of the People.

Burchenal: Folk Dances and Singing Games.

Chalif: Chalif Text-book of Dancing.

Corsan: At Home in the Water.

ART.

THEORY AND PRACTICE.

56. A. Representation.

(1) *Pencil and Charcoal Drawing:*

The proper handling of the lead pencil and charcoal.

The principles of drawing, (1) in outline, (2) in neutral tones to represent colour values, and light and shade.

The principles of elementary perspective.

The study of the effects of light and shade and shadow.

The study of the laws of composition in the pleasing arrangement of objects in small groups.

Freehand drawing, above and below the eye level, in outline, and in neutral tones, (1) from common manufactured objects of curvilinear and of rectilinear form, and (2) from natural forms, as flowers, fruits, plants, trees, insects, animals, etc.

Freehand drawing from memory.

(2) *Blackboard Drawing:*

DETAILS OF COURSES.

Practice in making rapid sketches on the blackboard to ensure its use by the student-teacher in teaching other subjects of school study besides art.

(3) *Modelling:*

Modelling in clay and in plasticine of simple forms.
Casting in plaster.

(4) *Water Colour Painting:*

The theory of colour; colour perception; spectrum standards; properties of colour (hue, value, intensity); colour harmony (complementary, analogous, contrasted, and monochromatic scales).

Construction of colour charts.

Brushwork in monochrome.

Water colour painting from common manufactured objects, and from natural forms, of a single object and of small well-composed groups.

B. DESIGN AND LETTERING.

(1) *Decorative Design:*

The principles of decorative design.

The use of geometric and of natural forms in design.

The making of decorative designs and applying them to useful purposes.

The completion of decorative designs in balanced neutral tones and in harmonious colour schemes.

(2) *Lettering:*

The principles of lettering.

Lettering with the freehand and with mechanical aids.

The adaptation of lettering in exercises in applied design.

C. ART APPRECIATION AND THE HISTORY OF ART:

Pictorial Composition: The essential artistic qualities of pictures—in line, tone, and colour.

The study of masterpieces.   Essays.

Illustration of given themes.

Visits for study to the Museum and the Gallery of Art.

The study of home and school furnishings and decoration.

An outline of the History of Art.

D. METHODS OF TEACHING ART IN HIGH AND CONTINUATION SCHOOLS:

The Regulations of the Department of Education.

The real objects to be sought in the teaching of Art, involving a consideration of its relation to the life of the student and to the interests of the community.

The organization and equipment of classes.

The care of materials and of drawings.

—36

DETAILS OF COURSES.

The courses of study. A natural order and method of development of the subjects and the principles of these courses.

Methods of teaching form (including proportion and perspective), tone, colour, composition, decorative design, handling of mediums, and the appreciation of pictures.

The preparation of studies for class work.

The division of the time given to Art. The correlation of Art with other studies.

Conducting examinations in Art. Points to stress in criticising and valuing drawings.

A discussion of teaching difficulties and methods of overcoming them.

A description of teaching helps and information as to how and where they may be secured.

Books of Reference:

Ontario Teachers' Manual: Art.
Branch: Illustrated Exercises in Design.
Caffin: A Guide to Pictures.
Caffin: How to Study Pictures.
Cross: Colour.
Cross: Light and Shade.
Low: Composition.
Hatton: Perspective.
Norton: Freehand Perspective and Sketching.
Prang's Art Education for High Schools.
Reinach: Apollo—Story of Art throughout the Ages.
Seaby: Blackboard Drawing.
Simonds: Modelling in Clay and Wax.
Strange: Handbook of Lettering.
Taylor: Elementary Art Teaching.

COURSE FOR ORDINARY CERTIFICATES IN HOUSEHOLD SCIENCE.

PURPOSE.

The course for Interim Ordinary certificates in Household Science prepares candidates therefor in the theory and art of organizing, governing, and instructing in Household Science the pupils of the Public, Separate, and High Schools of Ontario.

CONDITIONS OF ADMISSION.

A candidate for admission to the course for the Interim Ordinary certificate in Household Science should make application, not later than September 26th, on a form to be obtained from the Secretary of the Ontario College of Education and should submit with this application:

(1) A certificate from a competent authority that she is a British subject.

(2) A certificate from a clergyman or other competent authority that she is of good moral character.

(3) A certificate from a physician that she is physically able for the work of a teacher and, especially, that she is free from serious pulmonary affection and from defective eyesight or hearing.

(4) A statement signed by herself to the effect that she intends, when opportunity offers, to teach the subject of Household Science.

(5) One of the following:

(a) A Second-Class or First-Class Public School or an Ordinary High School certificate.

(b) A Kindergarten-Primary or a Kindergarten Director's certificate together with Normal Entrance, Faculty Entrance, or equivalent certificates under other names.

FEES.

(1) The annual fee, which shall include tuition, laboratory supplies, and the use of the library shall be $25.00.

(2) At the beginning of the session, a deposit of $4.00 will be required from each student. This deposit, less the cost of equipment and apparatus that may have been destroyed, will be returned at the close of the session.

(3) If a student who has been granted an Ordinary Certificate teaches the subject of Household Science in a school in the Provincial system during the year following the examination, the fee of $25 will be returned to her on the report to the Minister of Education by the Inspector of Household Science that the work has been satisfactorily performed. Applications for such refunds should be made to the Deputy Minister of Education.

COURSES IN HOUSEHOLD SCIENCE—*Continued.*

COURSE OF STUDY.

The Course of Study for the Ordinary certificate in Household Science includes the following:

, PART I

FOODS.

Economics.—Marketing; points to be considered in selection; factors determining cost; saving of materials, fuel, and labour in preparation; care in the home; utilization of left-overs.

Food Values.—Composition of foods; requirements to maintain the body in health; factors influencing diet; digestion of foods; menu planning; diets for infants, children, and adults; special diets for use in the home care of the sick.

Preparation.—Scientific principles underlying methods of preparation; application of these principles by preparing food materials; practical and theoretical demonstration work; meal preparation (children's meals, home meals, the rural school lunch, etc.).

Table Service and Manners.

Special Schoolroom Methods.

CLOTHING.

Selection.—Origin and manufacture of cotton, linen, wool, and silk; their properties and value in relation to their manufacture; identification of textile materials (names, widths, prices, uses).

Construction.—Handsewing (constructive processes applied to simple articles); use and care of sewing machine and its attachments; use of home and commercial patterns; cutting and making of simple garments.

Care.—Daily, weekly, and seasonal; removal of stains; repairing.

Special Schoolroom Methods.

HOUSEHOLD MANAGEMENT.

The House.—Planning; furnishing; care (study of reagents, cleaning of metals, woods, textiles, laundry work); demonstrations; household administration (problems and technical procedures in the management of the modern home).

Sanitation.—Effect of environment on health; sanitary control of surroundings; disposal of waste.

Home Nursing.—Care of the infant, child, and adult; emergencies; bandaging.

Special Schoolroom Methods.

COURSES IN HOUSEHOLD SCIENCE—*Continued.*

ELEMENTARY APPLIED SCIENCE.

Chemical composition and reaction of household materials; physiological values of foods and changes which they undergo in digestion, putrefaction, etc.; testing of water, carbohydrates, proteins, fats, vegetables, flours, cereals, baking powders, beverages, etc.

GENERAL METHODS IN HOUSEHOLD SCIENCE.

Aims in teaching Household Science; scope of Household Science; relation to other subjects; methods of presentation in different types of schools; planning of courses; equipment; cost of lessons, etc. General discussions.

PART II.

Observation and Practice-teaching will be provided in the Public and High Schools of Toronto and will include a minimum of six practice lessons per student with an equal number of periods for observation lessons.

EXAMINATIONS.

(1) Candidates for Ordinary certificates shall pass in each of Parts I and II under the following conditions:

(*a*) Part I.

The following shall be the subjects in Part I with the maximum value for each subject:

Foods	(200)
Clothing	(200)
Household Management	(200)
Elementary Applied Science	(100)
General Methods in Household Science	(100)

The standing of candidates in the subjects of Part I will be determined by the sessional records and the final written examinations.

The sessional records, to which shall be allotted one-half the maximum value assigned above to each subject, shall consist of the daily credits and of the results of oral, written, and practical tests given throughout the session.

The final written examinations, to which shall be allotted the remaining half of the maximum value assigned above to each subject, shall include the following papers:

Foods, 2 papers.
Clothing, 2 papers.
Household Management, 2 papers.

COURSES IN HOUSEHOLD SCIENCE—*Continued.*

Elementary Applied Science, 1 paper.

General Methods in Household Science, 1 paper.

The pass standard in Part I shall be 50% of the marks assigned to each subject.

(*b*) Part II.

The standing of candidates in Part II shall be determined wholly by the sessional records. For this purpose the maximum value assigned to practice lessons shall be 300, and to observation lessons, 100.

The pass standard in Part II shall be 60% of the aggregate of the marks for the practice lessons and for the observation lessons respectively.

(2) (*a*) Candidates who pass in Part II and fail in not more than two subjects of Part I will be exempted from further attendance.

(*b*) All other candidates who fail to obtain the necessary final standing will be required to attend another session, beginning after the Christmas vacation.

(3) (*a*) Candidates who are exempt from attendance under (2) (*a*) above may complete their standing for a certificate by taking, at one annual examination, or, separately, at different annual examinations the examination, written or practical or both, in the subject or subjects in which they failed.

(*b*) The pass standard for candidates not in attendance will be the same as that for candidates in attendance, but no allowance will be made for sessional work in the case of those not in attendance.

CERTIFICATES.

A candidate who takes the subjects and passes the examinations therein prescribed above shall be entitled to an Interim Ordinary Household Science certificate which shall be valid in these subjects in any Public, Separate, or High School of the Province, and will be made Permanent on the report of the Inspector or Inspectors concerned that the holder thereof has taught successfully the subjects thereof for at least two years.

The Interim Certificate may be renewed under conditions satisfactory to the Minister.

COURSES FOR DEGREES IN PEDAGOGY.

The Ontario College of Education offers courses of instruction for the degrees in Pedagogy during the regular College Sessions and during Summer Sessions.

DEGREE OF BACHELOR OF PEDAGOGY (B.PAED.).

The degree of Bachelor of Pedagogy (B.Paed.) will be awarded under the following conditions:

1. The candidate shall hold an approved degree in Arts, Science, Agriculture, Engineering, or Commerce.

2. The candidate shall be in attendance at the Ontario College of Education two regular College Sessions or three Summer Sessions. A High School Assistant's, or First Class, or Second Class certificate valid in Ontario or a regular course in an approved training school for teachers will be accepted in lieu of attendance during one of these regular sessions or of one of the Summer Sessions.

3. The course shall consist of three subjects to be taken in any order and to be selected from the following:

Group A.—Science of Education, Educational Psychology.

Group B.—History of Education, Educational Administration.

Not more than two of these subjects shall be taken during a regular Session and not more than one during a Summer Session.

Candidates who, under Section 2 above, are exempted from attendance during one regular Session or one Summer Session will be exempted also from the instruction and examination in one of the three subjects, provided that the degree be awarded only to candidates who have taken the instruction and examinations in at least one subject in each of the two groups of subjects.

4. The examinations shall be held in May at the University of Toronto or in any other locality in the Province chosen by the candidate and approved by the Senate and under a presiding examiner appointed by the Senate, provided the candidate thereat defray the cost of the local examinations. The candidate shall send notice not later than the 15th day of March of his intention to take the examinations and of the locality he has chosen for such examinations.

5. The fee for registration is $5. The fee for the Summer Session is $10, the fee for the regular Session, which shall include the examination and library fees, is $25. The fee for examination is $3 for each subject. The fee for the degree is $20. All fees shall be paid to the Bursar with the application for registration or examination, as the case may be.

6. The standard for a Pass degree shall be 60 per cent. of the marks assigned to each subject. The candidate who obtains 60 per cent. of the marks of each subject, and 66 per cent. of the aggregate of marks, shall be awarded a degree with Second Class Honours. The candidate who obtains 60 per cent. of the marks of each subject and 75 per cent. of the aggregate of marks shall be awarded a degree with First Class Honours. On the report of the instructors concerned, a maximum of 40 per cent. of the marks in any subject may be assigned to the term work of the candidate.

7. Subjects of Instruction and Examination.

(a) The Science of Education, including a study of the philosophical, ethical, and sociological bases of education. (Two papers.)

(b) Educational Psychology. (Two papers.)

(c) The History of Education in Western Europe and North America in modern times, with special reference to Ontario, Great Britain, and the United States. (Two papers.)

(d) Educational Administration in Great Britain, the United States, France, and Germany, with special reference to the administration and organization of education in Ontario. (Two papers.)

8. Candidates who registered under former regulations may (a) complete their courses under those regulations provided that they do so not later than May, 1923, or (b) transfer to the present courses. On application before May, 1923, credit may be given in the new courses for examinations taken under former regulations, provided the candidate has attended a Summer Session or its equivalent in the subject or subjects in which he seeks credit.

DEGREE OF DOCTOR OF PEDAGOGY (D.PAED.).

The degree of Doctor of Pedagogy (D.Paed.) will be awarded under the following conditions:

1. The candidate shall hold an approved degree in Arts or Science or in the applied sciences of Agriculture, Engineering, or Commerce.

2. The candidate shall be in attendance at the Ontario College of Education during three regular College Sessions or four Summer Sessions. A High School Assistant's, First Class, or Second Class certificate valid in Ontario, or a regular Course in an approved training school for teachers will be accepted in lieu of the attendance during one of these regular Sessions or of one of the Summer Sessions.

3. The Course shall consist of the four subjects and a thesis as defined in Sections 5 and 7. The subjects may be taken in any order, provided that not more than two be taken in any regular Session and not more than one in any Summer Session. Candidates who, under Section 2, are exempted from attendance during one regular Session or one Summer

Session will be exempted also from the attendance and examinations in one of the four subjects. Candidates who have been credited with one or more subjects of the B.Paed. course as defined in the regulations of 1921 will be exempted from the attendance and examinations in said subject or subjects.

4. The examinations shall be held at such times and under such conditions as to date of application, place of examination, percentages, etc., as obtain with the Bachelor's degree.

5. The candidate, after passing the prescribed examinations, shall also submit on or before March 1st a thesis on some educational topic selected with the approval of the Ontario College of Education. In valuing this thesis literary excellence, as well as the discussion of the subject, will be taken into account. After the examiners have reported in favour of the candidate's examinations and thesis, and before the degree of D.Paed. is conferred, the candidate shall furnish the Registrar of the University with five copies of the thesis.

6. The fee for registration, if not already registered in the B.Paed. Courses, is $5. The fee for the Summer Session is $10; that for the regular Session, which shall include the examination and library fees, $25. The fee for examination is $3 for each subject. The fee for the degree is $25. All fees shall be paid to the Bursar with the application.

7. Subjects of Instruction and Examination.

(a) The Science of Education, including a study of the philosophical, ethical, and sociological bases of education. (Two papers.)

(b) Educational Psychology. (Two papers.)

(c) The History of Education in Western Europe and North America in modern times, with special reference to Ontario, Great Britain, and the United States. (Two papers.)

(d) Educational Administration in Great Britain, the United States, France, and Germany, with special reference to the administration and organization of education in Ontario. (Two papers.)

8. Candidates registered under former regulations may (a) complete the examinations under those regulations provided that they do so not later than May, 1923 or (b) transfer to the present Courses. On application before May, 1923, a candidate may be given credit in the new Courses for examinations taken under former regulations provided he has attended a Summer Session or its equivalent in the subject or subjects in which he seeks credit.

FACULTY OF FORESTRY.

ENTRANCE REQUIREMENTS

For the Session 1921-22 candidates for the Degree must have passed the Junior Matriculation Examination of the University in English, History, Mathematics, and in three·of Latin, Greek, German, French, Spanish, Experimental Science (Physics and Chemistry). The pass standard in this examination is 40 per cent on each paper and 60 per cent on the average.

For the Session 1922-1923 the standard for entrance requirements will be raised to Honour Matriculation in English, Mathematics and one language, preferably a modern language.

Admission may also be secured by candidates who (1) possess a degree in Arts, from any Canadian, British or American university of approved· standing; (2) come from other institutions whose certificates are recognised by the University of Toronto as ·equivalent to the above entrance requirements, and will be accepted *pro tanto;* or (3) have completed a year, or the examinations for the year, with satisfactory standing, in the Faculties of Arts, Medicine or Applied Science.

In addition to the academic requirements, a robust physique and good eyesight are essential in the practice of the profession, and candidates markedly deficient in these will be advised not to proceed. Deficiency in eyesight will be found a particular handicap in future practical employment.

Persons, not candidates for a degree, who are not less than 21 years of age, and who give evidence of sufficient ability, and especially of practical experience, to enable them to carry on with profit University courses in the subjects of the Faculty, although partly deficient in the regular matriculation requirements, may be admitted by the Faculty as *Non-Matriculated Students* on such conditions as the Faculty may determine. Such students may be required to complete matriculation and qualify for the degree within a prescribed period of time.

Occasional Students may be admitted to not more than three forestry subjects.

REGISTRATION AND ENROLMENT

Applications for admission, together with matriculation or equivalent certificates, should be forwarded to the Registrar of the University at as early a date as possible.

Students must complete their registration in person on or before the first day of the session, September 27th. On the same or the preceding day students will enrol with the instructors in their various courses.

Students who have not complied with the regulations for registration and enrolment may be admitted only upon petition to the Faculty and for good reasons. They may be refused enrolment with classes unless the head of the department is satisfied that they are able to go on with the class. A charge will be made for late registration.

No student will be allowed to continue who does not attend regularly, who wilfully disobeys rules and regulations, or whose presence is otherwise considered prejudicial to the interests of the University.

FEES

Regular Students in Forestry

First, Second, Third and Fourth Years. Annual fee, including instruction, main library, laboratory supply, and one annual examination, $80.00.

If paid in full in October...................... $80.00

By instalments:—

First instalment, if paid in October................ 40.00

Second instalment, if paid in January............ 41.00

Combined Courses in Arts and Forestry

First, second, third, fourth, fifth, and sixth years. Annual fee, including tuition, library, laboratory supply, and one annual examination. The College fee in each of the first, second, and third years is $30:—

If paid in full in October $70.00

By instalments:—

First instalment, if paid in October 35,00

Second instalment, if paid in January 36.00

Occasional Students

The fee for occasional students is $5.00 for the term for each course taken.

After October 31st, a penalty of $1.00 per month will be imposed upon tuition fees until the whole amount is paid. In the case of payment by instalments the same rule as to penalty will apply.

Students attending Fall Practice Camp will be allowed until November 15th to pay fees. Fees for Practice Camp, however, are due September 1st.

General Fees

Annual deposit for the departmental library....... $ 1.00

Supplemental Examinations..................... $10.00

Admission ad eundem statum................... $10.00

Degree of B.Sc.F............................. $10.00

Degree of F.E................................ $20.00

To defray expenses of spring nursery work a deposit of approximately $30.00 will be required from Third Year students, and for fall practice work approximately $80.00 from Fourth Year students.

Foresters' Club

Annual fee..$2.00

*Hart House, Students' Administrative Council and
Physical Training*

Hart House, annual fee......................... $8.00
Students' Administrative Council, annual fee...... 3.00
Physical Training, annual fee.................... 5.00

Every male student in attendance, proceeding to the degree of Bachelor of the Science of Forestry, is required to pay to the Bursar at the time of the entry of his name with the Registrar the above annual fees.

All fees are payable in advance.

A student will not be admitted to any of the University lectures or laboratories who is in arrears for his fees.

DEGREES

The satisfactory completion of the four-year course leads to the degree of Bachelor of the Science of Forestry (B.Sc.F.).

Graduates holding the degree of B.Sc.F., upon furnishing evidence of three years' practical employment in forestry work and the presentation of an acceptable thesis, the subject to be approved by the Faculty, will be given the degree of Forest Engineer (F.E.).

GEORGE E. BOTHWELL MEDAL

The friends and classmates of Lieut. George E. Bothwell, who was killed in action September, 1916, have established the George E. Bothwell medal for proficiency in Silviculture. This medal will be awarded upon the recommendation of the staff.

SIX-YEAR COURSE

Besides the regular four-year course to which the above requirements and degrees refer, there is offered a six-year course, combining with the regular four-year course certain humanistic and arts subjects, this combination being intended to give a broader education than can be attained by the shorter, purely professional course. This course leads to degrees in both Arts and Forestry at the end of six years.

Entrance to this course is secured by the same matriculation as is prescribed for the Faculty of Arts, namely, in the following subjects: Latin, English, History, Mathematics, and any two of the following: Greek, German, French, Spanish, Experimental Science, preferably two languages.

PHYSICAL TRAINING

By order of the Board of Governors each male student proceeding to a degree must take Physical Training in the first and second years of his attendance. He must first undergo a medical examination by the Physical Director of the University in order to determine the character of his training.

It is specially desired that students obtain training in swimming.

EXAMINATIONS AND STANDING

No student will be allowed to write on the annual examination who has not paid all fees and dues for which he is liable. A student who fails to perform the work in his course in a manner satisfactory to his instructors will not be allowed to present himself at the final examinations except by special permission of the Council.

The standard for pass in these examinations in all courses, whether taken in the Faculty of Forestry or any other Faculty, is 50 per cent of the marks for each subject. For students in the six-year course this has reference only to subjects in common with the regular course.

In making up the final standing of each candidate much consideration will be given to the character of his work through the term, including attendance, laboratory and field work, reports and term examinations.

Candidates who *fail* at the annual examinations *in more than two subjects,* of which *only one may be a forestry or biology subject,* cannot proceed to the next year unless they have attained at least 70 per cent on the average in all other subjects, when their case will be specially considered.

Candidates who fail in one or two subjects at the annual examinations, only one of which may be a forestry or biology subject, may be allowed to take supplemental examinations in such subjects. These supplemental examinations must be taken in Arts subjects in September at dates set by the Faculty of Arts, in forestry subjects before December 15th. Students who are prevented by fieldwork or by sickness from writing in September may be permitted to write in January.

Candidates are required to send to the Secretary of the Faculty at least three weeks before the date of supplemental examinations, notice in writing of their intention to take such examinations, and at the same time the fee of $10 (both September and January supplemental examinations) must be paid to the Bursar, and no student will be allowed to write who has failed to pay this fee.

If a candidate fail to pass a supplemental examination in a subject which is not basic to other subjects, he may carry it upon petition until the next examination, but if it be a subject fundamental to a subject of the year to which he wishes to advance he must take the subject over again (and if he fail in any three subjects he will be obliged to repeat the year). A student failing in laboratory work must repeat the same.

No candidate for a degree will be allowed to pass into the next higher year who has not fulfilled all the requirements of the next lower year.

PLAN OF INSTRUCTION

The regular course leading to the degree of Bachelor of the Science of Forestry is a four-year course, the first two years of which are mainly devoted to the study of the fundamental subjects. The last two years are mainly occupied with forestry subjects, there being also time allowed, especially in the last year, to add general educational subjects and to specialize in different directions under advice of the Dean.

Students are required to take either French or German and the language chosen must be continued for three years.

The courses are distributed through the four years as follows:—

Note.—Numbers after the subjects refer to numbers of the courses as designated in the Calendars of the Faculties of Arts, Forestry, and Applied Science and Engineering. The work is stated in terms of the number of lecture or laboratory periods per week.

1 Year

1. Mathematics:
   Algebra, Plane Trigonometry, Analytical Geometry (1*a*, 1*b*, 1*c*, or 1*g*, 1*k*, 1*l*). Three lectures through the session.

2. Physics:
   Elementary Physics (28): Two lectures and one laboratory period through the session.

3. Chemistry:
   Elementary Chemistry (1, 14). Two lectures and one laboratory period through the session.

4. Botany:
   Elementary Botany (5 and 6). Two lectures and two laboratory periods, first term.

5. Zoology:
   Elementary Zoology (5 and 6). Two lectures and two laboratory periods, second term.

6. Forestry:
   a. *Synoptical Course* (1). One lecture through the session.
   b. *Forest Botany* (2*a*). One lecture, two laboratory hours and field-work through the first and four hours, second term.

7. French (1*b*) or German (1*b*).

Summer Work

8. Employment on Forest Survey.

II Year

1. Chemistry:
   Elementary Organic Chemistry (3). Two lectures through the session.

2. Geology:
> *Elementary Geology* (150*). One lecture a week through the session.

3. Mineralogy:
> (159 and 161*). Twenty-five lectures and forty hours laboratory.

4. Surveying, Plane, and Map Drawing (205*). One lecture and two laboratory periods through the session.

5. Forestry:
> a. *Forest Mensuration* (7). Two lectures and one day field or laboratory work through the session.
>
> b. *Forest Botany* (2b). Two lectures through the session.
>
> c. *Biological Dendrology* (5). Two lectures and two laboratory periods through the session.

6. French (2b) or German (2b).

SUMMER WORK

7. Employment on Forest Survey.

III YEAR

1. Geology:
> *Glacial Geology and Physiography* (13). One lecture through the session.

2. Political Economy:
> a. *General introduction to the study of Political Economy* (5). Two lectures through the session.
>
> b. *Commercial Law* (8). One lecture through the session.

3. Surveying, Topographical, and Map Drawing. (Corresponding to Courses 206 and 207, Calendar Applied Science and Engineering.) One lecture and three laboratory periods through the session.

4. Forestry:
> a. *Silviculture* (6). Three lectures through the session and occasional field excursions as practicable; one week at nurseries.
>
> b. *Forest Geography* (3). Two lectures through the session.
>
> c. *Forest Utilization and Forest Engineering* (8). Three lectures through the session and visits to woodworking establishments one afternoon weekly in the second term.

---

*Calendar, Faculty of Applied Science and Engineering.

—37

5. French (3a) or German (3a).

Summer Work

6. Employment on Forest Survey.

IV Year

1. Chemistry:

   Applied Chemistry (12). One lecture through the session.

2. Botany:

   Plant Pathology (25). Fifty hours lecture and laboratory work.

3. Zoology:

   Economic Entomology (34), including Elementary Systematic Entomology. Two lectures and two laboratory periods through the second term.

4. Forestry:

   a. *Forest Organization* (11). Three lectures through the session.

   b. *Forest Valuation and Finance* (12). One lecture through the session.

   c. *History of Forestry* (13). One lecture through the session.

   d. *Forest Administration* (14). Two lectures through the session.

   e. *Forest Protection* (10). One lecture through the session.

   f. *Timber Physics and Wood Technology* (4). Three lectures and two laboratory periods through the second term.

   g. *Business Methods in the Lumber Trade* (9). One lecture through the session.

Field Work

Arrangements will be made with lumbermen to permit Third and Fourth Year students to spend a week or ten days of the Christmas vacation in lumber camps for the purpose of becoming acquainted with the methods of their management. A report on the results of such inspection visits will be required.

Six weeks at the beginning of the Fourth Year will be spent at the Forest School Practice Camp. During this time timber estimating, tree measurements, studies of rate of growth, forest description and forest survey, for the making of working plans, and other practical woods work will occupy the students. The students must report at the Camp on September 1.

At or near the end of the spring term the government nurseries at St. Williams, Ontario, will be visited for a week for practice in nursery work and planting by the Third Year students in connection with the course in Silviculture. This work forms an integral part of the course and constitutes a requirement for the degree.

SCHEDULE FOR SIX-YEAR COURSE

Combined Forestry and Arts

This schedule may, with the concurrence of the Faculties concerned, be varied in order to meet the exigencies of the time-table.

First Year

Latin, 1a, or Greek, 1a.
English, 1a, 1b.
German, 1a, or French, 1a.
Mathematics, 1a, 1b, 1c, or 1j, 1k, 1l.
Mechanics, 1 and Physics, 1, 2, 18.

Zoology, 5, 6.
One of Greek and Roman History, 1; or Religious Knowledge, 1a, or 1b or 1c.
Forestry, 1.

Second Year

English, 2a, 2b.
German, 2a, or French, 2a.
History, 2a.
Chemistry, 1, 14.
One of Latin, 2a or Physics, 3b, or Military Studies, 1.

Botany, 5, 6, 9.
One of Religious Knowledge, 2a, or 2b, or 2c, or 2d; or Geology, 1.
Forestry, 2a.

Third Year

English, 3a, 3b.
German, 3a, or French, 3a.
Chemistry, 3.
Mathematics, 2j, or Actuarial Science, 3.
Geology, 150*.
Mineralogy, 160*.

Surveying, Plane, and Map Drawing 205*.
Botany, 7, 17.
One of Religious Knowledge, 3a, or 3b, or 3c, or 3d, or 3e, or World History, 1, or 2, or 3, or Military Studies, 2.
Forestry, 2b, 7.

*Calendar of the Faculty of Applied Science and Engineering.

Fourth Year

Geology and Physiography, 13.

Surveying, Topographical and Map Drawing 206*, 207*.

History, 4a.

Chemistry, 4, or Physics, 4, 5, or Philosophy, 3b

One of Religious Knowledge, 4a, or 4b, or 4c, or 4d, or 4e, or World History, 1, 2, 3.

Forestry, 6, 9.

Nursery work

Fifth Year

English, 4a, 4b.

Political Economy, 1, 1b, 3.

Law, 4.

One of Philosophy, 4a, or Science, to be arranged.

Botany, 25.

Zoology, 32.

Forestry, 3, 4, 5, 7, 11.

Practice Camp

Sixth Year

Chemistry, 12a.

Political Economy, 33.

Engineering, to be arranged.

Botany, 24

Philosophy, 4b.

Forestry, 10, 12, 13, 14

DESCRIPTION OF FORESTRY COURSES

1. *Synoptical Course.* An introduction to the subject of forestry and a survey of the economic and political aspects of timber land management. This course, carried on in seminary style, is designed also for students of political economy and all those who desire a general knowledge of forestry problems. 25 hours.

2. *Forest Botany.* A taxonomic study (2a) of the forest trees (dendrology) and (2b) of the minor forest flora of North America and forage plants, laying special stress on the characteristics which lead to the recognition of the species in the field, with practice work in securing familiarity with morphological and other characteristics for identifying Canadian and exotic trees and shrubs, tree seeds and seedlings. 150 hours and field work.

3. *Forest Geography.* The geographical distribution, botanical composition and character of forests of the world, and of Canada in particular, with special reference to the ecological factors, climate and soil, influencing forest growth. Field practice in recognizing forest types and in making forest descriptions. 50 hours.

4. *Timber Physics and Wood Technology.* Study of the histology of wood with a view to identification of the different woods, recognition of their normal and abnormal physical characteristics and defects. Mechanical and technical properties of wood and the various technological uses dependent thereon. Lectures and laboratory work. 125 hours.

---

*Calendar of the Faculty of Applied Science and Engineering.

5. *Biological Dendrology.* Life history, laws of growth of trees, their dependence on ecological factors and silvicultural requirements of different species. Lectures and laboratory work. 150 hours.

6. *Silviculture.* Principles and practice of the art of forest production and forest improvement, nursery practice, planting, and methods of natural reproduction. 75 hours. Practice work in addition.

7. *Forest Mensuration.* Methods of ascertaining volume of felled and standing trees, of whole forest growths, timber estimating, determining increment of trees and stands. 100 hours, including practice work.

8. *Forest Utilization and Forest Engineering.* Methods and means employed in the harvesting of forest.products, logging, transportation, milling, preparation for market, and engineering problems. 100 hours, including visits to manufacturing plants.

9. *Business Methods in the Lumber Trade.* Description of usages in shipping, receiving and selling forest products; inspection and grading; financial methods. 25 hours.

10. *Forest Protection.* Methods of guarding against trespass, loss from fires, insects (applied entomology) and other damage to forest crops. 25 hours.

11. *Forest Organization.* Principles and methods underlying the preparation of working plans for continuous wood and revenue production. 75 hours.

12. *Forest Valuation and Finance.* Methods of ascertaining money value of forest growths and application of the principles of finance to forest management. 25 hours.

13. *History of Forestry.* Historical development of the economic and technical features of modern forestry at home and abroad. 50 hours.

14. *Forest Administration.* Principles and methods employed in the administration of forest properties. 50 hours.

OPENINGS FOR FORESTERS

To meet the many inquiries of students contemplating the choice of forestry as a profession the following statements may serve:

Openings for foresters may be found in four or five directions, namely, government employ, private employ, private enterprise, teaching, other business.

The Dominion Forestry Branch, which has charge of the Dominion timber lands in Alberta, Saskatchewan, Manitoba, part of British Columbia, and the unorganized territories, is employing graduates to do the technical work in exploring and classifying lands for forest reservations, surveying, mapping and determining contents of such reservations; organizing a forest fire service, controlling the grazing, timber sales and logging, and generally providing for an administration of forest reservations, of which there are now a dozen, under supervisors. These will have to work out the details of a forest management.

The Forestry Branch maintains large nurseries from which plant material is distributed for planting in the prairies; a staff of experts attend to the growing and distribution of plants, and inspect the planting.

Other field work with the Dominion Forestry Branch consists in silvicultural investigations.

Statistical and technological investigations are carried on and results published at the main office in Ottawa and its Forest Products Laboratories at Montreal.

Besides the permanent employment for graduates by the Dominion Forestry Branch undergraduates find their services required for the summer season as assistants, chiefly in reconnaissance survey. Such summer work is also offered by the Provincial Forestry Branch of Ontario.

Salaries for graduates run, at present, from $1,320 upwards; for undergraduates, $75 to $100 per month, according to experience.

During the summer of 1912, the British Columbia government instituted a full-sized Forest Branch, requiring a large staff of professional men, to do similar work to that of the Dominion B anch, and this organization employs graduates.

The Provincial Forestry Branch of Ontario has a staff of foresters, and assistants are added from time to time as the work develops.

The Quebec government has for some time organized and developed a forest service, but it provides its own technical men.

Private employment has been developed in several directions. The Canadian Pacific Railway Company maintains a staff of foresters, mainly investigating timber conditions on their holdings, but eventually, no doubt, will also administer the same as forest properties for tie purposes, and otherwise.

A number of paper manufacturing companies have for some years availed themselves of the services of foresters, to survey, map, and plan operations of their forest properties. Timber limit holders have employed such for similar purposes, and the time is not far distant when there will be a more general development in this direction.

At least one firm of consulting forest engineers has found for several years most lucrative business, employing a number of assistants. In the United States about half a dozen such firms are operating. Some of these are doing work in Canada.

Altogether, however, it needs to be understood that there will always be only a limited demand for high grade professional men, at least for some time to come; and only those with a special love and aptitude for the arduous work which is largely involved should enter the profession.

Besides the directions above outlined as offering employment for foresters, the education of foresters is such as to prepare them for transfering readily into other employment, such as park superintendents, landscape architects, nursery work, horticulture, and lumberman's business in its various phases.

FACULTY OF MUSIC.

LOCAL EXAMINATIONS IN MUSIC

In view of the fact that the Toronto Conservatory of Music has now
come under the direction of the Board of Governors of the University of
Toronto the Local Examinations in Music will after June, 1921, be conducted by that Conservatory. All information pertaining thereto may be
secured by applying to the Registrar, Toronto Conservatory of Music,
135 College Street, Toronto.

DEGREE OF BACHELOR OF MUSIC

The degree of Bachelor of Music (Mus. Bac.) will be conferred by the University of Toronto upon students of music, on compliance with the requirements of the curriculum in music which may from time to time be prescribed by the Senate.

Matriculation.

The subjects for matriculation in Music are English and two of: Greek, Latin, German, French, Italian.

The courses of study prescribed for matriculation in each of these subjects will be found in the Curriculum for Junior Matriculation, a copy of which may be obtai ed on application to the Registrar of the University.

A candidate for the degree of Bachelor of Music must complete his matriculation prior to admission to the examination of the final year.

The pass standard is the same as that for pass Junior Matriculation.

A candidate who has obtained the average of sixty per cent. on all the six papers but has failed to obtain forty per cent. in at most two of these papers may complete Junior Matriculation by passing on these papers at any one subsequent examination.

A candidate who has obtained forty per cent. on each of at least four papers, with an average of sixty per cent. on the same, will be credited with these papers. In order to complete his Matriculation, he must obtain at one subsequent examination, forty per cent. on each of the remaining papers, with an average of sixty per cent.

A candidate who is actually engaged in a mercantile, industrial or other occupation may proceed to pass Matriculation under special conditions to be found in the Curriculum for Junior Matriculation.

Special application for Matriculation may be dealt with by the Senate.

Registration.

Every student shall, in each year of his course, register his name with the Secretary of the Faculty of Music not later than the first of November.

After the first of November registration can be effected only by petition to the Faculty and on payment of a fine of One Dollar a month for each month after October.

Undergraduate Course.

In addition to Matriculation the candidate must have passed three examinations before the degree of Bachelor of Music shall be granted.

First Year.

1. Harmony in three and four parts.
2. Counterpoint in two and three parts.
3. The History of Music from 1600 to 1800.

Second Year.

1. Harmony in not more than four parts.
2. Strict Counterpoint (including the treatment of the various species in combination) in not more than four parts.
3. Double Counterpoint at the octave, in two parts.
4. Canon in two parts.
5. Fugue as far as subject and answer.
6. The History of Music from 1800 onwards.
7. Musical Form as far as the simple forms and analysis of the musical sentence.

Final Year.

I. THEORY OF MUSIC:—

1. Harmony in not more than five parts, including some original work.
2. Counterpoint, strict and free, in not more than five parts.
3. Canon in two and three parts.
4. Double Counterpoint at the octave, 10th, 12th, and 15th.
5. Imitation and Fugue up to four parts.
6. A general survey of the History of Music from the earliest times to the present. (Text-book recommended, Bonavia Hunt's History of Music, but see also list of text-books on page 11).
7. Elements of Acoustics.
8. Musical Form in general.

9. Orchestration.

10. Viva voce:—Analysis of the full orchestral score of some classical work or works. 1922: Beethoven's Symphony, No. 7, or Brahms' Symphony, No. 2, or Liszt's Les Préludes.

11. There will also be required an original composition, either sacred or secular, containing at least four movements and sufficiently long to occupy from fifteen to twenty minutes in performance. This must be

(a) A chorus in five parts, with a short instrumental introduction.

(b) A recitative and solo.

(c) A quartette or quintette for voices only.

(d) A four part vocal fugue.

Numbers (a), (b) and (d) must have accompaniments for string band only.

This composition must be sent to the Secretary of the Faculty not later than April 1st accompanied by a declaration that it is the candidate's own unaided work.

Candidates for the degree may defer presenting this composition until a subsequent annual examination, in which case the fee for examination shall be $10.

II. PRACTICAL MUSIC:

Candidates shall be required to play—on the piano or some orchestral instrument—or sing:—

Two or three compositions (or portions of them), selected by the examiner. They shall also be required to play, at the keyboard, the following tests, etc.:—

1. Transposition.

2. Extemporization upon a given theme.

3. Modulation.

Equivalent tests will be imposed for singers, or players upon orchestral instruments.

In the case of those candidates who have obtained Licentiate standing in the University of Toronto or in the Toronto Conservatory of Music requirements (11) and (II) will not be exacted but there will be required instead a short original composition in one of the following forms:

(a) A Solo Song with Pianoforte Accompaniment.

(b) A Four-part Vocal Composition.

(c) An Instrumental Composition (other than a Dance) for the Pianoforte or Organ, or for any Stringed or Wind Instrument with Pianoforte or Organ Accompaniment.

The Senate may admit *ad eundem statum* undergraduates of other Universities after due inquiry as to the requirements demanded by the institutions in which the candidates obtained their standing.

Examinations.

The examinations will take place at times to be fixed by the Senate.

Applications must be transmitted to the Secretary of the Faculty before the first of April, and at the time of application the proper fee must be paid to the Bursar.

The total number of marks necessary to pass on any subject is 60, second class honours, 70; first class honours, 80, maximum 100.

Fees.

Matriculation..................................	$10.00
Registration and Lecture Fees (Annual)....$5.00 each	10.00
Each examination subsequent to matriculation......	10.00
For admission *ad eundem statum*..................	10.00
Degree of Mus. Bac.............................	20.00
Lecture Fee for Occasional Students, $2.00 for each subject, covering all subjects, fee.............	5.00

Text-Books.

Stainer's Treatise of Harmony; Prout's Harmony; Hiles' Grammar of Music, Books I. and II.; Bannister's Music; Bridge's Primer of Counterpoint; Prout's Counterpoint; Richter's Counterpoint (Franklin Taylor's edition); Cherubini's Counterpoint, Canon and Fugue; Prout's Double Counterpoint and Canon; Jadassohn's Canon and Fugue; Albert Ham's Rudiments of Music and Elements of Harmony; Pearce's Student's Counterpoint; Pearce's Modern Academic Counterpoint; Higgs' Primer of Fugue; Prout's Fugue; Stainer's Primer of Composition; Prout's Musical Form; Ouseley's Musical Form; Prout's Fugal Analysis; Prout's Primer of Instrumentation; Niemann's Catechism of Musical Instruments; Berlioz on Instrumentation; Stone's Primer on Scientific Basis of Music; Sedley Taylor's Sound and Music; Sedley Taylor's Science of Music; Tyndall on Sound; Bonavia Hunt's History of Music; Naumann's History of Music; Parry's Summary of Musical History (Primer); Rockstro's History of Music; Articles in Grove's Dictionary of Music and Musicians bearing on the various subjects for examination.

Candidates are not restricted to the above list, which is only suggested. The paper work is judged irrespective of any particular author or school.

DEGREE OF DOCTOR OF MUSIC

Candidates for the degree of Doctor of Music must be Bachelors of Music of this or another university of at least three years' standing. Every candidate shall register his name with the Secretary of the Faculty not later than the first of November.

Candidates must present a musical exercise by the first day of April for submission to the examiners in Music, the approval of which is a necessary preliminary to further examination.

The exercise must be of the nature of a Cantata, sacred or secular, scored for full orchestra, and requiring from 40 to 60 minutes for its performance. The cantata must include an overture and parts for one or more solo voices, in addition to choruses.

If the exercise be approved the candidate must undergo an examination of a more advanced character than is involved in the Mus. Bac. examination in Harmony, Counterpoint, Fugue, Musical Form, Orchestration, and Musical History.

The fee for the examination is fifty dollars, divided as follows: Reading exercise, twenty-five dollars; practical and theoretical examinations, twenty-five dollars.

The fee for the degree is thirty dollars.

The examinations will take place at times to be fixed by the Senate.

Applications must be transmitted to the Secretary of the Faculty before the first of April, and at the time of application the proper fee must be paid to the Bursar.

DEPARTMENT OF SOCIAL SERVICE.

THE DEPARTMENT OF SOCIAL SERVICE.

In 1914 the University of Toronto established, in its Department of Social Service, the first university training school in Canada for social workers; and in 1920 it founded the first university chair of Social Science.

The Department, in planning its courses, has in view the following kinds of students:

1. Those intending to make social service a life work.

2. Those already doing some form of social work, but desiring more knowledge, either in their own or some related subject, or in the general setting of social service.

Last year these part time students included nurses, missionaries, Y.M. and Y.W.C.A. workers, deaconesses, teachers, students taking other university courses.

3. Volunteer workers wishing to increase their effectiveness and understand the problems with which they come in contact.

4. Those desirous of exercising their trusteeship on committees of social agencies, or administrative boards.

5. Those wishing to know more about the problems of the community to which they owe the responsibility of citizenship.

THE SOCIAL SERVICE BUILDING.

Is at the corner of the East Entrance to the University grounds, on the north side of College Street, just west of University Avenue.   Its Library, through the generosity of the McCormick Fund, possesses a good and growing collection of books, reports, periodicals, and bulletins on social subjects.   Students pay a library fee of $1.00, and the use of the library and reading-room is extended to social workers.   The staff welcomes enquiries for information on social matters, and does its best to meet them.

THE DIPLOMA COURSE.

The Diploma Course is covered in two years, but a certificate can be given on satisfactory completion of one year's work.

Men and women are admitted as students.   Part time students are admitted to any course or courses (except where specially noted in the list of courses below).

ADMISSION

A. *Full-time students* will be admitted on the following qualifications:

1. Graduation from university or college.   This, though not essential, is the most desirable preparation for entrance; both from the point of view of the work itself, and for eventual leadership in social service.

2. Matriculation is the minimum entrance requirement. The Department is open to consider applications from non-matriculants, but only if their experience has been educationally (not necessarily academically) more than equal to matriculation. Wherever possible, those who intend to train for social service should at least complete their matriculation.

3. Applicants with previous experience of social work will have special consideration, if they show sufficient general training to be able successfully to handle the work, and if their experience has been such as to give reasonable warrant of their fitness for the vocation.

4. Only in special cases will students be admitted over 35 or under 21.

(a) Applicants over the age limit will be admitted if their social experience and prospects of successful training warrant.

(b) Intending applicants under the limit are urged to spend one or more years in university work, giving voluntary service in settlements or clubs. The Department will gladly assist, if desired, in the choice of courses, looking to the time when students leaving school intending to train for social work (but not to follow a degree course), will take two years of selected courses in the University, thus completing with the Diploma a carefully planned 4 years of university education.

5. The full time work of the second year is open to those who have completed the requirements of the regular one-year course, or who have taken its equivalent in an accepted institution elsewhere.

6. Intending applicants who wish to take advantage of the interval before entering can be advised as to reading or practice; such preliminary work is always an advantage.

7. Application forms may be obtained from the Secretary, to whom they should be returned as soon as possible, and before September 1 if personal consultation is desired.

8. All full-time students are admitted on probation. Any student who is, in the opinion of the staff, very unlikely to succeed in social work, will be advised to withdraw.

B. *Part-time students* are admitted to any course or courses (except where otherwise specified) without question, unless the accommodation for the class is filled. Admission to certain courses of the Second Year requires evidence of sufficient previous knowledge to be able to follow the instruction.

FEES.

The tuition fee for the regular full-time course is $40 for each year.

The fee for part-time students is $5 for each regular course covering two terms and $2.50 for one term.

All fees are payable to the Bursar of the University within 30 days of the beginning of the course. Students whose fees remain unpaid at the end of this period are liable to be asked to withdraw.

The Library fee of $1 is payable at the beginning of the session to the Librarian of the Department.

RANKING

In Theoretical Work the pass mark is 60% on the total of all papers and 50% on each paper.

First Year students may be conditioned in two subjects if their general average is 60% or over.

Second Year students may be conditioned in two subjects if their general average is 70% or over.

In Field Work students are classified A, B, C, and D.

For a pass in either year a minimum standing of C is required. Standing is based on:

1. Weekly reports.
2. Attendance at all assignments.
3. Reports from supervisors and agencies.

Final Ranking.—On the combined results of practical and theoretical work students are classified:

Class I.—75% or over.

Class II.—60% or over.

SPECIAL COURSE FOR WORKERS WITH BOYS

There is an increasing demand for Boys' Work Secretaries; the Young Men's Christian Association, local churches, settlements and Boys' Work Boards are in constant need of more and better trained men than are available. As an effective and satisfying form of social service, as well as a promising field for a vocation, specialized work with boys makes one of the strongest claims.

At the beginning of the college year 1920-1921 the Department inaugurated a special two year course in Boys' Work. The subjects covered are English Bible, Religious Education, Sociology, English Literature, Social Economics, Psychology, Modern Industry, Community Organization, Public Speaking, Society and the Boy, Boy Behaviour and Methods of Boys' Work. These courses are open to students in other departments of the University who are interested in Boys' Work either as a life-work or as an outlet for volunteer leisure time service. In addition to class-room work full-time students are required to engage regularly in some form of active service in connection with some of the many agencies in the city that deal with boys.

In carrying out this work the Department co-operates closely with the Faculty of Theology of Victoria College, the Educational Department of the National Boys' Work Board, the National Council of the Y.M.C.A. and the city agencies engaged in Boys' Work. The fees are the same as for the regular Diploma Course.

SPECIAL LECTURES.

Special courses of lectures have in many cases been arranged to meet the needs of various organizations. For example, in addition to the Medical Social Course, a course was given, 1920-21, for the Neighbourhood Workers' Association and the Big Sisters combined, dealing with the following subjects: New Child Welfare Legislation in Ontario, Uncommercialized Recreation in Toronto, Unemployment Relief, Cycles of Unemployment, A Domestic Relations Court, Legal Aid, Co-operation in Case Records, The Adolescent Delinquent. A course was also given for the National Council for Combating Venereal Disease, dealing with the moral and psychological, medical, legal and educational aspects of the problem. Each course was composite, representing a co-operation of expert studies. For each a registration fee of 50 cents was charged.

Special single lectures are given to which the public are invited.

INFORMATION.

For further information address *The Department of Social Service, University of Toronto.* Those who are within reach will find a personal consultation at the office desirable.

COURSES OF INSTRUCTION.

In each year the training falls into three parts:

I. Courses in the fundamental conditions and principles of social life and development.

II. Courses in the specific conditions and problems of social service.

III. Field Work—providing by actual contact, (a) the illustration of lecture courses; (b) a widening of the student's understanding of living and working conditions, and community organization to improve these; and (c) experience in methods of social work. The following means are employed:

1. Visits of observation: (a) To institutions and agencies doing social work; (b) to factories, departmental stores and plants of public utilities.

2. Attendance at public meetings, conferences, forums, legislative assemblies, deputations, art galleries, museums, etc.

3. Apprentice work under supervision in agencies carefully selected for the facilities they offer for training.

FIRST YEAR COURSES.

A minimum of ten hours of lecture and class-room instruction a week is required of all full-time students, and an equal amount of field work. They take all courses under 1 (unless specially exempt), together with courses 5, 6, 7, and 8, with two others chosen in consultation with the Department. Additional courses can be taken only by special permission.

Courses marked with an asterisk are not open to part time students except by special permission.

I.

*1. Evolution of Modern Industry.

A course dealing with the Industrial Revolution, tracing the development of modern capitalism, the factory system, associations of capital and of labour, industrial legislation, and explaining in general the social and political reactions of modern industrial changes.

Mr. Innis.

*2. Social Economics.

A course on the elementary principles of economics; value, utility, wealth individual and national, the relation of wealth to welfare, competitive and anti-competitive forces; followed by certain applications to the problems of the wage-system and its alternatives, trade-unionism, unemployment, women in industry, juvenile labour, conditions of industrial work, and the distribution of wealth and poverty.

Professor MacIver.

3. General Introduction to Psychology.

Perception, imagination and memory in the child and the adult. The relation of instinct and emotion to behaviour. Reasoning, volition and motive in everyday life. Mental attitudes and psychological reactions of social significance.

Professor Smith.

4. Social Ethics.

The course will deal with the basal conceptions in Ethics, and their application to the problems of personal conduct and social relations. The basis of morals in human nature; the influences of heredity and environment; standards, motives, and sanctions of conduct; moral education; the sphere of morals in community life.

Professor Robinson.

II.

5. The Social Treatment of Poverty.

A course dealing with the technique of social case-work (investigation, diagnosis and treatment). The main causes of poverty and their inter-relations (ill-health; low wages; unemployment; physical, mental or moral defects; industrial accidents; old age, widowhood; desertion; large family). Public and private relief agencies and their relation. The Social Service Exchange.

Mr. Stapleford.

6. Community Organization.

The nature and development of social forms, associations and institutions, within community. The extension and development of community life. Its focal points: home, school, church, club, union, the organization of industry; of philanthropy. Experiments in social organization, the community centre, the health centre, the "city unit", the garden city, etc.

Professor Dale.

7. HYGIENE AND PUBLIC HEALTH.

A lecture course dealing with the principles of Public Hygiene, including a discussion of preventable diseases and preventable deaths. The communicable diseases are classified and their modes of infection and methods of control, elucidated. Community control of Tuberculosis, Venereal Diseases and Infant Mortality are emphasized. Industrial Hygiene, Vital Statistics and the activities of Governmental and Voluntary Health Promoting Agencies are considered.

PROFESSOR FITZGERALD.

8. THE ESSENTIALS OF CASE-WORK. DISCUSSION COURSE,

Case treatment of Special types. Study of Social Agencies and their relations. The use of Social data. The Survey Method.

MR. STAPLEFORD.

9. THE MUNICIPALITY: ITS WORK AND PROBLEMS.

The nature of a municipality. Types of municipal organization. Municipal organization in Toronto, Hamilton and Ottawa. Functions of a city organization. Transportation. Sanitation. Health. Protection of life and property. Corrections. Housing. Recreation. Relation of city government to education. Citizen organization. Social and governmental surveys.   •

DR. BRITTAIN.

10. RECREATION AND PLAYGROUND WORK.

The playground and recreation centre movement, history, organization and administration. The playground supervisor. Community organization and recreation. Mental, moral and physical value of recreation.

Part of the course will be devoted to the practice and teaching of organized games, folk dancing and musical games, suitable for both adults and children.

MISS HODGKINS.

11. CHILD WELFARE.

The child and the family. Child education, child recreation, child labour. Vocational direction. Dependent and defective children. Child placing and children's societies. Institutional care. Juvenile delinquency and the development of the juvenile court. Probation and parole methods.

MISS BROOKING.

*12. INDUSTRIAL PROBLEMS.

This course is designed as an introduction to the study of social questions as they centre in industry, and will include some discussion of industrial conditions, industrial relations and labour legislation. Working conditions, including wages, hours, personal relations in the shop, and other matters relating to the health, safety, stability, and welfare of the workers will be subjects of study.

PROFESSOR MacIVER.

13. Society and the Boy.

A study, based upon an investigation of individual boys, of the effects of our social institutions on boy life. The home, church and Sunday school, public school; social and industrial conditions; recreational facilities. Students taking this as part of a full-time Boys' Work course will be in charge of actual groups or clubs of boys.

Dr. Hayward.

14. Medical Social Work.

Arranged for the Nurses' Training Committee, and in charge of Miss Emory. In 1920-21, the course was given in series:

1. The place of Medical (or Hospital) Social Work in the general field of social work; 3 lectures by Professor Dale.

2. Public Health Nursing; 14 lectures by leading exponents of its various branches.

3. Closely Related Social Problems; 2 lectures by Mr. Stapleford on housing and social legislation; 4 on poverty, education and recreation, and a resumè of the course, by Professor Dale.

15. Literature.

The intention is to share an hour a week in the pleasure and refreshment of literature rather than in its study. Much of the time will be devoted to reading aloud prose and verse, chosen for its beauty and truth. No rigid syllabus will be followed: the guides will be 'the taste of the leaders, and the interest of the class.

Professor Dale and Dr. Pratt.

III.

16. Field Work (Discussion Course).

Relation of Field Work to lectures. Consideration of current events. Assignment of special reports. Occasional discussions led by representative social workers in order to widen understanding of various types of work and give vocational guidance. Discussion of problems arising out of field experience.

Miss McGregor.

SECOND YEAR COURSES.

Courses under I are required of all full-time students. One course must also be selected under II. Additional courses may be selected by the student in consultation with the department.

I.

17. SOCIAL EVOLUTION.

Primitive society, types and stages. Early kinship' and marriage relations. Family, clan, tribe and nation. The evolution of institutions. The various modes of competition and co-operation. Various conceptions of the state and society, with special reference to contemporary discussions and experiments in reconstruction.

The psychological bases of social evolution: the instincts in society, self-realization and repression; personality and community; the individual and his environment; adaptation and maladjustment.

PROFESSOR DALE.

18. SOCIAL ECONOMICS.

Economic wealth and social welfare. An examination of the present economic organization in view of its direct and indirect influences on social welfare. Economic wealth as a necessary basis of all social welfare. Waste and conservation. Social and anti-social uses and forms of wealth. The control of the state over economic life, its object, conditions, and limitations. The state in relation to poverty, economic exploitation, private property, competition, combination, and free enterprise in general.

PROFESSOR MICHELL.

19. SOCIAL ETHICS.

The ethical development of society, and the relation of the individual to it; nature of social progress and the forces controlling it; the relation of the individual to the state, and the grounds of civic obligation; modern social conditions and problems in their ethical aspects.

PROFESSOR ROBINSON.

20. CASE WORK: SEMINAR.

The social case-work method, with particular reference to its application to child welfare work. The technique of child placing. Study of standards of social work for neglected, dependent, delinquent and illegitimate children. Study of child-caring institutions. Admissions and field work. Ontario Child Welfare legislation.

MR. STAPLEFORD.

II.

21. MENTAL TESTING.

Relation of experimental psychology to the measurement of intelligence. History of mental tests. Problems of standardization. Norms and variations. The Binet-Simon scale with revisions. Application of methods to juvenile and adult intelligence. Correlation of mental abnormality with moral delinquency. Discussion of social problems involved.

DR. PRATT.

22. HOUSING AND IMMIGRATION.

(a) *Immigration (before Christmas).*

Motives for migration; countries receiving immigrants; supervision and control; "old" and "new" immigration; racé in industry; relation of immigrants to wage-rates, the trade-cycle and unemployment; Asiatic immigration.

PROFESSOR JACKSON.

(b) *Housing (after Christmas).*

Historical introduction. Social and industrial aspect. Attempts at solving the problems (a) in England; (b) in America. The garden city. The garden suburb. The stabilization of land values—(a) by zoning; (b) by taxation. Civic beautification versus housing. Community and individual gardens. The fundamental principles of town planning. The necessity for a Town Planning Act.

MRS. DUNINGTON-GRUBB.

23. PSYCHIATRY.

Definitions of fallacious sense perceptions, such as hallucinations, illusions, delusions, etc. Symptoms—Cause and treatment of mental diseases. Mental deficiency, epilepsy, heredity. Clinical demonstrations and examinations. History and case taking. Relations of Social work to psychiatry.

DR. CLARKE.

24. THE INDUSTRIAL REHABILITATION OF THE HANDICAPPED.

1. *Society and the cripple.* From the dawn of civilization to the 16th century. The Middle Ages. From the 16th Century to the beginning of Workmen's Compensation. The war disabled. From Rome and Athens to the break up of the Feudal system. The rise of professional armies. Pension systems. The great war and the new social conscience.

2. *Science and rehabilitation.* Invalid occupation as a therapy. As a humanitarian measure. Its economic aspects. Occupational Therapy as a measurement of intelligence and capabilities. Psychological factors in Vocational Guidance of the cripple and the mentally handicapped.

MR. BURNETTE.

25. INDUSTRIAL LEGISLATION.

Modern tendencies in the industrial order. State-help and self-help. Canadian movements. The principle of minimum standards, in wages, hours and working conditions. Development of social insurance throughout the world. Unemployment. Industrial casualties. Sickness. Old age. The framing of laws. Their administration.

PROFESSOR MACMILLAN.

26. BOY BEHAVIOUR AND METHODS OF BOYS' WORK.

(*a*) The physical, mental, social and religious development of the boy through the various stages of life.

(*b*) Plans and programmes of work for the Boys' Division of a local Y.M.C.A.; the secretary's duties to a Boys' Work Board and in the community as a whole.

DR. HAYWARD.

III.

27. FIELD WORK.

It is expected that in the second year the student's impulse towards service has become articulate and that a definite branch of work may be selected for intensive experience. Field work for the Diploma student will, therefore, give opportunity for this intensive experience, and thus for the building up of technique. It will also aim to develop a proper sense of perspective in relating this chosen work to social work generally.

MISS MCGREGOR.

CURRICULA AND REGULATIONS

FOR DEGREES AND DIPLOMAS.

LAW,

DENTISTRY,

PHARMACY,

AGRICULTURE,

PHYSICAL TRAINING,

VETERINARY SCIENCE

CURRICULUM IN LAW.

DEGREE OF LL.B.

Candidates for the degree of LL.B. must have:

    (a) produced satisfactory certificates of conduct;

    (b) matriculated in the Faculty of Law;

    (c) passed the prescribed examinations;

    (d) attained the age of twenty-one years.

Any person having the degree of Bachelor of Arts or of Master of Arts in the University of Toronto; or any person having the degree of Bachelor of Arts or of Master of Arts of another University, who has been admitted *ad eundem gradum* in the University of Toronto; or any person who has been admitted to the Bar by the Law Society of Upper Canada, or any person who has been admitted a student at law by the Law Society of Upper Canada, and who has passed his Intermediate Examinations as required by the said Society, provided that before he be entitled to receive the degree of LL.B. he shall have been admitted as a Barrister by the said Law Society, may enter the Faculty of Law at the Third Year of the course of study in that Faculty; but prior to presenting himself for the final examination in the course of the degree of LL.B. he shall pass in addition to the examinations of the Third and Fourth Years in the Faculty of Law, the following examinations in the Faculty of Arts, viz.:—

1. ENGLISH CONSTITUTIONAL HISTORY: Honour examinations of the Second and Third Years.

2. ENGLISH CONSTITUTIONAL LAW: Honour examination of the Third Year.

3. COLONIAL CONSTITUTIONAL LAW: Honour examination of the Third Year.

4. ROMAN LAW: Honour examination of the Third Year.

5. HISTORY OF ENGLISH LAW: Honour examination of the Third Year.

6. POLITICAL ECONOMY: Honour examinations of the Second or Third Year.

7. JURISPRUDENCE: Honour examination of the Fourth Year.

8. INTERNATIONAL LAW: Honour examination of the Fourth Year.

9. CANADIAN CONSTITUTIONAL HISTORY: Honour examination of the Fourth Year.

10. FEDERAL CONSTITUTIONAL LAW: Honour examination of the Fourth Year.

Undergraduates in the Faculty of Arts, who intend to proceed to the degree of LL.B., may take these examinations either during their Arts course or during the Third and Fourth Years of their Law course.

Matriculation.

The Matriculation examination in the Faculty of Law shall be identical with the examination of the First Year in the Undergraduate Pass Course: English; Latin; one of Greek, French, German, Hebrew, Italian *or* Spanish; a second optional language, *or* Science; Algebra and Geometry; Ancient History *or* Trigonometry *or* Religious Knowledge.

First Year.

The subjects of examination in the First Year in the Faculty of Law are as follows:—

(*a*) Subjects of the Pass Course in the Faculty of Arts in which Pass standing will be required:—

1. English of the Third Year including English Composition.
2, 3. Any two of the following subjects of the Second Year, viz.:— Latin, Greek, French, German, Hebrew, Physics, Zoology, Botany, Chemistry, Geology of which one must be a language.
4. History of the Second Year.
5. Ethics of the Third Year.
6. History of Philosophy of the Third Year.

(*b*) Subjects of the Political Science Course, in which Honour standing will be required:—

1. English Constitutional History of the Second and Third Years.
2. English and Colonial Constitutional Law of the Third Year.
3. Political Economy of the Third Year.
4. History of English Law of the Third Year.
5. History of Roman Law of the Third Year.

Second Year.

The subjects of examination in the Second Year in the Faculty of Law shall be as follows, viz.:—

(*a*) Subjects in the Faculty of Arts in which Pass standing will be required:—

1. English of the Fourth Year of the Pass Course.
2, 3. Any two of the following languages of the Third Year of the Pass Course:—Latin, Greek, French, German, Hebrew.

(*b*) Subjects of the Political Science Course, in which Honour standing will be required:—

1. Modern History of the Third Year.
2. Canadian Constitutional History of the Fourth Year.
3. Public Finance of the Fourth Year.
4. Political Philosophy of the Fourth Year.
5. Jurisprudence of the Fourth Year.
6. Public International Law of the Fourth Year.
7. Federal Constitutional Law of the Fourth Year.

Third Year.

1. Common Law.................... Broom's Common Law.
2. Personal Property............. Williams.
3. History of the Law of Real
     Property.................. Digby.
4. Contracts.................... Anson.
5. Medical Jurisprudence.......... Rees.

6. Equity...................... { Maitland's Lectures on Equity.
                              Smith's Principles of Equity.

7. Roman Law of "*Obligationes*"... { Justinian, Institutes 3.13-4.5.
                              Gaius, Institutes 3.88-3.225.
                              Mackintosh, Roman Law of Sale

8. Canadian Constitutional Law.   Clement.

Additional subjects for candidates for the American Law Book Company's Prize:—

9. The Law of Companies........ { Palmer's Company Law.
                              Robson and Hugg's Leading Cases
                                on Company Law.

10. Municipal Corporation Law. The Powers of Municipal Corporations to make contracts, and the manner in which they may contract; the general principles governing the exercise of these powers to pass by-laws; and their powers to create or establish highways and their liabilities with respect to the same when created. The Municipal Act (R.S.O. 1914, c. 192); Meredith and Wilkinson's or Robson and Hugg's Municipal Manual; and Robson and Hugg's Leading Cases; so far as they relate to the named subjects.

Each candidate for the American Law Book Company's Prize must present a thesis upon some subject relating to either of the additional subjects on or before the 31st of March in the year in which he presents himself for examination in his Third Year in the Faculty of Law. The subject of the thesis for the Prize for 1921 is "The advantages and disadvantages from a legal point of view and otherwise of the government of cities by Commission under special Act, as compared with the present system under the Municipal Act".

Fourth Year.

1. Law of Torts................. { Salmond, English ed.
                              Pollock

2. Law of Real Property.......... Armour's Real Property.

3. Commercial Law.............. { Chalmers' Sale of Goods, with
                                the Ontario Act of 1920.
                              Falconbridge's Banking and Bills
                              of Exchange, Book II.

4. Conflict of Laws.................	Dicey's Conflict of Laws, or Westlake's Private International Law.
5. Law of Companies...............	Masten and Fraser's Canadian Law of Companies. Robson and Hugg's Leading Cases on Company Law.
6. Construction and Operation of Statutes.....................	Craie's Hardcastle on Statutes.
7. Criminal Law...................	Harris's Criminal Law or Kenny's Outline of Criminal Law. Stephen's General View of the Criminal Law.
8. Domestic Relations............	Eversley, Parts 1, 2 and 3.

Each candidate for the degree of LL.B must present a thesis satisfactory to the examiners in Law, upon some subject embraced in the curriculum, on or before the 31st March in the year in which he presents himself for examination in his Fourth Year in the Faculty of Law, or on or before the said date in any subsequent year. The subject of the thesis will be prescribed by the Senate, and will be announced at least eight months before the date upon which it is due. An oral examination on the subject of the thesis may be required at the option of the examiners in Law. Candidates for the degree may defer presenting the thesis until a subsequent annual examination, in which case the fee for examination shall be $10.

Fees.

The following fees must be paid :—

For matriculation or entrance.......................	$10.00
For each examination after matriculation.............	10.00
For each supplemental examination.................	10.00
For the degree of LL.B............................	20.00
For admission *ad eundem gradum*, LL.B..............	20.00

A candidate will not be admitted to an examination unless he has paid all the fees due from him. A candidate who fails to pay his examination fees on or before the fifteenth of March—the last day for receiving fees prior to the May examination—must pay an additional fee of one dollar.

A candidate who fails to send his application for examination by the day appointed for receiving such applications must pay an additional fee of one dollar.

Examinations.

The examinations will take place in the month of May.

Every student who purposes presenting himself at any examination is required to send to the Registrar, not later than March 15th, a paper

—39

(according to a printed form which will be provided on application) stating his standing, and whether he is a candidate for Honours or otherwise.

Candidates who at any examination have failed in not more than two subjects may, with the consent of the Senate, present themselves for examination in such subjects at the next ensuing Supplemental examinations.

Undergraduates below the Fourth Year in the Faculty of Law, who have been rejected or who have been prevented from attending the Annual examinations in May by sickness or other cause beyond their control, may, with the consent of the Senate, present themselves in September, at the time of the Supplemental examinations in Arts.

Candidates in the Faculty of Law shall not be required to pass an examination on those subjects in which they have already passed the required examination in the University of Toronto, or an equivalent examination in the course of studies prescribed by the Law Society of Upper Canada.

Candidates who have taken the course at the Law School are required to present to the Registrar a certificate from the Secretary of the Law Society, showing the subjects in the Law School curriculum on which the candidate has passed examinations at the said school, and such certificates shall entitle the candidate to exemption from examination on the subjects mentioned in said certificate, where said subjects are included in the University curriculum in Law.

Subject of Thesis.

The following is the subject for Thesis for candidates for LL.B. for the year 1922, viz.:—

The powers respectively of the Dominion Parliament and Provincial Legislatures over the interchange of commodities by export and import between the Provinces.

DEGREE OF LL.M.

Candidates for the said Degree must have been admitted to the Degree of Bachelor of Laws, must be of the standing of one year from admission to the Degree of Bachelor of Laws, must have presented a thesis satisfactory to the examiners in Law, and to the special examiners of such thesis appointed by the Senate, on some branch of law or of the history or philosophy of law, and must have passed the following examinations in the Faculty of Law, viz.:—

1. Roman Law.................. Gaius and Ulpian, edition Muirhead. Roby's Roman Private Law in the times of Cicero and the Antonines.

2. Criminal Law: Stephen, History of the Criminal Law (omitting chapters on History of Procedure, Summary Jurisdiction, and Indian Criminal Law).

3. History of English Law: Pollock and Maitland, History of English Law.

4. English Constitutional Law: Gneist, History of the English Constitution; Select Cases in Constitutional Law—Broom, Constitutional Law, Part II. (Relation of the Subject to the Executive); and Part III. (Relation of the Subject to Parliament); Todd, Parliamentary Government in England.

5. Canadian Constitutional Law: Lefroy on Legislative Power in Canada; and subsequent reported cases on the subject.

6. International Law: Oppenheim, International Law, Third Edition. Constitution of the League of Nations. The British Orders in Council, 1914-1917, relating to the Declaration of London and to maritime retaliation, together with the related documents of other governments. Stowell and Munro: International Cases.

7. Jurisprudence: Salmond, Jurisprudence; Bryce, Studies in Jurisprudence; Hall, Foreign Jurisdiction of the British Crown.

8. Civil Code of Lower Canada.

Candidates shall have the option of taking the examination in two groups—subjects 1 to 4 and subjects 5 to 8—the groups being taken in any years after the necessary LL.B. standing has been attained. The thesis may be presented in the year of the second examination or in any subsequent year. A candidate taking the eight subjects together, and failing, shall be awarded standing in either group if he shall have attained the standard for the group, the thesis being returned not read.

The thesis must be sent to the Registrar in typewritten or printed form, not later than the thirty-first day of March.

The Senate may appoint special examiners for the whole or any part of the work prescribed for examinations for said degree.

The fee for the said degree shall be thirty dollars ($30.00).

Certificates of Honour.

Certificates of Honour will be given at each examination to those students who have been placed in Honours. The fee for such certificates shall be one dollar.

Prizes.

The Edward Thompson Company's Prize of the first twenty-five volumes of the American and English Annotated Cases will be awarded to that undergraduate of First Year standing who as a candidate for the examination of the Second Year submits the best thesis on some branch of the law of Personal Property, of Contracts or of Trusts. The subject for 1922 is "A study of the law of Trusts in relation to personal property".

The Canada Law Book Company's Prize of a set of Halsbury's Laws of England will be awarded to that graduate of this University who having completed his course in the department of Political Science, and having passed the First Year examination at Osgoode Hall, has written a thesis on some portion of the work prescribed in the first examination at Osgoode Hall.   The subject for 1922 is "A comparative study of the constitutions of Canada and Australia".

The award of these two prizes shall be made to the candidate who obtains the highest aggregate number of marks on all the subjects of the second examination and also the highest number of marks for the thesis and is recommended for the Prize by the regular and special examiners in Law.   The thesis shall be sent to the Registrar, in typewritten or printed form, not later than the thirty-first of October, signed by the candidate's pseudonym, and shall be submitted to the special examiners for adjudication and report to the Senate.   The special examiners shall, before the day of examination, fix the maximum number of marks to be allowed, and the minimum number of marks which must be obtained on the thesis.   In determining the merit and value of the thesis, the examiners shall attach special importance to the literary qualities, and to the amount of original thought, research and investigation, which have been shown by the candidate in his treatment of the subject of the thesis.

The American Law Book Company's Prize of a complete set of their Cyclopædia of Law and Procedure will be awarded to the successful candidate in the Third Year who shall have obtained the highest aggregate number of marks in all the subjects of examination prescribed in the curriculum for said year, and also in the additional subjects of the Law of Companies and Municipal Law, prescribed for the said Prize, including a thesis upon some subject relating to either of those two additional subjects, and who shall be recommended for said prize by the examiners in Law and by the special examiners appointed to examine the thesis submitted by such candidates.

The Edward Thompson Company's Prizes of the American and English Encyclopædia of Law and of the Encyclopædia of Pleading and Practice will be awarded to the candidates for LL.B. who shall have receivedthe highest and second highest aggregate number of marks at the examinaion for that degree in the Faculty of Law in all the subjects prescribed for the Fourth Year, including the thesis upon a legal subject, required of such candidates, and who shall be recommended for the Prizes by the examiners in Law, and the special examiners appointed to examine the thesis submitted by such candidates.

, The American Law Book Company's Prize of a complete set of their Cyclopædia of Law and Procedure will be awarded to the successful candidate for LL.M. who shall have obtained the highest aggregate number of marks at the examination in subjects 5 to 8 for the said degree, including a thesis upon some branch of Law or of the history of philosophy of Law, and who shall be recommended for the said prize by the examiners in Law and by the special examiners to be appointed by the Senate to examine the theses submitted by such candidates.

Standards.

The standing for passing shall in the case of Arts subjects be fifty per cent., and in the case of the Law subjects be fifty per cent. on each subject of an examination, with an average of sixty per cent. on the whole. The standard for Honours shall be an average of seventy-five per cent. of the marks assigned to all the subjects of the Year.

Works of Reference.

American and English Annotated Cases, American and English Encyclopædia of Law, Cyclopædia of Law and Procedure, Encyclopædia of Pleadings and Practice, Halsbury's Laws of England, the English and Empire Digest.

CURRICULUM IN DENTISTRY.

DEGREE OF DOCTOR OF DENTAL SURGERY.

Matriculation.

A candidate for admission to the course in Dentistry will be entitled to the status of an undergraduate who possesses either of the following qualifications:

1. A certificate issued by the Ontario University Matriculation Board, of standing as for Pass Matriculation in the subjects of English, History, Mathematics, Latin and Experimental Science (Physics and Chemistry).

2. A certificate of Junior Matriculation or Normal Entrance with Latin of the Province of Ontario.

3. A certificate of matriculation in the Faculty of Arts of a British or Canadian University.

4. A certificate, accepted by the General Medical Council of Great Britain for registration as a student of Medicine or Dentistry.

5. A degree in Arts (not being an honorary degree) from some recognized University.

The following certificates may be accepted pro tanto for matriculation:—

Ontario—Normal Entrance and Entrance to the Faculties of Education as well as certificates of the same standards under titles no longer in use.

Prince Edward Island—First or Second Class Teacher's Licence. Honour, First or Second Class Ordinary Diplomas, as issued by the Prince of Wales College, P.E.I.

Nova Scotia—Teacher's Licence, Grade A or B, or Grade A or B Leaving Certificate; issued by the Council of Public Instruction.

New Brunswick—Superior and Grammar School Teachers' Licences; also Normal Entrance Certificates of the First and Second Class.

Quebec—Associate in Arts.

Manitoba—First and Second Class Teachers.

Saskatchewan—First and Second Class Teachers.

Alberta—Grade 11 or 12.

British Columbia—Intermediate or Senior Grade.

A certificate of standing as an unconditioned student of a University in the United States, may be accepted, but it must be on the basis of a complete four years' course in a High School accredited by the said University. Such a certificate must include Latin for at least two years.

Certificates other than those previously mentioned will be considered in determining the status of applicants as undergraduates.

A candidate must hold the full entrance qualifications before he can be admitted.

Curriculum.

Pre-Dental Year.

Lectures—Inorganic Chemistry, Physics, Biology, English, French.

Laboratory—Biology, Modelling, Art, Inorganic Chemistry, Physics, Manual Training.

Freshman Year.

Lectures—Inorganic Chemistry, Human Anatomy, Dental Anatomy, Comparative Dental Anatomy, Histology, Embryology, Biology, Prosthetic Dentistry, Physiology, Applied Dental Physics, Ethics.

Laboratory—Dental Anatomy, Histology, Prosthetic Dentistry, Physics, Chemistry, Dissection.

Sophomore Year.

Lectures—Organic and Physiological Chemistry, Anatomy, Physiology, Materia Medica and Pharmacology, Elementary Bacteriology, Operative Dentistry, Prosthetic Dentistry, Crown and Bridge, Special Histology.

Laboratory—Dissection, Inorganic, Organic and Physiological Chemistry, Operative Dentistry, Prosthetic Dentistry, Crown and Bridge, Physiology, Pharmacology.

Junior Year.

Lectures—Bacteriology and Pathology, Pharmacology, Anaesthetics, Exodontia, Operative Dentistry, Preventive Dentistry, Orthodontia, Prosthetic Dentistry, Metallurgy, Crown and Bridge, Dental Economics, Applied Dental Physics.

Laboratory—Applied Dental Physics, Bacteriology and Pathology, Metallurgy, Pharmacology, Operative Dentistry, Prosthetic Dentistry, Crown and Bridge, Orthodontia, Clinical Dentistry.

Senior Year.

Lectures—Medicine, Surgery, History of Dentistry, Ethics, Dental Jurisprudence, Electro-Therapeutics, Dental Pathology, Orthodontia, Operative Dentistry, Prosthetic Dentistry, Crown and Bridge, Preventive Dentistry, Dental Economics, Exodontia, Anaesthesia and Analgesia, Periodontia.

Laboratory—Pathology, Operative Dentistry, Prosthetic Dentistry, Crown and Bridge, Orthodontia, Oral Surgery, Preventive Dentistry, Medicine and Surgery (General Hospital), Clinical Dentistry.

Examinations and Standards.

The standard for pass for all years and subjects and all sections or parts of subjects shall be 50 per cent. of possible marks.

No student will be permitted to enter a higher year without having first completed all the subjects of the lower year. A student who fails to meet this requirement must repeat the lower year.

All examinations are connected under the joint direction of the Board and of the University. The term work done by the student in each subject may count as high as 50 per cent. of the examination, and is reported by the instructor in charge of each subject. The report of the examiners may count as high as 50 per cent. of the examination.

Supplemental Examinations.

Supplemental examinations are held at convenient times for removing conditions. All conditions must be removed before a student may enter a higher year than the one in which he is conditioned. Applications, together with the fee to write or take a supplemental examination, must be in the hands of the Superintendent of the College at least fifteen days before the date set for the examination.

Fees.

The following fees are payable to the Royal College of Dental Surgeons for transmission to the University.

Supplemental examination for each paper $10.00
For Degree of Doctor of Dental Surgery............... 10.00
Admission ad eundem gradum....................... 20.00

CURRICULUM IN PHARMACY.

DEGREE OF BACHELOR OF PHARMACY.

Matriculation.

Candidates for the degree of Bachelor of Pharmacy must either:—

1. Possess a degree in Arts (not an Honorary degree) from some recognized University; or

2. Have already matriculated in the Faculty of Arts in this or some other University in Canada; or

3. Be matriculants in the College of Physicians and Surgeons of Ontario; or

4. Have passed the Junior or Senior Teachers' examinations of the Education Department of Ontario in which Latin has been taken.

Provided always that all candidates registered as apprentices of the Ontario College of Pharmacy, or who have received the diploma of the College of Pharmacy up to the first day of July, A.D. 1898, shall be admitted as matriculants in the Department of Pharmacy on payment of the registration fee of five dollars.

Regulations.

Undergraduates (candidates for the degree) resident in the Province of Ontario must have complied with all the requirements prescribed from time to time by the Council of the Ontario College of Pharmacy for admission to examination for a diploma licensing to practise Pharmacy in Ontario, and must have received from the Registrar of the Ontario College of Pharmacy a certificate of having passed the final examination of that College.

Candidates for the degree, not resident in Ontario, must have devoted at least four years (not being engaged in any other business) to the study of Pharmacy, being apprenticed during that time to a regularly qualified Pharmaceutical Chemist; must have attended the full courses of lectures embracing all the subjects of the curriculum, the length of each course being not less than that required from time to time by the Council at the Ontario College of Pharmacy, and including practical work of some College of Pharmacy recognized by this University; the last of which courses must be taken at the Ontario College of Pharmacy.

All candidates who have, prior to August 15th, 1892, received the diploma of the Ontario College of Pharmacy will not be required to conform to the above, but will be allowed their degree on passing the examination on the subjects hereinafter given.

Examinations.

Candidates for the degree must pass an examination to be held in the month of May of each year—hour and date of commencing to be hereafter given—must present to the Registrar satisfactory certificates covering all the requirements relating to undergraduates as given above, and of having passed the final examination of the Ontario College of Pharmacy.

The subjects of the examination shall be as follows — · :
1. Botany and Microscopy.
2. Theory and Practice of Chemistry and Toxicology.
3. Materia Medica, including Posology and Pharmacognosy.
4. Theory and Practice of Pharmacy, including interpretation of Prescriptions and Dispensing.

These examinations shall be partly written, partly oral and partly practical.

No candidate shall be considered as having passed the examination who has not obtained fifty per cent. of the marks allotted; nor shall a candidate be considered as having passed in any subject who has not obtained at least forty per cent. of the marks allotted to such subject.

Fees.

For matriculation or registration of matriculation....... $5.00
For annual examination (each)....................... 10.00
For each practical examination...................... 0.50
For the degree of Phm.B............................ 10.00

No fee shall be charged for transference from any Faculty of this University to the Department of Pharmacy.

CURRICULUM IN AGRICULTURE.

DEGREE OF B.S.A.

For many years students successfully completing the Two Year Course at the Ontario Agricultural College for the Associate Diploma, who have obtained 50 per cent. general proficiency and 60 per cent. average in English subjects, have been admitted to Third and Fourth Year Courses of study leading to the Degree of Bachelor of the Science of Agriculture. Commencing with the work of the First Year in the Session 1920-21 the Two Year Course for the Associate Dipoma and the Four Year Course for the Degree of B.S.A. became entirely separate and distinct Courses. Applications for admission to the Course leading to the Degree will be considered on the basis of "Qualifications for Admission" stated below. Students who have taken at least one year of the Course as it formerly existed, shall complete their Course under the old regulations.

Qualifications for Admission.

All candidates for admission to the Course leading to the Degree of B.S.A.

(a) Must be eighteen years of age on or before the opening day of college.

(b) Must produce satisfactory evidence as to moral character and physical ability.

(c) Must produce certificate of having spent at least one year at work on a farm, and must have a practical knowledge of ordinary farm operations, such as harnessing and driving horses, plowing, harrowing, drilling, etc. When it is thought necessary, this knowledge will be tested by an examination at entrance or at any subsequent date.

(d) Must at the request of the college physician submit to vaccination unless certificate of successful vaccination within two years is furnished.

(e) Must pay in advance tuition fees and laboratory charges and make the required deposits on account of board, contingencies and other fees.

(f) Must produce with application for entrance Ontario Pass Matriculation Certificate in Arts or Science or Normal Entrance except as defined in sub-sections 1 and 2 below.

　　(1) Credits of candidates whose education has been obtained outside of the Province of Ontario will be considered by special committee of the college staff.

(2) Any students who have entered the Associate Course at the O.A.C. or elsewhere, and who later desire to transfer to the degree course, may be allowed certain credits on the work which they have already covered.

General Regulations.

A student taking the Agricultural Option must have at least three years' practical farm experience before entering the Third Year.

A student taking the Dairy Option must have spent one season at practical work in a Cheese Factory or Creamery, and must have taken the full Course (Cheese and Butter) in a Dairy School, or have spent two years on a Dairy Farm before entering the Third Year.

COURSES OF STUDY.

First Year.

Agriculture—Animal Husbandry, Field Husbandry, Dairy Husbandry, Horticulture, Apiculture, Poultry, Farm Economics, Farm Mechanics.
Agricultural Economics.
Bacteriology.
Botany.
Chemistry.
English.
Physics.
Zoology.

Second Year.

Agriculture—Animal Husbandry, Field Husbandry, Dairy Husbandry, Horticulture, Apiculture, Poultry, Farm Mechanics.
Bacteriology.
Botany.
Chemistry.
English.
Entomology.
Genetics.
Physics.

Examination Standards.

The following standards shall apply to all First and Second Year Examinations:—

First Class Honours.................................... 75%
Second Class Honours.................................. 60%
Third Class Honours................................... 40%
General Proficiency on the total of all subjects of a year.. 50%

ADMISSION TO THIRD YEAR STANDING.

An Associate of the College is admitted to third year standing and allowed to proceed with the work of Third and Fourth Years:—

(1) Provided he has taken rank in his Associate Course satisfactory to the College Staff, 60 per cent. of the marks in English and 50 per cent in general proficiency.

NOTE.—In addition to the above, candidates intending to take the *Agriculture Option* must present satisfactory evidence of having spent at least two years at practical work with a good farmer; those entering for the *Dairy Option* must have spent one season at practical work in a cheese factory and one in a creamery, or have spent one season in a cheese factory or creamery, and have taken the full course (cheese and butter) in a Dairy School, or have spent at least two years on a dairy farm; and those entering for the *Horticulture Option* must have spent at least one year at practical work with a good fruit grower, market gardener, or florist.

A graduate or undergraduate in Arts and Science of any reputable University, having had the necessary training in farm work, may proceed to the degree, upon presenting certificates of standing satisfactory to the head of the department to which the certificate relates, and approved by the President, and passing examinations on subjects not covered by his certificates.

The work done previously by such a candidate will be accepted *pro tanto* for any part of the work prescribed for the degree, provided he submits to the President all credentials and records of standing from other institutions.

Third Year (for the B.S.A. Degree).

Attendance and Term Work for Third and Fourth Years.

NOTE.—Any candidate before being passed on any examination must have attended at least seventy-five per cent. of the lectures and seventy-five per cent. of the laboratory periods in each subject, and must have obtained at least fifty per cent. of the marks for term work in each department and sixty per cent. in all departments together. "Attendance" and "Term Work" rank as separate subjects.

The Course of Study.

Botany   { Cryptogamic.
              { Plant Physiology.

Chemistry   { Inorganic.
              { Qualitative Analysis.
              { Organic.
              { Quantitative Analysis.

English   { Composition.
              { Literature.
              { Public Speaking.

Entomology.
French.
Geology.

Physics   { Heat.
              { Cold Storage.
              { Meteorology.

Animal Husbandry.
Bacteriology.
Horticulture.
Economics.

NOTE.—The time allotted to each subject *per week* is indicated as follows:

"L" represents a lecture period of 50 minutes.

"Lab." represents a laboratory period of one hour and a half.

1. BOTANY.—[2 "L" and 2 "Lab." fall and winter terms.]

(1) Physiology and Histology.—Duggar, Plant Physiology, or Percival, Agricultural Botany.

(2) Cryptogamic.—A study of the chief types, Coulter, Barnes and Cowles, Vol. 1.

2. CHEMISTRY.—[3 "L" and 4 "Lab." fall and winter terms.]

(1) Historical Chemistry.—(8 lectures.)

(2) Inorganic Chemistry.—Text-book, Newth.

(3) Qualitative Analysis.—A comprehensive laboratory course during the fall term. Text-book: Mason, Notes on Qualitative Analysis.

(4) Organic Chemistry. — Text-book: Cohen, Theoretical Organic Chemistry.

(5) Quantitative Analysis. — Laboratory practice in gravimetric and volumetric analysis. Reference: Lincoln and Walton, Elementary Quantitative Analysis.

Reading.—As assigned.

3. ECONOMICS.—[2 "L" fall and winter terms.] A study of the conditions of Canadian Agriculture. The factors of Agricultural Production. It is the aim to familiarize the student with the resources of Canada, and with the part played by Canada in the world's food supply. Markets, Transportation, International Trade and Tariffs are discussed with special

reference to Canada. A study of the farmer's relation to the general problems of industrial development.

4. ENGLISH.—[3 "L" fall term.]
[3 "L" and a "Lab." winter term.]

(a) Journalism.—Lectures and practice in the writing of news, press bulletins, etc.

(b) Public Speaking.—A continuation of the practice in public speaking as outlined under second year English.

(c) English Poetry from 1600-1830. Text: Representative Poetry.

(d) English Prose.—Macaulay: Essay on Johnson; Addison, Sir Roger de Coverley; Swift, Gulliver's Travels.

5. ENTOMOLOGY.—[2 "L" and 2 "Lab." fall and winter terms.]

(a) Economic Entomology.—Detailed study of injurious and beneficial insects and the best methods of preventing the ravages of the former. Sanderson, Insect Pests of the Farm, Garden and Orchard; Slingerland and Crosby's Manual of Fruit Insects.

(b) Systematic Entomology.—A laboratory and lecture course in the identification and classification of insects. Each student is required to collect and mount at least 150 insects representing as many orders as possible. From these collections the Department reserves the right to appropriate specimens of any species not represented in the College collection. Sanderson's and Jackson's Elementary Entomology; Comstock's Manual for the Study of Insects.

6. FRENCH.

(a) Grammar.—Selected lessons from the Ontario High School French Grammar.

(b) Translation.—Part I, Super's French Reader.

7. GEOLOGY.—[2 "K" fall and winter terms.] Economic Geology of Canada, Archaean, Glacial and Stratigraphical Geology and Physiography. Works of reference: Scott, An Introduction to Geology; Chamberlain and Salisbury, Geology; Reports of the Geological Survey of Canada and of the Bureau of Mines of Ontario.

8. PHYSICS.—[2 "L" and 2 "Lab." fall and winter terms.]

(a) Heat, Text: Scarlet, Course in Heat; (b) Meteorology. Reference: Milham. (c) Ventilation and Cold Storage. Texts: Ventilation; Cooper, Practical Cold Storage.

9. BACTERIOLOGY.—[2 "L" fall term.] Bacteriological technique; cultural studies of various molds, yeasts and bacteria; microscopic preparations; staining methods; bacterial analysis of milk, water, soil, diseased plants, etc.

10. ANIMAL HUSBANDRY.—[1 "L" fall and winter terms.] For students intending to take the Agricultural Option during the Fourth Year. Text: Vaughan, Types and Market Classes of Live Stock.

11. HORTICULTURE.—[1 "L" fall and winter terms.] For students intending to take the Horticultural Option during their Fourth Year.

NOTE.—Students intending to take the Fourth Year shall select their option not later than the 1st of April in the Third Year, after consultation with the head of the department concerned; and shall then notify the President of their selection and its approval by the Head above referred to.

Fourth Year (for the B.S.A. Degree.)

One of the following options:—

1. Agriculture
2. Bacteriology.
3. Biology.
4. Chemistry and Physics.
5 Dairy.
6. Horticulture.

Standard for Pass and Honours in Fourth Year Examinations.

Major Subjects: I. 75 per cent.
II. 66 per cent.
III. 40 per cent.

Each student must obtain an average of 50 per cent. on all major subjects.

Minor Subjects: A. 75 per cent.
B. 50 per cent.
C. 33 per cent.

Fees.

Each examination.....................................$10.00
Degree..10.00

Thesis.

Each fourth year student is required to prepare a Thesis on some branch or.department of the work in his special course under the direction of the Professor or Instructor in whose department the work is done. The subject is to be chosen not later than the end of the third year, and submitted for the approval of the Staff on or before April 1st. The Thesis must be based on original work. It must be typewritten on letter-sized paper of good quality, allowing one and a half inches on the left side of each page and one inch on the other three sides to allow for binding. Maps, charts, photographs, etc., must have one inch margin on the left side. All theses must be handed to the Committee of Adjudication on or before the 1st of April of the fourth year.

Agriculture Option.

See note under "Admission to Third Year Standing", page 15 of this calendar; also Attendance and Term Work for third and fourth year students, page 16.

NOTE.—The time allotted to each subject per week is indicated as follows:

"L" represents a lecture period of 50 minutes.

"Lab." represents a laboratory period of one hour and a half.

MAJORS:

1. ANIMAL HUSBANDRY.— [2 "L" and 4 "Lab." fall term.]
[2 "L" and 5 "Lab." winter term.]

(a) Horses, cattle, sheep and swine. Characteristics of the principal breeds; lectures and practical work in judging. Texts: Plumb, Types and Breeds of Farm Animals; Curtis, Live Stock Judging and Selection.

(b) Pedigrees and live stock catalogues.

(c) Principles and practice of stock breeding. Text-books: Davenport, Principles of breeding; Marshall, Breeding Farm Animals; Punnett, Mendelism; Mumford, The Breeding of Animals.

(d) Feeding and Management of Live Stock. Text-book: Henry and Morrison, Feeds and Feeding.

(e) Poultry.—[1 "Lab." fall term, 1 "L" spring term.] Buildings, feeding and management; principal breeds. Text: Lippincott, Poultry Production.

Each student shall be required to operate at least one incubator, to rear one brooder of chicks to four weeks of age, to feed and care for one pen of laying hens for one month, and to crate, fatten, kill and dress one dozen birds.

Reading.—As assigned.

2. FIELD HUSBANDRY.—[2 "L" fall term and 2 "L" and 1 "Lab." winter term.]

Advanced course in field crops: systematic breeding of cereals, legumes, etc.; agricultural organization throughout the world; experiment stations and their work; results of field experiments; practical judging of seeds, roots, potatoes, grasses and clovers; study of fanning mills, grading machines, generators, seed testers, etc.

Reading.—As assigned.

3. CHEMISTRY.—[3 "L" and 4 "Lab." fall term.]
[2 "L" and 4 "Lab." winter term.]

(a) Soil Chemistry.—As outlined in Chemistry and Physics Option, Section 1, Part B.

(b) Animal Chemistry.—As outlined in Chemistry and Physics Option, Section 1, Part D.

(c) Laboratory Work.—A comprehensive course of analysis of soils, manures, fodders, condimental and stock foods.

(d) Chemistry of Insecticides and Fungicides [Minor].

Reading.—As assigned.

4. PHYSICS.—[2 "L" and 2 "Lab." fall and winter terms.]

(a) Climatology as under Physics, Section A, in the Chemistry and Physics Option.

(b) Soils as under Physics, Section B, in the Chemistry and Physics Option.

—40

(c) Tillage and Drainage as under Physics, Section C, in the Chemistry and Physics Option.

(d) Light as under Physics, Section D, in the Chemistry and Physics Option.

Reading.—As assigned.

5. THESIS.—As outlined on page 18.

MINORS:

1. ENGLISH.—[2 "L" fall and winter terms.]

(a) Journalism.—A continuation of the work outlined in the third year course; technical reports, interviews, editorials, etc.

(b) English Poetry.—The Victorian Era. Text: Manley's English Poetry.

(c) English Prose.—Carlyle, Heroes and Hero Worship; Ruskin, Crown of Wild Olive; Stevenson, Selected Essays.

2. ECONOMICS.—[1 "L" fall and winter terms.] Instruction in the principles underlying Economics, especially Rural Economics, Land, Capital, Labour, Taxation, Money, etc. Ways of getting a living—farming as distinguished from other ways. Management as a factor in Agricultural Production. Problems of Buying and Selling, Credit, Distribution of the agricultural income. The social side of rural life. Co-operation.

3. BACTERIOLOGY.—[2 "L" fall term.] Infectious diseases of animals, modes of infection, prevention and eradication; bacterial diseases of plants; micro-organisms in the soil; the relation of bacteria to the handling of milk and other phases of bacteriological science as met with on the farm. Text: Marshall, Microbiology.

4. FRENCH.—[3 "L" fall and winter terms.]

(a) Translation.—Parts II and III in Super's French Reader.

(b) Grammar.—Selected lessons from the Ontario High School French Grammar. (Course of Third Year continued).

(c) Sight Translation.—Selected passages from Super's Anecdotes, Faciles.

5. BOTANY.—[1 "Lab." fall term.]
[2 "L" winter term.]

(a) Systematic botany: grasses, weeds and forage crops; (b) fungi and fungous diseases; (c) Field Botany.—The identification of common trees, weeds and field plants. The examination in this subject will include the identification of trees, weeds and common plants found in the neighbourhood of the College. Texts: Percival, Agricultural Botany; Duggar, Fungous Diseases of Plants.

COLLECTIONS.—*Fifty specimens (25 of which are to be grasses or forage plants, and 25 to be fungi, representing the diseases of vegetables and cereal crops), specimens to supplement the collections of the second and third year, and not to repeat them.*

Fourth Year (for the B.S.A. Degree).
Bacteriology Option.

See note under "Admission to Third Year Standing", page 15 of this calendar; "Attendance and Term Work" for third and fourth year students, also time allotted to each subject per week.

MAJORS:

1. BACTERIOLOGY.—[12 "L" and 6 "Lab." fall and winter terms.]

(a) Microscopical Methods.—A study of the morphology of micro-organisms by the examination of living cultures and various staining methods: preparation of morbid specimens, embedding of tissues and section cutting.

(b) Cultivation Methods.—Apparatus, principles of sterilization, preparation of culture media, and various means employed in the cultivation of different types.

(c) Systematic and Physiologic Bacteriology.—Chemical composition, nutrition, circumstances affecting growth, products of growth, chromogenic, zymogenic, toxic and pathogenic bacteria. Studies in symbiosis, metabiosis and antagonism. Studies in enzymes.

(d) Examination of Air, Water, Soils and Foods.

(e) Hygienic Bacteriology.—Infectious diseases; anthrax, symptomatic anthrax, tuberculosis, glanders, typhoid fever, hog cholera, diphtheria, actinomycosis, pyemia, fowl and insect diseases; toxins and antitoxins, susceptibility and immunity, attenuation of virus, protective inoculation; serum-therapy.

(f) Fermentation Bacteriology.—Micro-organisms of fermentation, enzymes; fermentations: alcoholic, acetic, lactic, butyric, ammoniacal, putrefactive; nitrification, dentrification.

(g) Agricultural Bacteriology.—Relation of micro-organisms to tillage of the soil; management of the compost heap; bacteria and the farm water supply; disposal of sewage; bacteria and pure milk production.

(h) Dairy Bacteriology.—The relation of micro-organisms to dairying; the fermentation of milk; pure culture system in butter and cheese making; pasteurization and sterilization; the bacteriological analysis of milk, butter and cheese; sanitary milk production; diseases conveyed by dairy products.

2. Chemistry of Fruits, Vegetables and Fermentations. As in Sect. I.

Part F. Chemistry and Physics Option.

3. THESIS.—As outlined on page 18.

MINORS:

1. ENGLISH.—As in the Agriculture Option.

2. ECONOMICS.—As in the Agriculture Option.

3. FRENCH.—As in the Agriculture Option.

4. BOTANY.—[2 "L" and 2 "Lab." fall term.] Section 1, Parts D and E, in the Biology Option.

5. Zoology.—[2 "L" and 1 "Lab." fall and winter terms.]   Section 2, Parts A, B, D, F, in the Biology Option.

6. Physiology.—As in 3 F, Biology Option.

7. Chemistry.—Animal Chemistry as in Section 1, Part D, Chemistry and Physics Option.

Fourth Year (for the B.S.A. Degree).
Biology Option.

· See note under "Admission to Third Year Standing", page 16 of this calendar; "Attendance and Term Work" for third and fourth year students; also time allotted to each subject per week.

Majors:

1. Botany.—[3 "L" and 6 "Lab." fall term.]
[5 "L" and 6 "Lab." winter term.]

(a) Systematic.—Lectures and Laboratory work on the chief orders of flowering plants; including grasses and the identification of grass, clover, and other seeds. *A mounted collection of 100 plants and 50 specimens of weed seeds.* Texts: Gray, New Manual of Botany; Strasburger.

(b) Structural and Histological.—Lectures and laboratory work on the organs of the plant; mounting, examining and drawing vegetable cells and tissues. Strasburger; Chamberlain; Stevens, Plant Anatomy.

(c) Physiological.—An advanced seminary course. Strasburger; Green; Duggar; Jost.

(d) Fungi and Plant Pathology.—(i) *Laboratory* course with occasioual lectures in which are studied the injurious fungi affecting orchard, garden, greenhouse, and farm crops; (ii) *a collection of 50 injurious fungi.* Texts: Reports and Bulletins; Duggar, Fungous Diseases of Plants; Stevens and Hall, Diseases of Economic Plants.

(e) Cryptogamic.—Laboratory study of the chief types covering the thallophytes, bryophytes and pteridophytes. Coulter, Barnes and Cowles, Vol. 1; Strasburger; Campbell; Massee, Text-book of Fungi.

Reading.—As assigned.

2. Zoology.—[2 "L" and 2 "Lab." fall term.]
[4 "L" and 4 "Lab." winter term.]

(a) Invertebrate.—A systematic study of the lower animals with reference to structure, function, development and relationship, the student using as types the amoeba, paramecium, vorticella, sponge (commercial and grantia), fresh water hydra, corals, campanularian hydroid, tapeworm, liver fluke, starfish, earthworm, crayfish, spider, grasshopper and mussel.

Text-books: McMurrich, Invertebrate Morphology; Parker and Haswell, Invertebrate Zoology.

(b) Vertebrate.—This course is chiefly a study of comparative anatomy, the student using as types the amphioxus, fish, frog, snake, or turtle, pigeon, and cat or rabbit.

Text-books: Parker and Haswell, Vertebrate Zoology, Vol. II; Kingsley, Comparative Anatomy of Vegetables.

(c) Economic.—A lecture course on the identification, habits, life histories and economic importance of animals, giving special attention to Ontario forms.

. Reading.—Jordan and Enerman, American Food/and Game Fishes; Bulletins and Reports of U.S. Department of Agriculture, Ontario Fish and Game Association, and Canadian Commission of Conservation, etc.

(d) Vertebrate Histology.—A laboratory course in the theory and use of the microscope and its accessories; the study of the animal cell, its multiplication and contents, and the normal histology of the various tissues and organs of vertebrates with particular reference to Mammalia.

Text-book: Hill, Manual of Histology and Organography. Reference books; Piersol, Normal Histology; Stohr, Text-book of Histology; Clarkson, Text-book of Histology.

(e) Insect Histology, Physiology and Morphology.—A laboratory and lecture course on the anatomy and physiology of insects with special reference to biological aspects. Methods and practice in the preparation of microscopical sections of insect tissue and in photomicrography.

Reading.—Folsom, Entomology with reference to Biological and Economic Aspects. Packard, Text-book of Entomology.

(f) Animal Physiology.—The study of the functions of the different organs and parts. Lectures and demonstrations are given on the cell, blood, circulation, respiration, digestion and absorption, secretion and excretion, general metabolism and animal heat and force.

Text-book: Howell, Text-book of Physiology. Reference books: Kirke, Handbook of Physiology (Nineteenth English edition); American Text Book of Physiology.

3. ENTOMOLOGY.—[1 "L" and 2 "Lab." fall term.]
[2 "L" and 2 "Lab." winter term.]

(a) Systematic.—A laboratory course in the identification and classification of insects. Where material and literature will permit this classification is carried through to genera and species. Each student is required to collect and mount at least 300 insects representing as many orders as possible. This collection the student should have as thoroughly classified as time will permit. Comstock, Manual for the Study of Insects; Blatchley, Coleoptera of Indiana; Williston, North American Diptera; Blatchley, Orthoptera of Indiana.

(b) Economic.—A careful study of injurious and beneficial insects with special attention to the most practicable and economical methods of control of the former; study of spray mixtures, spray outfits, and best methods of spraying. Each student is required to work out for himself the life histories of at least five different species of insects; take careful records of all data obtained in so doing, and hand in these along with a concise typewritten account of each life history. He must also hand in

Riker mounts or other suitable cases containing the different stages of the insects reared. These will be retained by the Department. Sanderson, Insect Pests of Farm, Garden and Orchard; Slingerland and 'Croy, Manual of Fruit Insects; Saunders, Insects Injurious to Fruits; OKane, Injurious Insects. Reports and Bulletins.

Reading.—As assigned.

4. THESIS.—As outlined on page 18.

MINORS:

1. ENGLISH.—As in the Agriculture Option.
2. ECONOMICS.—As in the Agriculture Option.
3. FRENCH.—As in the Agriculture Option.
4. BACTERIOLOGY.—As in the Agricultural Option.
Reading.—As assigned.
5. CHEMISTRY OF INSECTICIDES AND FUNGICIDES.—
   [2 "L".]
   [4 "Lab". ½ winter term.]

Fourth Year (for the B.S.A. Degree).

Chemistry and Physics Option.

See note under "Admission to Third Year Standing", page 15 of this calendar, "Attendance and Term Work" for third and fourth year students, page 16; also time allotted to each subject per week.

MAJORS:

1. CHEMISTRY.—[6 "L" and 8 "Lab." fall term.]
                [8 "L" and 8 "Lab." winter term.]

   (a) Inorganic Chemistry.—Newth, Advanced course.

   (b) Soil Chemistry.—Atmosphere, soils, reactions occurring in soils, fertilizers, the plant, its characteristics and relation to soil and atmosphere. Storer, Ingle, Hall.

   (c) Organic Chemistry.—Lectures and preparation of organic compounds. Cohen, Organic Chemistry.

   (d) Animal Chemistry.—Foods, their composition and digestibility; food constituents and their function; physiological value of the nutrients; selecting and compounding of rations. Armsby, Jordan, Ingle, Wolff, Kellner.

   (e) Chemistry of Insecticides and Fungicides.—Short course dealing with the Chemistry and the preparation of the principal insecticides and fungicides.

   (f) Chemistry of Fruits, Vegetables and Fermentations.

   (g) Laboratory Work.

   1. Qualitative Analysis. Text-book: Jones, Qualitative Chemical Analysis.
   2. Volumetric Analysis. Text-book: Coblentz.
   3. Polariscope and Sugar Determinations.

4. Analysis. Of water, soil, fertilizers, fodders, etc

5. Preparation of Organic Compounds.

Reading.—As assigned.

2. PHYSICS.—[4 "L" and 4 "Lab." fall and winter terms.]

(a) Climatology.—A general study of conditions that influence climate; particular study of Canadian climate; climatic factors in relation to agriculture; climate limits in Canada for the agricultural and horticultural products. Text: Hann, Climatology.

(b) Soil Physics.—Movements of air and water in the soil; soil temperatures; conditions affecting tilth; analysis and microscopic examinations of types. References: Warrington, Physical Properties of the Soil. King, Soil Management; Soils, Lyon, Fippin and Buckman.

(c) Tillage and Drainage.—Spring and autumn tillage; relation of various implements to air, moisture, warmth and tilth of soil; management of different types of soil; principles of drainage; preliminary surveys; systems of drainage; preparing plans for drainage; principles and methods of irrigation. Reference: Elliott, Engineering for Land Drainage.

(d) Light.—Nature and measurement of light, velocity, reflection, refraction, diffusion, interference, spectrum, images, optical instruments.

(e) Logarithms and Trigonometry.—Theory and use of logarithms, trigometrical ratios, and relations between them; solutions of triangles. Texts: Hall and Knight, Higher Algebra; Hall and Knight, Elementary Trigonometry.

(f) Electricity.—Telephones, principles, installation and care; telegraphy, metallic circuit and wireless; generators, direct and alternating; transmission of electricity; motors, direct and alternating; electric lighting; wiring; installation of plants for farm use.

(g) Sound.—Nature, propagation, velocity, pitch, musical scales, laws of vibration, resonance, consonance, Doppler's principle; Thomson and Poynting. Sound.

3. THESIS.—As outlined on page 18.

MINORS.

1. ENGLISH.—As in the Agriculture Option.

2. ECONOMICS.—As in the Agriculture Option.

3. FRENCH.—As in the Agriculture Option.

4. FIELD HUSBANDRY.—[2 "L" fall and winter terms.] As outlined in Section 2: Major portion of Agriculture Option.

Fourth Year (for the B.S.A. Degree).

Dairy Option.

See note under "Admission to Third Year Standing", page 15 oy fah calendar; "Attendance and Term Work" for third and fourth sst-ieutr dents; also time allotted to each subject per week.

Majors:

1. Dairy Husbandry.—[5 "L" and 6 "Lab." fall and winter terms.]

(a) Farm Dairy work and milk-testing; theory, practice and lectures, with Fleischmann, The Book of the Dairy.

(b) Lectures, in the winter term, with Stocking, Manual of Milk Products; Vanslyke and Publow, Science and Practice of Cheesemaking, Part III; Larsen and White, Dairy Technology.

(c) Laboratory course of experiments in cheese-making, butter making, cream separators and milk-testing, relating to the latest practices in dairy operations. Time amounting to two days a week, throughout the year, one being Saturday, will be devoted to this experimental work.

Reading.—As assigned.

2. Bacteriology.—[2 "L" fall term.]
[1 "L" and 6 "Lab." winter term.]

Dairy bacteriology, and such general bacteriology as is necessary for a thorough understanding of the work of dairying.

Reading.—As assigned.

3. Chemistry.—[2 "L" and 5 "Lab." fall term.]

(a) Dairy Chemistry.—(i) A chemical study of milk, butter, cheese, and the by-products of the dairy; (ii) Laboratory work, analysis of the products of the dairy, preservatives, adulterants, water and colouring material—Richmond.

(b) Animal Chemistry.—As outlined in the Chemistry and Physics Option, Section 1, Part D.

Reading.—As assigned.

4. Thesis.—As outlined on page 18.

Minors.

1. English.—As in the Agriculture Option.

2. Economics.—As in the Agriculture Option.

3. French.—As in the Agriculture Option.

4. Soil Chemistry.—[3 "L" fall term.] As outlined in the Chemistry and Physics Option, Section 1, Part B.

5. Field Husbandry.—[2 "L" fall term.] Advanced course in field crops, emphasizing hay, pasture and fodder crops. Lectures and laboratory work.

Fourth Year (for the B.S.A. Degree).
Horticulture Option.

See note under "Admission to Third Year Standing", page 15 of this calendar; "Attendance and Term Work" for third and fourth year students; also time allotted to each subject per week.

Majors:

1. Horticulture.—[6 "L" and 3 "Lab." fall term.]
[8 "L" and 2 "Lab." winter term.]

(a) POMOLOGY.

Lectures.—The theory and practice of nursery work and fruit growing cost of production; systems of selling; systematic classification of Canadian fruits and identification of varieties.

Text-books: Waugh, Systematic Pomology; Beach, Apples of New York; Hedrick, Grapes of New York; Bailey, Principles of Fruit Growing; Bailey, Pruning Book; Bailey, Nursery Book; Card, Bush Fruits; Sears, Productive Orcharding; Kains, Plant Propagation; Brown, Fruit Tree Propagation.

Practical Work.—Stratification and planting of seeds and pits; budding, root and cleft grafting; making cuttings; pruning and spraying; picking, grading, packing; selection of fruit for exhibition purposes; judging; studies of varieties and commercial packages at exhibitions.

(b) VEGETABLE GARDENING.

Lectures.—Theory and practice of truck gardening under glass and out-doors; greenhouse construction and management. Canning factory crops and methods of canning; seed growing; spraying, fumigating, etc.

Practical Work.—Selection and testing of seeds; preparation of vegetables for exhibition and market; judging; greenhouse management. Text-books: Watts, Vegetable Gardening; Lloyd, Productive Vegetable Gardening; Corbett, Garden Farming.

(c) FLORICULTURE.

Lectures.—Theory and practice of commercial plant and flower production; plant Ecology relative to plant culture; culture of outdoor and indoor decorative plants; greenhouse management.

Demonstrations and Practical Work.—Propagation of special florist's crops; greenhouse management; visits to leading commercial establishments. Text-books: Bailey, Manual of Gardening; White, Principles of Floriculture; Bailey, Nursery Book; Robinson, The English Flower Garden.

(d) LANDSCAPE GARDENING.

Lectures.—History and development; principles underlying rural and civic improvement; planning public and private grounds, etc.

Practical Work.—Study of landscape materials; preparation of plans. Text-books: Waugh, Maynard; Van Rensselaer, Art out of Doors; Parsons.

(e) PLANT BREEDING.

Lectures.—Studies of theory and practice of plant improvement with special reference to fruits, flowers and vegetables. Text-books: Walter, Genetics; Punnett, Mendelism; Bailey and Gilbert, Plant Breeding.

Reading.—As assigned.

2. BIOLOGY.—[4 "Lab." fall and winter terms.]

(a) Plant Pathology.—Identification and classification of fungous diseases affecting orchard, garden and greenhouse crops, prevention and remedies. A collection of 50 injurious fungi required. Texts: Duggar, Fungous Diseases of Plants; or Stevens and Hall, Diseases of Economic Plants.

(b) Economic Entomology.—Special study of injurious and beneficial insects, especially those affecting fruit, vegetables and green-house crops. Study of mouth parts, ovipositors and external anatomy; life histories and treatment; spray mixtures and methods of spraying. Each student is required to collect specimens of at least 40 of the injurious insects studied, to mount these neatly and place labels on them with the name and the date and place of capture. The student is also required to work out for himself the complete life history of at least two species of insects, to preserve the different stages in some suitable case, such as a Riker mount, and hand these into the Department along with an orderly and concise typewritten record of the life history. Such mounts and records will be retained by the Department.

(c) Plant Histology and Physiology.—An advanced seminary course dealing particularly with the histology and physiology of horticultural crops. Texts: Duggar, Plant Physiology; Green, Vegetable Physiology.

3. CHEMISTRY.

(a) Chemistry of Insecticides and Fungicides.—[2 "L" and 4 "Lab." ½ winter term.]

(b) Chemistry of Fruits, Vegetables and Fermentations.—[2 "L" and 4 "Lab." ½ winter term.]

Reading.—As assigned.

4. THESIS.—As outlined on page 18.

MINORS:

1. SYSTEMATIC BOTANY.—[1 "Lab." fall and winter terms.]

Lectures and laboratory work on the chief orders of flowering plants, with special references to cultivated forms. *A mounted collection to be made of 100 cultivated plants.* Text-book: Gray, Field, Forest and Garden Botany; with Leavitt's Outlines.

2. PHYSICS.—[2 "L" fall and winter terms.]

Soil Management.—Movements of air and water in the soil; soil temperature; conditions affecting tilth; spring and autumn tillage; management of different types of soils; principles of drainage.

3. SOIL CHEMISTRY.—[3 "L" and 2 "Lab." fall term.]—As under Chemistry, Part 1, Section B, in the Chemistry and Physics Option.

4. ENGLISH.—As in the Agriculture Option.

5. ECONOMICS.—As in the Agriculture Option.

6. FRENCH.—As in the Agriculture Option.

7. POULTRY.—As in the Agriculture Option.

CURRICULUM FOR DIPLOMA IN PHYSICAL TRAINING.

A diploma will be granted to students of the University who shall have completed to the satisfaction of the Senate the following courses for teachers of Physical Training:—

First Year.

Theory:

ANATOMY—Composition and classification of bones; classification of joints, description of movable joints; varieties, origin, insertion and action of muscles; anatomy of circulatory, respiratory, digestive and nervous systems.

PHYSIOLOGY—Oxidation and waste, metabolism; mechanism of respiration; physiology of muscle; function of digestive juices; lymph; nutrition and absorption; animal heat.

FIRST AID—Shock, wounds, bleeding, burns, exposure to cold, frost bite, fractures, sprains, dislocations, choking, foreign bodies in eye and ear, unconsciousness, fainting, apoplexy, heatstroke, epilepsy, hysteria, poisons, bandaging.

Practice:

FOR MEN—Mutual instruction in calisthenics, dumb bells, wands, clubs and freehand; elementary exercises on the horse, mats, vaulting bar, and buck; indoor games: basket ball, indoor baseball and volley ball and elementary gymnasium games as tag, follow the leader; playground games— outdoor athletics: starting, sprinting, running, broad jump, high jump, shot put, hurdles; swimming.

FOR WOMEN—Elementary Swedish exercises; corrective exercises; marching tactics, figure marching; exercises and drills with wands, dumb bells and clubs; exercises on vaulting horse, suspended ladder, parallel bars, Swedish stall bars, parallel rings; junior technique of dancing, rhythmic steps, aesthetic, folk and national dances; ball, singing and miscellaneous active games; swimming.

Second Year.

Theory:

HYGIENE—School, dwelling and gymnasium ventilation; personal hygiene; baths and bathing; immunity.

PHYSIOLOGY OF EXERCISE—Combustion, fatigue, breathlessness, stiffness, overwork, effect of training, mental work.

ANTHROPOMETRY—Card index system, value of measurements, average physique, ideal physique, instruments, prescription of exercise.

Practice:

FOR MEN—Mutual instruction in calisthenics; first and second grade exercises on the horse, mats, parallel bars, horizontal bar, bar, ladder, rings.

Outdoor Games: baseball, hockey, lacrosse, rugby, soccer.

Swimming: life saving methods, Schafer method of resuscitation; Boxing, Bayonet and Singlestick, Playground games.

FOR WOMEN—Continuation of Swedish Exercises; corrective exercises; marching tactics, figure marching; advanced exercises and drills with wands, dumb bells and clubs; Exercises on apparatus, vaulting horse and buck, vaulting bar; parallel bars, suspended travelling rings, Swedish stall bars; senior technique of dancing, aesthetic, classic rhythmic movement, folk and national dances; gymnastic, ball, and miscellaneous games; basket ball; swimming.

Third Year.

Theory:

ANTHROPOMETRY—Laws of growth; comparative measurements; height, weight; lung capacity; acceleration and retardation of growth.

PHYSICAL DIAGNOSIS—Normal body, detection of defects, method of examining heart, lungs, inspection palpation, percussion, auscultation.

PRESCRIPTION OF EXERCISE—Exercise as a therapeutic agent according to needs of the individual.

Practice:

FOR MEN—Mutual instruction in calisthenics; second and third grade exercises on the horse, mats, parallel bars, horizontal bar, rings; advanced boxing and fencing; wrestling; swimming, life saving methods, diving; further practice in indoor and outdoor games for coaching and officiating purposes.

FOR WOMEN—Continuation of Swedish exercises and gymnastics; remedial exercises and medical gymnastics; marching tactics; apparatus; fencing; single stick drill; dancing; swimming, and life saving; dancing, senior technique, solo and interpretive dances.

Fourth Year.

Theory:

PRESCRIPTION OF EXERCISE—Remedial gymnastics; spinal curvature; special apparatus; massage and thermal agents.

PHYSICAL DEPARTMENT METHODS—Organization, administration, gymnasium construction and equipment, swimming pools, playgrounds, extension work.

HISTORY OF PHYSICAL EDUCATION—

Practice:

FOR MEN—Pedagogy: Common faults in teaching, assignment of exercise for classes of various grades; nomenclature: calisthenics, apparatus; gymnastic and athletic competition: rules of competition scoring; practical extension work: supervision of classes outside the University.

FOR WOMEN—Pedagogy: Supervision of classes outside of the University; mutual instruction in Swedish exercises and gymnastics; calisthenics; apparatus, technique of dancing; marching tactics; gymnastic and athletic games; continuation of class instruction in artistic drills; fencing; swimming and life saving.

Text Books and Works of Reference: Barton, Physical Training; Corsan, At Home in the Water; The Syllabus of Physical Exercises for Elementary Public Schools (Strathcona Trust); Hastings, Manual for Physical Measurements; Seaver, Anthropometry; Le Grange, Physiology of Exercise; Gray, Anatomy; Fisher, Physiology; Poore, Medical Gymnastics; Lovett, Lateral Curvature; Gymnasti Nomenclature (Y.M.C.A.); Skarstrom, Gymnastic Kinesiology; E. Burchenal, Folk-Dances and Singing Games; E. Burchenal, The Dances of the People; Marè Hofer, Popular Folk Games and Dances; Louis H. Chalif, Text-Book of Dancing, Part I and II; J. Brancroft, Games for the Playground, Home, School, and Gymnasium; Magazines, American Physical Education, Review, Playground.

CURRICULUM IN VETERINARY SCIENCE

DEGREE OF B.V.Sc.

The course leading to the Degree of Bachelor of Veterinary Science (B.V.Sc.), shall extend over a period of four academic years, of not less than seven months each.

Matriculation

The standard adopted for the entrance requirement is based upon the successful completion, or the equivalent, of a high school course of four years in a Collegiate Institute, High School or Continuation School.

Candidates for admission to the Course in Veterinary Science must therefore, submit either—

1. A Normal Entrance of Junior Matriculation Certificate of Ontario.

2. A Certificate, equivalent in standard, of any Province of Canada, of any part of the British Empire, or of the United States of America.

3. Certificates other than those mentioned will be considered by the Senate in determining the status of applicants as undergraduates.

4. A Certificate of having passed a qualifying examination in English Composition, English Literature, British and Canadian History, Ancient History, Algebra, Geometry, Physics, and Chemistry, similar to the Normal Entrance examination of Ontario and represented in general by the Second Class Teacher's examinations of the Provinces of Canada.

To qualify for such a certificate candidates may present themselves at an examination centre in any Province of the Dominion at the time when the Department of Education of that Province holds its regular annual examinations, and at such other times and centres as may be approved by the Senate.

Admission to Advanced Standing

A student of a recognized veterinary college, or agricultural college, may he admitted to standing on conditions to be determined in each case by tbe Senate upon the report of the Ontario Veterinary College.

Curriculum

Candidates for the Degree shall ordinarily complete the courses of instruction and examinations of the first, second and third years at the Ontario Veterinary College. The subjects of instruction and examination for the fourth year are as follows:

Veterinary Medicine and Surgery.
Infectious and Contagious Diseases of Animals.
Obstetrics and Hygiene of Breeding Animals.
Animal Husbandry.
Veterinary Materia Medica and Therapeutics.
Pathology.
Bacteriology.
Meat and Milk Hygiene.
Jurisprudence and Veterinary Sanitary Service Laws.

Examinations at the end of the fourth year shall be conducted by examiners appointed by and under regulations approved by the Senate.

The standard of passing shall be fifty per cent. in each subject with an average of sixty per cent. of the total number of marks assigned to the subjects.

The first class honour standard is seventy-five per cent. and the second class sixty per cent.

Any student failing in not more than three of the above subjects may take supplementary examinations in these subjects, and upon passing the same shall be entitled to receive the Degree.

Upon the successful passing of the examinations in the above subjects the students shall be entitled to receive the Degree of Bachelor of Veterinary Science (B.V.Sc.).

Doctor of Veterinary Science.

The degree of Doctor of Veterinary Science is intended to be conferred under such conditions as will denote its receipt only by those distinguished for professional eminence.

A candidate for this degree shall be a graduate in Veterinary Science (B.V.Sc.) of the University of Toronto of at least three years' standing. He must present a thesis embodying the results of an original investigation conducted by himself on some subject approved by the Senate not later than the first of January.

The thesis must be based upon either:

(a) The results of a special research.

(b) The results of professional experience in a designated field allied to the live stock industry.

(c) The results of a special course of study extending over at least one year.

In order to be qualified for admission to the degree at the Annual Commencement in June, the thesis must be in the hands of the Registrar of the University not later than the first of May.

Fees.

(Subject to change).

A deposit fee of $5.00 may be assessed students by the University to guard against breakages and waste in their laboratories. Members of the graduating class will require to pay a fee of $10.00 for examinations and the degree of Bachelor of Veterinary Science (B.V.Sc.). This fee is to be paid to the Bursar of the University before writing the final examinations. The fee for the degree of Doctor of Veterinary Science (D.V.Sc.), shall be $15.00, which shall be paid on presentation of the thesis for the said Degree.

FEDERATED AND AFFILIATED COLLEGES.

WYCLIFFE COLLEGE.

Wycliffe College was founded in 1877 and incorporated in 1879. In 1885 it was affiliated with the University of Toronto, and federated in 1890 upon the proclamation of the Federation Act.

Its object is the Theological training of candidates for the ministry of the Church of England in Canada, and for the foreign missionary field.

In the University and University College its students receive instruction in the prescribed subjects of the Arts Course, as preliminary to the special study of Theology. The Theological course extends over a period of three years, and leads up to the degree of B.D., and D.D.

Part of the first year of the Theological Course may be taken concurrently with the Arts work of the University by means of the Theological options, and by following the schedule laid down in the Calendar of the College.

The first building of the College was erected in 1882. The work is now carried on in the second building erected in 1891, and added to in 1902, 1908, and in 1911, on the University Grounds and immediately adjoining the new Hart House. It contains rooms for 98 students, Convocation hall, lecture rooms, library, chapel, dining hall, etc.

Students are members of the Hart House, with gymnasia and club rooms, and have all the privileges of the University.

The Faculty.

REV. T. R. O'MEARA, LL.D., (*Principal*), *Professor of Practical Theology, Homiletics and Pastoral Theology.*

REV. DYSON HAGUE, M.A., D.D., *Professor of Liturgics.*

REV. W. T. HALLAM, M.A., D.D., *Professor of New Testament Literature and Exegesis.*

REV. E. A. McINTYRE, M.A., B.D., *Professor of Systematic Theology and Apologetics.*

REV. C. V. PILCHER, M.A., B.D., *Professor of Old Testament Literature and Exegesis.*

REV. H. W. K. MOWLL, M.A., *Professor of Ecclesiastical History.*

JOHN D. FALCONBRIDGE, ESQ., M.A., *Honorary Lecturer in Canon Law.*

MIRIAM W. BROWN, *Lecturer in Reading and Voice Culture.*

President and Chairman of the Council
N. W. HOYLES, ESQ., B.A., K.C., LL.D.,

Representatives on the University Senate
THE PRINCIPAL, N. W. HOYLES, ESQ., B.A., K.C., LL.D.
J. D. FALCONBRIDGE, ESQ., M.A.

Secretary to the Faculty
REV. W. T. HALLAM, M.A., D.D.

Dean of Residence
REV. H. W. K. MOWLL, M.A.,

Librarian
REV. E. A. McINTYRE, M.A., B.D.

Bursar and *Registrar*
H. MORTIMER, ESQ. C.A.

KNOX COLLEGE.

Knox College was established at Toronto in 1844, as a theological seminary in connection with the Synod of the Presbyterian Church of Canada (Free Church), which had been organized in the same year. In 1858 it was incorporated by Act of Parliament. In 1861, in consequence of the union of the Synod of the Free Church and that of the United Presbyterian Church, as the Synod of the Canada Presbyterian Church, Knox College and the Theological Institute of the United Presbyterian Synod were united.

After several changes of location the buildings on Spadina Avenue were erected in 1875 and were occupied until 1914 when the College moved to the beautiful new buildings facing on the University Lawn. Knox College was affiliated with the University of Toronto in 1885, and federated in 1890, upon the proclamation of the Federation Act. In the University and University College such of its students as are not proceeding to a degree receive instruction during three sessions in English, Latin, Greek, History, Logic, Mathematics, Chemistry, Biology, Physics, Psychology, Mental and Moral Philosophy and Hebrew. The Regular University Course leading to the degree of B.A. is the preparation expected of entrants in Theology. The course in Theology extends over three years. In addition to the required course, a special course of study leads to the degree of B.D. A number of scholarships and prizes are offered for competition in each year. Religious Knowledge options may be taken by students of the University in any year of their course, and Theological options taken in the Third and Fourth years may be counted as part of the regular course in Theology. Courses of study in the New Testament are provided in Knox College for every year of the Undergraduate course, and may be taken as Religious Knowledge options for the University degree.

The College is governed by "The Board of Management": Mr. J. K. Macdonald, Chairman; Rev. R. C. Tibb, B.A., Secretary; The Treasurer of the Presbyterian Church in Canada is the Treasurer of Knox College. The "Board" consists of thirty-five members, appointed annually by the General Assembly of the Presbyterian Church in Canada.

The Faculty.

Rev. Alfred Gandier, M.A., D.D., LL.D., *Principal and Professor of Pastoral Theology, Christian Missions and the English Bible.*

Rev. James Ballantyne, B.A., D.D., *Professor of Church History and Church Government.*

Rev. T. B. Kilpatrick, D.D., S.T.D. (Hart.), *Professor of Systematic Theology.*

Rev. William Manson, M.A., B.A.,(Oxon.), *Professor of New Testament Literature and Exegesis.*

Rev. Richard Davidson, M.A., Ph.D., D.D., *Professor of Old Testament Literature and Exegesis.*

Rev. Hugh Matheson, LL.B., *Librarian.*

Rev. R. C. Tibb, B.A., *Secretary of Senate.*

Rev. J. A. Turnbull, LL.B., D.D., *Chairman of Board of Examiners.*

Mr. F. H. Kirkpatrick, *Teacher of Elocution.*

Prof. Peter Sandiford, Ph.D., *Lecturer in Child Psychology and Pedagogy.*

Rev. Alexander MacMillan, D.D., *Lecturer on Hymnology and Church Music.*

VICTORIA UNIVERSITY.

Faculty of Theology.

The Faculty of Theology in Victoria College was established in 1871 for the purpose of training candidates for the ministry of the Methodist Church. Its classes and degrees have, however, always been open to candidates for the ministry in any Church, and are now open to members in good standing in any Christian Church.

.Instruction is provided in the various courses of study leading up to ordination in the Methodist Church, viz., the B.D. Course, the Course for Graduates in Arts, and the Course for Non-graduates.

Undergraduates in Arts, whether candidates for the ministry or not, have the privilege of taking certain subjects in Theology as options in Religious Knowledge in the several years of their course, as indicated in this Calendar in the prescriptions of the Arts Courses..

For further information as to courses of study, fees, honours, prizes, scholarships and regulations, see the Theological Calendar of Victoria College, or apply to the Rev. Professor J. F. McLaughlin, B.A., D.D., Dean of the Faculty of Theology.

The Faculty.

REV. A. H. REYNA, M.A., LL.D. } *Professores Emeriti.*
REV. F. H. WALLACE, M.A., D.D., }

REV. J. F. McLAUGHLIN, B.A., D.D., *Professor of Old Testament Exegesis and Literature.*

REV. R. P. BOWLES, M.A., D.D., LL.D., *Professor of Systematic Theology.*

W. B. LANE, M.A., PH.D., *Professor of Ethics and Didactics.*

W. H. GREAVES, M.A., *Professor of Public Speaking.*

REV, A. J. JOHNSTON, B.A., *Professor of Homiletics and Pastoral Theology and of Church History.*

REV. J. W. MACMILLAN, B.A., D.D., *Professor of Sociology.*

REV. J. H. MICHAEL, M.A., *Professor of New Testament Exegesis and Literature.*

REV. W. A. POTTER, M.A., B.D., *Associate Professor of Old Testament Exegesis and Literature.*

REV. F. W. LANGFORD, B.A., M.R.E. *Associate Professor of Religious Pedagogy.*

W. T. BROWN, M.A., PH,D., *Associate Professor of Ethics and Apologetics.*

REV. W. B. CASWELL, B.A., *Special Lecturer in History of Preaching.*

ROYAL COLLEGE OF DENTAL SURGEONS OF ONTARIO.

This is the corporate name of the Profession of Dentistry in the province of Ontario, incorporated in 1868, with power to examine, and issue license to practise as a dentist in the Province. In connection with the College, a School of Dentistry was established in 1875 for the instruction of students in their professional work.

The Faculty.

Administrative Officers.

ALBERT E. WEBSTER, L.D.S., D.D.S.,   WALLACE SECCOMBE, L.D.S., D.D.S.
M.D., *Dean.*   *Superintendent.*
W. E. WILLMOTT, L.D.S., D.D.S.,
Secretary of Faculty.

Professors.

G. R. ANDERSON, B.A.Sc., M.A., *Professor of Physics.*

HAROLD KEITH BOX, L.D.S., D.D.S., PH.D., *Professor of Dental Pathology and Periodontia.*

F. A. CLARKSON, M.B., *Professor of Physiology, Hygiene and Medicine.*

F. J. CONBOY, L.D.S., D.D.S., *Professor of History of Dentistry.*

J. W. CORAM, L.D.S., D.D.S., *Professor of Dental Ceramics.*

THOMAS COWLING, L.D.S., D.D.S., *Professor of Metallurgy.*

W. E. CUMMER, L.D.S., D.D.S., *Professor of Prosthetic Dentistry; Professor of Applied Physics.*

B. O. FIFE, L.D.S., D.D.S., *Professor of Clinical Operative Dentistry.*

JOSEPH S. GRAHAM, M.B., M.R.C.S., *Professor of Histology, Bacteriology and Pathology.*

G. G. HUME, L.D.S., D.D.S., *Professor of Orthodontia.*

H. M. LANCASTER, B.A.Sc., *Professor of Chemistry.*

A. D. A. MASON, L.D.S., D.D.S., *Professor of Operative Dentistry.*

R. G. McLAUGHLIN, L.D.S., D.D.S., *Professor of Dental Jurisprudence and Ethics.*

A. J. McDONAGH, L.D.S., *Professor of Periodontology.*

E. W. PAUL, L.D.S., *Professor of Anaesthesia, Exodontia.*

F. D. PRICE, L.D.S., D.D.S., *Professor of Electro Therapeutics.*

F. E. RISDON, L.D.S., D.D.S., M.B., *Professor of Surgery.*

T. A. ROBINSON, M.D., C.M., *Professor of Anatomy.*

WALLACE SECCOMBE, L.D.S., D.D.S., *Professor of Preventive Dentistry; Professor of Dental Economics.*

A. A. STEWART, L.D.S., D.D.S., *Professor of Crown and Bridge Work.*

R. D. THORNTON, L.D.S., D.D.S., *Professor of Dental Anatomy and Comparative Dental Anatomy.*

A. E. WEBSTER, L.D.S., D.D.S., M.D., *Professor of Operative Dentistry, Dental Pathology and Therapeutics.*

W. EARL WILLMOTT, L.D.S., D.D.S., *Professor of Clinical Prosthetic Dentistry; Professor of Materia Medica and Pharmacology.*

Associate Professors.

G. R. ANDERSON, B.A.Sc., M.A., *Associate Professor, Applied Physics.*

I. H. ANTE, L.D.S., D.D.S., *Associate Professor, Prosthetic Dentistry.*

J. A. BOTHWELL, L.D.S., D.D.S., *Associate Professor, Clinical Prosthetic Dentistry.*

THOMAS COWLING, L.D.S., D.D.S., *Associate Professor of Chemistry.*

G. H. CORAM, L.D.S., D.D.S., *Associate Professor of Clinical Operative Dentistry.*

NORMAN T. MACLAURIN, M.B., *Associate Professor of Bacteriology.*

W. C. SMITH, L.D.S., D.D.S., *Associate Professor of Clinical Operative Dentistry.*

Lecturers.

G. N. BRAMFITT, B.A., *Lecturer in English.*

J. B. WALLACE, B.A., *Lecturer in French.*

L. E. WESTMAN, B.A.Sc., *Lecturer in Chemistry.*

J. L. BANKS, *Demonstrator in Modelling.*

W. J. BEATTY, R.C.A., *Demonstrator in Art.*

Clinicians.

C. A. CORRIGAN, L.D.S., D.D.S., *Clinician, Orthodontia.*

B. R. GARDINER, L.D.S., D.D.S., *Clinician, Anaesthesia and Exodontia.*

H. A. HOSKIN, L.D.S., D.D.S., *Clinician Patients' Examination.*

F. C. HUSBAND, L.D.S., D.D.S., *Clinician, Preventive Dentistry.*

C. A. KENNEDY, L.D.S., D.D.S., *Clinician, Orthodontia.*

L. F. KRUEGER, L.D.S., D.D.S., *Clinician, Operative Dentistry.*

Demonstrators.

G. D. BEIERL, L.D.S., D.D.S., *Demonstrator, Dental Anatomy.*

A. B. BABCOCK, L.D.S., D.D.S., *Demonstrator, Operative Dentistry.*

H. G. BEAN, L.D.S., D.D.S., *Demonstrator, Dental Laboratory.*

W. EASSON BROWN, M.B., *Demonstrator, Osteology, Anatomy.*

E. H. CAMPBELL, L.D.S., D.D.S., *Demonstrator, Dental Laboratory.*

F. W. CLEMENT, M.B., *Demonstrator, Osteology and Anatomy.*

F. L. COLE, L.D.S., D.D.S., *Demonstrator, Dental Anatomy.*

W. H. COON, L.D.S., D.D.S., *Demonstrator, Prosthetic Dentistry.*

S. S. CROUCH, L.D.S., D.D.S., *Demonstrator, Dental Laboratory.*

L. R. DAVIDSON, L.D.S., D.D.S., *Demonstrator, Dental Laboratory.*
L. D. DREW-BROOK, L.D.S., D.D.S., *Demonstrator, Histology.*
J. H. DUFF, L.D.S., D.D.S., *Demonstrator, Dental Laboratory.*
D. M. FLETT, L.D.S., D.D.S., *Demonstrator, Histology.*
R. J. GODFREY, L.D.S., D.D.S., *Demonstrator, Dental Laboratory.*
E. A. GRANT, L.D.S., D.D.S., *Demonstrator, Dental Laboratory.*
H. H. HALLORAN, L.D.S., D.D.S., *Demonstrator, Dental Laboratory.*
HOWARD HARRISON, M.D., F.R.C.S., (Eng.), *Demonstrator, Anatomy.*
H. W. HOAG, L.D.S., D.D.S., *Demonstrator, Dental Labotarory.*
W. T. HOLMES, L.D.S., D.D.S., *Demonstrator, Dental Laboratory.*
W. L. HUGILL, L.D.S., D.D.S., *Demonstrator, Dental Laboratory.*
J. W. INGRAM, L.D.S., D.D.S., *Demonstrator, Dental Laboratory.*
W. E. MARTIN, M.B., *Demonstrator, Anatomy.*
G. E. OLDHAM, L.D.S., D.D.S., *Demonstrator, Dental Laboratory.*
B. M. OTT, L.D.S., D.D.S., *Demonstrator, Dental Laboratory.*
J. A. PRIESTMAN, L.D.S., D.D.S., *Demonstrator, Dental Laboratory.*
A. C. PYE, L.D.S., D.D.S., *Demonstrator, Dental Laboratory.*
S. M. RICHARDSON, L.D.S., D.D.S., *Demonstrator, Infirmary Laboratory.*
MISS W. C. RIDDLE, B.A., *Demonstrator, Histology, Bacteriology and Pathology.*
J. L. ROBINSON, M.D., C.M., *Demonstrator, Osteology and Anatomy.*
H. A. ROSS, L.D.S., D.D.S., *Demonstrator, Dental Laboratory.*
J. M. SHELDON, L.D.S., D.D.S., *Demonstrator, Dental Laboratory.*
R. B. STEWART, M.A., M.D., *Demonstrator, Chemical Laboratory.*
W. G. SWITZER, L.D.S., D.D.S., *Demonstrator, Dental Laboratory.*
VICTOR THOMSON, *Demonstrator, Chemical Laboratory.*
W. G. TRELFORD, L.D.S., D.D.S., *Demonstrator, Senior Laboratory.*
R. R. WALKER, L.D.S., D.D.S., *Demonstrator, Dental Laboratory.*
R. M. WATSON, L.D.S., D.D.S., *Demonstrator, Dental Laboratory.*
R. S. WOOLLATT, L.D.S., D.D.S., *Demonstrator, Dental Laboratory.*

Librarian and Curator of Museum.

C. A. KENNEDY, L.D.S., D.D.S.

Honorary Clinicians.

W. B. AMY, L.D.S., D.D.S.
W. L. CHALMERS, L.D.S., D.D.S.
HAROLD CLARK, L.D.S., D.D.S.
CHAS. E. PEARSON, L.D.S., D.D.S.
A. S. THOMSON, L.D.S., D.D.S.

The Royal College of Dental Surgeon was affiliated with the University of Toronto in 1888, and shortly thereafter an examination for the degree of Doctor in Dental Surgery was instituted in the University. See Curriculum in Dentistry elsewhere in this volume.

ONTARIO COLLEGE OF PHARMACY.

The Council of the College of Pharmacy, the biennially-elected governing body of the practising pharmacists of the Province of Ontario, began in 1882 to give instruction in the various subjects necessary for license for druggists. The College Building, situated in St. James' Square, was erected in 1886, and the Faculty reorganized and extensive additions made to the building in 1891. In the same year affiliation was entered into with the University of Toronto. For curriculum, see p. 593. For details as to laboratory and other courses, preliminary qualifications, etc., see Annual Announcement of the College, which may be had by addressing W. B. Graham, Registrar-Treasurer, Ontario College of Pharmacy, Toronto, Ontario.

The Faculty.

Charles F. Heebner, Ph.G., Phm.B., *Dean, Professor of Theory and Practice of Pharmacy and Dispensing, Director of the Pharmaceutical and Dispensing Laboratories.*

Graham Chambers, B.A., M.B., *Emeritus Professor of Chemistry.*

John T. Fotheringham, B.A., M.D., C.M., *Emeritus Professor of Materia Medica.*

Paul L. Scott, M.B., *Professor of Biology.*

George A. Evans, Phm.B., *Professor of Chemistry and Physics, Director of the Chemical Laboratory.*

R. O. Hurst, Phm.B., *Lecturer on Latin and Materia Medica.*

ONTARIO AGRICULTURAL COLLEGE.

Faculty of Instruction.
1920-1921.

(All except the President arranged in order of seniority).

J. B. REYNOLDS, M.A., *President.*
H. H. DEAN, B.S.A., *Professor of Dairy Husbandry.*
C. A. ZAVITZ, B.S.A., *Professor of Field Husbandry.*
J. HUGO REED, V.S., *Professor of Veterinary Science.*
WADE TOOLE, B.S.A., *Professor of Animal Husbandry.*
O. J. STEVENSON, M.A., D.PAED., *Professor of English.*
R. HARCOURT, B.S.A., *Professor of Chemistry.*
MISS OLIVE CRUIKSHANK, *Director of Home Economics.*
JOHN EVANS, *Professor of Manual Training.*
W. R. GRAHAM, B.S.A., *Professor of Poultry Husbandry.*
W. C. BLACKWOOD, B.A.Sc., *Professor of Physics.*
J. W. CROW, B.S.A., *Professor of Horticulture.*
J. E. HOWITT, M.S.A., *Professor of Botany.*
D. H. JONES, B.S.A., *Professor of Bacteriology.*
L. CAESAR, B.A., B.S.A., *Associate Professor of Entomology.*
W. J. SQUIRRELL, B.S.A., *Associate Professor of Field Husbandry.*
H. H. LeDREW, B.S.A., *Lecturer in Economics.*
F. E. MILLEN, B.S.A., *Lecturer in Apiculture.*
E. W. KENDALL, *Lecturer in Manual Training.*
H. L. FULMER, B.S.A., *Lecturer in Chemistry.*
R. R. GRAHAM, B.A., B.S.A., *Lecturer in Physics.*
R. E. STONE, B.Sc., PH.D., *Lecturer in Botany.*
G. H. UNWIN, B.S.A., *Lecturer in English and French.*
A. C. WHEATLEY, *Lecturer in Chemistry and Geology.*
A. W. BAKER, B.S.A., *Lecturer in Entomology.*
F. L. FERGUSON, B.S.A., *Lecturer in Physics.*
T. H. LUND, B.S.A., *Lecturer in Bacteriology.*
J. P. SACKVILLE, B.S.A., *Associate Professor of Animal Husbandry.*
MISS H. THEODORA JOB, *Instructor in Normal Methods.*
MISS M. A. PURDY, *Demonstrator in Chemistry.*
MISS JEAN RODDICK, *Instructor in Domestic Science.*
MRS. F. DOUGHTY, *Domonstrator in Domestic Art.*
MISS GRACE CONNOVER, *Demonstrator in Domestic Science.*
MISS ALTA V. DICKEY, *Instructor in Domestic Art.*
E. S. SNYDER, B.S.A., *Demonstrator in Poultry Husbandry.*
D. R. SANDS, B.S.A., *Lecturer in Botany.*

MISS BELLE MILLAR, *Demonstrator in Dairying.*
MISS JEAN BRADLEY, *Demonstrator in Laundry and Household Adminis-
tration.*
G. J. SPENCER, B.S.A., *Demonstrator in Entomology.*
S. H. GANDIER, B.S.A., (temporary position), *Fellow in Chemistry.*
K. W. FORMAN, *Instructor in Athletics.*
R. C. FRITH, *Resident Master and Instructor in English.*

College Officers.

J. B. REYNOLDS, M.A., *President.*
S. SPRINGER, *Bursar.*
A. M. PORTER, B.S.A., *Secretary.*
R. C. FRITH, *Resident Master.*
MISS J. GARDINER, *Librarian.*
MISS A. O. HALLETT, *Assistant Librarian.*
W. O. STEWART, M.D., *Physician.*
MRS. K. L. GALBRAITH, *Matron.*
MISS M. MONTGOMERY, *Dietitian.*

THE ONTARIO VETERINARY COLLEGE.

In 1862, through the efforts of the late Hon. Adam Ferguson of Woodhill and the late George Buckland, Professor of Agriculture in the University of Toronto, Professor Andrew Smith, a graduate of the Edinburgh Veterinary College, was appointed to give instruction in Veterinary Studies in the Province of Upper Canada. The Veterinary College thus established was later taken over by the Government of the Province of Ontario and affiliated with the University of Toronto, from which graduates of the College may receive the degree of Bachelor of Veterinary Science and Doctor of Veterinary Science. See Curriculum in Veterinary Science elsewhere in this volume.

College Staff and Subjects Taught, 1920-21.

C. D. McGilvray, V.S., M.D.V., *Contagious Diseases, Special Therapeutics.*

J. N. Pringle, M.R.C.V.S., B.V.Sc., *Sporadic Diseases, Dentistry.*

R. A. McIntosh, M.D.V., *Disesaes of Cattle, Obstetrics.*

W. J. R. Fowler, B.V.Sc., *Surgery, Surgical Therapeutics, Restraint.*

J. A. Campbell, V.S., *Canine and Feline Diseases.*

H. D. Nelson, V.S., D.V.Sc., *Anatomy.*

H. B. Collet, M.R.C.V.S., B.V.Sc., *Veterinary Hygiene, Surgery.*

R. G. Gwatkin, V.S., B.V.Sc., *Bacteriology, Milk Hygiene.*

H. E. Batt, V.S., *Histology, Laboratory Pathology.*

C. McIntosh, B.V.Sc., *Meat Inspection.*

D. King Smith, M.B., V.S., *Pathology.*

E. A. McCulloch, B.A., M.B., *Parasitology.*

Paul L. Scott, M.B., *Pharmacy.*

C. A. Temple, M.D., C.M., *Materia Medica.*

F. C. Bailey, B.S.A., *Animal Husbandry.*

Professor J. J. R. MacLeod, University of Toronto, *Physiology.*

Professor J. Hunter, University of Toronto, *Biochemistry.*

Professor R. B. Thomson, University of Toronto, *Botany.*

Professor E. F. Burton, University of Toronto, *Physics.*

Professor F. B. Allan, University of Toronto, *Chemistry.*

Dyce W. Saunders, K.C., *Jurisprudence.*

F. H. Kirkpatrick, Ph.D., *Public Speaking.*

H. W. Brown, B.A., *Civics, Economics.*

APPENDIX

FACULTY OF ARTS.

UNIVERSITY COLLEGE.

First Year.

The names of students registered in the Course in Commerce are printed in italics.

Allan, W........Winnipeg, Man.
Allison, Miss J. L......Walkerville
Anderson, Miss C. E. H...Toronto
Andrews, J..............Toronto
Ansley, E. C..Medicine Hat, Alta.
Archibald, D. A...........Elora
Armitage, Miss D........Toronto
*Armstrong, A..........Armitage
Armstrong, J. W.........*Allandale*
Armstrong, W. M...Fort William
Asman, Miss M. L.......Toronto
Ayer, H. M........Okotoks, Alta.
Babbitt, G. M. W........Toronto
Bagley, Miss M. M.......Toronto
Ball, Miss H. M. ....Harriston
Barnhardt, E. H......Oro Station
Barrett, Miss M. L........Ottawa
Beadle, G. G..............(Ob.)
Beck, F. A.....Penetanguishene
Belger, L...............Mildmay
Bell, J. E..............Priceville
Bell, W. G........Britannia Bay
Belyea, G. H. V....St. John, N.B.
Benn, L................Toronto
Bennett, C. H..........Toronto
Bennett, Miss M. U......Toronto
Berger, J. J.............Toronto
Billings, A. B.......*Vernon, B.C.*
Binning, R. D....Moose Jaw, Sask.
Blackburn, Miss M. E.....Toronto
Blackwell, L. E..........Toronto
Blair, B. D...........Hintonburg
Blugerman, N............Toronto
Booth, J. H. K..........Toronto
Booth, W. G............Toronto
Boothe, A. E...........Toronto
Boucher, G. R.............Carp
Bovaird, Miss G.......Brampton
Bowen, L. N............Toronto
Boyd, W. K..........Flesherton
Boyle, J................Toronto
Brisbin, Miss J. M......Harriston
Brittain, A. C..........Ottawa
Brock, Miss G., Medicine Hat, Alta.
Brodie, W. M..........Sudbury

Brown, Miss A. J........Toronto
Brown, N. P. H.........Toronto
Buffam, Miss M. C. W.....Perth
Burns, D. K..........Pembroke
Burton, Miss B. E......Toronto
Bustard, Miss I. H.......Toronto
Caldwell, K. H......North Gower
Calvert, L. P...........Toronto
Campbell, W. N. M....Oro Station
Carmichael, Miss M. F....Toronto
Carr, D. G..............Sarnia
Carroll, T. E., Loughgall, Armagh,
                Ireland
Carson, J. A.........Gamebridge
Carswell, Miss M........Toronto
Cathcart, S. V........Courtright
Chaikoff, I.............Toronto
Chambers, Miss E. C.....Toronto
Charles, Miss G........Toronto
Chisholm, Miss D. B...Chatsworth
Chisholm, Miss R. E.....Oakville
Clark, J. F..............*Ottawa*
Cohen, Miss E...........Toronto
Coleman, H. R.....St. John, N.B.
Coleman, Miss T. L.......Weston
Coles, G. E.............Toronto
Coles, Miss M. E........Toronto
Conboy, Miss V. L.......Toronto
Conn, Miss M. D.........Sarnia
Conrad, Miss D. V., Detroit, Mich.
Copeland, P. A..........Toronto
Copping, Miss M. E...Fort William
Cowan, Miss E. J.........Drumbo
Cowan, F. P.............Sarnia
Creighton, Miss M. E.,
              Alameda, Sask.
Crombie, Miss J. M......Toronto
Cronyn, T..............London
Cross, T. L.....Edmonton, Alta.
Crossen, W. V..........Cobourg
Crow, Miss L. E........Chatham
Crozier, A. R...........Toronto
Crozier, E.............Fairbank
Cryer, G...........Charing Cross
Cryer, J...........Charing Cross

* In attendance Michaelmas Term only.

Crysdale, J. P............Toronto
Cuddy, Miss W. E...Amherstburg
Currie, P. N. W...........Ottawa
Dack, J. O.......Los Angeles, Cal.
*Dalrymple, A. J.........Toronto
Davis, A. E. N.........Welland
Davis, J. A.....Grand Forks, B.C.
Davison, Miss D. A....Unionville
Deans, Miss M. G......Dundalk
Dewar, Miss K. L......Oil Springs
Dilworth, R. W. E........Toronto
Dingman, R. E..........Toronto
Doig, W. P............Wroxeter
Donaldson, Miss M. C....Toronto
Doxsee, M. I.............Toronto
Duff, G. A..............Drayton
Dunbar, Miss K. S.......Guelph
Easton, C. G.......Smith's Falls
Edmonds, Miss M. B..St. Thomas
Edwards, Miss M. S...Gananoque
Eickler, H..............Toronto
Ellis, Miss O. E.........Toronto
English, Miss F. P.......Toronto
Fairbairn, Miss H........Toronto
Fawcett, W. L............Sarnia
Field, A. C. H..........Cobourg
Finlayson, R. A......Campbellton
Fitzgerald, F. G.....St. Catharines
Fleming, Miss A. B.........Galt
Fleming, R. H..........Grimsby
Flynn, Miss A......St. Catharines
Foex, Miss B. M........Chatham
Fogal, H. R.............Toronto
Foran, Miss M. L......St. George
Forster, L. C.......St. Catharines
Foster, Miss M. G......Listowel
Fraser, Miss M. E. F.....Toronto
Fulford, R. T.........Brockville
Fuller, Miss A. L.........Sarnia
Fuller, W. E..........Peterboro
Gardiner, Miss A. C. E.,
                    Mount Forest
Gash, A. B..............Toronto
Gavin, Miss E. G........Toronto
Getty, G. S....Moose Jaw, Sask.
Gibson, Miss F. E. P....Oakville
Gibson, H. J..........Newcastle
Gilchrist, N. M..........Toronto
Gilfillan, Miss V. G........Orono
Gillelan, H. W.......Milton West
Giller, I. E..............Toronto
Glassey, C..............Toronto
Gogo, Miss J. L. M......Cornwall
Golding, Mrs. A. J.....Bracebridge
Gooderham, Miss V. L....Toronto

Goold, E. M...........Brantford
Gordon, K. S...........Pembroke
Gould, Miss E. C. S......Toronto
Graham, Miss L. G.....Bothwell
Grant, W. G.....Port of Spain,
                Trinidad, B.W.I.
Green, Miss E. W........Toronto
Greig, F. C. W..........Toronto
Greig, Miss J. G.........Toronto
Griffith, Miss B. M......Toronto
Griffith, J. L.......Niagara Falls
Griffith, Miss M. I.......Toronto
Gullette, Miss B. A......Toronto
Gulston. C. S............Toronto
Haines, Miss F. L......Wingham
Haines, J. A............Toronto
Halford, Miss K. M......Toronto
Hall, H. G.............Toronto
Hambly, Miss D. S.......Ottawa
Hampson, Miss D...St. Catharines
Hanes, C. S............Willowdale
Hardy, Miss F. S........Toronto
Hargreaves, Miss F. I......Toronto
Harkness, Miss J. W......Toronto
Harris, Miss C............Toronto
Harris, Miss D. K........Ottawa
Harris, G. E. M.....Brandon, Man.
Harris, Miss L. A........Toronto
Harris, Miss R. C........Toronto
Hastie, W. J. A. .....Sheguindah
Hatheway, C. M....St. John, N.B.
Haywood, K. D..........Toronto
Heinonen, Miss V. S.,
                Helsinki, Finland
Hewetson, H. W.........Toronto
Hewitt, C. J.............Toronto
Higgins, Miss E. A......Clinton
Hislop, Miss E. B........Stratford
Hogg, D. A........Chefoo, China
Hollinrake, Miss P. I.....Toronto
Holmes, W. M....Moose Jaw, Sask.
Hornal, J..............Muirkirk
Horne, Miss H. M........Toronto
Horrell, Miss J. I.......Midland
Howell, Miss M. K........Toronto
Howson, Miss G.........Toronto
Huband, A. R............Ottawa
Huddart, Miss M. G....Hamilton
Hugill, H. R............Toronto
Hulme, Miss D. A.,
                Vancouver, B.C.
Hunter, Miss A. B.......Toronto
Hurst, Miss H. J.........Toronto
Huth, Miss M. I.........Stayner
Hwang, L. T......Kashing, China

* In attendance Michaelmas Term only.
—42

Hyde, J......Pincher Creek, Alta.
Innes, Miss J. B..........Toronto
Irvine, W. K..............Toronto
Jack, J. C................Toronto
James, A. G. B.,
    Aronca, Trinidad, B.W.I.
James, C.................Toronto
Joffe, Miss E....Rochester, N.Y.
Johnston, C. H...........Toronto
Johnston, Miss D. M......Toronto
Johnston, J..............Toronto
Kaplan, J................Toronto
Kaye, W. A..........Bracebridge
Keast, R. W..............Toronto
Keenleyside, Miss H. A.,
    Regina, Sask.
Keens, Miss M. M........Toronto
Keith, W. S..............Toronto
Kelly, J. G., Charlottetown, P.E.I.
Kelso, M. M.............Toronto
Kennedy, Miss B. H.....Wingham
Klotz, Miss M. E.........Ottawa
Knowles, Miss M. V.......Sarnia
Korman, Miss A. M.......Toronto
Lackey, A. O.......Lachute, Que.
Laird, A. M..............Norval
Lane, R. W.........Halifax, N.S.
Lash, K. M...............Toronto
Lasher, G. A......Richmond Hill
Law, C. A. G.............Toronto
Lawson, F. S., Yuanchow, Ki, China
Leary, A. E..............Toronto
Leigh, G. F............Chapleau
Lem, F. Y...............Toronto
Lewis, M................Toronto
Lifchitz, A..............Toronto
Litster, Miss M. I....Burk's Falls
Littlejohn, R. H.........Toronto
Lowden, Miss J. G.......Toronto
Luke, M. C..............Ottawa
Luxton, J. H............Jessopville
McAllister, S............Toronto
McConkey, Miss E. A. M.,Toronto
McConnell, Miss K. B....Toronto
McCready, Miss M. L....Toronto
McCready, Miss F. K., Wallaceburg
McCubbin, Miss C. A.....Chatham
McCullagh, E. C.........Toronto
McCullough, W. S........Toronto
McDonagh, Miss J. A.....Toronto
Macdonald, Miss I. M....Markham
McDougall, J. E..........Toronto
McElroy, Miss E. L. M....Ottawa
McFarlane, Miss C. I....Hamilton
McGeachy, Miss M. A.....Sarnia
McIlwraith, A. K........Toronto

McIntosh, G. A.........Guelph
McKay, D. D...........Toronto
Mackay, Miss E. L......Ingersoll
McKay, K. R............Annan
McKay, W. S........St. Thomas
McKean, H..........Collingwood
McKean, Miss V. A...Collingwood
McKenzie, L. M.........Guelph
Maclaren, Miss J. D...Brockville
MacLaren, Miss M. M....Toronto
McLean, J. L............Ottawa
MacLean, L. A. B.......Bradford
Maclennan, Miss H. M....Toronto
MacLennan, Miss M. C.,
    Alameda, Sask.
McLeod, Miss C. G......Toronto
McMurchie, Miss J........Clinton
McNichol, Miss D. E. L...Toronto
MacQuaker, Miss V. C.,
    Owen Sound
MacRae, F. J............Toronto
MacTaggart, Miss J. E....Toronto
MacTaggart, K. W........Toronto
Madill, Miss D. M...St. Catharines
Malcolm, R. T........Owen Sound
Mallon, J. G.............Toronto
Marshall, W. P..........Belleville
Martin, H. E............Toronto
Matenko, P..............Toronto
Mather, Miss H. C.......Toronto
Matthew, Miss D. A..Georgetown
Matthews, A. S..........Toronto
Maybee, G. E.........Port Credit
Mearns, Miss H. M......Toronto
Meldrum, Miss K........Weston
Melhuish, Miss G. I......Toronto
Milkin, M...............Toronto
Millar, H. M............Toronto
Miller, Miss A. M........Toronto
Miller, B...............Toronto
Miller, W. R............Toronto
Mills, Miss A. C.....Wallaceburg
Mills, Miss M. L........Hamilton
Milner, J. B............Toronto
Mitchell, G. C........Flesherton
Mitchell, W. B............Sarnia
Mollins, Miss F. N...Burgessville
Monypenny, Miss C. F....Toronto
Morden, Miss A. M., Niagara Falls
Morrison, J. A..........Iroquois
Morrison, W. K........Richwood
Mowat, W. H......Peterborough
Mustard, Miss E. M.....Chatham
Mutchmor, H. A..........Dixie
Nettelfield, J. B.........Toronto
Niblock, J. N...........Toronto
Nicholson, G. W.........Toronto

Noble, D..............Toronto
Northey, R. V...........Toronto
Oake, C. M.............Toronto
O'Brian, Miss M. J.....Franklin
O'Brian, P. D..........L'Orignal
Park, Miss I. M.........Toronto
Parker, Miss M. D.......Toronto
Parrott, Miss O.........Uxbridge.
Pemberton, J. T..........Toronto
Penman, W. M......St. Catharines
Percy, J. L.............Toronto
Phin, D. E.............Hamilton
Phippen, B. C.............Sarnia
Pidgeon, A. L...........Toronto
Plaxton, H. A. W........Toronto
Pocock, L. V..........Brockville
Potter, C. E.............Toronto
Pritchard, J. E. ....Harriston
Rachlin, H.............Toronto
Raikes, Miss E. G........Barrie
Rappaport, L. C.........Toronto
Ratz, H. G.............Toronto
Read, Miss M. A.....Peterborough
Reid, Miss B. M.........London
Relyea, F. B..............Perth
Rhodes, J. B...........Toronto
Richardes, G. C..........Toronto
Riddell, Miss H. G...St. Catharines
Ritchie, H. S.............Toronto
Robb, I. M.............Toronto
Robbins, Miss H. E.....Windsor
Roberts, C. A. M.......Toronto
Robinson, Miss H........Toronto
Rochester, R. B.........Toronto
Romm, A...............Toronto
Rose, G. F...............Toronto
Rose, Miss M. J.........Toronto
Ross, Miss H. I.........Toronto
Ross, R. W. J........Woodbridge
Rotenberg, H. D.........Toronto
Rowan, G. M...........Toronto
Rowan, Miss K. G.......Toronto
Rumac, J..............Toronto
Rutherford, Miss H. C...Toronto
Ryckman, E. B..........Toronto
Ryrie, J...............Toronto
Sadowski, Miss E........Toronto
Salter, P. E............Toronto
Sanderson, A. L.........Wroxeter
Sanderson, Miss J......Agincourt
Saylor, W. C............Trenton
Schell, Miss E. M........Stayner
Schell, Miss G..........Stayner
Schoenchen, Miss M. G....Toronto
Schroeder, G. D.........Hanover
Scilly, A. J......Welland Junction
Scott, Miss B. C........Alliston

Scott, H. C.............Galt
Scott, R. K...........Pakenham
Secord, Miss M. L.......Toronto
Seim, I. E.........Mount Forest
Shadick, H. E......London, Eng.
Shaw, H. G.......Kamloops, B.C.
Sher, D................Toronto
Sherlock, F. M.......Scarborough
Shortill, Miss I. J........Toronto
Shute, E. V.............Windsor
Silverthorn, R. F........Islington
Sims, H. des B.......Thistletown
Skelton, Miss J. E...Mimico Beach
Smith, Miss A. M. B.....Toronto
Smith, Miss E. G........Toronto
Smith, Miss H. A........Toronto
Smith, Miss H. M......St. Thomas
Smith, L L.............Winona
Smith, S. A.............Toronto
Smyth L. G.............Toronto
Snelgrove, E. C..........Toronto
Solomon, Miss D. F. ....Brighton
Somerville, J...........Toronto
Spence, Miss M.........Toronto
Staley, H. J.........Wolfe Island
Stanley, A. A...........Toronto
Steen, Miss E. G.......Ridgetown
Stephenson, E. A., Myrtle Station
Stewart, J. A. M....Buffalo, N.Y.
Stirrett, A. G............Petrolia
Struthers, Miss J. F......Toronto
Sumberg, S. L..........Toronto
Sutherland, A. B........Bradford
Sutherland, H. R.........Toronto
Tait, C. E........Port Dalhousie
Tallman, F. F.....Red Deer, Alta.
Tanton, Miss M. L.......London
Tate, F. J............Bluevale
Taylor, C. H..........Mansfield
Taylor, R. C...........Toronto
Teskey, C. H...........Orillia
Thompson, Miss M. S.....Toronto
Thompson, S. M..........Toronto
Thomson, J..........Dobbington
Thomson, R..........Dobbington
Torrance, J. C...........Toronto
Torrance, W. C..........Laurel
Tory, J. S. D...........Toronto
Totton, Miss J. A........Toronto
Trent, Miss F. E.........Toronto
Trott, G. T............Oil City
Trumpour, Miss M. G....Napanee
Tuer, J. E...........St. Mary's
Tustin, Miss E. A.....Limehouse
Van de Water, E. B.......Picton
Varty, J. A............Markdale
Vennels, G. W.....Regina, Sask.

Vickers, W. M...........Toronto
Waddell, F. F..........Hamilton
Waddell, W. L. M......Ballinafad
*Wade, Miss M. G.....Brighton
Waldron, K. S..........Hamilton
Walfish, C.............Toronto
Walker, Miss F. E.......Toronto
Walker, R. B. ....Hay
Wallace, Miss G. M.,
            Osgoode Station
Wallace, Miss M. V......Toronto
Ward, Miss M. B........Toronto
Wardell, Miss H. G......Toronto
Warren, Miss J. L., St. Catharines
Watkins, W. W. R.......Toronto
Watson, L. A..........Thamesville
Watt, Miss I. K.........Toronto
Waugh, Miss I. L........Toronto
Weatherhead, Miss D....Toronto
Weir, Miss M. A.........Toronto
Weir, Miss N. P.........Toronto

Weissbrod, Miss M. E.....Toronto
Wells, Miss K. B........Toronto
West, Miss G. A.........Toronto
West, Miss J. R.........Toronto
White, E. F.............London
White, W. A............Toronto
Whitton, W. C..........Alvinston
Wiancko, Miss F. H......Toronto
Willson, D. H ....Ridgetown
Wilson, D. F............Toronto
Wilson, Miss E. D......Seaforth
Wong, Y. T............Arnprior
Worthington, Miss E. M...Toronto
Wyke, D. A......Port of Spain,
            Trinidad, B.W.I.
Wylie, I. M.............Toronto
Young, D. A............Toronto
Young, Miss F. A. A.......Sarnia
Young, Miss M.....Scarborough
Younger, Miss R. E......Toronto
Zybach, Miss M. P., Niagara Falls

Second Year.

Alexander, Miss G. W.....Guelph
Alford, Miss E...........Toronto
Allen, C. E.......Mount Forest
Anderson, Miss H. E......Toronto
Ashworth, C. G..........Toronto
Austin, Miss A. M., Sturgeon Falls
Baker, W. R............Toronto
Ball, Miss K...........Harriston
Balmer, H. F............Toronto
Bannister, Miss E...New Liskeard
Bastedo, J. B.......Bracebridge
Beatty, G. B...........Toronto
Begg, Miss E. M.....North Bay
Bell, Miss E. H............Paris
Bemrose, Miss J. H......Toronto
Bennett, Miss E. I., Mille Roches
Bergoine, Miss D. I.......Toronto
Bird, J. N...........Georgetown
Blake, V. B...........Toronto
Boles, Miss M. H.........Simcoe
Bond, L. B.............Aurora
Bone, R. C.............Toronto
Bone, Miss R. M........Toronto
Bowman, Miss G. L......Toronto
Braid, J. L. ....Windsor
Brennand, C. G..........Toronto
Brodey, A..............Toronto
Brodie, Miss L. T.........Toronto
Brooks, Miss B. I.......Rockwood
Bryce, G. M...........Toronto

Bryson, G. G............Toronto
Cameron, Miss J. T....St. Thomas
Campbell, Miss H. C. S...Toronto
†Campbell, Miss W. M..Tottenham
Carson, Miss E. E......Toronto
*Carson, Miss N. I.......Toronto
Chaikoff, J............Toronto
Chambers, Miss M. L. Fenelon Falls
Chesters, Miss M. H....Brampton
Clapson, W. J..........Kettleby
Clark, Miss E. M......Teeswater
Clark, Miss M. I. H......Toronto
Clothier, W. J. K.........Ottawa
Clougher, Miss E. J......Toronto
Cohen, Miss C. P........Toronto
Colwill, Miss M. B.......Arthur
Comay, S...............Toronto
Connal, Miss M. E., Peterborough
Cooper, J. M..........Sudbury
Coulter, Miss J. I........Alliston
Coulthard, H. S.........Toronto
Creelman, G. R..........Toronto
Cronk, Miss E. E......Pickering
Cryan, W. C...........Stratford
Crysler, A. C......St. Catharines
Currie, C. M........Smith's Falls
Curtis, Miss B. S.......Havelock
Cushnie, J.........Mount Forest
Dagger, Miss E. M. A.....Toronto
Dalton, E. W........Walsingham

   * In attendance Michaelmas Term only.
   † In attendance Easter Term only.

Dandy, J. P............Toronto
Davidson, Miss M. E. G.,
     Mimico Beach
Davidson, S. W..........Toronto
Day, D. J...............Toronto
Dean, Miss H. M........Toronto
Deeton, W. L...........Toronto
Denton, S. B. G.........Toronto
Dinsmore, Miss R. F...St. Mary's
Donaldson, J. S. R., Grand Forks,
       B.C.
Doole, Miss A. I.........Toronto
Douglas, Miss F. I.......Toronto
Douglas, J. W...........Toronto
Edge, Miss M. F........Seaforth
Efreim, S...............Toronto
Elliot, Miss O. E..........Toronto
Elsley, W. B........Campbellville
Entwistle, A. W.........Guelph
Farrar, Miss P. I.......Cornwall
Fawcett, Miss M. J.......Toronto
Ferguson, D. H.......St. Thomas
Ferguson, R. I...........Toronto
Findlay, D. K.....Carleton Place
Fingland, F...........Londesboro
Fisher, Miss K. G........Toronto
Fitzgerald, Miss E. K...Petrolia
Foster, Miss E. W.......Toronto
Fraser, G. A.........Niagara Falls
Fraser, Miss M. B........Toronto
Freyseng, W. P..........Toronto
Fry, Miss A. C..........Dunnville
Furniss, Miss P. H. B.....Brechin
Gillies, A.............Cedarville
Gogo, Miss M. O........Cornwall
Gold, Miss S. M.........Toronto
Gordon, R. G..........Pembroke
Graham, G. M.....Victoria, B.C.
Graham, J. L. L.........Toronto
Graham, Miss M. E......Ottawa
Granatstein, Miss R......Toronto
Grant, Miss C. W........Toronto
Grant, D. I.............Toronto
Grant, E. W...........Belleville
Guthrie, D. P...........Guelph
Haines, Miss D. F.....Thornhill
Halliday, C. P..........Toronto
Hambly, W. J..........Toronto
Hanlan, J. D...........Toronto
Hanley, H. G...........Milton
Hanna, F. J..........Ottawa
Hathway, E. G..........Toronto
Hetherington, Miss H. E...Toronto
Hewitt, G. W...........Toronto
Hilliard, W. L.........Waterloo
Holmes, S. D..........Picton
Hough, H. B. T.....Amherstburg

Hunt, Miss D. B........Toronto
Hunter, J. R...........West Hill
Hurwich, S. B...........Toronto
Hutton, J. C...........Wingham
Ingram, Miss H., Moose Jaw, Sask.
Irwin, Miss M. O........Wingham
Jackson, Miss E. M. O....Toronto
Jamieson, R. A.........Almonte
Jephcott, Miss A. B......Toronto
Jephcott, C. M..........Toronto
Jolly, J. E............Hamilton
Keeler, J. W...........Toronto
Kennedy, Miss E. J......Toronto
Kennedy, Miss K. O...Stratford
Kennedy, Miss S. K......Toronto
Kennedy, W. A..........Toronto
Kerr-Lawson, D. E.......Toronto
Kidd, Miss M.....Burritt's Rapids
Kilbourn, Miss R. M......Toronto
King, G. G......Vancouver, B.C.
Kirkwood, K. P.....London, Eng.
Kiteley, Miss M. E......Bradford
Klie, D. R.............Harrow
Krug, C. W............Chesley
Krug, Miss F...........Chesley
Larkin, Miss M. H.....Seaforth
Larkin, S..............Toronto
Lauder, Miss M. F.......Toronto
Lavine, Miss T. D.......Toronto
Lee, L. C.............Toronto
Leighton, E. R........Cannington
Leitch, Miss M. M....Port Arthur
Lennox, H.............Markdale
Levy, H. H............Hamilton
Lightbourn, G. O.........Oakville
Ludwig, Miss H.........Toronto
Lutman, Miss M. E......London
Lyons, L. S............Weston
MacAlpine, N. A........Toronto
McCandless, J. C.......Brampton
McClenahan, Miss O. I.,
     Milton West
McCluskey, Miss M. E.,
     Collingwood
McCool, B. S.........Walkerton
McDerment, R...........Milton
MacDonald, C. C....Muirkirk
McDonald, P. W........Colborne
McDonnell, Miss M. P....Toronto
MacDougall, Miss J. V....Toronto
McFadden, A. P., Sault Ste. Marie
MacFarlane, Miss J. C.,
    Lake Saskatoon, Alta.
McGirr, E. J............Durham
McInnis, E. W., Charlottetown,
      P.E.I.
McKague, A. E........Teeswater

MacKay, H. H.....:.....Goderich
MacKay, L. A............Hensall
McKeown, J. J. F.........Toronto
MacLaren, D. F...........Barrie
McLaren, Miss E. C.,
          St. Catharines
McLaurin, A. C...........Toronto
Maclean, Miss G. V......Napanee
MacLellan, Miss M. E...Claremont
McMurchie, Miss M. A....Clinton
MacNamara, Miss B......Toronto
McNeely, Miss C. A.,
          Carleton Place
McNish, Miss J...........Toronto
Macpherson, Miss J. H. K. Toronto
Mahon, Miss M..........Toronto
Marr, R. B............Dorchester
Maxwell, Miss J. G.....St. Mary's
Meredith, E. R.........Peterboro
Millar, D. L......Sault Ste. Marie
Miller, S................Toronto
Mitchell, Miss P. E......Toronto
Mitchell, R. S.........St. Mary's
Mitchell, W. H...Weihwei, Honan,
          China
Mitchener, E. H.........Toronto
Morrell, C. A...........Hamilton
Moyes, Miss M. C.......Toronto
Mueller, Miss F. H.....Waterloo
Muir, Miss E. J....Summerstown
Murray, R. H...........Toronto
Naylor, Miss E. M.......Toronto
Nieghorn, Miss A........Toronto
Nodwell, W. E.........Hillsburg
O'Reilly, C..............Toronto
Orr, M. D..............Toronto
Park, B. E.........Peterborough
Parker, Miss D. A.......Toronto
Payne, Miss W. M.......Toronto
Peaker, Miss I. M.......Toronto
Petrie, Miss P. A.......Clarkson
Petry, Miss M. A........Toronto
Phillips, Miss L. I.......Toronto
Poland, G. W..........Dunnville
Pringle, Miss J. A.........Selby
Quirie, Miss V. J........Weston
Rance, H. P............Clinton
Reburn, H. E. G.........Toronto
Rice, Miss M. R. ......Welland
Richards, L. W., Campbellton, N.B.
Riggs, Miss M. J.......Listowel
Robertson, D. G........Hamilton
Robertson, Miss P. A.....Barrie
Robertson, S. G........Belleville
Robinson, C. W. T.......Toronto

Robinson, Miss F. M., Walkerville
Robinson, R. H..........Fergus
Rogers, H. M......St. Catharines
Rotenberg, H............Toronto
Rothwell, T. J. H........Lanark
Ruddy, R. K..........Brantford
Rutherford, Miss K. M.,
          Owen Sound
Sauerbrei, C.....,......Kenora
Schatz, M. H............Toronto
Scott, Miss E. L.........Clifford
Scott, R. B. Y..........Toronto
Sheppard, Miss E. M.....Toronto
Shipley, M. A............Clinton
Sidey, W. J. K.........Harwood
Simpson, Miss E. A., Campbellville
Sinclair, Miss J. H.......Toronto
Smith, M. D..........Unionville
Sneddon, H. R..........Toronto
Sparks, M. I............Toronto
Sparling, E. M...........Goring
Stacey, Miss D. E.......Toronto
Stanton, O. L...........Toronto
Stark, Miss E. M.......Chatham
Stark, Miss L. J.........Chatham
Steele, Miss M. I.......Tavistock
Stewart, A. G.........Stouffville
Stewart, R. A...........Toronto
Stone, T. A...........Chatham
Strachan, I. T.......:.....Toronto
Sutherland, J. L........Brantford
Sweitzer, C. W.........Kitchener
Taylor, E. I.............Toronto
Taylor, Miss G. M. P.....Stratford
Taylor, J. W.............Guelph
Taylor, N. W............Toronto
Taylor, Miss V. A........Toronto
Taylor, W. E...........Pefferlaw
Telford, Miss M. E...Owen Sound
Thomas, H. F. S.........Toronto
Thomas, J. C..........Streetsville
Thomas, Miss M. R......Toronto
§Thomson, J. C.......Teeswater
Tuck, G. I.............Breslau
Tucker, Miss V. J........Toronto
Tudhope, J. B...........Orillia
Ulrich, Miss A. G., Springfield, Ill.
Vaughan, A. H..........Swansea
Waldman, H. J..........Toronto
Waldron, L. F........Hamilton
Wales, H. G...........Markham
Walmsley, Miss M. H.....Toronto
Walton, Miss E..........Toronto
Warne, W. H............Oshawa

§ Dispensation.

Wasson, E. L., Young's Cove R'd., N.B.
Webber, R. P..............Paris
Weber, C. R............Windsor
Weir, Miss E. M...........Paris
Wharton, T. V...........Cayuga
Wheadon, Miss M.......Toronto
Whealy, J. A............Toronto
Wheler, Miss E. R....Tignall, Ga.
Whitaker, F. C........Brantford
White, Miss I. G., Moose Jaw, Sask.

Whitfield, H. G.......Fraserville
Wilkins, S. R............Toronto
Wilkinson, F. H.........Toronto
Williamson, Miss W....Beaverton
Wilson, J. L......Kamloops, B.C.
Wilson, Miss L. A.......Midland
Winnett, F. V.........Oil Springs
Wodehouse, Miss G. M....Toronto
Wright, E. N.............Toronto
Wright, Miss T. D.......Toronto

Third Year.

Adams, Miss A. M...Peterborough
Alexander, W. A.........Toronto
Allan, Miss P. M.........Picton
Allen, S.,...............Toronto
Anderson, C. M.....Wilton Grove
Armstrong, J. C..........Ottawa
Arthur, Miss D. L........Sudbury
Baker, C. C..............Ottawa
Baker, W. A.....Moose Jaw, Sask.
Barfoot, W. F........Collingwood
Beecroft, Miss C. I.......Toronto
Bell, D. W..........Shakespeare
Bell, Miss G...Indian Head, Sask.
Brown, Miss A. M. H.....Toronto
Bird, Miss G. R............Barrie
Bredin, W...............Toronto
†Brierly, Miss E. G.......Toronto
Broadbridge, Miss R. P...Toronto
Brubacher, C. S........Kitchener
Bull, F. L...............Weston
Campbell, W. S.......Cheltenham
Carswell, Miss H. M......Toronto
*Carver, L. D.......Peterborough
Cave, Miss V. B., Barbados, B.W.I.
Clarke, Miss M. E....Palmerston
Cochrane, Miss H. M....Toronto
Cordingley, Miss K. D....Toronto
Cowan, J. A............Toronto
Crawford, A. R...........Toronto
Cray, Miss M. B.........Guelph
Crombie, J. K. B....St. Catharines
Currie, J. E............Wingham
Curry, A. G.........Windsor, N.S.
Curtis, C. A........Smith's Falls
Darby, T. J.......Pangman, Sask.
Darker, G. D.........Streetsville
Dickie, W. C.....Edmonton, Alta.
Doran, Miss E. M.......Iroquois
Doran, Miss M. V......Iroquois
Dow, Miss L. M.........Toronto

Eakins, C. G. ....Napanee
Elliott, B. V............Norwich
Ewart, Miss A. A........Toronto
Fair, G. L..............Toronto
Fair, Miss M. E.....Collingwood
Ferriss, A. M.........Windsor
Fink, H. J. V....Cranbrook, B.C.
Fisher, F. W............Toronto
Fleming, Miss M...........Perth
Fletcher, C. L.........Melbourne
Flynn, M. J............Hamilton
Forster, F. C...........Toronto
Foster, J. W...........Toronto
Fraser, Miss F........York Mills
Fried, Miss M. H........Toronto
Gault, T. S...........Deseronto
Gavin, Miss D. G........Toronto
Geddes, H. H..........Strathroy
Gee, R. J..............Selkirk
Gemmill, C. D..........Toronto
Glazebrook, G. P. de T....Toronto
Glover, C.....Southfield, Hessle, Yorks., Eng.
Gordon, A. R............Toronto
Gordon, J. A. H.,
New Westminster, B.C.
Gordon, Miss M. F.......Toronto
Gray, Miss N. E.......Coldwater
Griffiths, Miss G. M.......Fonthill
Halliday, Miss F. F.......Toronto
Hamilton, F. C..........Toronto
Harkness, W. J. K.,
Vineland Station
§Hassard, Miss M. G...Springfield
Hele, Miss S. E..........Mimico
Hickson, Miss B. N......Toronto
Hill, D. C..............Ottawa
Hodgins, Miss D. C....Stratford
Home, Miss R. M.......Welland
Hoover, G. I............Weston

* In attendance Michaelmas Term only.
† In attendance Easter Term only.
§ Dispensation.

Hudson, A. D............Toronto
Hume, Miss A. K.........Toronto
Hutchison, F. L...:......Mitchell
Inwood, Miss J. S........Toronto
Jackson, J. A.........Leamington
Jamieson, Miss M. J......:Oshawa
Jasperson, F. K........Kingsville
Johnston, H. W.........Toronto
Johnston, M. C..........:...Toronto
Johnstone, J. E. A.......Toronto
Jones, C. O.............:.Toronto
Kastner, Miss F.........Stratford
Kearney, Miss M. B......Toronto
Keens, Miss C. H.........Toronto
Kitchen, C. E.............Toronto
Langworthy, Miss E. M.,
                    Port Arthur
Lewis, Miss G. V.........Toronto
Littlefield, C. G..........Toronto
Lowther, A. A............Toronto
McCormick, N. A....Walkerville
McCullough, Miss J. J., Harriston
Macdonald, Miss A. H. G.,Toronto
MacIntyre, A. L..........Lindsay
Mackenzie, A. A..........Guelph
McKeown, Miss H......Belleville
McKnight, Miss M. B.....Simcoe
McLaughlin, Miss M. A....Oshawa
MacLean, Miss H. M.....Toronto
McLean, Miss M.........:Toronto
MacLennan, F. A....Gould, Que.
MacLennan, H. A.......Hamilton
MacMillan, Miss J. R.....Toronto
*McMillan, Miss M. V...Hillsburg
MacNamara, W. G......Toronto
McQueen, Miss J. C......Toronto
Maitland, Miss M..........Elora
Martin, J. B......Langford, B.C.
Martyn, M.............Ripley
Matchett, H. B..........Toronto
Maxwell, W. D.........Pembroke
Maybee, Miss A. L., Port Credit
Millar, Miss K. M........Toronto
Moran, Miss M..........Toronto
Morrison, Miss H. K., Edmonton,
                        Alta.
Morson, Miss H. W.......Toronto
Muir, W. S.........Niagara Falls
Mustard, J. T...........:.Toronto
Mustard, W. M........Uxbridge
Needler, Miss M. C......Toronto
Paterson, Miss I. L......Ingersoll
Pearl, Miss M. J.........Toronto

Pidgeon, Miss M. A......Toronto
Pratt, Miss F. P.........Toronto
Prentice, J. L...........Toronto
Purcell, G. M............Guelph
Raney, Miss G. C ......Renfrew
Reid, Miss M. E.........London
Reoch, A................Nottawa
Reoch, Miss A.........Nottawa
Rhodes, Miss M. E......Brockville
Rickaby, H. C...........Orono
Rosebrugh, Miss M......Toronto
Rosenthal, H............Toronto
Ross, J. L..............Erindale
Roulston, W. A..........Toronto
Ryrie, R................Toronto
Saunders, H. E......Fort William
Schorman, Miss K. S.....Toronto
Scott, R. H............Alliston
Scott, W. J.........Owen Sound
Shaw, Miss E. A. J.......London
Sher, A................Toronto
Sherrin, Miss M. H. M....Toronto
Sinclair, Miss H. I.......Toronto
Smillie, J. M............:.Toronto
Smith, Miss A. J.........Chatham
Solway, J. B............Toronto
Spaidal, Miss M. G......Toronto
Sparrow, W. H..........Toronto
Stagg, Miss E. J........Brockville
Stanley, Miss G.........:.Toronto
Steacy, R. G............Wiarton
Steele, T. M...........Stratford
Stewart, R. A...........Brussels
Stewart, S. R...........Toronto
Stillwell, W. A..........Toronto
†Stuart, Miss M. M.......Guelph
Stuart, Miss R. G........Mitchell
§Suttie, G. L. P.........Toronto
Swan, W. J. M..........Toronto
*Swift, Miss E. W......Watford
Tait, R. G...........Port Sydney
Taylor, A. C.........Indore, India
Taylor, Miss A. L., Edmonton, Alta.
Taylor, Miss N. C.......Toronto
Telfer, Miss M. L.....Collingwood
Terryberry, W. W........Dundas
Thomson, W. G..........Toronto
Trick, H. W............Oshawa
Twitchell, Miss M. C..... Toronto
Valentine, Miss C. F....Waterloo
Wells, D. C............Toronto
West, Miss L. B.........Toronto
Wheaton, H. B..........Toronto

* In attendance Michaelmas Term only.
† In attendance Easter Term only.
§ Dispensation.

Wilkinson, R.E.,
       Yellow Grass, Sask.
Wilson, Miss J. A........Toronto
Wilson, W. G..........Midland
Wood, Miss D. M......Brantford

Wood, J. D.............Toronto
Wood, R...............Listowel
Woodland, F. A. L.......Toronto
Wright, Miss M. C.......Toronto

Fourth Year.

Adamstone, F. B.........Toronto
Allen, R. A...............Toronto
Armstrong, E. C......Science Hill
Atkinson, Miss M. E. F....Toronto
Ballantyne, L. R.........Atwood
Beasley, Miss J. E......Sandwich
Beasley, J. H............Toronto
Bell, A. D. ....:Sarnia
Belton, Miss A. M.....Thorndale
Bentley, A. W............Sarnia
Best, C. H....West Pembroke, Me.
Billings, Miss G. M......Toronto
Bogart, E. C.........Newmarket
Borsook, H..............Toronto
Breithaupt, Miss F. C., Kitchener
Bristol, Miss J. T.........Toronto
Brown, Miss U. K........Toronto
Bryans, Miss H. L........Toronto
Bryce, W. A.............Toronto
Bussell, W. F............Toronto
Cale, Miss F. M.........Toronto
Campbell, Miss B. L..........Oro
Chant, Miss E. H........Toronto
Clarke, Miss E. M. B...Tottenham
Clark, Miss M. L......Stouffville
Connell, Miss M. I.......Lucknow
Connolly, Miss M. A.....Toronto
Cook, Miss G. M........Toronto
Cornette, Miss C. L.....Dundalk
Coutts, J. M..........Thamesville
Cowan, Miss K. L......Seaforth
Creery, Miss I. V......Woodham
Cringan, Miss E. R......Toronto
Crumb, Miss J. H.........Toronto
Davis, O................Toronto
Dingle, Miss D. A.......Toronto
Duggan, A. M. S........Toronto
Eldon, F. I..............Toronto
Enushevsky, Miss B......Toronto
Faichney, T. T.........Hamilton
Findlay, D. M...........Toronto
Findlay, Miss H....Carleton Place
Finlayson, Miss B. M.....Toronto
Folsetter, Miss H. J..........Paris
Forsyth, E. W.........Stouffville
Fox, Miss E. G.........Cainsville
Gallagher, D. H.........Toronto
Gallagher, E. O..........Barrie
Gamble, Miss M. E.rantB..fdor..

Geddes, W. R.........Strathroy
Glazier, Miss E. A. E....Brockville
Grant, Miss A. A........Toronto
Gray, Miss K. H.........Toronto
Graydon, A. R...........Toronto
Green, W. E....Moose Jaw, Sask.
Hamilton, K. A...Moose Jaw, Sask.
Hammond, G. S.........Preston
Harbert, Miss E. M.,
       Montreal, Que.
Hardy, Miss D. S.........Toronto
Hearst, Miss I...........Toronto
Henry, Miss E. M......Stratford
Hill, Miss E. M..........Toronto
Hobden, Miss D. M......Toronto
Hodgins, B. A..........:.London
Hunter, Miss L. M......Bradford
Jackson, Miss I. V....Downsview
Jennison, J. D., New Glasgow, N.S.
Johnson, E. M..........Hamilton
Jones, C. G..............Toronto
Knox, L. A...............Alma
Lane, Miss J. V..........Ottawa
Leggett, Miss E. G......Newboro
Lehman, S..............Toronto
Leonard, Miss A.........Toronto
Levi, Miss M.............Toronto
Lindsay, Miss E. I........Weston
Little, G. D.............Toronto
Lockhart, Miss H. I......London
Loggie, Miss D. C., Chatham, N.B.
Lorriman, F. R..........Thorold
Lucas, G. H. W......Middlemiss
Lyle, Miss E. H.......:.St. Thomas
Lyle, Miss L. M....Smith's Falls
McCowan, Miss M. J.,
       Winnipeg, Man.
MacDonald, Miss E. M...Toronto
McDougall, F. M.........Ottawa
McDougall, J. L. ....Ottawa
MacGregor, Miss K......Clinton
McHenry, E. W..........Toronto
Maclennan, Miss J. E. H..Toronto
McLeod, C. H.......Collingwood
MacMillan, H. A.......Lucknow
McMurtry, Miss L. J. L.,
       Moose Jaw, Sask.
MacPherson, Miss G.....Dutton
McTaggart, Miss M......Clinton

Main, Miss A. I........Hamilton
Marsh, H. H..............Lindsay
Marshall, G.............Puslinch
Matthew, Miss E. P. ...Gananoque
Matthews, W. J......Port Arthur
Maxwell, Miss H. M., St. Mary's
Millen, Miss M. K........Toronto
Morden, J. R. ....Hamilton
Morrell, J. A...........Hamilton
Mulvihill, Miss M. B....Arnprior
Murphy, Miss G. M....Mt. Forest
Mustard, Miss M. I.....Uxbridge
Noble, E. C..............Toronto
Noble, W. H.............Toronto
O'Meara, Miss M. M......Ottawa
Paisley, A. B..........Stouffville
Pearen, Miss E. M......Rockwood
Petrie, P. A...........Brucefield
Phillips, Miss L. M.......Toronto
Porter, D. H.............Toronto
Porter, Miss N...........Toronto
Rae, Miss J..................Toronto
Richardson, Miss S. L. A...Toronto
Robertson, Miss M. I.....Ottawa
Robertson, R. M.....Hagersville
Rogers, Miss J............Toronto
Ross, Miss R. W..........Ottawa
Russell, J. B..........Hillsburg
Russell, J. W..........Waterford
Russell, Miss M. E.......Fergus
Schell, Miss H. C.....Woodstock
Scott, Miss B. M........Toronto
Scott, Miss E. H........Seaforth
Scott, Miss E. R.......Uxbridge
Scott, Miss R. V.........Toronto
Scrimgeour, Miss G....Stratford
Shafner, Miss H. D.,
            Annapolis Royal, N.S.
Shaw, H. F. R...........Clinton

Sheard, T...............Toronto
Sheppard, Miss E. M. P.,
            Waubaushene
Simpson, Miss J. I.......Toronto
Smilovitz, Miss R. L......Quebec
Smith, H. G.............Toronto
Smith, Miss J. H..........Lucan
Snell, Miss M. E.......Seaforth
Soward, F. H............Toronto
Sowers, R. V.............London
Speers, Miss L......Yorkton, Sask.
Stanton, Miss C. J........Toronto
Stewart, H. J. F.......Brockville
Stirrett, J. R............Petrolia
Struchen, J. M.........Gananoque
Szammers, Miss R. A....Toronto
Taylor, Miss E. M.......Toronto
Thomson, E. W......Dobbinton
Tilley, Miss D. L.........Toronto
Tracy, H. L.............Toronto
Troop, G. R. F............Ottawa
Turnbull, W. L...........Dundas
Twigg, Miss A. E. M. ....Toronto
VanVelzer, Miss A. A., Dunboyne
Vaughan, W. S.,
            Niagara-on-the-Lake
Vining, C. M............Toronto
Wallace, W. L...........Toronto
Weatherall, Miss M. B.,
            Southampton
Webb, Miss A. M.......Bradford
Webster, Miss M. G., Beirut, Syria
Whitelaw, Miss F.....Woodstock
Wiley, Miss L. Y......Brantford
Wilson, J. T.............Ottawa
Wright, J. H............Toronto
Young, Miss A. M.......Toronto
Young, Miss W. A.....Brantford

Occasional Students.

Alfsen, Miss D. H........Toronto
Asman, Miss K. M.......Toronto
Atkinson, B.............Toronto
Barlow, W........St. Catharines
Bennett, G............Kincardine
Bentum, A. V...........Toronto
Bond, B. C............Caledonia
Brown, Miss E. W......Wyoming
Budd, Miss M. F........Toronto
Burke, J. V.............Toronto
Butler, E. P.............Toronto
Chamberlain, Miss M. L...Toronto
Clark, Miss M. L.........Toronto
Collins, Miss W. C...St. Catharines
Cooper, Miss B..........Toronto

David, Miss W. M........Toronto
Dyer, C. L..............Toronto
Eaton, Miss E. E........Toronto
Gray, B. G..............Toronto
Gray, Miss I. M.........Toronto
Gurd, Miss J. W...St. Clair, Mich.
Hanna, W. G............Toronto
Hedges, Miss I..........Toronto
Hudson, Miss D. M......Toronto
Hudson, Miss W. D......Toronto
Ibbott, J. T................York
Jeffrey, Miss I. M........Toronto
Johnstone, Mrs. I. B.....Toronto
Kennedy, V.............Toronto
Krieger, Miss C.........Toronto

Lamb, C. J.........St. Catharines
Lawson, J. S.............Guelph
Le Bel, E. C..............Toronto
Lee, E. G..............,.Toronto
Loughrane, L. B..........Toronto
McCrimmon, Miss H. M...Toronto
McGrath, Miss E., St. John's, Nfld.
McIntyre, J. V..........Brantford
Mallon, Miss M. F.......Toronto
Mallon, J. P.............Toronto
Medland, Miss M. L......Toronto
Meen, H................Toronto
O'Connor, G. L..........Sudbury
O'Malley, Miss I. F......Toronto
O'Reilly, J. B.......Seattle, Wash.
Ormsby, Miss O. A. M....Toronto
Oxley, Miss D...........Toronto

Primrose, Miss O. C.......Toronto
Ray, Miss M. D.........Toronto
Riddell, J...............Chatham
Scarff, H. A.............Windsor
Servais, F. J..........Port Arthur
Smart, W. L. B...........Toronto
Stott, Miss E. I..........Toronto
Templeton, Miss M. H. J..Toronto
Tolhurst, Miss F. E.......Toronto
Tuffy, Miss C...........Toronto
Unsworth, J............Brantford
Vahey, T. J..............Toronto
Wass, S. W.............Toronto
Wheaton, Miss I.........Toronto
Wuilleumier, Miss H. H...Toronto
Zeidman, M. ....Poland

SUMMARY—UNIVERSITY COLLEGE.

First Year................. 457
Second Year............... 293
Third Year............... 189
Fourth Year............... 168
Occasional Students......... 63

Total.................. 1170

VICTORIA COLLEGE.

First Year.

The names of students registered in the Course in Commerce are printed in italics.

Adams, Miss N. G.......Toronto
Adney, T. H.............Toronto
Allin, Miss A. M........Lindsay
Atchison, Miss I R.,
               Winnigeg, Man.
Attridge, C. G.........Waterdown
Augustine, Miss H. G.,
            Port Colborne
Baker, Miss G. A.........Toronto
Bannerman, G. F.........Toronto
Bartlett, F. L...........Toronto
Bartrem, F. W...........Toronto
Bauslaugh, Miss H. B...Brantford
Beach, M................Toronto
Becker, R. P............Toronto
Beecroft, E. A..........Whitby
Bennett, Miss R. J...Parry Sound
Bennett, Miss S. M......Toronto
Blair, J. W. K...........Arthur
Boyle, Miss E. J.........Toronto
Brown, Miss A. M. B.....Toronto
Burgar, W. J............Toronto
Campbell, J. A.....Niagara Falls
Carswell, J. A...........Toronto
Carter, Miss R. A.........Galt
Cocks, Miss L. A.........Winona
Colbeck, L. H.....Grand Valley
Cooke, J. P............Fullarton
Cotton, Miss L..........Toronto
Couch, H. N.......Quebec, Que.
Coulter, D..............Toronto
Creighton, D. G.........Toronto
Culham, Miss M.........Toronto
Cutbush, G. W..........Toronto
Daly, E. A..............London
Darke, C. T.........Regina, Sask.
Davidson, Miss S. M., Regina, Sask.
Davies, Miss K. M.......Toronto
Depew, Miss Margaret E...Paris
Depew, Miss Mary E......Paris
Dixon, R. M.........Peterborough
Domm, G. O.............Ayton
Douglas, L. H...........Toronto
Elliot, Miss J. B...Peterborough
Elliott, Miss K. E., New York City
Endicott, N. J...........Toronto

Evans, W. H..........Beaverton
Fairfield, Miss A. A.,
            Lethbridge, Alta.
Fairles, Miss R........Stouffville
Fawcett, Miss M. B. R....Toronto
Fenwick, Miss M. M.,
            St. John's, Nfld.
Ferguson, J. D...........Toronto
Foster, C. W.............Moira
Franks, W. R......Regina, Sask.
Fulford, G. T.........Brockville
Gibbons, J. G......Regina, Sask.
Gillan, Miss E. S.......Pakenham
Gosse, R. E........Petites, Nfld.
Goulding, Miss R. G.....Toronto
Graham, E. H...........Toronto
Gray, Miss A. M........Listowel
Guy, H. L..............Toronto
Hanna, Miss J. V........Toronto
Harker, G. C...........Toronto
Harron, L. S............Toronto
Hart, E. W..............Essex
Hill, A. S. H...........Windsor
Hilliard, Miss A. M....Morrisburg
Hillaird, T. A.........Kitchener
Hislop, Miss E. E.......Toronto
Hoidge, Miss A. M.......Toronto
Hone, P. W.............Petrolia
Hooker, W.............Toronto
Hope, H. B..............Milliken
Howson, Miss L. C......Norwood
Hudson, F. E............Toronto
Hull, Miss E. G. A........Toronto
Hunt, Miss M. K.........Lanark
Irwin, Miss I. F.........Toronto
Jackson, Miss D. B......Toronto
Johnston, Miss M. W....Hamilton
Jones, Miss V. I......Parry Sound
Junkin, W. R............Toronto
Keene, J.............Eagle Place
Keenleyside, E. A...Regina, Sask.
Kirby, F. B.............Toronto
Kitching, O. C. H.....Woodstock
Knox, Miss K. D........Toronto
*Knox, W. J. S........Brucefield
Langstone, T. W..........Toronto

* In attendance Michaelmas Term only.

Lennox, A. M........Shallow Lake
Lilly, Miss M. M. E......Toronto
Little, Miss R. M...Proton Station
Luke, Miss S. M..........Toronto
McColl, D. B........Regina, Sask.
McKay, Miss H. G......Toronto
MacKinnon, Miss M. G.,
                    Sillery, Que.
McRoberts, Miss R. D.,
                    Port Arthur
Maitland, Miss J. A. B....Toronto
Malott, Miss M. P....Leamington
Mann, W. E............Brantford
Matthews, N. W......Rockwood
Mellow, H. A...........Napanee
Mix, I. W..............Ottawa
Moir, Miss K. V......Oxbow, Sask.
Monkman, Miss O......Toronto
Moody, Miss M. E.,
                    Winnipeg, Man.
Morgan, L. S...........Toronto
Mundy, Miss L. E.......Toronto
Murphy, L. C..........Colborne
Narraway, L. W.........Ottawa
Neal, Miss F. L.........Toronto
Neill, Miss A. C....Peterborough
Nelson, Miss A. G.,
                    Huntingdon, Que.
O'Hara, Miss M. L........Madoc
Ottewell, A.............Wiarton
Panabaker, W. C.......Hespeler
Patterson, Miss M. R....Toronto
Pearson, Miss D. M......Weston
Percival, Miss M. D.....Toronto
Philp, C. R.............Colborne
Philp, R. W.............Arthur
Philp, W. R............Colborne
Pickett, A. E.....Twin Falls, Ida.
Plyley, Miss D. E.......Toronto
Pyne, Miss W. M........Toronto
Reid, Miss M. M. J......Toronto
Reinke, F. G...........Ancaster
Reynolds, V. E..........Beeton
Reynolds, W. B.........Guelph
Ririe, W. B.............Toronto
Rivers, F. S...........Goderich
Robertson, H...........Chatham
Ruttle, Miss M. L., Yorkton, Sask.
Sanders, H. A........Stouffville

Schlichter, Miss N. M.....Bright
Scott, A. W........Calgary, Alta.
Shortt, J. E. R..........Toronto
Sine, Miss P. L...Gananoque
Singleton, Miss M. E. V...Toronto
Sissons, Miss M. H....Thornhill
Slater, Miss P. E......Waterdown
Smith, D. M......Campbellcroft
Smith, Miss H. K......Brantford
Snyder, W. B..........Toronto
Sparling, P. H............Gorrie
Stalter, O. R............Oshawa
Stewart, Miss R. J.......Toronto
Stone, Miss G. A......St. Mary's
Strangways, F. B........Toronto
Studholme, Miss B. G.,
                    Edmontom, Alta.
Sutton, R. E............Lindsay
Sykes, Miss A. L.,
                    Swift Current, Sask.
Terryberry, Miss M. L...Toronto
Thomas, Miss A. M., Niagara Falls
Toye, Miss G. E..........Toronto
Trask, R.................Alma
Trewin, R. F............Toronto
Tuck, C. P.............Oakville
Tuck, Miss G. E......Waterford
Tufford, F. D.........St. Thomas
Walkom, W. F.........Mitchell
Walton, Miss W. G...Parry Sound
Watson, C.............Loretto
Watson, Miss M. B...Oxbow, Sask.
Wedlake, G. N.........Brantford
Westlake, C. W...........Bethany
Westman, Miss E. M......Toronto
White, Miss Marion A.....Lindsay
White, Miss Marjorie A....Oshawa
Williams, B. H..........Toronto
Williams, P. E..........Toronto
Wingfield, Miss M. M....Hamilton
Wise, Miss E. C........Toronto
Wood, B. F., Prince Albert, Sask.
Woolnough, Miss V. G.,
                    Niagara Falls
Wright, H. L...........Hamilton
Wright, Miss M. M.,
                    Richmond Hill
Wyllie, Miss M. A. Kamloops, B.C.
Young, Miss R. L........Toronto

Second Year.

Addison, Miss L. M......Toronto
Aikins, L. H..........Wallaceburg
Alexander, Miss E. A....Woodstock
Anderson, J. C..........Napanee
Armstrong, W. T.......Lucknow
Ashbourne, E. G.........Toronto

Bailey, Miss M. G.........Arner
Balfour, G. R............Toronto
Banbury, P......Wolseley, Sask.
Beaman, Miss M. B.,
                    Monrovia, Cal.
Bell, M. S..............Ingersoll

Booth, M. W............Ottawa
Bòyle, Miss B. E...... ..Toronto
Boyle, C. C.... .:.....Brampton
†Brewer, F. W....Glanford Station
Brewster, Miss M. W..Brantford
Broddy, H. H. ....Toronto
Burns, A. G............Toronto
Burwash, Miss C. F. Lachute, Que.
Caldwell, Miss M. A.,
        Currie's Crossing
Carnahan, Miss R..Campbellford
·Chisholm, Miss A. M.....Toronto
Chisholm, Miss E. M....Toronto
Clare, Miss M. E..Little Britain
Clarke, S. H............Toronto
Coburn, Miss L. M......Toronto
Coker, Miss W. A. J.....Toronto
Cowan, R. B......Peterborough
Cox, Miss G. E.....Leamington
Cox, Miss V. M.....Leamington
Craig, Miss M. E...North Gower
Crawford, Miss G. M...Brampton
Crawford, H. S.... ....Sarnia
Crosby, Miss K. G.......Weston
Cummings, R. C.......Toronto
Day, G. S. ....Toronto
Delahay, Miss H. F......Ottawa
Delahey, N. A..........Ottawa
Dingman, C. D........Stratford
Dorsey, M. C. C.....Cookstown
Doxsee, J. E. R....Regina, Sask.
Dunbar, Miss A......Newington
Dynes, F. C............Toronto
Elgie, Miss A. C., Sault Ste. Marie
Emberson, Miss D. M....Weston
Endicott, J. G..........Toronto
Evans, E. S............Clinton
Flavelle, W. G........Lindsay
Greene, Miss F. B......Toronto
Hambley, G. H., Swan Lake, Man.
Hamer, Miss M. L.......Aurora
Hamilton, J. R......Waterdown
Harley, Miss M. E. E.....Burford
Hastings, Miss M. D....Aurora
Haver, M. J.......Luella, Sask.
Hay, Miss D. M.....Brockville
Hazlewood, H. E.......Clifford
Hilborn, H. W...........Blair
Hiltz, W. L............Toronto
Hinchey, R. R.....Shannonville
Hogarth, Miss M. V...Hamilton
Howard, Miss E........Toronto
Howey, H. J. S......Owen Sound
Hughes, Miss K. H.,
        Moose Jaw, Sask.

Ireland, J. A...........Toronto
Jackson, Miss C. M......Whitby
Jeffs, Miss K. L........Toronto
Keffer, F. R...........Hespeler
Kell, J. A. C........Cookstown
Kelly, G. C............Hamilton
Kendrick, Miss R. V.....Athens
Kerr, J. W............Hamilton
Lavell, Miss N.,.......Toronto
Learn, B. C......Aylmer (West)
Leonard, A. K.........Clinton
Lindsay, J. H.....Aylmer (West)
Lister, Miss C. I.....Beamsville
Luckey, L. E. R.......Toronto
Lyons, Miss B. E....Newmarket
MacGillivray, Miss E. B.,
        Shanghai, China
McGregor, Miss H. D., Waterdown
McKerlie, J .E.......Waterford
Marr, E. C..........St. Thomas
Marshall, Miss H. W...Brantford
Mathers, S. J.........Palmerston
Metzler, S. J...........Napanee
Millar, Miss D. E......Thorold
Minore, Miss A. J......Norwood
Morgan, Miss P. L.......Lindsay
Neal, H. B..........Port Hope
Nelson, J. F............Orillia
Nephew, Miss E. G.......Finch
Odell, Miss J. M. D....Cobourg
Oke, C. C.............Toronto
Partridge, B. O..........Barrie
Perkins, I. G.......Owen Sound
Perry, Miss E. K.......Toronto
Pook, Miss E..........Ingersoll
Rowe, C. L.......Regina, Sask.
Shannon, Miss D. E.,
        Sault Ste. Marie
Shaver, C. B...........Ottawa
Shelton, B. M.....Peterborough
Sheridan, Miss D. G...Brockville
Slater, Miss F. R.....Waterdown
Smale, A. J............Highgate
Smart, Miss F. P....Collingwood
Smith, H. A...........Hamiltou
Smith, Miss H. M......Grimsby
Smith, L. V...........Brantford
Smith, Miss M. B.......Toronto
Smith, Miss M. S......Sandford
Smith, W. E. L.........Toronto
Snider, Miss W. H....St. Jacob's
Staples, Miss K. M........Orono
Start, R. G......Currie's Crossing
Stewart, Miss N. H.....Toronto
Stone, A. R............Highgate

† In attendance Easter Term only.

Taylor, J. R. ....Clinton
Taylor, Miss M. V. L.,
    St. Catharines
Thompson, A. L........Hamilton
Toye, Miss D. E........Toronto
Trethewey, W. H.....Woodville
Trewin, R. F...........Toronto
Van Alstyne, Miss H. G. Napanee
VanLuven, Miss D. M. D.,
    Hamilton
Wallace, Miss O. M......Toronto

Walton, Miss M. B., Parry Sound
Walwyn, A. G.........Meaford
Ward, F. G............Toronto
Webster, W. L.....Shediac, N.B.
Weston, W. J. L........Toronto
Whaley, D. W..........Toronto
Whittington, Miss E. R., Toronto
Wiggins, Miss G. E., Kemptville
Wilkinson, T. C.........Ripley
Yeomans, Miss N. A....Belleville

Third Year.

Allan, P. C.............Toronto
Allin, S. J..............Ilderton
Armstrong, Miss S. G...Markdale
Avery, C. L.............Toronto
Baycroft, Miss H. M.....Aurora
Bell, H. J..........Peterborough
Bennett, Miss K. E.,
   Swift Current, Sask.
Binkley, G. A............Dundas
Brown, G. G............Toronto
Brown, L. W.........Crediton
Burrows, Miss K. F.....Seaforth
Cayley, M. A.........Stratford
Chant, S. N. F.....St. Thomas
Chantler, W. E......Mt. Dennis
Christie, K. A.......Winchester
Cline, C. W............Hannon
Colley, A. K...........Toronto
Couch, J. H........Quebec, Que.
Crossen, E. P.......Sunderland
Daly, Miss F. D. .....London
Daly, Miss K. B. .....Napanee
Dewey, H. W........St. Mary's
Drew, Miss K.,
   New Westminster, B.C.
Eastcott, J. C. .....Pembroke
Everson, Miss M. A.....Oshawa
Fallis, Miss F. A.......Toronto
Ferguson, E.............Sarnia
Fisher, D. B............Toronto
Fitzpatrick, Miss B. M...London
Forman, J. H.........Woodville
Gallaway, Miss E. A.,
   Estevan, Sask.
Gay, A. G............Belleville
Gibson, D. F.......Tillsonburg
Gilroy, A. E. T....Mount Forest
Goodwyn, Miss H. F.. .Arnprior
Goulding, Miss M. L.....Toronto
Grudeff, J.............Toronto
Guillet, E. C...........Cobourg

Hanna, Miss M. I......Toronto
Harries, I. C..........Toronto
Hassard, Miss G. G.....Toronto
Henry, W. C..........Markdale
Hobbs, Miss J. E.....Thorndale
Horwood, E. C..........Toronto
Hubbell, Miss R. A., Smith's Falls
Irvine, L. C........St. Mary's
Lawson, O. G...........London
Luck, J. M............Brantford
McAndrew, H. O......Hamilton
McClenaghan, Miss J. V., Ottawa
MacDougall, R. A.......Sarnia
McNeely, J. V.........Norwood
Maines, W. J...........Blyth
Manning, T. P.........Sarnia
Menzies, A. E. A........Sarnia
*Miller, L. H.........Milliken
Milliken, Miss R. M.,
   Saskatoon, Sask.
Mullet, C. L...........Toronto
Nourse, R. E.......Downsview
Oaks, Miss M. B........Preston
Pakenham, F. R.......Norwood
Patterson, Miss E. F.,
   Niagara Falls
Phillips, J. T.........Hamilton
Potter, H. F............Clinton
Prentice, G. T.........Nottawa
Ray, Miss M. V........Woodville
Rehder, Miss A. K........Paris
Sanders, H. F.....Calgary, Alta.
Sayles, F. A..........Brantford
Scarrow, C. E.........Creemore
Stewart, R. P......Buffalo, N.Y.
Strangway, W. E.......Petrolia
Uren, Miss A. M.......Mitchell
Van Allen, Miss B. G., Morrisburg
Vipond, F. E..........Hamilton
Wallis, Miss G. E.......Clinton
Williams, Miss F. V.....Athens

* In attendance Michaelmas Term only.

Wilson, Miss M. M......Toronto
Wilson, R. L.............Delhi

Wright, Miss A. M......Toronto
Wright, W. J. A........Dundalk

Fourth Year.

Allen, R. O.............Toronto
Annis A. F..............Tyrone
Austin, A. M...........Renfrew
Ayearst, M. J..........Toronto
Baine, F. J.............Toronto
Balfour, Miss I. K......Toronto
Bott, G. E..........Blackwater
Broughton, T. R. S....Corbetton
Brown, H. D..........Brampton
Bush, Miss S. E.....Morrisburg
Butcher, Miss E. M.....Toronto
Button, J. W...........Walton
Cameron, Miss J. D.....Welland
Chappell, Miss M. J.,
                Tokyo, Japan
Congdon, E. P........Hamilton
Cox, Miss T. M.....Leamington
Creighton, J. H.........Toronto
Dafoe, Miss E. C........Madoc
Dales, Miss W. M.......Toronto
Davidson, Miss J. G.,
                Regina, Sask.
Davis, Mrs. M. E.,
                St. John's Nfld.
Denton, Miss R.........Toronto
Dewey, Miss H. J....St. Mary's
Dickinson, C. H......St. Mary's
Duggan, D. W........Brampton
Elliott, Miss M. L......Norwood
Fisher, Miss H. E......Toronto
Follick, Miss L. M. B., Port Perry
Gilley, Miss M. E.,
                New Westminster, B.C.
Golding, Miss H. R....Brampton
Graydon, W. J. G.....Brampton
Greene, Miss M. E.....Toronto
Hall, E. R.............Guelph
Hames, C. F. W........Toronto
Hampson, A...........Toronto
Harrison, Miss M. L.....Madoc
Harstone, R. H......St. Mary's
Hukins, G. R.....Yorkton, Sask.
Irwin, Miss H. M......Grimsby
Irwin, W. A............Toronto
Johnston, S. R..........Gorrie
Keeling, W. L..........Toronto
Keenleyside, Miss N. J. D.,
                Regina, Sask.

Kimura, S......Shigakben, Japan
Langford, W. F....Calgary, Alta.
Laughton, N. B........Walker's
Lawson, Miss M. R...Chesterville
Linton, J. G. H.......Bright
Locke, L. S., ...Brampton
McGregor, Miss L. N., Waterdown
McLaughlin, Miss E. M., Toronto
McVitty, G. C..........Toronto
Marshall, Miss M. E. Owen Sound
Murgatroyd, F. R.....Smithville
Mutart, L. C......Niagara Falls
Neff, Miss E. U........Toronto
Noble, W. G........Leamington
Oaten, B. W. L.........Toronto
Pearson, V. W.........Guelph
Pentland, A. E. C.....Maidstone
Powell, C. E...........Lucan
Powell, H. W...........Ottawa
Powers, Miss M. H. R., Beamsville
Price, H. W............Toronto
Rentner, L. W.....Collingwood
Robinson, M. R........Toronto
Rodman, Miss F. E.....Toronto
Rossiter, Miss J. E.,
                Sault Ste. Marie
Rutherford, Miss G. L., Brampton
Ryan, Miss E. M.......Oakville
Scarrow, Miss A. A. V....Toronto
Shepley, Miss J. E...Amherstburg
§Smith, H. A. L.......Toronto
Smith, J. L.............Toronto
Smith, L. G., ...Grimsby
Smith, R. G.......... Hickson
Smith, W. C. ....Woodville
Swann, H. F.....Vancouver, B.C.
Swanson, W. L........St. Mary's
Tane, W. F...........Oshawa
Trimble, G. E.............Erin
Unger, D. B.........St. Williams
Uren, Miss M. F.......Toronto
Wallen, Miss E. J.....Unionville
Westman, A. E. R........Ottawa
Williams, Miss E. M....Toronto
Wismer, K. L.....Humberstone
York, Miss J. E........Toronto

§ Dispensation.

Occasional Students.

Bradford, W. H............Orillia
Brett, A. F....Springdale, Nfld.
Butt, W. S....Western Bay, Nfld.
Campbell, G. W. W. A...Toronto
Chamberlain, C. O...St. Thomas
Evans, Miss H. P......Sudbury
Fowler, J. H............Toronto
Gardiner, F. J.....Regina, Sask.
Hambley, Miss L. H.,
                Tzchintsing, China
Hargrave, O. L...........Udney
Harris, Miss J. H........Madoc
Lamb, J. B............Toronto
MacDonald, R........Lakefield

Miller, C. C...............Bath
Moores, H......Blackhead, Nfld.
Moote, S. A............Toronto
Munro, W. F.......Pictou, N.S.
Osborne, W. H.....Galgary, Alta.
Oshima, R.........Tokyo, Japan
Patterson, W. R........Toronto
Reid, Miss H. E..Vancouver, B.C.
Rogers, E. E......Delburne, Alta.
Southcott, R. E.........Exeter
Stewart, S. W...........Toronto
Trueblood, A. S.......Trafalgar
*Waite, A. D.....Qu'Appelle, Sask.
Wilson, H. C..........Goderich

SUMMARY—VICTORIA COLLEGE.

First Year...........178
Second Year.........136
Third Year..........81
Fourth Year.........88
Occasionals..........27

Total..........510

TRINITY COLLEGE.

First Year.

The names of students registered in the Course in Commerce are printed in italics.

Arthur, R. K............Sudbury
Beaumont, H......Glen Williams
Bell, J. A. M......Humberstone
Belt, Miss V. E........Oshawa
Bettes, Miss H. T.
           Jacksonville, Fa.
Cayley, H. C...........Toronto
Conn, Miss J. E.........Ottawa
Deacon, G. S.....Vancouver, B.C.
DeLom, T. C. B....Bruce Mines
Doctor, Miss G. M......Toronto
Ellis, J. D...........Mt. Forest
Fairweather, Miss M. L...Ottawa
Ferguson, S. C......Macleod, Alta.
Garrow, Miss M. M.....Goderich
Gillard, Miss A. E..Melville, Sask.
Goodison, Miss V. F..Streetsville
Graham, G. C...........Toronto
Grout, Miss A. E........Arnprior
Harper, S. E.......St. Catharines
Haryett, Miss A. L.
          Peace River, Alta.
Herbert, R. H...........Preston
Hill, L. C.............Hespeler

Huston, Miss M. D.....Glencoe
Irwin, R. P............Hamilton
Kembar, A. K........Creemore
King, D. B.....Vancouver, B.C.
Klaehn, J. O..........Stratford
Lawson, Miss H. W......Barrie
Mackenzie, Miss M. G...Toronto
MacPherson, Miss M. G.
          Port Stanley
Mitchell, D. R..........Oshawa
Mitchell, Miss R. H.....Lucknow
Ponsford, Miss V. I...St. Thomas
Pritchard, Miss M. R.....Ottawa
Ramsbottom, Miss M. S....Conn
Sanders, Miss D. M......Norwich
Saunders, Miss A. L......Ottawa
Serson, C. M.......Trenton, N.J.
Smith, F. A. W....... Cataraqui
Smith, L. H............Ottawa
Spencer, L. A...........Hamilton
Washington, C. F.,
          Cummings Bridge
Wheeler, T. J...........Toronto
Wilson, D.............Oakville

Second Year.

Adams, W.........Peterborough
Benore, Miss M. L...Campbellford
Berry, F. B............Meaford
Bonnycastle, R. H. G.,
          Dauphin, Man.
Burns, Miss M. A........Oshawa
Campbell, Miss M......Thorold
Coate, Miss D.........Chatham
Collip, Miss R. E......Belleville
Day, J. F..............Toronto
Dewdney, D. R........Toronto
Ditchburn, Miss E. S.....Rosseau
Graham, H.............Toronto
§Grew, R..............Ottawa
Harshaw, E. B..........Ottawa
Hazlewood, Miss A. L.,
          Bowmanville
Hope, Miss H. J........Toronto
Jameson, A. E........St. Mary's
Jones, J. R............Brighton

Ketchum, J. D..........Toronto
Ketchum, P. A. C......Toronto
Lee, W. E. M..........Goderich
Luxton, G. N.....Mount Forest
McGillivray, D. J........Whitby
M'Gonigle, R. H....Newmarket
MacMillan, A. W.,
          Niagara-on-the-Lake
Mathews, R. B.........Toronto
Messervy, Miss E.
          Charlottetown, P.E.I.
Mikel, Miss A.........Belleville
Nanton, E. A...Winnipeg, Man.
Philip, J. A.............Galt
Pickford, B. C. W.....Brighton
Pickford, Miss M. A.....Brighton
Preston, A. V........Orangeville
Roderick, J. H.....Stoney Creek
Ross, D. G.............Toronto

§ Dispensation.

†Sargeant, Miss V. M.,
Sault Ste. Marie
Sloggett, Miss L. H...Warkworth
Smith, H. H. W........Toronto

Thompson, Miss F. M...Belleville
Weaver, E. L. ....Hespeler
Wilkes, Miss M. E...Gravenhurst
Williams, M. G. B.....Havelock

Third Year.

Abbott, H.J.E., Bound Brook, N.J.
Ambrose, A. L.........Hamilton
Brown, W. A...........Hamilton
Burpee, Miss R. M. ......Ottawa
Burwash, Miss F. M....Arnprior
Dwelly, R. T. C. ....Toronto
Ewart, Miss M. B........Ottawa
Ferguson, Miss J. E., Port Stanley
Gee, A. H............Hamilton
Gladman, Miss E.G., Peterborough
Hill, K. W.............Toronto
Izzard, Miss E. W....Woodstock
Ketchum, H. F..........Toronto
Lawrence, W. H. R.....Toronto

Lowe, J...............Toronto
Luxton, W. G......Mount Forest
M'Gonigle, Miss E. M.,
Newmarket
Mason, F. H...........Toronto
Moore, A. B...........Toronto
Morse, Miss M. S.......Toronto
Nation, J. S. D.........Toronto
Pittman, Miss B....Topsail, Nfld.
Potts, Miss G. H. ......Lindsay
Stanley, S. W...........Guelph
Stowe, H. J.............Toronto
White, J. R. ....Ottawa
Wilson, H. A...........Toronto

Fourth Year.

Child, P. A...........Hamilton
Coulson, Miss N. I...Brantford
Davidson, J. F.....Peterborough
dePencier, J. C., Vancouver, B.C.
Dixon, Miss E. F......Brantford
Galt, Miss M. C.......Goderich
Humphries, Miss J. B....Glencoe

†Lucas, G. H..........Markdale
Nevill, Miss R. M.....Bartonville
Patterson. A. S........Hamilton
Phillips, C. E..........Toronto
Pridham, Miss E. M....Goderich
Smith, Miss M. L.....Millbrook
Snelgrove, O. H........Toronto

Occasional Students.

Coate, Miss D. E.......Rosseau

Oakley, Miss M........Toronto

SUMMARY—TRINITY COLLEGE.

First Year...........44
Second Year.........42
Third Year..........27
Fourth Year.........14
Occasionals.......... 2
___
Total..........129
___

† In attendance Easter Term only.

ST. MICHAEL'S COLLEGE.

First Year.

The names of students registered in the Course in Commerce are printed in italics.

Barnett, L. F......St. Catharines
Bauer, Miss A. M.......Waterloo
Beaudoin, G...........Toronto
Begley, C. J........Peterborough
Blanchard, Miss C. M....Lindsay
Bolger, J. P.............Dundalk
Burke, Miss E...........Ottawa
Burke, J. V.............Toronto
Butler, E. P...........Toronto
Campbell, Miss M. R...Hamilton
Chalue, Miss D. M......Toronto
Cloutier, A. L........North Bay
Cosgriffe, J. J.........Hamilton
Costello, Miss M. A......Toronto
Dillon, Miss C. M.......Toronto
Dobell, Miss M. M......Toronto
Dolan, L. J............Toronto
Donnelly, C. J........Pinkerton
Dooley, Miss K. L. M....Guelph
Dunnigan, Miss E. C.....Toronto
Dwan, Miss W. L........Toronto
Dwyer, H. C............Toronto
Ellard, B. A............Toronto
English, Miss E. M......Toronto
Flanagan, P. J..........Toronto
Fleury, Miss D.........Toronto
Garden, Miss M. E. C.,
                Peterborough
Gavard, W..............Thorold
Good, R. J............Toronto
Griffin, J. J............Toronto
Grosso, A............Huntsville
Hayes, Miss A. T.......Toronto
Healy, T. L...........Atherley
Houlahan, Miss G......Toronto
Hylinger, Miss M. A.,
                Buffalo, N.Y.
Irvine, Miss E. A.......Toronto
James, Miss C. F........Toronto
Kastner, Miss E. C.....Toronto
Kavanagh, Miss A. M.,
                Penetanguishene
Kelly, C. M. ....Toronto
Keogh, G. B...........Toronto
Killen, J..............Lindsay

Knowlton, A. J.........Toronto
Kramer, Miss Miss H.....Guelph
Leahy, J. P.............Douro
LeBel, E. C............Toronto
Lee, E. G.............Toronto
*Loughrane, L. B.........Toronto
McCabe, D. A..........Toronto
McCool, J. A...........Toronto
McCormick, Miss M....Toronto
McDonald, Miss A. E....Toronto
McDonald, W. F........Toronto
McDonnell, Miss C......Toronto
McDonnell, Miss H......Toronto
McGahey, J. E. ....Toronto
McGuire, P. J..........Toronto
McKeon, F. J.........Hamilton
McKeown, L.........North Bay
McNab, E. B...........Chepstow
McNally, H. J........Westport
Mallon, Miss E. M.......Toronto
Miller, Miss C. M. R.,
                Niagara Falls, N.Y.
Mogan, F..............Toronto
Mulvihill, Miss J. E.....Arnprior
Murphy, J. P......Fort William
Murtha, T. J............Lindsay
O'Boyle, B. J...........Dundas
O'Boyle, Miss M. A.,
                Sault Ste. Marie
*O'Connor, G. L.........Sudbury
O'Connor, W. L.........Whitby
O'Neail, Miss K. M....Brantford
O'Reilly, D. O......Copper Cliff
Pineau, Miss A. C......Windsor
Quinlan, M. J......Trout Creek
Redican, F. W..........Toronto
Roach, Miss M. G........Arthur
Runstadler, Miss M......Toronto
Servais, F. J......Port Arthur
Sullivan, Miss M. E....Hamilton
Thompson, V. A........Toronto
Vahey, T. J...........Toronto
Walsh, Miss M. M.......Lindsay
Welsh, E. A........Peterborough

* In attendance Michaelmas Term only.

Second Year.

Agnew, Miss D. L.......Toronto
Ashbrook, Miss V. C.,
　　　　　　　Washington, Pa.
Ballard, Miss A. B..Niagara Falls
Bench, Miss M.........Toronto
Cleary, L. A............Hastings
Connelly, E. D.........Toronto
Coumans, M. J........Chepstowe
Curtin, L. F.......West Monkton
Dawson, Miss E. M......Toronto
Deloughery, F. J.......Pembroke
Ducharme, Miss E. A. M.,
　　　　　　　　Stratford
§Forner, B. M.....Houston, Texas
Garey, J. L.........Moira, N.Y.
Gendron, W. H., Penetanguishene
Gibbons, Miss L. M.....Toronto
Gravelle, Miss E.........Toronto
Hannan, Miss A. A.....Toronto
Hughes, Miss A........Toronto
Kelly, Miss M. A.......Renfrew
Kennedy, V............Toronto
Lanphier, C. B.........Toronto
Latchford, Miss L.......Toronto
Legris, Miss D..........Renfrew

Lenahan, N............Toronto
Lynch, P. J........Peterborough
MacDonald, T. A......Sandwich
MacDonnell, Miss M. H. I.,
　　　　　　　　Toronto
McIntyre, J. V........Brantford
McNab, C. M.........Walkerton
Mallon, Miss M. F......Toronto
Morrow, J. E...........Colgan
Mulligan, M. J.........Toronto
Mulville, E. E.........Westport
Murray, Miss E. M.....Toronto
Nash, A. J. W.........Hamilton
O'Brien, A. D..........Toronto
O'Connor, J. J.........Hastings
†O'Toole, A. L......Peterborough
Pagé, A. M............Windsor
Pickett, Miss M. M.,
　　　　　　　Mount Forest
Pickett, O........Mount Forest
Theobold, J. C....Peterborough
Vale, P.............Toronto
Wheeler, W. R.........Toronto
Williams, Miss L...Niagara Falls
Wood, Miss C..........Toronto

Third Year.

Bart, P. J..............Toronto
Carroll, W. T..........Guelph
Collins, Miss W. C., St. Catharines
Coughlin, Miss C. E.....Toronto
Dobell, R. J...........Toronto
Dore, J. W. ....Hamilton
Doyle, Miss E. S........Toronto
Dunbar, J............Priceville
Ford, J. A............Hamilton
Garland, Miss M........Toronto
Gibson, Miss N. J..Chicapee,Mass.
Guinane, Miss H. M.....Toronto
Hannan, Miss M. A.....Toronto
Henry, Miss M. A...New Toronto
Lassaline, H. J.........Windsor
Lee, Miss K. K.........Toronto
Longeway, Miss T. E. M.,
　　　　　　　　Stratford
McCardle, Miss M. M...Linwood
McDermott, F. T........Toronto

McGrath, Miss E., St. John's Nfld.
Mackintosh, Miss E. N...Toronto
McMahon, E. J...........Delhi
Malone, B. P.......... Toronto
Mullett, Miss A. K.,
　　　　　　　Carleton Place
O'Donnell, A........Merrickville
O'Donnell, Miss M......Toronto
O'Donohue, F. E......Brantford
O'Leary, Miss K. G.....Parkhill
†O'Shea, M. A..........Norwood
Ryan, Miss M. A........Toronto
Simpson, Miss A. C.,
　　　　　　　Port McNicoll
Simpson, F. R.....Port McNicoll
Stock, L. J........Mimico Beach
Sullivan, L. D. J........Hamilton
Troy, M. L......Chatham, N.B.
Tuffy, Miss C..........Toronto

Fourth Year.

Coghlan, Miss C. V.,
　　　　　　Vancouver, B.C.
Collins, F. T.....Westmount, Que.

Daley, Miss M. T.......Toronto
Donnelly, F. J.........Pinkerton
Gough R. P............Toronto

† In attendance Easter Term only.
§ Dispensation.

Leacy, A. T...........Pembroke
McBrady, Miss L. ......Toronto
McCormick, Miss S. F....Toronto
McGuire, J. F....,....Ennismore
McKeon, W. H........Hamilton
Mallon, J. P............Toronto
Malone, A. J...........Toronto
Melady, T. S............Dublin
Mullett, Miss H. F.,
     Carleton Place

O'Brien, Miss F. D.,
     New York City
O'Brien, Miss M. K......Toronto
O'Connell, Miss K. L....Toronto
O'Malley, Miss. I. F.....Toronto
O'Meara, Miss E........Toronto
O'Reilly, J. B......Seattle, Wash.
Overend, J.............Toronto
Ray, P. J...............Toronto
Sheehy, M. T ...:..Peterborough
Watson, F. T. W.......Toronto

Occasional Students.

Black, H. A........Peterborough
Blanchard, H. L........Toronto
Carty, W. H..............Elgin
Caufield, J. A. A.......Monteith
Corkery, V. J......Peterborough
Fitzgerald, R. W...Peterborough
Gibbs, Miss M. V........Toronto
James, A. P............Toronto

Killen, J. Q.........Peterborough
McCarney, W. C....Peterborough
Moreau, D .....Penetanguishene
Mulqueen, Miss E. M....Toronto
Munroe, H. J............Ottawa
Simpson, D. D........Hamilton
Sullivan, V. S.........Ennismore
Toomey, T. F. Niagara, Falls, N.Y

SUMMARY—ST. MICHAEL'S COLLEGE.

First Year Students... 84
Second Year Students. 46
Third Year Students.. 36
Fourth Year Students. 24
Occasional Students... 16
      ——
Total..............206

SUMMARY IN THE FACULTY OF ARTS.

(a) By Colleges.

University of Toronto......... 189
University College........... 1170
Victoria College............. 510
Trinity College............. 129
St. Michael's College......... 206
Duplicates.................. 11
       ——
Total.................. 2193

(b) By Years.

First Year........... 763
Second Year......... 517
Third Year.......... 333
Fourth Year........ 294
Occasionals, Summer
 Session, etc......... 286
      ——
Total...........2193

FACULTY OF MEDICINE.

REGISTER OF STUDENTS, 1920-21.

First Year.

Bain, T..................Toronto.
Baker, L. L...............Toronto
Barker, N. J.............Toronto
Bates, Miss J. L..........Toronto
Beckett, M. B..........Brantford
Bell, E. G.............Copper Cliff
Bennett, D. S............Toronto
Bennett, S. R......St. Catharines
Black, L. W.............Hespeler
Borron, R. W............Toronto
Boye, J. H...............Toronto
Brebner, W. B...........Toronto
Bright, W. G.............Wiarton
Brintnell, F. B..........Colborne
Bronstein, N. W.........Toronto
Brown, H. R.............Toronto
Bull, F. B............Brampton
Burt, C. F.............Brantford
Butters, H. L......Niagara Falls

Cairo, Miss M. R........Toronto
Cameron, H. M..........Ottawa
Campbell, C. A. L......Hamilton
Campbell, I..............Toronto
Campbell, I. P......Grand Valley
Campbell, J. G..........Toronto
Carr, C. W.............Thornton
Carson, W. H..........Chatsworth
Clarke, L...............Toronto
Clark, R..........Yorkton, Sask.
Cleland, S. G............Toronto
Coburn, W. A......Nanaimo, B.C.
Connolly, W. G.........Brechin
Cudmore, W. E..........Bronte

Dell, C. A. O.......Niagara Falls
Derbyshire, W. J...Sunnyside, Eng.
Dowsley, G. A......Mallorytown
Dreyer, J. F.............Toronto

Easton, N. L..............Ayton
Esdale, W. R.............Ottawa
Fairfield, A. B........Beamsville
Farnsworth, J. F..........Selby

Ferguson, J. G...........Toronto
Fidler, K. A.............Toronto
Fine, J. M..............Toronto
Flahiff, E. W.............Paris
Fleming, Miss E. W......Toronto
Fleming, F. J..........St. Marys
Flommerfelt, T. E......Thorold
Forde, J. H.............Toronto
Fowler, A. C.............Perth
Fowler, C. J..........Kingston
Fralick, F. T..........Thornhill

Gardiner, W. J.........Midland
Gies, A. H.............Hamilton
Goodchild, S. F.........Toronto
Goodwin, J. C......Niagara Falls
Gordon, M. K.........Caledonia
Gordon, S. D.........Agincourt
Graham, C. B..........Oakwood
Grant, R. C.............Toronto
Griffith, J. R. I.........Toronto
Guay, A. J. L..... Calgary, Alta.
Guthrie, J. A. T.........Toronto

Hain, C. W.............Toronto
Hakstian, A.............Brantford
Hall, G. W...........Sunderland
Ham, A. W............Brantford
Harvie, D. A..........Midland
Hassard, C. E. A........Toronto
Hatfield, W. H....Vancouver, B.C.
Hayes, F. A. M...........Guelph
Hemond, C. J..........Windsor
Henderson, J. G..........Troy
Hershey, J. M........Owen Sound
Higgs, W. D...Albert Head, B.C.
Hisey, R. F...........Creemore
Hobson, J. P......Niagara Falls
Hoffman, B.............Toronto
Hooey, L..............North Bay
Hooper, G. G............Brandon
Hooper, L. N........Little Britain
Houser, G. F........Humberstone
Huddart, Miss V. G......Toronto

Hudson, L.............Toronto
Huff, R. G.........Peterborough
Huggard, L. H. A. R...Vancouver, B.C.
Hutton, D. V..........Brantford
Hyland, H. H...........Toronto

Ingham, C. J..........Stratford
Irwin, D. A.............Toronto

James, A. P.............Toronto
James, G........Vancouver, B.C.
Jeffries, C. N............Toronto
Jones, A..............Toronto
John, T. P..........Bridgetown, St. Vincent, B.W.I.
Jones, G. H...........Claremont

Kamitakahara, E., Vancouver, B.C.
Kelly, J. A.........Long Branch
Kennedy, A. S...........Beeton
Kenney, W. G. C...........Acton
Kirk, C. M.......Antigonish, N.S.
Kyles, N. B...........Toronto

Landau, J.............Toronto
Laughton, J. L.........Walkers
Leaver, L. R............Toronto
Le Drew, F.............Toronto
Little, J. L.............Guelph
Lloyd, P. F.......Brewer's Mills
Lively, F. M.......New Liskeard
Lowrey, H. E. D........St. David's

Mackam, T. W.....St. Catharines
Manaceveth, B.A. ....Toronto
Manaceveth, G..........Toronto
Mason, L. W.............Simcoe
Mason, P. W.............Simcoe
Matheson, G. E.........Sudbury
Matheson, J. A......Granum, Alta.
Mayne, J. E............Drayton
Miller, J. M.....Moose Jaw, Sask.
Milne, J. E.............Elmwood
Moir, H. B.............Preston
Moir, H. K.............Toronto
Mortimer, G. H.........Toronto
Mulligan, T. J..........Sudbury
Mulock, Miss G. E., St. Catharines
Murray, S. S............Dundas

McCallum, J. D.......Lloydtown
McCannel, W. A........Chesley
McCombs, R. D........Lowbanks
McDonald, D. F......Sutton West
McDonald, Miss E.......Sudbury

McDonald, L. R....Regina, Sask.
McGee, A. R...........Norwood
McKay, J. B.....Owen Sound
McKeown, L....Moose Jaw, Sask.
McLellan, R. F........Harriston
McMullen, R. E.........Toronto
Macnamara, A. R........Toronto
MacNicoll, W. T........Hamilton
MacNiel, A. C..........Oakville
McNiven, E. L. ...Victoria, B.C.
Nicholson, T. F..........Toronto

Oakes, W. A.............Guelph
O'Donnell, J............Mimico

Paul, H. A...........Haileybury
Pearson, N. D..........Stayner
Peart, H. E..........Burlington
Peeler, D. B...........Toronto

Potter, C. W..........Southend
Pratt, D. W............Toronto

Raiter, L............Hamilton
Reeve-Newson, T.........Toronto
Riddell, F............Beaverton
Robertson, R............Toronto
Robinson, Miss H. S....Kleinburg
Rogow, H. A............Toronto
Rosen, N..............Toronto
Ross, J. R.............Toronto
Ruby, R. A..........Kemptville
Ryall, D. B.......Nanaimo, B.C.

Scher, J. N.............Toronto
Shaver, C. G. ...'......Ancaster
Sidenberg, I. I..........Toronto
Silverthorne, L. N.....St. Thomas
Silverton, T. L..........Toronto
Sinclair, G. A.........Burlington
Sinclair, J. W......Regina, Sask.
Sisley, E. B............Toronto
Small, W. R..........Sandwich
Smith, Miss F. M., Glanford Station
Smith, J. A..........Nashville
Smith, W. E...........Hamilton
Snitman, M.............Toronto
Soskin, S.............Toronto
Sparling, G. P. M.....Washington, D.C.
Stahl, H. F...........Kitchener
Stahl, O. J............Kitchener
Stevens, E............Chesley
Struthers, J. N. P.........Galt

Stuart, K. . . . . Simcoe
Sullivan, J. T. A. . . . . Toronto
Swart, H. A. . . . . Simcoe
Sweet, T. A. . . . . Hamilton

Taube, E. L. . . . . Toronto
Taube, N. . . . . Toronto
Teney, H. F. . . . . Toronto
Thaler, A. F. . . . . Elmwood
Thomas, Miss M. I. . . . . Toronto

Uren, J. L. . . . . Toronto

Verity, G. E. . . . . Brantford
Verner, T. B. . . . . .St. Catharines
Vivian, R. P. . . . . Barrie

Waddington, H. . . . . Brantford
Wagner, R. A. . . . . Hamilton
Walden, W. D. . . . . Thedford
Watson, J. L. . . . . Toronto
Watt, G. L. . . . . Brantford
Webb, A. J. M. . . . . Hamilton
Welsh, W. K. . . . . Scotland
White, A. W. M. . . . . Chatham
Whittier, Miss C. L. . . . .Elmsdale, N.S.
Wigle, Miss R. M., Sackville, N.B.
Wilcox, L. F. . . . . Beeton
Wilson, A. . . . . .Oakville
Wilson, A. K. . . . . . . .R.g n , Sask.
Wilson, J. A. . . . . .æ.i.Thorold
Wylie, J. H . . . . Almonte

Second Year, Six Years' Course.

Abell, R. S. . . . . Owen Sound
Ainslie, Miss M. E. . . . . .St. Marys
Alexander, H. J. . . . . Norwich
Allin, R. F. . . . . Toronto
Amyot, G. F. . . . . Ottawa
Armstrong, J. C. . . . . Ottawa

Barclay, L. T. . . . . Claremont
Bicknell, H. E. . . . . Toronto
Biehn, S. L. . . . . Parry Sound
Birch, J. R. . . . . Calgary, Alta.
Booth, C. S. . . . . Mallorytown
Boyd, J. . . . . Hamilton
Brillinger, F. . . . . .Stouffville
Brummitt, R. B., Vancouver, B.C.
Burgess, J. H. . . . . Ottawa

Cameron, J. M. . . . . Toronto
Campbell, Miss G. A., Blytheswood
Campbell, G. D. G. . . . . Toronto
Carscadden, W. G. . . . . Lindsay
Catherwood, W. L. . . . . Hagersville
Childs, H. H. . . . . London
Chu, P. Y. Y. . . . . . . Vancouver, B.C.
Clark, D. V. . . . . Toronto
Couch, J. H. . . . . Quebec, P.Q.
Coutts, G. S. . . . . Bradford
Cowie, G. A. . . . . Brantford
Croll, L. D. . . . . . .Saskatoon, Sask.
Cumming, G. S. . . . . Turnerville

de Souza, M. G. . . .New Amsterdam, Berbice, B.G.
Deyell, J. S. . . . . Peterborough
Dickson, B. R. . . . . Thamesville
Dill, J. L. . . . . .Dublin
Doran, Miss M. V. . . . . . . .Iroquois
Duncan, A. H. . . . . Toronto
Duncan, Miss J. R. . . . . . Chatham

Ely, C. W. . . . . Beamsville

Fair, G. L. . . . . Toronto
Falconer, J G. . . . . Toronto
Fielden, E. C. . . . . Toronto
Fleck, Miss M. . . . . Toronto
Fletcher, W. R. . . . . Toronto
Forrest, S. J. . . . .Summerville, N.J.
Forster, Miss M. B. . . . . . .Watford
Fraser, Miss F. H. . . . . .York Mills
Fried, J. S. . . . . .Toronto

Gerow, H. G. . . . . Colborne
Graham, W. L. . . . . .Galt
Gray, H. M. . . . . Toronto
Green, J. . . . . Toronto
Greer, H. J., Port Coquitlam, B.C.
Gung, E. B. . . . . .Victoria, B.C.

Hacking, L. C., New Westminster, B.C.
Hamilton, F. C. . . . . Toronto
Hare, M. A. . . . . . . Rosetown, Sask.
Heaton, T. G. . . . . .Toronto
Heggie, D. C. . . . . Brampton
Henderson, D. N. . . . . Toronto
Henne, F. R. . . . . Gananoque
Hill, W. V. . . . . Toronto
Hodd, D. G. . . . . Hamilton
Horton, C. B. . . . . Toronto
Hume, T. W. K. . . . . Toronto

Jackson, J. E. . . . . Auburn
Johnston, W. C. . . . . Kippen

Kelly, A. D. . . . . Toronto
Knowlton, C. E. . . . . Toronto

Lambert, A. G. . . . . Rosseau
Landsborough, A. M., Port Credit
Lang, A. . . . . Kitchener
Lantsevitsky, N. . . Brest-Litovsk,
                    Russia
Lathrope, C. D. . . . . . . Bowmanville
Laxton, J. E. . . . . Toronto

Mark, E. C. . . . . Hong Kong, China
May, C. R. . . . . Melfort, Sask.
Middlebro, J. P. . . . . . . Owen Sound
Millar, B. O. . . . . Smith's Falls
Millar, J. W. . . . . Castleton
Miller, W. H. . . . . Toronto
Milliken, J. . . . . Renfrew
Mills, Miss G. . . . . Toronto
Milne, R. E. A. . . . . Niagara Falls
Mitchell, C. L. . . . . Victoria, B.C.
Mitchell, H. D. . . . . . . Victoria, B.C.
Monaghan, H. J. . . . New Hamburg
Muir, W. S. . . . . Niagara Falls
Murchison, E. B. . . . . Cambray
Murray, L. L., Guy's Hill, Jamaica,
                    B.W.I.

McCarthy, K. C. . . . . Toronto
McCormick, N. A. . . . . Walkerville
McFadden, J. L. . . . . . Victoria, B.C.
MacGowan, G. A. . . . . Toronto
McGregor, G. W. . . . . . . Inglewood
McGuire, C. T. . . . . Merriton
McIntosh, J. S. . . . . . St. Catharines
Mackay, R. P. . . . . Toronto
MacLean, D. L. . . . . Harriston
McLean, G. C. . . . . Collingwood

Naden, J. R. . . . . Victoria, B.C.
Nicholson, Miss M. A., . . Lucknow

O'Gorman, J. T. . . . . Toronto
Omerod, M. J. . . . . Toronto

Park, J. H. . . . . Mitchell
Paterson, J. C. . . . . Sarnia
Patry, F. L. . . . . Toronto
Pember, F. R. . . . . Toronto
Perry, Miss F. E. . . . Victoria, B.C.

Potter, H. F. . . . . Clinton
Plewes, D. F. . . . . Toronto
Reid, Miss M. E. . . . . London
Roach, C. J. . . . . . . Vancouver, B.C.
Robinson, L. E. . . . . Aurora
Rudd, M. S. K. . . . . . Parry Sound
Rumball, W. C. . . . . St. Catharines
Russell, W. H. . . . . Toronto

Schwab, J. . . . . Toronto
Scott, R. F. . . . . Toronto
Scott, W. C. M. . . . . Omemee
Seltzer, I. E. . . . . Toronto
Senn, J. N. . . . . Caledonia
Sher, Miss L. . . . . Toronto
Singer, Miss M. . . . . Toronto
Smith, A. G. . . . . Toronto
Soanes, E. P. . . . . Aurora
Steele, T. M. . . . . Stratford
Stillman, I. . . . . Toronto
Strain, F. A. . . . . Gore Bay
Strangway, W. E. . . . . Petrolia
Strebig, D. L. M. . . . . Toronto
Stringer, F. H. . . . . . Dawson, Y.T.
Sutherland, L. J. . . Holland Centre
Syer, G. E. . . . . Fraserville

Taylor, A. C. . Indore, Central India
Teasdale, H. R. . . . . Massey
Trick, H. W. . . . . Oshawa

Vine, G. D. . . . . Atwood
Vokes, H. A. S. . . . . Toronto

Wade, C. W. . . . . . Vancouver, B.C.
Walker, J. E., New Westminster,
                    B.C.
Wallis, Miss G. E. . . . . Clinton
Westman, E. R. . . . . Toronto
White, C. O. . . . . Toronto
Wiley, W. R. . . . . Toronto
Wilkins, W. R. . . . . Toronto
Williamson, F. M. . . . . . . Priceville
Wilson, C. H. . . . . St. George
Wilson, Miss M. E. . . . . . . Toronto
Wolfson, H. . . . . Collingwood
Wyndham, C. . . . . Oakville

Second Year, Five Years' Course.

Adams, J. H. F. . . . . Toronto
Aitchison, D. B. . . . . Hamilton
Anderson, O. W. . . . . . . Sundridge
Armstrong, B. C. . . . . Calgary
Atkinson, W. L. . . . . Guelph

Baker, F. E. . . . . Belleville
Baker, Miss F. M. . . . . . . Toronto

Ball, W. M. . . . . Sault Ste. Marie
Barlow, H. S. . . . . Toronto
Barr, Miss C. A. . . . . Merlin
Beasley, J. H. . . . . Toronto
Beatty, S. R. . . . . Thomasburg
Bell, A. M. . . . . Priceville
Best, C. H., West Pembroke, Maine

Best, C. J..........Peterborough
Bigelow, L. H.............Bethany
Black, G. N...........Springfield
Borsook, H.....;.......Toronto
Boyce, R. W..........Belleville
Briant, T. E............Toronto
Brown, M. H............Trenton
Buchanan, W. P............Galt
Bull, F. L.............Weston
Byrne, U. P....New Westminster, B.C.
Caldwell, W. S...........Ottawa
Campbell, G. E........Hamilton
Campbell, S. M...........Toronto
Caple, H. H...... Vancouver, B.C.
Carmichael, Miss A. I. Peterborough
Chant, Miss E. H........:Toronto
Charlton, W. H. M.......Weston
Chisholm, G. B.........Oakville
Clifford, C. H...........Toronto
Code, D. B.............Ottawa
Cousland, P. A. C....Edinburgh, Scotland
Coyne, D. R...........Leamington
Cray, J. F.............Guelph
Currie, G. C.......Little Current
Currie, M. A......Little Current

Dales, C. W.............Drayton
Dalrymple, Miss L. A...Waskada, Man.
Davison, R. R............Dundas
Day, A.............Orillia
d'Easum, L. G. C., New Westminster, B.C.
Delamere, H. D........Toronto
Devins, W. P...........Barrie
Dinniwell, O. C.........Wiarton
Duncombe, K. L......Waterford
Dunlop, R. W...........Kintore

Elliott, G. A.........Nelson, B.C.
English, S. S.............Hamilton
Everist, W. C...........Toronto

Faulkner, Miss I. G....Duntroon
Fawcett, J. T...........Mitchell
Fenton, W. K..........Toronto
Ferguson, T. G.........Toronto
Fetterly, Miss M. E....Winchester
Finlay, H. H......Yorkton, Sask.
Fleming, D. R.....New Liskeard
Fletcher, G. M..........Toronto
Foster, F. H.............Toronto
Fraser, J. L............Petrolia

Gauld, R. L.............Mimico

Gilchrist, R. A...New Westminster, B.C.
Glenney, W. R.....Little Britain
Gossage, C. D...........Toronto
Gray, F. E.............Listowel
Gray, T. W. A.........Millbrook
Gray, W. G............Courtright
Griffin, B. M..........Coldwater
Grove, J. H.............Toronto
Gunn, Miss I. G..........Clinton

Hall, J. L.............Phelpston
Hames, C. F. W........Oakville
Hamilton, K. A..Moose Jaw, Sask.
Hardy, A. W............Oakwood
Hawkins, W. D..........Toronto
Heaslip, P. T..........Dunnville
Heath, T. R.............Orton
Henderson, W. W...Regina, Sask.
Henry, A. T.............Toronto
Henry, G. G...........Markdale
Herold, R. E..........Shakespeare
Hershey, J. H.......Owen Sound
Hilliar, H. K.......Burk's Falls
Hodgins, B. A............London
Howse, G. O.............Aylmer
Hunter, Miss D. L...Kuangning, Manchuria
Hurlburt, W. E..........Toronto

Janes, E. C.............Watford
Jaquith, L. E...........Toronto
Jennings, H. N......Hagersville
Johnstone, B. I.............Tara
Junkin, C. I.............Toronto

Keener, W. C...........Kitchener
Keith, H. M............Toronto
Kelly, A. B.............Toronto
Kenyon, B. B.............Blair
Kerr, H. T.............Toronto
Kinkead, J. C...........Britton
Kinsman, R. H........Hamilton

Laing, J. W.............Wyevale
Lang, H. B.............Toronto
Latimer, R. H.........Beaverton
Liddy, F. J.............Toronto
Lefurgey, J. A...North Bedeque, P.E.I.
Lockhart, J. L.........Midland
Lyon, L. A.............Oakville

Madoo, S. C. V....Port of Spain, Trinidad
Maltby, E. J............Toronto

Meehan, Miss G. B. . . . .Rochester, N.Y.
Meekison, D. M...Vancouver, B.C.
Menzies, F. H........Burks Falls
Michell, G. E...........Toronto
Miller, J. B............Toronto
Mitchell, H. C...........Toronto
Montgomery, R. C.......Toronto
Mount, H. T. R.........Toronto
Munro, F. W............Toronto
Murphy, W. M......Owen Sound
Mustard, J. M.........Uxbridge

McAlister, H. R........Hamilton
McAllan, N. R.........Woodstock
McAteer, J.............Toronto
McBain, R. W....Hamiota, Man.
McCartney, T. G.......Bethany
McClinton, J............Goderich
McCosh, R. A.......Kincardine
MacDonald, N....:.....Atherley
MacDonald, P. G........Oilli a
McDonald, T. A...Deloraine, Man.
Macdonell, R.-V...Dalhousie Mills, P.Q.
McGarvey, M. R.......Petrolia
McGill, W. L............Toronto
MacKay, A. F.......Truro, N.S.
McKay, D. R..........Stayner
McKinnon, A. L.........Orton
MacLachlan, Miss S. R....Toronto
McLaughlin, P. B........Toronto
McLellan, T. G..........Toronto
McLeod, A. M........Kincardine
MacPherson, Miss G.......Dutton

Neelin, W. E. E...Richmond West
Neilson, J. R...........Stratford
Nichols, T. R..........Stratford
Noble, E. C.............Toronto
Noble, J. H.....London, England

O'Donnell, B. A. P.......Toronto
Ogden, C. E.............Toronto
Orr, Miss J. S..........Toronto
Owens, Miss M......Grenville, P.Q.

Paton, W. M...........Toronto
Phillips, M.............Dundalk
Pinchin, A. H..........Toronto
Pratt, C. H.............Chesley
Price, H. W............Toronto
Proud, R. H................Tara
Purdy, A. D. T..........Toronto

Richards, C. A.........Millbrook

Ridge, W. W...........Hamilton
Riley, R. C...........Welland
Robert, J. T...........Chatham
Robinson, J. T. H......Belgrave
Ross, J. C.........Zealandia, Sask.
Rowley, A. E...........Toronto
Rynard, W. M. W.......Zephyr

Sands, G. E.............Corunna
Scarlett, E. P., Portage la Prairie, Man.
Scott, D. E............Belleville
Sexsmith, E. L..........Oakville
Sharpe, W. C..........Toronto
Shaw, E. S.............Guelph
Sherman, S............Toronto
Simpson, Miss R. R. M....Toronto
Sinnott, J. A..........Hamilton
Sloan, S. G............Chatham
Smith, H. M...........Chatham
Smith, R. G...........Hickson
Spaulding, H. E........Aurora
Spratt, E. H..........Ottawa
Standen, C. W....Penticton, B.C.
Stewart, D. W..........Toronto
Stokes, L. S........Mount Albert
Stott, S. J............Toronto
Sykes, A. V.......Calgary, Alta.

Taylor, W. H.........Guelph
Thompson, C. E....Stony Creek
Thompson, R. A.........Zephyr
Thompson, T. W.....Port Credit
Truax, A. J............Toronto
Tyrrell, J. D...........Hamilton

Urquhart, A. M.........Oakville
Urquhart, C. H.........Toronto
Urquhart, D............Toronto

Vanderburgh, A. W., West Summerland, B.C.

Waddell, R. R..........Hamilton
Wansborough, R. M..Grand Valley
Warner, O. M..........Toronto
Weaver, R. T., Red Pheasant, Sask.
Welsh, H. E.............Moira
Westcott, D. B......Collingwood
White, C. C............Chatham
White, M. F............Lindsay
White, Miss K. M.....Rothesay Park, Moose Jaw, Sask.
Wilcox, F. A............Toronto
Wildfang, E. J..........Elmwood
Wilkins, A. R..........Toronto

Williams, J. E.............Toronto
Williams, W. O..........Cardinal
Williamson, G. S........Beaverton

Wylie, W. A..............Markham

Young, Miss A. M........Toronto

Third Year.

Adams, Miss D...........Toronto
Anderson, E. S...........Toronto
Anderson, W. K..........Chatham
Arbuckle, D. S...........Toronto

Baker, Miss G............Chatham
Baker, S. E..............Toronto
Ballantyne, P. M.........Toronto
Barnes, L. S.............Toronto
Barton, E. R.............Toronto
Batson, H. H............Brantford
Beaton, C...............Owen Sound
Beattie, O. M.............Batteau
Bell, J. K........Kamloops, B.C.
Belyea, C. C..............Kenora
Bennett, A. E......Grand Valley
Binning, G.G.T., Moose Jaw, Sask.
Bishop, C. A.............Toronto
Blott, R. D..............Dunnville
Bochner, M..............Toronto
Bochner, T. N............Toronto
Borland, T. H...........Innerkip
Boulding, C. R...........Putnam
Boulter, L. W...........Picton
Boyden, R. W............Ottawa
Brady, F. A..............Toronto
Brewster, W. R..........Brantford
Brodie, Miss M. H.....Stouffville
Bronstein, Miss R.......Toronto
Brown, G. W................Lyn
Buckley, H. R......Niagara Falls
Burridge, Miss M. F., Victoria, B.C.

Cameron, H. G....Saskatoon, Sask.
Campbell, D. M.........Strathroy
Carrie, D. S...........St. Thomas
Carruthers, Miss H. R....Toronto
Carson, J. E.............Desboro
Carson, R. J.............Orillia
Carter, J. J.............Clifford
Caven, W. R.............Toronto
Challener, R. E. S.......Toronto
Cheney, Miss M. J........Ottawa
Clysdale, E. S. ....Mooretown
Cohen, J. L.............Toronto
Cohen, W. A.............Toronto
Cole, M. S.............Brantford
Colvin, L. T. ....Picton
Comisky, Miss E. H.,
                     Richmond Hill
Cook, Miss S. M. L.......Toronto

Copeman, E. S..............Paris
Copp, E. F. F............Clinton
Couch, A. J..............Toronto
Crowe, L. L.....Bridgetown, N.S.

Denison, L..............Toronto
Devitt, F. B.............Toronto
Dimitroff, T.............Toronto
Douglas, H. S.........Springfield
Drummond, H. A........Toronto
Dunning, G. W......Cumberland
Dunton, A. S..............Paris
Dusseau, C..............Toronto
Dyer, H. F..............Allandale

Evans, G. F...........St. Mary's
Ewing, C. H..............Fergus

Fallon, J. T............North Bay
Farley, J. W............Trenton
Fatum, O............Gowanstown
Fisher, M. M............Kippen
Fisher, R. S. M......Georgetown
Fitzgerald, G. J...........Vasey
Ford, J. R..............Dutton
Fortune, C. W........Walkerton
Foster, G. V............Toronto
Fowler, M. N..........Hamilton
Frank, F. W............Toronto

Gamble, J. E. D.......Brantford
Gauld, Miss F. M.......Toronto
Gay, Mrs. St. C. R.
                    New York, N.Y.
Gebirtig, T.............Toronto
Gemmel, J. G.............Ayr
Gilbertson, R. L........Simcoe
Glass, S. J.............Toronto
Gleeson, H. J...........Napanee
Golberg, L.............Toronto
Golden, I. M............Toronto
Gordon, G.............Toronto
Graham, J. D...........Toronto
Graham, R. W..........Toronto
Graham, W.L.............Lobo
Gratz, C. M....Sunnyslope, Alta.
Greenberg, D. Y........Windsor
Greenberg, J. H.........Toronto
Grierson, N. B..........Hanover
Grieve, J. G........Millbank
Griffin, F. R.........St. Thomas

Hall, G. C. R........Little Britain
Hall, S........Pyong Yang, Korea
Hanley, E. G........... Midland
Hardie, G. C.........Victoria, B.C.
Harkins, E. B............:.Toronto
Harold, R. L.......Caron, Sask.
Harris, C. S..............Toronto
Hayes, J. J.............Phelpston
Hazen, G. M. T..Saskatoon, Sask.
Henderson, W. S...........Sarnia
Henry, L. L.........Niagara Falls
Hipwell, R. E............Alliston
Hunt, V. G.........Galgary, Alta.
Hynes, B. J.........St. Catharines

Ireland, G. I.............Trenton

Jessel, L.................Toronto
Johnston, J. A.............Kars
Johnston, J. L...........Inwood
Johnston, W. V..........Auburn
Jones, E. M.............Hamilton
Judson, F. M..............Lyn

Kenny, W. G..........Hamilton
Kernick, M.............:..Toronto
Kilgour, D. G............Guelph
Knight, E. W...........Toronto
Kohan, M...............Toronto

Large, R. G....Port Simpson, B.C.
Lavine, I................Toronto
Levin, S. J.............Windsor
Levinson. R. M..........Kenora
Lewis, F. I...........Orangeville
Long, E. C.............Listowel
Luke, W. R. F..........Toronto
Lyon, E. K...............Blyth

Maginley, H. D.
        Lyons, Antigua, B.W.I.
Mahaffy, A. F.........Cromarty
Maitland, C. W.........Toronto
Manning, R. F...........Forest
Markowitz, J............Toronto
Miller, H. R.............Selkirk
Miner, H. B........:Humberstone
Moffat, G. F............Weston
Montogmery, A. E.......Tiverton
Monypenny, Miss A. D....Toronto
Moore, W. N..........Uxbridge
Morgan, A. E............Toronto
Morton, W. R............Proton
Mowat, H. F,.............Acton
Murray, L. M...........Toronto
McCallum, A. P..........Dutton

McCluskey, E. R........Alliston
McCormick, Miss H. H....Toronto
McCormick, W. K.... Amherstberg
McEachern, J. M. Winnipeg, Man.
McInnis, T. J......Regina, Sask.
Mackay, D. A.....Ingersoll, Ont.·
McKee, W. A...........Millbank
McKenzie, R. D..... Hanley, Sask.
McMaster, E. A.:..........Utopia
McMurray, W. J....Niagara Falls

Neelands, R. J.............Forest
Nichol, K. D...........Brantford

O'Connor, M. J..........Toronto
Oke, Miss I. R.....St. Catharines
O'Neill, C. N.........Clandeboye
Crechkin, L............Windsor

Page, N. A.............Brockville
Papish, A................Toronto
Parnell, H. M......St. Catharines
Parry, G. O.............Toronto
Patterson, J. A.........:..Walkers
Pauley, G. E..........Gananoque
Perkin, F. S.............Toronto
Philp, D. P.............Toronto
Philp, W. G.............Toronto
Polack, S. S.............Toronto
Price, C. K....:........·..Toronto
Pritchard, J. R., North Wakefield,
                              P.Q.

Radcliffe, E. J.:..........Toronto
Rahner, H. R....Rochester, N.Y.
Ranta, O. O.............Toronto
Rhodes, Miss G..Bergerville, P.Q.
Richer, Miss F....Lachute, P.Q.
Riddell, J. R............Newton
Robertson, Miss E. M.....Toronto
Robinson, A. J..........Toronto
Ross, A. C.............Kirkfield
Ross, J.............:....Toronto
Ross, J. W.............Stratford
Ross, S. G..............Toronto
Rowen, E. H............Guelph
Ruskin, S. H............Windsor

Sackin, I. J.............Toronto
St. John, H. F..........Uxbridge
Scott, J. F..............Barrie
Serles, H. R........Niagara Falls
Shaver, E. O............Toronto
Shaw, A. E............Bluevale
Shields, W. L..........Coboconk
Silverman, N............Kenora
Singleton, A. C.........Toronto
Slaughter, C. B. P.......Toronto

Smart, J. B.............Brockville
Smylie, C. H.........New Liskeard
Snell, G. C................Toronto
Snell, J. W...............Dutton
Snider, D. I.............Windsor
Spence, C. A.............Toronto
Spence, J. E...........Orangeville
Spratt, L. M..........Caledonia
Stone, A. L..........Hawkestone
Stone, W................Toronto
Streets, C. W.........Bridgeburg
Suffel, S. C.........Smith's Falls
Summerfeldt, Miss P. F...Toronto
Swan, D. C. S............Toronto
Switzer, W. A. W.....Science Hill
Symington, J. B......Camlachie

Taylor, O. L.............Bolton
Temes, J. H.............Toronto
Temes, S................Toronto
Teskey, L...............Toronto

Thomas, C. H............Forest
Torrance. A. M.........Listowel
Trimble, F. R............Cottam
Tufford, N. G........St. Thomas

Urquhart, J. L..........Uxbridge

Veale, W. T..........Bowanville
Volinsky, I. R...........Toronto

Walker, R. J........Smith's Falls
Walters, W. R............Toronto
Walton, G. R............Toronto
Watson, G. H........Port Credit
Wellwood, G. R....Richmond Hill
Wilson, W. H............Toronto
Wilson, W. S............Toronto
Wolseley, R. G.....Campbellville
Woodrow, W. H......Coldwater
Woolfson, J..........Toronto
Wright, F. W.........Tottenham

Young, Miss P. V....Peterborough

Fourth Year.

Allan, F. N.............Wroxeter
Anderson, J. O..........Toronto
Andrew, O..............Oakville
Appel, S...............Toronto
Armstrong, G. W.......Uxbridge

Balfe, T. H............Hamilton
Bates, J. E..............Toronto
Bell, E. C..............Stayner
Bell, J. W.............Harrow
Benson, J. G.........Wellington
Bicknell, E. A..........Toronto
Bird, E. S.............Ganaoque,
Bird, H. G...........Gananoque
Boley, J. P.........Huntsville
Bowyer, Miss M. E......Toronto
Boyes, T. L.............Hamilton
Bradley, B. V..........Toronto
Bryan, C. G............Toronto
Bull, R. C..............Weston
Burrows, Miss D. J....Harriston
Byers, J. W. R........Bailieboro

Carrow, G. W...........Toronto
Carruthers, W. L........Elmvale
Carson, R. A............Barrie
Case, G. E.........Dungannon
Cavanagh, J. L......Owen Sound
Chase, Miss L. A...Greenwich, N.S.
Chester, J. F. V........Toronto
Chung, Miss V.....Victoria, B.C.
Claridge, V. O......Grand Valley
Cleghorn, I. M.....Baldur, Man.

Clendenan, D. G........Toronto
Cosgrove, K. W.....Asheville, N.C.
Crowley, L. J............Gadshill
Cruickshank, F..........Weston
Cumming, J. F.......Turnerville

Danard, B. P.........Owen Sound
Dickson, J. A......Niagara Falls

Eisen, D................Toronto
Ellis, E. G.............Sarnia

Farquharson, R. F......Agincourt
Ferrier, C. W. G.........Mimico
Fine, H. P.............Toronto
Fleming, E. G...........Cobourg
Forrest, J. A...........Toronto
Francis, A......Vancouver, B.C.
Garratt, Miss G. C......Toronto
Gauld, W. H.....Tamsui, Formosa
Gill, D. G......Victoria Harbour
Gordon, H...Riversdale, S. Africa
Gordon, R. I...........Stratford
Graham, A. H...Denver, Colorado
Grainer, M..............Toronto
Gray, W. H..............Toronto
Green, N. H..........Agincourt
Grigg, V. S.........Bruce Mines

Hale, A. S..............Stratford
Hamill, F. C...........Meaford
Hamlin, L. E.........Kincardine
Harcourt, J. A. A........Cayuga

Hare, R. B.......Rosetown, Sask.
Harris, G. W.............Rodney
Hart, H................Omemee
Harvey, M. C.............Arthur
Harvey, W. H.........Princeton
Haskett, F. H...........Watford
Heard, K. M.........St. Thomas
Helston, G. E............Toronto
Hendry, J. R.............Toronto
Henry, C. R.............Drayton
Hetherington, H. W.
                    St. Catharines
Hewgill, J. C............Toronto
Hopkins, J. E........Stony Creek
Hubbard, J. P............Forest
Hutchison, J. H....Kinley, Sask.
Hutton, F. T.........St. Mary's

Ireland, F. A......St. Catherines
Ives, R. E.............Colborne

Jackson, J. L....Edmonton, Alta.
Jennings, G. H........Brantford
Jewell, R. M............Toronto
Johnston, J. H..........Kenora
Junkin, F. L............Toronto

Kilgour, A. J...........Cornwall
Kiteley, P............Glen Allan
Kreiner, J. H,.........Kitchener

Laing, W. C...........Brantford
Lancaster, W. E. G....Kingsville
Lang, R. S...............Orono
Lee, W. W..............Toronto
Lehrman, D.............Toronto
Linklater, E. W.........Wingham
Logan, H. D........Niagara Falls
Lowrie, R. J............Toronto

Mackersie, W. G........Atherley
Markowitz, C. A.........Toronto
Martin, C. A.........Milton West
Martin, G. G......Campbellford
Merifield, R. C.
                  Swift Current, Sask.
Merritt, E. G...........Chatham
Minns, J. E..............Tweed
Montgomery, S. R. P....Toronto
Morris, R. H....Middleton, N.S.
Mounce, A. R. E........Oshawa
Myers, F. C..........St. Mary's

McClelland, J. C......Brampton
McClure, R. B.
         Tsinan, Chantung, China
McClure, W. B........Brampton

McCormack, O. L.........Toronto
Macdonald, Miss F..Pinette, P.E.I.
McDonald, J. J. A........Orillia
McDonald, R. H.......Lakeside
MacDonald, W. G.......Toronto
MacFarlane, J. A...Nokomis, Sask.
McFaul, A. M......Collingwood
McGarry, J. R......Niagara Falls
McGarvah, A. W..,......Windsor
McLatchie, Miss L. D.
                    Calgary, Alta.
McLean, A. L............Toronto
McLellan, C.......Mount Forest

Nesbitt, Miss E....Hartshorn, Alta.
Nickle, F. J.............Malone
Nodwell, G. R......Grand Valley

Ogilvie, J. M............Toronto
O'Leary, F. J............Orillia

Palmer, W. S............Toronto
Pamphilon, W. M........Toronto
Patterson, F. R. C.........Perth
Perfect, F. R............Toronto
Phillips, H. S......Smith's Falls
Pollack, J...............Toronto
Pratt, R. S..............Laurel
Prendergast, D. J........Toronto

Riddell, W. R..........Beaverton
Robinson, P. J..........Toronto
Running, D. H........Agincourt
Russell, Miss M. P.......Toronto

Sansone, A. J..........Hamilton
Sarvis, E. S......Bindloss, Alta.
Scott, H. R...........Maxville
Shaul, N................Toronto
Shaul, S................Toronto
Shaw, Miss V. A........Windsor
Shier, L. V.............Toronto
Shoniker, H. J..........Toronto
Sievenpiper, S. H.......Toronto
Simpson, R. N.........Thornhill
Sinclair, K. Y...........Toronto
Skinner, H. A. L.........Guelph
Skipper, S. C..........Kingsville
Smith, C. G........Sydney, N.S.
Speck, J. T.............Toronto
Speers, Miss F. E.......Toronto
Stanley, A. M...........Lucan.
Stephens, R. W.........Wiarton
Stoddart, W. O........Woodville
Sullivan, O. P...........Orillia

Taylor, R. E.........Woodstock
Templin, Miss M. I.......Fergus

Thomas, M. E. . . . . .Toronto
Thompson, A. A..Penetanguishene
Tom, Miss M. I. . . . . .Goderich
Trapp, Miss D. M.
New Westminster, B.C.
Truscott, R. S. . . . . .Hamilton
Tucker, W. L. . . . . .St. Thomas

Underhill, F. W. . . . . .Aurora

Watson, M. C. . . . . .Bolton
Weir, N. A. . . . . .Toronto
Wells, J. G. . . . . .Rutland, Sask.
Wellwood, M. B. . .Richmond Hill
Wigle, D. St. J. . . . . .Windsor
Williams, C. V. . . . . .Toronto
Wilson, W. . . . . .Toronto
Wrong, H. A. . . . . .Aylmer

Fifth Year.

Anderson, A. L. . . .Saskatoon, Sask.
Armstrong, A. G. . . . . .Warkworth

Atwell, W. C. . . . . .Toronto
Ayer, Mrs. I. T. . . . Okotoks, Alta.

Bartley, Miss K. M. . . . . . .Toronto
Bastow, D. C. . . . . .Toronto
Bird, G. L. . . . . .Brighton
Birrell, R. G. . . . . .Pinkerton
Blatz, W. E. . . . . .Hamilton
Blye, R. A. . . . . .Trenton

Brady, H. A. . . . . .Toronto
Bromley, A. J. . . . . .Toronto
Brown, Miss C. A. . . . . . . .Toronto
Bulmer, F. M. R. . . . . .Toronto
Bulmer, H. R. . . . . .Toronto

Campbell, F. C. . . . . .Hepworth
Carlisle, A. M. . . . . .Peterborough
Chambers, G. L. . . . . .Toronto
Charteris, W. F. . . . . .Chatham
Clark, H. G. . . . . .Toronto
Crehan, W. H. . . . . .Calgary, Alta.
Cryderman, W. J. . . .Niagara Falls

Dales, M. G. . . . . .Drayton
Danby, S. L. E. . . . . .Ottawa
Danis, J. T. . . . . .Ottawa
Dawson, L. E. . . . . .Toronto
Dollar, G. L. . . . . .Toronto
Dow, W. W. . . . . .Toronto
Doyle, R. H. . . . . .Toronto
Duncan, W. S. . . . . .Port Credit

Eadie, G. S. . . . . .Toronto
Edmonds, W. B. . . . . .Toronto
Edwards, J. C. R. . . . . .Cannington
Ellis, E. W. . . . . .Torono
Ewart, E. W. . . . . .Bolton

Feader, F. N.   Toronto
Ferguson, J. S. . . . . .Chatham
Folinsbee, Miss M. E. . . . . .Toronto
Fraser, G. M. . . . . .Toronto
—44

Gallaugher, L. C. . . . . .Lisle
Gillrie, R. B. . . . . .Drayton
Glasgow, G. K. . . . . . .Tupperville
Glassberg-Volpe, A. . . . . . .Toronto
Gordon, A. C. . . . . .Toronto
Grady, Miss L. R. . . . .Peterborough
Graham, J. A. . . . . .Toronto
Green, C. O. P. . . . . . .Port Hope

Hain, G. R. . . . . .Toronto
Harris, C. W. . . . . .Toronto
Harrison, Miss E. D. . . . . .Toronto
Hepburn, J. . . . . . .Vancouver, B.C.
Hill, C. E. . . . . .Richmond Hill
Hobson, W. J. . . . . .Milford
Hopkins, H. E. . . . . .Toronto

Johnston, H. W. . . . . .Drayton

Kilborn, L. G.
Chengtu, Szechwan, China

Latchford, J. K. . . . . .Toronto
Laughlin, E. R. . . . . .Belleville
Lehman, E. J. . . . . .North Bay
Lee, P. A. . . . . .Kingsville
Linton, J. A. . . . . .Belle River

Malcolmson, A. S..St. Catharines
Mallin, D. . . . . .Toronto
Martin, A. D. . . . . . . .St. Mary's
Martin, R. C. . . . . .Newburgh
Mayne, C. H. . . . . .Drayton
Middleton, R. H. . . . . . .Caledonia
Mills, O. G. . . . . .Tottenham
Mitchell, N. H. . . . . .Hamilton
Moffat, W. W. . . . . .Teeswater
Moon, H. R. . . . . .Sydenham

Montgomery, R. C. . . . . .Harriston
Mooney, Miss A. M.
Grand Coulee, Sask.
Morris, N. D. . . . . .Orillia
Murray, D. W. G. . . . . . .St. Paul's
Murray, J. K. P. . . . . .Toronto

McCart, H. W. D........Toronto
McCarter, A. B....Dawson, Y.T.
McCorvie, C. R........Chatham
McDonald, J. G. L.
　　　　　　　　Little Current
Macdonald, J. H. A......London
McGarry, J. M......Niagara Falls
McHugh, M. J...........Orillia
McKenzie, W. L.........Toronto
McKinnon, N. E........Toronto
McLeod, J. H.
　Kingstown, St. Vincent, B. W. I.
Macnamara, H. O........Toronto
McPherson, R. J...........Galt
MacQueen, M. D.........Comber

McQuitty, M...........Douglas

Newhouse, J. A........Snelgrove
Noonan, W. T......Mount Forest

O'Brien, J. M.........Erinsville

Pedley, W. H........Woodstock
Pennock, G. M..........Ottawa
Phillips, T. G. W........Toronto
Price, Miss R......Libau, Russia

Ratz, R. G.............Toronto
Richardson, R. N. C.....Toronto
Ruskin, I. W...........Windsor

Sauder, P.........Richmond Hill
Seymour, R. A.....Vancouver, B.C
Sheppard, R. J........Queenston

Shunk, E. S. M.........Toronto
Slocombe, G. W......Port Dover
Smylie, R. T......New Liskeard
Sneath, P. A. T..........Toronto

Stover, I...............Chatham
Sutherland, J. L....St. Catharines
Swan, W. D...........Brucefield
Switzer, J. W.........St. Mary's

Thompson, I. B..........Harrow
Thomson, Miss A. E.
　　　　　　　　Yonkers, N.Y.
Tice, J. W.............Oshawa
Tipping, C. E...........Toronto
Trackman, J. A..........Toronto
Turnbull, A............Canfield

Van Wart, A. F...Fredericton, N.B.

Walden, A. P............Guelph
Walters, A. G......Niagara Falls
Walwyn, W. M.........Meaford
Watson, C. H............Bolton
Watson, G. F...........Elmira
Weissgerber, L. A.
　　　　　　Nielson, Montana, U.S.
Wilkinson, F. W.........Toronto
Williams, Miss M. M.....Beeton
Williamson, Miss A. B....Toronto
Wilson, F. H..........Stouffville
Wladowsky, Miss M.....Toronto
Woodhouse, W. W...Niagara Falls

Zwick, F. F.............Stirling

POST GRADUATE STUDENTS.

Archibald, M. G., M.D., C.M.........................Kamloops, B.C.
Birks, W. H., M.D..........................Chungchow, West China
Burris, H. L., M.B...............................Kamloops, B.C.
Hogg, A., M.D., C.M...............................Chefoo, China
Rogers, K. F., M.D..................................Toronto
Simpson, E. K., M.D.........................Junghsien, West China
Speers, Ada B., M.B..........................Chengtu, West China

DIPLOMA OF PUBLIC HEALTH STUDENTS.

Berry, E. G., M.B...Toronto
Cruickshank, H. L., M.B....................................Toronto
Fraser, D. T., B.A., M.B..........................York Mills, Ont.
Graham, W. A., M.B...Toronto
Hazelwood, J. F., M.B......................................Toronto
Jackson, G. P., M.B..Toronto
McClenahan, R. R., B.A., M.B...............................Toronto
Naismith, A. G., M.B........................Straffordville, Ont.
Phair, J. T., M.B..Toronto
Wodehouse, R. E., M.D., C.M................................Toronto
Woodhouse, Catharine F., B.A., M.B.........................Toronto

OCCASIONAL STUDENTS.

Bowie, D. J.......................................Midland, Ont.
Fielding, E. M. V............................Niagara Falls, Ont.
Mahoney, F. O..Toronto

Summary.

First Year Students.............................   208
Second Year, Five Year Course Students...........   212
Second Year, Six Year Course Students............   148
Third Year Students..............................   233
Fourth Year Students.............................   174
Fifth Year Students..............................   131
Post Graduate Students...........................   7
Diploma of Public Health Students................   11
Occasional Students..............................   3

                                                   1,127

FACULTY OF APPLIED SCIENCE.

REGISTER OF STUDENTS, 1920-1921.

First Year.

1 Adams, H. C. . . . . Lindsay
2 Adamson, J. C. . . Lambton Mills
6 Agnew, E. A. . . . . Toronto
7 Almond, J. R. . . . . Toronto
7 Archibald, T. A. . . . . . Woodstock
6 Armstrong, G. C. . . . . Warkworth
6 Baker, H. N. . . . . Toronto
6 Barbour, A. D.   . . . . Toronto
7 Barley, E. B. . . . . Toronto
6 Barrett, H. A. . . . . . Collingwood
7 Baxter, L. H. . . . . Drumbo
7 Baxter, W. J. F. . . Niagara Falls
7 Beaman, A. E. . . . . . North Gower
2 Beattie, J. . . . . Galt
7 Becker, W. A. . . . . . . St. Thomas
3 Bell, J. W. . . . . Corunna
3 Bell, W. T. A. : . . . . . Thornbury
3 Boake, W. R. . . . . Toronto
1 Boswell, F. B. . . . . Toronto
3 Boyes, J. W. . . . . Hamilton
3 Brittain, C. L. . . . . Toronto
2 Browne, L. M. . . . . Toronto
6 Buck, L. G. . . . . Brantford
7 Burbank, J. D. . . . . Toronto
6 Buschlen, H. C. . . . . . Port Elgin
7 Cameron, G. D. W. . . Peterboro
7 Campbell, L. De V. . . . . King
7 Capel, A. J. . . . . Collingwood
4 Carswell, W. E. . . . . Toronto
3 Catto, C. E. . . . . York Mills
1 Chadwick, A. R. . . . . . . Toronto
1 Chaffe, R. S. S. . . . . . . Waterdown
1 Chambers, H. J. A. . . . . . Toronto
2 Chowen, W. R. . . . . Clinton
6 Christman, C. W. . . . . . . Windsor
6 Chute, G. M. . . . . Toronto
7 Clark, H. S. . . . : . . . . . . Toronto
7 Clark, W. H. D. . . . . Toronto
4 Coleman, E. M. . . . . . North Bay
1 Collison, L. S. . . . . . Leamington
2 Colman, A. R. . . . . Toronto
6 Conners, W. M. . . . . Smiths Falls
1 Connolly, H. J. . . . . Toronto
2 Cooper, W. C. . . . . : Clinton
3 Cowan, W. R. . . . . Toronto
1 Crane, A. . . . . Aylmer
3 Crossgrove, G. M. . . Copper Cliff
6 Davidson, P. C. . . . . Toronto
3 Davis, C. R. . . . . Welland
7 Davis, F. . Valleyfield, B.B., Nfld.
4 Deacon, P. A. . . . . Toronto
7 Dean, G. F. . . . . Toronto

7 DeCou, D. D. . . . . . . Strathroy
3 Dill, R. H. . . . . Nelson, B.C.
1 Dillane, C. W. . . . . . Kemptville
6 Dow, J. A. . . . . Toronto
1 Drummond, C. H. P. . . . . Toronto
3 Drummond, J. M. E. . . Toronto
3 Dymond, J. M. . . . . Toronto
3 Elder, J. G. . . . . Toronto
7 Elliott, W. K. . . . . . St. Thomas
1 Emerson, T. R. . . . . Toronto
8 Enushevsky, M. I. . . . . Toronto
7 Findlater, J. R. . . . . Ayr
4 Finlay, W. E. . . . . Norwood
7 Firth, H. E. . . . . Orangeville
6 Forward, F. A. . . . . Ottawa
3 Gannon, L. J. . . . . Ottawa
6 Gilmore, L. E. . . . . Toronto
3 Goldstein, A. . : . . . . Toronto
7 Good, E. F. . . . . Blair
6 Gordon, R. A. . . . . Wallaceburg
2 Grabill, D. L. . . . . Toronto
3 Graham, T. C. G. . . . Inglewood
7 Greenwood, A. H. . . . Palmerston
7 Grenzebach, S. L. . . . Woodstock
2 Griffin, K. . . . . Toronto
4 Haggans, H. H. . . . . Toronto
3 Hamilton, F. W. . . . . . Hamilton
6 Hammond, H. J. . . . . . . Toronto
1 Hardcastle, S. . . . . Toronto
1 Harman, W. J. . . . . Zephyr
7 Hawkins, R. M. . . . . . . Exeter
1 Hazell, H. F. . . . . Hamilton
7 Hendershott, R. W. . . Kingsville
1 Henderson, G. G. . . . . . . Toronto
7 Heyland, K. V. . . . . Toronto
1 Hill, A. J. . . . . Toronto
1 Ings, J. H. . . . . Toronto
6 Jackson, L. C. . . . . Brussels
7 Jackson, T. W. . . . . Toronto
4 Johnson, J. A. . . . . Toronto
3 Keefer, R. H. . . . . Toronto
3 Kellough, J. Y. . . . . Almonte
6 Kerr, R. S. . . . . Toronto
3 Kerr, R. B. . . . . Brantford
6 Kilmer, G. E. . . . . . Southampton
1 Kingston, T. M. S. . . . . . Toronto
1 Laine, D. . . . . Toronto
2 Lang, H. O. . . . . Toronto
6 Langton, J. M. . . . . Toronto
7 Laurie, R. M. . . . . Hamilton
3 Lavender, F. J. . . . . Dundas
4 Lawson, A. W. P. . . . . . Leaside

6 Lindsay, T..............Weston
7 Little, E. M.....Iroquois Falls
6 Littlejohn, E..........Toronto
7 Lowry, C. A.......Bridgeburg
6 Lowry, E. F..........Listowel
3 MacEwen, B. P.....Craik, Sask.
3 MacKendrick, D. E.....Toronto
3 MacLeod, M. P. ∘......Toronto
1 MacQuarrie, E. M.
      Sault Ste. Marie
1 MacQuarrie, J. D......Merlin
3 Mason, H. R..........Toronto
1 Matson, B. C..........Toronto
3 Maus, J. H...........Paris
3 McAndless, F. W.....Ilderton
7 McDowell, W. O.......Toronto
3 McIntosh, H. A....Port Arthur
7 McKenzie, B. J......Wawanesa
2 McKenzie, J..........Toronto
7 McKillop, V. A.....West Lorne
2 McLean, D. J...........London
6 McVicker, P..........Toronto
7 Millikin, G. I.........Midland
7 Mitchell, J. H..........Toronto
7 Moffatt, B. F..........Weston
7 Moon, A. M..........Wiarton
1 Mueller, E. K.......Hamilton
7 Muirhaed, S. R...Regina Sask.
3 Noonan, W. H..........Toronto
7 Norman, R. M. ....Galt
3 Osbourne, W. A.
  Ramelton, Co. Donegal,Ireland
4 Palmer, G. V..........Toronto
7 Patience, A. M........Toronto
7 Pedder, J. F.......Trout Creek
6 Petry, H. H.........Port Hope
1 Pickford, G. S..........Toronto
7 Pike, J. G..........Todmorden
8 Piper, R. L.......Calgary, Alta.
3 Pugsley, H. J........Kitchener
7 Ratcliffe, L. C........Oshawa
3 Rattle, C. H...........Milliken
7 Reid, W. J. H....Cardale, Man.
3 Robertson, G. D.....Petrolea
7 Robinson, F. H........Toronto
3 Rowat, G. H..........Toronto

6 Rowland, S. A....Mount Albert
3 Rugg, H...............Toronto
7 Rumble, G............Hillsdale
6 Russell, N. E..........Toronto
1 Sabiston, G. P.....Owen Sound
7 Samuel, N. M..........Toronto
8 Saunders, T. D........Toronto
1 Sharpe, C. T..........Toronto
3 Shibley, L. K.......Haileybury
7 Shields, S..........Ft. William
7 Simpson, W. C.......Elmvale
7 Sirrs, R. R............Toronto
7 Smart, G. W..........Toronto
7 Smith, J. D..........Pt. Hope
7 Smith, V. G..........Toronto
4 Smyth, A. R..........Toronto
3 Sneyd, C. S...........Preston
7 Sorby, W. O...........Guelph
1 Story, C. A.........Morrisburg
3 Strickland, V. D.....Hamilton
4 Sullivan, F. G.........Toronto
7 Switzer, R. H.........Toronto
3 Take, P. H........Orangeville
3 Taniyama, S..Hososhenia, Japan
7 Taylor, J. C..........Toronto
7 Tomlinson, G. K........Simcoe
7 Tomsinsky, W.........Toronto
7 Turner, H. E........Brantford
7 Vanderburgh, W. A.
      Richmond Hill
7 Voaden, G. H.....St. Thomas
3 Wagner, J. F.......Kitchener
7 Waite, G. G.........Colborne
3 Wales, C. C...........Toronto
6 Walton, W. W.........Toronto
7 Wanless, G. A........Windsor
6 Watson, W. W.......Pt. Hope
2 Wheatley, W. P.......Toronto
3 Wilford, J. R........Lindsay
6 Willard, M. V.........Toronto
2 Williams, C. S........Toronto
3 Williams, J. A.........Toronto
1 Wilson, F. E..........Toronto
6 Woodburn, C..........Toronto
6 Yeats, F. B..........Stirling
6 Young, C. M..........Toronto

Second Year.

1 Abernethy, W. W......Beeton
3 Acres, W. P..........Toronto
3 Albertson, R. G...Niagara Falls
3 Anderson, E. B.......Lindsay
2 Anderson, W. St. C...Oil Springs
1 Baird, E. L...........Toronto
1 Baird, E. M.....Scarboro Jct.
7 Baird, H. P...........Toronto

1 Ball, F. C..............London
7 Barbour, Miss J. E.....Meaford
7 Bateman, J. W.........Tweed
7 Beckett, R. W.......Hamilton
3 Bedford, H. F.........Toronto
3 Bedford, P. S..........Toronto
1 Beecroft, G. W........Toronto
7 Beger, A. R......New Hamburg

6	Begg, E. M............Toronto	2	Duncan, G. G.........Toronto
6	Bell, A. A.............Toronto	1	Dunlop, C......Saskatoon, Sask.
7	Bell, H. B........Georgetown	2	Dunlop, P. J.........Pembroke
1	Bennett, W. E.........Ottawa	3	Dyer, J. W...........Goderich
6	Berner, G. T..........Toronto	1	Earle, M. D...........Toronto
3	Blackburn, R. G..Regina, Sask.	6	Edwards, P. S.....Buffalo, N.Y.
3	Boake, V. E...........Toronto	7	Elliott, F. W..........Toronto
6	Bonham, L. J...........Dutton	7	Ellis, F. A.*..........Toronto
3	Booz, F. B............Toronto	1	Erwin, R. B........Waterford
2	Bowyer, C. M..........Simcoe	7	Evans, M. G..........Toronto
2	Boyd, O. H...........Toronto	6	Ewing, C. W..........Toronto
3	Boyle, G. E......Pt. Colborne	3	Fairbairn, R. A........Toronto
7	Bruels, C. P.........Belhaven	7	Fardoe, H. R....Brandon, Man.
4	Brown, F. B..........Toronto	7	Faris, E. M. ....Aurora
7	Brown, R. J............Acton	3	Farley, J............Toronto
7	Browne, J. H......Haileybury	2	Farncomb, H. L......Trenton
6	Bruce, V. N..........Toronto	7	Fawcett, W. W.....Hamills Pt.
6	Buchan, J. E...........Sarnia	7	Ferrier, W. G. ......Markham
2	Bull, W. J............Weston	7	Fiddes, G. H.......Elmwood
7	Bunting, W. R...St. Catharines	7	Finley, R. A..........Meaford
7	Burke, J. P...........Ottawa	6	Fitzgerald, A. D.....Lakefield
3	Butler, F............Toronto	3	Forster, I. H..........Toronto
7	Butter, R............Ancaster	7	Franks, S. T......Regina, Sask.
3	Button, E. W............Galt	3	Fraser, J. M..........Aurora
1	Byram, A. T..........Toronto	2	French, H. E........Midland
7	Cain, L. A...........Toronto	7	Galbraith, R. A. H......Toronto
6	Campbell, L. S........Toronto	7	Gardner, L. S........Windsor
7	Campbell, T. L.......Elmvale	7	Garrow, K. A. C....Chesterville
3	Carew, A. W.........Lindsay	7	Gillmor, J..........North Bay
3	Carley, F. C..........Consecon	7	Gillmor, T..........North Bay
6	Carnahan, E. H...Campbellford	4	Givens, H. F.........Beaverton
1	Carp, M..............Toronto	3	Goldie, J. E.
7	Carr, W. H...........Barrie		North Vancouver, B.C.
1	Carruthers, V. H. H.	6	Graham, H. F....:.Owen Sound
	Foremost, Alta.	1	Graham, H. J.......Brampton
6	Carson, C. T.......Oakville	6	Grant, N. S........Stratford
7	Carson, R. W.........Toronto	7	Gray, A. S...........Toronto
4	Catto, D. E...........Toronto	2	Gray, K. C.........Coldwater
7	Chadwick, N. B........Toronto	6	Greey, S. M..........Toronto
8	Chambers, A. J........Toronto	1	Griesbach, R. J.....Collingwood
3	Chambers, F. W..Hamiota, Man.	7	Guenther, W. F.....Brantford
1	Church, J. A......Smiths Falls	6	Hamilton, K. C..........Galt
7	Churchill, T. C. D.....Toronto	3	Hanning, J. R.........Preston
1	Clappison, H. G.....Hamilton	6	Harston, J. C.........Toronto
2	Cockshutt, C. F.....Brantford	1	Hawkins, W. J. H.....Islington
8	Cohoe, J. E...........Welland	1	Hayman, H. L.........London
7	Colter, J. L...........Petrolea	7	Hayward, A. E........Toronto
6	Conklin, A. N.........Toronto	7	Hepburn, D......Milton West
6	Coulter, H. J.........Windsor	6	Hewgill, R...........Toronto
3	Cowan, E..........Pt. Arthur	1	Higbee, J. C..........Toronto
4	Crawford, A. S.......Hamilton	1	Hitchon, L. E......Brantford
3	Crowe, G. F.......Truro, N.S.	7	Howell, D. R..........Toronto
7	Doherty, A. H........Meaford	3	Hueston, R. M....:...Ingersoll
6	Duffill, W. H.........Toronto	8	Huggins, F. W........Toronto
8	Drummond, P. R......Toronto	7	Ickler, C. H...........Chesley
2	Dumbrille, J. C....Kemptville	7	Inglis, J. G...........Atwood
2	Dunbar, W. R.........Ethel	8	Ironside, J. G.........Simcoe

1 Irwin, K. W...........Oshawa
3 Ives, V. E...........Colborne
1 Jackson, C. H..........Toronto
6 Jackson, H. A.........Ilderton
7 Jackson, W. C......Port Perry
7 Jaques, C. A.........Woodstock
3 Jennings, W. B..........Sarnia
3 Jewett, W. D..........Toronto
1 Johnson, J. L............Arthur
7 Johnson, N. F............King
7 Johnston, A. M...St. Catharines
7 Johnston, D...........Guelph
3 Johnston, J. G.........Toronto
6 Johnston, O. D...Billings Bridge
1 Joy, C. B............Toronto
6 Kay, G. F............Toronto
3 Keenleyside, H. B......London
1 Keith, W. H........Newmarket
3 Kelly, F. R..........Lindsay
1 Kelly, M. C........Hamilton
3 Kennedy, H. L.........Parkhill
3 Kennedy, W. M........Toronto
1 Kenney, W. E....Pt. Maitland
7 Kent, W. H.........Hamilton
6 Kesteven-Balshaw, H...Toronto
6 Kinsman, D. A.........Toronto
3 Kischel, G. H.........Toronto
6 Kramer, H. O.....Humberstone
7 Lappin, W. D..........Toronto
1 Langlois, W. L........Toronto
7 Laurie, W. L.........Agincourt
7 Lawton, F. L..........Toronto
1 Learoyd, E. S.........Scarboro
6 Lebeau, A. M.....Calgary, Alta.
1 Leslie, R. C...........Swansea
1 Lewis, C. E...........Toronto
3 Lindsay, G. E..........Toronto
2 Logan, H. J..........Dunnville
3 Longworthy, W. O..Regina, Sask.
6 Low, R. St. C:.........Toronto
7 Lucas, C. H..........Toronto
2 Lyle, F. J..........Brantford
2 Lyle, V. B..........Peterboro
1 Lyons, R. T..........Toronto
6 MacBeth, D...........Toronto
6 MacDougall, H. A.....Toronto
3 MacKendrick, J. N......Galt
1 Mackenzie, W. J..Port Robinson
7 Macklin, W. H........Milliken
7 MacLellan, J.......Claremont
1 Macqueen, C. B.......Toronto
6 Maedel, H. C.........Norwich
4 Magee, J. G...........London
2 Maguire, W. S.........Toronto
1 Martin, G. A..........Toronto
7 Martyn, E. R.........Ripley
1 McAllister, D. G.......Toronto

6 McBride, E. W.:......Toronto
7 McBroom, H. E........Toronto
6 McBurney, W. G..Niagara Falls
7 McCabe, R. H.....Tottenham
6 McClellan, G. E..Vancouver B.C.
3 McCrae, G. W.........Lindsay
3 McCulloch, H. L.........Galt
1 McIntosh, D. N.......Simcoe
6 McIntosh, J. H....Victoria B.C.
4 McIntyre, H. A........Toronto
1 McIntyre, V. H.......Toronto
1 McKay, H. A........Seaforth
7 McKenzie, H. B.......Toronto
1 McLelland, W. J.....Hamilton
3 McMahon, T. J......Maitland
2 McMaster, J. A......Toronto
6 McMillan, R. J......Stratford
3 McMullen, A. W......Toronto
8 McMurrich, J. R......Toronto
7 McQueen, A. W. F....Nottawa
6 McQueen, M. V.......Toronto
7 Meikle, M............Midland
3 Menendez, C. G...
           Nassau, Bahamas
6 Meredith, H. J..Vancouver, B.C.
7 Miller, W. H............Galt
7 Miller, W. L...Lawrence Station
7 Mills, C. A.........Orangeville
3 Monkman, F. C.....Brampton
7 Moon, G. D........Port Hope
1 Morris, H. M.........Petrolea
8 Morris, R. V.........Toronto
7 Morrish, J. S....Highland Creek
2 Morrison, R. G. K.
           Edmonton, Alta.
2 Morton, C. O.........Toronto
7 Morwick, E. I.......Jerseyville
1 Moss, F. W..........Toronto
7 Murphy, F. A........Wardsville
6 Murphy, G. H...New York, N.Y.
6 Murray, C. A.
     Costra Rica, Central America
3 Murray, J. R..........Toronto
1 Murtha, L. J.........Lindsay
8 Mutch, G. C..........Toronto
7 Nablo, H. W..........Cayuga
7 Nahrgang, A. R..New Hamburg
7 Nattress, D. I...Sault Ste. Marie
2 Nethercott, F. A......Stratford
1 Nettleton, C. A........Toronto
6 Norman, R. E.........Toronto
1 Norris, C. A...........Toronto
4 Oldford, R..Musgravetown Nfld.
6 Oliver, C. W...........Belton
8 O'Shaughnessy, T. J.....Cobalt
7 Paget, J. A.........Huntsville
6 Parrett, A. E. J.......Toronto

6 Parrett, R. E..........Toronto
3 Plewes, R. V............Sarnia
3 Potvin, L. J...........Ottawa
7 Pôrter, W. J..........Powassan
6 Price, L. M........St. Thomas
6 Pritchard, H. S.........Toronto
3 Purvis, W. F...........Toronto
7 Ratz, H. W......New Hamburg
1 Reid, A. M............Toronto
6 Relyea, R. C..........Cornwall
6 Robertson, G. H.......Toronto
6 Robertson, H. F......Brantford
2 Robson, W. T..........Toronto
7 Rogers, E. S...........Toronto
3 Rolph, E. G...........Toronto
7 Romm, N.............Toronto
1 Rose, A. A.........Ailsa Craig
1 Rose, H. G...........Ottawa
4 Ross, D. M. M........Toronto
7 Rossiter, R. E...Sault Ste. Marie
7 Ruby, E. A.........Kitchener
7 Rundle, W. L..........Dundalk
2 Russell, W. J.........Unionville
1 Sanders, F. W.......Stouffville
3 Schinbein, E. E......Conestogo
1 Schultz, F. H.......Brantford
7 Scott, F. A..........Orangeville
7 Scott, G. D........Claremont
6 Seaborne, F. S.........Toronto
4 Seeli, E. S. S............Lucan
6 Shaffer, B...........Welland
7 Sharp, R. A...........Sudbury
1 Siddall, K. C........Islington
3 Simson, F. T...........Toronto
1 Smith, G. W...........Weston
1 Smith, J. M...........Durham
6 Smye, G. R..............Galt
7 Snow, R. B. L.......Juddhaven
6 Snyder, A. L..........Toronto

4 Sproatt, C. B. ....Toronto
7 Stevens, E. C...........Toronto
3 Stevenson, H. J........Toronto
2 Stewart, H. E....Montreal, Que.
7 Stewart, W. D.........Toronto
1 Stokes, L. F...........Sombra
7 Story, R. A..........Claremont
3 Stott, F. W........St. Thomas
6 Stuart, A. F..........Ottawa
3 Strudley, D. B.......Stratford
8 Thomson, G. A........Toronto
7 Thomson, G. A......Agincourt
3 Timmins, W. W. ......Toronto
6 Tofflemire, R. H......Windsor
2 Tomlinson, F. C......Langstaff
3 Tuckey, F. E.....Victoria, B.C.
6 Turner, J. W........Craighurst
6 Upper, F. A.....Niagara Falls
6 Veals, R. C............Toronto
7 Vernon, A............Toronto
6 Wade, C. A. G........Grimsby
7 Walker, S. W.......Streetsville
1 Walker, W. H........Stratford
1 Walks, J. D..........Chesley
6 Ward, N. F..........Hamilton
6 Warren, A. R.........Hespeler
3 Wells, C. M..........Toronto
1 Welsh, D. T.........Hamilton
7 West, G. R........Northwood
7 White, W. A.........Toronto
3 Whiteside, J. J....Little Brittain
7 Wilkinson, G. I.....Wallenstein
6 Williams, B. I.........London
2 Williams, W. F......Markham
3 Wingfield, H. E......Dunnville
7 Wolsey, M............Toronto
7 Wright, W. E.....Cadogan, Alta.
6 Zadnoff, M...........Toronto

Third Year.

3 Ahara, E. V...........Toronto
1 Anderson, A. M.......Toronto
1 Archibald ,S. W.......Seaforth
3 Armstrong, E. F.......Iroquois
1 Ashcroft, C. C......York Mills
1 Aykroyd, G. C.......Toronto
7 Benson, W. R.........Toronto
7 Bishop, W. V.......Kimberley
6 Bongard, G. R........Toronto
6 Breithaupt, C. L.....Kitchener
6 Broughall, G. M.......Toronto
2 Brown, E. L..........Toronto
7 Bryant, G. F........Midland
7 Burns, D...........Brantford

3 Bysshe, H. A.
         Springfield, Vermont
6 Campbell, W. A.......Toronto
1 Carruthers, K. L......Toronto
6 Carslake, C. H........Toronto
6 Chantler, H. McD...Mt. Dennsi
1 Chater, W. N.........Toronto
1 Clairmont, W. L....Gravenhurst
2 Clarke, A. R..........Toronto
1 Clarke, T............Toronto
1 Cockerline, E. W......Toronto
7 Coles, F. B..........Brantford
2 Coo, C. W............Toronto
1 Cook, R. H. B.........Aurora

7 Coulter, S. L..........Windsor
6 Crawford, J. J..........Toronto
6 Day, G. A..............Guelph
6 Dignam, H. M.........Toronto
6 Dilworth, H. M........Toronto
1 Dougall, C. H.........Hamilton
7 Doran, J.Y............Toronto
2 Drybrough, J..........Sudbury
3 Dunbar, P. G........St. Thomas
7 Duncan, W. C. C......Toronto
3 Dunn, E. A............Chatham
3 Elliott, W. B.....St. Catharines
3 Evans, G. F...........Bradford
3 Evans, M. M..........Bradford
6 Everest, T. E..........Toronto
3 Everson, S. F...........Oshawa
6 Fair, A. E. H..........Midland
7 Fenwick, J. R..........Toronto
7 Fitzgerald, W. W.......Toronto
1 Foley, W. ....Ottawa
6 Fotheringham, D. T....Toronto
1 Fry, C................Chesley
7 Fuller, G. B............Arkona
3 Gardner, J. W........Hamilton
1 Gibbs, J. W. S.......Kincardine
1 Glover, T. S....Hessle, England
7 Goodwin, J. E..........Toronto
6 Grant, W. J...........Toronto
6 Gray, F. M............Toronto
3 Greig, A. K...........Toronto
7 Graves, H. P..........London
1 Guscott, A. G..........Toronto
6 Haldenby, C. N........Toronto
6 Hamilton, C...........Toronto
3 Harlow, R. H..........Toronto
1 Hayman, H. G.........Toronto
6 Heatley, A. H........Brampton
2 Heisey, K. B.........Markham
3 Helliwell, A. L..........Toronto
4 Helme, J. B........Smiths Falls
2 Henry, R. J..........Grimsby
3 Henry, S. W..........Stratford
7 Houston, F. C. A.......Toronto
7 Howden, H. E.........Caledonia
3 Hume, A. G...........Toronto
6 Johnson, A.............Orillia
7 Johnston, B. H........Toronto
7 Johnston, J. W........Uxbridge
6 Kay, J. A. C.........Stratford
3 Kerr, H. H...........Seaforth
3 Kirkconnell, H. R.....Lindsay
3 Kirkconnell, J. R......Lindsay
2 Lawson, H. H.........Toronto
2 La Ronde, H. J.......Toronto
7 Langford, J. A....Calgary, Alta.
7 Lidkea, H. J.........North Bay
1 Little, A. M. ....Toronto

6 Lindsay, A........Dover Centre
3 MacAllister, J. S. E.....Toronto
2 Mackle, W. P..........Toronto
8 Mallett, G. S..........Toronto
7 Mayberry, J. S.......Stratford
1 McClintock, G. A.
          St. Andrews East, Quebec
1 McGrath, R. J........Toronto
7 McHaffie, R. P..Nokomis, Sask.
6 McKeown, C. J. W..Mono Road
6 McLaughlin, R. R......Toronto
7 McLean, G. E......Thornbury
1 McMurtry, L. C.......London
2 McNiven, J. G..........Acton
8 Mellish, A. H.........Brantford
6 Meyer, H. B.........Brantford
7 Miller, B. H..........Stouffville
7 Milne, J. W..........Toronto
7 Montemurro, M. M..North Bay
6 Moor, H. H...........Toronto
6 Mueller, H. H.........Toronto
3 Mummery, C. R.....Hamilton
3 Murphy, A. R.......Wardsville
1 Nash, A. L. S.......Dunnville
4 Norcross, M. A.
              Lennoxville, Que.
4 Noxon, K. F...........Toronto
2 Oaks, H. A.............Preston
3 Park, R..............Hamilton
6 Parker, R. E........Tavistock
6 Parker, R. R..........Stirling
1 Paul, R. J..........Sunderland
3 Pearce, W. R..........Toronto
6 Pearen, C. B..........Toronto
2 Perry, J. C...........Uxbridge
7 Philip, E. B..........Islington
3 Philp, H. J...........Nestleton
1 Pollock, F. J..........Almonte
1 Powell, H. R....Grenfell, Sas.
3 Powell, M. V........Petreboro
1 Pratt, D. L..........Midland
1 Ramsay, W. B...Lumsden, Sask.
6 Reynolds, H..........Toronto
6 Richardson, W. R........Essex
7 Ridout, G. S......Montreal, Que.
8 Robertson, W. G....Palmerston
2 Robinson, L. J.........Toronto
7 Rosebrugh, D. W......Toronto
7 Ross, M. D..........Chatham
7 Ruddy, T. F.........Brantford
3 Sanderson, A. C........Toronto
7 Scadding, S. C.....Humber Bay
6 Schemnitz, D. A........Toronto
6 Sherk, W. S..........Sherkston
7 Shockley, H. M.
              Prince Rupert, B.C.
7 Smillie, S. S...........Toronto

6 Spence, F. S...........Toronto
7 Spotton, J. G...........Guelph
1 Stewart, M. D:.........Toronto
3 Stewart, V.....Milestone, Sask.
2 Stratford, A. H.........Toronto
3 Stuart, G. L.............Toronto
7 Thomlinson, J. F.......Toronto
3 Thompson, H. G........Belmont
7 Thompson, R. J........Toronto
7 Trent, E. E.............Toronto
7 Weldon, H. S.........Oakwood
1 West, J. A..............Simcoe

6 Westren, J. H.........Toronto
7 White, R. E.............Ottawa
3 Wilford, H. J. D........Lindsay
1 Williams, R. H......Burlington
3 Williams, S.............Toronto
7 Williamson, R. J.......Toronto
6 Winter, L. A. G........Toronto
3 Woelfle, E. J............Chesley
6 Wass, F. L...........St. Marys
6 Wynne-Roberts, R. I....Toronto
3 Yack, W. L..........Walkerton
1 Zealand, E. L.........Hamilton

Fourth Year.

6 Affleck, J. K...........Toronto
1 Angus, J. C.............Toronto
1 Augustine, W. P..Port Colborne
1 Baker, G. H.............Toronto
6 Barry, T. M.........Hamilton
2 Beck, C. M.....Penetanguishene
5 Bell, J. C. ....Toronto
3 Blue, A. C.........Wallacetown
3 Booth, G. E.............Toronto
1 Bowman, N..........Kitchener
7 Brace, G. A............Toronto
1 Breen, J. M........Long Branch
6 Brody, D...............Toronto
1 Burton, H. R...........Toronto
3 Chaikoff, S.............Toronto
5 Churchill, J. W...........Toronto
1 Coulter, W. D.....Port Robinson
2 Craigie, D. E............Toronto
3 Crane, H. C.............Toronto
1 Culliton, P. J...........Stratford
3 Dickenson, M. E......Hamilton
7 Doherty, W. A.........Toronto
2 Doner, G. B............Stayner
5 Downey, F. P..........Toronto
1 Downie, R. W...........Toronto
3 Dunton, F. W........Brampton
7 Durbrow, P. A.........Renfrew
3 Eckert, R..............London
7 Eley, F. C.............Toronto
5 Elliott, C. R...........Toronto
1 Elliott, H. J.............Toronto
6 Emory, V. H...........Toronto
5 Fair, H. A.............Toronto
5 Fasken, J. E............Kippen
2 Fawcett, T. C.....Gravenhurst
1 Ferris, C. B............Toronto
5 File, R. R..............Toronto
7 Flynn, J. P..........Merritton
5 Fraser, A. D. R........Toronto
3 Galbraith, S. L....Macleod, Alta.
4 Gallanough, R.........Toronto
1 Gillespie, J............Seaforth

1 Gilley, J. R.
    New Westminster, B.C.
5 Goldstick, D...........Toronto
4 Gouinlock, G. R.......Toronto
1 Graham, D. S.......Inglewood
7 Graham, H. C.........Elmvale
6 Gundy, J. V.........Windsor
5 Haberman, W. U......Toronto
4 Haldenby, E. W.......Toronto
4 Hall, R. W..........Brampton
7 Hamilton, A. E........Toronto
3 Hamilton, J. B.
    Fort Qu Appelle, Sask.
2 Hannan, B. T.........Toronto
3 Henry, S. E...........Stratford
7 Hepburn, G............Milton
3 Herold, W. H.........Shakespeare
3 Hulfish, B. W.........Toronto
8 Irwin, A. L............Toronto
3 Keenleyside, R. D......London
6 Knight, H. A...........Guelph
5 Lailey, C. P...........Toronto
3 Laird, C. H...........Hamilton
7 Landsberg, M. A........Toronto
3 Lawrence, A. M........Toronto
1 Legate, J. H........Owen Sound
4 Livingston, A. H......Brantford
5 Logan, I. M......Niagara Falls
7 Lyon, G. M...........Toronto
3 Macdonald, D. M..
    Edmonton, Alta.
2 MacKenzie, A. P......Toronto
1 MacLean, C. H........Toronto
7 MacLean, H. K........Toronto
1 Marsh, E. J............Grimsby
3 Maunder, W. F........Toronto
1 Maxwell, G. D........Toronto
7 McClelland, J. P........Arthur
3 McDonald, F. R.......Toronto
1 McGee, G. L...........Toronto
8 McIntrye, P. F..........Perth
6 McLean, B. M.........London

1 McLean, J. R.......... Toronto
7 McLellan, J. D......... Toronto
3 McNaughton, L. T..... London
1 Meader, J. C....'.... Toronto
1 Mitchell, J. C.......... London
1 Monteith, J. C........ Stratford
4 Niece, H. P.......... Preston
1 Nixon, W. H.......... Toronto
2 O'Brien, A. E......... Toronto
1 Parker, W. J.......... Toronto
1 Pepler, S. H.......... Toronto
6 Phillips, J. F.......... Toronto
1 Pinel, W. G.......... Toronto
7 Prendergast, R. M..... Toronto
5 Presgrave, R.......... Toronto
7 Preston, H. E......... Midland
1 Proctor, W. D.......... Satnia
2 Purdy, H. E......... Port Perry
7 Ratcliff, J. H......... Stouffville
1 Rayner, G. V......... Hamilton
3 Relyea, J. De W...... Prescott
1 Richardson, F. C.
                  Montgomery, Wales
2 Roph, E. A.......... Toronto
5 Sale, C. P............. Ford
6 Schierholtz, O. J........ Elmira
7 Shephard, G. R........ Toronto
8 Shepard, H. M....... Hamilton

3 Shortt, J. E. B......... Toronto
3 Simmers, J. A......... Toronto
2 Simpson, F. W....... Thornhill
1 Smith, C. T......... St. Thomas
7 Smith, W. M........ Brantford
3 Spencer, H. S.......... Picton
3 Stafford, M. C......... Toronto
7 Stalker, W. D.......... Simcoe
1 Steel, G. E............ Toronto
1 Taylor, F. H.......... Toronto
7 Tracey, G. F.......... Toronto
1 Vardon, L. M......... Toronto
3 Voaden, V.......... St. Thomas
1 Waddell, F. M....... Brantford
7 Wallace, J. S. M.......... Galt
7 Ward, J. W............ Simcoe
1 Warwick, R. S........ Brussels
5 Weelands, J. E........ Toronto
3 West, T. M.......... Toronto
7 Wilson, A. S........ Woodstock
4 Wilson, W. S...... Owen Sound
1 Wimperly, C. C....... Oakville
6 Wingfield, A. H...... Hamilton
4 Wright, B. H.......... Toronto
2 Wyllie, W. J..... Kamloops, B.C.
2 Young, J. F............ Toronto
4 Toung, T. J............ Toronto

Occasional.

Wilson, A. E.................................. Toronto

Summary.

First Year Students	192
Second Year Students	316
Third Year Students	162
Fourth Year Students	135
Occasional	1
Total	806

Scholarship.

Awarded by the Boiler Inspection and Insurance Co. of Canada for General Proficiency in the Third Year in Mechanical Engineering.

1912. A. S. Anderson
1913. E. D. W. Courtice
1914. C. G. Davey
1915. L. L. Youell
1916. A. M. Snider

1917. W. D. Robertson
1918. T. W. Campbell
1919. J. L. Chambers *and* M. L. Weir
1920. H. C. Crane

FACULTY OF EDUCATION.

LIST OF STUDENTS REGISTERED FOR SESSION, 1920-1921

Course for the Ordinary High School Certificate.

Aitken, W. E. M......Courtright
Baldwin, Anah M..........King
Beasley, A. Gertrude.....Toronto
Bell, R. L.............Ingersoll
Braithwaite, G. E........Toronto
Cameron, Jean B...Carleton Place
Cameron, Marguerite A.,
              Carleton Place
Cameron, Myrtle W. L...L'Orignal
Coatsworth, Helen R......Toronto
Cronin, C. Dorothy......Toronto
Cruikshank, N. Leslie...Hamilton
Cummiford, L...........Windsor
Daviss, A. E............Toronto
Day, Helen G..........Callander
Dickinson, Mary A......Toronto
Dippell, L. W.........Walkerton
Dunlop, J. J........Williamstown
Fair, Marjorie W.......Kingston
Fell, Jean H...........Gore Bay
Fines, E. A............Camilla
Floody, Lily M......Haileybury
Franklin, Florence A.....Simcoe
Fraser, G. E...........Ottawa
Galbraith, Flossie P...Bridgeburg
Gardiner, A. B......Thamesville
Gardiner, Myrtle E......Toronto
Gilbert, A. F. S.....Peterborough
Graham, J. K..........Hamilton
Graham, W. T..........Toronto
Greene, Edith A.,
          Newton Robinson
Hall, E. O.............Oshawa
Hambly, Ila H..........Napanee
Harrison, R. Alberta....Uxbridge
Horwood, R. B..........Toronto
Houghton, C. W.,
          Newton Robinson
Howarth, Isabel N.......Toronto

Kerr, Helen M........Hamilton
Langford, H. D..........Toronto
Long, Irene M..........Toronto
Mabee, Helen A.....Gananoque
Magee, H. E............Toronto
Mallagh, Marjorie E. F....Toronto
Mallory, G. H.........St. Thomas
Massecar, Ethelyn.....Dunnville
McArton, Margaret H.,
          Carleton Place
McGugan, Mary C.,
         Mount Brydges
McNaughton, J. L...Martintown
Medcof, W. T........Hartington
Miller, H. M............Rodney
Murphy, Teresa N.......Toronto
Norman, Clara H....Kincardine
Oaten, Beryl E.........Toronto
Orr, Wilma N. ....Stratford
Pearce, Marion.......Waterford
Powell, F. C..........Toronto
Quigley, Emily M......Penetang
Quinn, E. Lillie.........London
Rowan, Jean C.........Toronto
Ryan, J. B............Hamilton
Saunders, Alice I...Smith's Falls
Self, A. R.............Toronto
Sherican, Edith G.....Brockville
Sinclair, A............Batteau
Smith, Lylla E.........Toronto
Sonley, J. A.......Blackwater
Stillwell, Mabel W....Owen Sound
Stuart, Norma K.......Mitchell
Summerhays, R. V........Paris
Summers, Doris M.......Toronto
Thompson, Helen I...Warkworth
Thompson, Muriel H..Georgetown
Wood, Rachel E........Toronto
Wright, Jennie.........Dundalk

Courses for Specialist Certificates.

Brown, H. D..........Brampton
Brown, L. A..........Toronto
Campbell, A. D........Kerwood
Chrysler, H. W.......Brantford
Currie, J. E...........Wingham
Edgar, Margaret.......Stratford
Foley, R. S...........Toronto

Hardy, J. H..............Galt
Ireland, N. J..........Whitby
Jackson, A. B..........Elmira
Keeling, W. L.........Toronto
Kehoe, M. B.........Stratford
MacDonald, Jessie H...Dalkeith
McArthur, Annie.......Alliston

Messer, Cora M.........Toronto
Oatway, G. A......Carleton Place
O'Brian, Mabel B.......L'Orignal
Philp, J. H..........Reaborough
Rosewarne, Winnifred G...Ottawa

Russell, J, W.........Waterford
Saunders, Lucy A......Strathroy
Vrooman, Agnes S.......London
Wallen, Elizabeth J....Unionville
Whitelaw, Florence M..Woodstock

Course for the Ordinary Certificate in Household Science.

Arnold, Edith M.......Hamilton
Doan, Lila M..........Keswick
Donaldson, Vesta A. M....Guelph
Gray, Irene L...........Toronto
Heaslip, Cora.........Hagersville
King, Lilian E.......Terrace, B.C.
Kirby, Carolyn M......Braeside
Langford, Margaret I.Thamesville
Leslie, Elizabeth E....Georgetown

McKibbon, Edna R......Milford
Newton, Adelaide H.....Hamilton
Noble, Zilpha M.....Oxbow, Sask.
Oaten, Beryl E..........Totonto
Rooney, Norma.......St. Thomas
Ryley, Alice E...........Bethany
Stickwood, Alice M...Newmarket
Watchorn, Bessie B..Calgary, Alta.

Courses for Degrees in Pedagogy.

Althouse, J. G...........Oshawa
Anderson, F. H.,
　　　　　Indian Head, Sask.
Armstrong, G. H........Toronto
Armstrong, W. E...Weyburn, Sask.
Ashall, Frances M.......Toronto
Axford, B. W............Toronto
Bannister, J. A.......North Bay
Barnes, C. L............Toronto
Beech, W. K....Vancouver, B.C.
Benson, J. E...........Windsor
Bramfitt, G. N.........Toronto
Brown, G. A...Prince Albert, Sask.
Buchanan, Florence M.,
　　　　　Medicine Hat, Alta.
Buchanan, F. G.,
　　　　　Medicine Hat, Alta.
Caldwell, A............Cornwall
Cameron, M............Watford
Campbell, J. D..........Ottawa
Charles, F.............Toronto
Chisholm, W. I..........Toronto
Clarke, T. E...........London
Cowles, J. P...........Toronto
Daniher, E. L..........Toronto
Doan, A. W. R..........Toronto
Dunlop, W. J. ....Toronto
Edward, W. G...........Toronto
Evans, G. E..........Port Hope
Ferguson, J. G.....Empress, Alta.
Finlayson, D. K., Grand River, N.S.
Firth, J. W.............London
Firth, T...............Lindsay
Froats, J..............Finch

Froats, W. C.......Carleton Place
Fuller, E. L....Wainwright, Alta.
Goldring, C. C..........Toronto
Goldstick, I............London
Gray, J. E.............Toronto
Greer, V. K............London
Haward, W........Regina, Sask.
Hofferd, G. W..........London
Hughes, T. J...........Toronto
Hume, W. E............Toronto
Hunter, J. H...Sherbrooke, Que.
Jenkins, R. S..........Colborne
Jennings, W. A.........Toronto
Jones, C. D............Dundas
Jones, G. M............Toronto
Kay, E. W............Hamilton
Keillor, J.............Toronto
Kelly, W. J.....Edmonton, Alta.
Kerfoot, H. W...........Picton
Kerr, M. W...........Hamilton .
King, H. B......Vancouver, B.C.
Lock, E. H....New Westminster,
　　　　　　　　　B.C.
Long, J. A...........Walkerton
Lord, G. S....Fort Saskatchewan,
　　　　　　　　　Alta.
Lougheed, W. J..........Toronto
Macdonald, A.......Peterborough
MacDonald, D. D.......Toronto
Macpherson, F. F......Hamilton
Madill, A. J.......Peterborough
Martyn, H. G.........Stratford
Matthew, Frances.......Toronto

McCool, J.............Walkerton
McDonald, G........Regina, Sask.
McEachern, J. G...........London
McFadden, R. W. E....Brantford
McGill, G. W...........Toronto
McIntosh, H. W..........Toronto
McIntyre, A. J...Lucky Lake, Sask.
McKellar, J.............Toronto
McLellan, J. C..........Toronto
McLellan, R. F..........Toronto
Menzies, L. P...........Toronto
Mills, J. S.......Saskatoon, Sask.
Misener, G. D....Edmonton, Alta.
Mitchell, R. A.....Weihwei, China
Mitchener, J. L..........Cayuga
Montgomery, J. E.......Toronto
Moshier, D. D...........Toronto
Mulloy, C. W...........Aurora
Munro, P. F...........Toronto
Murch, N. L...........Toronto
Newland, H. C...Edmonton, Alta.
Niddrie, J. G....Edmonton, Alta.
Nivins, C......Prince Albert, Sask.
Ogilvie, A. I.......Fort William
Patterson, A. M.........Toronto
Patterson, W. J..........London

Perry, S. W.............Toronto
Quance, F. M......Regina, Sask.
Quirk, E. L..............Toronto
Radcliffe, S. J...........Toronto
Richardson, R. P....Craik, Sask.
Ryan, Agnes ....Lindsay
Sabine, E. L.....Sault Ste. Marie
Scott, W..........Hardisty, Alta.
Seaton, E. T..........Hamilton
Shales, W. E........Hawkesbury
Smith, A.................Toronto
Sorsoleil, M. A....... ....Toronto
Stevenson, W. E...Balcarres, Sask.
Tamblyn, J. W. J........Toronto
Teeter, C. G............Toronto
Tench, G. R........Tokyo, Japan
Thomas, G. H...........Toronto
Trask, J. A............Hamilton
Tuck, J. R........Camrose, Alta.
Tucker, Mary C.........Toronto
VanEvery, J. F..........Toronto
Walker, D.....Peterborough
Walmsley, L. C.........Milford
White, E. T.........:....London
Williams, W. H.........Toronto

Summary.

Ordinary High School course.. 73
Course for specialist certificates 24
Course for the Ordinary certifi-
   cate in Household Science.. 17
Course for degrees in Pedagogy 113

227

FACULTY OF FORESTRY.

REGISTER OF STUDENTS, 1920-1921

First Year.

Acklom, R. de R. D., New York, U.S.
Ardenne, M.............Toronto
Batt, C. A.............Toronto
Burk, A. H...........Thessalon
Fensom, K. G....Westmount, Que.
Fenwick, A. R...........Toronto
Greenwood, W. B......Ohsweken
Higgins, W. A...........Toronto
Hosie, R. C.............London

Jones, E. C.............Toronto
Kensit, N. M...........Ottawa
Kingston, G. A..........Ottawa
Laschinger, E. J...New Hamburg
McCreath, D. O......Kincardine
McKenzie, A. R....Brandon, Man.
Stewart, J. V............Toronto
Whitelaw, W. A...Edmonton, Alta.
Willson, R. M...........Aurora

Second Year.

Brodie, J. A..........Newmarket
Brown, J. D.........Brockville
Commins, M. J..........Toronto
Cosens, G. G...........Toronto
Cram, W. D. .....Carleton Place
Crosbie, H. W.....Chatham, N.B.
Druce, E.........Winnipeg, Man.
Faulkner, W. T....Enderby, B.C.
Foote, C. E...........Rosseau
Haddow, W. R..........Toronto

Heaven, H. C. G.......Hamilton
Jenkins, F. T............Ottawa
MacDougall, F. A., Carleton Place
MacFarlane, J. D. B., Mscdonald College, Que.
Munro, D. J...........Wroxeter
Turnbull, J. F...........Toronto
Walton, J. R.............Toronto
Westland, C. E..........Toronto

Third Year

Doran, A. B..............Toronto
Irwin, C. H.............Toronto
Irwin, J. C. W...........Toronto
McDonald, J. H..........Guelph
Marritt, I. C...........Keswick

Pepler, W. A. E.........Toronto
Reid, L. H. ....England
Stewart, K. A..........Toronto
Thrupp, A. C....Kamloops, B.C.
VanVamp, J. L..........Toronto

Fourth Year

Alexander, J. L......Mono Road
Carman, R. S..........Iroquois
Clarke, T. A............Toronto

Eisler, H. P............Mitchell
Hughson, H. M..........Ottawa

Occasional or Special

Baker, F. W. C. Elliott-...Toronto
Mowat, R. H...Campbellton, N.B.

FORESTRY AND ARTS.

First Year
Campbell, W. N. M...Oro Station

Sixth Year
Bentley, A. W..........Sarnia

Summary

First Year Students........................	19
Second Year Students.....................	18
Third Year Students......................	10
Fourth Year Students.....................	5
Sixth Year Students.......................	1
Occasional Students......................	1
Special Students..........................	1
	55

FACULTY OF MUSIC.

REGISTER OF STUDENTS, 1920-21

First Year

Bird, Miss A. C..........................Toronto
Curtis, Miss A..........................Bronte
Evans, Miss H. P. ....Sudbury
Fisher, Miss M. I. ....Toronto
Goldhang, D. C.........................Toronto
Reed, E................................Toronto
Record, H. J...........................Weyburn, Sask.
Robinson, R. C.........................Belmont, Mass.
Solway, J. B...........................Toronto
White, E. F............................London

Second Year

Hermon, E. W..........................Toronto
Kenny, J. L............................Hamilton
Wilkinson, F. H........................Toronto

Third Year

Campbell, Mrs. G. H....................Toronto
Horwood, F. J..........................Norham
Rees, L. P.............................Toronto
Wilson, G. A...........................Brooklyn, N.Y.

Occasional

Prittie, Miss E. K. ....Toronto

Summary.

First Year.................... 10
Second Year..................   3
Third Year...................   4
Occasional   1
                               —
    Total.................... 18

DEPARTMENT OF SOCIAL SERVICE.

Session 1920-21.

FULL-TIME STUDENTS.

First Year.

Aiman, J. S........Calcutta, India
Aird, Miss W. E.........Toronto
Bond, Miss M. A........Toronto
Bronstein, Miss J.........Toronto
Burnham, Miss M. V......Toronto
Cameron, Miss W. C., Halifax, N.S.
Chisholm, Miss D. M....Oakville
Christopherson, Miss D. J.,
                        Gowganda
Creighton, Miss M. H.,
                    Dartmouth, N.S.
Curley, Miss M. V........Sudbury
Curtis, Miss I. M.........Aylmer
Doran, Miss J. E........Toronto
Godfrey, Mrs. E. L......Toronto
Griffin, Miss H. R.....St. Thomas
Gurney, Miss G..........Toronto
Hamilton, Miss B. E....,.Oakville
Harris, Miss A. E......Pictou, N.S.
Jaffray, Miss M. F..........Galt
Johnston, Mrs. J. L........Toronto
Lasby, Miss O. M........Toronto
Lawson, Miss M. C.....Hamilton
Lightbourn, Miss M. D...Oakville
Lightbourn, Miss S. M...Oakville
Livingstone, Miss S...Georgetown
McDowell, Mrs. K. H.....Toronto
McIlraith, Miss M. M.....Durham
MacKenzie, Miss C. E. V.,
                    Scotsburn, N.S.

MacQuarrie, Miss M. J.,
                Barss' Corners, N.S.
Master, Miss O. K.......Weston
Meyer, Miss L. L.....Gowanstown
Mooney, Miss G. S......Toronto
Murray, Miss D. M. E.,
                        Halifax, N.S.
Nelles, Miss H. E....Niagara Falls
O'Gorman, Miss L. C....Toronto
Pearson, Miss E. J.,
                Upper Brighton, N.B.
Roberts, Miss H. G.....Hamilton
Ryrie, Miss G. M........Toronto
Ryrie, Miss M...........Toronto
Sarjeant, Miss M. L........Orillia
Scadding, Miss B. H......Toronto
Smith, Miss J. G.....Port Credit
Sommer, F..............Toronto
Stretton, Miss S. B.......Toronto
Tonkin, Miss G..........Toronto
Townsend, Miss M. S.....Toronto
Tye, Miss C. DeN.......Watford
White, Miss H. M.,
                    Vancouver, B.C.
Whitman, Miss K. H.....Ottawa
Wilkinson, Miss M. E....Toronto
Willans, Miss A. E.......Toronto
Wishart, Miss E. T......Toronto
Yeigh, Miss M. A........Toronto

Second Year.

Jackson, Miss K. R.......Orillia
MacInnes, Miss M. I.,
                Midnapore, Alta.
MacPherson, Miss J. M...Tiverton

Sawyer, Mrs. M. O.....Churchill
Serson, Miss M. R...Trenton, N.J.
Sher, Miss B. B..........Toronto
Valentine, Miss M.....Waterloo

PART-TIME STUDENTS

Agnew, Miss M. A......Cookstown
Alford, Miss L. M.......Toronto
Algie, Miss B............Toronto
Algie, Miss J............Toronto
Allward, Miss I. M........Barrie
Anderson, Miss J. R., Waubaushene
Avery, Miss J. O.........Ottawa

Aylward, Miss K.........Toronto
Bailey, Miss A............Madoc
Balfour, Miss A. E......Hamilton
Barnett, Miss H.........Toronto
Barton, Miss A. L......Uxbridge
Bateman, Miss M........Stirling
Beahan, Miss R. E.......Toronto

Bell, Miss A. O......Regina, Sask.
Bellman, Miss G. M., Bowmanville
Bickell, Miss N. B.............Galt
Bing, Mrs. E..............Toronto
Blair, Miss H........Kincardine
Bowles, Rev. N. E........Toronto
Boyce, Miss I. M.........Toronto
Boyd, Miss M. A.....Bobcaygeon
Brandt, Miss G...........Elmira
Brodie, Miss C. M........Toronto
Brown, Miss F. E........Toronto
Brown, Miss M. M.......Toronto
Brown, Miss M. F. P.....Alliston
Brunet, Miss A...Valleyfield, Que.
Burns, Miss M.......Port Perry
Burgess, Miss M. T...Leamington
Butchart, Miss M. E.....Toronto
Cameron, Miss R........Toronto
Campbell, Miss F. O.....Toronto
Cane, Miss G. B......Newmarket
Capling, Miss F. H....St. Mary's
Cardwell, Miss V.....Frazerville
Carnegie, Miss F........Toronto
Carscallen, Miss F.....Tamworth
Carson, Miss M. F.......Toronto
Cass, Miss A. H.........L'Original
Chaffee, Mrs. M. P......Toronto
Chamberlain, C. O.....St. Thomas
Charlebois, Miss H,
                    Penetanguishene
Cherry, Miss C. L....Bowmanville
Christie, Miss E. M...Owen Sound
Chute, Miss F. M.......Belleville
Clapp, Miss J. A.....Mount Forest
Clark, Miss C. R...........Galt
Clarke, Miss G. E.....Schomberg
Cohen, Miss A. E........Toronto
Cohen, J. W.............Toronto
Coles, Miss M. I. G......Colborne
Connell, Miss M.......Kingston
Connor, Miss E. K.,
                    Moosomin, Sask.
Coulter, Miss N. M...Port Perry
Cowan, Miss J. M...Yorkton, Sask.
Cowling, Miss D.........Toronto
Davidson, Miss M. J......Delta
Dawson, P. W.....Melfort, Sask.
Derbyshire, Miss A.....Westport
Dix, Miss M. E..........Fergus
Doherty, Miss M. H., Dalhousie,
                    N.B.
Dunnigan, Miss B.......Toronto
Durie, Miss E...........Toronto
Dwan, Miss F...........Toronto
Eatough, Miss M. O.......Galt
Eckersville, Miss M. P...Clifford
Elliott, Miss J. W., Penetanguishene

Empey, Miss J. L........Napanee
Ellis, Miss M. A.....Peterborough
Essery, Miss F. M....Palmerston
Fensom, Miss M. K......Toronto
Fernley, Miss E. G.......Toronto
Firman, Miss G. E........Barrie
Folsetter, Miss H. J........Paris
Fowler, J. H.....New York, N.Y.
Fraser, Miss I. M.....Hawkesbury
Fulton, Miss A. J........Toronto
Galilee, Miss D. L......Hamilton
Gardiner, Miss C........Toronto
Garrow, Miss R.......Chesterville
Gauld, Miss G. L. V.,
                    Tamsui, Japan
Geiger, Miss F. L......Brockville
Gier, Miss G. G........Waldemar
Gilbert, Miss I .H.......Toronto
Gillespie, Miss A. F.......Roslin
Gillies, Miss L. J...Campbellton,
                    N.B.
Gordon, Miss E. L.......Toronto
Gough, Miss B. M........Toronto
Goulding, Miss F....Burk's Falls
Gow, Miss J. M..........Guelph
Graham, Miss E. M......Lindsay
Greaves, Miss W. C......Toronto
Grimshaw, Miss M. L.....Toronto
Hagerman, Mrs. O. M.....Toronto
Haly, Miss H. L.........Toronto
Hall, Miss M. C.....Peterborough
Halpern, Miss S.........Toronto
Ham, Miss L. M.........Fergus
Hamilton, Miss E........Toronto
Hamilton, Miss H........Toronto
Hammil, Miss M........Sudbury
Harcourt, C. C..........Toronto
Hardy, Miss M..........Toronto
Harrington, Miss H....Wellington
Harrison, Miss A. R., Mount Albert
Harrold, A. W...........Toronto
Harstone, Miss M....Peterborough
Harvey, Miss H. M....Deseronto
Heffernan, Miss H........Guelph
Hendrie, Miss A. B. D.,
                    Galston, Scotland
Hewitt, Miss I..Jamaica, B.W.I.
Hind, Mrs. N. P.........Winona
Hodson, Miss N..........Alton
Hogg, Miss F. I..........Galt
Holmes, A..............Toronto
Hopper, Miss P. A......Chapleau
Horne, Miss E. H........Toronto
Hounsom, Miss D. M.....Toronto
Houston, Miss L. M......Toronto
Howe, Miss A.....St. Catharines
Hughes, Miss H.........Toronto

Hugill, Miss H. C........Toronto
Huntley, Miss T. C........Toronto
Hutchinson, Mrs. E. C....Toronto
Ingham, Miss A. M......Toronto
Ings, Miss O............Toronto
Jackson, Miss A. L........Toronto
Jackson, Miss L. E........Toronto
Jackson, Miss............Toronto
James, Miss A. P........Toronto
Jarvis, Mrs. E..........Toronto
Jay, Miss E............Toronto
Jenkins, Miss F. G........Toronto
Jennings, Miss I...Montreal, Que.
Johnson, Miss B......Millbrook
Johnston, Miss M. H......Toronto
Jones, Miss L. G...Kuling, China
Jones, Miss M. L........Toronto
Joyce, Miss J. C........Napanee
Keith, Miss F. A.....Parry Sound
Kelly, Miss L. E.........London
Kernahan, Miss C......Maxwell
Kerr, Miss M. H.........Toronto
King, Miss L. L.......Toronto
Land, Miss H. D.......Hamilton
Langdon, Miss C. E......Toronto
Latter, Miss B....Winnipeg, Man.
Laurie, Miss A. M. .....Toronto
Ledoux, Miss J..........Toronto
Lee, Miss K. L...Murrayville, B.C.
Lillie, Miss M............Orillia
Loftus, Miss A.........Phelpston
Longman, Miss M. I.....Iroquois
Lowe, Miss J. S. M...Bracebridge
Loy, Miss M.........North Bay
McBeath, Miss A. E........Madoc
McConnell, Miss M. E....Toronto
McCrimmon, Miss C. F., Woodville
MacDonall, Miss V......Toronto
McDougall, Miss R...Burk's Falls
McEachern, Miss G. M....Toronto
Macfarlane, Miss A. M.,
       Campbell's Bay, Que.
McFarlane, Mrs. F......Toronto
McGarity, Miss G. M.....Toronto
McGill, Miss B..........Toronto
McGuinness, Miss C.....Toronto
McIntosh, Miss I...Honan, China
MacIvor, Miss A. M....Toronto
MacIvor, Miss E.,
       South Cove, N.S.
McKay, Miss A. M. E...Welland
MacKenzie, Mrs. S......Toronto
MacKinnon, Miss M.,
       Peters Road, P.E.I.
McLaren, Miss A. G....Toronto
McLaren, Miss K. A.....Toronto
McLaren, Miss S. F.......Sarnia

McLaughlin, Mrs. E.....Toronto
McLelland, Miss M. E...Bellwoods
MacLennan, Miss M,
       Detroit, Mich.
McMillard, Miss M. E...Port Hope
Macnamara, Miss E. R...Hamilton
McNeilly, Miss W.......Toronto
McRorie, Miss E....Durban, Man.
MacQuarrie, Miss M., Sydney, N.S.
Maddell, Miss L.........Toronto
Malcolm, Miss C. W.....Orillia
Manning, Miss L........Toronto
Marks, Miss C...........Toronto
Marr, Miss H. M. O.......Barrie
Marrin, Miss L..........Mimico
Marsden, Miss L. W....Tottenham
Marshall, Miss B.......Eversley
Martin, Miss M. E....St. Thomas
Maryln, Mrs. M. J.......Toronto
Mason, Miss O...........Canton
Meader, Miss K.........Toronto
Mears, Miss F. O........Toronto
Meikle, Miss M. W...Mount Forest
Meiklejohn, Miss E. M...Toronto
Menzies, Mrs. A. B., Honan, China
Miell, Miss H. M........Toronto
Millar, Miss L..........Wiarton
Millman, Miss M. B.....Toronto
Mitchell, Miss E. H...Mono Road
Morley, Miss M. M....Chesley
Morrison, Miss E........Mildmay
Morton, Miss E. L.......Keswick
Moulton, R. F...........Toronto
Mounce, Miss R. L......Oshawa
Mountjoy, Miss A.......Toronto
Mowat, Miss D. M.,
       Campbellton, N.B.
Moyer, Miss G....Jordan Station
Mullen, Miss M.........Toronto
Murray, Miss M. V......Tavistock
Murray, Miss W.........Toronto
Naisbitt, Miss M. E.,
       Rapid City, Man.
Nelson, Miss A. L.......Paisley
Newton, Miss I. ....Toronto
Noble, Miss O. M......Brampton
O'Connor, Miss V. J....Hamilton
O'Gorman, Miss F. M....Toronto
Oliver, Miss L. M........Maple
Osborne, W. H....Calgary, Alta.
Paisley, Miss C. B.....Stouffville
Parkin, Miss D. R.......Toronto
Passmore, Miss J. C.....Toronto
Patten, Miss B., Grand Bank, Nfld.
Payne, Mrs. C...........Toronto
Peacock, Miss E. E......Toronto
Pearse, Miss F. I............Galt

Perrie, Miss M.........Wingham
Pettit, Mrs. E. P........Toronto
Phillips, Miss J..........Toronto
Pickles, Miss F. E.......Toronto
Pinchin, Miss J. V.......Toronto
Playle, Miss E. G...Dunkirk, N.Y.
Porter, Miss E. O....St. Paul's
Powers, Miss D. M. M....Picton
Poyntz, Miss A. J...Regina, Sask.
Quinlan, Miss M. L...Peterborough
Raphael, Miss A. L.,
Vancouver, B.C.
Ratz, Miss E. M.........Toronto
Reid, Miss D............London
Riordan, Miss M. A.....:.Toronto
Robinson, Miss M.......Toronto
Rogers, E. E.....Delburne, Alta.
Root, Miss J............Toronto
Rose, Miss A. M.....Urbania, N.S.
Ross, Miss M..........Toronto
Rotenberg, Miss M......Toronto
Rumball, Miss E. P......Toronto
Russell, Miss M. V......Toronto
Ryde, Miss G. K........Toronto
Salkeld, Miss F. A.......Toronto
Schell, C. A............Toronto
Schofield, Miss J. C...St. John,
N.B.
Scott, Mrs. M. C...Indore, India
Scrimgeour, Miss G....Stratford
Secrett, L. C...........Ottawa
Sheckleton, Miss M. L....Toronto
Shembrook, Miss O. E.,
Regina, Sask.
Shepherd, Miss E. P., Alexandria
Sheppard, Miss E. M.,
Waubaushene
Sheridan, Miss A. P......Toronto
Sherin, Miss D. M......Lakefield
Shipman, Miss R. V.....Ottawa
Simpson, Miss M. A.....Toronto
Sinclair, Miss A. E...Gordon Bay
Sloane, Miss M....Leslie, Sask.

Smith, Miss B. N.....Queensville
Smith, Miss E. E., Westmount, Que.
Smith, Miss J. M.....Kemptville
Smith, Miss W. B........Toronto
Smithson, Miss M........Weston
Steacy, Miss E. M......Napanee
Stevenson, Miss M. B.,
Peterborough
Stevenson, Miss L. E.....Listowel
Stover, Miss G. L...Iroquois Falls
Sutherland, Miss V. L.,
Lockport, N.S.
Tait, Miss V. E..........Toronto
Taylor, Miss F. G........Toronto
Thompson, Miss A. L....Chapleau
Thompson, Miss D. I. E.,
Tillsonburg
Thompson, Miss H. M.,
Elmsdale, N.S.
Thomson, Miss A.....Tillsonburg
Tod, Miss O. L.....Bowmanville
Trotter, Miss G. D........Toronto
Wallace, Rev. T. G......Toronto
Walton, Miss E. L...Mount Albert
Ward, Miss H. B........Deloro
Washburn, Miss E. M...Toronto
Wass, S. W........London, Eng.
Watterton, Miss M.......Toronto
Watts, Miss J. V.........Toronto
Webster, Miss I. M., Marie, P.E.I.
Weldon, Miss O. E......Oakwood
Wellington, Miss K., Malden, Mass.
West, Miss M.......Campbellford
Wheeler, Miss M. A......Toronto
White, Vivian..........Coboconk
Wilkins, Miss M. E.....Norwood
Wilson, Mrs. M..........Toronto
Woodrow, G. E......Woodstock
Woods, Miss R..........Toronto
Wright, Miss B..........Toronto
Wright, Miss D. M.,
Naigara-on-the-Lake
Zimmerman, Miss R. M...Toronto

SUMMARY.

Full time Students:
First Year................ 52
Second Year............. 7
——
59
Part time Students......... 307
——
366

PUBLIC HEALTH NURSING.

REGISTER OF STUDENTS FOR THE YEAR 1920-1921

Bain, Elsie C.........................Toronto.
Barnes, Florence H....................Toronto.
Beatty, Atholia L.....................Peterborough.
Beck, Anna D..........................Sault Ste. Marie.
Blackstock, Barbara...................Toronto.
Boyd, Annie B.........................Hamilton.
Bryden, Jean D........................Flora, Ill.
Campbell, Annie L.....................Georgetown.
Cameron, Anna McD.....................Hamilton.
Cross, Dorothy........................Toronto.
Cryderman, Ethel......................Niagara Falls.
Dawson, Winnifred.....................North Bay.
Dickison, Alison......................Ottawa.
Eckert, Claudia P.....................Toronto.
Fenton, A. Edith......................East Toronto.
Fletcher, Mary E......................Paisley.
Forbes, Agnes C.......................Waterdown.
Galbraith, Lillian E..................Toronto.
Galbraith, M. Flora...................Toronto.
Gamble, Laura A.......................Ottawa.
Gridley, Mary E.......................Ottawa.
Henderson, Alma F.....................Toronto.
Henderson, Viola......................Mimico Beach.
Hindley, Alice........................Rockwood.
Hughes, Edna E........................Mimico Beach.
Jackson, Josephine....................Brantford.
King, Josephine.......................Hamilton.
Lovell, M. Gordon.....................Toronto.
Lyle, Robina C........................St. Thomas.
MacGregor, Dell G.....................Dundarve P. O. West Vancouver.
McKinnon, Emma D......................Ottawa.
Manchester, A. S. Louise..............Ottawa.
Manning, Elvira.......................Toronto.
Marshall, Annie J.....................Embro.
Martin, Muriel A......................Toronto.
Morrison, Marion I....................Chatham, N.B.
Murray, Mabel J.......................Tavistock.
Nettleton, Constance H................Penetanguishene.
Nodwell, Mabel........................Grand Valley.
Oram, Anna M..........................Burlington.
Papst, Nora I.........................Avonmore.
Pike, Ada.............................Toronto.
Price, Elizabeth R....................Toronto.
Raymond, Edythe L.....................London.
Reid, Gertrude E......................Peterborough.
Roberts, Pansy E......................Port Hope.
Ross, Barbara A.......................Toronto.
Ruddy, Eva............................Brantford.
Stovel, Mamie.........................Stratford.
Wood, Grace E.........................Toronto.

OCCASIONAL STUDENTS 1920-1921.

Allison, Miss J. T.........Department of Public Health, Toronto.
Blackmore, Miss G........Department of Public Health, Toronto.
Bone, Miss A.............Department of Public Health, Toronto.
Budge, Miss A. O.........Board of Education, Toronto.
Burns, Miss A. A.........Victorian Order of Nurses, Toronto.
Butchart, Miss M. L......Department of Public Health, Toronto.
Butterfield, Miss E. M.....Department of Public Health, Toronto.
Clarke, Miss E. deV......Department of Public Health, Toronto.
Chisholm, Miss C.........Social Service Department, Toronto Genera
    Hospital, Toronto.
Coker, Miss C. E.........Department of Public Health, Toronto.
Conlin, Miss I............Department of Public Health, Toronto.
Conlin, Miss L. M.........Department of Public Health, Toronto.
Crickmore, Miss I. M......Victorian Order of Nurses, Toronto.
Daniel, Miss G. M........Department of Public Health, Toronto.
Devaney, Miss D.........Victorian Order of Nurses, Toronto.
Dewey, Mrs. M...........Social Service Department, Toronto General
    Hospital.
Dowdell, Miss L. B........Department of Public Health, Toronto.
Dunn, Miss E.............Department of Public Health, Toronto.
Elliot, Miss E. F..........Victorian Order of Nurses, Toronto.
Elliott, Miss B. C.........Department of Public Health, Toronto.
Ferriman, Miss M. A.......Department of Public Health, Toronto.
Fraser, Miss M. B........Victorian Order of Nurses, Toronto.
Galbraith, Miss M........Department of Public Health, Toronto.
Gardner, Miss M. E......Department of Public Health, Toronto.
Goodman, Miss J. L......Department of Public Health, Toronto.
Green, Miss E...........Victorian Order of Nurses, Toronto
Gregg, Miss A...........Victorian Order of Nurses, Toronto.
Haliburton, Miss M. L....Department of Public Health, Toronto.
Hamilton, Miss S.........Social Service Department, Toronto General
    Hospital.
Hanna, Miss R. M........Department of Public Health, Toronto.
Harrington, Miss H.......Department of Public Health, Toronto.
Hefferman, Miss H.......Department of Public Health, Toronto.
Hopkins, Miss L. M.......Victorian Order of Nurses, Toronto.
Husband, Miss M. S......Department of Public Health, Toronto.
Hutchison, Miss B. S......Department of Public Health, Toronto.
Hutchins, Miss E. E......Department of Public Health, Toronto.
Johnston, Miss E. M......Department of Public Health, Toronto.
Johnston, Miss I.........Victorian Order of Nurses, Toronto.
Jordon, Miss T. B........Department of Public Health, Toronto.
Kingstone, Miss M. A.....Dept. of Soldiers' Civil Re-establishment,
    Toronto.
Kirk, Miss M............Dept. of Soldiers' Civil Re-establishment,
    Toronto.
Kniseley, Miss M.........Social Service Department, Toronto General
    Hospital.
Laing, Miss M............Department of Public Health, Toronto.
Lilley, Miss E. E.........Victorian Order of Nurses, Toronto.
MacIntosh, Miss G.......Department of Public Health, Toronto.
Mackay, Miss M.........Hydro Electric Power Com. of Ontario.
MacLeod, Miss I.........Department of Public Health, Toronto.
Marrin, Miss T. M.......Department of Public Health, Toronto.

Marshall, Miss N. L.......Department of Public Health, Toronto.
Miller, Miss M...........Department of Public Health, Toronto.
Mowry, Miss B. M........Department of Public Health, Toronto.
Mutch, Miss J. G.........Department of Public Health, Toronto.
Patterson, Miss E. J.......Department of Public Health, Toronto.
Patterson, Miss G. E......Department of Public Health, Toronto.
Patton, Miss G...........Department of Public Health. Toronto.
Peterson, Miss F.........Department of Public Health, Toronto.
Porter, Miss V. B. M.....Victorian Order of Nurses, Toronto.
Roberts, Miss L. C.......Victorian Order of Nurses, Toronto.
Ross, Miss M............Department of Public Health, Toronto.
Rouse, Miss K. L.........Department of Public Health, Toronto.
Russell, Miss E. G........Department of Public Health, Toronto.
Schoales, Miss F. M.......Department of Public Health, Toronto.
Sketch, Miss R. B........Department of Public Health, Toronto.
Spanner, Miss G. L.......Dept. of Soldiers' Civil Re-Establishment,
                        Toronto.
Stewart, Miss M. E.......Department of Public Health, Toronto.
Sussex, Miss R. K.........Department of Public Health, Toronto.
Sutherland, Miss S. S......Department of Public Health, Toronto.
Tait, Miss M. E...........Victorian Order of Nurses, Toronto.
Walker, Miss D. M......Victorian Order of Nurses, Toronto.
Walker, Miss J. M.........Department of Public Health, Toronto.
Walsh, Miss B...........Department of Public Health, Toronto.
Wheeler, Miss M. E.......Department of Public Health, Toronto.
Willison, Miss E. M.......Department of Public Health, Toronto.
Wilson, Miss J. K.........Department of Public Health, Toronto.

The above are all engaged in public health nursing in Toronto, and the organization with which each is working has been listed.

General Summary.

Faculty of Arts:

University of Toronto	189	
University College	1,170	
Victoria College	510	
Trinity College	129	
St. Michael's College	206	
Registered twice	11	
		2,193
Graduate Courses		163
Faculty of Medicine		1,127
Faculty of Applied Science and Engineering		806
Faculty of Education		226
Faculty of Forestry		55
Faculty of Music		18
Department of Social Science		366
Department of Public Health Nursing		126
Registered twice		20
Grand Total		5,060

HISTORICAL SKETCH

The movement which ended in the establishment of the University of Toronto as the centre of the educational system of the Province of Ontario originated with General Simcoe, the first Governor of Upper Canada, who repeatedly expressed his conviction, both before his departure from England and also during his term of office (1792-1796), that the best interests alike of the Government and of the inhabitants demanded the establishment of a University in Upper Canada. It was not, however, during his administration that the project assumed a definite form.

In 1797 the Legislative Council and House of Assembly in a joint address to King George III. asked "that his Majesty would be graciously pleased' to direct his Government in the Province to appropriate a certain portion of the waste lands of the Crown as a fund for the establishment and support of a respectable Grammer School for each district thereof; and also a College or University for the instruction of youth in the different branches of liberal knowledge". To this address a favourable answer was transmitted, and the acting Lieutenant-Governor, the Hon. Peter Russell, was directed to determine the manner and character of the appropriation. In accordance with this request the Executive Council of Upper Canada reported on the 1st December, 1798, that an appropriation of 500,000 acres would be sufficient for the support and maintenance of four Grammer Schools and a University. For the foundation of the latter nothing was done until 1827, when a Royal Charter was granted for the establishment at or near York, as Toronto was then called, of a College, "with the style and privileges of a University", to be called "King's College", having for its endowment that portion of the grant of "waste lands" originally provided for the University in the report above referred to. These lands were in 1828 exchanged for 225,944 acres of Crown Reserves.

Owing not only to the character of the endowment, which required time for its realization in the form yielding an annual revenue, but also owing to the terms of the charter, which required all the members of the Faculty to be adherents of one particular religious denomination, the opening of the College was delayed for fourteen years. In consequence of public representations on the sectarian character of the College, all religious tests were abolished by an amended charter which passed the two Houses of the Provincial Legislature and received the Royal Assent in 1837. In 1842 the affairs of the University had assumed such a condition as to render its organization possible, and Faculties of Arts, Medicine, Law and Divinity were established. In that year the erection of the College Building was begun on the eastern portion of the site of the present Legislative Buildings. In 1843 the first matriculation of students took place, and inaugural addresses and lectures were delivered on the 8th and 9th of June of that year.

The agitation which resulted in the amended charter of 1837 had continued after the opening of the College in 1842, owing to the efforts made to defeat the purpose of the amendment, and in 1849 an Act of the Legislature effected important modifications in the constitution of King's College whereby all instruction in Divinity was discontinued, and a larger measure of public control of the affairs of the University instituted, through the formation of a Senate, of which a number of the members were appointed by the Crown. The name was now changed from that of "The University of King's College" to that of "The University of Toronto".

· . Three years afterwards the University underwent a further transformation, by which the Act of 1853 abolished the Faculties of Medicine and Law, and divided its functions between the two newly organized corporations of the "University of Toronto" and "University College." To the Senate were assigned the duties of framing the curriculum, holding examinations and admitting to degrees in Arts, Law and Medicine, while to the Presidents and Professors of University College, as a distinct and independent corporation with special powers, were assigned the teaching in Arts and the entire discipline and control of students. The models followed in the reorganization of the University, it claimed, were the University of London and University College, London, both of which had then been only recently established. For thirty-four years the University of Toronto and University College performed the functions respectively assigned to them by this Act.

During the early years of the University it experienced repeated changes in its local habitation. The faculty and students of King's College were at first temporarily accommodated in the Parliament Buildings until the erection of the east wing of King's College admitted of the occupation of their own building. From this they were anew transferred to the old Parliament Buildings in 1853, when, by a special Act, the site of King's College was appropriated for the proposed new buildings for the use of the Parliament of Upper and Lower Canada. On the return of the Legislature to Toronto, in 1856, the Faculty resumed the occupation of the old King's College Building, while one formerly in use by the Medical Faculty, situated on the site of the present Biological Building, was being adapted for their occupation. There accordingly the work of the College was carried on, pending the erection of the new University buildings. These buildings were begun in 1856, and on October 4th, 1859, the top stone of the main tower was placed in position by Sir Edmund Head, the Governor-General, an old Oxford professor, the value of whose sympathy and support at this critical period in the history of the University cannot be overestimated.

For thirty-four years the constitution of the University of Toronto and of University College remained unchanged. Other collegiate bodies, principally denominational schools of theology, entered into affiliation with the University, and, with regard to their especial requirements, the course of study in Oriental Languages was augmented, but the Faculty of University College continued to do the work of instruction for nearly all the students in Arts who presented themselves for examination. The candidates for examination and degrees in medicine were trained in medical schools in affiliation with the University, and for degrees in Law the examinations were based upon text-books prescribed by the Senate, without teaching.

In 1887 both the University of Toronto and University College were remodelled by the University Act. The main object of renewed legislation was to secure a more uniform standard of higher education by the union of the various denominational universities of Ontario with the Provincial University. Since the proclamation of the Act, Victoria University at Cobourg, representing the Methodist body, has entered into federation with the University of Toronto. The governing body of this institution is now represented on the Senate of the University of Toronto, its graduates elect representatives to the same body, and by the removal of the faculty and students of Victoria University to Toronto, where college buildings have been erected to the north of Queen's Park, the union of the two universities · has been effected. Under the Federation Act, the theological colleges, also formerly in affiliation with the University of Toronto, have become federated colleges, and enjoy increased representation on the Senate.

The Faculty of University College, by the Act 1887, consists of professors and lecturers in Classic Languages and Literature (including lectures in Ancient History), Oriental Languages, English, French, German and Moral Philosophy. All other portions of the Arts course are assigned to the Faculty of the University of Toronto, of which the lectures are made equally available to the students of University College, and those of all federating universities and colleges. For the maintenance of certain of the departments of science on a scale demanded by modern methods of research, special provision has been made by the erection of new and the enlargement of old buildings. In the new Biological Building every facility is now provided for practical training in Biology and Physiology. The Chemical Building was completed in 1895, and affords similar facilities for practical work in Chemistry.

A Faculty of Medicine in the University of Toronto was established immediately upon the passing of the Act in 1887, and teaching is imparted in all branches of medical science. All the advantages of the Faculty of Arts are available for students in Medicine, and the laboratories of the scientific departments are utilized equally by students in both faculties. In 1903 the new Medical Building was opened.

In 1888 a stimulus was given to the study of scientific methods of farming by the affiliation of the Ontario Agricultural College and the adoption of a curriculum of study for the degree of Bachelor of the Science of Agriculture. Similarly an examination for the degree of Doctor of Dental Surgery was instituted, as a consequence of the affiliation of the Royal College of Dental Surgeons of Ontario. The College of Pharmacy was subsequently admitted to affiliation and a curriculum in Pharmacy prescribed. On the affiliation of the Toronto College of Music a curriculum of study was prepared for the degree of Bachelor of Music. The School of

Practical Science was affiliated in 1889, and graduates of the School are specially eligible on certain conditions for the degree of Bachelor of Applied Science and of various degrees in Engineering in the University. By a recent enactment of the Senate a curriculum was prescribed leading to the degrees of Bachelor and Doctor of Pedagogy. In 1897 a course of study was established leading to the degree of Doctor of Philosophy in certain of the Arts departments. In 1897 the Ontario Veterinary College was also affiliated.

On February 14th, 1890, the Main University building was partly destroyed by fire. In the reconstruction thereby rendered necessary, opportunity was afforded for important improvements in lighting, heating and ventilation. Considerable extension was effected in the numbers, capacity and equipment of the lecture rooms and laboratories. A new library building was erected on plans embracing the most recent improvements suggested by the experience of leading universities in the United States and elsewhere. A building for the accommodation of the Gymnasium was erected in 1982, and additions to it were completed in 1894 for the accomodation of student societies.

One of the most important events of recent years was the federation of the University of Trinity College, which was proclaimed by His Honour the Lieutenant-Governor on the 18th of November, 1903, and came into effect on the 1st of October, 1904.

The passing of the University Act, 1906, is the latest and most important development in the history of the University. A short account of the changes of greatest importance will be found in the early portion of this calendar under the title "Constitution and Administration of the University".

As provided in the University Act of 1906, St. Michael's College was declared to be a College in the Faculty of Arts on the 8th of December, 1910 On November 11th, 1919, Hart House, the gift of the Massey Foundation, was formally opened by His Excellency the Duke of Devonshire, Governor-General of Canada. The building is the new Undergraduates Union of the University and contains completely equipped club rooms, including common rooms, dining hall, chapel, the offices of the various students societies, gymnasia and theatre.

THE ROYAL ONTARIO MUSEUM.

The Royal Ontario Museum was officially opened by Field Marshal His Royal Highness the Duke of Connaught, Governor-General of Canada, on the afternoon of Thursday, March 19th, 1914. This event marked a memorable occasion in the history of Art and Science in the Province of Ontario.

The Royal Ontario Museum was established under an Act of the Legislative Assembly of Ontario in the year 1912. According to the Act the purposes of the museum are:—

(a) The collection and exhibition of objects of every kind calculated to illustrate the natural history of Ontario, and thereby to aid in a knowledge of what this province is able to contribute to science and industry.

(b) The collection and exhibition of objects of any kind calculated to illustrate the natural history of the world and the history of man in all ages.

(c) Such other objects as may be authorised by the Lieutenant-Governor in Council.

The cost of the erection of the building and the maintenance thereof is borne in equal amounts by the Province of Ontario and the University of Toronto. The present building, inclusive of offices, is 360 feet long and 60 feet wide and was erected at a cost of about $400,000. The large section of University property lying between the present building and Avenue Road has been reserved by the Board for the extension of the Museum. The proposed plans show the building in the form of a hollow square with a handsome stone front facing Bloor Street.

Under Section 20 of the Museum Act the Board is empowered to establish various departments of the Museum which are to be designed "The Royal Ontario Museum of..............". In accordance with this by-law the Board has already established the Royal Ontario Museums of Archaeology, Geology, Mineralogy, Palaeontology and Zoology.

The establishment of this museum conjointly by the Province of Ontario and the University of Toronto is due in very large measure to the enthusiasm and leadership of Sir Edmund Walker, the Chairman of the Board of Trustees.

The Museum is governed by a Board of Trustees, a body corporate consisting of ten members. The Minister of Lands, Forests and Mines and the Minister of Education of the Province of Ontario, and the Chairman of the Board of Governors of the University of Toronto are ex-officio members of this Board. The other seven members are appointed— four by the Lieutenant-Governor in Council, and three by the Governors of the University of Toronto as follows,—

ARCHAEOLOGY.

The Royal Ontario Museum of Archaeology is under the direction of C. T. Currelly, and is designed to show the best work which was done in the different crafts by the people of the past. An attempt has been made to show the history of the development of each of the great arts which have made civilization possible, by exhibiting the best examples of the early stages of development, of the culminating point, and then of the decline.

For the Stone Age the collection is very large, almost world-wide. The use of the early metals (copper and bronze) in the evolution of important tools is shown by a series of examples grouped under the Last Pre-historic Collection.

A large Egyptian series and a smaller Babylonian collection exhibit the history of pottery, stone vases, weapons, jewelry, medicinal articles, tools, textiles, sculpture and objects connected with death and burial. These exhibits occupy three galleries.

Two large galleries are devoted to the exhibition of ancient works of art from Greece and Italy. These consist of vases that illustrate nearly all the stages of vase painting from the Aegean and the mainland, armour, statuettes, jewels, and sculpture.

The next gallery is devoted to a collection to illustrate the life of the common people at the time of Christ and the early Church. This ranges from rag dolls to weapons, and from combs and domestic articles to shoes and tunics. In this same gallery is a large collection mainly of pottery objects obtained from the tombs of Palestine, and extending in periods from the earliest times down to the periods of the Byzantine empire.

As the student is now brought through the great spread of civilization of the Roman period, the next exhibition is of those nations that have lagged behind, where pre-historic things may be illustrated more freely by peoples who have recently been in the stone age. Here are shown the weapons and implements of the Eskimos, Africans, and South Sea Islanders, and of other jpeoples in the stone age or other primitive conditions.

Parallel to this gallery runs the collection illustrating the life of the American Indian. This consists of a fine series of paintings, objects of the stone age, and survivals of early things in use by the present Indians. It is mainly devoted to North America, though several cases contain Peruvian and other South American objects.

The great central hall is packed with Chinese works of art, of which we are particularly rich in tomb objects, especially terracotta sculptures and early wares. The collection of stone sculpture is also considerable, and the collection of textiles, jades, bronzes, etc., quite large. The whole forms one of the best general collections of Chinese art in existence. No space is available for the large collection of very fine Chinese paintings possessed by the Museum.

South of the central hall are two galleries devoted mainly to furniture and rooms, but with a certain number of costumes, musical instruments, etc., put in because of lack of other space for them.

The cross gallery at the end contains the Japanese collections of pottery, bronzes, armour, carvings, paintings, etc.

Between the large central hall and the door are parallel galleries, one devoted to the history of faience, and filled in with velvets, glass, furniture, sculpture, etc.; the other one devoted to lace and embroideries, but with the general collection of arms and armour also packed into it.

The space immediately inside the door is at present filled with an exhibit that is to go into the new War Museum.

GEOLOGY.

The Museum of Geology is under the direction of Professor A. P. Coleman and occupies the gallery along the west front of the basement. The ten alcoves into which the gallery is divided are designed to exhibit material illustrating the mineral resources of Canada and Economic and Structural Geology in general. It is intended that this gallery should be devoted to ores rather than to minerals, and it depends for its advancement on the generosity of mining men throughout the country.

The more important collections now in position in this gallery are the Cobalt silver ores, specimens illustrating the geology and ore deposits of the Sudbury nickel field, the coals of Canada, the asbestos and mica mines, and most of the metalliferous mines of Canada and other parts of the world. A particularly valuable exhibit is one illustrating the occurrence of ice ages at different times in the history of the earth. The more important marble producing regions of America are represented by a fine series of pedestals.

The more important additions to the Museum of Geology during the year are as follows:

Large collection of iron ores and related rocks from the Marquette district, Michigan, obtained through the kindness of the Cleveland Cliffs Mining Co.

Complete series of the copper ores and related rocks of Keweenaw point, Michigan, obtained through the kindness of several of the large copper-mining companies and of Professor Seaman of Houghton, Mich.

Zinc ores and graphite. J. C. Biedelman, Montreal.

Sphalerite from Missouri. Professor Guess.

—46

Volcanic ash of postglacial age from Yukon, and set of zinc ores from Franklin Furnace, N. J. Professor T. L. Walker.

Copper ores from Japan. Kenzo Ikeda per Professor W. G. Miller.

Samarskite from North Carolina. Dr. W. F. Ferrier.

Various ores and decorative stones. Ward's Natural Science Establishment, Rochester, N.Y.

MINERALOGY.

In the mineral gallery, which is under the direction of Professor T. L. Walker, are found very extensive collections of minerals and rocks. The most generous benefactors of this section are the men connected with the mining industry. To make the collections useful to visitors, the large specimens contained in the high cases are provided with special explanatory labels. In the cases on the east wall of the gallery a special display of minerals of Canada is arranged. The Director appeals to friends of the University for contributions of minerals and rocks with a view to making these collections as complete as possible. Donations are acknowledged annually in the Calendar of the University.

PALAEONTOLOGY.

The Museum of Palaeontology is under the direction of Professor W. A. Parks, and occupies the middle section of the top floor of the building. The collection of fossils is very extensive and contains many rare and unique specimens. It has developed from a nucleus presented by Sir Edmund Walker some years ago. Among the more important exhibits are the type Cambrian fossils presented by Sir William MacKenzie, the fossil sea-lilies presented by Mr. Frank Springer of Burlington, Iowa, a large fossil reptile presented by Sir Edmund Walker, Sir Donald Mann, Sir Lyman Melvin Jones and others. Recently a very fine skeleton of the extinct moa of New Zealand was added, and the skeleton of a mastodon, obtained some years ago near Welland, was prepared and mounted.

A series of wall cases has been installed, in which the geology and palaeontology of Canada is illustrated in a continuous but restricted manner.

During the last few years a vigorous campaign has been conducted for the acquisition of fossil dinosaurs from the famous region on the Red Deer river, Alberta. The preparation of one nearly complete skeleton has been completed and the specimen has been placed on exhibition. The material already obtained contains several very fine examples on which work is now being done preparatory to placing them in the gallery.

The department is provided with commodious storage and preparation rooms equipped with the necessary appliances for cutting and polishing specimens.

ZOOLOGY.

The Museum of Zoology is under the direction of Professor B. A. Bensley, and occupies the north portion of the top floor of the building. The first installation of specimens took place in 1914, some time after the establishment of the remaining portions of the Royal Ontario Museum, the nucleus of the new collection having been formed chiefly from Canadian material previously housed in the Biological Museum of the University. Many new additions have been made through the generosity of individual donors and through the co-operation of the Provincial Government and the Parks Department of the City of Toronto. The exhibits illustrate especially the fauna of Canada, all groups of which are represented, though Birds, Mammals, and Insects predominate. Some foreign material, more especially of birds, mammal heads and molluscan shells, has been installed as the beginning of a more general collection which will be developed later when more extensive accommodation becomes available.

ADDITIONS TO COLLECTIONS.

ZOOLOGY.

The zoological collections, especially those of the Royal Ontario Museum, have been greatly enlarged through the addition of new material collected by the staff; also through the organization of the technical service, principally in the preparation of specimens for exhibition, and through many exchanges, loans and gifts. The collections now include a good representation of Canadian fishes in the form of casts, especially prepared to show the form and colouration to the best advantage. There has also been completed a series of twelve habitat groups of small birds and mammals, in which the animals are depicted in replicas of their natural environments. Two large collections, consisting for the most part of mounted insects have been purchased at very nominal figures from Mrs. C. A. Snazelle and Professor C. J. S. Bethune, late of the Ontario Agricultural College, Guelph. In addition to a large number of individual smaller specimens there have been presented to the Museum specimens of southern Atlantic fishes from Mr. W. H. Brouse, Toronto, a large Atlantic sturgeon and case from the Board of Trade of the City of Toronto, a valuable collection of mounted specimens and trophies from the Estate of the late Mr. W. R. Patton, Toronto, and many specimens of captive animals from Riverdale Park donated by the Parks Department of the City of Toronto.

BOTANY.

The following additions have been made to the Department during last year:—

A collection of drawings, water sketches, notes on mushroons from the late Mr. T. Langton, LL.B., and a number of plants from various contributors.

Specimens of fungi from Algonquin Park and from Rondeau Park—G. W. Bartlett.

A Loranthaceae gall, (wooden flower), from Guatemala—Albert Miles.

Collection of insect galls from Dr. A. Cosens.

Contributions of seaweeds from Mrs. A. I. Sargent, and the estate of Mrs. Treble Massey.

Collections of timber-destroying fungi and photographs from Dr. J. R. Weir, W. H. Long, Dr. E. P. Meinecke of the U.S. Forest Service, from the following centres respectively: Montana and Washington, California, and New Mexico.

Contributions of mycological and pathological material from Dr. J. S. Boyce, San Francisco; C. H. Kauffman, Ann Arbor; H. T. Güssow, Ottawa; A. W. McCallum, Ottawa; R. J. Blair, Montreal; Miss Clara Fritz; Miss Jennie McFarlane; Miss Isa Underhill; Professor G. F. Atkinson (collections made mostly from the south eastern States).

Collection of Plants from Labrador—Rev. W. G. Walton.

Collection of Ontario Plants—The late Wm. Scott.

Collections of Seeds from the Seed Branch, Ottawa; Department of Agriculture, New Zealand; India; Eli Lilly Co., Indianapolis,

Type material of wheat, barley, vetch from Svälof, Sweden.

Western types of wheat—W. P. Thompson, University of Saskatchewan.

Type material of wheat from C. E. Saunders, Ottawa.

Lantern Slides, prints and negatives of coffee, cocoa, and fungi from the late Dean W. H. Ellis.

Collections of seeds from St. Albans, England.

MINERALOGY.

During the past year the collections of the University and of the Royal Ontario Museum of Mineralogy have been increased by donations from a large number of friends. The Hon. Senator M. J. O'Brien of Ottawa presented a very large specimen of silver ore from the Miller Lake O'Brien mine at Gowganda. This specimen is a section across a vein nearly two feet wide and weighs about one ton. It is very rich in silver and is one of our handsomest donations. Several mining men in Sudbury and Cobalt have presented much valuable material. An extensive series of minerals has been obtained from the government of Brazil.

Exchanges have been arranged with museums in Sweden, India, Denmark, France and the United States.

Large collections from Cobalt, Gowganda, Quebec, Nova Scotia and New Brunswick were made by the Director during the summer of 1920.

The material added by purchase is small, owing to limited means, when compared with what is received by presentation, collection and exchange. The Museum in thanking friends for past assistance looks to the general co-operation of the public for its future expansion.

PALAEONTOLOGY.

The more important acquisitions during the past year are as follows.—

Large collections of fossils from the local rocks at Toronto—Professor Parks and students.

Several more or less perfect dinosaurs from the Belly River formation of Alberta—Museum Expedition of 1920.

Fossils from Idaho, Wyoming, and Utah—Dr. W. F. Ferrier.

Mastodon bones from St. Catharines, Ont.—Miss Stewart.

Fossils from the Peace River district—Mr. A. H. Bell.

Fossils from Devonian of Great Slave lake—Mr. Warren.

Fossils from New Mexico—Professor Coleman.

Petrified tree from Arizona.

Set of specimens from Giants' Causeway—Mr. James Crowther.

Various collections purchased from Ward's Natural Science Establishment, Rochester, N.Y.

Two specimens of Coccosteus decipiens—Buffalo Society of Natural History.

DONATIONS OF BOOKS.

Since the destruction of the University Library by fire in 1890, upwards
of 50,000 volumes have been presented by various persons and organizations. For a complete list of the latter see Appendix to Calendars since
1893. The following is a list of donors for the year ending December 31st,
1920.

Government of Australia.

           Belgium.
           Brazil.
           British Columbia.
           Buitenzorg.
           Canada.
           Egypt.
           France.
           Holland.
           India.
           Indiana.
           Ireland.
           Italy.
           Java.
           Kansas.
           Manitoba.
           Maryland.
           Mexico.
           Michigan.
           New Brunswick.
           New Jersey.
           New South Wales.
           Nova Scotia.
           Ohio.
           Ontario.

Philippine Islands.
Prince Edward Island.
Quebec.
Saskatchewan.
Scotland.
Texas.
Uruguay.
United States.
Detroit, Board of Commerce.
Montreal, Harbour Commissioners of.
Richmond, Governor's Office.
Toronto, Bureau of Municipal Research.
Aberdeen, University of.

Academie Royale des Sciences de Denmark.
Academy of Natural Sciences of Philadelphia.
Adelaide, South Australia, Public Library of.
Adelbert College, Cleveland.
Adelbert College, Western Reserve University.
Aix-en-Provence, University of.
Akita Mining College, Japan.
Albany Medical College.
Alberta, University of.
Alliance Française, Paris.
American Antiquarian Society.
American Association for International Conciliation.
American Catholic Historical Society.
American Geographical Society.
American Law Book Company.
American Mining Congress.
American Museum of Natural History.
American Pediatric Society.
American Philosophical Society.
American Red Cross, Washington.
American School of Oriental Research.
American Union Against Militarism.
American Wood Preservers' Association.
Amherst College.
Amherst Graduates' Quarterly.
Ann Arbor, University of.
Argentina, Buenos Aires, Escuola Industrial.
Association for International Conciliation.
Association of American Physicians.
Association of Collegiate Alumni.
Association of Insurance Presidents.
Association of Life Insurance Medical Directors.
Athens, University of.
Auburn Theological Seminary.
Australia, Institute of Science and Industry.
Australian Museum, Sydney, N.S.W.
Bâle, University of.
Bergens Museum.
Berne, University of.
Bodleian Library.
Boston Public Library.
Boston, University of.
Bowdoin College.
Brandon College.
British Columbia, University of.
British Museum.

British Museum, Natural History.
Brooklyn Academy of Arts and Sciences.
Brooklyn Institute of Arts and Sciences, Museum.
Brussels, University of.
Bryn Mawr College.
Buenos Aires, University of.
Buffalo Historical Society.
Buffalo Society of Natural Sciences.
Calcutta University, the Registrar.
California State Library.
California, University of.
Cambridge Observatory.
Cambrigde Philosophical Society, England.
Cambridge Philosophical Society, Mass.
Cambridge, University of, Solar Physics Observatory.
Canadian Bank of Commerce.
Canadian Engineering Standards Association, Ottawa.
Canadian Journal of Medicine and Surgery.
Canadian Manufacturers Association, Toronto.
Canadian Practitioner and Review.
Canadian Reconstruction Association, Toronto.
Canadian Society of New York.
Canterbury College, Christchurch, N.Z.
Canton Christian College.
Cardiff Naturalists' Society.
Carnegie Endowment for International Peace.
Carnegie Foundation for the Advancement of Teaching.
Carnegie Institution of Technology.
Carnegie Institution of Washington.
Carnegie Institution of Washington, Dept. of Historical Research.
Carnegie Museum, Pittsburgh.
Carnegie Trust for the Universities of Scotland.
Case School of Applied Science.
Casualty Actuarial and Statistical Society.
Catholic Historical Review, Washington.
Chase National Bank, New York.
Chicago Board of Education.
Chicago Historical Society.
Chicago School of Civics and Philanthropy.
Chicago, University of.
Cincinnati.
Cincinnati Observatory.
Clarendon Press, The, Oxford.
Clarkson College of Technology.
Coimbra, University of.
College of Industrial Arts, Denton, Texas.

College of Physicians of Philadelphia.
Colombo Museum, Ceylon.
Colorado College.
Colorado, University of, Boulder.
Columbia University.
Commission Météorologique du Touks.
Commission of Fine Arts, Washington.
Comité Catholique de Propagande Française.
Consul Général de France, Montreal.
Copenhagen, K. Bibliotek.
Copenhagen, Store Kongel. Bibliotek.
Cordoba, Academia Nacional de Ciencias.
Cornell University.
Dalhousie University.
Dante Society.
Deutsche Dendrologische Gesellschaft.
Doninion Astrophysical Observatory.
Dublin University.
Dundee, University of.
Durham University, Philosophical Society.
École Libre des Sciences Politiques, Paris.
École Française des Hautes Études, Paris.
Edinburgh, University of, Library.
Eli Lilly and Co., Research Department.
Episcopal Theological School, Cambridge.
Eugenics Record Office.
Essex Institute.
Federated Malay States Medical Entomologist.
Field Museum of Natural History.
Forbes Library.
Friends of Ukraine.
Geographical Society of Philadelphia.
George Washington University.
George Williams Hoofer Foundation for Medical Research.
Gesellschaft für Erdkunde zu Berlin.
Glasgow City Library.
Glasgow Natural History Society.
Glasgow, University of.
Grand Rapids Public Library.
Grand Trunk Railway, General Advertising Agent.
Grenoble, University of.
Hamburgische Botanische Staatsinstitute.
Hamburgische Institut für Allgemeine Botanik.
Hartford Seminary Foundation.
Harvard College.
Harvard College, The Librarian.

Harvard College Observatory.
Havana, University of.
Heidelberg University.
Heye Museum.
Historić Landmarks Association of Canada.
Hongkong, Royal Observatory.
Hudson's Bay Company, Montreal.
Hudson's Bay Company, Winnipeg.
Hydro-Electric Power Commission.
Illinois Catholic Historical Society.
Illinois State Historical Society.
Illinois State Natural History Survey, Urbana.
Illinois, University of.
Illinois, University of, College of Medicine.
Imperial Cancer Research Fund, London.
India, Agricultural Adviser to the Government.
Indiana Academy of Science.
Indiana University.
Indicator Publishing Company.
Institut Botanique Léo Errera, Bruxelles.
Institut Central de Météorologie, Stockholm.
Institut d'Estudis Catalans, Barcelona.
Institut Océanographique de Monaco.
Institute for Crippled and Disabled Men.
Institute of Chemistry of Great Britain and Ireland.
Institute of Public Health, London, Ont.
Institution of Civil Engineers, Sec. Action Committee.
Institution of Mechanical Engineers, London.
Instituto Geological de Mexico.
Insurance Institute of Toronto.
Inter-America.
Inter-Fraternity Conference, Secretary, New York.
International Free Trade League, Boston.
International Health Board, Rockefeller Foundation.
Investment Bankers' Association of America.
Iowa, Historical Department of.
Iowa State Historical Society.
Iowa, University of.
Italian Consul, Toronto.
Jardin Botanique de l'État a Bruxelles.
John Crerar Library.
John Rylands Library.
Johns Hopkins University.
Joint War Committee of the British Red Cross Society and the Order of
    St. John of Jerusalem.
King Edward VII Sanatorium, Medhurst, Sussex.

K. Preussische Akad. der Wissenschaften, Berlin.
Kgl. Danske Videnskabernes Selskab, Copenhagen.
Kgl. Norske Videnskabers Selskab, Trondhjem.
"Kosmos".
Kyoto Imperial University.
La Plata, University of.
Lusanne, University of.
Laval University, Quebec.
League of Nations, London.
Lewis Institute, Chicago.
Libr. Honore Champion, Paris.
Library of the Committee of the Corporation of the City of London, Guild
    Hall.
Lick Observatory.
Liverpool University.
Lloyd Library.
Lloyd Publishing Company, Los Angeles.
London and Middlesex Historical Society.
London School of Economics.
London, University of.
Louisville Free Public Library.
Lund, University of.
McCormick Theological Seminary.
McGill University.
McMaster University Monthly,
Manchester Steam Users' Association.
Manchester University.
"Maria Immaculata", Hunfeld.
Marine Biological Association.
Massachusetts General Hospital, Cambridge.
Medical Research Committee, London.
Melbourne, University of.
Meteorological Office, Toronto.
Miami Conservatory District, Engineering Dept.
Miami University.
Michigan Agricultural College.
Michigan College of Mines.
Michigan Historical Commission.
Michigan University of.
Milwaukee City Public Museum.
Minnesota Historical Society
Minnesota, University of.
Mississippi Agricultural and Mechanical College.
Mississippi Valley Historical Association.
Missouri Botanical Gardens, St. Louis.
Missouri State Historical Society.

Missouri, University of.
Missouri, University of, School of Mines and Metallurgy.
Museu Paulista, San Paula.
Muséum d'Histoire Naturelle, Paris.
Museum of Comparative Zoology at Harvard University.
Museum of Comparative Zoology, Cambridge.
Museum of the American Indian, Heye Foundation.
Municipal Tuberculosis Sanitàrium, Chicago.
National Academy of Sciences, Washington.
National Advisory Committee for Aeronautics, Washington.
National Association of State Universities.
National Bank of Commerce in New York.
National City Bank of New York.
National Federation of Remedial Loan Associations.
National Institute for Medical Research.
National Polish Committee of America.
National Research Council, Washington.
Nebraska, University of.
New England Society of Brooklyn.
New Mexico State School of Mines.
New Mexico, University of.
New Philosophy, The.
New York Association for Medical Education.
New York Public Library.
New York School of Social Work.
New York Zoological Society.
Newberry Library.
Niagara Historical Society.
North Carolina, University of, Studies in Philology.
North Dakota, University of.
North Wales, University College of.
Nova Scotia Historical Society.
Nova Scotian Institute of Science.
Oberlin College.
Observatoire National de Besançon.
Observatorium, Breson, Helsingsfr. Denmark.
Observatory, Cape of Good Hope.
Ohio Archaeological and Historical Society.
Ohio Historical and Philosophical Society.
Ohio State University.
Okanagan United Fruit Growers, Vernon.
Oklahoma, University of.
Oneida Historical Society.
Ontario Agricultural College.
Ontario Historical Society.
Osborn Botanical Laboratory, Yale University.

Oxford, University of, Observatory.
Pan-American Union.
Paris, University of.
Pekin Union Medical College.
Pennsylvania Museum and School of Industrial Art.
Pennsylvania, University of, Botanical Hall.
Pennsylvania State College.
Philippines, University of the.
"Popular Astronomy".
Porto, University of.
Presbyterian College, Halifax.
Princeton University.
Puget Sound Biological Station, University of Washington.
Purdue, University of.
Purdue, University of, Engineering Experiment Station.
Quebec Geographical Society.
Queen's University, Kingston.
Queenlsand Museum.
Radcliffe Library, Oxford.
  . Academia de la Historia.
  . Accad. dei Lincei.
  . Accademia delle Scienze, Torino.
  . Accademia delle Scienze Fisiche e Matemat. di Napoli.
  . Accad. Virgiliana di Mantova.
  . Scuola Superiore di Agricultura.
R. Sociedad Espanola de Historia Natural.
Recife, Faculdade de Direito.
Research Laboratory Glass Container Association of America.
Revista de Archivos, Madrid.
Revue de l'Université de Bruxelles.
Revue Trimestrielle Canadienne.
Rhode Island State College.
Rio de Janeiro, Jardin Botanico.
Riverside Public Library.
Rochester, University of.
Rockefeller Foundation, New York.
Rockefeller Institute for Medical Research.
Rod and Gun.
Rose Polytechnic Institute.
Royal Academy of Amsterdam.
Royal Academy of Medicine in Ireland.
Royal Air Force of Canada, Historical Section.
Royal Astronomical Society, London.
Royal Astronomical Society of Canada.
Royal Botanic Gardens, Kew.
Royal Botanic Society, London.

Royal Canadian Institute.
Royal College of Dental Surgeons.
Royal College of Physicians of London.
Royal College of Surgeons of London.
Royal Colonial Institute.
Royal Dublin Society.
Royal Geographical Society, London.
Royal Historical Society.
Royal Observatory, Greenwich.
Royal Observatory, Hongkong.
Royal Scottish Geographical Society.
Royal Society of Edinburgh.
Royal Society of London.
Royal Society of London, Metric Committee, Board of Science Society.
Russian Liberation Committee, London.
Ryerson Public Library, Grand Rapids.
St. Andrews, University of.
St. Joseph's College, University of.
St. Louis Public Library.
St. Louis, University of.
St. Stephen's College.
Scripp's Institution for Biological Research.
Senckenbergische Naturforschende Gesellschaft.
Smithsonian Institution, Washington.
Social Service Council of Canada, Toronto.
Sociedad Cientifica "Antonio Alzate".
Sociedad de Estudios Vaseos, San Sebastian.
Société de l'Histoire des Colonies Francaises.
Société Francaise de Physique.
Société Technique des Experts en Écritures, Paris.
South Dakota, School of Mines.
South Wales, University College of.
Southern California, University of.
Station Suisse de Recherches Forestières, Zurich.
Stazione Sperimentale per le Malattie Infettive del Bestiame, Naples.
Sternwarte des Eidgenoss. Polytechnikums, Zurich.
Stevens Institute of Technology.
Stockholm University, Laboratoire de Physique.
Stockholm, K. Vitterhets Historie och Antikvitets Akademien.
Strassbourg, University of, Faculty of Medicine.
Structural Materials Research Laboratory, Lewis Institute.
Superintendent, The, University of Toronto.
Syracuse University.
Tasmania, University of.
Tennessee, University of.
Texas State Historical Association.

Thayer School of Civil Engineering.
"The New Philosophy".
Tohoku Imperial University.
Tokyo, University of.
Tokyo Zoological Society.
Toronto Public Library.
Toulouse, University of.
Union des Associations Internationales, Brussels.
Union Panatlantique, Paris.
Union Theological Seminary.
United States Pan American Union.
Université Internationale, Bruxelles.
Universitets Zoologische Museum, Copenhagen.
Universities Bureau of the British Empire.
University College Hospital Medical School, London.
University of the South.
Uppsale, University of.
Utah, University of.
Vassar College.
Vassar College Library.
Verein f. Schlessische Insektenkunde, Breslau.
Vermont Historical Society.
Victoria and Albert Museum.
Vienna, K. Preuss. Akad. der Wissenschaften.
Virginai, University of.
Warren Academy of Sciences.
Washington University State Historical Society.
Waterloo Historical Society.
Wellesley College.
Wellesley Hall.
Wentworth Historical Society.
Western Reserve University.
Western University Medical Dept.
Winnipeg Board of Trade.
Wisconsin State Historical Society.
Wisconsin, University of.
Woman's Hopsital, New York.
Women's Canadian Historical Society of Ottawa.
Women's Canadian Historical Society of Toronto.
World Peace Foundation.
Yale University.
Yorkshire Philosophical Society.
Zentralbeurau der International enErdmessung (Berlin).
Zoologisches Museum in Hamburg.
Zoological Society of London.
Zurich, University of.

Individual Donations.

Baird, A. B., Winnipeg.
Balch, Thos., W. Philadelphia.
Borden, Sir Robert.
Cacciapuoti, Rev. N., Toronto.
Carbonnel, M. Émile, New York.
Cassels, Mrs. Hamilton, Toronto.
Chalmers, A. J., Khartoum.
Champion, H., Paris.
Clercq, P. de, Veenwouden, Nederland.
Coleman, W. M., Trumpington, Cambridge.
Cooke, R. B., Cornell University.
Coolidge, Mrs. C. A., Boston.
Croft, Dr. A. J., Chicago.
Cullen, Dr. Thos. S., Boston.
Danmar, W., Jamaica, N.Y.
Dehaut, M. E. G., Paris.
Dutèns, Mme. Alfred, Paris.
Eaton, Dr., Boston.
Falconer, Sir Robert, Toronto.
Ferres, Jas., Montreal.
Fields, Prof. J. C., Toronto.
Fish, U.S., Cleveland.
Garneau, M. Hector, Montreal.
Gejsbeek, J. B., Denver.
Gooch, F. H.
Hall, Dr. T. Proctor, Vancouver.
Hamilton, L., Berlin.
Harrower, Henry R., Glendale, Cal.
Kellaway, William, Los Angeles.
Kenney, J. F., Public Archives, Canada.
Kerry, Miss E., Montreal.
Langton, H. H., Toronto.
Larson, Prof. A., Copenhagen.
Lindsay, R., Montreal.
Little, A. D., Cambridge.
Lloyd, Prof., Montreal.
Martin, Chester, University of Manitoba.
Montijn, A. M. M., The Hague, Holland.
Morgan, J. P., New York.
Nimmo, D. C., Detroit.
Norris, Frank H.
Osborn, H. F., American Museum of Natural History.
Pijoan, Prof., Toronto.
Powell, Dr. N. A., Toronto.

Rauschenberger, Dr. Walther, Frankfurt.
Robbins, R. C., North East Harbour.
Roddick, Lady, Montreal.
Snow, A. H., Washington.
Squair, Prof., Toronto.
Street, Mrs. W. P. R., Toronto.
Taylor, William, Son & Co.
Thompson, Edward, Northport, L. I.
Thompson, Slason, Chicago.
Thum, William, Publisher, Pasadena.
Tsolainos, M. Kyriakos P., Athens.
Vander Laeuw, H. J., Rotterdam.
Wallace, W. S., Toronto.
White, A. V., Toronto.
Williams, E. H., Woodstock, Vermont.
Windle, Sir Bertram, Toronto.
Wolbach, Dr. S. B., Harvard Medical School.
Wood, Dr. Casey, Stanford University, Cal.
Wrong, Prof. G. M., Toronto.
Yu, Lan-Tien, Peking.

PORTRAITS AND WORKS OF ART.

The following portraits and works of art have been presented to the University:

1. A portrait of the late Hon. William Hume Blake (oil painting by T. Hamel), presented by the Hon. Edward Blake.

2. A portrait of the Hon. Edward Blake, Chancellor 1876-1900 (oil painting by E. Wyly Grier), presented by graduates and friends.

3. A portrait of Professor E. J. Chapman (oil painting by Miss Frances Sutherland), presented by the artist.

4. A portrait of the late Professor Henry Holmes Croft (oil painting by A. Dickson Patterson), presented by friends of Professor Croft.

5. A portrait of the late President, Dr. McCaul (oil painting by A. Dickson Patterson), presented by the artist.

6. A portrait of the late Hon. Thomas Moss, Chief Justice of Ontario, Vice-Chancellor 1875-1881 (oil painting by Miss C. S. Berthon, copy of oil painting by M. Berthon), presented by the Hon. Charles Moss, Chief Justice of Ontario, Vice-Chancellor of the University.

7. A portrait of the late Right Reverend Bishop Strachan (oil painting copy), presented by the Council of University College.

8. A portrait of the late President, Sir Daniel Wilson (oil painting by A. Dickson Patterson), presented by friends of Sir Daniel Wilson.

9. A portrait of Professor E. J. Chapman (oil painting by A. Dickson Patterson), presented by graduates and friends.

10. A marble bust of the late Professor George Paxton Young (by Hamilton McCarthy), presented by friends of Professor Young.

11. A portrait of the late Professor George Paxton Young (oil painting by W. Allaire Shortt), presented by the artist.

12. A steel engraving of Sir John Colborne, afterwards Lord Seaton, Lieutenant-Governor of Upper Canada from 1830 to 1838, presented by Mr. Henry Hutchison.

13. "The Call to Duty" (oil painting by Paul Giovanni Wickson), presented to the Medical Faculty by the artist.

14. "The Marriage of the Duke of York" and "The King of Denmark's First Visit," commemorative medals, presented by the Town Clerk of London, Eng.

15. A bronze medal commemorative of the sesquicentennial anniversary of the founding of the College of New Jersey (Princeton University), presented by the trustees of Princeton University.

16. A bronze medal commemorative of the 150th anniversary of the capture of Louisbourg in 1745, presented by the Louisbourg Memorial Committee of the General Society of Colonial Wars.

17. A bronze medal commemorative of the 50th anniversary of Sir George Gabriel Stokes' appointment to a professorship in the University of Cambridge.

18. Busts of Dr. W. T. Aikins, Dr. J. H. Richardson, and Dr. H. H. Wright, by the Medical Faculty and other friends.

19. A bust of the late Hon. George Brown, and a portrait of the late Professor Croft, by Dr. Reeve.

20. Portraits of their Royal Highnesses the Prince and Princess of Wales, presented by their Royal Highnesses as a souvenir of their visit to the University in 1901.

21. A portrait of the Hon. Sir William Mulock, LL.D., ex-Vice-Chancellor of the University, presented by members of the Senate and other friends.

22. A steel engraving after Turner, by the late Sir Daniel Wilson, presented by Charles James Heywood, Esq., Manchester, Eng.

23. A collection of medals and coins, bequeathed by the late Dr. Scadding.

24. A portrait of Professor Goldwin Smith, presented by J. Ross Robertson, Esq.

25. A portrait of Dr. John Hoskin (oil painting by Robert Harris), presented by members of the Board of Governors and of the Senate and other friends.

26. A portrait of Dr. Maurice Hutton, Principal of University College (oil painting by William Cruikshank), presented by the Board of Governors.

27. A portrait of Sir Daniel Wilson, late President of the University of Toronto (oil painting by Sir George Reid), presented by members of the Board of Governors and of the Senate and other friends.

28. A portrait of Dr. R. A. Reeve (oil painting by Curtis Williamson), presented by members of the Board of Governors and of the Senate and other friends.

29. A portrait of Dr. John Galbraith (oil painting by J. W. L. Forster), presented by graduates of the Faculty of Applied Science.

30. A portrait of Dr. James Loudon, ex-President of the University of Toronto (oil painting by William Orpen), presented by the members of the Senate and other friends.

31. A portrait of Dr. James Loudon (oil painting by Frederick Victor Poole), presented by Mrs. Loudon.

32. A portrait of the Hon. Sir William Ralph Meredith, LL.D., Chancellor of the University (oil painting by William Strang),

presented by members of the Board of Governors and of the Senate and other friends.

33. A portrait of the late Hon. Joseph Curran Morrison, Chancellor of the University of Toronto, 1860-1876 (oil painting by Charles Hayward) presented by Judge Hardy of Brockville.

34. A portrait of Dr. William Henry van der Smissen, Professor Emeritus of German in University College (oil painting by Professor Philip Otto Schafer), presented by Mrs. van der Smissen.

35. A bronze medal commemorative of the 300th Anniversary of the founding of the University of Groningen.

36. A portrait of the late John Langton, M.A., Vice-Chancellor of the University of Toronto, 1856-1861 (oil painting by E. Wyly Grier) presented by his surviving sons, W. A. Langton, John Langton and H. H. Langton.

37. A portrait of the late Larratt William Smith, D.C.L., K.C., Vice-Chancellor of the University of Toronto, 1873-1875 (oil painting by G. T. Berthon), presented by his family.

38. "C'est l'Empereur" (oil painting by H. de T. Glazebrook), presented by the artist.

39. A portrait of the late William Oldright, M.A., M.D., Professor of Hygiene in the University of Toronto, 1887-1910 (oil painting by E. Wyly Grier), presented by his children.

40. A portrait of James Mavor, Ph.D., Professor of Political Economy in the University of Toronto (oil painting by Horatio Walker, Esq., LL.D.), presented by the artist.

41. A portrait of Charles Vincent Massey, M.A., a member of the Board of Governors of the University (oil painting by F. H. Varley), presented by friends of Mr. Massey.

42. A portrait of Robert Ramsay Wright, M.A., D.Sc., LL.D., Vice-President and Dean of the Faculty of Arts of the University of Toronto, 1901-1812, and Professor Emeritus of Biology (oil painting by Arnesly Brown), presented by the Board of Governors.

43. A portrait of Alfred Baker, M.A., LL.D., Dean of the Faculty of Arts of the University of Toronto, 1912-1919, Professor Emeritus of Mathematics (oil painting by E. Wyly Grier), presented by members of the Board of Governors of the Senate and other friends.

44. A portrait of William Hodgson Ellis, M.A., M.B., LL.D., Dean of the Faculty of Applied Science and Engineering of the University of Toronto, 1914-1919, and Professor Emeritus of Applied Chemistry (oil painting by E. Wyly Grier), presented by the members of the staff of the Faculty of Applied Science and Engineering.

45. Fifteen water-colour sketches of Canada and Edinburgh by Sir Daniel Wilson, purchased by the Board of Governors.

46. A portrait of Chester Daniel Massey, a member of the Board of Governors of the University from 1906 until 1920 (oil painting by F. H. Varley), presented to the University by the Board of Governors.

47. A collection of engravings of Old Montreal, done by the late Mr. Learmont, from paintings by H. Bunnett, and presented by Mrs. Learmont, of Montreal.

UNIVERSITY STUDIES.

The following is a list of studies published up to January, 1921:

HISTORY AND ECONOMICS.

Review of Historical Publications relating to Canada, edited
by Professor GEORGE M. WRONG and H. H. LANGTON.
Vol. I.-XXII, Publications of the years 1896-1917.

Vols. 2, 3, 5-18 (in cloth), each $1.50
Vols. 1 and 4 .... o.p
Index to Vols. I.-X. 1.00
Index to Vols. XI.-XX. 1.50

The Review of Historical Publications has ceased to appear,
being merged in a new publication, The Canadian Historical Review, a quarterly, annual subscription 2.00

History and Economics, Vol. I. comprising

1. Louisbourg in 1745, the anonymous "Lettre d'un Habitant de Louisburg,' 'edited and translated by Professor GEORGE M. WRONG 0.75
2. Preliminary stages of the Peace of Amiens, by H. M.
BOWMAN 0.75
3. Public debts in Canada, by J. ROY PERRY 0.50

Vol. II. comprising

1. City government in Canada, by S. MORLEY WICKETT.
Westmount, a municipal illustration, by W. D. LIGHT-
HALL. Municipal government in Toronto, by S. MORLEY
WICKETT 0.50
2. Municipal Government in Ontario, by A. SHORTT.
Municipal government in Ontario, by K. W. McKAY.
Bibliography of Canadian municipal government by S.
MORLEY WICKETT 0.50
3. Municipal history of Manitoba, by ALAN C. EWART.
Municipal government in the North-West Territories,
by S. MORLEY WICKETT. Municipal institutions in the
Province of Quebec, by R. STANLEY WEIR. Bibliography
supplementary), by S. MORLEY WICKETT 0.50
4. Evolution of law and government in the Yukon Terri-
tory, by J. N. ELLIOTT BROWN. Local government in
British Columbia, by S. MORLEY WICKETT. Local government in the Maritime Provinces, by WALTER C. MUR-
RAY. Local government in Newfoundland, by D. W.
PROWSE. Some notes on the charters of Montreal and
related statutes, by the Hon. R. STANLEY WEIR... The

civic administration of Montreal, by the Hon. PAUL
G. MARTINEAU. City government in Ottawa, by FRED
COOK. Present conditions, by S. MORLEY WICKETT.
Bibliography (supplementary), S. MORLEY WICKETT 1.50
Vol. II. complete (cloth binding) 3.50
Vol. III. No. 1: A colony of Emigrés in Canada, 1789-1816,
by LUCY ELIZABETH TEXTOR 1.00
No. 2: The Maseres Letters, 1766-68, edited with in-
troduction, notes and appendices by W. STEWART WAL-
LACE.
Extra volume: Early trading companies of New France, by
H. P. BIGGAR .... o.p.
Extra volume: Roman economic conditions, by E. H. OLIVER. 1.50

PHILOLOGY.

No. 1: The Anglo-Saxon Scop, by L. F. ANDERSON $0.50
No. 2: George Ticknor's Travels in Spain, edited by G. T.
NORTHUP 0.50
No. 3: Beginnings of the English Essay, by W. L. McDONALD. 1.0€
No. 4: Dio Cassius, Historia Romana, Bk. 53, with notes by
H. W. DUCKWORTH 1.00
No. 5: John Galt, by R. K. GORDON 1.00
Extra volume: Golding's A Tragedie of Abraham's Sacrifice,
edited with an introduction, notes and an appendix con-
taining the Abraham Sacrifiant of Theodore Beza, by M.
W. WALLACE 2.50
Extra volume: The Gest of Robin Hood, by W. H. CLAWSON 1.00
Extra volume: Calderon's La Vida es Sueno, edited by MIL-
TON A. BUCHANAN, Vol. O.: Text (cloth) 1.25
Extra volume: Theban Ostraca, transcript from the originals
with translations and plates 5.00

PSYCHOLOGY.

Vol. I., comprising
1. Spatial threshold of colour, by W. B. LANE, with ap-
pendices 0.75
2. A contribution to the psychology of time, by M. A.
SHAW and F. F. WRINCH .... } 0.75
3. Experiments on time relations of poetical metres,
by J. S. HURST and JOHN MCKAY .... }
4. Conceptions and laws in aesthetics, by Professor A.
KIRSCHMANN. Experiments on the aesthetic of life and
colour, by EMMA S. BAKER. Experiments with school-
children on color combination, by W. J. DOBBIE 1.50

Vol. II., comprising

1. The conception and classification of art from a psychological standpoint, by Professor O. KULPE. Spectrally
pure colours in binary combinations, by EMMA S.
BAKER. On colour-photometry and the phenomenon
of Purkinje, by R. J. WILSON. Experiments on the
function of slit-form pupils, by W. J. ABBOTT 1.50

2. Combinations of colours and uncoloured light by SUSIE
A. CHOWN. The complementary relations of some sys-
tems of coloured papers, by D. C. McGREGOR and D.
S. DIX. Some photometrical measurements, by W. G.
SMITH. Stereoscopic vision and intensity, by T. R.
ROBINSON 1.50

3. Combinations of colours with tints and with shades,
by F. LOUIS BARBER. Stereoscopic vision and intensity
(second paper), by T. R. ROBINSON 1.50

4. Combinations of colours with tints and with shades
(second paper), by F. LOUIS BARBER 1.50

Vol. III., No. 1: Complementarism, physical, by D. S. DIX   1.00

Vol. IV., Studies in Industrial Psychology, No. 1: A Point of
View, by E. A. BOTT. No. 2, Juvenile employment
in relation to Public Schools and Industries in Toronto   1.00

PHILOSOPHY.

No: 1: Light from the East, studies in Japanese Confucian-
ism, by R. C. ARMSTRONG $1.50

BIOLOGY.

No. 1: The gametophyte of Botrychium Virginianum, by E.
C. JEFFREY .... o.p.

No. 2: The anatomy of the Osmundaceae, by J. H. FAULL   o.p.

No. 3: On the identification of Meckelian and mylohyoid
grooves in the jaws of Mesozoic and recent mammalia,
by B. ARTHUR BENSLEY .... o.p.

No. 4: The megaspore-membrane of the Gymnosperms, by R.
B. THOMSON 1.00

No. 5: The homologies of the stylar cusps in the upper mo-
lars of the Didelphyidae, by B. ARTHUR BENSLEY   0.50

No. 6: On polystely in roots of Orchidaceae, by J. H. WHITE   0.50

No. 7: An early anadidymus of the chick, by Professor R.
RAMSAY WRIGHT 0.25

No. 8: The habits and larval state of Plethrodon Erythrono-
tus, by W. H. PIERSOL 0.50

ANATOMY.

PHYSIOLOGY.

No. 28: The action of adrenalin on the kidneys, by F. A. HART-MAN and R. S. LANG 0.25

No. 29: Some recent work on the control of the respiratory centre, by J. J. R. MACLEOD 0.25

No. 30: Studies in the regeneration of denervated mammalian muscle, by F. A. HARTMAN, W. E. BLATZ and L. G. KILBORN 0.50

No. 31: The functional pathology of surgical shock, by J. J. R. MACLEOD 0.25

No. 32: On ventilation, by J. J. R. MACLEOD 0.25

No. 33: Observations on the glycogen content of certain invertebrates and fishes, by L. G. KILBORN and J. J. R. MACLEOD 0.25

No. 34: The behavior of the respirations after decerebration in the cat, by J. J. R. MACLEOD 0.25

No. 35: On the formation of hydrochloric acid in the gastric tubules of the vertebrate stomach, by J. B. COLLIP...... 1.50

PATHOLOGY.

No. 1: Studies upon the influence of tension in the degeneration of elastic fibres of buried aortae, by W. H. HARVEY 0.25

No. 2: A case of acute phlegmonous gastritis, by Professor J. J. MACKENZIE ....

No. 3: Phlegmonous gastritis—report of a case, by CHARLES J. WAGNER .... } 0.25

No. 4: Report of the experimental production of chronic nephritis in animals by the use of uranium nitrate, by ERNEST C. DICKSON 0.25

MEDICAL RESEARCH FUND.

No. 1: On the haemolytic properties of fatty acids and their relation to the causation of toxic haemolysis and pernicious anaemia, by W. F. McPHERDRAN........

No. 2: Biological curves obtained during the onset and course of tuberculous infection, by A. H. CAULFIELD and F. S. MINNS ....

No. 3: Tuberculin treatment based upon clinical and biological data, by A. H. CAULFEILD and F. S. MINNS.... } 1.00

No. 4: The excretion of nitrogen in fever, by N. C. SHARPE and K. M. B. SIMON ....

No. 5: On fatty changes in the liver, heart, and kidney, by C. G. IMRIE ....

No. 6: On the fat in the blood in a case of lipaemia, by C. G. IMRIE ....

No. 7: A spectroscopic examination of the colour reactions of certain indol derivatives and of the urine of dogs after their administration, by ANNIE HOMER........

No. 8: A method for the estimation of the tryptophane contents of proteins involving the use of baryta as a hydrolyzing agent, by ANNIE HOMER .... } 1.00

No. 9: The relations between the administration of tryptophane to dogs and the elimination of kynurenic acid in their urine, by ANNIE HOMER ....

No. 10: A suggestion as to the cause of the lessened production of indol, etc., by ANNIE HOMER 0.25

No. 11: Experimental endocarditis, by H. K. DETWEILER and W. R. ROBINSON 0.25

GEOLOGY.

No. 1: The Huronian of the Moose River basin, by W. A. PARKS 0.50

No. 2: The Michipicoten iron ranges, by Professor A. P. COLEMAN and W. A. WILLMOTT 1.00

No. 3: The geology of Michipicoten Island, by E. M. BURWASH 1.00

No. 4: The stromatoporoids of the Guelph formation in Ontario, by Professor W. A. PARKS 1.00

No. 5: Niagara stromatoporoids, by Professor W. A. PARKS.... 1.00

No. 6: Silurian stromatoporoids of America, by Professor W. A. PARKS 1.00

No. 7: Ordovician stromatoporoids, by Professor W. A. PARKS 1.00

No. 8: A Cervalces antler from the Toronto Interglacial, by B. A. BENSLEY 0.25

No. 9: Palaeozoic fossils from a region s. w. of Hudson Bay, by W. A. PARKS 1.00

No. 10: Mineralogy from the H. B. Mine, Salmo, B.C., by T. L. WALKER 0.50

No. 11: The osteology of the trachrodont dinosaur kritosaurus incurvimanus, by W. A. PARKS 1.00

MATHEMATICS.

No. 1: Extension of results concerning the derivatives of an algebraic function of a complex variable, by S. BEATTY 0.50

PAPERS FROM THE PHYSICAL LABORATORIES.

The "Papers from the Physical Laboratories," issued as a special series of University of Toronto Studies, date from the year 1900. Nos. 1-17 were published by the Physical Department in a very limited edition and are no longer in print. For the sake of a complete record the numbering of the Papers, as forming a series of University of Toronto Studies, is made continuous with the earlier series and commences with No. 18. The earlier numbers, except those given below, are not now available either for sale or gift.

No. 73: The absorption of gases by carbonized lignites, by
　　STUART MCLEAN 0.25
No. 74: The destiny of absorbing materials, by STUART MC-
　　LEAN 0.25
No. 75: On the permeability of thin fabrics and films to
　　Hydrogen and Helium, by J. C. MCLENNAN and W. W.
　　SHAVER 0.25
No. 76: On the electrical conductivity of copper fused with
　　mica, by A. L. WILLIAMS 0.25

PAPERS FROM THE CHEMICAL LABORATORIES.

The papers from Chemical Laboratories, issued as a special series of University of Toronto Studies, date from the year 1895. No. 1-39 were published by the Chemical Department in a very limited edition, and are no longer in print. For the sake of a complete record the numbering of the papers as forming a series of University of Toronto Studies is made continuous with the earlier series and begins with No. 40. The earlier numbers are not now available either for sale or gift.

No. 40: The oxalates of bismuth, by F. B. ALLAN 0.25
No. 41: The economic admission of steam to water gas pro-
　　ducers of the Lowe type, by G. W. MCKEE 0.25
No. 42: The rate of formation of iodate in alkaline solutions
　　of iodine, by E. L. C. FORSTER 0.25
　　by Professor W. LASH MILLER and T. R. ROSEBRUGH.... 0.50
No. 43: Numerical values of certain functions involving e^{-n}
No. 44: A reaction whose rate is diminished by raising the
　　temperature, by CLARA C. BENSON 0.25
No. 45: On the decomposition of benzene at high temperature,
　　by G. W. MCKEE 0.25
No. 46: The action of liquefied ammonia on chromic chloride,
　　by Professor W. R. LANG and C. M. CARSON. Note on
　　the action of methylamine on chromic chloride, by Pro-
　　fessor W. R. LANG and C. M. JOLLIFFE 0.25
No. 47: A mechanical model to illustrate the gas laws, by
　　FRANK B. KENRICK 0.25
No. 48: The rate of the reaction between iodic and hydriodic
　　acids, by S. DUSHMAN 0.25
No. 49: The electrolysis of acid solutions of aniline, by
　　LACHLAN GILCHRIST 0.25
No. 50: Some compounds of chromic chloride with substituted
　　ammonia, by Professor W. R. LANG and C. M. CARSON 0.25

—48

No. 111: The effect of chlorine on periodic precipitation, by
MISS A. W. FOSTER 0.25
No. 112: The scattering of light by dust-free liquids, by W.
H. MARTIN 0.25
No. 113: Friedel and Crafts' reaction—nitrophthalic anhy-
drides and acetylaminophthalic anhydrides with ben-
zene and aluminum chloride, by W. A. LAWRANCE 0.25
No. 114: Toxicity and chemical potential, by W. LASH
MILLER 0.25
No. 115: The toxicity towards anthrax and staphylococcus
of solutions containing phenol and sodium chloride,
by J. S. LEMON 0.25
No. 116: Some phenomena observed in electric furnace arcs,
by J. KELLEHER 0.25

Theses Accepted for the Degree of Doctor of Philosophy.

FREDERICK HUGHES SCOTT. 1900.
The Structure, Micro-Chemistry and Development of Nerve
Cells, with special reference to their nuclein compounds. Uni-
versity of Toronto Studies, Physiological Series No. 1, 1900.
Transactions of the Canadian Institute. 1898-99, Vol. 6, Parts
1 and 2, pp. 405-438.
JOHN CUNNINGHAM MCLENNAN. 1900.
Electrical Conductivity in Gases Traversed by Cathode Rays.
1900. Philosophical Transactions of the Royal Society of Lon-
don. Series A, Vol. 195, pp. 49-77.
WILLIAM ARTHUR PARKS. 1900.
The Huronian of the Basin of the Moose River. University of
Toronto Studies, Geological Series, No. 1, 1900.
FRANCIS BARCLAY ALLAN. 1901.
The Basic Nitrates of Bismuth, 1901. American Chemical
Journal, Vol. XXV., No. 4, April, 1901, pp. 307-315.
ROSS GEORGE MURISON. 1902.
The Mythical Serpents of Hebrew Literature, 1902.
RICHARD DAVIDSON. 1902.
The Semetic Permansive-Perfect, 1902.
WALTER REUBEN CARR. 1903.
On the Potential Difference required to produce electrical
discharges in gases at low pressure, an extension of Paschen's
Law. Transactions of the Royal Society of Canada, Second
Series, 1902-03. Vol. VIII, section III., pp. 161-182. 1902.
On the Laws governing electric discharges in gases at low
pressures. Philosophical Transactions of the Royal Society of
London, Series A, Vol. 201, pp. 403-433.

EMMA SOPHIA BAKER. 1903.

Experiments on the Æsthetic of Light and Colour. University of Toronto Studies, Psychological Series, Vol. I., No. 4.

Spectrally Pure Colours in Binary Combinations. University of Toronto Studies, Psychological Series, Vol. II., No. 3. 1902.

GEORGE GALLIE NASMITH. 1903.

The Chemistry of Wheat Gluten.

University of Toronto Studies, Physiological Series, No. 4.

The Transactions of the Canadian Institute, Vol. VII. 1903.

CLARA CYNTHIA BENSON. 1903.

The Rates of Reactions in Solutions containing Ferrous Sulphate, Potassium Idolide and Chromic Acid.

The Journal of Physical Chemistry, May, 1903, pp. 356-388.

WILLIAM EDINGTON TAYLOR. 1903.

The Ethics and Religious Theories of Bishop Butler.

Toronto: The Bryant Press. 1903.

THOMAS EAKIN. 1905.

The Text-book of Habakkuk, chap. I. 1-II. 4.

Toronto: E. D. Apted, n.d.

THOMAS RUTHERFORD ROBINSON. 1906.

Stereoscopic Vision and its relation to Intensity and Quality of Light Sensation. University of Toronto Studies. Psychological Series. Vol. II., Nos. 2 and 3. Reprint. n.d.

JOHN RANSON ROEBUCK. 1906.

The rate of the Reaction between Arsenious Acid and Iodine in Acid Solution; the rate of the reverse Reaction; and the Equilibrium between them.

The Journal of Physical Chemistry, Vol. VI., p. 365, and Vol. IX., p. 727. Reprint. n.d.

MAITLAND CREASE BOSWELL. 1907.

The Course of the Oxidation of α-Naphthoquinone to Phthalic Acid and the Detection and Estimation of α-Naphthoquinone, β-Naphthoquinone, Phthalonic Acid and Phthalic Acid.

Toronto: The University Press. n.d.

RALPH EMERSON DELURY. 1907.

The Rate of Oxidation of Arsenous Acid by Chromic Acid and the Induction of Arsenious Acid by the Reaction between Chromic and Hydriodic Acids.

The Journal of Physical Chemistry, Vol. XI. Reprint. n.d.

DAVID STRATHY DIX. 1908.

Complementarism; Physical and Psychical. University of Toronto Studies. Reprint. n.d.

AUSTIN PERLEY MISENER. 1909.

The Place of Hosea I.-III. in Hebrew Literature.

Toronto: E. D. Apted. n.d.

JOHN FRANCIS MACKEY. 1909.
  Part I.: Some Esters of Arsenious Acid.
  Part II.: Some Esters of Antimony Trioxide. Reprint. n.d.
CALVIN ALEXANDER McRAE. 1910.
  The Hebrew Text of Ben Sira (Ecclesiasticus).
  Toronto: Queen Printing Co. n.d.
WILLIAM ROBERT TAYLOR. 1910.
  The Originality of the Hebrew Text of Ben Sira in the light
  of the Vocabulary of the Versions.
  Toronto:. E. D. Apted. n.d.
WALTER DANIEL BONNER. 1912.
  Experimental Determination of Binodal Curves, Plait Points,
  and Tie Lines in Fifty Systems, each consisting of Water
  and Two Organic Liquids.
ELI FRANKLIN BURTON. 1910.
  On the Physical Aspect of Colloidal Solution. University of
  Toronto Studies, Physical Series, No. 36.
SAUL DUSHMAN. 1912.
  The Behaviour of Copper Anodes in Chlorine Solutions.
  The Journal of Physical Chemistry, Vol. XIV. Reprint. n.d.
JOSEPH ROY SANDERSON. 1812.
  The Relation of. Evolutionary Theory to Ethical Problems.
ABSALOM COSENS. 1913.
  A Contribution to the Morphology and Biology of Insect Galls.
VIVIAN ELLSWORTH POUND. 1913.
  I. The Absorption of the Different Types of Beta Rays to-
      together with Study of the Secondary Rays excited by
      them.
  II. On the Secondary Rays excited by the Alpha Rays from
      Polonium. Part I.
  On the Secondary Rays excited by the Alpha Rays from Polo-
      nium. Part II.
PERCIVAL WILSON SPENCE. 1913.
  Moray Transitions in Israel Between 1200 and 700 B.C.
EDWARD MOORE JACKSON BURWASH. 1914.
  The Geology of Michipicoten Island.
ROBERT CORNELL ARMSTRONG. 1914.
  Light from the East, Studies in Japanese Confucianism.
SAMUEL BEATTY. 1915.
  Extensions of Results Concerning the Derivatives of an Alge-
  braic Function of a Complex Variable.
ROY BALMER LIDDY. 1915.   ....
  The Relation of Science and Philosophy.
JAMES BERTRAM COLLIP. 1916.
  On the Formation of Hydrochloric Acid in the Gastric Tubules
  in the Vertebrate Stomach.

HARDY VINCENT ELLSWORTH. 1916.

A Study of Certain Minerals from Cobalt, Ontario.

WILLIAM HARVEY MCNAIRN. 1916.

. Growth of Etch Figures.

EDWIN JOHN PRATT. 1917.

Studies in Pauline Eschatology and its Background.

HENRY FRANKLIN DAWES. 1918.

Image Formation by Crystalline Media.

A Lens Refractometer.

On the Ionisation by Collision in the gases Helium and Argon.

RAYMOND COMPTON'DEARLE. 1919.

Some Investigations in the Infra-Red Regions of the Spectrum.

ELLIS INGHAM FULMER. 1919.

The Action of Certain Poisons and of Ammonium Fluoride on Yeast.

ARCHIBALD BRUCE MACALLUM. 1919.

The Relation of Vitamines to the Growth of Young Animals.

MOSSIE MAY WADDINGTON. 1919.

The Development of British Thought from 1820 to 1890.

JAMES HERBERT WHITE. 1919.

On the Biology of Fomes Applanatus.

FULTON HENRY ANDERSON. 1920.

Substance in John Locke's Theory of Knowledge.

HAROLD KEITH BOX. 1920.

Dental and Associated Tissues.

EDWARD HORNE CRAIGIE. 1920.

On the Relative Vascularity of Various Parts of the Central Nervous System of the Albino Rat.

ROBERT KAY GORDON. 1920.

John Galt.

KENNETH HAY KINGDON. 1920.

Low Voltage Ionisation.

Phenomena in Mercury, Vapour.

The Magnetisation' of Ships and its Application to the Operation of Magnetic and Electro-magnetic Devices External to the Ship.

NORMAN ASHMELL CLARK. 1921.

The Growth Rate of Yeast.

WALTER ALBERT LAWRENCE. 1921.

(1) Friedel and Crafts' reaction—intrphthalic anhydrides and acetylaminophthalic anhydrides with benzene and aluminium chloride. (2) Friedel and Crafts' reaction.

MAURICE EDWARD SMITH. 1921.

"Friedel and Crafts' Reaction—the carbmethoxy—benzoyl chlorides with aromtic hydrocarbons and aluminium chloride."

EXTENSION LECTURES.

These lectures are offered to the public so that it may be possible for those interested, in any part of Ontario, to avail themselves of either single lectures or short courses of lectures on literary and scientific subjects. *If requests are made for lectures not found on the present list, an effort will be made to provide them.*

Most benefit results, as a rule, from a carefully arranged course of lectures on some topic with, if possible, collateral reading by the members of the organization taking the course. This procedure is strongly recommended.

In order that the members of the staff who give these Extension lectures should receive some recognition for their work, the Board of Governors of the University has decided that the organization arranging for such lectures should pay five dollars and the lecturer's travelling expenses for each lecture. For the encouragement of this work the Board has set aside a sum of money which is calculated to pay the lecturer the same amount as he receives in fees from the local organization.

All correspondence with regard to lectures, and all money paid for lectures, or for lecturer's expenses, should be sent to the Director, University Extension, University of Toronto.

Professor E. F. Burton—
1. The Properties of Collodial Solutions.
2. Commercial Applications of Liquid Air.
3. Relativity.
4. The Structure of the Atom.

Professor C. A. Chant—
Single lectures on various astronomical subjects or short courses of three to five lectures. (Illustrated).

Dr. A. P. Coleman: (Dean of the Faculty of Arts.)—
1. Geology: The Ice Age, Mountain Building, the Tooth of Time, Volcanoes, Ancient Ice Ages.
2. Geography: The Rocky Mountains, Labrador, Gaspé, South America, South Africa, Australia and New Zealand, India and the Far East, Scandinavia and Spitsbergen, Mexico. (All illustrated.)

Dr. W. H. Clawson—
1. "Shakespeare's Theatre." (Illustrated.)

Professor Cameron—
1. French Art. (Illustrated.)

Professor W. A. Clemens—
1. The Life of our Inland Waters. (Illustrated.)

Professor G. A. Cornish—
1. History of the Great Lakes.
2. History of Niagara Falls.
3. Our Greatest Travellers (Bird Migration). (With slides.)
4. The Japanese and their Industries. (With slides.)
5. The New Europe.

Professor E. A. Dale—
1. Algernon Charles Swinburne.
2. The Roman Plays of Shakespeare and of Jonson Compared.
3. Ballad Poetry.
4. Some English Mystical Poets.
5. Greek Tragedy and the Greek Theatre.
6. Salvation in Greek Religion.
7. Theories of the Primitive Life and Development of Man in Greek and Latin Literature.
8. The Value of the Greek and Latin Classics to the Modern World.
9. The Vanishing Art of Reading Aloud—What to Read and How to Read It.
10. The Roman World in the Early Days of Christianity.

Professor Saint-Elme de Champ—
1. Alsace-Lorraine.
2. French Women before, during, and after the War.
3. The Religious Question in France.
4. The attitude of France towards the Treaty of Versailles.

Professor J. G. Fitzgerald—
Single Lectures:
1. Public Health Education, its bearing on community welfare.
2. The Preparation of Antitoxins used in preventing and treating communicable diseases (illustrated with lantern slides).
3. The Value of the Public Health Laboratory to the community.

Courses of Lectures:
1. Etiology, Methods of Spread and means of Control of some of the important communicable Diseases. (Six lectures.)
2. Official and Voluntary Health Promoting Agencies. (Three lectures.)
3. How man protects himself against harmful bacteria. (Two lectures.)

Professor L. Gilchrist—
1. X-Rays and Radioactive-Radiations, and their applications.
2. Light Waves and their Uses.
3. The Production of Colour in Insects and Birds.

Dr. C. D. Howe—
1. The making of a Tree. (Illustrated.)
2. The Making of a Forest. (Illustrated.)
3. Nature's Forest and Man's Forest. (Illustrated.)
4. Forest Conditions in Canada. (Illustrated.)
5. The Work of the Various Forestry Organizations in the Dominion. (Illustrated.)

Professor Maurice Hutton—
1. German and British Ideals.
2. Greece and the Great War.
3. Kipling—(One or two lectures).
4. Thucydides.
5. Herodotus—(One or two lectures).
6. Romans, Greeks, English and French. (One or two lectures.)
7. The Antigone of Sophocles. (One, or a series of five or six lectures.)

Professor V. E. Henderson—
1. A Brief History of Architectural Development in Europe.
2. A Comparison of French and English Architecture during the period from 1000-1500 A.D.
3. A Comparison of the Nervous Systems and the Accompanying Habits of Some of the Lower Animals.
4. Czecho-Slovakia, its history and development.

Professor L. E. Horning—
1. A Course on English Life and Literature (also as single lectures.)—(a) Old England and Alfred. (b) The Normans and the Court of Henry II. (c) The Triumph of English: Chaucer and Wycliffe. (d) Elizabethan England. (e) The Stuarts. (f) Romanticism. (g) The Early Victorians. (h) The Later Victorians. (i) 1890-1910. (j) To-day and To-morrow.
2. Canadian Topics—
(a) Oldest Canada. (b) Salient Features of Canadian History. (c) Canadian Literature. (d) Canadian Citizenship.
3. Our Mother-Tongue. (Two or five lectures.)
4. Goethe and his Faust. (One to five lectures.)
5. European Topics—
(a) The Everlasting Balkans. (b) Teuton and Slav: an age-long problem. (c) Russia. (d) The French Revolution and Europe. (e) Europe: 1815 to 1878. (f) Europe: 1878-1914. (g) The Peace of Versailles—1919 and the Future. (h) Italy and the near East.

6. Miscellaneous—
    (a) The Growth of Freedom. (b) War Poetry. (c) Nationalism, Imperialism, Internationalism. (d) Melting-Pots—Europe and America.

Professor J. Gibson Hume—
1. Some Educational Problems in Ontario:
    (a) Problems of the Public Schools (Urban and Rural).
    (b) Problems of the High Schools and Technical Schools.
    (c) Problems of the University.
2. Problems of the Pupil:
    (a) The Choice of a Life Work. (b) How to Think. (c) The Training of the Memory. (d) The Training of the Imagination. (e) Life's Problems and Life's Ideals (Individual and Social).

Professor W. T. Jackman—
1. Government Ownership of Railways.
2. The Railway Situation in Canada.
3. Relation of the Railways to the National Welfare (Course of lectures).
4. Motor Truck Transportation in Relation to Rural Development.
5. Rural Re-organization. (Courses of lectures.)
6. Rural Credits.

Professor G. M. Jones—
1. The Imperial Conference.
2. The Growth of Democracy in Great Britain.
3. The Romance of Canadian History. (Illustrated.)
4. Tennyson's "In Memoriam."

Professor F. C. A. Jeanneret—
1. Prieux and the Modern French Drama.

Professor D. R. Keys—
1. American Humour—Its Genesis and Exodus.
2. King Alfred the Great.
3. Chaucer and his Times. (Illustrated.)
4. The English Novel as a Guide to Conduct.
5. Folk Lore.
6. Shakespeare and his Time.
7. The Modern Novel.
8. The Historical Method: the greatest discovery of the 19th Century.
9. Toronto—Past, Present, and Future.
10. World Problems of Our Day.

Professor W. B. Lane—
1. Pragmatism and Idealism—one lecture, or a series.
1. Ethical Features of the Modern Flux Philosophy (Bergson), (one lecture, or a series).
3. Ethics of Kant (or J. S. Mill or Green), one lecture, or a series.
4. Nietzsche's Immoralism. One lecture.

Professor R. M. MacIver—
1. The Present Economic Situation.
2. The Wealth of a Nation.
3. Evolution away from War.
4. Selective Agencies in Modern Society.
5. The Formation of Public Opinion.
6. One of a series of lectures on Nationality, including such subjects as its meaning, historic development, dangers, the place of internationalism, etc.
7. One of a series of lectures on the problems and tasks of Representative Government.
8. One of a series of lectures on fundamental economic questions, such as capital and labour, the wage system, the production of wealth and the distribution of wealth, the relation of wealth and poverty, the conservation of wealth in Canada, etc.

Professor J. F. McLaughlin—
1. History and Monuments of Ancient Egypt.
2. History and Monuments of Ancient Mesopotamia.
3. Mohammed and his Koran.
4. Poetry and Religion of the Arabs.
5. The Hebrew Prophets.
6. The Hebrew Poets.
7. Modern Movements and Changes in Palestine.

(Nos. 1, 2 and 7 can be illustrated. Nos. 5 and 6 can be given in short courses of five or six lectures).

Professor H. McTaggart—
1. X-Rays and Crystal Structures.

Professor H. S. McKellar—
1. Dr. Drummond, the Habitant Poet (one lecture).
2. A Glimpse of Paris (with illustrations) one lecture (in French, if desired, for High Schools).
3. Victor Hugo:
(a) His Life (with illustrations); (b) His Poems and Novels; (c) His Dramas.

Professor Moraud—
1. (a) Three Modern French Novelists (or one lecture on each). (b) Anatole France as a representative of

French liberalism. (c) A Defender of the French
Traditions, Maurice Barrés. (d) The Spokesman of
the Middle Classes, René Bazin.

2. France of To-day.
(a) The Press (one lecture). (b) The Political Parties and their Platforms (one lecture). (c) The Present French Foreign Policy (one lecture).

Professor G. H. Needler—
1. Landmarks in the Political History of Germany.
2. The Constitution of the New German Republic.
3. Single lectures or a series of lectures on any authors or
movements in German literature as called for.

Dr. W. Pakenham (Dean, Ontario College of Education)—
1. The Ontario School of Sixty Years Ago.
2. The Physical Well-being of Pupils.
3. Schools of To-morrow.
4. A Citizen of London in 1660.

Dr. W. A. Parks—
1. The Great Fossil Reptiles of Alberta. (Lantern.)
2. The Origin and Development of the Mammalia. (Lantern.)
3. Northern Ontario—Geological Geography. (Lantern.)
4. Trilobites—an extinct race. (Lantern.)
5. The Development of the Science of Geology.
6. The Surficial Geology of Ontario.

(Please note that these lectures will be given to adult audiences
only. Sunday school and similar organizations are quite unsuited
to this type of lecture.)

Professor Peter Sandiford—
1. Educational Problems of Canada and their proposed solutions. (One or six lectures.)
2. Aspects of Child Life, being lectures to teachers and parents. (One to twelve lectures.)
3. Measurements of Intelligence. (Lectures and demonstrations.)

Professor C. B. Sissons—
1. Ancient and Modern Imperialism.
2. Athenian and American Democracy.
3. Socrates, Citizen and Teacher.
4. The Status of the French Language in Canada.
5. Peculiar Peoples in the Canadian West—A Study of Immigration—(Illustrated).
6. The Rise of the Co-operative Movement.

Dr. John Satterly—
1. Soap Bubbles and the Forces that mould them.
2. The Law of Gravitation.
2. Conduction of Heat.
4. Radiation of Heat.
5. The Elements of the Thermodynamics of a Steam Engine.
6. The Liquefacation of Gases.
7. Radioactivity.
8. The Laws of the Continuity of State.
9. The Second Law of Thermodynamics.
10. The Effect of Pressure on Change of State.
11. Meteorology (including Weather Forecasts).
12. Osmotic Pressure and Osmosis.
13. Gyroscopes and Spinning Tops.
14. The different forms of Energy.
15. Capillarity.
16. The Elastic Properties of Metals.

Professor H. B. Sifton—
1. Poisonous Plants. (Illustrated)—one or a series of lectures).
2. Poisonous Seeds in Feeds. (Illustrated)—one lecture.
3. Weeds. (Coloured Illustrations)—one lecture.

Professor G. O. Smith—
1. Roman Occupation of Britain.

Professor R. B. Thomson—
1. Insectivorous Plants (Illustrated)—one lecture.
2. Plant Breeding (Illustrated)—one, or several lectures.
3. Botanic Gardens and Their Value to the Public. (One lecture.)
4. Sphagnum (peat-bog moss) for surgical dressings. (One lecture.)

Professor W. S. Wallace—
1. The Growth of Canadian National Feeling. (One lecture, or a course of lectures).
2. The First White Men in America. (One lecture.)

Professor J. S. Will—
1. Mediaeval Saints and Modern Sinners (a lecture on religion in France).
2. France of To-day and Yesterday.
3. Renaissance and Reform (one or more lectures).
4. French Painters. (Illustrated.)
5. Illustrious French Women (one or more lectures).
6. Intellectual Liberty.
7. French Thought in the Nineteenth Century.
8. Canada's Debt to France.

Professor A. H. Young—

1. Land Granting in Upper Canada.
2. Major-General Simcoe, the first Lieutenant-Governor of Upper Canada.
3. Dr. Samuel Peters—The Loyalist who did not become Bishop of Upper Canada.
4. Dr. John Stuart of Kingston—The first schoolmaster in Upper Canada.
5. Getting a University for Upper Canada.
6. John Strachan, D.D., first Bishop of Toronto and founder of King's College, Toronto, and of Trinity College.

UNIVERSITY EXTENSION.

The following statute relating to University Extension work was passed by the Senate in April, 1894:

1. A standing committee of seven members of Senate shall be appointed annually for the purpose of carrying on "University Extension" work of a kind similar to that carried on under the same designation in connection with the Universities of Cambridge and Oxford.

2. The committee shall have authority to appoint a secretary, define his duties and fix his remuneration.

3. No part of the expenses incurred for teaching and examining done at "local centres" of instruction, or for secretarial work done under the authority of the Committee, or for any other purpose connected with University Extension shall be a charge on the ordinary revenue of the University.

4. It shall be the duty of the Committee, subject to ratification by the Senate, to appoint teachers and examiners for approbed or prescribed courses of study at local centres, and to grant certificates to such students as may have passed the final examinations in each course and complied with other conditions prescribed from time to time by the Committee.

5. It shall be the duty of the Secretary to keep a register, in which shall be entered the name and address of each student who obtains a certificate with a description of the course of study in which he has passed, and such other particulars as the Committee may from time to time order to be inserted.

CATALOGUE OF SPECIAL EVENTS, 1920-21.

1920.

Aug. 10—1.30 p.m.—Luncheon in the Great Hall, Hart House, given in honour of the members of the Imperial Press Conference, by the Governors of the University.

3.00 p.m.—Special Convocation at which the degree of Doctor of Laws was conferred upon the following members of the Imperial Press Conference.

Robert Donald, Esq.,

Geoffrey E. Fairfax, Esq.,

Sir Robert Bruce,

Rt. Hon. Sir Gilbert Parker, Bart., P.C.

Oct. 3—University Sermon by Sir Robert Falconer, K.C.M.G., M.A., LL.D., D.Litt.

Oct. 10—University Sermon by Dr. Wilfred T. Grenfell.

Oct. 24—University Sermon by Major G. G. D. Kilpatrick, D.S.O.

Oct. 30—Lecture in the Physics Building, by Robert Mond on "Recent Discoveries in Egypt."

Oct. 31—University Sermon by Dr. James Endicott.

Nov. 2—Organ Recital by Mr. F. A. Mouré, University Organist.

Nov. 5—Special Convocation in the Music Room of Hart House when the portrait of Mr. Chester D. Massey was presented to the University and when the Honourary Degree of Doctor of Laws was conferred on Mr. Massey.

Nov. 7—University Sermon by Dr. H. Symonds.

Nov. 9-13—Presentation of "Matsuo" and "Rasmus Montanus" by the Players' Club of the University.

Nov. 14—University Sermon by Canon F. G. Scott, D.S.O.

Nov. 16—Organ Recital by Mr. F. A. Mouré, University Organist.

Nov. 21—University Sermon by Bishop W. F. McDowell.

Nov. 28—University Sermon by Dr. E. C. Cayley.

Nov. 30—Organ Recital by Mr. F. A. Mouré, University Organist.

Dec. 5—University Sermon by R. E. Welsh.

Dec. 6—University visited by the Royal Commission on University Finances.

Dec. 7-11—Presentation of Bernard Shaw's "You Never Can Tell" by the Players' Club of the University.

Dec. 12—University Sermon by C. R. Brown.

—49

Dec. 14—Organ Recital by Mr. F. A. Mouré, University Organist.
Dec. 22-24—Presentation of "The Chester Mysteries" by the Players' Club of the University.

1921.

Jan. 5—Lecture by Sir Bertram Windle, LL.D., on Britain in the Ages before the Roman Occupation—the first of his series on "The Roman Occupation of Britain."

Jan. 5-26—Conference on "Recent Advances in Physics" held in the Physics Building.

Jan. 8—Illustrated Lecture by Professor F. J. Foakes Jackson, D.D., on Margaret Catchpole, a Study in East Anglian Life and in Literary Criticism.

Jan. 9—University Sermon by Professor W. Manson.

Jan. 11—Organ Recital by Mr. F. A. Mouré, University Organist.

Jan. 12—Lecture by Sir Bertram Windle, LL.D., on "Caesar's Invasion of Britain."

Jan. 15—Lecture by W. D. Woodhead, M.A., "The Case for Greek.'

Jan. 16—University Sermon by Dr. A. N. Marshall.

Jan. 19—Lecture by Sir Bertram Windle, LL.D., on "The Military Organization of the Romans in Britain."

Jan. 23—University Sermon by J. H. Oldham.

Jan. 25—Organ Recital by Mr. F. A. Mouré, University Organist.

Jan. 26—Lecture by Sir Bertram Windle, LL.D., on "Roman Travel etc.," the fourth lecture of his series.

Jan. 29—Lecture by Professor Andrew Hunter, M.B., on "Digestion."

Jan. 30—University Sermon by Rev. Dr. Frere.

Feb. 2—Lecture by Sir Bertram Windle, LL.D., the fifth of his series on "The Roman Occupation of Britain."

Feb. 5—Lecture by Professor C. T. Currelly, M.A., on Recent Developments in our Knowledge of Chinese Arts.

Feb. 8—Organ Recital by Mr. F. A. Mouré, University Organist.

Feb. 8-12—Presentation of "Alcestis" by the Players' Club of the University.

Feb. 9—Lecture by Sir Bertram Windle, LL.D., the sixth of his series on "The Roman Occupation of Britain."

Feb. 12—Lecture by Professor M. A. Buchanan, Ph.D., on "Lope de Verga and the Spanish Drama."

Feb. 13—University Sermon by Dean E. I. Bosworth.

Feb. 16—Lecture by Sir Bertram Windle, LL.D., the seventh of his series on "The Roman Occupation of Britain."

Feb. 19—Lecture by Professor J. G. Fitzgerald, M.B., on "The Practice of Preventive Medicine."

Feb. 20—University Sermon by Dr. Trevor Davies.

Feb. 22—Organ Recital by Mr. F. A. Mouré, University Organist.

Feb. 23—The Keats' Centenary Commemoration in Hart House Theatre, the speakers being B. C. Scott, Prof. W. J. Alexander, Prof. Pelham Edgar. Songs by J. Campbell McInnes.

Feb. 23—Lecture by Sir Bertram Windle, LL.D., the eighth of his series on "The Roman Occupation of Britain."

Feb. 26—Lecture by Professor Pelham Edgar, Ph.D., on the "Novels and Poems of Thomas Hardy."

Feb. 27—University Sermon by Professor J. B. Reynolds.

Mar. 2—Lecture by Sir Bertram Windle, LL.D., the ninth of a series on "The Roman Occupation of Britain."

Mar. 5—Lecture by the Rev. Abbé Dimnet on the "Coming Men in French Literature."

Mar. 6—University Sermon by Canon Renison.

Mar. 8—Organ Recital by Mr. F. A. Mouré, University Organist.

Mar. 8-12—Presentation of "The Romancers" by the Players' Club of the University.

Mar. 9—Lecture by Sir Bertram Windle, LL.D., the tenth of a series on the "Roman Occupation of Britain."

Mar. 13—University Sermon by Rev. Dr. W. Sparling.

Mar. 16—Lecture by Sir Bertram Windle, LL.D., the eleventh of a series on "The Roman Occupation of Britain."

Mar. 20—University Sermon by R. Bruce Taylor.

Mar. 22—Organ Recital by Mr. F. A. Mouré, University Organist.

Mar. 23—Lecture by Sir Bertram Windle, LL.D., the twelfth of his series of "The Roman Occupation of Britain."

Apr. 5-9—Presentation of Three Canadian plays by the Players' Club.

June 7-11—Presentation of "Cymbeline" by the Players' Club of the University.

June 9—Special Convocation at which the following honorary degrees were conferred:—

Doctor of Laws.

The Right Honourable Arthur Meighen, K.C., B.A., (in absentiâ).

The Right Honourable Jan Christian Smuts, P.C., (in absentiâ).

The Honourable Ernest Charles Drury, B.S.A.

The Honourable Louis Alexandre Taschereau.

The Honourable Newton Wesley Rowell, K.C., M.P.

Francis Walter Merchant, M.A., D.Paed.

Doctor of Letters.

Wilfred Pirt Mustard, M.A.
Duncan Campbell Scott, F.R.S.C.

Doctor of Science.

John Morrice Roger Fairbairn.
Robert Alexander, Ross, E.E.
An address was delivered by the Honourable Mr. Tasch-
erau.

UNIVERSITY OF TORONTO ASSOCIATIONS AND SOCIETIES

1920-1921.

ALUMNI ASSOCIATION.

The University of Toronto Alumni Association was organized in 1900. It has thirty-five branches in various parts of Canada and the United States. Its official organ is *The University of Toronto Monthly.*

Honorary President—Sir John Gibson.

President—The Hon. Mr. Justice Masten.

Vice-Presidents—Angus MacMurchy, J. H. Coyne, The Hon. Mr. Justice Kelly, W. J. K. Vanston, S. S. Silcox, Carl Riordon, A. L. MacCredie, James Chisholm, C. H. Mitchell, Walter J. Francis, S. J. McLean, H. M. Darling.

Board of Directors—The Hon. Mr. Justice Masten, Sir Robert Falconer, J. J. Gibson, P. H. Mitchell, J. Bone, H. D. Scully, Professor McMurrich, Angus MacMurchy, D. B. Gillies, Miss McDonald, Miss Helen Dafoe, C. E. Macdonald, W. C. James, Dr. George Wilson. Charles McInnes, Samuel King, W. R. P. Parker.

Secretary-Treasurer—W. N. MacQueen.

HART HOUSE.

Warden—W. F. Bowles.

Secretary-Treasurer and Librarian—H. P. Bell.

Director of Theatre—Roy Mitchell.

Stewards—Sir Robert Falconer, W. F. Bowles, Vincent Massey, G. M. Smith, V. E. Henderson, I. R. Pounder, J. W. Barton, J. Jennings, R. H. Rickard, W. E. Blatz, Med., R. W. Downey, Sc., G. S. Eadie, Med., C. M. Beck, Sc., H. Borsook, U.C., G. A. Elliott, Med., A. D. Bell, U.C., H. P. Bell, Secretary.

Finance Committee—M. A. Mackenzie, Vincent Massey, V. E. Henderson, C. R. Young, W. F. Bowles, H. P. Bell, Secretary.

House Committee—S. G. Bennett, M. W. Wallace, R. H. Rickard, J. W. Barton, F. C. Houston, Sc., J. A. Langford, Sc., C. M. Gratz, Meds., J. A. Sinnott, Meds., G. V. Rayner, Sc., G. F. Amyot. Med., H. E. Hopkins, Med., S. F. Everson, Sc., W. L. Yack, Sc., W. F. Bowles, G. S. Eadie, Med., Secretary.

Hall Committee—P. G. Gillespie, R. H. Williams, I. R. Pounder, W. W. Woodhouse, Med., A. M. Carlisle, Med., J. C. Bell, Sc., D. M. Campbell, Med., J. A. West, Sc., J. W. Gardner, Sc., W. D. Coulter, Sc., C. H. Best, U.C., J. L. McDougall, U.C., W. F. Bowles, C. M. Beck, Sc., Secretary.

FACULTY UNION.
Organized 1901.
Officers.

President—Sir Robert Falconer, K.C.M.G.
Secretary—I. R. Pounder.
House Committee—S. Beatty, J. R. Cockburn, G. R. Cornish, G. H. Duff, A. Hunter, K. B. Jackson.

STUDENTS' ADMINISTRATIVE COUNCIL.

The Students' Administrative Council has developed from the Parliament of Undergraduates which was organized in 1105 with a large membership to afford students of all the Colleges and Faculties the privilege of discussing in open debate questions of interest to them. During the last few years the membership of the Parliament has been reduced as the work became more executive. The Council, as now recognized by the University authorities, has the following duties:—

To represent the students on all public occasions and in all matters pertaining to their interests.

To afford a recognized means of communication between the students and the University or Civic authorities.

To promote inter-university relationships and to cultivate a University "esprit de corps" among the students of all Colleges and Faculties.

An important step in the growing power of the Council was accomplished during the Session 1914-15, when the Caput of the University delegated to the Council full authority to deal with all matters concerning student discipline within the University.

Another isnovation is the Students' Council fee, collected by the Bursar, for the use of the Council. This makes possible the employment of a salaried permanent secretary and provides a working capital by means of which a greater efficiency in the management of the various organizations can be attained.

The Council is responsible for Theatre Night, the Glee Club, the University Musical Society, and Inter-University Debating, and jointly responsible wiht the Women Students' administrative Council for the publication of THE VARSITY, TORONTONENSIS, and the STUDENTS' DIRECTORY.

Students' Administrative Council Officers, 1920-21.

President, F. G. Lightbourn.
Vice-President, N. E. McKinnon
General Secretary-Treasurer,
    F. C. Hastings.
"Torontonensis" Representative,
    E. B. Harshaw.
"Varsity" Representative,
    R. A. Williams
Vice-President Athletic Directorate, W. E. Blatz.
President Medical Society,
    W. S. Duncan
President Federal Exec. U. of T., Y.M.C.A., H. Kemp.
Convenor Students' Court, J. R. McLean.
Convenor Musical Organizations, D. H. Porter.
Convenor Literary Organizations, E. L. Wasson.
University College: W. J. Mathews, F. L. Hutchison, D. F.

McLaren, I. M. Wylie.
Victoria College: J. L. Smith, A. Hampson, C. W. Cline.
Trinity College: E. B. Harshaw.
St. Michael's College: J. P. Mallon.
Medicine: C. V. Williams, G. E. Pauley, A. G. Smith, G. E. Sands, W. B. Brebner.
Applied Science: R. W. Downie, H. G. Thompson, A. A. Bell, W. A. Osbourne.
Education: B. Cummiford.
Forestry: A. W. Bentley.
Wycliffe: E. L. Wasson.
Dentistry: L. M. Martin, A. A. Cameron, J. A. Deitrich, F. C. Simms.
Pharmacy: J. D. B. Hatchwell.
Ontario Veterinary College: L. M. Heath, A. W. Munson.

WOMEN STUDENTS' ADMINISTRATIVE COUNCIL.

Executive.

President, Miss A. B. Williamson, Med.
Vice-Pres., Miss G. M. Billings, U.C.
Varsity Rep., Miss M. J. Chappell, Vic.

"Torontonensis" Rep., Miss E. F. Dixon, Trin.
St. Michael's Rep., Miss K. L. O'Connell.
Gen. Sec.-Treas., Miss A. E. M. Parkes, B.A.

Representatives.

University College: Misses G. M. Billings, D. S. Hardy, A. L. Maybee, M. F. Edge, M. Spence.
Victoria College: Misses M. J. Chappell, E. F. Patterson, A. C. Elgie.
Trinity College: Misses E. F. Dixon, E. G. Gladman.

St. Michael's College: Misses K. L. O'Connell, W. C. Collins.
Medicine: Misses A. B. Williamson, H. H. McCormick.
Education: Miss E. G. Sheridan.
Social Service: Miss H. E. Roberts.

THE VARSITY.

Editor-in-Chief, J. W. Gardner.

Women's Editor, Miss E. R. Cringan.

Managing Editors, W. J. Scott, Miss D. Hardy.

Business Manager, F. C. Hastings.

Sporting Editor, H. A. MacLennan.

Asst. Sporting Editors, J. B. Tudhope, G. R. Creelman, Miss A. Brown.

New Editors, H. H. Geddes, H. R. Sutherland.

Dramatic Editor, C. E. Tait.

Exchange Editor, A. C. McLawrin.

TORONTONENSIS BOARD, 1920-21.

Editor-in-Chief ....R. V. Sowers

Business Manager ....F. C. Hastings

Representatives.

University College: W. F. Bussell, Miss I. Hearst, Miss N. Porter, F. H. Soward.

Victoria College: Miss H. R. Golding, Miss F. E. Rodman, L. G. Smith.

Trinity College: Miss Marion Neville, O. H. Snelgrove.

St. Michael's College: T. S. Melady, Miss Helen Mullett, F. T. Watson.

Medicine: Wm. Blatz, Miss L. R. Grady, N. E. McKinnon,

M. C. MacQueen, R. G. Ratz.

Applied Science: H. J. Elliott, B. M. McLean, W. M. Smith, W. S. Wilson.

Knox: W. J. Preston.

Ontario Veterinary College: L. M. Heath.

Wycliffe: C. C. Harcourt.

Dentistry: R. G. Agnew, B.A., C. A. Elliot, C. B. Wilson, J. Zimmerman.

Pharmacy: T. S. Brandy.

Forestry: T. A. Clarke.

YOUNG MEN'S CHRISTIAN ASSOCIATION.

The object of the Association is to lead the men in the University of Toronto to acknowledge Jesus Christ as Lord and Master, and to have them decide on a life's work in His name; to promote Christian character; to develop and train men for aggressive Christian work and service, and generally to promote the physical, mental and spiritual welfare of the student body.

Y.M.C.A. FEDERAL CABINET.

President, H. R. Kemp, M.A.

Vice-President, W. M. Walwyn.

Recording Secretary, W. E. Meldrum.

Assistant Treasurer, F. R. Murgatroyd.

General Secretary, R. H. Rick-

ard, B.A.

Associate Secretary, H. A. MacMillan.

Asso. Sec. of Medicine, R. B. MacLure.

Asso. Sec. of Dentistry, T. R. Marshall.

PRESIDENTS OF COLLEGE ASSOCIATIONS.

University College: H. A. Mac-Millan.
Victoria College: H. F. Swan.
Medicine: J. T. Speck.
Applied Science, F. W. Dunton.
Dentistry, T. R. Marshall.

Veterinary College, G. Baker.
Pharmacy, Clyde Shaw.
O. C. E., A. R. Self.
Forestry: J. L. VanCamp.
McMaster University: H. Carr.

Convenors.

Voluntary Study, K. P. Kirkwood.
Campus Service, R. J. Neelands.

Community Service, W. S. McKay.
Missionary, J. S. Ditchburn.
University Sermons, W. M. Walwyn.

CANADIAN OFFICERS' TRAINING CORPS.

University of Toronto Contingent.

Officer Commanding, Lt.-Col. W. R. Lang, late Gen. Staff, C.E.F.
Second in Command, Major T. R. Loudon, late Can. Eng., C.E.F.
Adjutant, Major H. H. Madill, late C.E.F.
Quartermaster, Lieut. V. C. Kerrison, late C.A.S.C., C.E.F.
Paymaster, Lieut. T. A. Reed.
Musketry Officer,

Contingent Sergeant-Major, S. M. W. Hunt, late Royal Welsh Fusiliers.
Company Officers, Major W. S. Wallace, Capt. J. R. Cockburn, M.C., Lieuts. N. U. Jones, B. H. Miller, F. G. Lightbourn, B. H. Miller.
Attached for Duty, Lieut. H. F. Balmer, C.A.F.; Lieut. A. M. Duggan, C.A.F.

THE UNIVERSITY OF TORONTO ATHLETIC ASSOCIATION.

The Athletic Association is now the paramount body in University athletics, and has entire jurisdiction over the athletic clubs using the University name, and over their finances, members and policy, subject to the University authorities. Henceforth no financial agreement can be entered into by any such club without the sanction of the Directorate. No expenditure of any kind in connection with any such club can be made without the written order of the Secretary-Treasurer of the Directorate.

—50

Officers, 1920-21.

Hon. President, Sir Robert Falconer.

President, Professor M. A. Mackenzie.

Vice-President, W. E. Blatz, M.A.

Sec.-Treas., T. A. Reed.

Physical Director, J. W. Barton, M.D.

Directors: Professor C. H. C. Wright, A. F. Barr, M.A., W. A. Dafoe, M.B., F. C. A. Houston, K. L. Carruthers, P. F. McIntyre, J. W. Douglas.

Rugby Football Club, 1920-21.

Hon. President, W. C. Foulds, B.A.Sc.

Hon. Vice-President, L. R. Shoebottom, B.A.Sc.

President, P. A. C. Ketchum.

Vice-President, K. A. Hamilton.

Sec.-Treasurer, A. S. Malcolmson.

Hon. Coach, Hamilton Cassels, Jr.

Capt. 1st Team, J. M. Breen.

Manager 1st Team, W. E. Blatz.

Capt. 2nd Team, J. C. Paterson.

Manager 2nd Team, C. G. Littlefield.

Manager 3rd Team, H. A. MacLennan.

Captain 1920-21 *1st Team,* G. G. Duncan.

Track Club Officers, 1920-21.

Hon. President, F. J. Halbus.

Hon. Vice-President, Dr. L. J. Sebert.

President, L. D. Croll.

Vice-President, G. F. Leigh.

Sec.-Treasurer, J. E. Buchan.

Asst. Sec.-Treasurer, B. O'Donnell.

Manager (Provisional), R. A. Williams.

Association Football Club Officers, 1920-21.

Hon. President, Prof. F. C. A. Jeanneret.

Hon. Vice-President, J. A. Woodward.

President, S. W. Archibald.

Vice-President, A. G. Rintoul.

Sec.-Treasurer, H. F. Swan.

Manager, B. I. Johnston.

Gymnasium Club Officers, 1920-21.

Hon. President, R. D. Huestis, B.A.Sc.

Hon. Vice-President, J. B. Ridley, B.A.

President, P. J. Robinson.

Vice-President, J. H. F. Adams.

Secretary and Manager, S. T. Glover.

Gymnasia.

The Physical Department has now five gymnasia. The main floor, 100 x 50 feet, is fitted up with the latest apparatus for all round class and individual work. The upper gymnasium 80 x 40 feet, is known as the Games Room, where the interfaculty contests in basketball, indoor baseball and volley ball are played. The teams of the various faculties and colleges have practice hours allotted to them on this floor. There are also the three small gymnasia, each 50 x 30 feet for boxing, wrestling and fencing, respectively. These three rooms are also fitted up with basketball goals and afford extra practice floors in an emergency.

All the male students of the University are examined by the Physical Director and placed in categories according to their physical fitness. Some form of physical training is compulsory for every student of the first and second years. Students in Category "A," that is physically fit, can elect the form of exercise in which they wish to engage. Students in Category "B," (hardly up to "A" standard physically), can elect in the same manner, but are limited to certain forms of exercise as recommended by the Physical Director. Students in Category "C" must take the form of exercise recommended by the Physical Director.

Two gymnasium instructors are in attendance from 9 a.m. to 6 p.m. Classes are held at various hours throughout the day. The Swimming Instructor is in attendance at the pool from 9 a.m. to 6 p.m. Swimmers may use the pool at any time. Non-swimmers must attend at the hours set for them. Students may consult the Physical Director on all matters pertaining to their health.

The Gymnasium Feee is now merged in the Hart House Fee of Ten Dollars, payable to the Bursar, and compulsory in all male students.

Basketball Club Officers, 1920-21.

President, D. G. Gill. *Secretary-Treasurer*, J. D. Graham.
Vice-President, R. G. Stewart.

Boxing, Fencing and Wrestling Executive, 1920-21.

Hon. President, Prof. T. R. Loudon.
Hon. Vice-President, Dr. Flett.
President, A. H. Livingstone.
Vice-President, W. G. Grey.

Secretary, G. W. Hewitt.
Manager, C. W. Steele.
Assistant Managers: F. Seaborne, S. H. Pepler, L. R. Dodds.

Hockey Club Executive, 1920-21.

Hon. President, Dr. A. B. Wright.

Hon. Vice-President, Conn Smythe, B.A.Sc.

President, P. F. McIntyre.

Vice-President, E. N. Wright.

Secretary, F. R. McDonald.

Hon. Coach, Dr. W. A. Dafoe.

Captain 1st Team, Bruce West. B.A.

Manager 2nd Team, R. T. Weaver.

Man. 3rd Team, A. B. Moore.

Swimming Club Executive, 1920-21.

Hon. President, Prof. F. C. A. Jeanneret.

President, G. Lindsay.

Vice-President, K. Ruddy.

Sec.-Treasurer, J. B. Tudhope.

Manager, L. E. Blackwell.

Coach, T. R. Earl.

Tennis Executive, 1920-21·

President, H. S. Spencer.

Secretary, T. Sheard.

Asst. Secretary, C. Thornton.

Lacrosse Club.

Hon. President, Dr. F. S. Park.

President, J. D. McClure.

Vice-President, J. Geoghegan.

Sec.-Treasurer, J. McLennan.

Harrier Club Executive, 1920-21.

Hon. Vice-President, Dr. E. H. Campbell.

Hon. Vice-President, Rev. P. J. Dykes.

President, G. F. Leigh.

Vice-President, L. D. Croll.

Secretary, A. Brodey.

THE PLAYERS' CLUB.

Technical Staff.

Stage Manager, Mr. Alan Coventry (Univ. Staff).

Regisseur, Mr. Elton Johnson (Univ. Coll.)

Electrician, Mr. Arthur S. Wilson (Fac. App. Sc.)

Master Mechanician, Mr. J. Lorne Graham (Univ. Coll.)

Master of Properties, Mr. Donald McKay (Univ. Coll.)

Syndics.

Walter F. Bowles.

Ernest A. Dale (President)

George H. Locke (President, 1919-20)

Vincent Massey (President, 1914-15.)

Dixon Wagner

Alice Vincent Massey

G. Frank McFarland

Leslie H. Reid

J. D. Robins

Arthur S. Wilson

Officers.

Secretary-Treasurer .... E. O. Mitchell, B.A.

Director .... Roy Mitchell

MATHEMATICAL AND PHYSICAL SOCIETY.

Hon. President, Prof. Lachlan Gilchrist, M.A., PH.D.

President .... A. B. Paisley '21

Vice-President, J. T. Phillips '22

Secretary, Miss M. McLean '22

Treasurer .... W. Webster '23

Corr. Secretary

Miss E. M. Henry '21

Representatives

Fourth Year, L. W. Rentner '21

Third Year, E. C. Horwood '22

Second Year .... M. S. Bell '23

First Year, Miss G. Bovaird '24

CHESS CLUB.

Hon. President..Maurice Hutton

President .... A. Turnbull

Sec.-Treas .... A. C. Thrupp

Rep. Staff Mem., W. M. Threadgold.

Rep. Graduate Mem., C. E. H. Freeman.

Representatives.

University College: N. P. H. Brown.

Victoria College: L. W. Narraway.

Applied Science: A. H. Greenwood.

Dentistry: R. V. Weston.

COMMERCE AND FINANCE CLUB.

Hon. Pres., Prof. M. A. Mackenzie.

President .... W. L. Turnbull

Vice-Pres............ G. R. F. Troop

Secretary.................. Ross Ryrie

Treasurer...... F. A. L. Woodland

3rd Year Rep...... H. B. Wheaton

2nd Year Rep....... S. R. Wilkins

1st Year Rep............ W. G. Booth

MENORAH SOCIETY.

Hon. Pres., Sir Robert Falconer
Hon. Vice-Pres., Prof. W. R. Taylor, Ph.D.
Advisor, Rabbi B. R. Brickner, Ph.D.
Pres., D. Eisen, Medicine, 2T1
1st Vice-Pres., J. Markus, B.A.
2nd Vice-Pres. ......Miss M. Levi, U.C. 2T1.
Gen. Sec., J. M. Stuchen, U.C. 2T1.
Rec. Sec. .... B. Caplan

Treasurer, W. Goldstick, S.P.S. 2T1.
Arts Rep., Miss T. Levine, U.C. 2T2.
Med. Rep., J. Greenberg, Med. 2T2.
School Rep., M. Zaduoff, S.P.S. 2T4.
Osgoode Rep.......:........ I. B. Levine
Dent. Rep., J. Zimmerman, Dent. 2T1.

THE SKETCH CLUB.

The University of Toronto Sketch Club was formed in 1917 and reorganised for active work in 1920. It has a home in Hart House. The purpose of the Club is to encourage the practice and study of the Fine Arts, particularly the Graphic Arts, in the University of Toronto and to establish an Art centre in the University by collecting works of Art and publications thereon.

The 1920-21 Executive is as follows:—

Hon. President, C. W. Jefferys, A.R.C.A.
President, G. R. Gouinlock, Science.
Vice-Pres., T. J. Young, Science
Secretary, J. B. Helme, Science
Treasurer, J. L. VanCamp, Forestry.

Curator, C. B. Sproatt, Science
Graduate Rep., H. H. Madill, B.A. Sc.
Councillors, J. C. Jack, Arts; C. A. Elliott, Dentistry; G. R. Walton, Medicine.

UNIVERSITY COLLEGE STUDENTS SOCIETIES.
1919-20.

YOUNG MEN'S CHRISTIAN ASSOCIATION.

The Association was organized in 1873 and incorporated in 1892.

The objects of the Association are:

To unite the men of the Institution for the maintenance of a positive moral and religious atmosphere.

To develop and conserve in all our men a complete Christian manhood.

To lead them to become disciples of Jesus Christ in life and service.

To lead them to unite with and promote the Christian Church.

To enlist them in the extension of Christ's Kingdom throughout the world.

Membership in the Christian Association consists of all those in the Colleges who approve of the objects of the organization and declare it their purpose to live and work for the extension of the Kingdom of Righteousness among men, especially the men of this University.

Officers.

Hon. Pres.......Prof. W. R. Taylor
President............H. A. MacMillan
Vice-President.......R. A. Stewart

Secretary..................G. M. Graham
Treasurer..................J. C. Stone

Convenors.

Bible Study...............E. C. Bogart
Campus Service, H. J. F. Stewart.
Community Service.......A. Gillies

Missionary Service..... ....G. Fair
Publicity Service, H. J. McQuillan.

WOMEN'S STUDENT CHRISTIAN MOVEMENT.

President ....Dorothy C. Loggie
Vice-Pres......... Agnes M. Brown
Secretary Margaret J. Jamieson
Treasurer, Jessie H. MacPherson.
Convenors, Helen D. Shafner,

Elizabeth H. Chant, Janet H. Smith, Isabel L. Patterson, Marjorie C. Twitchell, Adelaide H. MacDonald, Lilian T. Brodie, Marion H. Larkin, Genevieve Brock.

LITERARY AND SCIENTIFIC SOCIETY.

Hon. Pres. Prof. M. W. Wallace
President .... G. E. Jackson
Vice-Pres............. W. J. Mathews
Curator .... H. F. R. Shaw.
Rec. Sec.............. J. L. MacDougall

Corr. Sec. .... C. Glover
Treasurer .... J. B. Martin
2nd Year Councillors, L. A. MacKay, W. R. Klim.
1st Year Councillors, H. des B. Sims, L. A. C.-MacLean.

WOMEN'S LITERARY SOCIETY.

Executive 1920-21.

Hon. Pres. Mrs. G. H. Needler
President.. Eleanor M. Harbert
Vice-President.... Jennie V. Lane
Critic..... Marguerite E. Gamble
Rec. Sec.................... Myra McLean
Corr. Sec., Marguerite A. Gogo
Treasurer........... Gladys V. Lewis

4th Year Rep. Mary K. Millen
3rd Year Rep. Marjorie C. Twitchell.
2nd Year Rep. Margaret E. MacLellan.
1st Year Rep. M. Ferga Carmichael.

WOMEN'S UNDERGRADUATE ASSOCIATION.

Hon. Pres. Mrs. M. A. Buchanan
President...... Miss G. M. Billings
Vice-Pres., Miss M. McTaggart

Head Girl of Queen's Hall, Miss A. I. Main.
Secretary........ Miss J. A. Wilson
Treasurer........... Miss M. E. Reid

CLASS SOCIETIES.
1921.

President .... D. H. Porter
1st Vice-Pres., Miss M. J. McCowan.
2nd Vice-Pres........... W. A. Bryce
Treasurer................ A. M. Duggan
Rec. Sec...................... H. J. Stewart
Corr. Sec. .... J. D. Jennison
Musical Directress, Miss C. L. Cornette.

Poetess .... Miss D. S. Hardy
Prophetess, Miss E. Maclennan
1st Historian, Miss R. W. Ross
2nd Historian.......... W. H. Noble
Gentleman Councillor, J. R. Stirrett.
Lady Councillor, Miss E. A. Cringan.

Permanent Executive.

President.................. F. H. Soward
Vice-Pres..... Miss E. R. Cringan
Sec.-Treas. .... G. D. Little

Lady Councillor, Miss A. Leonard.
Gentleman Councillor, A. D. Bell

1922.

President..... F. Lorne Hutchison

Vice-President. Miss A. H. Mac-donald.

Secretary...... Mr. W. D. Maxwell

Treasurer, Mr. J. C. Armstrong

Athletic Director, Mr. G. M. Purcell.

Athletic Directress, Miss G. Stanley.

Scribe.......... Miss J. C. McQueen

Musical Directress, Miss J. R. MacMillan.

Lady Councillor, Miss M. H. Sherrin.

Gentleman Councillor, Mr. W. M. Mustard.

1923.

President.......... D. F. MacLaren

1st Vice-President, Miss H. E. Anderson.

2nd Vice-Pres.......... H. M. Miller

Secretary .... I. T. Strachan

Treasurer .... L. B. Bond

1st Historian, Miss E. E. Carson

2nd Historian .... H. Booth

Musical Directress, Miss N. I. Carson.

Poetess .... Miss P. A. Petrie

Athletic Rep.... J. L. Sutherland

Judge .... J. Armstrong

Critic .... G. Graham

1st Lady Councillor, Miss W. D. Hudson.

2nd Lady Councillor, Miss J. G. Maxwell.

Prophetess........ Miss E. M. Begg

Orator .... R. A. Stewart

1924.

President .... Ian Wylie

Secretary........... J. E. McDougall

CLASSICAL ASSOCIATION.

Executive Committee, 1920-21.

Hon. President, Prof. W. D. Woodhead.

President .... H. L. Tracy, '21

Vice-Pres., Miss M. Needler, '22

Secretary, L. A. MacKay, '23

Treasurer, J. E. A. Johnstone, '22.

4th Year Councillor, Miss J. H. Crumb, '23.

2nd Year Councillor, Miss M. Edge, '23.

1st Year Councillor, A. K. McIlwraith, '24.

1st Year Councillor, Miss M. V. Knowles, '24.

MODERN LANGUAGE CLUB.

President.......... Miss G. M. Cook

1st Vice-Pres., J. L. McDougal

2nd Vice-Pres., J. Burns Martin

Rec. Sec........... Miss D. L. Arthur

Corr. Sec. .... H. E. Saunders

Treasurer..... J. J. F. McKeown

Business Manager of Plays, C. L. Fletcher.

2nd Year Rep., Miss D. E. Stacey.

1st Year Rep. Miss M. P. Zybach

1st Year Rep., N. P. H. Brown

WOMEN'S ATHLETIC ASSOCIATION.

Hon. Pres. ...... Miss. M. Peterkin
President, Miss M. McTaggart
Vice-Pres............. Miss N. E. Gray

Sec.-Treas..... Miss H. W. Morson
Rep. to Directorate, Miss E. H. Chant.

Curators.

Tennis .... Miss D. M. Wood
Hockey   Miss G. Stanley
Swimming...... Miss H. L. Bryans
Basketball .... Miss M. E. Fair
Gymnasium... *Miss M. H. Bowles*
1st Year Rep............. Miss M. E. Fraser.

Sen. Rep. to Federal, Miss N. E. Gray.
Jun. Rep. to Federal, Miss M. H. Bowles.
Athletic Rep. to Directorate, Miss E. H. Chant.

VICTORIA COLLEGE STUDENT SOCIETIES.

THE VICTORIA MEN'S COUNCIL.

President.... J. Lavell Smith, '21

Vice-Pres.......... A. Hampson, '21

Secretary...... A. E. T. Gilroy, '22

Treasurer, C. D. Daniel, Theol.

Councillors.

W. H. Moss, B.A.; C. W. Cline, '22; N. J. Endicott, '24; W. G. Graydon, '21; J. G. Endicott, '23; D. M. Guest, Theol.

WOMEN'S UNDERGRADUATE ASSOCIATION.

President, Miss Jean Chappell, '21.

Vice-Pres.... Miss Jean Cameron, '21.

Secretary...... Miss Kathleen Bennett, '22.

Treasurer, Miss Mildred Taylor, '23.

3rd Year Rep... Miss Ethel Patterson, '22.

2nd Year Rep... Miss Ann Elgie '23.

1st Year Rep............ Miss Minnie O'Hara, '24.

UNION LITERARY SOCIETY.

	Fall Term.	Spring Term.
President	E. P. Congdon.	H. F. Swann.
Vice-President	J. C. Eastcott.	A. E. Gilroy.
Critic	R. S. Hosking, B.A.	R. J. Irwin, B.A.
Leader of Government,	C. H. Dickinson.	H. F. Sanders.
Secretary	A. J. Smale.	J. A. C. Kell.
Treasurer	M. A. Cayley.	J. V. McNeely.

WOMEN'S LITERARY SOCIETY.

President, Miss J. G. Davidson.

Vice-President, Miss Jean D. Cameron.

Rec. Secretary, Miss Grace Armstrong.

Cor. Secretary, Miss Dorothy Shannon.

Treasurer, Miss Jessie Odell.

Pianist, Miss Dorothy Emberson.

1st Year Councillor, Miss Irene Irwin.

Leader of Government, Miss Essa Dafoe.

Leader of Opposition, Miss Jennie Harris.

Critic, Miss Lillian Elliott.

Assistant Critic, Miss Frieda Daly.

Literary Editor Acta, Miss Harriet Dewey.

Personals, Miss Emily McLaughlin.

Locals, Miss Margaret Uren.

Athletics, Miss Marjorie Oaks.

Asst. Circulation Manager, Miss Blanche Van Allen.

Cabinet:

VICTORIA COLLEGE ATHLETIC CLUB.

Hon. President, Mrs. C. B. Sissons.

President, Jean Rossiter.

Secretary - Treasurer, Gertrude Wallis.

4th Year Rep., Mary Marshall.

3rd Year Rep., Marjorie Oaks.

2nd Year Rep., Vera Hogarth.

1st Year Rep., Maud Johnston.

Basket Ball Curator, Helen Irwin.

Tennis Captain, Hannah Golding.

Hockey Curator, Muriel Everson.

Swimming Captain, Kathleen Drew.

ACTA VICTORIANA.

Editorial Staff, 1920-21.

Editor-in-Chief, J. G. H. Linton, '21·

Literary Editors, C. H. Dickinson, '21; Miss H. J. Dewey, '21·

Personals and Exchanges, J. C. Eastcott, '22; Miss E. M. McLaughlin, '21.

Locals Editors, S. J. Allin, '22; Miss A. M. Uren, '22·

Athletics Editors, S. N. F. Chant, '22; Miss M. B. Oaks, '22.

Scientific Editor, W. G. Noble, '21·

Missionary and Religious, H. C. Wolfraim, B.A.

Board of Management.

Business Man., A. F. Annis, '21·

Circulating Manager, D. F. Gibson, '22·

Asst. Circulation Manager, Miss B. G. VanAllen, '22·

Advisory Board.

Prof. C. E. Auger, B.A.

George H. Locke, M.A.

MEN'S STUDENT CHRISTIAN ASSOCIATION.

Hon. President, Prof. W. T. Brown.

President, H. F. Swann.

Voluntary Study, Vice-Pres., H. S. Hosking, B.A.

Missionary Vice-Pres., H. D. Brown.

New Member Vice-Pres., J. M. Luck.

Community Service Vice-Pres., S. N. F. Chant.

Pres. Student Volunteer Band, F. A. Sayles.

Treasurer, J. G. Endicott.

Secretary, Chas. D. Daniel.

WOMEN'S STUDENT CHRISTIAN ASSOCIATION.

Cabinet:

Hon. President, Miss M. C. Rowell, B.A.

President, Miss Gertrude Rutherford.

Vice-President, Miss Kathleen Bennett.

Secretary, Miss Margaret Uren.

Treasurer, Miss Nina Yeomans.

Missionary Convener, Miss Irene Balfour.

Social Service Conveners, Miss Hannah Golding, Miss Ruth Lawson.

Bible Study Convener, Miss Emily McLaughlin.

Conference Convener, Miss Evelyn Butcher.

Publicity Convenor, Miss Rose Wittington.

Pianist, Miss Marion Hilliard.

ATHLETIC UNION.

Hon. President, Prof. C. B. Sissions.

President, H. D. Brown.

1st Vice-President, S. N. F. Chant.

2nd Vice-President, F. L. Bartlett.

Secretary, J. R. Hamilton.

Treasurer, W. G. Graydon.

GLEE CLUB.

Hon. President, Prof. L. E. Horning.

President, W. H. Moss, B.A.

Vice-President, M. A. Cayley, '22.

Business Manager, B. L. Oaten, '21.

Secretary, O. G. Lawson, '21.

Librarian, F. R. Keffer, '23.

Reporter, H. F. Sanders, '21.

THE CHORAL SOCIETY.

President, Miss Mary Marshall.

Vice-President, Miss G. Armstrong.

Secretary, Miss H. Goodwyn.

Treasurer, Miss V. Hogarth.

Librarian, Miss G. Studholme.

Business Manager, Miss I. Balfour.

VICTORIA COLLEGE ORCHESTRA.

Hon. President, Miss M. E. T. Addison, B.A.

President, F. J. Baine, '21.

Vice-President, Miss M. R. Lawson, '21.

Secretary, Miss A. M. Chisholm, '23.

Treasurer and Business Manager, M. Cayley, '23.

Librarian, Miss B. Fitzpatrick, '22.

Conductor, Frank Blachford.

THE COLLEGIANS' DEBATING CLUB.

President, H. E. Hazlewood, '23·   *Secretary*, S. J. Mathers, '23·
Vice-President, N. H. Endicott,   *Treasurer*, J. P. Cooke, '24·
'24·

Year Representatives.

H. S. Crawford, '23·   C. R. Philp, '24·
W. H. Trethewey, '23·   S. W. Stewart, Theol.
J. D. Ferguson, '24·   H. A. Mellow, Theol.

THE CLASSICAL ASSOCIATION.

President, T. R. S. Broughton.   *Secretary*, Miss I. F. Irwin.
Vice-President, C. E. Scarrow.   *Treasurer*, Miss D. E. Toye.

DRAMATIC SOCIETY.

Director, Prof. W. H. Greaves.   *Business Manager*, Miss Francis
Hon. Pres., Prof. S. H. Hooke.   Uren.
President, Miss Mabel Davis.   *Costume Convener*, Miss Jean
1st Vice-Pres., Miss Muriel   McClenaghan.
  Everson.   *Asst. Convener*, Miss Marion
2nd Vice-President, Miss Jean   Wylie.
  Keenleyside.   *Stage Manager*, Miss Ardeth
Secretary, Miss Gladys Wig-   Hull.
  gins.   *Asst. Stage Manager*, Miss K.
Treasurer, Miss J. H. Harris.   E. Elliott.

TRINITY COLLEGE STUDENT SOCIETIES.

HEAD OF COLLEGE—1920-21.

F. H. Paul, L.Th.

SCRIBE OF EPISKOPON—1920-21.

J. F. Davidson, '21·

The Literary Institute.

The Institute exists for the encouragement of debating, essay writing and reading. It meets on Friday evenings throughout the two terms. The fee is $3.00 per annum and is payable with the College bills.

1920-1921.

Speaker—J. F. Day, '23·

President, N. Clarke Wallace, '12·

1st *Vice-Pres.,* J. F. Davidson, '21·

2nd *Vice-Pres.,* P. A. C. Ketchum, '21·

Secretary, J. A. Philip, '23·

Debating Secretary, J. R. White, '23·

Treasurer, K. W. Hill, '20·

Librarian, W. E. M. Lee, '23·

Curator, W. L. Elliott, '23·

1st Year Councillor, C. de Lom, '24.

Opposition Committee.

T. F. W. de Pencier, '17·
H. F. Ketchum, '22·

E. L. Weaver, '23·

Officers for 1920-21.

Hon. President, Prof. Cosgrave.

Hon. Vice-Presidents, Prof. Brett, Prof. Kirkwood, Prof. Owen.

President, P. A. Child, '19·

Vice-President, H. R. Lawrence, '20·

Secretary, A. L. Ambrose, '22·

Treasurer, S. M. Adams, M.A.

Asst. Treasurer, J. L. Johnson, '17·

Reporter, E. B. Harshaw, '23·

Committee: P. A. C. Ketchum, '21; R. H. L. Grew, '23; H. F. K. Ketchum, '22; C. A. Bender. '19·

Freshman Representative, S. Harper, '24·

Captains for 1920-1921.

Rugby—H. F. Ketchum, '22·
Hockey—H. R. Lawrence, '20·
Basketball—J. Lowe, '20.
Harriers—J. F. Davidson, '21·
Tennis—H. A. Wilson, '22·

Badminton—C. A. Martin, '21·
Indoor Baseball—P. A. Child, '19·
Track—G. S. Deacon, '23·

THE REVIEW.

The "Trinity College Review" is published once a month throughout the academic year. The annual subscription is $1.50, payable with the College bills.

Board of Management for 1920-1921.

Editor-in-Chief, P. A. Child, '19
Business Mgr., F. H. Mason, 22.
Associate Editors, T. F. W. de Pencier, '17; J. Lowe, '20; H. J. E. Abbott, '22; A. H. Gee, '22; H. A. Wilson, '22; J. A.

Philip, '23; E. B. Harshaw, '23; J. R. White, '23·
Convocation and Consulting Editor. and Chairman, Professor Young.

THE GLEE CLUB.

Officers for 1920-1921.

Hon. Pres.......... Professor Young
Hon. Vice-Presidents, Prof. Cosgrave, E. J. Brethour, '15; R. N. Smith, '17·
Pres......... T. F. W. dePencier, '17
Vice-Pres. Miss E. F. Dixon, '21

Secretary...... H. F. Ketchum, '22
Treasurer......... S. W. Stanley, '21
Curator......... R. T. C. Dwelly, '22
Committee, Miss J. B. Humphries, '21; Miss N. Coulson, '22; E. L. Weaver, '23·

THE DRAMATIC SOCIETY.

Officers for 1920-1921.

Hon. President, The Reverend the Provost.
Hon. Vice-Presid'ts, Mr. Adams, Mr. Simpson, Mr. Owen.
Pres.................. H. J. E. Abbott, '22
Vice-Pres....... A. L. Ambrose, '22

Secretary.................. A. H. Gee, '22
Treasurer.................. Mr. Kittredge
Asst. Treas......... R. T. C. Dwelly
Curator.......... J. S. D. Nation, '22
Committeeman, J. L. W. Laurie, '21·

THE SCIENCE CLUB.

Officers for 1920-1921.

Hon. Pres., The Rev. Wm. Rollo

Hon. Vice-Pres. P. S. Warren, '16.

President............ A. H. Gee, '22

Vice-Pres............. C. A. Martin, '21

Secretary............ J. H. Roderick, '23

Treasurer...... S. C. Ferguson, '23

Curator........ R. H. M'Gonigle, '23

Asst. Curator D. R. Mitchell, '24

TRINITY COLLEGE STUDENTS' MISSIONARY ASSOCIATION

Committee, 1920-1921.

Pres............. J. S. Ditchburn, B.A.

Sec.-Treas......... W. A. Brown, '19

Vice-Pres...... H. F. Ketchum, '22

BROTHERHOOD OF ST. ANDREW.

Officers for 1920-1921.

Chaplain, The Rev. the Provost

Hon. Director.. A. N. Hoath, '20

Director.......... J. F. Davidson, '21

Vice-Dir. R. T. C. Dwelly, '22

Sec.-Treas..... B. C. W. Pickford, '23.

Convenor of Bible Classes, T. F. W. dePencier, '17.

THE THEOLOGICAL SOCIETY.

Officers for 1920-1921.

Hon. Vice-Presidents, The Members of the Teaching Staff in Divinity.

President............ F. H. Paull, '16

Vice-Pres. A. B. Browne, '23

Sec.-Treas....... G. N. Luxton, '23

Councillors, J. R. Jones, 23; W. A. Brown, '19.

1st Year Rep......... D. Wilson, '24

ST. HILDA'S COLLEGE STUDENT SOCIETIES.

HEAD OF COLLEGE—1920-1921.
Miss E. F. Dixon, '21·

SCRIBE OF EPISKOPON—1920-1921.
Miss J. B. Humphries, '21·

LITERARY SOCIETY—1920-1921.

Hon. Prs. Miss Cartwright, B.A.
1st Hon. Pres., Miss W. F. Scott B.A.
2nd Hon. Pres., Miss V. M. Crossley, '20·
Pres.   Miss M. C. Galt, '21
Vice-Pres., Miss N. I. Coulson, '21.

Rec. Sec., Miss M. B. Ewart, '21
Cor. Sec., Miss E. G. Gladman, '22.
Treas. Miss E. M. M'Gonigle, '22
Ex-officio, Miss M. Campbell, 23
1st Year Councillor, Miss A. E. Grout, '24·

INTER-COLLEGE DEBATING UNION—1920-1921.

Sr. Rep... Miss E. W. Izzard, '22   *Jr. Rep.*.......... J. E. Ferguson, '22

ATHLETIC ASSOCIATION—1920-1921.

Hon. Pres. Miss M. A. Boyd, B.A
Hon. Vice-Pres. Miss M. I. Tom, B.A.
Pres....................... Miss D. Trapp
Vice-Pres. Miss J. B. Humphries '21.
Secretary. Miss N. I. Coulson, 21
Treasurer...... Miss R. Burpee, '22
Head of Tennis, Miss M. C. Galt '21·

Head of Hockey, J. B. Humphries, '21·
Head of Basketball, Miss M. B. Ewart, '21·
Curator of Swimming, Miss F. M. Burwash, '22·
Sen. Rep. to Federal, Miss M. C. Galt, '21·
Jun. Rep. to Federal, Miss P. Young.

UNIVERSITY ATHLETIC LEAGUE—1920-1921.

Representatives.......... Miss M. C. Galt, '21; Miss P. Young

THE CHRONICLE—1920-1921.

Editor-in-Chief, Miss M. L. Smith, '21·

1st Sub-Editor, Miss R. M. Nevill, '21·

2nd Sub-Editor, Miss G. H. Potts, '22·

Business Manager, Miss E. G. Gladman, '22·

Asst. Bus. Manager, Miss M. Campbell, '23·

Advertising Manager, M. G. Mackenzie, '24·

Graduate Notes, Miss M. L. Bradfield, B.A.

Literary Notes, Miss E. M. M'Gonigle, '22·

Athletic Notes, Miss N. I. Coulson, '21·

St. Hilda's Notes, Miss E. W. Izzard, '22·

Y.W.C.A. Notes, Miss J. E. Ferguson, '22·

Rep. on the Varsity, Miss M. A. Burns, '23·

Rep. to Rebel, Miss G. H. Potts, '22·

Editor of St. Hilda's Notes, Trinity Review, Miss M. Campbell, '23·

YOUNG WOMEN'S CHRISTIAN ASSOCIATION.
1920-1921.

Head of Extension Work, Miss E. M. Pridham, '21·

Head of Red Cross Work, Miss F. Macdonald.

Poster Committee, Miss L. M. Ireland; Miss G. H. Potts, '22

President, Miss R. M. Nevill, '21

Vice-Pres., Miss E. Pridham, '21

Sec....... Miss J. E. Ferguson, '22

Treas....... Miss M. L. Benore, '23

Head of Mission Study, Miss B. Pittman, '22·

Head of Exten. Work, Miss M. S. Morse, '21·

Head of Red Cross Work, Miss F. Macdonald.

Poster Committee, Miss G. H. Potts, '22; Miss E. M. Anderson, '23·

Reps. at Summer Conf., 1920, Miss M. C. Galt, '21; Miss P. V. Young, Miss M. A. Burns, '23; Miss M. A. Pickford, '23·

ST. HILDA'S COLLEGE ALUMNAE ASSOCIATION.
Officers 1920-1921.

Hon. Pres., Miss M. Cartwright, B.A.

Pres....... Miss L. C. Scott, M.A.

1st Vice-Pres., Mrs. P. J. Dykes, B.A.

2nd Vice-Pres., Mrs. Britton Osler, B.A.

Sec.-Treas., Miss H. J. Martin, B.A.

Executive Com., Miss H. A. McClung, M.A., Miss R. M. Grier, B.A.; Miss M. A. Fortier, B.A.

Rep. to Local Council, Miss M. M. Waddington, Ph.D.

Rep. to United Alumnae Assoc., Miss M. Cartwright, B.A.

Editor Graduates' Notes in Chronicle, Miss M. L. Bradfield, B.A.

FACULTY OF MEDICINE.

MEDICAL SOCIETY.

President .... W. S. Duncan
Vice-President........R. H. Morris
Secretary.............. W. W. Moffat
Treasurer............: J. E. Carson
Curator ...... A. R. Wilkins
Ass't Sec......................... A. D. Kelly
Musical Director C. G. Smith

1921.

President........................... O. G. Mills
Vice-President............ E. W. Ellis
Secretary....... W. W. Woodhouse
Treasurer .... A. Turnbull

1922.

President .... R. I. Gordon
Vice-Pres J. A. A. Harcourt
Secretary...................... C. G. Bryan
Treasurer....... D. J. Prendergast

1923.

President .... D. M. Campbell
Vice-President....... R. L. Harold
Secretary............... Miss D. Adams
Treasurer .... H. F. Mowat

1924.

President .... B. I. Johnstone
Vice-President....: A. F. MacKay
Secretary.......... Miss K. M. White
Treasurer..................... D. B. Code

1925 (Six Years Course).

President .... A. G. Smith
Vice-President.......... C. B. Harton
Secretary............... Miss M. Singer
Treasurer.......... J. L. McFadden

1925 (Five Years Course).

President................... I. L. Johnstone
Secretary........ Miss K. M. White

YOUNG MEN'S CHRISTIAN ASSOCIATION.
(Medical).

Hon. President, Prof. J. J. R. MacLeod.
President .... J. T. Speck
Vice-President....... A. S. Dunton
Treasurer .... D. A. MacKay
Secretary .... R. B. McClure

The year representatives are as follows:—

5th Year, H. A. Brady, I. Stover
4th Year, J. T. Speck, W. L. Carruthers.
3rd Year, D. A. MacKay, A. S. Dunton.

2nd Year (5-year Course), E. P. Scarlett, H. A. S. Vokes.
2nd Year (6-year Course) J. R. Birch, J. E. Jackson.
1st Year, E. G. Bell, P. F. Lloyd

FACULTY OF APPLIED SCIENCE AND ENGINEERING.

THE ENGINEERING SOCIETY—1920-1921.

The Society meets every second Wednesday during the academic year (except April), beginning with the third Wednesday in October. Papers are read, and discussions are held on engineering subjects. The Society publishes a journal yearly, containing the best papers read at the meetings. A supply department is conducted by the Society, on a co-operative plan, through which instruments, drafting supplies, stationery, etc., may be purchased at a low cost. The Society is divided into five clubs for the purpose of affording a medium of study of matters relating in particular to the different departments of engineering.

Executive of Engineering Society.

1920-1921.

President .... R. W. Downie *Corr. Sec.* .... B. H. Miller
Vice-Pres. .... K. L. Carruthers *Treasurer* .... J. A. Langford
Rec. Sec. .... J. Farley *Curator* .... W. E. Bennett

Year Representatives.

4th Year ......,........ J. R. McLean *2nd Year*................. A. A. Bell
3rd Year .... H. G. Thompson *1st Year*.............. W. A. Osborne

Club Representatives

Civil .... P. J. Culliton *Chemical* .... A. D. R. Fraser
Mining ....A. E. O'Brien *Architecture* .... T. J. Young
Elect. & Mech......M. C. Stafford

INDUSTRIAL CHEMICAL CLUB.

Hon. Chairman, Prof. J. W. Bain.
Hon. Vice-Chairman, Prof. E. G. R. Ardagh.
Chairman .... A. D. R. Fraser
Vice-Chairman, C. E. J. McKeown.

Sec. .... H. Kesteven-Balshaw
Curator .... H. N. Baker
4th Year Rep............. C. P. Lailey
3rd Year Rep. .... H. B. Meyer
2nd Year Rep. .... E. M. Begg
1st Year Rep. ...... R. A. Gordon

ELECTRICAL AND MECHANICAL CLUB.

Hon. Chairman, Prof. R. W. Angus.

Hon. Vice-Chairman, Prof. H. W. Price.

Chairman .... M. C. Spafford

Vice and 4th Year Rep., G. A. Brace.

Secretary and 3rd Year Rep., B. H. Johnson.

Treas. and 2nd Year Rep., A. W. F. McQueen.

Curator and 1st Year Rep., G. W. Smart.

CIVIL ENGINEERING CLUB.

Hon. Chairman, Prof. C. R. Young.

Chairman.................. P. J. Culliton

Vice-Chairm'n, E. W. Cockerline

Sec.-Treas............ C. B. MacQueen

4th Year Rep............ H. J. Elliott

3rd Year Rep. .... W. J. Foley

2nd Year Rep. .... M. C. Kelly

1st Year Rep....... J. R. Emerson

Varsity Rep. .... F. S. Glover

MINING AND METALLURGICAL CLUB.

Hon. Chairman, Prof. G. A. Guess.

Chairman .... A. E. O'Brien

Vice-Chairman............ C. M. Beck

Sec.-Treas. .... R. J. Henry

2nd Year Rep. .... V. B. Lyle

1st Year Rep. .... J. Beatty

Chairman Entertainment Committee, A. Mackle.

THE DEBATING CLUB.

Chairman .... G. A. Brace

Secretary ...... D. W. Rosebrugh

4th Year Rep. .... J. D. Relyea

3rd Year Rep. ...... A. L. S. Nash

2nd Year Rep. ....F. A. Murphy

1st Year Rep........ G. P. Sabiston

Eng. Soc. Rep...... W. E. Bennett

THE ARCHITECTURAL CLUB.

President .... T. J. Young

Vice-Pres.......... E. W. Haldenby

Secretary .... A. S. Crawford

Treasurer .... M. A. Norcross

3rd Year Councillor, J. B. Helme

2nd Year Coun. .... J. G. Magee

1st Year Coun. ..... A. R. Smythe

APPLIED SCIENCE ATHLETIC CLUB.

President .... F. R. McDonald

Vice-Pres. .... G. W. Duncan

Sec.-Treas. .... W. S. Sherk

4th Year Rep. .... R. Parker

3rd Year Rep. .... J. C. Perry

2nd Year Rep. .... G. Johnson

1st Year Rep. .... E. Littlejohn

COLLEGE OF EDUCATION.

CLASS EXECUTIVE.

Hon. Pres. .... Dean Pakenham
President .... Alex. Sinclair
1st *Vice-President*, Miss M. A. Cameron.
2nd *Vice-President*, Miss I. M. Hambly.
Secretary... Miss M. H. McArton
Treasurer... ...... C. W. Houghton

Convenor of Soc. Com., R. L. Bell.
Convenor of Prog. Com., Miss H. A. Mabee.
Convenor of Educ. Com., W. T. Medcof.
Convenor of Dramatic Com., J. J. Dunlop.

ATHLETIC ASSOCIATION.

Hon. President, Professor H. J. Crawford.
President .... G. E. Fraser

Secretary .... L. W. Dippell
Treasurer .... J. B. Ryan
Director .... Frank Halbus

STUDENT CHRISTIAN ASSOCIATION.

Hon. Pres............. Dr. P. Sandiford
President .... A. R. Self
Vice-Pres............. Miss B. E. Oaten
Secretary .... H. D. Langford
Treas. ...... Miss M. E. Gardiner

Convenor of Bible Study, J. K. Graham.
Convener of Sociology, Miss L. M. Floody.
Pianist .... Miss H. A. Mabee

FACULTY OF FORESTRY.

THE FORESTERS' CLUB.

President .... H. M. Hughson
Vice-President ...J. L. VanCamp
Secretary .... J. L. Alexander
Treasurer .... E. Druce

Students' Council Rep., A. W. Bentley.
Athletic Committee, R. S. Carman, A. C. Thrupp, J. H. Duff.

INDEX.